# College Algebra
## A Narrative Approach
### Second Edition

**Stephen Majewicz**
**Kingsborough Community College**

**PEARSON**
Custom
Publishing

Printed in the United States of America

25 24 23 22

ISBN 0-536-44720-9

2007360777

KC

Please visit our web site at *www.pearsoncustom.com*

PEARSON CUSTOM PUBLISHING
501 Boylston Street, Suite 900, Boston, MA 02116
A Pearson Education Company

To my wife, Annemarie

# A Note to the Instructor

This book was written to aid the students in succeeding in Mat 9 and to prepare them for future mathematics courses such as precalculus and calculus. As you know, Mat 9 is a college algebra course which contains many of the topics that are traditionally taught in an algebra course. There are two fundamental resources of any mathematics course which students need to take advantage of in order to succeed, a good instructor and a good textbook. It is your job to be a good instructor. By providing the students with a clear lecture and thorough notes, you are supplying them with the necessary background that they need in order to succeed. The job of the textbook is to provide the student with clear explanations of worked examples, plenty of exercises for the students to work on, and comfortable reading material which the student can understand. This book contains such qualities.

"College Algebra: A Narrative Approach" provides the student with clear explanations of worked examples, plenty of exercises and material which supplements the notes given by the instructor. Each chapter is divided into sections. Whenever a new topic is discussed, it is accompanied by an exhaustive number of worked examples, along with in-depth detailed explanations. At the end of each section (or chapter), there is a set of examples (called 'Try These') for the student to try out. The solutions to these examples are given at the end of the text. Each chapter (or section) concludes with numerous exercise problems, as well as a multiple choice quiz on the material from the chapter. The exercise problems vary in their level of difficulty and the solutions to the odd numbered problems are given in detail at the end of the text. The quizzes will prepare the student for taking a multiple choice exam, hence, prepare them for taking the Mat 9 exit exam. The text is reader friendly and, when reading, a student will feel as if he/she were being taught by the instructor one on one (hence, the material is narrated).

This textbook is a supplement to your lessons. It has numerous exercise problems which make excellent homework problems. The quizzes and 'Try These' problems should be assigned to the students as well. The text will provide you with the adequate teaching material for Mat 9 and, possibly, some teaching tips for certain topics. It is important that your students get enough practice in order to succeed in Mat 9. Since there is only so much that you can do in the classroom, the text is the students' instructor outside of the classroom. Provided by homework problems and reading material, they will be guided in the right direction. I hope that this book serves your needs in teaching Mat 9.

Professor Stephen Majewicz

# A Note to the Student

Algebra may seem very difficult and confusing when you begin learning it because there are fancy symbols and weird looking expressions with letters in them. In fact, it can be discouraging when you encounter a topic which makes no sense to you whatsoever. At this point, you may want to give up and forget all about algebra. These emotions that you feel are very common and I've seen them expressed by many students in the past. In order to succeed in algebra, you must have confidence and patience. You cannot accomplish your goals (such as passing a math class) without being confident that you can succeed. When things become tough, it is very easy to just back off and quit. Patience is the key; you need to assess the problem or topic which you are stuck on and try again. Without patience, you may be too quick to give up. Don't! You will succeed in this course if you have the proper attitude and approach to learning the topics.

The two resources at your disposal which will aid you in doing well in this course are the lectures and the textbook. It is important to attend class regularly and take notes. The instructor will be able to explain something to you that you do not understand. Ask questions when an explanation is not clear to you. Don't be afraid and don't ever think that your question is stupid. Every question is a good one. Remember that the instructor is there to help you. The textbook contains all of the material that you will need to learn in the course. It has plenty of worked out examples for you to read. After looking over the examples, you should do the 'Try These' examples to convince yourself that you understand the material. Make sure that you do all of the homework assignments that your instructor assigns. Homework can be time consuming, but it is given to you for a reason. No one can become good in algebra by just attending class; don't think that you are such a person. By doing homework, you are strengthening your mathematics skills, as well as becoming a disciplined student. Such skills and discipline are key necessities for success in your college career, as well as in your life. After completing each chapter of the text, you should try the 'Try These' examples once more and the 'End of Chapter Quiz'. The quiz is designed to prepare you for the final exam known as the 'exit exam'. If you read over your notes, read the book, and do your homework regularly, you will do well in the class.

I wish you the best of luck in Mat 9. Remember to have confidence and patience. You will succeed!

Professor Stephen Majewicz

# Table of Contents

# Acknowledgments

I would like to thank Professors Stanley Rabinowitz, Eric Rothenburg and Dale Siegel of Kingsborough Community College for reviewing several sections of the book and for their suggestions and comments. I would also like to thank Professor Isaac Garber and Mr. David Greenberger for having pointed out some mistakes that were made in the first edition of this text.

The solutions portion of the text was done by Ms. Mary Greene and Ms. Danielle Heckman and the index was organized by Mr. William Greene (not related to Mary Greene). Their assistance saved me an enormous amount of work and time. I am very grateful for their help.

I would like to thank Professor Ed Martin of Kingsborough Community College for the 'crash course' in working with graphics in Microsoft Excel. I would also like to thank Mr. Daniel Collins for his advice on improving the visual aspects of the text.

I would like to thank the Mat 9 committee of Kingsborough Community College for their support of this text: Professors Aleksandr Davidov, Susan Hom, Robert Putz, Stanley Rabinowitz, Dale Siegel, Richard Staum, and Rachel Sturm.

I would like to extend a special 'Thank you' to Professor Rina Yarmish, Chair of the Mathematics Department at Kingsborough Community College, for giving me the opportunity to use my work for the Mat 9 course. She has been very supportive and encouraging during the preparation of this text.

# Chapter 1:    The Real Numbers and an Introduction to Algebra

In order to succeed in algebra, you must be familiar with the set and properties of real numbers, as well as the arithmetic computations performed with such numbers. As you are learning about different types of algebraic expressions and methods of solving equations, you will encounter situations in which the properties of real numbers help in solving such problems. When we study algebra, we use letters (called **variables**) in our algebraic expressions to represent real numbers. Consequently, the properties of real numbers will be helpful in working with such expressions. For this reason, understanding the properties of the real numbers is a prerequisite to learning algebra.

In this chapter, we will study the real numbers and the properties which they satisfy. In Section 1.1, we will learn how to build the set of real numbers by taking the set of natural numbers and enlarging it by adding numbers to it. In this way, the set of real numbers will emerge. We will also recall some basic arithmetic, such as converting a fraction to a decimal. Section 1.2 contains a review of arithmetic for the real numbers. We will recall the rules for the signs (without proving why these rules work the way they do) and how to work with fractions. In Section 1.3, we will briefly recall how to round off and truncate a decimal to a specified decimal place (this is called an **approximation** of a number). In Section 1.4, we will look at how to evaluate an arithmetic problem containing several operations in it. We will learn the order of operations, which basically tells us in what order we need to do the problem. Section 1.5 is devoted to a discussion of the properties which the real numbers satisfy. These properties will be seen throughout this book, so you should build a strong understanding of them. Sections 1.6 and 1.7 deal with graphing real numbers on a number line, comparing two numbers using the inequality symbol and finding the distance between two numbers on the number line using absolute value. The chapter concludes with Section 1.8, an introduction to algebra and algebraic expressions. We will practice evaluating algebraic expressions by utilizing the order of operations. The reader should have seen this already in a previous math course. However, we will go over it from scratch.

## Section 1.1    The Classification of Numbers

Our goal in this section is to classify numbers. Let's begin with a definition of a **set** and how to write a set of elements symbolically.

**Definition:** A **set** is a collection of objects. The objects in a set are called the **members** or **elements** of the set.

The symbol that we use to write a set is the 'squiggly parentheses' (called **braces**) { }. For example, if we want to write the set of numbers 1, 2, and 3 symbolically, we simply write {1, 2, 3}. If we want to write the set of colors red, white, and blue, we write {red, white, blue}. In Chapter 9, we will talk more about sets.

### I) **The Natural Numbers** (or **Counting Numbers**)

The set of **natural numbers** is {1, 2, 3, ...}.

These are just the numbers which we use to count with. The three dots (called an **ellipsis**) after the comma indicates that this set of numbers continues without ever ending. Obviously, we couldn't continue to write down **all** of the numbers which follow 3, since there are too many (we say that there are **infinitely many**). Notice that the pattern which occurs in the set is 'add 1 to get the next element'. Hence, the next three numbers in the set will be 4, 5, and 6. Whenever you see the ellipsis, look for a pattern for which the numbers in the set satisfy.

## II) The Whole Numbers

The set of **whole numbers** is the set $\{0,\ 1,\ 2,\ 3,\ ...\}$.

Observe that the whole numbers is just the set of natural numbers together with the number 0.

## III) The Integers or The Signed Numbers

The set of **integers** (or **signed numbers**) is the set $\{...,\ -2,\ -1,\ 0,\ +1,\ +2,\ +3,\ ...\}$.

As you can see, an integer is formed by taking a whole number and putting a **sign** (either a **negative sign** '$-$' or a **positive sign** '$+$') in front of it. Notice that the number 0 has no sign. If an integer has a '$-$' sign, we call it a **negative integer**. If an integer has a '$+$' sign, we call it a **positive integer**. For example, $-3$, $-11$ and $-7$ are negative integers, whereas $+1$, $+9$, and $+16$ are positive integers. Whenever we have a positive integer, we may omit the '$+$' sign. For example, $+5 = 5$ and $9 = +9$.

Integers appear in many places in the real world. For example, when dealing with banking, an account with $+\$200$ means that you have $\$200$ in the bank, whereas an account with $-\$200$ means that you owe $\$200$ to the bank. Notice that $\$0$ means that you have no money in the bank and you owe no money to the bank. Another example of integers being used appears when talking about the weather. If you've taken a basic chemistry course, you know that the freezing temperature of water (in Celsius) is $0°C$. If you look at a thermometer, you'll notice that there are numbers above and below the number 0. If you take the temperature of a liquid and its measurement is below the value $0°$, say $10°$ below $0°$, we say that the temperature is $10°$ below zero and write this temperature as $-10°C$. On the other hand, if the temperature is above the value $0°$, say $35°$ above $0°$, we say that the temperature is $35°$ above zero (or just $35°C$) and write this temperature as $35°C$. In conclusion, the positive and negative signs are used to compare the temperature of an object to the freezing temperature of water (in Celsius). These are just a couple of examples of where integers are used.

Notice that the set of integers contains all of the whole numbers.

## IV) The Rational Numbers

To describe this set, I will use the letters (or **variables**) $p$ and $q$ to represent certain types of numbers.

The set of **rational numbers** is the set $\left\{\dfrac{p}{q},\ \text{where } p \text{ and } q \text{ are integers},\ q \neq 0\right\}$.

Hence, a rational number is a fraction whose numerator and denominator are integers, provided that the denominator is not zero. For example, the following are rational numbers:

$$\frac{1}{2},\ \frac{4}{-5},\ \frac{-9}{-18},\ \frac{0}{6},\ \frac{-26}{232},\ \text{and}\ \frac{12}{1}$$

However, the expressions

$$\frac{1}{0},\ \frac{-8}{0},\ \frac{0}{0},\ \text{and}\ \frac{15}{0}$$

are undefined. Notice that every integer, can be written as a rational number by writing

$$n = \frac{n}{1}.$$

In fact, there are infinitely many ways of writing an integer as a rational number. For example, we have

$$3 = \frac{3}{1} = \frac{6}{2} = \frac{9}{3} = \frac{12}{4} = ...$$

We call such rational numbers **equivalent** because they all reduce to the same number, 3. Since every integer can be written as a rational number, we see that the set of rational numbers contains the set of integers.

Now, recall that every rational number can be written as a decimal by dividing the denominator into the numerator. For example, to express $\frac{1}{2}$ as a decimal, we divide $1 \div 2$ as follows:

$$
\begin{array}{r}
0.5 \\
2\overline{)\,1.0} \\
-10 \\
\hline
0
\end{array}
$$

Remember that you can keep on working on this division problem by adding infinitely many more 0's after the 1.0. However, if you do this, your answer will just be 0.5 with infinitely many more 0's following the 5:

$$
\begin{array}{r}
0.5000... \\
2\overline{)\,1.0000...} \\
-1\,0 \\
\hline
0
\end{array}
$$

Therefore, we simply write $\frac{1}{2} = 0.5$. Writing the answer as 0.500000... would not change the value, but just make it look different. A decimal which has infinitely many 0's after a certain decimal place and no other numbers is called a **terminating decimal**. Other examples of terminating decimals are 0.12, 0.7, 3.14, and $-5.11193$. Now let's express $\frac{25}{99}$ as a decimal. We divide $25 \div 99$ as follows:

$$
\begin{array}{r}
0.2525... \\
99\overline{)\,25.00000...} \\
-19\,8 \\
\hline
520 \\
-495 \\
\hline
250 \\
-198 \\
\hline
520 \\
-495 \\
\hline
25
\end{array}
$$

Notice that this division problem contains a repeating pattern. After we perform the first two subtraction steps, we get the number 25, the same number we began with. If we keep adding more 0's after 25.00000, the answer will contain the same **block** of digits, namely 25. In other words, we will obtain $\frac{25}{99} = 0.252525252525...$ Since the '25' repeats itself forever, we call this a **non-terminating, repeating decimal**. It is non-terminating because you will never get 0's at the end of the decimal and it is repeating since the block of 25's always appears. Since the decimal is repeating, we write $0.252525252525... = 0.\overline{25}$ for short. The 'bar' symbol is put above the repeating block. For another example, if we write $\frac{1}{6}$ as a decimal, we will obtain $0.16666... = 0.1\overline{6}$. This time, only the 6 gets the bar since it is the repeating number and not the 1. Here's one for you to verify on your own:

$$
\frac{3}{7} = 0.428571428571... = 0.\overline{428571}
$$

So, why do we care about all of this? Well, it turns out that **every** rational number can be expressed as one of these two types of decimals.

Every rational number can be expressed as either a
**terminating decimal** or a **non-terminating, repeating decimal**.

Similarly, by using algebraic techniques, the following can be shown.

> Every decimal which is either terminating or non-terminating,
> repeating can be expressed as a **rational number**.

We conclude from the above that a rational number can be represented in either fractional form (with integers in the numerator and denominator and no zero in the denominator) or in decimal form as one of the types mentioned above. Now, there is one type of decimal which wasn't mentioned yet, namely a decimal which is **non-terminating and non-repeating**. Such a decimal **cannot** be expressed as a rational number. These numbers make up our next set.

## V) The Irrational Numbers

The set of **irrational numbers** is the set {non-terminating, non-repeating decimals}.

**Examples.** The following are irrational numbers.

1) $\pi$ is irrational. I will assume that you have seen this symbol (pronounced as 'pi') before. If not, the number represented by this symbol is the ratio of the circumference of a circle to its diameter. If this is still unclear, don't worry. We will see $\pi$ occur later on in this book. Most of the time, it is approximated to either 3.14 or $\frac{22}{7}$ (we write $\pi \approx 3.14$ or $\pi \approx \frac{22}{7}$). However, the actual value of $\pi$ could not be written down in full, nor with the repeating 'bar' symbol.

2) The number 5.72772777277772... is irrational. It is non-terminating because there will always be 7's and 2's in its decimal if you continued the pattern. It is also non-repeating because the pattern which arises is to increase the number of 7's by one once you go past 2. There will never be a repeating block, since there will always be one more 7 tossed in as you continue the pattern.

3) There is a number, $n$, for which $n \times n = 2$. The number $n$ is irrational. For those of you who learned about square roots before, we write this number as $n = \sqrt{2}$ and read it as 'the square root of 2'. We will learn about square roots in Chapter 5.

We will learn later on that there are infinitely many irrational numbers which come from square roots. What I want you to understand for now is that an irrational number is a non-terminating, non-repeating decimal and that such decimals really do exist. Now, if we put all of the rational numbers and all of the irrational numbers together in one set, we get the set of real numbers.

## VI) The Real Numbers

The set of **real numbers** is the set {rational numbers and irrational numbers}. More simply put, the set of real numbers contains every possible decimal that you can think of. These are the numbers which we will be concerned with.

**Try These (Set 1):**

1) Express each fraction as a decimal. State whether it is terminating or non-terminating, repeating.

   a) $\dfrac{3}{4}$       b) $\dfrac{3}{8}$       c) $\dfrac{7}{9}$       d) $\dfrac{0}{12}$

2) Which of the following real numbers are integers?

   a) $-7$       b) $4.612$       c) $\sqrt{2}$       d) $14\frac{1}{5}$       e) $10$

3) Which of the following real numbers are rational?

   a) $\dfrac{4}{-11}$       b) $3.0801$       c) $\pi$       d) $-5$       e) $+9$

4) Which of the following are irrational numbers?

   a) $-5$       b) $2.838338333...$       c) $\pi$       d) $\dfrac{-6}{-18}$       e) $\dfrac{24}{0}$

# Section 1.2   Arithmetic of Real Numbers

In this section, we will review the rules for doing arithmetic with real numbers. We'll begin by recalling the different ways in which the operations of arithmetic can be written. To do this, I will use variables to represent real numbers. We will review how to do arithmetic of integers, followed by arithmetic of rationals. As we do these arithmetic problems, you will see the rules for arithmetic show up (for example, how to add two negative numbers). If you remember how these rules work, you may just want to skim through this section. I will not go into detail as to how to obtain the different rules, although they are interesting to learn. I will only demonstrate how they work. Later in this chapter, I will mention some of the properties which give us these rules.

## Operations Used in Arithmetic

### 1. Addition
When doing an addition problem, the 'plus' symbol, $+$, is used. We can read the mathematical sentence '$x + y$' as '$x$ plus $y$', '$x$ added to $y$', or 'the sum of $x$ and $y$'.

### 2. Subtraction
When doing a subtraction problem, the 'minus' symbol, $-$, is used. We can read the mathematical sentence '$x - y$' as '$x$ minus $y$', '$y$ subtracted from $x$', '$x$ take away $y$', 'the difference between $x$ and $y$' or '$x$ less $y$'.

### 3. Multiplication
There are various ways to write a multiplication statement. If we want to multiply $x$ and $y$, we can write it as

$$xy, \ (x)(y), \ x(y), \ (x)y, \ x \cdot y, \ (x) \cdot (y), \ x \cdot (y) \text{ or } (x) \cdot y.$$

Notice that I didn't use the traditional multiplication symbol, '$\times$', because it can easily be confused with the variable $x$. Of course, if my variables were called $u$ and $v$ instead, then I could certainly write $u \times v$ for the product of $u$ and $v$. We can read the mathematical sentence '$xy$' as '$x$ times $y$', '$x$ multiplied by $y$', 'the product of $x$ and $y$' or '$x$ by $y$'.

**4. Division**

If we want to divide $x$ by $y$, we can write

$x \div y$ (recall that ' $\div$ ' is called the **division**, or **quotient symbol**), $(x) \div y$, $x \div (y)$, $(x) \div (y)$, $\dfrac{x}{y}$ or $x/y$.

We can read the mathematical sentence '$x \div y$' as 'the quotient of $x$ and $y$' or '$x$ divided by $y$'.

**5. Exponentiation**

If you've never learned about exponents before, don't worry. I will only mention the definition at this point and present a couple of examples. Suppose you want to multiply a real number by itself several times. Rather than writing down a long product, we can express the product using an exponent.

**Definition:** Suppose $n$ is a natural number and $a$ is any real number. Then

$$\underbrace{a \cdot a \cdots a}_{n \text{ of these}} = a^n$$

We read the expression '$a^n$' as '$a$ raised to the $n^{th}$ power' or '$a$ to the power $n$'. We call '$a$' the **base** and '$n$' the **exponent** of the expression. If the exponent is 1, then we write $a^1 = a$.

For example,

$$5^2 = \underbrace{5 \times 5}_{\text{The exponent is 2.}} = 25, \quad 2^4 = \underbrace{2 \times 2 \times 2 \times 2}_{\text{The exponent is 4.}} = 16 \text{ and } 9^1 = 9.$$

Chapter 2 is devoted to the study of exponents and the properties they satisfy. For now, I just want you to know what the 'little number upstairs' (the exponent) means.

## Arithmetic with Integers

We know from grade school how to do arithmetic with whole numbers, so I won't waste time going over how to add $4 + 8$ or multiply $45 \times 37$. What I do want to go over is how to work with negative integers. Once again, I am assuming that you have learned this before. This is just meant to be a review. To begin with, let me mention a definition which comes from some properties that we will learn about later in this chapter. For starters, recall that if $x$ is a positive number, then $-x$ represents the number $x$ with a negative sign in front of it. For example, if $x = 7$, then $-x = -7$.

**Definition:** Suppose that $a$ is any real number and $b$ is a positive number. Then $a - b = a + (-b)$.

This definition states that if we want to subtract a positive number from any real number, we can think of it as an addition problem instead. In fact, we will soon see that $b$ can represent **any** real number once we understand what $-b$ means when $b$ is a **negative** number.

We can establish the rules for adding and subtracting real numbers (integers, in particular) by using this definition, along with the real number line (we will look at the real number line soon). Let's remind ourselves of these rules by looking at the following examples.

**Examples.** Add or subtract.

1) $(-3) + (-4) = -7$

Remember that when you **add two negative numbers**, you add them as if they were positive instead. When you get your answer, you put a negative sign in front. In other words, you figure out $3 + 4 = 7$. After putting a negative in front, you get $-7$.

2) $(-2) + (+5) = +3 = 3$

Remember that when you **add two real numbers of different signs**, you make believe the numbers are both positive and subtract the larger minus the smaller. The answer that you obtain will then take the same sign as that of the larger number. In other words, you take $5 - 2$, forgetting that the 2 is really $-2$. You obtain 3, which will be $+3$ because the sign of the larger number, $+5$, is positive.

3) $(-14) + 8 = -6$

The larger minus the smaller (without worrying about their signs) will be $14 - 8 = 6$. Since the larger number, 14, is really $-14$, the sign of the answer will also be negative. Hence, the answer is $-6$.

4) $-8 - 7 = -15$

By the definition above, we can write the problem as $-8 + (-7)$, which is the sum of two negatives. Now we add them just like in the first example.

5) $5 + (-5) = 0$

6) $(+23) + (-30) = -7$

7) $7 - 13 = -6$ (since $7 - 13 = 7 + (-13)$ by definition)

Let's now recall how to multiply and divide integers. The rules for multiplication (and division) which we often memorize without questioning come from several properties. We will take them for granted here although I will mention their origins later in this chapter. An important definition which allows us to relate division and multiplication is

**Definition:** Suppose that $a$ and $b$ represent two real numbers and $b \neq 0$, then $a \div b = \dfrac{a}{b} = a \left( \dfrac{1}{b} \right)$.

This definition says that you can always interpret a division problem as a multiplication problem and vice versa. From this definition, as well as some properties that we will soon learn about, we have the following rules for multiplication and division:

$$
\begin{aligned}
(+)(+) &= + &\qquad (+) \div (+) &= + \\
(+)(-) &= - &\qquad (+) \div (-) &= - \\
(-)(+) &= - &\qquad (-) \div (+) &= - \\
(-)(-) &= + &\qquad (-) \div (-) &= +
\end{aligned}
$$

The following property is important to know.

---

**Property I:**   If $a$ is any real number, then $-(-a) = a$.

---

For example, $-(-1) = 1$ and $-(-5) = 5$. As you can see, the negative signs cancel each other out. Notice that we can also write $-(-a) = -1(-a)$ since $1(-a) = -a$. In Section 1.5, we will see why this property holds. By the way, we now have that $a - b = a + (-b)$ makes sense for **any** real numbers, $a$ and $b$. Let's see why.

**Examples:** Evaluate.

1)     $\underbrace{3 - (-2) = 3 + [-(-2)]}$     $= 3 + 2 = 5$
Let $a=3$, $b=-2$, then use $a-b=a+(-b)$.

A shortcut to doing this is to remember that the two negative signs cancel out each other and we obtain a positive sign. Hence,

$$\underbrace{3 - (-2) = 3 + 2}_{\text{The } -\text{'s cancel out.}} = 5.$$

In the following examples, try them by using the short-cut. I've done them the long way.

2)     $\underbrace{7 - (-11) = 7 + [-(-11)]}$     $= 7 + 11 = 18$
Let $a=7$, $b=-11$, then use $a-b=a+(-b)$.

3) $-5 - (-8) = -5 + [-(-8)] = -5 + 8 = 3$

4) $-9 - (-9) = -9 + [-(-9)] = -9 + 9 = 0$

5) $-6 - (-4) = -6 + [-(-4)] = -6 + 4 = -2$

Another useful property to remember is

---

**Property II:**   If $a$ and $b$ are any integers and $b \neq 0$, then $\dfrac{-a}{b} = \dfrac{a}{-b} = -\dfrac{a}{b}$.

---

This says that if you have a negative sign present in a fraction, you may put it in the numerator, the denominator, or outside of the fraction. For example, the fractions $\dfrac{-2}{3}$, $\dfrac{2}{-3}$, and $-\dfrac{2}{3}$ are all equivalent (that is, they all have the same value). Let's do some examples with multiplication and division.

**Examples.** Multiply or divide.

1) $(3)(-4) = -12$, since a positive times a negative is a negative.

2) $(-7)(6) = -42$, since a negative times a positive is a negative.

3) $(-8)(-2) = 16$, since a negative times a negative is a positive.

4) $(+5)(+6) = 30$ (remember that the positive sign may be left out).

5) $-2(-3) = 6$, since $-2(-3) = -[2(-3)] = \underbrace{-[-6] = 6}_{\text{by Property I}}$.

6) $36 \div (-4) = -9$, since a positive divided by a negative is a negative.

7) $(-50) \div (-10) = 5$, since a negative divided by a negative is a positive.

8) $\dfrac{-16}{2} = -8$, since a negative divided by a positive is a negative.

9) $\dfrac{-27}{-9} = 3$, since a negative divided by a negative is a positive.

10) $-(-7) = 7$ by Property I.

**Try These (Set 2):** Evaluate (the word **evaluate** designates that your answer will be numerical).

1) $5 + (-2)$      4) $-1 - 3$      7) $(8)(-4)$      10) $(-15) \div 3$

2) $(-8) + (-16)$      5) $0 - 12$      8) $(-3)(-7)$      11) $(-64) \div (-16)$

3) $9 - 21$      6) $-16 - (-5)$      9) $-(-20)$      12) $\dfrac{35}{-5}$

## Arithmetic with Rational Numbers

### I) Adding and Subtracting

Recall that in order to add (or subtract) two fractions, you need to have common denominators. Once you have common denominators, you can combine the fractions by combining their numerators. In other words,

$$\text{if } A, B, \text{ and } C \text{ are any integers but } C \neq 0, \text{ then } \frac{A}{C} + \frac{B}{C} = \frac{A+B}{C} \text{ and } \frac{A}{C} - \frac{B}{C} = \frac{A-B}{C}.$$

Sometimes, as you know, you may have to change the denominators in a given problem to get what is called the **least common denominator** (or **LCD**). For example, to add $\dfrac{1}{6} + \dfrac{3}{8}$, you find the LCD of the denominators 6 and 8, which is 24 (since both 6 and 8 are divisors of 24, that is, they both divide into 24 without a remainder). You now rewrite your fractions into equivalent ones which have denominator 24 and add the fractions as follows:

$$\frac{1}{6} + \frac{3}{8} = \frac{1(4)}{6(4)} + \frac{3(3)}{8(3)} = \frac{4}{24} + \frac{9}{24} = \frac{13}{24}$$

Let me mention that another name for the LCD of the denominators in the example $\dfrac{1}{6} + \dfrac{3}{8}$ is the **least common multiple** (abbreviated as **LCM**) of the numbers 6 and 8. I will assume that you know how to find the LCM of 2 natural numbers.

**Examples.** Add or subtract.

1) $\underbrace{-\dfrac{2}{9} + \dfrac{1}{3}}_{\text{The LCM of 9 and 3 is 9.}} = \dfrac{-2}{9} + \dfrac{1(3)}{3(3)} = \dfrac{-2}{9} + \dfrac{3}{9} = \dfrac{-2+3}{9} = \dfrac{1}{9}$

2) $-\dfrac{3}{5} + \left(-\dfrac{1}{7}\right) = \dfrac{-3(7)}{5(7)} + \dfrac{-1(5)}{7(5)} = \dfrac{-21}{35} + \dfrac{-5}{35} = \dfrac{-21 + (-5)}{35} = \dfrac{-26}{35}$

<u>                 </u>
The LCM of 5 and 7 is 35.

3) $\dfrac{1}{4} - \dfrac{5}{6} = \dfrac{1(3)}{4(3)} - \dfrac{5(2)}{6(2)} = \dfrac{3}{12} - \dfrac{10}{12} = \dfrac{3 - 10}{12} = \dfrac{-7}{12}$ or $-\dfrac{7}{12}$

<u>                 </u>
The LCM of 4 and 6 is 12.

4) $\dfrac{9}{-10} - \dfrac{5}{6} = \dfrac{-9(3)}{10(3)} - \dfrac{5(5)}{6(5)} = \dfrac{-27}{30} - \dfrac{25}{30} = \dfrac{-27 - 25}{30} = \dfrac{-52}{30} = -\dfrac{26}{15}$

<u>                 </u>
Make the denominator positive.

5) $\dfrac{8}{15} + \left(-\dfrac{8}{15}\right) = \dfrac{8}{15} - \dfrac{8}{15} = 0$

6) $-\dfrac{10}{11} + \left(+\dfrac{10}{11}\right) = \dfrac{-10}{11} + \dfrac{10}{11} = \dfrac{-10 + 10}{11} = \dfrac{0}{11} = 0$

7) $\dfrac{1}{6} - \left(-\dfrac{5}{18}\right) = \dfrac{1(3)}{6(3)} - \left(-\dfrac{5}{18}\right) = \dfrac{3}{18} - \left(\dfrac{-5}{18}\right) = \dfrac{3 - (-5)}{18} = \dfrac{3 + 5}{18} = \dfrac{8}{18} = \dfrac{4}{9}$

8) $-\dfrac{4}{9} - \left(-\dfrac{1}{9}\right) = \dfrac{-4 - (-1)}{9} = \dfrac{-4 + 1}{9} = \dfrac{-3}{9} = -\dfrac{1}{3}$

## II) Multiplying and Dividing

To multiply or divide two rational numbers, remember the following properties:

> **Multiplication.**   If $A$, $B$, $C$, and $D$ are integers and both $B, D \neq 0$, then $\dfrac{A}{B} \cdot \dfrac{C}{D} = \dfrac{AC}{BD}$.

> **Division.**   If $A$, $B$, $C$, and $D$ are integers and $B, C, D \neq 0$, then $\dfrac{A}{B} \div \dfrac{C}{D} = \dfrac{A}{B} \cdot \dfrac{D}{C} = \dfrac{AD}{BC}$.

So, to multiply two rational numbers, multiply numerators and then multiply the denominators (recall that you may be able to simplify first, then multiply). To divide two rational numbers, 'flip over' (or take the **reciprocal** of) the second fraction and change the division problem into a multiplication problem. Note that the division problem $\dfrac{A}{B} \div \dfrac{C}{D}$ can also be written as $\dfrac{\frac{A}{B}}{\frac{C}{D}}$. An expression of this form is called a **mixed quotient**, or **complex fraction**. We will see that our examples are written as in the first case, using the division symbol '$\div$'. We will study mixed quotients in Chapter 4.

**Examples.** Multiply or divide.

1) $\left(-\dfrac{1}{3}\right)\left(\dfrac{2}{5}\right) = -\dfrac{2}{15}$

6) $\left(\dfrac{9}{2}\right) \div \left(-\dfrac{6}{7}\right) = \left(\dfrac{\overset{3}{\cancel{9}}}{2}\right)\left(-\dfrac{7}{\underset{2}{\cancel{6}}}\right) = -\dfrac{21}{4}$

2) $\left(\dfrac{6}{7}\right)\left(-\dfrac{2}{7}\right) = -\dfrac{12}{49}$

7) $\left(-\dfrac{8}{15}\right) \div (-12) = \left(-\dfrac{8}{15}\right) \div \left(-\dfrac{12}{1}\right) = \left(-\dfrac{\overset{2}{\cancel{8}}}{15}\right)\left(-\dfrac{1}{\underset{3}{\cancel{12}}}\right) = \dfrac{2}{45}$

3) $\left(-\dfrac{3}{8}\right)\left(-\dfrac{1}{7}\right) = \dfrac{3}{56}$

8) $1 \div \left(-\dfrac{1}{4}\right) = 1\left(-\dfrac{4}{1}\right) = -4$

4) $\left(-\dfrac{10}{11}\right)\left(\dfrac{3}{20}\right) = \left(-\dfrac{\overset{1}{\cancel{10}}}{11}\right)\left(\dfrac{3}{\underset{2}{\cancel{20}}}\right) = -\dfrac{3}{22}$

5) $(5)\left(-\dfrac{2}{15}\right) = \left(\dfrac{\overset{1}{\cancel{5}}}{1}\right)\left(-\dfrac{2}{\underset{3}{\cancel{15}}}\right) = -\dfrac{2}{3}$

**Try These (Set 3):** Evaluate.

1) $\dfrac{4}{5} + \left(-\dfrac{1}{3}\right)$

4) $\dfrac{-1}{8} - \dfrac{1}{6}$

7) $\dfrac{1}{16} \div \left(-\dfrac{3}{20}\right)$

2) $\dfrac{2}{9} - \left(-\dfrac{1}{3}\right)$

5) $\left(-\dfrac{9}{10}\right)\left(\dfrac{5}{6}\right)$

8) $(-18) \div \left(+\dfrac{20}{21}\right)$

3) $-\dfrac{4}{7} - \dfrac{6}{7}$

6) $(-3)\left(\dfrac{7}{8}\right)$

9) $1 \div \dfrac{8}{9}$

To end this section, I would like to mention a few more properties which we will use throughout the text.

***

**Property III:** If $a \neq 0$ is a real number, then $\dfrac{0}{a} = 0$.

***

For example, $\dfrac{0}{2} = 0$, $\dfrac{0}{-5} = 0$, and $\dfrac{0}{18} = 0$. Notice that $\dfrac{0}{0}$ is undefined.

***

**Property IV:** If $a$ is any real number, then $\dfrac{a}{0}$ is undefined.

***

For example, $\dfrac{1}{0}$, $\dfrac{-3}{0}$, and $\dfrac{9}{0}$ are undefined.

***

**Property V:** If $a \neq 0$ is a real number, then $\dfrac{a}{a} = 1$.

***

For example, $\dfrac{6}{6} = 1$, $\dfrac{-12}{-12} = 1$, and $\dfrac{-4}{-4} = 1$.

---

**Property VI:** If $a$ is any real number, then $a \cdot 0 = 0$.

---

For example, $5 \cdot 0 = 0$, $\dfrac{2}{5}(0) = 0$, and $0 \cdot 0 = 0$.

## Section 1.3   Approximation of a Decimal

A decimal which is non-terminating can never be written down entirely since the digits in the decimal go on forever. What we can do, however, is to 'cut down' the number of digits in the decimal, using only part of it. This is known as **approximating** a decimal or **decimal approximation**. There are two ways a decimal can be approximated. One method is called **rounding off** to a specified decimal place. The other is called **truncation** to a specified decimal place. Let me discuss how these methods work.

When you want to round off a decimal to a certain decimal place (say, the nearest tenth or nearest thousandth), you first find the digit in the place which you want to round off to. If the next digit is less than 5, you delete everything after the digit which you are rounding off to. On the other hand, if the next digit is 5 or more, you increase the digit which you are rounding off to by 1 and then delete everything after it. For example, suppose you want to round off the decimal 6.249093 to the nearest tenth (or to 1 decimal place). Notice that after the tenths place, a 4 appears. Since 4 is less than 5, you leave the digit in the tenths place (the 2) as it is and delete everything afterwards. By doing this, we get 6.2. Let's now round off $\pi = 3.14159...$ to the nearest thousandth (or to 3 decimal places). In the third decimal place, there is a 1. We go to the next digit and observe that it is a 5. We now increase the previous digit (the 1) by 1 and delete everything after it. By doing this, we obtain the decimal 3.142.

When you want to truncate a decimal to a certain decimal place, all you need to do is to delete everything that comes after the decimal place which you are truncating to. For example, to truncate the decimal 0.333333... to the nearest ten-thousandth (that is, to 4 decimal places), just throw away all the digits which come after the fourth decimal place. By doing so, we obtain 0.3333. Notice that this is the same thing that we would obtain if we were rounding off to the nearest ten-thousandth. You may wonder whether or not truncating a decimal will always give the same answer as rounding off. Let's see an example where the two are different. Let's truncate the decimal 9.81223 to the nearest whole number (that is, to 0 decimal places). If we delete everything after the whole number, we obtain $9.0 = 9$. However, if we round off the decimal 9.81223 to the nearest whole number, we need to examine the digit following the whole number. This digit, 8, is more than 5 and, consequently, we must increase the 9 by 1. By doing this, we obtain $10.0 = 10$ and so the truncation is different from the rounded off answer.

**Examples.** Round off the following to one decimal place and to two decimal places:

1) $2.94105 = 2.9$ to one decimal place and $2.94105 = 2.94$ to two decimal places.

2) $3.7603 = 3.8$ to one decimal place and $3.7603 = 3.76$ to two decimal places.

3) $10.1853 = 10.2$ to one decimal place and $10.1853 = 10.19$ to two decimal places.

4) $23.9861 = 24.0$ to one decimal place and $23.9861 = 23.99$ to two decimal places.

5) $0.0137 = 0.0$ to one decimal place and $0.0137 = 0.01$ to two decimal places.

**Examples.** Truncate the following to one decimal place and to two decimal places:

1) $3.1174 = 3.1$ to one decimal place and $3.1174 = 3.11$ to two decimal places.

2) $12.0558 = 12.0$ to one decimal place and $12.0558 = 12.05$ to two decimal places.

3) $9.00632 = 9.0$ to one decimal place and $9.00632 = 9.00$ to two decimal places.

4) $31.965 = 31.9$ to one decimal place and $31.965 = 31.96$ to two decimal places.


**Try These (Set 4):** Round off and truncate to three decimal places.

1) 3.24109          3) 24.60009          5) 60.101808
2) 7.90583          4) 9.222777          6) 0.1491625


# Section 1.4  The Order of Operations

Whenever you have to do a computation with several arithmetic operations involved, there is a specific order that you need to follow in order to evaluate the expression. This order is known as the **order of operations**. In this section, we will discuss the order of operations.


The following rules for the order of operations must be obeyed when evaluating an arithmetic problem:


    1. Start by working out what is in the **parentheses**, beginning with the innermost and working outward.
    2. Next, work out any **exponentiation**.
    3. Perform any **multiplications** and **divisions**, going from left to right.
    4. Perform any **additions** and **subtractions**, going from left to right.


To help you remember this ordering, it is useful to remember the initials **PEMDAS**, where **P** is **parentheses**, **E** is **exponentiation**, **M** is **multiplication**, **D** is **division**, **A** is **addition**, and **S** is **subtraction**. A phrase that students sometimes remember with the same initials is

**P**lease **E**xcuse **M**y **D**ear **A**unt **S**ally

Take a look at the following set of examples. I worked out each one step by step, following the PEMDAS order.


**Examples.** Evaluate.

1) $\underbrace{4(3)}_{12} + 7 = 12 + 7 = 19$

2) $\underbrace{4(3 + 7)}_{10} = 4(10) = 40$

3) $5 - \underbrace{6 \times 3}_{18} = 5 - 18 = -13$

4) $\underbrace{(5 - 6)}_{-1} \times 3 = (-1) \times 3 = -3$

5) $(-6) + \underbrace{12 \div 3}_{4} = (-6) + 4 = -2$

6) $\underbrace{(-6 + 12)}_{6} \div 3 = 6 \div 3 = 2$

7) $\underbrace{(5 - 7)^2}_{-2} + 16 = \underbrace{(-2)^2}_{4} + 16 = 4 + 16 = 20$

8) $\underbrace{-23 - 4}_{-27} + 18 = -27 + 18 = -9$

9) $-23 - \underbrace{(4 + 18)}_{22} = -23 - 22 = -45$

10) $\underbrace{45 \div 9}_{5} \cdot 2 \div 10 \cdot 9 = \underbrace{5 \cdot 2}_{10} \div 10 \cdot 9 = \underbrace{10 \div 10}_{1} \cdot 9 = 1 \cdot 9 = 9$

11) $\underbrace{(-3 - 1)}_{-4}\underbrace{(-4 + 12)}_{8} - 5 \times 6 = \underbrace{(-4)(8)}_{-32} - 5 \times 6 = -32 - \underbrace{5 \times 6}_{30} = -32 - 30 = -62$

12) $\underbrace{6^2}_{36} - \underbrace{(1 + 3)^2}_{4} \times 3 + 8 = 36 - \underbrace{4^2}_{16} \times 3 + 8 = 36 - \underbrace{16 \times 3}_{48} + 8 = \underbrace{36 - 48}_{-12} + 8 = -12 + 8 = -4$

13) $5 + 2\{3 - 7(10 - 12)\} = 5 + 2\{3 - 7(-2)\} = 5 + 2\{3 + 14\} = 5 + 2\{17\} = 5 + 34 = 39$

14) $\dfrac{-2 + 5(3 + 7)}{15 - 3^2} = \dfrac{-2 + 5(10)}{15 - 9} = \dfrac{-2 + 50}{6} = \dfrac{48}{6} = 8$

In Example 14, notice that the numerator and denominator were worked out before dividing. Think of the numerator and denominator as being in parentheses when you get such an example.

**Try These (Set 5):** Evaluate.

1) $7 - 2(3 + 1)$

2) $-1 - 2 - 3 - 4$

3) $5 \cdot 8 \div (1 + 3)$

4) $4^2 - 8 + 6(2)$

5) $-1 - (5^2 - 2^3)$

6) $36 \div 2 + 18 \div 9$

7) $14 - 9(2 - 3)^2 + 3$

8) $(-3 - 1)^2 \cdot \{4 + 2(-6)\}$

9) $\dfrac{3 \times 8 - 12}{-2 \cdot 3}$

10) $-2 + 3[5 + 6(2 - 4)] - 1$

11) $(1 + 2)(1 - 5) \cdot (4 - 7)(0)$

12) $10 - 10 + 10 \cdot 10 - 10$

# Section 1.5  Properties of the Real Numbers

Now we will learn about some properties which the real numbers satisfy. It is these properties which give us the rules for doing arithmetic with real numbers.

---

### The Commutative Properties

Suppose that $a$ and $b$ are any real numbers. Then

$$a + b = b + a$$

and

$$ab = ba$$

---

For example, $5 + 8 = 8 + 5$ and $7 \times 2 = 2 \times 7$. Notice that the commutative property only works for addition and multiplication. For example, observe that $9 - 1 \neq 1 - 9$ and $16 \div 2 \neq 2 \div 16$.

---

 **BEWARE:** $a - b \neq b - a$ and $a \div b \neq b \div a$

---

### The Associative Properties

Suppose that $a$, $b$ and $c$ are any real numbers. Then

$$(a + b) + c = a + (b + c) = a + b + c$$

and

$$(ab)\, c = a\,(bc) = abc$$

---

For example, $(2 + 3) + 7 = 5 + 7 = 12$ and $2 + (3 + 7) = 2 + 10 = 12$ as well. As for multiplication, observe that $(4 \times 5) \times (-3) = 20 \times (-3) = -60$ and $4 \times (5 \times (-3)) = 4 \times (-15) = -60$ as well. Note that the associative property only works for addition and multiplication. For example, you can check and see that $(0 - 4) - 6 \neq 0 - (4 - 6)$ and $(50 \div 10) \div 2 \neq 50 \div (10 \div 2)$ by using the order of operations (remember to work out the parentheses first).

---

 **BEWARE:** $(a - b) - c \neq a - (b - c)$ and $(a \div b) \div c \neq a \div (b \div c)$

---

### The Distributive Property

Suppose that $a$, $b$ and $c$ are any real numbers. Then

$$\overset{\frown}{a\,(b + c)} = ab + ac$$

and

$$\overset{\frown}{(a + b)\,c} = ac + bc$$

---

For example, if we want to evaluate $6\,(4 + 5)$, we should work out the sum in the parentheses first, obtaining

$$6\,(4 + 5) = 6\,(9) = 54.$$

We can also compute this by using the distributive property as follows:

$$6\,(4+5) = 6\,(4) + 6(5) = 24 + 30 = 54$$

as before. Clearly, it is easier to do it using the order of operations rather than the distributive property. However, when we learn how to multiply algebraic expressions, the distributive property will come in handy. For example, if we want to multiply $9\,(x+3)$, we cannot add $x$ and $3$ together into a single expression since we don't know what $x$ equals. Nevertheless, we can multiply the two expressions together by using the distributive property as follows:

$$9\,(x+3) = 9(x) + 9(3) = 9x + 27$$

Recall that Property I of Section 1.2 states that if $a$ is any real number, then $-(-a) = a$. Let's see why this is true. Consider the expression $-1\,((-a)+a)$. Since $(-a)+a = -a+a = 0$, we have $-1\,((-a)+a) = -1\,(0) = 0$. On the other hand, the distributive property gives us

$$-1\,((-a)+a) = -1\,(-a) + (-1)\,(a) = -(-a) - a.$$

Therefore, we have

$$0 = -(-a) - a$$

and when we add $a$ to both sides of the equation, we obtain

$$a = -(-a).$$

---

### The Additive and Multiplicative Identities

The number 0 is called the **additive identity**, and it satisfies the following property:

If $a$ is any real number, then $a + 0 = 0 + a = a$.

The number 1 is called the **multiplicative identity**, and it satisfies the following property:

If $a$ is any real number, then $a \cdot 1 = 1 \cdot a = a$.

---

For example, $6 + 0 = 6$ and $\dfrac{4}{5} \cdot 1 = \dfrac{4}{5}$.

---

### The Additive and Multiplicative Inverse Properties

1. Suppose that $a$ is any real number. Then $-a$ is called the **additive inverse** of $a$, and it satisfies

$$a + (-a) = (-a) + a = 0.$$

2. Suppose that $a \neq 0$ is a real number. Then $\dfrac{1}{a}$ is called the **multiplicative inverse** (or **reciprocal**) of $a$, and it satisfies

$$a\left(\frac{1}{a}\right) = \left(\frac{1}{a}\right)a = 1.$$

---

The additive inverse of a real number is just the number itself with the opposite sign. The reciprocal of a number (written in fraction form) is obtained by 'flipping over' the fraction.

**Examples.** Find the additive inverse and reciprocal.

1) 3 has additive inverse $-3$ and reciprocal $\dfrac{1}{3}$ $\left(\text{write } 3 = \dfrac{3}{1} \text{ and flip over } \dfrac{3}{1} \text{ to obtain the reciprocal, } \dfrac{1}{3}\right)$.

2) $-8$ has additive inverse 8 and reciprocal $\dfrac{1}{-8} = -\dfrac{1}{8}$.

3) $-\dfrac{6}{11}$ has additive inverse $\dfrac{6}{11}$ and reciprocal $-\dfrac{11}{6}$.

4) $5\dfrac{3}{4} = \dfrac{23}{4}$ has additive inverse $-\dfrac{23}{4}$ and reciprocal $\dfrac{4}{23}$.

5) 0 has additive inverse 0 and no reciprocal, since $\dfrac{1}{0}$ is undefined.

6) 1 has additive inverse $-1$ and reciprocal 1.

**Try These (Set 6):**

I) State the property being used.
1) $7 + 9 = 9 + 7$                   3) $(13)(-5) = (-5)(13)$
2) $(1 + 2) + (-6) = 1 + (2 + (-6))$    4) $2(x - 7) = 2(x) + 2(-7)$

II) Find the additive inverse and reciprocal of 9 and $-\dfrac{3}{16}$.

III) True or False:  $x - y = y - x$ for any real numbers $x$ and $y$.

IV) Multiply.
1) $4(x + 4)$        3) $a(b - 2)$
2) $-8(a + 5)$       4) $-1(12 - x)$

# Section 1.6   The Real Number Line and Inequalities

We learned that the set of real numbers consists of the rational numbers (numbers which are expressible as either terminating or non-terminating, repeating decimals), together with the irrational numbers (the set of non-terminating, non-repeating decimals). What we will do is to develop a picture, or geometrical representation, of the set of real numbers. To do so, we take a line (which we will draw horizontally) and label the integers on it as follows:

As you can see from the previous number line, each integer corresponds to a point on the line. We say that the integer is the **coordinate** of the point on the line which it corresponds to and we call the point the **graph** of the integer. For example, the point labelled $A$ on the line above has coordinate 3 and point $A$ is the graph of 3. Clearly, we can't label (or **graph**) all of the integers, so we use the 'arrows' to denote the fact that there are more integers on the number line even though we haven't labelled them. Notice that the integers have been placed on the number line in increasing order from left to right (recall that a negative integer is always smaller than a positive integer). We call the number 0 the **origin**. Now, if we want to find the location of **any** real number on the number line, whether it be rational or irrational, we find the pair of integers which it lies in between and label the number accordingly. To do this, however, you will have to approximate its location. Several numbers have been located on the number line below.

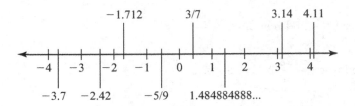

The number line is a graphical representation of the set of all real numbers. For this reason, we call it the **real number line.** No matter which real number you choose, it will have a home on the real number line.

Now, suppose you are given two real numbers, say $a$ and $b$, and you are interested in knowing which one is the larger (or smaller) of the two. Since the real number line is constructed in such a way that the numbers get larger from left to right, we can find the location of $a$ and $b$ on it and see which of the two is on the right-hand side of the other. The number on the right is always larger than the number on the left. When comparing two numbers, we use one of the **inequality symbols**, written as either $>$ or $<$ . The sentence $a < b$ is read "$a$ is **less than** $b$" and the sentence $a > b$ is read "$a$ is **greater than** $b$". As usual, if the two numbers are equal to each other, we use the **equality symbol** $=$ . The following law for comparing two numbers always holds:

---

### The Law of Trichotomy

If $a$ and $b$ are any two real numbers, then exactly one of the following holds:

$$a > b, \ a < b \text{ or } a = b$$

---

Graphically, this is saying that if you pick two numbers, then one number will be on the right-hand side of the other, unless the two numbers are equal to each other. Let's now recall how to compare numbers. We will do this **without** using the real number line.

**Examples.** Compare the numbers.

1) $4 < 8$ should be easy to figure out.

2) $\dfrac{3}{8} > \dfrac{1}{3}$

To obtain this, you could either rewrite the fractions as equivalent ones with the same denominator and compare their numerators or write each fraction as a decimal and compare the decimals instead. For the first method, notice that the LCM of 8 and 3 is 24 and, so $\dfrac{3(3)}{8(3)} = \dfrac{9}{24} > \dfrac{8}{24} = \dfrac{1(8)}{3(8)}$. As for the second method, notice that $\dfrac{3}{8} = 0.375$ and $\dfrac{1}{3} = 0.333....$ We have $0.375 > 0.333...$ since the second digit of $0.375$ is larger than the second digit of $0.3\overline{3}3....$

3) $0.6565 < \dfrac{65}{99}$

Observe that $\dfrac{65}{99} = 0.\overline{65} = 0.656565...$, which is a non-terminating, repeating decimal. When we compare $0.6565 = 0.6565000...$ to $0.656565...$, we see that the fifth digit of $0.656565...$ is greater than the fifth digit of $0.6565000....$ Therefore, $0.6565 < 0.\overline{65} = \dfrac{65}{99}$.

4) $0 < 7$ is obvious, since zero is less than any positive number.

5) $0 > -2$ is also obvious, since zero is greater than every negative number.

6) $-11 < -3$

One way of comparing two negative numbers is to first compare the numbers WITHOUT the negative signs. Then reverse the inequality. In this example, we have $11 > 3$. Therefore, $-11 < -3$. Another way of comparing them is to use the real number line to notice that $-3$ is closer to zero than $-14$ is.

7) $-0.334 < -\dfrac{1}{3}$

To compare these, you should first compare $0.334$ and $\dfrac{1}{3}$. Observe that $\dfrac{1}{3} = 0.\overline{3} = 0.3333...$ and, consequently, $0.334 > \dfrac{1}{3}$ (by comparing the third digit of each decimal). Therefore, you reverse the inequality and obtain $-0.334 < -\dfrac{1}{3}$.

8) $-\pi > -4$

Recall that $\pi \approx 3.14$ and so $\pi < 4$. Therefore, $-\pi > -4$.

9) $-\dfrac{1}{8} > -\dfrac{1}{4}$

First, compare $\dfrac{1}{8}$ and $\dfrac{1}{4}$. Observe that $\dfrac{1}{8} < \dfrac{2}{8} = \dfrac{1}{4}$. Hence, $-\dfrac{1}{8} > -\dfrac{1}{4}$.

10) $-17 < 2$

Comparing a positive number to a negative number is simple: the positive number is always greater than the negative number.

**Try These (Set 7):**

I) Locate the numbers on the real number line:

1) 3         3) $\dfrac{2}{3}$      5) $2\dfrac{1}{2}$      7) $-\dfrac{7}{5}$      9) 4.2

2) $-1$      4) $-3.5$      6) $-\pi$      8) $-2.\overline{412}$      10) 0.39

II) Fill in the space with the inequality symbol $<$ or $>$.

1) 5___2      3) $\dfrac{1}{6}$___$\dfrac{1}{5}$      5) $-8.\overline{5}$___$8.\overline{5}$      7) $-1.5656$___$-\dfrac{155}{99}$

2) $-7$___$-20$      4) $-3.022$___$-3.0225$      6) $\pi$___3.16

# Section 1.7  Absolute Value

In the last section, we saw that the real number line is a graphical representation of the set of all real numbers. By using an inequality (or equal) symbol, you can write down a mathematical sentence which compares two numbers. In this section, we will learn how to find the distance between two numbers on the real number line.

**Definition:** Let $n$ represent any real number. The **absolute value** of $n$ written as $|n|$ is the distance between 0 to $n$ on the real number line.

**Examples.** Find the absolute value.

1) $|5| = 5$

By using the real number line, you can see that the number 5 is 5 units away from 0 (see picture below).

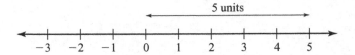

It turns out that $|n| = n$ for any positive number $n$ (which is the same as saying that $n > 0$).

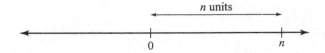

2) $|-4| = 4$

Once again, you can see that the number $-4$ is 4 units away from 0 (see picture below).

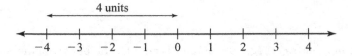

Notice that the answer that we obtained is just the number $-4$, but without the negative sign. We can write this algebraically as

$$|-4| = -(-4) = 4.$$

In general, if $n$ is any negative number (which is the same as saying that $n < 0$), then $|n| = -n$.

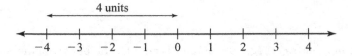

3) $|0| = 0$

This makes perfect sense. The distance between 0 and 0 on the real number line is just 0.

If we summarize the 'rules' mentioned above algebraically, we have

$$|n| = n \text{ if either } n > 0 \text{ or } n = 0 \qquad \text{and} \qquad |n| = -n \text{ if } n < 0.$$

By the way, instead of writing '$n > 0$ or $n = 0$', we can simply write $n \geq 0$. Don't worry too much about the algebraic interpretation written above at the moment. Just make sure that you know that the absolute value of a positive number is the number itself and the absolute value of a negative number is the number, but **without** the negative sign. The absolute value of zero is zero. Let's continue with our examples.

4) $|9| = 9$

5) $|-6.32| = 6.32$

6) $\left|\dfrac{12}{17}\right| = \dfrac{12}{17}$

7) $\left|-\dfrac{20}{23}\right| = \dfrac{20}{23}$

8) $\left|-11\dfrac{5}{6}\right| = 11\dfrac{5}{6}$

9) $\left|8\dfrac{1}{2}\right| = 8\dfrac{1}{2}$

10) $|2.\overline{341}| = 2.\overline{341}$

11) $|-\pi| = \pi$

12) $|4 - 16| = |-12| = 12$

13) $|4| - |16| = 4 - 16 = -12$

14) $|-2| \cdot |7| = 2 \cdot 7 = 14$

15) $|(-2)(7)| = |-14| = 14$

By definition, the absolute value of a number tells us the distance between 0 and the number on the real number line. Suppose we want to find the distance between any two real numbers on the real number line. The following formula tells us how to do this.

## The Distance Formula

If $A$ and $B$ are two points on a real number line with coordinates $a$ and $b$, respectively, then the distance, $d$, between $A$ and $B$ is:

$$d = |b - a|$$

**Examples.** Find the distance between the points whose coordinates are given.

1) 2 and 9

It doesn't matter which number you label as $a$ or $b$, since the distance between $a$ and $b$ is the same as the distance between $b$ and $a$. Let's choose $a = 2$ and $b = 9$. Then

$$d = |b - a| = |9 - 2| = |7| = 7.$$

Therefore, the distance is 7.

2) $-5$ and $-2$

Let $a = -5$ and $b = -2$. Then

$$d = |b - a| = |-2 - (-5)| = |-2 + 5| = |3| = 3.$$

Therefore, the distance is 3.

3) $\dfrac{3}{4}$ and $-\dfrac{5}{6}$

Let $a = \dfrac{3}{4}$ and $b = -\dfrac{5}{6}$. Then

$$d = |b - a| = \left| -\frac{5}{6} - \frac{3}{4} \right| = \left| -\frac{5(2)}{6(2)} - \frac{3(3)}{4(3)} \right| = \left| -\frac{10}{12} - \frac{9}{12} \right| = \left| \frac{-19}{12} \right| = \frac{19}{12}.$$

Therefore, the distance is $\dfrac{19}{12}$.

Here are some properties of absolute value. Some of these properties will come in handy later on.

## Properties of Absolute Value

Suppose that $a$ and $b$ are any two real numbers. Then

**Property 1.** $|a| \geq 0$

**Property 2.** $|a|^2 = a^2$

**Property 3.** $|a \cdot b| = |a| \cdot |b|$

**Property 4.** $|-a| = |a|$

**Property 5.** $\left| \dfrac{a}{b} \right| = \dfrac{|a|}{|b|}, b \neq 0$

**Property 6.** $|a + b| \leq |a| + |b|$

Property 6 is called the **Triangle Inequality**.

Observe that $|a^2| = \underbrace{|a \cdot a| = |a| \cdot |a|}_{\text{by Property 2}} = |a|^2$. Consequently, we have

**Property 7.** $|a^2| = a^2$

More generally,

**Property 8.** $|a^n| = a^n$ if $n$ is even and $|a^n| = |a|^n$ if $n$ is odd.

**Examples.** Simplify.

1) $|x|^2 = x^2$ by Property 2

2) $\underbrace{|4a| = |4| \cdot |a|}_{\text{by Property 3}} = 4|a|$

3) $|x^3| = \underbrace{|x^2 \cdot x| = |x^2| \cdot |x|}_{\text{by Properties 3 and 7}} = x^2|x|$

4) $\underbrace{\left| \dfrac{-3}{t} \right| = \dfrac{|-3|}{|t|}}_{\text{by Property 5}} = \dfrac{3}{|t|}$ (assuming that $t \neq 0$)

5) $\underbrace{\left|\dfrac{b^2}{7}\right| = \dfrac{\left|b^2\right|}{|7|}}_{\text{by Properties 5 and 7}} = \dfrac{b^2}{7}$

**Try These (Set 8):**

I) Evaluate.

1) $|6|$          3) $|-12|$          5) $\left|-\dfrac{9}{10}\right|$          7) $-|-17+3|$

2) $|-9|$          4) $|25|$          6) $\left|4.217\overline{3}\right|$          8) $-\left(8 + \left|5 - 3^2\right|\right)$

II) Find the distance between the given numbers on the real number line.

1) 8 and $-3$          3) $-6$ and $-13$

2) 17 and 4          4) $\dfrac{-3}{4}$ and $\dfrac{5}{3}$

III) Simplify.

1) $|y|^2$          4) $\left|\dfrac{5}{x}\right|, \ x \neq 0$

2) $|-14x|$          5) $\left|-\dfrac{y}{8}\right|$

3) $\left|3a^2 b\right|$          6) $\left|\dfrac{a^2 b^3}{-2}\right|$

# Section 1.8  Introduction to Algebra

As we have already seen, we can use letters (called **variables**) to write mathematical statements or sentences. For example, when we wrote down the distance formula for two numbers on the real number line, we actually used variables to write the formula:

$$d = |b - a|$$

In this formula, the letters $a$, $b$, and $d$ are the variables and the equality symbol is used to tell us how these variables are related to one another. When we used this formula to figure out some distance problems, we plugged the given values for $a$ and $b$ into the formula and computed $d$. In algebra, we are interested in working with formulas, expressions, and equations which contain variables. Throughout this text, you will encounter such algebraic objects and be required to know how to perform a computation involving the replacement of a variable by a specified value. As you will now see, it just boils down to using the order of operations.

**Examples.** Evaluate each expression if $x = 5$, $y = -2$, and $z = 1$.

1) $x + y + 2z$

The first thing you should do is to put parentheses around each of your variables. By doing this, you will avoid making mistakes with signs (I've seen such mistakes made numerous times before). After inserting the parentheses, you replace each variable with the given value and use the order of operations to compute the answer. Here, we obtain:

$$(x) + (y) + 2(z) = (5) + (-2) + 2(1) = 3 + 2 = 5.$$

2) $3x - 5y$

$$3(x) - 5(y) = 3(5) - 5(-2) = 15 + 10 = 25$$

3) $-4xz + 2yz - z^2 + 2$

$$
\begin{aligned}
-4(x)(z) + 2(y)(z) - (z)^2 + 2 &= -4(5)(1) + 2(-2)(1) - (1)^2 + 2 \\
&= -20 + (-4) - (1) + 2 \\
&= -20 - 4 - 1 + 2 \\
&= -23
\end{aligned}
$$

4) $\dfrac{z - 2x}{-8y + 11}$

$$\frac{(z) - 2(x)}{-8(y) + 11} = \frac{(1) - 2(5)}{-8(-2) + 11} = \frac{1 - 10}{16 + 11} = \frac{-9}{27} = -\frac{1}{3}$$

5) $x^2 + x - 2 + \dfrac{3}{x}$

$$
\begin{aligned}
(x)^2 + (x) - 2 + \frac{3}{(x)} &= (5)^2 + (5) - 2 + \frac{3}{(5)} \\
&= 25 + 5 - 2 + \frac{3}{5} \\
&= 28\frac{3}{5}
\end{aligned}
$$

6) $\left| 3y - 7x - z^2 \right|$

$$
\begin{aligned}
\left| 3(y) - 7(x) - (z)^2 \right| &= \left| 3(-2) - 7(5) - (1)^2 \right| \\
&= \left| -6 - 35 - 1 \right| \\
&= \left| -42 \right| = 42
\end{aligned}
$$

7) $(9z - 2x)(y + 2x)$

$$
\begin{aligned}
(9(z) - 2(x))((y) + 2(x)) &= (9(1) - 2(5))((-2) + 2(5)) \\
&= (9 - 10)(-2 + 10) \\
&= (-1)(8) = -8
\end{aligned}
$$

Sometimes you may be working with an algebraic expression which does not allow certain numbers to be plugged into it. For example, if we plug $x = 7$ into the expression $\dfrac{1}{x - 7}$, then we obtain

$$\frac{1}{(x) - 7} = \frac{1}{(7) - 7} = \frac{1}{0}$$

which is undefined. We must, therefore, be concerned with which numbers can be plugged into an expression that give us a well-defined answer. We call the set of values that a variable can equal the **domain**

**of the variable.** For $\dfrac{1}{x-7}$, the only 'bad' number is $x = 7$ (since this is the only number for which $x - 7 = 0$, an undefined answer). We say that the domain of $x$ is the set of all real numbers **except** 7. Let's see some examples on finding domains.

**Examples.** Find the domain of $x$ in each expression.

1) $\dfrac{2}{x-3}$ is undefined when the denominator, $x - 3$, equals 0. Well, let's find out which $x$-value does this (I'll assume that you know how to solve some basic equations).

$$
\begin{array}{rl}
x - \cancel{3} = & 0 \\
+\cancel{3} & +3 \\
\hline
x \quad\; = & 3
\end{array}
$$

So, if $x = 3$, the expression is undefined. This means that the domain of $x$ is the set of all real numbers except 3.

2) $\dfrac{-8}{x+6}$ is undefined when $x + 6 = 0$. Let's find the value of $x$.

$$
\begin{array}{rl}
x + \cancel{6} = & 0 \\
-\cancel{6} & -6 \\
\hline
x \quad\; = & -6
\end{array}
$$

This means that if $x = -6$, the expression is undefined. The domain of $x$ is, therefore, the set of all real numbers except $-6$.

3) $\dfrac{5}{9-x}$ is undefined when $9 - x = 0$. Let's find the value of $x$.

$$
\begin{array}{rl}
9 - \cancel{x} = & 0 \\
+\cancel{x} & +x \\
\hline
9 \quad\; = & x
\end{array}
$$

$x = 9$ makes the expression $\dfrac{5}{9-x}$ undefined. This means that the domain of $x$ is the set of all real numbers except 9.

**Try These (Set 9):**

I) Evaluate the following if $a = -2$, $b = 3$, and $c = -4$:

1) $2a + 3b$      3) $\dfrac{ab+c}{7a+3b}$      5) $\dfrac{1}{a} + \dfrac{1}{c}$

2) $c\,(a - 4b)$      4) $1 - b - c^2$      6) $b^2 - 4ac$

II) Find the domain of $x$ in each expression.

1) $\dfrac{2}{x-1}$      2) $\dfrac{10}{x+8}$      3) $\dfrac{-7}{-x+12}$

**Exercise 1**

In Exercises 1-12, place a check mark in the correct columns. Exercises 1 and 2 have been done for you.

| | Number | Natural Number | Integer | Rational Number | Irrational Number |
|---|---|---|---|---|---|
| 1. | 6 | ✓ | ✓ | ✓ | |
| 2. | $-\dfrac{2}{3}$ | | | ✓ | |
| 3. | $+10$ | | | | |
| 4. | $-8$ | | | | |
| 5. | $-4.18\overline{6}$ | | | | |
| 6. | $3.\overline{524}$ | | | | |
| 7. | $12.1963$ | | | | |
| 8. | $\dfrac{12}{49}$ | | | | |
| 9. | $18.131331333...$ | | | | |
| 10. | $\pi$ | | | | |
| 11. | $23.0$ | | | | |
| 12. | $5.29183$ | | | | |

In Exercises 13-42, express the fraction as either a terminating or non-terminating, repeating decimal.

13. $\dfrac{1}{4}$     14. $\dfrac{2}{5}$     15. $\dfrac{3}{2}$     16. $\dfrac{3}{4}$     17. $\dfrac{1}{8}$

18. $\dfrac{7}{8}$     19. $-\dfrac{1}{10}$     20. $-\dfrac{9}{10}$     21. $\dfrac{17}{3}$     22. $\dfrac{22}{3}$

23. $-\dfrac{1}{9}$     24. $-\dfrac{5}{9}$     25. $\dfrac{18}{5}$     26. $\dfrac{16}{5}$     27. $\dfrac{16}{99}$

28. $\dfrac{28}{99}$     29. $\dfrac{100}{999}$     30. $\dfrac{2}{999}$     31. $\dfrac{209}{990}$     32. $\dfrac{33}{990}$

33. $-\dfrac{7}{15}$     34. $-\dfrac{12}{25}$     35. $\dfrac{35}{6}$     36. $\dfrac{52}{7}$     37. $\dfrac{18}{3}$

38. $\dfrac{27}{3}$     39. $\dfrac{0}{14}$     40. $\dfrac{0}{9}$     41. $\dfrac{59}{59}$     42. $\dfrac{-33}{-33}$

In Exercises 43-66, add or subtract.

43. $5 + (+8)$     44. $12 + (+3)$     45. $(-7) + (-8)$     46. $(-13) + (-6)$

47. $(-25) + (+9)$     48. $(-19) + (+5)$     49. $(-2) + (+16)$     50. $(+15) + (-3)$

51. $31 + (-16)$     52. $22 + (-9)$     53. $-9 + 17$     54. $-30 + 8$

55. $-21 + 6$     56. $-10 + 13$     57. $-12 - 3$     58. $-4 - 17$

59. $-5 - 15$     60. $-19 - 6$     61. $7 - 15$     62. $10 - 14$

63. $16 + (-16)$     64. $21 + (-21)$     65. $-26 + 26$     66. $-19 + 19$

In Exercises 67-98, multiply or divide.

67. $(+7)(-4)$     68. $(-5)(+3)$     69. $(-8)(+6)$     70. $(+2)(-12)$

71. $(3)(-16)$        72. $(6)(-11)$        73. $(-9)(5)$        74. $(-4)(13)$

75. $(-5)(-6)$        76. $(-4)(-8)$        77. $(-3)(-2)$        78. $(-14)(-4)$

79. $(+36) \div (-9)$     80. $18 \div (-6)$        81. $(-64) \div 4$        82. $(-42) \div 7$

83. $45 \div (-5)$       84. $(+36) \div (-9)$    85. $(-35) \div (-5)$    86. $(-81) \div (-9)$

87. $(-60) \div (-10)$   88. $(-56) \div (-7)$   89. $\dfrac{-63}{+9}$        90. $\dfrac{-38}{+2}$

91. $\dfrac{-14}{+7}$        92. $\dfrac{-55}{+11}$        93. $\dfrac{-26}{2}$        94. $\dfrac{-48}{4}$

95. $\dfrac{-28}{-7}$        96. $\dfrac{-90}{-10}$        97. $\dfrac{-64}{-16}$        98. $\dfrac{-121}{-11}$

In Exercises 99–138, add or subtract.

99. $\dfrac{4}{7} + \dfrac{3}{7}$        100. $\dfrac{1}{11} + \dfrac{3}{11}$        101. $\dfrac{9}{13} - \dfrac{6}{13}$        102. $\dfrac{16}{5} - \dfrac{14}{5}$

103. $\dfrac{2}{9} + \dfrac{1}{9}$        104. $\dfrac{7}{16} + \dfrac{1}{16}$        105. $\dfrac{21}{10} - \dfrac{17}{10}$        106. $\dfrac{11}{15} - \dfrac{1}{15}$

107. $\dfrac{1}{2} + \dfrac{1}{4}$        108. $\dfrac{1}{4} + \dfrac{1}{8}$        109. $\dfrac{1}{3} + \dfrac{1}{6}$        110. $\dfrac{1}{5} + \dfrac{1}{10}$

111. $\dfrac{1}{4} - \dfrac{1}{12}$        112. $\dfrac{1}{6} - \dfrac{1}{18}$        113. $\dfrac{1}{8} - \dfrac{1}{16}$        114. $\dfrac{1}{7} - \dfrac{1}{14}$

115. $\dfrac{2}{7} + \dfrac{1}{3}$        116. $\dfrac{1}{8} + \dfrac{2}{3}$        117. $\dfrac{5}{6} + \dfrac{3}{8}$        118. $\dfrac{3}{10} + \dfrac{5}{8}$

119. $\dfrac{2}{3} - \dfrac{3}{5}$        120. $\dfrac{7}{11} - \dfrac{1}{2}$        121. $\dfrac{7}{10} - \dfrac{1}{4}$        122. $\dfrac{8}{9} - \dfrac{5}{6}$

123. $\left(-\dfrac{4}{5}\right) + \dfrac{1}{5}$        124. $\left(-\dfrac{5}{7}\right) + \dfrac{4}{7}$        125. $\dfrac{8}{13} + \left(-\dfrac{3}{13}\right)$        126. $\dfrac{4}{15} + \left(-\dfrac{2}{15}\right)$

127. $\left(-\dfrac{1}{4}\right) + \left(-\dfrac{3}{4}\right)$        128. $\left(-\dfrac{3}{8}\right) + \left(-\dfrac{5}{8}\right)$        129. $\left(-\dfrac{2}{5}\right) + \left(-\dfrac{3}{10}\right)$

130. $\left(-\dfrac{7}{20}\right) + \left(-\dfrac{1}{5}\right)$        131. $-\dfrac{1}{8} - \dfrac{1}{8}$        132. $-\dfrac{1}{6} - \dfrac{1}{6}$

133. $-\dfrac{2}{21} - \dfrac{5}{14}$        134. $-\dfrac{5}{24} - \dfrac{1}{3}$        135. $-\dfrac{1}{6} - \dfrac{1}{12}$

136. $-\dfrac{5}{12} - \dfrac{3}{16}$        137. $-\dfrac{6}{7} + \dfrac{6}{7}$        138. $-\dfrac{5}{12} + \dfrac{5}{12}$

In Exercises 139–196, multiply or divide.

139. $\left(\dfrac{2}{5}\right)\left(\dfrac{1}{3}\right)$        140. $\left(\dfrac{1}{4}\right)\left(\dfrac{3}{4}\right)$        141. $\left(\dfrac{7}{10}\right)\left(\dfrac{3}{4}\right)$        142. $\left(\dfrac{8}{9}\right)\left(\dfrac{2}{5}\right)$

143. $\left(\dfrac{4}{7}\right)\left(\dfrac{21}{8}\right)$     144. $\left(\dfrac{6}{11}\right)\left(\dfrac{22}{3}\right)$     145. $\left(\dfrac{8}{15}\right)\left(\dfrac{30}{24}\right)$     146. $\left(\dfrac{9}{14}\right)\left(\dfrac{7}{6}\right)$

147. $\left(-\dfrac{1}{6}\right)\left(\dfrac{1}{7}\right)$     148. $\left(-\dfrac{1}{2}\right)\left(\dfrac{1}{5}\right)$     149. $\left(\dfrac{2}{3}\right)\left(-\dfrac{2}{5}\right)$     150. $\left(\dfrac{6}{7}\right)\left(-\dfrac{8}{5}\right)$

151. $\left(-\dfrac{9}{10}\right)\left(\dfrac{15}{8}\right)$     152. $\left(-\dfrac{12}{13}\right)\left(\dfrac{5}{8}\right)$     153. $\left(\dfrac{10}{11}\right)\left(-\dfrac{7}{8}\right)$     154. $\left(\dfrac{1}{16}\right)\left(-\dfrac{10}{3}\right)$

155. $(15)\left(\dfrac{2}{3}\right)$     156. $(18)\left(\dfrac{5}{6}\right)$     157. $(-6)\left(\dfrac{4}{9}\right)$     158. $(-12)\left(\dfrac{7}{8}\right)$

159. $\left(-\dfrac{7}{12}\right)\left(-\dfrac{6}{7}\right)$     160. $\left(-\dfrac{11}{7}\right)\left(-\dfrac{21}{11}\right)$     161. $\left(-\dfrac{5}{9}\right)(-21)$     162. $\left(-\dfrac{9}{16}\right)(-10)$

163. $\left(-\dfrac{3}{4}\right)\left(-\dfrac{10}{21}\right)$     164. $\left(-\dfrac{12}{13}\right)\left(-\dfrac{26}{27}\right)$     165. $\dfrac{1}{3} \div \dfrac{2}{3}$     166. $\dfrac{2}{5} \div \dfrac{3}{5}$

167. $\dfrac{2}{7} \div \dfrac{4}{5}$     168. $\dfrac{7}{8} \div \dfrac{14}{3}$     169. $\dfrac{9}{10} \div \dfrac{3}{4}$     170. $\dfrac{12}{5} \div \dfrac{4}{3}$

171. $\dfrac{1}{2} \div 8$     172. $\dfrac{1}{5} \div 3$     173. $6 \div \dfrac{2}{3}$     174. $8 \div \dfrac{4}{7}$

175. $\left(-\dfrac{3}{4}\right) \div \dfrac{1}{8}$     176. $\left(-\dfrac{8}{11}\right) \div \dfrac{1}{22}$     177. $\left(-\dfrac{1}{2}\right) \div \dfrac{1}{2}$     178. $\left(-\dfrac{1}{5}\right) \div \dfrac{1}{5}$

179. $\dfrac{5}{6} \div \left(-\dfrac{1}{3}\right)$     180. $\dfrac{2}{7} \div \left(-\dfrac{8}{9}\right)$     181. $\dfrac{4}{5} \div (-5)$     182. $\dfrac{7}{10} \div (-2)$

183. $\left(-\dfrac{4}{7}\right) \div \left(-\dfrac{1}{7}\right)$     184. $\left(-\dfrac{9}{10}\right) \div \left(-\dfrac{1}{10}\right)$     185. $\left(-\dfrac{1}{6}\right) \div \left(-\dfrac{2}{9}\right)$     186. $\left(-\dfrac{3}{8}\right) \div \left(-\dfrac{1}{12}e\right)$

187. $(-2) \div \left(-\dfrac{1}{2}\right)$     188. $(-6) \div \left(-\dfrac{1}{12}\right)$     189. $\left(-\dfrac{5}{7}\right) \div (-5)$     190. $\left(-\dfrac{8}{15}\right) \div (-3)$

191. $\left(-\dfrac{1}{2}\right) \div (-1)$     192. $\left(-\dfrac{7}{8}\right) \div (-1)$     193. $1 \div \left(-\dfrac{7}{16}\right)$     194. $1 \div \left(-\dfrac{3}{8}\right)$

195. $0 \div \left(-\dfrac{3}{20}\right)$     196. $0 \div \left(-\dfrac{5}{12}\right)$

In Exercises 197–260, evaluate.

197. $5(2) + 6$     198. $8(3) + 12$     199. $9(-3) + 16$     200. $8(-5) + 23$

201. $3(-7) - 2$     202. $5(-5) - 5$     203. $6 - 5 \times 7$     204. $2 - 6 \times 3$

205. $6(2 + 8)$     206. $9(7 - 3)$     207. $(7 - 12) \times 3$     208. $(4 + 9) \times 2$

209. $(10 + 6) \times (-4)$     210. $(5 - 12) \times (-3)$     211. $(-1) + 24 \div 8$     212. $(-5) + 6 \div 6$

213. $-11 - 8 \div 4$     214. $-3 - 24 \div 3$     215. $(-11 - 9) \div 4$     216. $(-3 - 24) \div 3$

217. $7 - 12 - 3 + 4$     218. $6 + 2 - 12 - 5$     219. $12 \times 4 \div 2 \times 3$     220. $28 \div 2 \times 14 \div 7$

221. $(7-12)-(3+4)$        222. $(6+2)-(12-5)$        223. $(12\times 4)\div(2\times 3)$        224. $(28\div 2)\times(14\div 7)$

225. $5^2+4$        226. $6^2-7$        227. $(5+4)^2$        228. $(6-7)^2$

229. $7+6\times 3-5\times 2$        230. $12-18\div 3+6\times 2$        231. $(7+6)\times(3-5)\div 2$

232. $(12-18)\div 3+6\times 2$        233. $(4+2)^2(5-7)$        234. $(14-8)^2(2-3)$

235. $-10-(-5)^2\times 2$        236. $(-6)^2\div 18-9$        237. $\dfrac{1+2(4-15)}{2^2+3}$

238. $\dfrac{(6-14)^2}{2-(5-7)}$        239. $-1+5\{2-8(9-7)\}$        240. $8-3\{1+2(6\div 3)\}$

241. $12+(4+1)^2\cdot(-2)$        242. $5\cdot 9-3(2)^2$        243. $(-4)\left(\dfrac{1}{6}\right)\left(-\dfrac{9}{10}\right)$        244. $(-6)\left(-\dfrac{3}{4}\right)\left(\dfrac{1}{2}\right)$

245. $5+3\left(-\dfrac{1}{12}\right)$        246. $-6+2\left(-\dfrac{1}{4}\right)$        247. $(5+3)\left(-\dfrac{1}{12}\right)$        248. $(-6+2)\left(-\dfrac{1}{4}\right)$

249. $\dfrac{4}{5}-\dfrac{1}{30}-\dfrac{2}{3}$        250. $\dfrac{5}{24}-\left(\dfrac{1}{6}-\dfrac{3}{4}\right)$        251. $\dfrac{4}{5}-\left(\dfrac{1}{30}-\dfrac{2}{3}\right)$        252. $\left(\dfrac{5}{24}-\dfrac{1}{6}\right)-\dfrac{3}{4}$

253. $\dfrac{1}{2}+10\div\dfrac{5}{7}$        254. $\dfrac{1}{3}\times 3-\dfrac{4}{5}$        255. $\left(\dfrac{1}{2}+10\right)\div\dfrac{5}{7}$        256. $\left(\dfrac{1}{3}\times 3\right)-\dfrac{4}{5}$

257. $\dfrac{2}{5}+\dfrac{2}{5}-\dfrac{2}{5}\times\dfrac{2}{5}$        258. $\dfrac{7}{12}+\dfrac{1}{12}-\dfrac{1}{2}\times\dfrac{1}{2}$        259. $\dfrac{2}{5}+\left(\dfrac{2}{5}-\dfrac{2}{5}\right)\times\dfrac{2}{5}$        260. $\dfrac{7}{12}+\left(\dfrac{1}{12}-\dfrac{1}{2}\right)\times\dfrac{1}{2}$

In Exercises 261-276, round off and truncate to two decimals.

261. 0.273        262. 0.971        263. 6.1129        264. 8.8212

265. 14.3186        266. 19.1182        267. 123.65523        268. 67.38582

269. 1.19923        270. 28.69901        271. 0.0005        272. 0.001

273. 19.9992        274. 49.9981        275. 100.50505        276. 95.1151

In Exercises 277-294, replace the question mark (?) with the appropriate answer and state the property used.

277. $x+5=?+x$        278. $7+y=y+?$        279. $4(7+2)=4(7)+4(?)$        280. $5(x+1)=5(?)+5(1)$

281. $2\times(?\times 7)=(2\times 6)\times 7$        282. $1+(9+?)=(1+9)+5$        283. $(-4)[(2)(?)]=[(-4)(2)](-12)$

284. $(?)[(-3)(0)]=[(5)(-3)](0)$        285. $(?+5)y=6(y)+5(y)$        286. $(x-?)(8)=x(8)-3(8)$

287. $6+?=0$        288. $?+(-9)=0$        289. $(-7)(?)=1$        290. $(?)\left(\dfrac{2}{5}\right)=1$

291. $a+?=a$        292. $a(?)=1,\ a\neq 0$        293. $\left(\dfrac{7}{9}\right)(-5)=(?)\left(\dfrac{7}{9}\right)$        294. $(x)(?)=(-12)(x)$

In Exercises 295-316, fill in the space with the inequality symbol $<$ or $>$.

295. 7___16          296. 24___2          297. $\frac{1}{3}$—$\frac{1}{6}$          298. $\frac{2}{5}$—$\frac{1}{10}$

299. $-6$___13          300. 6___ $-13$          301. $-15$___ $-4$          302. $-12$___ $-31$

303. 0___ $-13$          304. $-5$___ $-2$          305. $\frac{1}{9}$___0.11          306. $\frac{2}{9}$___0.21

307. 0.333___ $\frac{1}{3}$          308. 0.622___ $\frac{62}{99}$          309. 0.17___ $\frac{17}{99}$          310. 0.434___ $\frac{43}{99}$

311. $-12.0115$___ $-12.011$          312. $-3.226$___ $-3.2262$          313. $-\frac{5}{9}$___ $-0.05$

314. $-\frac{2}{99}$___ $-0.0022$          315. $\pi$___3.1          316. $-\pi$___ $-3.1$

In Exercises 317-344, evaluate.

317. $|9|$          318. $|17|$          319. $|-7|$          320. $|-21|$

321. $|+25|$          322. $|-19|$          323. $|-30|$          324. $|+12|$

325. $\left|-\frac{5}{6}\right|$          326. $\left|+\frac{9}{13}\right|$          327. $|0.754|$          328. $|-28.1103|$

329. $|16-7|$          330. $|28-12|$          331. $|6-23|$          332. $|10-31|$

333. $|-5-5|$          334. $|-9-24|$          335. $|0-12+5|$          336. $|0+6-20|$

337. $|3|-|-4|$          338. $|-13|-|+3|$          339. $|-10|+|-18|$          340. $|+15|+|-18|$

341. $\left|-\frac{1}{2}-\frac{2}{7}\right|$          342. $\left|\frac{3}{4}+\left(-\frac{1}{5}\right)\right|$          343. $\left|-\frac{1}{2}\right|-\left|\frac{2}{7}\right|$          344. $\left|\frac{3}{4}\right|+\left|-\frac{1}{5}\right|$

In Exercises 345-356, find the distance between the given numbers on the real number line.

345. 9 and 2          346. 14 and 3          347. $-3$ and 0          348. 0 and $-12$

349. $-15$ and 17          350. 26 and $-5$          351. $-\frac{5}{6}$ and $\frac{3}{8}$          352. $\frac{7}{10}$ and $-\frac{3}{4}$

353. $-6$ and $-28$          354. $-1$ and $-30$          355. $-\frac{3}{16}$ and $-\frac{7}{6}$          356. $-\frac{8}{27}$ and $-\frac{4}{9}$

In Exercises 357-368, simplify (assume that all variables are non-zero).

357. $|4x|$          358. $|10y|$          359. $|-14a|$          360. $|-8b|$

361. $|5x^2|$          362. $|3y^2|$          363. $|-27a^2|$          364. $|-18b^2|$

365. $\left|\frac{6}{x}\right|$          366. $\left|\frac{9}{t}\right|$          367. $\left|\frac{-16}{x^2}\right|$          368. $\left|\frac{y^2}{-10}\right|$

In Exercises 369-386, find the value of the expression when $x = 4$, $y = -3$, and $z = 0$.

369. $3x - 2y + z$

370. $5z + y - 4x$

371. $2x^2 + y + 3z$

372. $-x + 3y^2 - z$

373. $3xy + 2yz - 7xz$

374. $-9xz - yx + 8yz$

375. $\dfrac{-2x + 3y}{-2y + 5z}$

376. $\dfrac{x - 7y}{z - 3x}$

377. $x^2 + 3x - 12$

378. $y^2 - 4y + 9$

379. $z^2 + z + 18$

380. $2 + 3x - 9z^2$

381. $\dfrac{1}{x} + \dfrac{1}{y}$

382. $\dfrac{1}{x + y}$

383. $|5x + 7y|$

384. $|-x + 12z|$

385. $|5x| + |7y|$

386. $|-x| + |12z|$

In Exercises 387-394, find the domain of the variable $x$.

387. $\dfrac{4}{x - 1}$

388. $\dfrac{2}{x - 3}$

389. $\dfrac{-8}{x + 7}$

390. $\dfrac{-14}{x + 9}$

391. $\dfrac{1}{5 - x}$

392. $\dfrac{10}{10 - x}$

393. $\dfrac{15}{3 + x}$

394. $\dfrac{6}{7 + x}$

395. The area, $A$, of a triangle (in square units) base is $b$ and height is $h$ is given by the formula $A = \frac{1}{2}bh$. Find the area of a triangle whose base is 8 inches and whose height is 4 inches.

396. The perimeter, $P$, of a rectangle whose length is $l$ and width is $w$ is given by the formula $P = 2l + 2w$. Find the perimeter of a rectangle whose length is 5 meters and whose width is 9 meters.

397. The volume, $V$, of a cube (in cubic units), each of whose edges measures $s$ units, is given by the formula $V = s^3$. Find the volume of a cube whose edges are 4 feet each.

398. The area, $A$, of a trapezoid (in square units) whose bases are $b_1$ and $b_2$ and height is $h$ is given by the formula $A = \dfrac{h}{2}(b_1 + b_2)$. Find the area of a trapezoid whose bases measure 1 yard and 7 yards and whose height is 6 yards.

399. The formula $C = \frac{5}{9}(F - 32)$ is used to convert degrees Fahrenheit, $F$, into degrees Celsius, $C$. Find the temperature, in Celsius, of the Fahrenheit temperature $212°F$.

400. The formula $F = \frac{9}{5}C + 32$ is used to convert degrees Celsius, $C$, into degrees Fahrenheit, $F$. Find the temperature, in Fahrenheit, of the Celsius temperature $-20°C$.

# END OF CHAPTER 1   QUIZ

1. Which of the following is an integer?

   a) $\dfrac{1}{3}$     b) $-4.91$     c) 5     d) $\pi$     e) $\dfrac{-9}{7}$

2. Which of the following is an irrational number?

   a) $-7$     b) $2.\overline{86}$     c) 0     d) $\pi$     e) $\dfrac{13}{36}$

3. Which set contains only rational numbers?

   a) $\left\{5, -\dfrac{2}{5}, \pi\right\}$     b) $\{-12, 4.232332333\cdots\}$     c) $\{\sqrt{2}, 8\}$     d) $\left\{\dfrac{1}{9}, -\dfrac{2}{11}, \dfrac{5}{0}\right\}$     e) $\left\{\dfrac{-8}{-15}, -\dfrac{3}{10}, -1\right\}$

4. $-\dfrac{2}{3} + \dfrac{4}{9} =$

   a) $\dfrac{2}{9}$     b) $-\dfrac{2}{9}$     c) $-\dfrac{10}{3}$     d) $\dfrac{-10}{9}$     e) $\dfrac{10}{9}$

5. $-\dfrac{7}{8} - \dfrac{5}{6} =$

   a) $-\dfrac{6}{7}$     b) $\dfrac{35}{48}$     c) $\dfrac{41}{24}$     d) $-\dfrac{41}{24}$     e) $-\dfrac{41}{48}$

6. $12\left(-\dfrac{4}{3}\right) =$

   a) $\dfrac{8}{3}$     b) $-16$     c) 16     d) $\dfrac{-1}{9}$     e) $-\dfrac{32}{3}$

7. $\left(-\dfrac{1}{2}\right) \div \left(-\dfrac{9}{8}\right) =$

   a) $\dfrac{4}{9}$     b) $-\dfrac{4}{9}$     c) $\dfrac{9}{16}$     d) $\dfrac{9}{4}$     e) $\dfrac{8}{11}$

8. $7 - (8 - 12) =$
   a) $-13$     b) 11     c) $-11$     d) 3     e) $-3$

9. $-4 + 2\left(3^2 - 5\right) =$
   a) $-2$     b) $-4$     c) 4     d) $-8$     e) 0

10. Which of the following demonstrates a commutative property?
    a) $2(x + y) = 2x + 2y$     b) $5 + (-5) = 0$     c) $1 + (a + 4) = (1 + a) + 4$
    d) $4(3) = 3(4)$     e) $\left(-\dfrac{1}{5}\right)(1) = -\dfrac{1}{5}$

11. Which of the following demonstrates an associative property?
    a) $7\left(\dfrac{1}{7}\right) = 1$     b) $6(x + 4) = 6x + 24$     c) $a + (b + 5) = (a + b) + 5$
    d) $9 + 0 = 9$     e) $x + y = y + x$

12. The number 21.771683, rounded off to 3 decimal places, is
 a) 21.772    b) 21.771    c) 21.7    d) 21.77    e) 21.7717

13. Which of the following is true?
 a) $1 > 7$    b) $-3 < 2$    c) $0 < -4$    d) $-19 > -2$    e) $6 < -6$

14. Which of the following is false?
 a) $6.3 > 6.03$    b) $-7 < -6.8$    c) $\frac{1}{3} = 0.33$    d) $\frac{1}{5} = 0.2$    e) $\pi < 4$

15. $|-5| + |2| =$
 a) $|-3|$    b) $-3$    c) $-7$    d) $7$    e) $3$

16. The distance between $2\frac{3}{4}$ and $-1\frac{5}{6}$ on the real number line is

 a) $4\frac{7}{12}$    b) $4\frac{5}{6}$    c) $\frac{11}{12}$    d) $-4\frac{7}{12}$    e) $3\frac{2}{3}$

17. The value of $a\left(b^2 - 3\right)$ when $a = -3$ and $b = 1$ is

 a) $-6$    b) $6$    c) $3$    d) $-4$    e) $1$

18. The value of $\dfrac{4x - 3y}{6x + y}$ when $x = 0$ and $y = -2$ is
 a) $4$    b) $\dfrac{5}{2}$    c) $3$    d) $-3$    e) $0$

19. Which of the following numbers is not in the domain of $x$ of the expression $\dfrac{x+2}{x-5}$?
 a) $2$    b) $-2$    c) $0$    d) $5$    e) $-5$

20. The area of a triangle whose base is 5 in. and whose height is 12 in. is
 a) 60 in$^2$.    b) 30 in.    c) 30 in$^2$.    d) 17 in.    e) $\dfrac{17}{2}$ in$^2$.

ANSWERS FOR QUIZ 1

| | | | | |
|---|---|---|---|---|
| 1. c | 2. d | 3. e | 4. b | 5. d |
| 6. b | 7. a | 8. b | 9. c | 10. d |
| 11. c | 12. a | 13. b | 14. c | 15. d |
| 16. a | 17. b | 18. d | 19. d | 20. c |

# Chapter 2: Integer Exponents

In this chapter, we will study integer exponents. Section 2.1 begins with the definition of an exponent which is a natural number. Numerous examples will be provided which will give us a good grasp on computing expressions containing exponents. Afterwards, we will look at a couple of properties which natural valued exponents satisfy. From these two properties, other definitions and properties will emerge. For example, we will define the zero exponent and the negative exponent (hence, exhausting all possible integers which can be exponents). Once this is established, more properties which hold for exponents that are natural numbers will be shown to hold for all integer exponents.

Section 2.2 will contain many examples pertaining to negative exponents. I will introduce the "flipping technique" which can be derived from the method involved in simplifying algebraic objects known as mixed quotients. We will study mixed quotients later on in this book, at which time I will show why the "flipping technique" really works. For now, we'll just take it for granted.

In the final section, Section 2.3, we will study scientific notation. Scientific notation appears in pretty much any field of science, among other places. I will demonstrate how to convert back and forth between the scientific notation of a number and its actual value. We will also see how to use the properties mentioned in Sections 2.1 and 2.2 to simplify expressions which are in scientific notation.

## Section 2.1  Definition and Properties of Integer Exponents

**Definition:** Suppose that $n$ is a natural number larger than 1 and $a$ is any real number. Then

$$\underbrace{a \cdot a \cdots a}_{n \text{ of these}} = a^n$$

We read the expression '$a^n$' as '$a$ raised to the $n^{th}$ power' or '$a$ to the power $n$'. We call '$a$' the *base* and '$n$' the *exponent* of the expression. By convention, we write $a^1 = a$.

Note: The expression '$a^2$' is often read as '$a$ squared'. The expression '$a^3$' is often read as '$a$ cubed'.

Exponents come in handy when we write a long multiplication problem of a number with itself. For example, instead of writing the expression $5 \times 5 \times 5 \times 5 \times 5 \times 5 \times 5$, one simply writes $5^7$. Instead of writing $x \cdot x \cdot x \cdot x \cdot x \cdot x \cdot x \cdot x \cdot x$, one simply writes $x^9$. It turns out that some properties that we know for multiplication, such as the associative and commutative properties, will allow us to come up with properties for handling computations with exponents. We will study these properties as we go along. First, let's look at some examples on doing numerical computations with exponents.

**Examples.** Evaluate.

1) $3^2 = 3 \times 3 = 9$

2) $4^3 = 4 \times 4 \times 4 = 64$

3) $\underbrace{(-7)^2 = (-7)(-7)}_{\text{Square the } -7.} = 49$

4) $\underbrace{-7^2 = -(7)(7)}_{\text{Square only the 7.}} = -49$

5) $\left(\dfrac{12}{13}\right)^1 = \dfrac{12}{13}$

6) $\left(\dfrac{1}{5}\right)^2 = \left(\dfrac{1}{5}\right)\left(\dfrac{1}{5}\right) = \dfrac{1}{25}$

7) $\left(-\dfrac{2}{3}\right)^4 = \left(-\dfrac{2}{3}\right)\left(-\dfrac{2}{3}\right)\left(-\dfrac{2}{3}\right)\left(-\dfrac{2}{3}\right) = \dfrac{16}{81}$

8) $\left(-\dfrac{2}{3}\right)^5 = \left(-\dfrac{2}{3}\right)\left(-\dfrac{2}{3}\right)\left(-\dfrac{2}{3}\right)\left(-\dfrac{2}{3}\right)\left(-\dfrac{2}{3}\right) = -\dfrac{32}{243}$

9) $(0.9)^3 = (0.9)(0.9)(0.9) = 0.729$

11) $\underbrace{(-5)^3 = (-5)(-5)(-5)}_{\text{The exponent applies to } -5.} = -125$

10) $(-3.7)^1 = -3.7$

12) $\underbrace{-5^3 = -(5)(5)(5)}_{\text{The exponent only applies to } 5.} = -125$

Notice that in Example 3, both the negative and the 7 get squared whereas, in Example 4, only the 7 gets squared and not the negative. The reason for this is because the $-7$ is in parentheses in Example 3 and not in Example 4. Examples 11 and 12 exhibit the same phenomenon. Remember the following rule:

> The exponent only applies to whatever is on the immediate left-hand side of it.

Another thing to remember is:

> $(-)^{\text{even number}} = +$   AND   $(-)^{\text{odd number}} = -$

**Try These (Set 1):** Evaluate (**without** using a calculator).

1) $7^2$

5) $\left(\dfrac{4}{3}\right)^2$

9) $-\left(\dfrac{6}{5}\right)^3$

2) $5^3$

6) $\left(-\dfrac{1}{3}\right)^4$

10) $(165)^1$

3) $(-2)^2$

7) $-\left(\dfrac{1}{3}\right)^4$

11) $(0.41)^2$

4) $-2^2$

8) $\left(-\dfrac{6}{5}\right)^3$

12) $(-0.03)^3$

Let us now discuss two properties of exponents which are natural numbers.

**Property I.**  Let $a$ be any real number and let $m$ and $n$ be any natural numbers. Then

$$\boxed{a^m \cdot a^n = a^{m+n}.}$$

Let's look at a demonstration of why this property should work. Let's multiply $a^4 \cdot a^3$. According to the property, the answer should be $a^{4+3} = a^7$. Let's see why this happens. Well, observe that $a^4 \cdot a^3$ is the same as $\underbrace{(a \cdot a \cdot a \cdot a) \cdot (a \cdot a \cdot a) = a \cdot a \cdot a \cdot a \cdot a \cdot a \cdot a}_{\text{By the associative property, we can remove the parentheses.}} = a^7$, which is what we hoped for.

Notice how the base, $a$, remains the same when using the property; only the exponents get added together. For example, $7^3 \cdot 7^5 = 7^{3+5} = 7^8$. A common mistake I see students make is that they tend to multiply the bases.

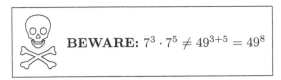

**BEWARE:** $7^3 \cdot 7^5 \neq 49^{3+5} = 49^8$

**Examples.** Multiply.

1) $x^2 \cdot x^9 = x^{2+9} = x^{11}$

2) $\left(a^5\right)\left(a^7\right) = a^{5+7} = a^{12}$

3) $\underbrace{y^3 \cdot (y^4 \cdot y) = y^3 \cdot y^4 \cdot y^1}_{\text{by the associative property}} = y^{3+4+1} = y^8$

4) $\left(x^8\right)\left(x^8\right)\left(x^8\right)\left(x^8\right) = x^{8+8+8+8} = x^{32}$

5) $\underbrace{\left(4a^3\right)\left(6a^2\right) = 4 \cdot 6 \cdot a^3 \cdot a^2}_{\text{by associative and commutative properties}} = 24a^{3+2} = 24a^5$

6) $\left(-9x^6 y^2\right)\left(5xy^7\right) = -45x^{6+1}y^{2+7} = -45x^7 y^9$

7) $\left(2x^2 y^4 z\right)\left(-4x^5 z^3\right)\left(-3x^3 y^5\right) = 24x^{2+5+3}y^{4+5}z^{1+3} = 24x^{10}y^9 z^4$

**Property II.**   Let $a$ be any non-zero real number and let $m$ and $n$ be any natural numbers. Suppose that $m > n$. Then

$$\boxed{\frac{a^m}{a^n} = a^m \div a^n = a^{m-n}.}$$

Let's look at a demonstration of why this property should work. Let's divide $\dfrac{a^7}{a^3}$ (notice that the exponent in the numerator is larger than the exponent in the denominator). According to the property, the answer should be $a^{7-3} = a^4$. Let's see why this happens. Well, observe that $\dfrac{a^7}{a^3}$ is the same as $\dfrac{\overset{1}{\cancel{a}} \cdot \overset{1}{\cancel{a}} \cdot \overset{1}{\cancel{a}} \cdot a \cdot a \cdot a \cdot a}{\underset{1}{\cancel{a}} \cdot \underset{1}{\cancel{a}} \cdot \underset{1}{\cancel{a}}} =$

$\dfrac{a \cdot a \cdot a \cdot a}{1} = \dfrac{a^4}{1} = a^4$, which is what we have hoped for.

Notice how the base, $a$, remains the same when using the property; only the exponents subtract from one another. For example, $\dfrac{8^6}{8^4} = 8^{6-4} = 8^2$. A common mistake I see students make is that they tend to cancel out the bases.

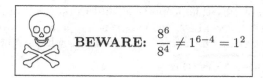

$$\textbf{BEWARE: } \frac{8^6}{8^4} \neq 1^{6-4} = 1^2$$

**Examples.**   Divide. Assume that all variables represent non-zero real numbers.

1) $\dfrac{a^{17}}{a^{12}} = a^{17-12} = a^5$

2) $\dfrac{x^8}{x} = x^{8-1} = x^7$

3) $y^{23} \div y^{14} = y^{23-14} = y^9$

4) $\dfrac{36a^{18}b^5}{18a^{17}b^2} = \dfrac{36}{18} \cdot \dfrac{a^{18}}{a^{17}} \cdot \dfrac{b^5}{b^2} = 2a^{18-17}b^{5-2} = 2a^1 b^3 = 2ab^3$

5) $\dfrac{-\overset{4}{\cancel{2}}4x^{10}y^{13}}{\underset{1}{\cancel{6}}x^7 y^2} = -4x^{10-7}y^{13-2} = -4x^3 y^{11}$

6) $\dfrac{\overset{10}{\cancel{40}}x^4 y^9 z^6}{\underset{3}{\cancel{12}}x^2 y^5} = \dfrac{10}{3}x^{4-2}y^{9-5}z^6 = \dfrac{10}{3}x^2 y^4 z^6 \text{ or } \dfrac{10x^2 y^4 z^6}{3}$

**Try These (Set 2):**

I) Multiply and Simplify.

1) $x^4 \cdot x^2$            4) $\left(-9x^{15}y^6\right)\left(-3y^8\right)$

2) $\left(y^3\right)\left(y^6\right)\left(y^8\right)$      5) $\left(2a^3b^2\right)\left(2a^4b\right)\left(-3b^6\right)$

3) $\left(5a^4\right)\left(-6a^{11}\right)$      6) $\left(3x^6\right)^3$  (remember: $a^3 = a \cdot a \cdot a$)

II) Divide. Assume that all variables represent non-zero real numbers.

1) $\dfrac{x^{16}}{x^{12}}$            4) $\dfrac{-16x^5y^9}{8y^7}$

2) $\dfrac{a^9}{a^8}$            5) $\dfrac{-15a^{10}b^{17}c^{12}}{-9a^7c^6}$

3) $\dfrac{42m^8n^{13}}{7m^2n^5}$      6) $\dfrac{9^{50}}{9^{48}}$

Recall that Property II works whenever the exponent in the numerater is greater than the exponent in the denominator. We would like to allow this property to work for **any** exponents in the numerator and denominator, provided that they are natural numbers. First, we will look at what happens when the exponents are equal. This will give us Property III. Afterwards, we will see what happens if the exponent in the denominator is larger than the exponent in the numerator. This will give us Property IV.

**Property III.** Let $a$ be any non-zero real number. Then we define

$$\boxed{a^0 = 1.}$$

Let's look at a demonstration of why this definition is valid. Let's consider the expression $\dfrac{a^n}{a^n}$, where $a$ is any non-zero real number and $n$ is any natural number. Then we know that $\dfrac{a^n}{a^n} = 1$, since everything in the numerator will cancel out everything in the denominator. However, we would like Property II to work for this situation. By Property II, we obtain $\dfrac{a^n}{a^n} = a^{n-n} = a^0$. Since $\dfrac{a^n}{a^n}$ simplifies to both 1 and $a^0$, it makes sense to define $a^0 = 1$ whenever $a$ is a non-zero real number. Notice that the expression $0^0$ is **not** a well-defined expression, since the fraction $\dfrac{0^n}{0^n}$ is **always** undefined.

**Examples.** Evaluate or simplify. Assume that all variables represent non-zero real numbers.

1) $5^0 = 1$            5) $x^0 = 1$

2) $9^0 = 1$            6) $(3a)^0 = 1$

3) $(-7)^0 = 1$        7) $3a^0 = 3(1) = 3$  (the exponent applies **only** to '$a$')

4) $-7^0 = -\underbrace{7^0}_{1} = -1$       8) $x^2y^7\left(y^8\right)^0 = x^2y^7(1) = x^2y^7$

**Try These (Set 3):** Evaluate or simplify. Each of your answers should not contain any zero exponents.

1) $6^0$         3) $(8x)^0$         5) $\left(-4a^2b\right)^0$         7) $(-5)^0$

2) $8x^0$         4) $\left(\dfrac{3}{2}\right)^0$         6) $-4a^2b^0$         8) $-5^0$

**Property IV.** Let $a$ be any non-zero real number and let $n$ be any whole number. Then we define

$$\boxed{a^{-n} = \frac{1}{a^n}.}$$

Recall that a whole number is any number from the set $\{0, 1, 2, 3, ...\}$. In Property IV, our exponent can be any such number.

Let's look at a demonstration of why this definition is valid. Consider the expression $\dfrac{a^0}{a^n}$, where $a$ is any non-zero real number and $n$ is any whole number. Then we know that $\dfrac{a^0}{a^n} = \dfrac{1}{a^n}$, since $a^0 = 1$ by Property III. However, we would like Property II to work for this situation as before. By Property II, we obtain $\dfrac{a^0}{a^n} = a^{0-n} = a^{-n}$. Since $\dfrac{a^0}{a^n}$ simplifies to both $\dfrac{1}{a^n}$ and $a^{-n}$, it makes sense to define $a^{-n} = \dfrac{1}{a^n}$ whenever $a$ is a non-zero real number and $n$ is a whole number. In fact, this property holds when $n$ is *any* integer. We will study the case when $n$ is a negative integer in the next section.

**Examples.** Evaluate or simplify. Assume that all variables represent non-zero real numbers.

1) $4^{-1} = \dfrac{1}{4^1} = \dfrac{1}{4}$         6) $(-8)^{-3} = \dfrac{1}{(-8)^3} = \dfrac{1}{-512}$ OR $-\dfrac{1}{512}$

2) $3^{-2} = \dfrac{1}{3^2} = \dfrac{1}{9}$         7) $-8^{-3} = -(8^{-3}) = -\dfrac{1}{8^3} = -\dfrac{1}{512}$

3) $5^{-3} = \dfrac{1}{5^3} = \dfrac{1}{125}$         8) $x^{-1} = \dfrac{1}{x^1} = \dfrac{1}{x}$

4) $(-7)^{-2} = \dfrac{1}{(-7)^2} = \dfrac{1}{49}$         9) $y^{-5} = \dfrac{1}{y^5}$

5) $-7^{-2} = -(7^{-2}) = -\dfrac{1}{7^2} = -\dfrac{1}{49}$         10) $a^{-13} = \dfrac{1}{a^{13}}$

Notice how the exponent applies to the number $-7$ in Example 4, but only to the number 7 in Example 5. Similarly, the exponent applies to the number $-8$ in Example 6, but only to the number 8 in Example 7. **Watch out for the parentheses!**

At this time, I would like to mention that Property I, $a^m \cdot a^n = a^{m+n}$, holds whenever $m$ and $n$ are **any** two integers. For example, observe that $a^{-4} \cdot a^6 = \dfrac{1}{a^4} \cdot \dfrac{a^6}{1} = \dfrac{a^6}{a^4} = a^{6-4} = a^2$, which is the same as $a^{-4} \cdot a^6 = a^{(-4)+6} = a^2$. If both exponents are negative, then Property I still works. For example, notice that $a^{-5} \cdot a^{-2} = \dfrac{1}{a^5} \cdot \dfrac{1}{a^2} = \dfrac{1}{a^{5+2}} = \dfrac{1}{a^7} = a^{-7}$, which is the same as $a^{-5} \cdot a^{-2} = a^{(-5)+(-2)} = a^{-7}$.

**Try These (Set 4):**  Evaluate or simplify. Each of your answers should contain positive exponents.

1) $8^{-2}$

2) $4^{-3}$

3) $6^{-1}$

4) $9^{-2}$

5) $(-2)^{-4}$

6) $-2^{-4}$

7) $x^{-6}$, $x \neq 0$

8) $y^{-4}$, $y \neq 0$

9) $(-3)^{-3}$

10) $-3^{-3}$

**Property V.**  Let $a$ be any real number and let $m$ and $n$ be integers. Then

$$\boxed{(a^m)^n = a^{mn}.}$$

Note that the only exception to this property is when $a = 0$ and either $m = 0$ or $n = 0$. In this case, we obtain $0^0$, which is undefined.

Let's look at a demonstration of why this property should work. Consider the expression $\left(a^7\right)^4$. According to the property, the answer should be $a^{(7)(4)} = a^{28}$. Let's try it **without** using the property. Well, observe that $\left(a^7\right)^4 = \underbrace{\left(a^7\right)\left(a^7\right)\left(a^7\right)\left(a^7\right)}_{\text{by Property I}} = a^{7+7+7+7} = a^{28}$, which is what we expected.

Let's take a look at another demonstration. Observe that

$$\left(a^{-3}\right)^3 = \left(\frac{1}{a^3}\right)^3 = \underbrace{\left(\frac{1}{a^3}\right)\left(\frac{1}{a^3}\right)\left(\frac{1}{a^3}\right)}_{\text{by Property I}} = \frac{1}{a^{3+3+3}} = \frac{1}{a^9} = a^{-9},$$

which is the same as $a^{(-3)(3)} = a^{-9}$. If both $m$ and $n$ are negative integers, then a demonstration of this property would require some knowledge of mixed quotients, which we will study later on. For example, $\left(a^{-2}\right)^{-6} = a^{(-2)(-6)} = a^{12}$ and $\left(a^{-1}\right)^{-1} = a^{(-1)(-1)} = a^1 = a$. At this time, we will take it for granted that it works.

**Examples.**  Evaluate or simplify. Assume that all variables represent non-zero real numbers.

1) $\left(a^3\right)^6 = a^{(3)(6)} = a^{18}$

2) $\left(x^7\right)^{-2} = x^{(7)(-2)} = x^{-14} = \dfrac{1}{x^{14}}$

3) $\left(y^{-4}\right)^{-1} = y^{(-4)(-1)} = y^4$

4) $\left(a^0\right)^5 = a^{(0)(5)} = a^0 = 1$

5) $\left(2^3\right)^2 = 2^{(3)(2)} = 2^6 = 64$

6) $\left[(-3)^2\right]^2 = (-3)^4 = 81$

**Try These (Set 5):**  Simplify. Assume that all variables represent non-zero real numbers.

1) $\left(x^3\right)^2$

2) $\left(t^5\right)^4$

3) $\left(y^{-1}\right)^{-7}$

4) $\left(a^{-2}\right)^{-2}$

5) $\left(b^0\right)^6$

6) $\left(x^4\right)^9$

**Property VI.**  Let $a$ and $b$ be any two real numbers and let $n$ be any integer. Then

$$\boxed{(ab)^n = a^n b^n.}$$

Notice that this property simply says that you can 'distribute the exponent' into the parentheses (not to be confused with the distributive property). The only exception to applying this property is when either $a = 0$ or $b = 0$ and $n = 0$. Such a situation produces $0^0$ which is undefined.

Let's look at a demonstration of why this property should work. Let's consider $(ab)^6$. According to the property, the answer should be $a^6 b^6$. Let's try it **without** using the property. Well, observe that $(ab)^6 = \underbrace{(ab)(ab)(ab)(ab)(ab)(ab) = abababababab}_{\text{by the associative property}} = a^6 b^6$ (obtained by commuting terms), which is what we expected. Let's look at another demonstration. Observe that

$$(ab)^{-3} = \underbrace{\left(\frac{1}{ab}\right)^3}_{\text{by Property IV}} = \underbrace{\left(\frac{1}{ab}\right)\left(\frac{1}{ab}\right)\left(\frac{1}{ab}\right) = \frac{1}{a^3 b^3}}_{\text{by the associative and commutative properties}} = a^{-3} b^{-3},$$

which is what the property yields. By the way, this property **doesn't** work if you are **adding** or **subtracting** in the parentheses.

 **BEWARE:** $(a+b)^n \neq a^n + b^n$ and $(a-b)^n \neq a^n - b^n$ (unless $n = 1$)

For example, $(3+2)^2 \neq 3^2 + 2^2$ and $(7-4)^2 \neq 7^2 - 4^2$.

**Examples.** Simplify.

1) $(xy)^4 = x^4 y^4$

2) $(ab)^5 = a^5 b^5$

3) $(3xy)^3 = 3^3 x^3 y^3 = 27 x^3 y^3$

4) $(-2a^5 b^7)^3 = (-2)^3 (a^5)^3 (b^7)^3 = -8a^{15} b^{21}$  (by Property V)

5) $(4x^6 y^2 z^8)^2 = 4^2 (x^6)^2 (y^2)^2 (z^8)^2 = 16 x^{12} y^4 z^{16}$  (by Property V)

6) $\left(\frac{2}{5} m^5 n\right)^3 = \left(\frac{2}{5}\right)^3 (m^5)^3 (n)^3 = \frac{8}{125} m^{15} n^3$  (by Property V)

**Try These (Set 6):** Simplify. Assume that all variables represent non-zero real numbers.

1) $(ab)^3$

2) $(5xy)^2$

3) $\left(-4x^2 y^6\right)^2$

4) $\left(3x^5 y z^3\right)^4$

5) $\left(-\frac{4}{7} a^4 b^7\right)^3$

6) $\left(2xy^5 z^2\right)^5$

**Property VII.**  Let $a$ be any real number, $b$ be any non-zero real number and $n$ any integer. Then

$$\left(\frac{a}{b}\right)^n = \frac{a^n}{b^n}.$$

Note that the only exception is when both $a = 0$ and $n \leq 0$. In this case, $0^n$ arises, which is undefined.

To demonstrate the validity of this property, let's simplify the expression $\left(\frac{a}{b}\right)^4$. Observe that $\left(\frac{a}{b}\right)^4 = \left(\frac{a}{b}\right)\left(\frac{a}{b}\right)\left(\frac{a}{b}\right)\left(\frac{a}{b}\right) = \frac{a^4}{b^4}$, which is what the property claims to give us. The property also holds if the exponent is a negative integer, which will be taken for granted at the moment.

**Examples.** Evaluate or simplify. Assume that all variables represent non-zero real numbers.

1) $\left(\dfrac{5}{8}\right)^2 = \dfrac{5^2}{8^2} = \dfrac{25}{64}$

4) $\left(\dfrac{6}{a^4}\right)^2 = \dfrac{6^2}{(a^4)^2} = \dfrac{36}{a^8}$ (by Property V)

2) $\left(-\dfrac{4}{5}\right)^3 = -\dfrac{4^3}{5^3} = -\dfrac{64}{125}$

5) $\left(\dfrac{x^3}{2y^4}\right)^5 = \dfrac{\left(x^3\right)^5}{(2y^4)^5} = \dfrac{x^{15}}{32y^{20}}$ (by Property V)

3) $\left(\dfrac{x}{y}\right)^5 = \dfrac{x^5}{y^5}$

6) $\underbrace{\left(-\dfrac{3a^7}{8b^5c^2}\right)^2 = \dfrac{3^2\left(a^7\right)^2}{8^2\left(b^5\right)^2\left(c^2\right)^2}}_{\text{by Properties VI and V}} = \dfrac{9a^{14}}{64b^{10}c^4}$

**Try These (Set 7):** Evaluate or simplify. Assume that all variables represent non-zero real numbers.

1) $\left(\dfrac{2}{7}\right)^2$   3) $\left(\dfrac{x^3}{9}\right)^2$   5) $\left(-\dfrac{x^7}{11y^2}\right)^2$

2) $\left(-\dfrac{1}{6}\right)^3$   4) $\left(\dfrac{4a^{10}}{b^3}\right)^3$   6) $\left(\dfrac{2m^0}{5n^4}\right)^3$

Let's now do some examples which use more than one property. For now, we will focus on nonnegative integer exponents only. Negative integer exponents will be studied extensively in the next section.

**Examples.** Simplify. Assume that all variables represent non-zero real numbers.

1) $\underbrace{3x^4\left(4x\right)^2 = 3x^4(16x^2)}_{\text{by Properties VI and I}} = 48x^6$

2) $\underbrace{\left(5a^2\right)^0\left(-5a^6\right) = 1\left(-5a^6\right)}_{\text{by Property III}} = -5a^6$

3) $\underbrace{\left(-2x^4y^3\right)^4\left(-3x^8y\right) = \left(16x^{16}y^{12}\right)\left(-3x^8y\right)}_{\text{by Properties VI, V and I}} = -48x^{24}y^{13}$

4) $\underbrace{\dfrac{7m^{10}}{2n^4}\left(\dfrac{2m^2}{5n^3}\right)^2 = \dfrac{7m^{10}}{\overset{1}{\cancel{2}}n^4}\left(\dfrac{\overset{2}{\cancel{4}}m^4}{25n^6}\right)}_{\text{by Properties VII, VI, V and I}} = \dfrac{14m^{14}}{25n^{10}}$

5) $\underbrace{\dfrac{4x^2\left(3x^3\right)^2}{-9x^7} = \dfrac{4x^2\left(\cancel{9}x^6\right)}{-\cancel{9}x^7} = \dfrac{4x^8}{-x^7} = -4x^1}_{\text{by Properties VI, V, II and I}} = -4x$

6) $\underbrace{\left(\dfrac{2x^8}{5y^9}\right)^2\left(-\dfrac{3x^0}{5y^3}\right) = \left(\dfrac{4x^{16}}{25y^{18}}\right)\left(-\dfrac{3}{5y^3}\right)}_{\text{by Properties VII, VI, V, III and I}} = -\dfrac{12x^{16}}{125y^{21}}$

7) $\underbrace{\left(-\dfrac{1}{4}x^3\right)^3\left(\dfrac{3}{2x^0}\right)^2 = \left(-\dfrac{1}{64}x^9\right)\left(\dfrac{3}{2}\right)^2}_{\text{by Properties VI, V and III}} = \left(-\dfrac{1}{64}x^9\right)\left(\dfrac{9}{4}\right) = -\dfrac{9}{256}x^9$

**Try These (Set 8):** Simplify. Assume that all variables represent non-zero real numbers.

1) $5a^2\,(2a)^3$

2) $(3x^5)^2\,(-7x^8)^0$

3) $(5x^2y)^2\,(-x^6y^{12})^3$

4) $\left(\dfrac{-3x^2}{-4y^6}\right)^3\left(\dfrac{5x}{3y^3}\right)^0$

5) $\dfrac{5s^3\,(3s^4t^6)^2}{(9t)^2}$

6) $\dfrac{(6a^7)\,(-4a^2)^2}{(5a^0)^3}$

To end this section, let's list all of the properties that we have learned so far. I will only summarize the properties in which the bases in each expression are non-zero. If we allow a base to equal zero, then we need to be careful with the exponents that we are using.

**Property I.** Let $a \neq 0$ be a real number and let $m$ and $n$ be any integers. Then

$$a^m \cdot a^n = a^{m+n}.$$

**Property II.** Let $a \neq 0$ be a real number and let $m$ and $n$ be any integers. Then

$$\frac{a^m}{a^n} = a^m \div a^n = a^{m-n}.$$

**Property III.** Let $a \neq 0$ be a real number. Then

$$a^0 = 1.$$

**Property IV.** Let $a \neq 0$ be a real number and let $n$ be any integer. Then

$$a^{-n} = \frac{1}{a^n}.$$

**Property V.** Let $a \neq 0$ be a real number and let $m$ and $n$ be integers. Then

$$(a^m)^n = a^{mn}.$$

**Property VI.** Let $a \neq 0$ and $b \neq 0$ be two real numbers and let $n$ be any integer. Then

$$(ab)^n = a^n b^n.$$

**Property VII.** Let $a \neq 0$ and $b \neq 0$ be two real numbers and $n$ any integer. Then

$$\left(\frac{a}{b}\right)^n = \frac{a^n}{b^n}.$$

## Exercise 2.1

In Exercises 1-43, evaluate.

1. $5^2$

2. $8^2$

3. $\left(\dfrac{3}{4}\right)^3$

4. $\left(\dfrac{9}{7}\right)^3$

5. $\left(-\dfrac{2}{11}\right)^2$

6. $(-6)^2$

7. $-6^2$

8. $\left(-\dfrac{1}{5}\right)^3$

9. $\left(-\dfrac{1}{3}\right)^5$

10. $(-4)^3$

11. $-4^3$

12. $3^4$

13. $7^0$

14. $\left(\dfrac{8}{9}\right)^0$

15. $(-10)^0$

16. $-10^0$

17. $\dfrac{5^6}{5^5}$

18. $\dfrac{2^8}{2^6}$

19. $\dfrac{(-3)^8}{(-3)^5}$

20. $\dfrac{(-2)^5}{(-2)^3}$

21. $\dfrac{4^6}{4^8}$

22. $\dfrac{6^3}{6^6}$

23. $\dfrac{(-5)^5}{(-5)^6}$

24. $\dfrac{(-7)^8}{(-7)^{10}}$

25. $6^{-1}$

26. $3^{-3}$

27. $9^{-2}$

28. $2^{-4}$

29. $5^{-3}$

30. $(-8)^{-2}$

31. $-8^{-2}$

32. $(-7)^{-3}$

33. $(-7)^{-3}$

34. $-6^{-1}$

35. $(-6)^{-2}$

36. $\left(2^3\right)^2$

37. $\left(3^2\right)^2$

38. $\left(5^2\right)^{-1}$

39. $\left(4^3\right)^{-1}$

40. $\dfrac{33^3}{11^3}$

41. $\dfrac{555^2}{111^2}$

42. $\dfrac{(-1,000)^4}{1,000^4}$

43. $\dfrac{1,000^5}{(-1,000)^5}$

In Exercises 44-111, simplify each expression using the properties discussed in this section. Assume that all variables represent nonzero numbers. Make sure that all of your answers contain **only** positive exponents.

44. $x^3 \cdot x^4$

45. $y^2 \cdot y^6$

46. $a^5 \cdot a$

47. $t \cdot t^8$

48. $\left(x^2\right)\left(x^2\right)\left(x^3\right)$

49. $\left(a^3\right)\left(a^7\right)\left(a^2\right)$

50. $\left(2x^3\right)\left(4x^7\right)$

51. $\left(-5x^2\right)\left(8x^3\right)$

52. $\left(x^3 y^{10}\right)\left(-3xy^2\right)$

53. $\left(6x^7 y\right)\left(x^3 y^2\right)$

54. $\left(7s^3 t^7\right)\left(4s^2 t\right)$

55. $\left(4a^4 b^3\right)\left(5a^2 b^5\right)$

56. $\dfrac{x^5}{x^2}$

57. $\dfrac{x^9}{x^4}$

58. $\dfrac{a^3 b^{13}}{-a^2 b^5}$

59. $\dfrac{-35s^7 t^4}{-5s^4 t}$

60. $\dfrac{12x^5 y^9}{-8x^4 y^4}$

61. $\dfrac{-24x^{15} y^{13}}{9x^{11} y^2}$

62. $(7x)^0$

63. $7x^0$

64. $8x^4y^3\left(6xy^8\right)^0$    65. $-2t^3\left(5s^6t^3\right)^0$    66. $x^{-2}$    67. $x^{-3}$

68. $-y^{-6}$    69. $-y^{-8}$    70. $a^{-1}\cdot a^{-2}$    71. $x^{-3}\cdot x^{-4}$

72. $t^5\cdot t^{-4}$    73. $t^{-6}\cdot t^{10}$    74. $\dfrac{x^3}{x^{-1}}$    75. $\dfrac{y^4}{y^{-6}}$

76. $\dfrac{x^{12}y^{-1}}{x^7y^0}$    77. $\dfrac{-15x^0y^{-1}}{-3x^5y^{-7}}$    78. $\left(x^2\right)^4$    79. $\left(x^5\right)^3$

80. $\left(y^2\right)^{-6}$    81. $\left(t^{-4}\right)^4$    82. $\left(a^0\right)^3$    83. $\left(x^0\right)^{-2}$

84. $(3y)^2$    85. $(2x)^4$    86. $\left(-9a^6b^3\right)^2$    87. $\left(-4x^2y^9\right)^3$

88. $(2x)^{-5}$    89. $(5t)^{-3}$    90. $\left(7xy^2\right)^{-1}$    91. $\left(8x^3y\right)^{-1}$

92. $\left(\dfrac{1}{4}m^7n^2\right)^2$    93. $\left(\dfrac{3}{7}a^2b^7\right)^2$    94. $\left(\dfrac{a}{b}\right)^4$    95. $\left(\dfrac{x}{y}\right)^8$

96. $\left(\dfrac{9}{x^3}\right)^2$    97. $\left(-\dfrac{5}{a^8}\right)^2$    98. $\left(\dfrac{x}{4y^2}\right)^3$    99. $\left(\dfrac{10x^4}{y^3}\right)^4$

100. $\left(-\dfrac{2x^5}{5y^8z^2}\right)^3$    101. $\left(-\dfrac{3m^7}{8n^{12}}\right)^2$    102. $2x^4(-3x)^3$    103. $-3a^4\left(4a^2\right)^2$

104. $\left(5a^6\right)^0\left(-6a^8\right)^2$    105. $\left(9x^4\right)^2\left(8x^5\right)^0$    106. $\left(-3a^5b^7\right)^2\left(2ab^2\right)^2$

107. $\left(m^3n^9\right)^3\left(-5mn^{14}\right)^3$    108. $\left(\dfrac{7x^2}{-y^4}\right)^0\cdot\left(\dfrac{7x^2}{12y^5}\right)^2$    109. $\left(\dfrac{-11a^5}{4b^2}\right)^2\cdot\dfrac{(-9a)^0}{2b^6}$

110. $\dfrac{14x^2\left(2x^5y^0\right)^2}{\left(6xy^2\right)^2}\cdot\left(\dfrac{x^{13}}{-9y^{12}}\right)^0$    111. $\dfrac{\left(-3x^0y^{12}\right)^2}{-2\left(9x^5y\right)^2}\cdot\dfrac{\left(-3x^0y^{12}\right)^0}{(-4x)^3}$

## Section 2.2  Negative Integer Exponents Revisited

In the previous section, we studied several properties for which integer exponents satisfy. We began with two natural properties (I and II) and then defined two new types of integer exponents, namely the zero exponent (III) and the negative exponent (IV). Recall that Property IV states that if $a$ is any non-zero real number and $n$ is any whole number, then

$$a^{-n}=\frac{1}{a^n}.$$

In this section, we will learn how to work with this property when negative exponents appear in a fraction and products are present in the numerator and/or denominator. The technique which we will apply will be referred to as the **flipping technique**. As mentioned in the introduction, the actual work which goes on in this technique will be overlooked, since it involves doing computations with mixed quotients and we have not yet learned about these algebraic objects. When we study mixed quotients, I will demonstrate why the flipping technique works. For now, we will use it freely.

Now, I will give a new property to add to our list of properties. It can actually be obtained from Property IV and vice-versa.

**Property VIII:** Let $a$ and $b$ be any two non-zero real numbers and let $n$ be any integer. Then

$$\left(\frac{a}{b}\right)^{-n} = \left(\frac{b}{a}\right)^{n} = \frac{b^n}{a^n}.$$

Notice that the negative exponent 'flips' (or takes the reciprocal of) the fraction $\frac{a}{b}$, giving us $\frac{b}{a}$. After flipping the fraction the negative sign disappears. Observe that Property IV can be obtained from Property VIII in the following way:

$$a^{-n} = \underbrace{\left(\frac{a}{1}\right)^{-n} = \left(\frac{1}{a}\right)^{n}}_{\text{by Property VIII}} = \frac{1^n}{a^n} = \frac{1}{a^n}, \text{ provided that } a \neq 0.$$

Establishing Property VIII from Property IV requires more work which will be left for later. Let's see some examples concerning negative integer exponents.

**Examples.** Evaluate.

1) $\left(\frac{2}{3}\right)^{-1} = \left(\frac{3}{2}\right)^{1} = \frac{3}{2}$

2) $\left(\frac{1}{7}\right)^{-2} = \left(\frac{7}{1}\right)^{2} = 7^2 = 49$

3) $\left(\frac{3}{5}\right)^{-3} \cdot \left(\frac{5}{6}\right)^{-2} = \left(\frac{5}{3}\right)^{3} \cdot \left(\frac{6}{5}\right)^{2} = \frac{5^3}{3^3} \cdot \frac{6^2}{5^2} = \frac{\overset{5}{\cancel{125}}}{\underset{3}{\cancel{27}}} \cdot \frac{\overset{4}{\cancel{36}}}{\underset{1}{\cancel{25}}} = \frac{20}{3}$

4) $\left(\frac{8}{3}\right)^{-2} + 4^{-3} = \left(\frac{3}{8}\right)^{2} + \frac{1}{4^3} = \frac{9}{64} + \frac{1}{64} = \frac{\overset{5}{\cancel{10}}}{\underset{32}{\cancel{64}}} = \frac{5}{32}$

5) $\dfrac{5^{-2}}{4^1} = \dfrac{1 \cdot 5^{-2}}{4^1} = \dfrac{1}{4^1 \cdot 5^2} = \dfrac{1}{4(25)} = \dfrac{1}{100}$

Notice that the negative exponent *flips* the $5^{-2}$ into the denominator and the $-2$ becomes 2.

6) $\dfrac{2^3}{7^{-2}} = \dfrac{2^3}{1 \cdot 7^{-2}} = \dfrac{2^3 \cdot 7^2}{1} = \dfrac{8\,(49)}{1} = \dfrac{392}{1} = 392$

Notice that the negative exponent *flips* the $7^{-2}$ into the numerator and the $-2$ becomes 2.

7) $\dfrac{6^{-1} \cdot 3^2}{5^3 \cdot 2^{-2}} = \dfrac{3^2 \cdot 2^2}{6^1 \cdot 5^3} = \dfrac{9(4)}{6(125)} = \dfrac{\overset{6}{\cancel{36}}}{\underset{1}{\cancel{6}}(125)} = \dfrac{6}{125}$

Notice that $6^{-1}$ *flips* to the denominator, whereas the $2^{-2}$ *flips* to the numerator. Consequently, both exponents become positive.

## Rules For Applying The Flipping Technique

Whenever you have a fraction whose numerator and denominator are factored, any factor in the numerator that is raised to a negative power *flips* down to the denominator and any factor in the denominator that is raised to a negative exponent *flips* up to the numerator. After the expression is *flipped*, the negative sign of the power disappears. For example, if all variables are non-zero, we have:

$$\frac{a^{-m}}{b^n} = \frac{1}{a^m b^n}, \quad \frac{a^m}{b^{-n}} = \frac{a^m b^n}{1} = a^m b^n, \quad \frac{a^{-m} b^n}{c^p} = \frac{b^n}{a^m c^p} \text{ and } \frac{a^m}{b^{-n} c^p} = \frac{a^m b^n}{c^p}.$$

8) $\dfrac{8^2 \cdot 3^{-1}}{4^2 \cdot 10^{-2}} = \dfrac{8^2 \cdot 10^2}{4^2 \cdot 3^1} = \dfrac{\overset{4}{\cancel{64}}(100)}{\underset{1}{\cancel{16}}(3)} = \dfrac{400}{3}$

9) $\dfrac{5^{-2} \cdot 2^{-1}}{5^{-3} \cdot 2^4} = \dfrac{5^3}{5^2 \cdot 2^4 \cdot 2^1} = \dfrac{\overset{1}{\cancel{5^3}}}{\underset{1}{\cancel{5^2}} \cdot 2^5} = \dfrac{5}{32}$

Note that the previous example can also be evaluated by using Property II. Observe that

$$\frac{5^{-2} \cdot 2^{-1}}{5^{-3} \cdot 2^4} = \frac{5^{-2}}{5^{-3}} \cdot \frac{2^{-1}}{2^4} = 5^{-2-(-3)} \cdot 2^{-1-4} = 5^1 \cdot 2^{-5} = \frac{5}{1} \cdot \frac{1}{2^5} = \frac{5}{32}$$

In my opinion, the flipping technique is easier.

10) $\underbrace{\dfrac{-7^2 \cdot 8^{-1}}{3^2 \cdot 4^{-2} \cdot 9^0} = -\dfrac{7^2 \cdot 8^{-1}}{3^2 \cdot 4^{-2} \cdot 9^0}}_{\text{Pull out the negative sign to avoid confusion.}} = -\dfrac{7^2 \cdot 4^2}{3^2 \cdot 8^1 \cdot 9^0} = -\dfrac{49 \cdot \overset{2}{\cancel{16}}}{9 \cdot \underset{1}{\cancel{8}} \cdot 1} = -\dfrac{98}{9}$

The same rules for 'flipping' apply when we have algebraic expressions containing negative exponents.

**Examples.** Rewrite **without** negative exponents.

1) $2(x+1)^{-1} = \underbrace{\dfrac{2(x+1)^{-1}}{1} = \dfrac{2}{(x+1)^1}}_{\text{Only } (x+1) \text{ flips.}} = \dfrac{2}{x+1}$

2) $4x^2(5x-2)^{-3} = \underbrace{\dfrac{4x^2(5x-2)^{-3}}{1} = \dfrac{4x^2}{(5x-2)^3}}_{\text{Only } (5x-2) \text{ flips.}}$

3) $\dfrac{6x^3}{(x-8)^{-1}} = \dfrac{6x^3(x-8)^1}{1} = 6x^3(x-8)$

4) $\dfrac{(y+3)^{-2}}{(7y+4)^3} = \dfrac{1}{(7y+4)^3(y+3)^2}$

5) $\dfrac{(t-1)^{-1}}{(2t+9)^{-4}} = \dfrac{(2t+9)^4}{(t-1)^1} = \dfrac{(2t+9)^4}{t-1}$

6) $\dfrac{4x^{-2}(x+2y)^2}{3^{-1}y^4(x-8y)^{-3}} = \dfrac{3 \cdot 4(x+2y)^2(x-8y)^3}{x^2y^4} = \dfrac{12(x+2y)^2(x-8y)^3}{x^2y^4}$

**Try These (Set 9):** Evaluate.

1) $\left(\dfrac{1}{3}\right)^{-2}$ 

4) $\dfrac{6^2}{5^{-1}}$ 

7) $\dfrac{3^2 \cdot 4^{-2}}{3^{-1} \cdot 4^{-1}}$

2) $\left(\dfrac{4}{9}\right)^{-3}$ 

5) $\dfrac{2^{-2}}{3^3}$ 

8) $\dfrac{9^0 \cdot 6^{-1}}{2^{-4} \cdot 4^0}$

3) $\left(\dfrac{2}{7}\right)^{-2} - \left(\dfrac{4}{5}\right)^{-1}$ 

6) $\dfrac{8^{-2}}{7^0}$ 

9) $\dfrac{(-10)^{-2} \cdot 2^3}{-3^2 \cdot 5^{-1}}$

Suppose that we are given an algebraic expression containing the zero exponent or negative exponents. We usually want to rewrite such an expression so that only positive exponents appear in the expression. We will do some examples which involve this rewriting process.

**Examples.** Rewrite each of the following as an expression with positive exponents only and simplify. Assume that all variables represent nonzero numbers.

1) $\underbrace{\left(\dfrac{2}{x}\right)^{-2} = \left(\dfrac{x}{2}\right)^2}_{\text{Property VIII}} = \dfrac{x^2}{2^2} = \dfrac{x^2}{4}$

2) $\underbrace{\left(\dfrac{x^2}{3}\right)^{-1} \cdot \left(\dfrac{x^4}{2}\right)^{-2} = \left(\dfrac{3}{x^2}\right)^1 \cdot \left(\dfrac{2}{x^4}\right)^2}_{\text{Property VIII}} = \left(\dfrac{3}{x^2}\right)\left(\dfrac{4}{x^8}\right) = \dfrac{12}{x^{10}}$

3) $\underbrace{a^5 b^{-5} = \dfrac{a^5 b^{-5}}{1}}_{\text{Create a fraction.}} = \dfrac{a^5}{b^5}$

4) $\underbrace{(a^5 b)^{-5} = \dfrac{(a^5 b)^{-5}}{1}}_{\text{Create a fraction.}} = \dfrac{1}{(a^5 b)^5} = \dfrac{1}{a^{25} b^5}$

5) $\underbrace{(6m^3 n^{-2})^2 = 36 m^6 n^{-4}}_{\text{by Properties VI and V}} = \dfrac{36 m^6 n^{-4}}{1} = \dfrac{36 m^6}{n^4}$

6) $\underbrace{(-3x^4 y^{-1})^{-3} = \dfrac{(-3x^4 y^{-1})^{-3}}{1}}_{\text{Create a fraction.}} = \underbrace{\dfrac{1}{(-3x^4 y^{-1})^3} = \dfrac{1}{-27 x^{12} y^{-3}}}_{\text{by Properties VI and V}} = \dfrac{y^3}{-27 x^{12}} \text{ or } -\dfrac{y^3}{27 x^{12}}$

7) $\underbrace{(4a^{-2} b^{-4})^3 = 64 a^{-6} b^{-12}}_{\text{by Properties VI and V}} = \dfrac{64 a^{-6} b^{-12}}{1} = \dfrac{64}{a^6 b^{12}}$

Flip $(-5x^4y^{-1}z^2)^{-1}$ and set $y^0=1$.

$$8)\ (-5x^4y^{-1}z^2)^{-1} \cdot (2x^{-1}y^0z^{-5})^2 = \overbrace{\frac{(-5x^4y^{-1}z^2)^{-1} \cdot (2x^{-1}y^0z^{-5})^2}{1}} = \frac{(2x^{-1}(1)z^{-5})^2}{(-5x^4y^{-1}z^2)^1}$$

$$= \underbrace{\frac{(2x^{-1}z^{-5})^2}{-5x^4y^{-1}z^2} = \frac{4x^{-2}z^{-10}}{-5x^4y^{-1}z^2}}_{\text{by Properties VI and V}} = \underbrace{\frac{4y^1}{-5x^2x^4z^2z^{10}}}_{\text{after flipping}} = -\frac{4y}{5x^6z^{12}}$$

$$9)\ \frac{\left(5a^3b^{-7}\right)^2}{(6a^2b^{-3})^0 \left(-5a^{-1}b^{-4}\right)^3} = \underbrace{\frac{\left(5a^3b^{-7}\right)^2}{(1)\left(-5a^{-1}b^{-4}\right)^3} = \frac{\overset{1}{\cancel{25}}a^6b^{-14}}{\underset{5}{\cancel{-125}}a^{-3}b^{-12}}}_{\text{by Properties VI and V}} = \underbrace{-\frac{a^6a^3b^{12}}{5b^{14}} = -\frac{a^9}{5b^2}}_{\frac{b^{12}}{b^{14}} = b^{12-14} = b^{-2} = \frac{1}{b^2}}$$

**Try These (Set 10):** Rewrite each of the following as an expression with positive exponents only and simplify. Assume that all variables represent nonzero numbers.

1) $\left(\dfrac{y}{9}\right)^{-2}$

2) $\left(\dfrac{7}{x^3}\right)^{-2} \cdot \left(\dfrac{x^5}{2}\right)^{-3}$

3) $8a^4b^{-3}c^0$

4) $\left(-8x^{-5}y^{-3}\right)^{-2}$

5) $(-2a^2b^3c^{-3})^0 \cdot (5a^{-6}b^4c^0)^{-3}$

6) $\dfrac{4x^3y^{-1}(3x)^2}{(10x^{-3}y)^0(8xy^{-2})^2}$

7) $\dfrac{\left(-s^{-3}t^5\right)^{-1}}{12s^2t^{-6}} \cdot \dfrac{2st^4}{(7s^2t^{-12})^0}$

8) $\left[(3x^2y^4)^{-1} \cdot \left(4x^{-1}y^0\right)^2\right]^{-2}$

**Exercise 2.2**

In Exercises 1-36, evaluate. Your answers should be simplified and without any exponents in them.

1. $\left(\dfrac{1}{2}\right)^{-1}$

2. $\left(\dfrac{1}{5}\right)^{-1}$

3. $\left(\dfrac{2}{3}\right)^{-1}$

4. $\left(\dfrac{5}{9}\right)^{-1}$

5. $\left(\dfrac{3}{7}\right)^{-2}$

6. $\left(\dfrac{8}{3}\right)^{-2}$

7. $\left(\dfrac{4}{7}\right)^{-3}$

8. $\left(\dfrac{9}{2}\right)^{-3}$

9. $\dfrac{4^2}{3^{-1}}$

10. $\dfrac{3^2}{5^{-1}}$

11. $\dfrac{2^{-3}}{4^2}$

12. $\dfrac{7^{-2}}{2^2}$

13. $\dfrac{(-9)^{-2}}{(-2)^1}$

14. $\dfrac{(-8)^{-1}}{(-7)^2}$

15. $\dfrac{5^{-2}}{3^{-4}}$

16. $\dfrac{8^{-2}}{7^{-3}}$

17. $\dfrac{(-9)^{-2}}{-4^{-3}}$

18. $\dfrac{-2^{-2}}{(-3)^{-5}}$

19. $\dfrac{7^1 \cdot 3^{-2}}{7^{-1} \cdot 3^2}$

20. $\dfrac{6^{-2} \cdot 5^{-1}}{6^{-1} \cdot 5^0}$

21. $\dfrac{9^{-3} \cdot 7^0}{9^{-2} \cdot 7^{-2}}$

22. $\dfrac{8^{-2} \cdot 5^{-1}}{8^1 \cdot 5^{-2}}$

23. $2^4 \cdot 3^0 \cdot 6^{-1}$

24. $4^2 \cdot 5^{-2} \cdot 10^0$

25. $\dfrac{5^0}{6^{-3}}$

26. $\dfrac{9^0}{3^{-5}}$

27. $\dfrac{5^{-2}}{4^0}$

28. $\dfrac{10^{-3}}{(-12)^0}$

29. $\dfrac{(-4)^{-2} \cdot 2^{-1}}{3^2 \cdot (-5)^{-1}}$

30. $\dfrac{7^{-2} \cdot 6^0}{(-6)^{-2} \cdot (-2)^{-1}}$

31. $\left(\dfrac{2}{3}\right)^{-2} + \left(\dfrac{4}{7}\right)^{-1}$

32. $\left(\dfrac{2}{3}\right)^{-3} - \left(\dfrac{8}{9}\right)^{-1}$

33. $\left(\dfrac{3}{4}\right)^{-3} - 2\left(\dfrac{9}{2}\right)^{-1}$

34. $\left(\dfrac{4}{5}\right)^{-2} + 3\left(\dfrac{2}{5}\right)^{-3}$

35. $\left(\dfrac{1}{9}\right)^{0} - \dfrac{7}{4}\left(\dfrac{3}{2}\right)^{-2}$

36. $\dfrac{7}{18}\left(\dfrac{5}{6}\right)^{-2} + \left(\dfrac{4}{7}\right)^{0}$

In Exercises 37-80, rewrite the given expression with positive exponents **only** and simplify. Assume that all variables represent nonzero numbers.

37. $\left(\dfrac{x}{9}\right)^{-1}$

38. $\left(\dfrac{y}{3}\right)^{-1}$

39. $\left(\dfrac{a}{8}\right)^{-2}$

40. $\left(\dfrac{t}{5}\right)^{-3}$

41. $\left(\dfrac{4a}{7}\right)^{-2}$

42. $\left(\dfrac{3}{4t}\right)^{-3}$

43. $\left(\dfrac{6}{5x^3}\right)^{-3}$

44. $\left(\dfrac{9}{4b^5}\right)^{-2}$

45. $\left(\dfrac{10m^2}{3n^{12}}\right)^{-2}$

46. $\left(\dfrac{11p^5}{2q^7}\right)^{-2}$

47. $5x^{-4}y^6z^0$

48. $8x^7y^0z^{-9}$

49. $\left(6a^6b^{-1}\right)^{-2}$

50. $\left(4a^{-3}b^5\right)^{-3}$

51. $\left(\dfrac{x^{-3}}{y^7}\right)^{-2}$

52. $\left(\dfrac{x^2}{y^{-9}}\right)^{-3}$

53. $\left(\dfrac{a^0}{b^{-5}}\right)^{-3}$

54. $\left(\dfrac{a^4}{b^0}\right)^{-9}$

55. $\left(\dfrac{3x^{-1}}{4x^0}\right)^{-1}$

56. $\left(\dfrac{7t^0}{12t^{-4}}\right)^{-1}$

57. $\left(\dfrac{x^2}{6}\right)^{-2} \cdot \left(\dfrac{x^4}{2}\right)^{-1}$

58. $\left(\dfrac{y^5}{5}\right)^{-1} \cdot \left(\dfrac{y^3}{3}\right)^{-3}$

59. $\left(\dfrac{12}{t^7}\right)^{-2} \cdot \left(\dfrac{t^5}{12}\right)^{-1}$

60. $\left(\dfrac{10}{m^3}\right)^{-3} \cdot \left(\dfrac{m^2}{100}\right)^{-1}$

61. $\dfrac{\left(x^3y^5\right)^{-1}}{2} \cdot \dfrac{x^4y^9}{3}$

62. $\dfrac{a^4b^7}{8} \cdot \dfrac{\left(ab^5\right)^{-1}}{4}$

63. $\dfrac{\left(s^6t^{-1}\right)^{-1}}{s^3t^4}$

64. $\dfrac{\left(m^3n^{-7}\right)^{-1}}{m^2n^{10}}$

65. $\dfrac{x^6y^{-2}}{\left(x^{-3}y^5\right)^{-1}}$

66. $\dfrac{x^9y^{-8}}{\left(x^{-2}y^{10}\right)^{-1}}$

67. $\dfrac{x^{-7}y^3}{\left(x^2y^{-4}\right)^{-1}}$

68. $\dfrac{x^{-8}y^5}{\left(x^7y^{-3}\right)^{-1}}$

69. $5x^6y^{-4}(2xy^2)^2$

70. $-3xy^{-2}(4x^4y)^2$

71. $(8x^4y^{-4})^0(-7x^2y^{-6})^2$

72. $(14a^{-3}b^4)^0(9a^{-8}b^3)^2$

73. $(12a^5b^{-2}c)^0(-2a^{-1}b^0c^2)^{-3}$

74. $(x^0y^{-4}z^2)^{-3}(-8x^{-6}y^{-2}z^3)^0$

75. $\dfrac{\left(9x^{-13}y\right)\left(2x^5\right)^2}{\left(x^3y^5\right)^0\left(2x^2y\right)}$

76. $\dfrac{\left(5x^8y^{-1}\right)^2\left(3x^0y\right)}{\left(xy^2\right)\left(-4x^6y^4\right)^0}$

77. $\dfrac{\left(s^4t^{-2}\right)^{-2}}{2s^5t^{-1}} \cdot \dfrac{4t^3}{\left(8s^3t^{-10}\right)^0}$

78. $\dfrac{9x^5}{\left(3x^2\right)^3\left(y^{-1}\right)^2} \cdot \dfrac{\left(4x^5y^{-9}\right)^0}{x^{-6}y^{-7}}$

79. $\left[\left(25x^3y^{-2}\right)^{-1}\left(5x^0y^{-5}\right)^3\right]^{-2}$

80. $\left[\left(-4a^7b^{-1}\right)^{-3} \cdot \left(\dfrac{a^{-2}b^0}{8}\right)^{-1}\right]^2$

# Section 2.3  Scientific Notation

When working with extremely large and extremely small positive terminating decimals like 7,120,301,000 and 0.00000061, it is often convenient to express such a number as a product of two factors, one factor being a real number which lies between 1 and 10 (this factor may equal 1, but never equals 10) and the other factor of the form $10^p$, where $p$ is some integer. In fact, *any* positive terminating decimal can be expressed in the form $m \times 10^p$, where $m$ lies between 1 and 10 and $p$ is some integer. When we express a positive terminating decimal in such a form, we say that it is written in **scientific notation**. We will begin this section by practicing converting back and forth between positive terminating decimals and their scientific notation. Afterwards, we will apply the properties of exponents to do computations with numbers written in scientific notation.

## I)  Converting A Positive Terminating Decimal To Scientific Notation

Suppose that $n$ is a positive terminating decimal. I will describe the method which enables us to convert $n$ into scientific notation. The procedure is divided into 4 cases.

**Case 1.** If $n < 1$, then you move the decimal point of your number to the **right** until it is to the right of the first **nonzero** digit. If this first nonzero digit, together with all other digits to the right of the moved decimal, is called $m$ and if you moved your decimal point $p$ places to the right, then $n = m \times 10^{-p}$.

**Examples.** Write in scientific notation.

1) $0.5 = 5 \times 10^{-1}$  (Move the decimal point 1 place to the right.)
2) $0.324 = 3.24 \times 10^{-1}$  (Move the decimal point 1 place to the right.)
3) $0.000411 = 4.11 \times 10^{-4}$  (Move the decimal point 4 places to the right.)
4) $0.000000000822215 = 8.22215 \times 10^{-10}$  (Move the decimal point 10 places to the right.)
5) $0.010101 = 1.0101 \times 10^{-2}$  (Move the decimal point 2 places to the right.)
6) $0.0038921 = 3.8921 \times 10^{-3}$  (Move the decimal point 3 places to the right.)

**Case 2.** If the number, $n$, is between 1 and 10, then we can always write it as $n = n \times 10^0$.

**Examples.** Write in scientific notation.

1) $5 = 5 \times 10^0$
2) $3.427 = 3.427 \times 10^0$
3) $9.012 = 9.012 \times 10^0$
4) $8.81562 = 8.81562 \times 10^0$

**Case 3.** If $n = 10$, then $10 = 1.0 \times 10^1$ is in scientific notation. We can also write $10 = 1 \times 10^1$.

**Case 4.** If $n > 10$, then you move the decimal point of your number to the **left** until it is to the right of the first digit. If this first digit, together with all other digits to the right of the moved decimal, is called $m$ and if you moved your decimal point $p$ places to the left, then $n = m \times 10^p$.

**Examples.** Write in scientific notation.

1) $234.781 = 2.34781 \times 10^2$  (Move the decimal point 2 places to the left.)
2) $17 = 17.0 = 1.7 \times 10^1$  (Move the decimal point 1 place to the left.)
3) $3,053,221.0955 = 3.0532210955 \times 10^6$  (Move the decimal point 6 places to the left.)

4) $10.80032 = 1.080032 \times 10^1$ (Move the decimal point 1 place to the left.)

5) $3,000,000,000,000 = 3.000000000000 \times 10^{12}$ or simply $3 \times 10^{12}$ (Move the decimal point 12 places to the left.)

6) $571,001,123.16652 = 5.7100112316652 \times 10^8$ (Move the decimal point 8 places to the left.)


**II) Converting From Scientific Notation To A Positive Terminating Decimal**

We will now discuss the method for converting a number from scientific notation to a positive terminating decimal.

**Case 1.** Suppose the given number is of the form $m \times 10^p$, where $p$ is a positive integer. To begin with, you locate the decimal point in the number $m$. Starting from the decimal point, count $p$ digits to the **right**, adding in additional zeros if necessary. After counting $p$ digits to the right and placing the decimal point in the end position, you end up with your answer.


**Examples.** Write each number as a terminating decimal.

1) $8.4 \times 10^3 = 8.400 \times 10^3 = 8,400.0 = 8,400$ (Move the decimal point 3 places to the right.)

2) $6 \times 10^2 = 6.00 \times 10^2 = 600.0 = 600$ (Move the decimal point 2 places to the right.)

3) $9.513 \times 10^5 = 9.51300 \times 10^5 = 951,300$ (Move the decimal point 5 places to the right.)

4) $1.014 \times 10^7 = 1.0140000 \times 10^7 = 10,140,000$ (Move the decimal point 7 places to the right.)

5) $5.0001 \times 10^1 = 50.0001$ (Move the decimal point 1 place to the right.)

6) $3.027718 \times 10^4 = 30,277.18$ (Move the decimal point 4 places to the right.)


**Case 2.** Suppose the given number is of the form $m \times 10^{-p}$, where $p$ is a positive integer. To begin with, you locate the decimal point in the number $m$. Starting from the decimal point, count $p$ digits to the **left**, adding in additional zeros if necessary. After counting $p$ digits to the left and placing the decimal point in the end position, you end up with your answer.


**Examples.** Write each number as a terminating decimal.

1) $3.257 \times 10^{-2} = 0.03257$ (Move the decimal point 2 places to the left.)

2) $5 \times 10^{-4} = 5.0 \times 10^{-4} = 0.0005$ (Move the decimal point 4 places to the left.)

3) $8.0917 \times 10^{-1} = 0.80917$ (Move the decimal point 1 place to the left.)

4) $6.4713 \times 10^{-3} = 0.0064713$ (Move the decimal point 3 places to the left.)

5) $9.7 \times 10^{-4} = 0.00097$ (Move the decimal point 4 places to the left.)

6) $1 \times 10^{-7} = 1.0 \times 10^{-7} = 0.0000001$ (Move the decimal point 7 places to the left.)


**Try These (Set 11):**

I) Convert into scientific notation.

1) $4,103$      4) $12,890.028$

2) $509.334$      5) $0.06992103$

3) $0.200078$      6) $1$

II) Convert to a terminating decimal.

1) $2.4 \times 10^2$      4) $6.43 \times 10^{-3}$

2) $9.0034 \times 10^4$      5) $7.005 \times 10^{-1}$

3) $1.87 \times 10^1$      6) $1 \times 10^{-8}$

Now that we have an understanding of how scientific notation works, let's see how our properties of exponents allow us to easily do computations when our expressions are in this notation.

**Examples.** Evaluate the following. Express the answer in scientific notation.

1) $\underbrace{\left(1.5 \times 10^2\right)\left(4 \times 10^2\right) = 6 \times 10^4}_{\text{by Property I}}$

2) $\underbrace{\left(7 \times 10^{-3}\right)\left(9 \times 10^{-1}\right) = 63 \times 10^{-4}}_{\text{by Property I}} = \underbrace{\left(6.3 \times 10^1\right) \times 10^{-4} = 6.3 \times 10^{-3}}_{\text{by the associative property and Property I}}$

3) $\dfrac{2.5 \times 10^{-1}}{2.5 \times 10^6} = \dfrac{2.5}{2.5} \times \dfrac{10^{-1}}{10^6} = 1 \times \underbrace{\dfrac{10^{-1}}{10^6} = 1 \times 10^{-1-6}}_{\text{by Property II}} = 1 \times 10^{-7}$

4) $\dfrac{\overset{2}{\cancel{8}} \times 10^9}{\underset{1}{\cancel{4}} \times 10^{-3}} = \dfrac{2}{1} \times \underbrace{\dfrac{10^9}{10^{-3}} = 2 \times 10^{9-(-3)}}_{\text{by Property II}} = 2 \times 10^{12}$

5) $\underbrace{\left(4 \times 10^6\right)^2 = 16 \times 10^{12}}_{\text{by Properties VI and V}} = \underbrace{\left(1.6 \times 10^1\right) \times 10^{12} = 1.6 \times 10^{13}}_{\text{by the associative property and Property I}}$

6) $\underbrace{\left(5 \times 10^{-8}\right)^2 = 25 \times 10^{-16}}_{\text{by Properties VI and V}} = \underbrace{\left(2.5 \times 10^1\right) \times 10^{-16} = 2.5 \times 10^{-15}}_{\text{by the associative property and Property I}}$

7) $\underbrace{\dfrac{\left(3 \times 10^3\right)\left(2 \times 10^{-5}\right)^2}{6 \times 10^4} = \dfrac{\left(3 \times 10^3\right)\left(4 \times 10^{-10}\right)}{6 \times 10^4} = \dfrac{12 \times 10^{-7}}{6 \times 10^4}}_{\text{by Properties VI, V and I}} = \dfrac{12}{6} \times \dfrac{10^{-7}}{10^4} = 2 \times 10^{-7-4} = 2 \times 10^{-11}$

**Try These (Set 12):** Evaluate the following. Express the answer in scientific notation.

1) $\left(1.2 \times 10^5\right)\left(5 \times 10^3\right)$

2) $\dfrac{0.8 \times 10^2}{3.2 \times 10^{-5}}$

3) $\left(9 \times 10^4\right)^3$

4) $\left(1 \times 10^{-12}\right)\left(1 \times 10^{-15}\right)$

5) $\left(7 \times 10^2\right)\left(3 \times 10^{-1}\right)^2$

6) $\dfrac{\left(1 \times 10^{-3}\right)\left(5 \times 10^{-2}\right)^{-1}}{2 \times 10^4}$

**Exercise 2.3**

In Exercises 1-24, write each number in scientific notation.

| | | | |
|---|---|---|---|
| 1. 0.3 | 2. 0.5 | 3. 0.00734 | 4. 0.0007229 |
| 5. 0.0001000101 | 6. 0.0000258 | 7. 8 | 8. 2 |
| 9. 4.18 | 10. 7.612 | 11. 3.14 | 12. 2.71828 |

13. 50

14. 23

15. 94.16

16. 27.04

17. 452.935

18. 202.84

19. 1, 726

20. 4, 101

21. 77, 829.003

22. 52, 009.33

23. 20, 437, 441.86

24. 599, 103, 612.0001

In Exercises 25-50, write each number as a terminating decimal.

25. $2 \times 10^1$

26. $4 \times 10^1$

27. $9.1 \times 10^2$

28. $4.2 \times 10^2$

29. $7.56 \times 10^1$

30. $3.71 \times 10^1$

31. $6.914 \times 10^4$

32. $1.1053 \times 10^3$

33. $5.62093 \times 10^4$

34. $8.145024 \times 10^4$

35. $4.0 \times 10^5$

36. $1.0 \times 10^7$

37. $3 \times 10^8$

38. $2.00 \times 10^{12}$

39. $2.61694 \times 10^8$

40. $9.730163 \times 10^9$

41. $7.42902 \times 10^1$

42. $6.0195 \times 10^1$

43. $5 \times 10^{-1}$

44. $8 \times 10^{-1}$

45. $1.903 \times 10^{-2}$

46. $7.3615 \times 10^{-3}$

47. $3.55562 \times 10^{-3}$

48. $4.112 \times 10^{-4}$

49. $1 \times 10^{-5}$

50. $1 \times 10^{-4}$

In Exercises 51-90, evaluate. Express the answer in scientific notation.

51. $\left(2 \times 10^1\right)\left(3 \times 10^2\right)$

52. $\left(4 \times 10^2\right)\left(2 \times 10^2\right)$

53. $\left(2.5 \times 10^4\right)\left(5 \times 10^3\right)$

54. $\left(3 \times 10^3\right)\left(4.1 \times 10^5\right)$

55. $\left(1 \times 10^{-5}\right)\left(2 \times 10^{-1}\right)$

56. $\left(3 \times 10^{-6}\right)\left(1 \times 10^{-2}\right)$

57. $\left(9 \times 10^{-5}\right)\left(8 \times 10^6\right)$

58. $\left(6 \times 10^{-2}\right)\left(3 \times 10^5\right)$

59. $\left(7 \times 10^{-6}\right)\left(9 \times 10^2\right)$

60. $\left(8 \times 10^7\right)\left(8 \times 10^{-3}\right)$

61. $\dfrac{4 \times 10^5}{2 \times 10^3}$

62. $\dfrac{9 \times 10^{13}}{3 \times 10^7}$

63. $\dfrac{120 \times 10^9}{2 \times 10^4}$

64. $\dfrac{450 \times 10^{12}}{50 \times 10^2}$

65. $\dfrac{65 \times 10^{-4}}{5 \times 10^3}$

66. $\dfrac{121 \times 10^{-8}}{11 \times 10^2}$

67. $\dfrac{144 \times 10^{-2}}{6 \times 10^{-7}}$

68. $\dfrac{240 \times 10^{-8}}{1 \times 10^{-13}}$

69. $\left(3 \times 10^2\right)^2$

70. $\left(2 \times 10^5\right)^2$

71. $\left(6 \times 10^5\right)^3$

72. $\left(5 \times 10^4\right)^3$

73. $\left(8 \times 10^{-4}\right)^2$

74. $\left(7 \times 10^{-3}\right)^2$

75. $\left(2 \times 10^{-2}\right)^{-2}$

76. $\left(2 \times 10^{-5}\right)^{-2}$

77. $\left(3 \times 10^5\right)\left(2 \times 10^4\right)^2$

78. $\left(4 \times 10^2\right)\left(3 \times 10^4\right)^3$

79. $\left(2 \times 10^5\right)^3\left(3 \times 10^{-6}\right)^2$

80. $\left(4 \times 10^{-11}\right)^2\left(2 \times 10^{-4}\right)^3$

81. $\dfrac{\left(4 \times 10^2\right)\left(5 \times 10^{-1}\right)^{-1}}{2 \times 10^0}$

82. $\dfrac{\left(6 \times 10^3\right)^{-1}\left(2 \times 10^{-5}\right)}{4 \times 10^0}$

83. $\dfrac{\left(3 \times 10^5\right)^2\left(6 \times 10^3\right)^1}{9 \times 10^7}$

84. $\dfrac{\left(5 \times 10^7\right)^1\left(4 \times 10^6\right)^2}{8 \times 10^9}$

85. $\dfrac{\left(2 \times 10^5\right)^{-3}}{\left(8 \times 10^7\right)^{-2}}$

86. $\dfrac{\left(2 \times 10^2\right)^{-3}}{\left(4 \times 10^4\right)^{-2}}$

87. $\dfrac{\left(1 \times 10^8\right)^{-2}}{1 \times 10^{-1}}$

88. $\dfrac{\left(1 \times 10^4\right)^{-2}}{1 \times 10^{-2}}$

89. $\dfrac{9 \times 10^3}{\left(3 \times 10^{-4}\right)^{-1}}$

90. $\dfrac{8 \times 10^4}{\left(7 \times 10^{-3}\right)^{-1}}$

## END OF CHAPTER 2 QUIZ

1. $(-5)^2 =$
   a) 25    b) $-25$    c) 10    d) $-10$    e) $-52$

2. $4^3 =$
   a) 12    b) 81    c) 64    d) 43    e) 7

3. $\left(-\dfrac{1}{2}\right)^3 - \left(\dfrac{1}{2}\right)^3 =$
   a) 0    b) $\dfrac{1}{4}$    c) $-\dfrac{3}{8}$    d) $-\dfrac{1}{4}$    e) $-\dfrac{1}{8}$

4. $x^3 \cdot x^4 =$
   a) $x^{12}$    b) $2x^7$    c) $x^7$    d) $2x^{12}$    e) $x^{14}$

5. $\left(4^3\right)\left(4^7\right) =$
   a) $4^{10}$    b) $16^{10}$    c) $4^{21}$    d) $16^{21}$    e) 336

6. $\dfrac{y^{19}}{y^{14}} =$
   a) $y^{33}$    b) $y^5$    c) 1    d) 0    e) 5

7. $\left(x^{12}\right)^4 =$
   a) $x^{48}$    b) $x^{16}$    c) $x^3$    d) $4x^{12}$    e) $x^{96}$

8. $3a^7b^{-6} =$
   a) $\dfrac{1}{3a^7b^6}$    b) $\dfrac{3}{a^7b^6}$    c) $\dfrac{1}{(3a^7b)^6}$    d) $\dfrac{b^6}{3a^7}$    e) $\dfrac{3a^7}{b^6}$

9. $x^6\left(x^2y^3\right)^{-4} =$
   a) $x^2y^{12}$    b) $\dfrac{x^2}{y^2}$    c) $\dfrac{y^2}{x^2}$    d) $\dfrac{1}{x^2y^{12}}$    e) $\dfrac{1}{y^{12}}$

10. $\dfrac{a^{-2}b^3}{a^{-9}b^8} =$
    a) $a^7b^5$    b) $\dfrac{a^7}{b^5}$    c) $\dfrac{a^{11}}{b^5}$    d) $\dfrac{1}{a^7b^5}$    e) $\dfrac{1}{a^{11}b^5}$

11. $\left(\dfrac{7}{4x^5}\right)^2 =$
    a) $\dfrac{49}{16x^7}$    b) $\dfrac{49}{8x^{10}}$    c) $\dfrac{49}{16x^{10}}$    d) $\dfrac{49}{4x^5}$    e) $\dfrac{7}{4x^{10}}$

12. $\left(\dfrac{8}{9}\right)^{-2} \cdot \left(\dfrac{4}{3}\right)^{3} =$

   a) $3$   b) $\dfrac{4,096}{2,187}$   c) $\dfrac{1}{3}$   d) $\dfrac{3}{2}$   e) $-3$

13. $\left(m^3 n^{-2}\right)^{-3} \left(m^{-1} n^3\right)^{0} =$

   a) $1$   b) $\dfrac{1}{n^5}$   c) $\dfrac{m^9}{n^6}$   d) $\dfrac{n^6}{m^9}$   e) $\dfrac{n^9}{m^{10}}$

14. $\left(\dfrac{4a}{3b^2}\right)^{3} \cdot \dfrac{3b}{(4a)^3} =$

   a) $\dfrac{9}{b^5}$   b) $\dfrac{64a^3}{9b^5}$   c) $9b^5$   d) $\dfrac{27}{9b^5}$   e) $\dfrac{1}{9b^5}$

15. $\dfrac{5^{-2} \cdot x^3}{4^2 \cdot x^{-9}} =$

   a) $\dfrac{1}{400x^2}$   b) $\dfrac{x^{12}}{400}$   c) $\dfrac{400}{x^{12}}$   d) $\dfrac{16x^2}{25}$   e) $\dfrac{-25x^{12}}{16}$

16. $\dfrac{u^{-4}v^{-3}w^0}{u^0 v^8 w^{-9}} =$

   a) $\dfrac{u^4 v^{11}}{w^9}$   b) $\dfrac{v^{11} w^9}{u^4}$   c) $\dfrac{u^4 w^9}{v^{11}}$   d) $\dfrac{w^9}{u^4 v^{11}}$   e) $\dfrac{1}{u^4 v^{11} w^9}$

17. $\left(-6x^{-2} y^7 z^0\right)^{-2} =$

   a) $-\dfrac{1}{36x^4 y^{14}}$   b) $\dfrac{y^{14}}{36x^4}$   c) $\dfrac{x^4}{36y^{14}}$   d) $\dfrac{x^4 z}{36y^{14}}$   e) $\dfrac{-36x^4}{y^{14}}$

18. $\left(3 \times 10^8\right) \times \left(2 \times 10^{-5}\right) =$
   a) $6 \times 10^{13}$   b) $60 \times 10^3$   c) $6 \times 100^3$   d) $6 \times 100^{13}$   e) $6 \times 10^3$

19. $7,314.118 =$
   a) $7,314 \times 10^3$   b) $7.314118 \times 10^3$   c) $7,314,118 \times 10^3$
   d) $7.314118 \times 10^4$   e) $7.314118 \times 10^{-3}$

20. $\dfrac{2 \times 10^{-9}}{4 \times 10^{-2}} =$
   a) $0.5 \times 10^{-8}$   b) $50 \times 10^{-8}$   c) $5 \times 10^{-8}$   d) $5 \times 10^{-7}$   e) $5 \times 10^{-10}$

ANSWERS FOR QUIZ 2   1. a   2. c   3. d   4. c   5. a
                     6. b   7. a   8. e   9. d   10. b
                     11. c   12. a   13. d   14. e   15. b
                     16. d   17. c   18. e   19. b   20. c

# Chapter 3: Polynomials

This chapter is devoted to the study of algebraic objects known as **polynomials**. In Section 3.1, we will develop a vocabulary list of new words and phrases which are often used when discussing polynomials. To help us adapt to this new algebraic language, many examples are provided. Sections 3.2, 3.3 and 3.4 discuss how to do algebraic manipulations with polynomials. These operations include addition, subtraction, multiplication, and division. In Section 3.5, we will learn how to factor a polynomial. As we learn more algebra, we will see that many algebraic expressions, such as rational expressions and radical expressions, are constructed from polynomials.

## Section 3.1  Definitions and Examples of Polynomials

We begin this section with some definitions relating to the 'building blocks' of polynomials, namely monomials.

**Definition 1:** A **monomial** is either a real number (called a **constant monomial**) or a product of a real number a variable (or variables).

Any real number is a monomial (a constant). For example, the numbers $4$, $-9$, $3.3351$, $0$, $-\frac{6}{23}$, and $\pi$ are all constant monomials. The expressions

$$4x, \ -3x^5, \ 7a^2b^4, \ \frac{9}{10}y^2, \ 12.7128ab^2, \ \text{and} \ \pi s^4 t^3$$

are all monomials since each is a product of a real number with variables.

Monomials are named according to the number of variables they contain. For example, the monomial $4x$ is called a **monomial in 1 variable,** $x$, and the monomial $7a^2b^4$ is called a **monomial in 2 variables,** $a$ and $b$. Notice that the expressions $\frac{5x^3}{7}$ and $\frac{y^6}{8}$ are also monomials because we can rewrite them as $\frac{5x^3}{7} = \frac{5}{7}x^3$ and $\frac{y^6}{8} = \frac{1}{8}y^6$. However, the expressions $\frac{1}{x^2}$ and $-\frac{6}{t^4}$ are NOT monomials because they cannot be expressed as a product of a number with variables. Notice that we can rewrite $\frac{1}{x^2} = x^{-2}$ and $-\frac{6}{t^4} = -6t^{-4}$. Both of the exponents of the variables are negative integers, which cannot occur in a monomial. In fact, the exponents of the variables in a monomial **must** be positive integers. Therefore, $9a^8b^3c^2$ is a monomial, whereas $2x^5y^{-1}z^2$ is not a monomial.

**Definition 2:** The number part of a monomial is called the **coefficient** of the monomial. The variable part of a monomial will be referred to simply as the **variable part.**

**Examples.** Find the coefficient and variable part of each monomial.

1) $3x$ has coefficient 3 and variable part $x$.

2) $-10a^4$ has coefficient $-10$ and variable part $a^4$.

3) $\frac{4}{5}x^2y^6$ has coefficient $\frac{4}{5}$ and variable part $x^2y^6$.

4) $4$ has coefficient 4 and no variable part (or **empty** variable part).

5) $y^5$ has coefficient 1 (since $y^5 = 1y^5$) and variable part $y^5$.

6) $-x^3y^2$ has coefficient $-1$ (since $-x^3y^2 = -1x^3y^2$) and variable part $x^3y^2$.

7) $\dfrac{7a^4b}{15}$ has coefficient $\dfrac{7}{15}$ and variable part $a^4b$.

**Definition 3:** The sum of the exponents of the variables of a monomial is called the **degree** of the monomial.

Any constant monomial (except 0) has degree 0. The monomial 0 has no degree (or undefined degree).

**Examples.** Find the degree of each monomial.

1) $3x$ has degree 1, since $3x = 3x^1$.

4) $\dfrac{7a^4b}{15} = \dfrac{7}{15}a^4b^1$ has degree 5 ($= 4 + 1$).

2) $-10a^4$ has degree 4.

5) $x^3yz^7 = x^3y^1z^7$ has degree 11 ($= 3 + 1 + 7$).

3) $\dfrac{4}{5}x^2y^6$ has degree 8 ($= 2 + 6$).

6) 8 has degree 0 since it is a constant monomial.

You should notice from the examples above that the degree just tells us how many variables are multiplying together. For example, notice that $\dfrac{4}{5}x^2y^6 = \dfrac{4}{5} \cdot \underbrace{x \cdot x \cdot y \cdot y \cdot y \cdot y \cdot y \cdot y}_{\text{8 variables altogether.}}$. Observe that a constant monomial (other than 0) doesn't contain any variables, so its degree is 0. Moreover, the degree of a monomial in 1 variable is simply the exponent. Hence, the degree of $5x^4$ is 4 and the degree of $9.142a^3$ is 3.

We are ready to define a polynomial and other mathematical words and phrases related to it. For now, we will focus **only** on polynomials in 1 variable. We will look at some definitions for polynomials in several variables afterwards.

**Definition 4: A polynomial in 1 variable** is a sum of monomials, each containing the same variable. We call each monomial in a polynomial a **term** of the polynomial.

Note that the definition also allows differences to appear in a polynomial, since every difference can be expressed as a sum. Put another way, we have

$$a - b = a + (-b)$$

for any monomials $a$ and $b$.

Some examples of polynomials in 1 variable are:

$$2x + 1, \quad 5x^2 - 3x + 1, \quad -t^5 - 7 + 4t^2 + t^3, \quad \dfrac{-3}{4}y^3 + 7.182y^2 - 4.93, \quad \text{and} \quad x^4 + 3x.$$

Notice that every monomial can be thought of as a polynomial. For example, we can write the monomial $2x$ as $2x + 0$, making it a polynomial with two terms. Furthermore, in order for an algebraic expression to be a polynomial, each of its 'building blocks' **must** be a monomial. Hence, the expression $5x^2 - x + \dfrac{2}{x^3}$ is not a polynomial, since $\dfrac{2}{x^3}$ is not a monomial. However, the expression $5x^2 - x + \dfrac{x^3}{2}$ is a polynomial, since $\dfrac{x^3}{2} = \dfrac{1}{2}x^3$ is a monomial.

Sometimes we may be given a polynomial which does not appear to be a polynomial. For example, $\dfrac{7x^2 + 5x - 14}{7}$ is a polynomial, since we have

$$\frac{7x^2 + 5x - 14}{7} = \frac{7}{7}x^2 + \frac{5}{7}x - \frac{14}{7} = x^2 + \frac{5}{7}x - 2.$$

We will encounter such expressions as we go along. Let's now look at some definitions.

**Definition 5:** A polynomial in 1 variable is in **descending order** if the degrees of its terms are decreasing when the polynomial is read from left to right.

As we will see in the next examples, every polynomial in 1 variable can be written in descending order.

**Examples.** Write the following polynomials in descending order.

1) $2x + 1$ is already in descending order, since $2x + 1 = \underbrace{2x^1}_{\text{degree 1}} + \underbrace{1}_{\text{degree 0}}$ and the degrees are decreasing.

2) $5x^2 - 3x + 1$ is already in descending order, since $5x^2 - 3x + 1 = \underbrace{5x^2}_{\text{degree 2}} - \underbrace{3x^1}_{\text{degree 1}} + \underbrace{1}_{\text{degree 0}}$ and the degrees are decreasing.

3) $-t^5 + 7 - 4t^2 + t^3$ is not in descending order, since the terms of $\underbrace{-t^5}_{\text{degree 5}} + \underbrace{7}_{\text{degree 0}} + \underbrace{(-4t^2)}_{\text{degree 2}} + \underbrace{t^3}_{\text{degree 3}}$ do not have degrees which are decreasing. However, by the commutative property, we can rewrite our polynomial as $-t^5 + t^3 - 4t^2 + 7$ and we have descending order.

4) $\dfrac{1}{2}y^2 - 8y^3 + 9$ is not in descending order, since $\underbrace{\dfrac{1}{2}y^2}_{\text{degree 2}} + \underbrace{(-8y^3)}_{\text{degree 3}} + \underbrace{9}_{\text{degree 0}}$ and the degrees are not decreasing.

By commuting the first two terms, we obtain $-8y^3 + \dfrac{1}{2}y^2 + 9$ and now the polynomial is in descending order.

Observe that when a polynomial is written in descending order, the exponents of the terms decrease from left to right. This happens because the degree of a monomial in 1 variable is just the exponent of the variable part.

**Definition 6:** A polynomial is **simplified** if its terms have different variable parts.

For example, $5x^2 - 6x$ is simplified since the variable parts of the terms, namely $x^2$ and $x$, are different. The polynomial $7a^3 + 3a^3 - 2a$ is not simplified, since the terms $7a^3$ and $3a^3$ have the same variable parts, $a^3$.

**Definition 7:** The left-most (non-zero) term of a simplified polynomial written in descending order is called the **leading term** of the polynomial.

**Examples.** Find the leading term of each polynomial.

1) $2x + 1$ has the leading term $2x$.

2) $5x^2 - 3x + 1$ has the leading term $5x^2$.

3) $\underbrace{-t^5 - 7 + 4t^2 + t^3}_{\text{not descending}} = \underbrace{-t^5 + t^3 + 4t^2 - 7}_{\text{is descending}}$ has the leading term $-t^5$.

4) $\underbrace{\frac{1}{2}y^2 - 8y^3 + 7}_{\text{not descending}} = \underbrace{-8y^3 + \frac{1}{2}y^2 + 7}_{\text{is descending}}$ has the leading term $-8y^3$.

5) $0x^5 - 4x^4 + 7x - 2 = -4x^4 + 7x - 2$ has the leading term $-4x^4$.

Notice that the leading term of a polynomial in 1 variable is just the term in the polynomial containing the largest exponent. Moreover, the leading term of a monomial is just the monomial itself. Hence, the leading term of $6a^2$ is $6a^2$ and the leading term of $-9$ is $-9$. By convention, the leading term of 0 is 0.

**Definition 8:** The coefficient of the leading term of a polynomial in 1 variable is called the **leading coefficient** of the polynomial.

**Examples.** Find the leading coefficient of each polynomial.

1) $2x + 1$ has the leading coefficient 2.    3) $-t^5 + t^3 + 4t^2 - 7$ has the leading coefficient $-1$, since $-t^5 = -1t^5$.

2) $5x^2 - 3x + 1$ has the leading coefficient 5.    4) $x^3 + 2x^2 - 7$ has the leading coefficient 1, since $x^3 = 1x^3$.

**Definition 9:** The **degree** of a polynomial in 1 variable is the degree of its leading term.

**Examples.** Find the degree of each polynomial.

1) $\underbrace{2x}_{\text{degree 1}} + 1$ has degree 1.    3) $\underbrace{-t^5}_{\text{degree 5}} + t^3 + 4t^2 - 7$ has degree 5.

2) $\underbrace{5x^2}_{\text{degree 2}} - 3x + 1$ has degree 2.    4) $\underbrace{x^3}_{\text{degree 3}} + 2x^2 - 7$ has degree 3.

You may have noticed that the degree of a polynomial is simply the largest of the degrees (or exponents) of the terms of the polynomial.

**Definition 10:** A polynomial in 1 variable is in **ascending order** if the degrees of its terms are increasing when the polynomial is read from left to right.

For example, the polynomials

$$6 + x, \ 3 - y - 4y^2, \ 5a - 3a^2 + 9a^4, \ \text{and} \ -4x - x^3 + 7x^4$$

are in ascending order. We can always express a polynomial in 1 variable in ascending order by commuting terms if necessary. We've seen this done before when we rewrote polynomials in descending order.

**Definition 11:** A **binomial** is a polynomial with 2 terms.

For example, the polynomials

$$x + 1, \ -5y + 3, \ 2.01x^2 - 10.431, \ \frac{6}{5}a^4 + 7a, \ \text{and} \ -t^2 - \frac{9}{20}$$

are binomials. Notice that the prefix of the word 'binomial' is 'bi', meaning 2.

**Definition 12:** A **trinomial** is a polynomial with 3 terms.

For example, the polynomials

$$2x^2 + 3x + 9, \quad -5y^2 + 4 - y, \quad \frac{9}{5}x^4 - \frac{3}{5}x^3 - \frac{6}{5}, \quad a^4 + 5.001a^5 + 0.162, \quad \text{and} \quad -t^2 - 9 + 4t$$

are trinomials. Notice that the prefix of the word 'trinomial' is 'tri', meaning 3.

**Definition 13:** A polynomial of degree 1 is called **linear**.

For example, the polynomials

$$x, \quad 5t, \quad 4x - 3, \quad 7 + 14b, \quad \frac{4}{11}t + 1, \quad \text{and} \quad -12 - \frac{5}{3}y$$

are linear polynomials. Notice that the number of terms in a polynomial does not determine whether or not it is linear. For instance, $x$ is a monomial, whereas $4x - 3$ is a binomial. Nevertheless, they are both linear. Examples of polynomials which are **not** linear are $x^2$, $5x^3 - 7$, and $-3x^4 + x^2 - 9x + 1$.

**Definition 14:** A polynomial of degree 2 is called **quadratic**.

For example, the polynomials

$$x^2, \quad 3y^2 - 5y, \quad 4t^2 + 8t - 1, \quad 4 + 12a - a^2, \quad \frac{-2}{7}x^2 - \frac{6}{5}x + 1, \quad \text{and} \quad -\frac{15}{16} - 9.01y^2$$

are quadratic polynomials. Notice that the number of terms in a polynomial does not determine whether or not it is quadratic. For instance, notice that $x^2$ is a monomial, $3y^2 - 5y$ is a binomial, and $4t^2 + 8t - 1$ is a trinomial. However, they are all quadratic. Examples of polynomials which are **not** quadratic are $x$, $-4x^3 + 6x^2 + 12$, and $a^4 - 5a^2 - 6$.

Let us now list a few definitions relating to polynomials in several variables.

**Definition 15:** A **polynomial in several variables** is a sum of monomials. If no two terms of a polynomial in several variables have the same variable part, then the polynomial is **simplified**.

**Examples.**

1) $5x^2 + 6xy - y^2$ is a polynomial in 2 variables, $x$ and $y$. It is simplified because the terms $5x^2$, $6xy$, and $-y^2$ have different variable parts.

2) $-a^3b + 7ab^2c^3 + 2a^3b - 3c$ is a polynomial in 3 variables, $a$, $b$, and $c$. It is **not** simplified since the terms $-a^3b$ and $2a^3b$ have the same variable part, namely $a^3b$.

3) $2x + \frac{3}{5}y + 4z - \frac{5}{2}xy - 5yz - 4xz + \frac{3}{10}wxyz$ is a polynomial in 4 variables, $w$, $x$, $y$, and $z$. It is simplified.

4) $5x^2y^2 - \frac{7x}{y^2}$ is not a polynomial in 2 variables since $\frac{7x}{y^2}$ is not a monomial.

Some of the definitions that we've learned for polynomials in one variable do not hold for several variables. For instance, there is no such thing as 'descending order' for a polynomial in several variables. Observe, for example, that there is no unique way of writing the polynomial

$$x^2 + xy - y^2 = \underbrace{x^2 + x^1y^1 - y^2}_{\text{Each term has degree 2.}}$$

in 'descending order' as we did before. The reason is that all 3 terms of the polynomial have the same degree and so there is no unique way of rearranging the terms so that the degrees decrease from left to right.

Therefore, there is no such thing as 'descending order' for polynomials in several variables. This means that there is no leading term and leading coefficient as well. However, there is a way of defining the degree of such a polynomial.

**Definition 16:** The **degree** of **any** (simplified) polynomial is equal to the largest of the degrees of its terms. If it so happens that some of the terms of a polynomial have the same largest degree, say $n$, then the degree of the polynomial is $n$.

**Examples.** Find the degree of the polynomial.

1) $4x^3 - 5xz^2 - z^4 = \underbrace{4x^3}_{\text{degree 3}} - \underbrace{5x^1z^2}_{\text{degree 3}} - \underbrace{z^4}_{\text{degree 4}}$ has degree 4.

2) $9a - 4a^3b^2 + b^2 - 9a^4b^2 = \underbrace{9a^1}_{\text{degree 1}} - \underbrace{4a^3b^2}_{\text{degree 5}} + \underbrace{b^2}_{\text{degree 2}} - \underbrace{9a^4b^2}_{\text{degree 6}}$ has degree 6.

3) $x^2 + xy - y^2 = \underbrace{x^2 + x^1y^1 - y^2}_{\text{Each term has degree 2.}}$ has degree 2.

4) $-12x^5 + 3x^4 + \dfrac{7}{8}x - 1$ has degree 5.

**Exercise 3.1**

In Exercises 1-12, find the coefficient and the degree of each monomial.

1. $4$
2. $-3$
3. $-5x$
4. $8t$
5. $7y^3$

6. $13a^5$
7. $8x^2y^3$
8. $-7s^4t^3$
9. $\dfrac{10x^6}{11}$
10. $\dfrac{4a^3}{9}$

11. $-\dfrac{5y^{12}}{3}$
12. $\dfrac{-x^8}{12}$

In Exercises 13-24, determine whether or not the expression is a polynomial. For those expressions which are polynomials list the coefficient of each term.

13. $3x^2 + 5x - 6$
14. $\dfrac{1}{4}a^3 - a^2$
15. $\dfrac{y^2}{9} - \dfrac{7y}{3} + 8$
16. $\dfrac{3x}{13} + \dfrac{x^2}{12} - \dfrac{1}{2}$

17. $-5t^4 + \dfrac{2}{t^2}$
18. $\dfrac{9}{x^4} - x + 6$
19. $\dfrac{2xy}{7} - \dfrac{3x^2}{7y}$
20. $\dfrac{5x + 3}{8}$

21. $\dfrac{6x^2 - 14}{3}$
22. $\dfrac{5b^4}{9a} + \dfrac{5ab^4}{9}$
23. $\dfrac{x^2 + 12y^2 - 24}{12}$
24. $\dfrac{-5a + b + 10c}{5}$

In Exercises 25-36, write the polynomial in descending order. Find the leading term, the leading coefficient, and the degree of each.

25. $4 + 6x$
26. $7 + 2a$
27. $8 - 3x$
28. $12 - x$

29. $5x^2 + 8 - 12x$      30. $-a + 6a^2 - 11$      31. $t^2 - 4t^3 + \dfrac{2}{7}$      32. $6x^2 - \dfrac{1}{5}x^4 + 9x$

33. $6 - \dfrac{8}{3}x - x^2$      34. $-\dfrac{14}{13} + 9t - 2t^2$      35. $\dfrac{8x^4}{13} + 3x - \dfrac{1}{10}x^3$      36. $\dfrac{-x^2}{3} - \dfrac{1}{4}x^5 + x^3$

In Exercises 37-56, find the degree of each polynomial and decide whether the polynomial is linear, quadratic or neither.

37. $5x$      38. $-8t$      39. $-4a$      40. $-b$      41. $3x^2$

42. $9t^2$      43. $2x - 5$      44. $-10a + 3$      45. $6 - 10x$      46. $-2 - 9x$

47. $7x + 4$      48. $-x + 3$      49. $y^2 + 6y - 2$      50. $-a^2 - 3a + 8$      51. $8 + 8x^2$

52. $7t + 7t^2$      53. $4x^2 + 8x + 9x^3$      54. $b - 7b^3 + 4b^2$

55. $\dfrac{2x^2 - 8x + 1}{2}$      56. $\dfrac{3a^3 + 12a^2 - 2a}{3}$

In Exercises 57-66, find the degree of each polynomial.

57. $x + 5y - 4x^2$      58. $4x^2 + 7x + 6y^2$      59. $6y^3 - x^3 - 7x$      60. $a^2 + b^2 - 3a^3$

61. $x^2 + 8x^2y - y^2$      62. $5a^2b + 7ab^2 + b$      63. $2s^4 + 8s^3t^3 + 9t^4$      64. $12x^7 - 5xy^3 + 3x^2y^3$

65. $a^3b^4 + 3bc^2 + 8a^3c^4 - a^2b^3c^4$      66. $-5x^6y^2 + 3xyz^4 + 7x^6 - y^2z^4$

## Section 3.2   Addition and Subtraction of Polynomials

Now that we know what a polynomial is let's start doing some algebraic manipulations with them. In this section, we will do some addition and subtraction of polynomials. We'll begin with addition and subtraction of the 'building blocks' of polynomials, namely monomials. Afterwards, we'll see how some of our properties from Chapter 1 allow us to add and subtract polynomials.

Suppose we want to combine two monomials into a single monomial, say $3x + 4x$. The first question to answer is "When can we combine two monomials?". Well, the answer to this question depends on the variable parts of our monomials. If the two monomials have the same variable parts, they can be combined into a single monomial. We have the following definition.

**Definition:** Two or more monomials are called **like terms** if they have the same variable parts.

In our example, $3x$ and $4x$ are like terms. Observe that $3x + 4x = (3 + 4)x = 7x$ which is just an application of the distributive property (read from right to left). Notice that all that we did to combine the monomials is combine the coefficients (3 and 4) and keep the same variable part. Let's look at some examples.

**Examples.** Combine into a single monomial (if possible).

1) $\underbrace{6a + 5a}_{\text{like terms}} = (6 + 5)a = 11a$

2) $\underbrace{-8xy + 3xy}_{\text{like terms}} = (-8 + 3)xy = -5xy$

3) $\underbrace{-7x^2y^3 - 11x^2y^3}_{\text{like terms}} = (-7 - 11)x^2y^3 = -18x^2y^3$

4) $\underbrace{-15st^2 + (-19st^2) =}_{\text{Remember that } a+(-b)=a-b} -15st^2 - 19st^2 = (-15 - 19)\,st^2 = -34st^2$

5) $9a^2 - 7a^2 + 13a^2 = (9 - 7 + 13)a^2 = 15a^2$

6) $-12x^3y - 2x^3y + 6x^3y + 8x^3y = (-12 - 2 + 6 + 8)x^3y = 0x^3y = 0$

7) $2a^4b^5 - 3a^5b^4$ don't combine into a single monomial (the terms aren't like terms)

Now, suppose we want to add the binomials $(2x + 3) + (-5x + 2)$. Well, by the associative property for addition, we can disregard the parentheses. Moreover, by the commutative property, we can collect like terms. Doing this, we obtain

$$2x + 3 + (-5x) + 2 = 2x + (-5x) + 3 + 2 = -3x + 5.$$

**Examples.** Combine.

1) $\underbrace{(4x - 2) + (6x + 8) = 4x - 2 + 6x + 8}_{\text{the associative property}} = 10x + 6$

2) $\underbrace{(-3x^2 + x - 9) + (5x^2 - 7x + 12) = -3x^2 + x - 9 + 5x^2 - 7x + 12}_{\text{the associative property}} = 2x^2 - 6x + 3$

3) $(5a^2 + 7b^2 - 3) + (-a^2 + 10ab + 9b^2) = 5a^2 + 7b^2 - 3 + (-a^2) + 10ab + 9b^2$
$$= 4a^2 + 16b^2 - 3 + 10ab$$

4) $(2y^3 - 7y^2 - 3) + (-9y^2 + 8y) + (8y^3 + 5y^2 - 7y) = 2y^3 - 7y^2 - 3 + (-9y^2) + 8y + 8y^3 + 5y^2 - 7y$
$$= 10y^3 - 11y^2 + y - 3$$

5) $\left(\dfrac{2}{3}x^2 - 6x + \dfrac{3}{8}\right) + \left(\dfrac{1}{9}x^2 + 13x + \dfrac{7}{12}\right) = \dfrac{2}{3}x^2 - 6x + \dfrac{3}{8} + \dfrac{1}{9}x^2 + 13x + \dfrac{7}{12}$
$$= \left(\dfrac{2}{3} + \dfrac{1}{9}\right)x^2 + (-6 + 13)\,x + \left(\dfrac{3}{8} + \dfrac{7}{12}\right)$$
$$= \left(\dfrac{6}{9} + \dfrac{1}{9}\right)x^2 + 7x + \left(\dfrac{9}{24} + \dfrac{14}{24}\right)$$
$$= \dfrac{7}{9}x^2 + 7x + \dfrac{23}{24}$$

Notice that the above problems were done while written horizontally. You can also add polynomials by writing the problem vertically. The way you do this is by writing your polynomials, one above the other, so that the 'columns' contain like terms. For example, let's add $4x^2 + 5x - 7$ and $-x^2 + 5x + 4$ vertically. Well, you need to rewrite the problem and add the columns up as follows:

$$
\begin{array}{r}
4x^2 + \ 5x - 7 \\
+ \quad -\,x^2 + \ 5x + 4 \\
\hline
3x^2 + 10x - 3
\end{array}
$$

By the commutative property for addition, it doesn't matter which polynomial goes on top. Observe that

$$
\begin{array}{r}
-x^2 + 5x + 4 \\
+ \quad 4x^2 + 5x - 7 \\
\hline
3x^2 + 10x - 3
\end{array}
$$

Let's see some more examples like this.

**Examples.** Add.

1) $6x - 4$ and $9x + 7$

$$
\begin{array}{r}
6x - 4 \\
+ \quad 9x + 7 \\
\hline
15x + 3
\end{array}
$$

2) $-5x^2 + 3xy + y^2$ and $7x^2 - 14xy - 8y^2$

$$
\begin{array}{r}
-5x^2 + 3xy + y^2 \\
+ \quad 7x^2 - 14xy - 8y^2 \\
\hline
2x^2 - 11xy - 7y^2
\end{array}
$$

3) $2a^2 - 3$ and $8a^2 + 16a - 7$

$$
\begin{array}{r}
2a^2 \qquad - 3 \\
+ \quad 8a^2 + 16a - 7 \\
\hline
10a^2 + 16a - 10
\end{array}
$$

4) $5xy^2 + 10x^2 + 14$ and $6y^2 - 12x^2 + 2y - 14$

$$
\begin{array}{r}
5xy^2 + 10x^2 + 14 \\
+ \quad 6y^2 \qquad - 12x^2 - 14 + 2y \\
\hline
6y^2 + 5xy^2 - 2x^2 \qquad + 2y
\end{array}
$$

5) $9a + 3b$, $-a + 4b$ and $-4b - 3a$

$$
\begin{array}{r}
9a + 3b \\
- \quad a + 4b \\
+ \quad -3a - 4b \\
\hline
5a + 3b
\end{array}
$$

You can add polynomials by writing the problem either horizontally or vertically. Pick the method that you are comfortable with. As we will see, both techniques are used, so make sure you get enough practice with each of them.

**Definition:** The **additive inverse** of a polynomial, $P$, is $-P$.

Observe that the sum of a polynomial and its additive inverse is 0, since $P + (-P) = 0$.

For example, the additive inverse of $8x - 1$ is $-(8x - 1) = -8x + 1$ and the additive inverse of $-6x^2 - 3x + 7$ is $-(-6x^2 - 3x + 7) = 6x^2 + 3x - 7$.

**Try These (Set 1):** Combine using any technique.

1) $(4y + 12) + (-2y + 8)$

4) $(8a + ab - 1) + (-7ab + a^2 - 3a)$

2) $(5x^2 - 2x + 9) + (6x^2 + 8x + 13)$

5) $(-16x^2 - 12) + (7x - 3)$

3) $(3x^2 - 7xy - 4y^2) + (-x^2 - 18xy + 16y^2)$

6) $\left(\frac{1}{2}t^2 - \frac{2}{5}t - 1\right) + \left(-\frac{2}{3}t^2 - \frac{4}{5}t + \frac{7}{6}\right)$

**Try These (Set 2):** Find the additive inverse.

1) $6x$      2) $5x^2 - x + 3$      3) $-7a^2 - 9ab^2$      4) $x^2 - y^2$      5) $\dfrac{-x}{6} + \dfrac{2x^2}{7}$

Let's now look at the example $(2x - 5) - (7x - 6)$. Subtraction of polynomials works differently than addition because there is no associative property for subtraction. Consequently, we can't just throw away the parentheses. Instead, we need to distribute the negative sign into the second set of parentheses. This will change the signs of all of the terms in the second parentheses. Once this is done, we may toss out both sets of parentheses and combine like terms. In other words, we have

$$(2x - 5) - (7x - 6) = \underbrace{2x - 5 - 7x + 6}_{\text{7x became } -7x \text{ and } -6 \text{ became } 6.} = -5x + 1$$

By the way, this all can be done because $(2x - 5) - (7x - 6)$ is really the same as $(2x - 5) + (-1)(7x - 6)$ and the $-1$ may be distributed into the second parentheses.

**Examples.** Combine the following.

1) $\underbrace{(8y + 2) - (3y + 12) = 8y + 2 - 3y - 12}_{\text{Distribute the } - \text{ sign and change the signs of } 3y \text{ and } 12.} = 5y - 10$

2) $\underbrace{(-6x^2 + 4x - 9) - (3x^2 - 7x + 2) = -6x^2 + 4x - 9 - 3x^2 + 7x - 2}_{\text{Distribute the } - \text{ sign and change the signs of } 3x^2, -7x, \text{ and } 2.} = -9x^2 + 11x - 11$

3) $\underbrace{(9a^2 - 3ab + 6b^2) - (-a^2 + ab - 7b^2) = 9a^2 - 3ab + 6b^2 + a^2 - ab + 7b^2}_{\text{Distribute the } - \text{ sign and change the signs of } -a^2, ab, \text{ and } -7b^2.} = 10a^2 - 4ab + 13b^2$

4) $\underbrace{(14s + 2st^2 - 10t^3) - (-9s^2 - 3s + t^3 + 7) = 14s + 2st^2 - 10t^3 + 9s^2 + 3s - t^3 - 7}_{\text{Distribute the } - \text{ sign and change the signs of } -9s^2, -3s, t^3, \text{ and } 7.}$

$$= 17s + 2st^2 - 11t^3 + 9s^2 - 7$$

As with addition, there is a way of subtracting two polynomials by aligning them up vertically in such a way that the columns consist of like terms. The major difference between addition and subtraction is that when subtracting, we change the signs in all the terms in the second polynomial and the subtraction problem **turns into** an addition problem. This is due to the fact that the $-1$ gets distributed into the second polynomial, similar to the above 'horizontal technique'. Before doing some subtraction problems 'vertically', let's review how to subtract one number from another. We know how to do subtraction when the problem is given to us mathematically, but sometimes it is given to us verbally. For example, suppose we want to subtract 3 from 12. Then we would write the subtraction problem as $12 - 3$ (not $3 - 12$). Notice that the second number, 12, goes first and 3 goes second. If we wanted to write this 'vertically', we would write

$$\begin{array}{r} 12 \\ - \quad 3 \\ \hline \end{array}$$

and work out the problem. The same thing happens when subtracting polynomials. For example, let's subtract $5x - 7$ from $12x - 3$. If we were to do this problem 'horizontally', then the subtraction problem would be written as $(12x - 3) - (5x - 7)$. Now, to do this 'vertically', we write

$$\begin{array}{r} 12x - 3 \\ - \quad 5x - 7 \\ \hline \end{array} \qquad \text{becomes} \qquad \begin{array}{r} 12x - 3 \\ + \; -5x + 7 \\ \hline 7x + 4 \end{array}$$

Notice that the subtraction problem turned into an addition problem and the signs of the terms of $5x - 7$ changed ($5x$ becomes $-5x$ and $-7$ becomes 7). Let's see some examples using this method.

**Examples.**

1) Subtract $3a + 5$ from $-a + 3$.

$$\begin{array}{r} -\;a + 3 \\ - \quad 3a + 5 \\ \hline \end{array} \qquad \text{becomes} \qquad \begin{array}{r} -\;a + 3 \\ + \; -3a - 5 \\ \hline -4a - 2 \end{array}$$

2) Subtract $-6x^2 - 8x$ from $4x^2 + 2x$.

$$\begin{array}{r} 4x^2 + \;2x \\ - \quad -6x^2 - \;8x \\ \hline \end{array} \qquad \text{becomes} \qquad \begin{array}{r} 4x^2 + \;2x \\ + \quad 6x^2 + \;8x \\ \hline 10x^2 + 10x \end{array}$$

3) Subtract $7y^2 - y + 10$ from $8y^2 - 12$.

$$\begin{array}{r} 8y^2 \quad\;\; - 12 \\ - \quad 7y^2 - y + 10 \\ \hline \end{array} \qquad \text{becomes} \qquad \begin{array}{r} 8y^2 \quad\;\; - 12 \\ + \; -7y^2 + y - 10 \\ \hline y^2 + y - 22 \end{array}$$

4) Subtract $-9t^2 + 5t$ from $15t^2 + 11$.

$$\begin{array}{r} 15t^2 \quad\;\; + 11 \\ - \quad -9t^2 + 5t \\ \hline \end{array} \qquad \text{becomes} \qquad \begin{array}{r} 15t^2 \quad\;\; + 11 \\ + \quad 9t^2 - 5t \\ \hline 24t^2 - 5t + 11 \end{array}$$

5) Subtract $-5x^2 - 3y^2$ from $8y^2 - 9xy$.

$$\begin{array}{r} 8y^2 - 9xy \\ - \quad -3y^2 \quad\;\; - 5x^2 \\ \hline \end{array} \qquad \text{becomes} \qquad \begin{array}{r} 8y^2 - 9xy \\ + \quad 3y^2 \quad\;\; + 5x^2 \\ \hline 11y^2 - 9xy + 5x^2 \end{array}$$

We will see that both methods shown above come in handy. You should get to know how to do both of them. Use the method which is easier for you.

**Try These (Set 3):** Subtract using any technique.

1) $(4x + 5y) - (-x + 13y)$
2) $\left(-6a^2 + 2ab - b^2\right) - \left(-6a^2 - 3ab + 10b^2\right)$
3) $\left(s^2 - 2t^2\right) - \left(3s^2 + 5st - t^2\right)$

4) Subtract $4m^2 + 12mn - 9$ from $3m^2 - 8mn - 6$
5) Subtract $5a^2 - a + 6$ from $-9a^2 + 16$
6) Subtract $x - 3xy$ from $y - 3yx$

## Exercise 3.2

In Exercises 1-48, combine using any technique.

1. $9x + 4x$    2. $6y + 2y$    3. $-8y^2 + 3y^2$    4. $-a^2 + 9a^2$

5. $-5x - 5x$    6. $-8p - 9p$    7. $4ab^3 + \left(-7ab^3\right)$    8. $\left(-12x^2y\right) + 3x^2y$

9. $(-16ab) - (-2ab)$    10. $(-2st) - (-4st)$    11. $4x^2 + 6x^2 - 13x^2$    12. $-6a^2b^2 - a^2b^2 + 9a^2b^2$

13. $3n - 7n + n + 9n$    14. $7q + 14q - 8q + q$    15. $(9a + 7) + (-3a + 1)$

16. $(b - 7) + (6b + 12)$    17. $\left(a^2 - 2a - 1\right) + \left(4a^2 - 5a + 3\right)$    18. $\left(4x^2 + 7x + 3\right) + \left(x^2 - 9x - 2\right)$

19. $\left(-x^2 - 2xy + 14y^2\right) + \left(-x^2 + 2xy - 8y^2\right)$    20. $\left(7m^2 - m + 6\right) + \left(-m^2 + 15m - 4\right)$

21. $(4a - 5b - 2) + (12b - 6ab + 4)$    22. $(p + 3q - 5) + (7 + 9p + 4pq)$

23. $\left(a^2 - b^2\right) + \left(a^2 + 11ab + b^2\right)$    24. $\left(9x^2 - z^2\right) + \left(4z^2 - 12xz + 9x^2\right)$

25. $(9x + 1) - (3x + 4)$    26. $(7a + 2b) - (2a + 3b)$    27. $(-3a + 8b) - (4a - b)$

28. $(-2p + 2q) - (7p - q)$    29. $\left(-x^2 + 10x + 3\right) - \left(3x^2 - 2x - 1\right)$

30. $\left(14a^2 - a - 7\right) - \left(9a^2 + 4a - 9\right)$    31. $\left(5a^2 - 7ab + b^2\right) - \left(-3a^2 + 9b^2\right)$

32. $\left(-s^2 - 2st^2 + t^2\right) - \left(s^2 - 7t^2\right)$    33. $\left(12p + pq - q\right) - \left(-3p + 2pq - 9q^2\right)$

34. $\left(8x^2 - 13xy - 15x\right) - \left(2xy - x - 6xy^2\right)$    35. $\left(-4x^2 + 12\right) - \left(12 - 3x^2 + 6y^2\right)$

36. $\left(p^2 - 5\right) - \left(-13q^2 + p^2 + 8\right)$    37. $(7x + y) + (5x - 3y) + (-2x + 2y)$

38. $(9a - 10) + (3a + 14) + (-a + 7)$    39. $\left(5x^2 - 9x\right) + \left(-x^2 + 7\right) + (8x + 9)$

40. $\left(2s^2 - 2\right) + \left(-t^2 + 3s^2\right) + \left(11s^2 + 15\right)$    41. $(8m + 3) + (9m - 1) - (-5m + 4)$

42. $(-x + 2) + (6x - 15) - (7x + 2)$    43. $\left(x^2 + 5x + 9\right) + \left(x^2 - 5\right) - (-8x + 16)$

44. $\left(4a^2 - 3a\right) + \left(-a^2 + 3\right) - (7a + 2)$    45. $\left(y^2 - 6\right) - \left(4y^2 + 2y - 2\right) + (y + 1)$

46. $\left(3b^2 + 5b\right) - \left(9b^2 - 12b + 10\right) + (2b - 5)$    47. $\left(6t^2 + 12\right) - \left(-t^2 - 11t\right) - (7t - 14)$

48. $\left(2x^2 - 8y\right) - (3xy - 6y) - \left(2x^2 + 15xy\right)$

In Exercises 49-56, find the additive inverse of the given polynomial.

49. $6x$             50. $-3a^2$         51. $2n - 7$        52. $-3x + 12$

53. $-a^2 + 2a - 3$     54. $7y^2 - 6y + 7$     55. $8t^2 + 3st - s^2$     56. $-x^2 - 9xy + 4y^2$

## Section 3.3   Multiplication of Polynomials

In this section, we will learn how to multiply polynomials together. We will begin by studying how to multiply a monomial by a polynomial. Afterwards, we will look at the product of two binomials, followed by the product of any two polynomials.

### 1. <u>Monomial × Monomial</u>

We have already learned how to multiply two monomials (see Chapter 2). Let's look at few examples for review.

**Examples.** Multiply.

1) $\left(5x^3y\right)\left(3x^7y^2\right) = 15x^{3+7}y^{1+2} = 15x^{10}y^3$

2) $\left(-2a^2b^5\right)\left(16ab^4\right) = -32a^{2+1}b^{5+4} = -32a^3b^9$

3) $\left(-\dfrac{2}{\overset{\;}{\underset{1}{\cancel{9}}}}x^7y^2z\right)\left(-\dfrac{\overset{2}{\cancel{18}}}{5}xy^4z^2\right) = \dfrac{4}{5}x^{7+1}y^{2+4}z^{1+2} = \dfrac{4}{5}x^8y^6z^3$

4) $\left(3x^2yz^3\right)\left(-8x^4y\right) = -24x^{2+4}y^{1+1}z^3 = -24x^6y^2z^3$

**Try These (Set 4):** Multiply.

1) $\left(-a^3\right)\left(-15a^4\right)$                  3) $\left(\dfrac{2}{7}y^4\right)\left(\dfrac{21}{8}x^2y^5\right)$

2) $\left(4x^6y^7\right)\left(-7x^3y\right)$              4) $\left(-\dfrac{4}{5}m^3n^8\right)\left(15m^3n^2\right)$

### 2. <u>Monomial × Polynomial</u>

To multiply a monomial by a polynomial, all that you need to use is the distributive property.

**Examples.** Multiply.

1) $4a^2\left(7a - 6\right) = 4a^2\left(7a\right) + 4a^2\left(-6\right) = 28a^3 - 24a^2$

2) $5\left(3x^2 - 2x + 7\right) = 5\left(3x^2\right) + 5\left(-2x\right) + 5(7) = 15x^2 - 10x + 35$

3) $2y\,(6y^2 + y - 2) = 2y\,(6y^2) + 2y(y) + 2y(-2) = 12y^3 + 2y^2 - 4y$

4) $-3x^2\,(4x^2 - 7x - 12) = -3x^2\,(4x^2) - 3x^2\,(-7x) - 3x^2\,(-12) = -12x^4 + 21x^3 + 36x^2$

5) $-9p^5q^3\,(-8p^2 + 7pq^3) = -9p^5q^3\,(-8p^2) - 9p^5q^3\,(7pq^3) = 72p^7q^3 - 63p^6q^6$

6) $-7a^3b^4\,(-3a^2b^2 - 4ab^2 + 7a^2b) = -7a^3b^4\,(-3a^2b^2) - 7a^3b^4\,(-4ab^2) - 7a^3b^4\,(7a^2b)$
$$= 21a^5b^6 + 28a^4b^6 - 49a^5b^5$$

In the next set of examples, the distributive property is used to simplify each.

**Examples.** Simplify.

1) $2(2x + 1) - 7 = 4x + 2 - 7 = 4x - 5$

2) $3a^2(-a + 2) + 12a^3 = -3a^3 + 6a^2 + 12a^3 = 9a^3 + 6a^2$

3) $2(x - 5) + 4(6x - 3) = 2x - 10 + 24x - 12 = 26x - 22$

4) $a(10 + 3a) - 4a(6 - 7a) = 10a + 3a^2 - 24a + 28a^2 = -14a + 31a^2$

5) $-3x(8x + 3y) + 12y(2x - 3y) = \underbrace{-24x^2 - 9xy + 24yx - 36y^2 = -24x^2 + 15xy - 36y^2}$
Note that $xy=yx$ by the commutative property.

6) $8k^2(7k^2 + k + 2) - 3k(-6k + 11) + 5k^4 - 3k = 56k^4 + 8k^3 + 16k^2 + 18k^2 - 33k + 5k^4 - 3k$
$$= 61k^4 + 8k^3 + 34k^2 - 36k$$

**Try These (Set 5):** Multiply.

1) $4x(x - 3)$

2) $-5y^2(y^2 + 4y - 9)$

3) $8a(3a^2 - 5ab - b^2)$

4) $-7p^3q^5(-2pq^3 + 7p^3q^2 + 8pq)$

**Try These (Set 6):** Simplify.

1) $3x(4x - 1) + 6x(7x + 3)$

2) $-5a(a^2 + 6a + 2) + 8a(3a^2 - a - 7)$

3) $2y^2(8y + 5x - 9) - 5x^2(-3y + x - 2)$

4) $-8x(2x + 3) - 3x(8x + 1) + x(x - 2)$

5) $3a(2a - 4b) + 5b(-7a + 2b) - ab(ab - 8)$

6) $9(-3 + 7x + 8y) - 5(-8 + 2y - x) - 10(x + 2)$

## 3. **Binomial $\times$ Binomial**

To multiply two binomials, say $(A + B)(C + D)$, we distribute both $A$ and $B$ into the second parentheses and combine. We obtain

$$(A + B)(C + D) = A(C + D) + B(C + D) = \underset{\text{First terms}}{AC} + \underset{\text{Outer terms}}{AD} + \underset{\text{Inner terms}}{BC} + \underset{\text{Last terms}}{BD}.$$

This method of multiplying two binomials is often referred to as the **FOIL method.** Take the first letter of the name of each of the above products and put it next to its neighbor.

**Examples.** Multiply the following.

1) $(\overset{\frown}{x+1})(\overset{\frown}{x+2}) = \underbrace{x(x)}_{\text{First}} + \underbrace{x(2)}_{\text{Outer}} + \underbrace{1(x)}_{\text{Inner}} + \underbrace{1(2)}_{\text{Last}} = x^2 + \underbrace{2x + x}_{\text{Combine.}} + 2 = x^2 + 3x + 2$

2) $(\overset{\frown}{x-3})(\overset{\frown}{x+8}) = \underbrace{x(x)}_{\text{First}} + \underbrace{x(8)}_{\text{Outer}} + \underbrace{(-3)(x)}_{\text{Inner}} + \underbrace{(-3)(8)}_{\text{Last}} = x^2 + \underbrace{8x - 3x}_{\text{Combine.}} - 24 = x^2 + 5x - 24$

3) $(2y - 5)(3y - 1) = 2y(3y) + 2y(-1) + (-5)(3y) + (-5)(-1) = 6y^2 - 2y - 15y + 5 = 6y^2 - 17y + 5$

4) $(7 + 9x)(2 - x^2) = 7(2) + 7(-x^2) + 9x(2) + 9x(-x^2) = \underbrace{14 - 7x^2 + 18x - 9x^3}_{\text{Nothing combines.}}$

5) $(3a - 8b)(-a - 4b) = 3a(-a) + 3a(-4b) + (-8b)(-a) + (-8b)(-4b)$
$$= -3a^2 - 12ab + 8ba + 32b^2 = -3a^2 - 4ab + 32b^2$$

6) $(-4x + 7xy)(4y - 8xy) = -4x(4y) + (-4x)(-8xy) + 7xy(4y) + 7xy(-8xy)$
$$= -16xy + 32x^2y + 28xy^2 - 56x^2y^2$$

7) $(2x + 10)(2x - 10) = 2x(2x) + 2x(-10) + 10(2x) + 10(-10) = 4x^2 - 20x + 20x - 100 = 4x^2 - 100$

8) $(8a + 3)^2 = (8a + 3)(8a + 3) = 8a(8a) + 8a(3) + 3(8a) + 3(3) = 64a^2 + 24a + 24a + 9 = 64a^2 + 48a + 9$

Next, I would like to list some special products which often appear. These can be verified by using the FOIL method. You should check these on your own.

---

**Special Products**

**I. The Difference of Two Squares:**   $(A + B)(A - B) = A^2 - B^2$
**II. The Square of a Sum:**  $(A + B)^2 = (A + B)(A + B) = A^2 + 2AB + B^2$
**III. The Square of a Difference:**   $(A - B)^2 = (A - B)(A - B) = A^2 - 2AB + B^2$

---

Some common mistakes which often arise involve the last two products. Let me tell you what they are:

---

   **BEWARE:** $(A + B)^2 \neq A^2 + B^2$, $(A - B)^2 \neq A^2 + B^2$, and $(A - B)^2 \neq A^2 - B^2$.

---

To avoid making these mistakes, I suggest that you remember how the products are written rather than memorizing the identities. After you get enough practice, you should memorize them.

**Examples.** Multiply.

1)    $\underbrace{(x + 3)(x - 3) = (x)^2 - (3)^2}_{\text{By special product I, letting } A=x \text{ and } B=3.} = x^2 - 9$

Note that if we do this without the formula, we get the same answer:

$$(x+3)(x-3) = x^2 \underbrace{-3x+3x}_{0} - 9$$
$$= x^2 + 0 - 9$$
$$= x^2 - 9$$

2)  $\underbrace{(y-7)(y+7) = (y)^2 - (7)^2}$   $= y^2 - 49$

Special product I, letting $A=y$ and $B=7$.

3)  $\underbrace{(5y+2)(5y-2) = (5y)^2 - (2)^2}$   $= 25y^2 - 4$

Special product I, letting $A=5y$ and $B=2$.

4)  $\underbrace{(3a-11)(3a+11) = (3a)^2 - (11)^2}$ $= 9a^2 - 121$

Special product I, letting $A=3a$ and $B=11$.

5) $(x+4)^2 = (x+4)(x+4) = x^2 + 4x + 4x + 16 = x^2 + 8x + 16$

6) $(b-8)^2 = (b-8)(b-8) = b^2 - 8b - 8b + 64 = b^2 - 16b + 64$

7) $(2t+6)^2 = (2t+6)(2t+6) = 4t^2 + 12t + 12t + 36 = 4t^2 + 24t + 36$

8) $(4-9x)^2 = (4-9x)(4-9x) = 16 - 36x - 36x + 81x^2 = 16 - 72x + 81x^2$

9) $\underbrace{(5x+1)^2 = (5x)^2 + 2(5x)(1) + (1)^2}$ $= 25x^2 + 10x + 1$

Special product II, letting $A=5x$ and $B=1$.

10) $\underbrace{(3a-10b)^2 = (3a)^2 - 2(3a)(10b) + (10b)^2}$ $= 9a^2 - 60ab + 100b^2$

Special product III, letting $A=3a$ and $B=10b$.

**Try These (Set 7):** Multiply.

1) $(x+7)(x-2)$     3) $(y^2+3y)(2y-9)$     5) $(4y+7)(4y-7)$

2) $(5a-3)(2a-4)$     4) $(12-5x)(2-x)$     6) $(5a+11)^2$

4.  **Polynomial × Polynomial**

Now it's time for the grand finale. How do we multiply **any** two polynomials? Well, it turns out that the distributive property is the thing to use, just as for the monomial × polynomial and binomial × binomial situations. Let's see how this works.

**Examples.** Multiply the following

1) $(x+3)(x^2+2x-3) = x(x^2) + x(2x) + x(-3) + 3(x^2) + 3(2x) + 3(-3)$

Distribute both the $x$ and the 3 into the 2nd parentheses.

$$= x^3 + 2x^2 - 3x + 3x^2 + 6x - 9 = x^3 + 5x^2 + 3x - 9$$

2) $(4a^2-5)(2a^2-3a+3) = 4a^2(2a^2) + 4a^2(-3a) + 4a^2(3) + (-5)(2a^2) + (-5)(-3a) + (-5)(3)$
$$= 8a^4 - 12a^3 + 12a^2 - 10a^2 + 15a - 15$$
$$= 8a^4 - 12a^3 + 2a^2 + 15a - 15$$

3) $(x+2y-1)(x-3y-1) = x(x) + x(-3y) + x(-1) + 2y(x) + 2y(-3y) + 2y(-1) + (-1)(x) + (-1)(-3y) + (-1)(-1)$

Distribute the $x$, $2y$, and $-1$ into the 2nd parentheses.

$$= x^2 - 3xy - x + 2yx - 6y^2 - 2y - x + 3y + 1$$
$$= x^2 - xy - 2x - 6y^2 + y + 1$$

4) $(2y - 3)^3 = \underbrace{(2y - 3)(2y - 3)}(2y - 3) = (4y^2 - 12y + 9)(2y - 3)$

         FOIL the first pair $(2y-3)(2y-3)$.

$\quad = 4y^2(2y) + 4y^2(-3) + (-12y)(2y) + (-12y)(-3) + 9(2y) + 9(-3)$
$\quad = 8y^3 - 12y^2 - 24y^2 + 36y + 18y - 27$
$\quad = 8y^3 - 36y^2 + 54y - 27$

5) $\underbrace{(6t + 1)(2t - 2)}(t + 3) = (12t^2 - 10t - 2)(t + 3) = 12t^3 + 36t^2 - 10t^2 - 30t - 2t - 6$

       FOIL $(6t+1)(2t-2)$ first.

$\quad\quad\quad\quad\quad\quad\quad\quad\quad\quad = 12t^3 + 26t^2 - 32t - 6$

6) $(4x + 1)^2 (4x - 1) = (4x + 1)\underbrace{(4x + 1)(4x - 1)} = \underbrace{(4x + 1)(16x^2 - 1) = 64x^3 - 4x + 16x^2 - 1}$

                 Use special product I.             Use the FOIL method.

The examples above could've been done by setting the problem up **vertically**. Let's see how this method works.

7) $(a + 2)\left(a^2 + 4a - 1\right) =$

$$
\begin{array}{r}
a^2 + 4a - 1 \\
a + 2 \\
\hline
2a^2 + 8a - 2 \\
a^3 + 4a^2 - a \\
\hline
a^3 + 6a^2 + 7a - 2
\end{array}
$$

       $\longleftarrow$ 2 times $a^2 + 4a - 1$
       $\longleftarrow$ $a$ times $a^2 + 4a - 1$

8) $(3y - 7)\left(-5y^3 - 3y^2 + 2\right) =$

$$
\begin{array}{r}
-5y^3 - 3y^2 + 2 \\
3y - 7 \\
\hline
35y^3 + 21y^2 \quad\quad - 14 \\
-15y^4 - 9y^3 \quad\quad + 6y \\
\hline
-15y^4 + 26y^3 + 21y^2 + 6y - 14
\end{array}
$$

       $\longleftarrow$ $-7$ times $-5y^3 - 3y^2 + 2$
       $\longleftarrow$ $3y$ times $-5y^3 - 3y^2 + 2$

9) $(x + 2y - 3)(2x - 3y + 5) =$

$$
\begin{array}{r}
x + 2y - 3 \\
2x - 3y + 5 \\
\hline
5x + 10y - 15 \\
-3xy - 6y^2 \quad\quad + 9y \\
2x^2 + 4xy \quad\quad - 6x \\
\hline
2x^2 + xy - 6y^2 - x + 19y - 15
\end{array}
$$

       $\longleftarrow$ 5 times $x + 2y - 3$
       $\longleftarrow$ $-3y$ times $x + 2y - 3$
       $\longleftarrow$ $2x$ times $x + 2y - 3$

You can choose whichever method you like. Both of these methods of multiplication will be used from this point on. The next thing I'd like to do is to mention two special products which will arise later on. They are numbered as a continuation of the previous set of special products.

---

**Special Products**

IV. The Sum of Two Cubes:   $(A + B)(A^2 - AB + B^2) = A^3 + B^3$

V. The Difference of Two Cubes:   $(A - B)(A^2 + AB + B^2) = A^3 - B^3$

---

Let's verify Special Product IV by using the vertical method:

$$A^2 - AB + B^2$$
$$\underline{\hspace{3cm} A + B}$$
$$A^2B - AB^2 + B^3$$
$$+ \quad \underline{A^3 - A^2B + AB^2 \hspace{2cm}}$$
$$A^3 \hspace{4cm} + B^3$$

I'll leave it for you to verify Special Product V.

**Try These (Set 8):** Multiply.

1) $(x + 2)\left(x^2 + 3x + 1\right)$          4) $(x - 4)^2 (x + 4)$

2) $(3y - 1)\left(y^2 - 7y + 2\right)$          5) $(3t - 2)^3$

3) $(5a + b)\left(3a^2 - 2ab - 2b^2\right)$          6) $\left(a^2 - 2a - 1\right)^2$

**Exercise 3.3**

In Exercises 1-86, multiply and simplify.

1. $\left(3x^2\right)\left(6x^3\right)$          2. $\left(-4x^3\right)\left(3x^3\right)$          3. $\left(-6a^5\right)\left(-9a^2\right)$          4. $\left(2t^4\right)(-12t)$

5. $\left(-\dfrac{5}{6}y^3\right)\left(\dfrac{12}{25}y^8\right)$   6. $\left(\dfrac{4}{7}t^2\right)\left(-\dfrac{14}{9}t^6\right)$   7. $(-8y^2)\left(\dfrac{-9}{16}y^2\right)$          8. $\left(\dfrac{2}{13}p^5\right)\left(26p^5\right)$

9. $\left(3a^3b^6\right)\left(-ab^2\right)$     10. $\left(-5s^{12}t^{10}\right)\left(-3s^2t^8\right)$   11. $\left(\dfrac{9x^{14}y^{19}}{8}\right)\left(\dfrac{-24x^5y^2}{11}\right)$   12. $\left(\dfrac{-6m^9n^2}{5}\right)\left(\dfrac{-9mn^{15}}{12}\right)$

13. $4a(5a + 7)$          14. $6y(7y + 8)$          15. $8x^3(9x^4 - 2x)$          16. $3t^4(5t^2 - 6t^3)$

17. $-3x^5(8x^2 - 10x^4)$          18. $-2p^3(-12p + 8p^3)$          19. $6x^3y^4(2x^2y^5 - 5xy^2)$

20. $7x^2y^8(-3xy^3 + 4x^5y^2)$          21. $5(3a^2 + 6a - 2)$          22. $4(7t^2 - t + 9)$

23. $8x^2(4x^3 - 5x^2 - 11)$          24. $2n^3(-7n^4 - n^3 + 2)$          25. $-3x^4y^3(5x^2 - 7x^2y^2 + 9y^2)$

26. $6x^2y^8(7x^3 - 2xy + 9y^2)$          27. $9a^3b^2(-a^4b^2 + 9a^2b^5 - 4a^6b^7)$          28. $-7p^2q^8(6p^4q - 4p^3q^3 - p^{12}q^{15})$

29. $2xy^4z^5(x^3y + 4xy^6 - 5yz^{10})$          30. $-6x^5y^2z(3z^6 - 5x^3yz^8 + 12x^5y)$

31. $(x + 4)(x + 1)$          32. $(x + 6)(x + 7)$          33. $(y - 3)(y + 8)$          34. $(a + 9)(a - 2)$

35. $(t - 7)(t - 8)$          36. $(b - 10)(b - 4)$          37. $(2y + 5)(3y + 1)$          38. $(2x + 1)(5x + 3)$

39. $(6x - 7)(2x + 3)$　　40. $(5t + 9)(3t - 4)$　　41. $(12 - 3n)(3 + 4n)$　　42. $(6 + 7a)(2 - 2a)$

43. $(8 - 7t)(2 - 3t)$　　　44. $(1 - 9x)(5 - 4x)$　　　45. $(4x^2 + 5x)(2x + 3)$　　46. $(2y^2 + 7y)(3y - 1)$

47. $(-6a^2 + 3)(8a - 3)$　　48. $(4t^2 - 7t)(-5t + 5)$　　49. $(n^3 - 7n)(6n - 2)$　　50. $(2p^3 + 5p)(-p + 7)$

51. $(x + 2)(x - 2)$　　52. $(x - 6)(x + 6)$　　　53. $(7 - y)(7 + y)$　　54. $(8 + a)(8 - a)$

55. $(3x + 1)(3x - 1)$　　56. $(5p - 4)(5p + 4)$　　57. $(10a - 3b)(10a + 3b)$　　58. $(2x + 7y)(2x - 7y)$

59. $(x + 1)^2$　　　60. $(y + 3)^2$　　　61. $(p - 7)^2$　　　62. $(x - 12)^2$　　　63. $(3y + 2)^2$

64. $(4n + 7)^2$　　65. $(5x - 8y)^2$　　　66. $(7m + 3n)^2$　　67. $(11 - 4x)^2$　　　68. $(5 - 12p)^2$

69. $(x + 3)(x^2 - 2x + 2)$　　　70. $(x - 1)(x^2 + 3x - 5)$　　　71. $(2y - 3)(y^2 - 2y - 1)$

72. $(5a + 1)(a^2 + 6a - 2)$　　　73. $(4b + 2)(16b^2 - 8b + 4)$　　74. $(3y - 4)(9y^2 + 12y + 16)$

75. $(x + 2y + 5)(6x - 5)$　　　76. $(8a - b + 3)(2b + 4)$　　　77. $(t - 2)^3$

78. $(x + 4)^3$　　79. $(2m + 3n)^3$　　80. $(5p - 2q)^3$　　81. $(x - 3)^2(x + 3)$

82. $(y + 6)^2(y - 6)$　　83. $(2a + 1)(3a - 2)(a + 2)$　　84. $(4s - 1)(s + 3)(5s - 2)$

85. $(2x - 3y + 1)^2$　　　86. $(-m + 3n + 8)^2$


In Exercises 87-107, simplify.

87. $2(5x + 3) + 8(2x - 1)$　　　　88. $-3(2y - 4) + 6(4y + 3)$　　　　89. $-7a^2(a - 5) + 6a^2(3a + 1)$

90. $-x^2(8x + 2) - 2x^2(9x - 3)$　　　　91. $2p^2(-p^2 + 4p - 2) - 5p(5p^2 - p)$

92. $4t(7t^2 - 2t + 8) + 6t^2(-3t^2 + t - 2)$　　　　93. $7x(4x - 1) + 4x(-x + 3) - 8(x^2 - 9)$

94. $-10y(3 - 2y) + 8y^2(y + 3) - 7(y^2 + 3)$　　　　95. $(x - 1)(x + 3) + (x + 9)(x + 2)$

96. $(t + 5)(t + 1) + (t - 3)(t - 4)$　　　　97. $(2a - 5)(a + 1) - (a + 2)(2a - 3)$

98. $(n + 3)(3n + 2) - (4n - 1)(2n - 5)$　　　　99. $(y - 5)(y + 5) + (y - 7)(y + 7)$

100. $(x + 8)(x - 8) + (x - 2)(x + 2)$　　　　101. $(2b - 3)(2b + 3) - (6 + 3b)(6 - 3b)$

102. $(x - 2)^2 + (x + 4)^2$　　103. $(x - 3)^2 + (x + 7)^2$　　　104. $(y + 5)^2 - (y - 1)^2$

105. $(x - 6)^2 - (x + 1)^2$　　106. $(y + 12)^2 + (y - 6)(y + 2)$　　107. $(2x - 5)^2 - (x + 1)(x - 4)$


# Section 3.4　Division of Polynomials

In this section, we will learn how to divide two polynomials. The section begins with a look at how to divide a monomial by a monomial. Afterwards, we will learn how to divide a polynomial by a monomial followed by the quotient of any two polynomials. We will also learn about the remainder of a quotient of two polynomials. As we will see, many of the features seen in the quotient of two polynomials correspond to the quotient of integers.

1. <u>**Monomial ÷ Monomial**</u>

We have already learned how to divide two monomials (see Chapter 2). Let's look at a few examples for the review. Recall that a division problem can be written in different ways. Notice that the following means the same thing:

$$a \div b = \frac{a}{b} = b\overline{)\,a\,}$$

**In this section, we will assume that all variables are non zero valued.**

**Examples.** Divide.

1) $(12x^7) \div (3x^3) = \underbrace{\dfrac{12x^7}{3x^3}}_{\text{Rewrite as a fraction.}} = 4x^4$   $\qquad$ 4) $(35pq^7) \div (-5pq^2) = \dfrac{35pq^7}{-5pq^2} = -7q^5$

2) $(-24a^4b^8) \div (8ab^5) = \dfrac{-24a^4b^8}{8ab^5} = -3a^3b^3$   $\qquad$ 5) $(8x^5y^9z^3) \div (28x^4y^2z) = \dfrac{\overset{2}{\cancel{8}}x^5y^9z^3}{\underset{7}{\cancel{28}}x^4y^2z} = \dfrac{2}{7}xy^7z^2$

3) $(-42x^2y^{12}) \div (-6xy^9) = \dfrac{-42x^2y^{12}}{-6xy^9} = 7xy^3$

Notice that all of the above answers are monomials. However, it is NOT always the case that the quotient of two monomials is a monomial. For example, notice that

$$(-16x^2) \div (8x^5) = \frac{-16x^2}{8x^5} = -\frac{2}{x^3}.$$

This is not a monomial since the denominator contains a variable.

**Try These (Set 9):** Divide.

1) $(8x^5) \div (2x^3)$   $\qquad$ 3) $(-32x^7y^{15}) \div (-16x^7y)$   $\qquad$ 5) $(42m^3n^{10}) \div (6m^5n^{11})$
2) $(-24a^9b^3) \div (4a^6b^2)$   $\qquad$ 4) $(15st^6) \div (-3s^2t^4)$   $\qquad$ 6) $(54x^2yz^3) \div (-9x^2yz^9)$

2. <u>**Polynomial ÷ Monomial**</u>

To divide a polynomial by a monomial, we will use the following properties:

$$\frac{A+B}{C} = \frac{A}{C} + \frac{B}{C} \quad \text{and} \quad \frac{A-B}{C} = \frac{A}{C} - \frac{B}{C}.$$

**Examples.** Divide.

1) $\left(18x^3 + 21x^2\right) \div (3x) = \dfrac{18x^3 + 21x^2}{3x} = \dfrac{18x^3}{3x} + \dfrac{21x^2}{3x} = 6x^2 + 7x$

2) $\left(25y^2 + 15y\right) \div (-5y) = \dfrac{25y^2 + 15y}{-5y} = \dfrac{25y^2}{-5y} + \dfrac{15y}{-5y} = -5y + (-3) = -5y - 3$

3) $\left(-6x^4y^6 - 8x^2y^{10}\right) \div \left(-6x^2y^4\right) = \dfrac{-6x^4y^6 - 8x^2y^{10}}{-6x^2y^4} = \dfrac{-6x^4y^6}{-6x^2y^4} - \dfrac{\overset{4}{\cancel{8}}x^2y^{10}}{\underset{3}{\cancel{-6}}x^2y^4}$

$$= x^2y^2 - \left(-\dfrac{4}{3}y^6\right) \quad = x^2y^2 + \dfrac{4}{3}y^6$$

4) $\left(-32a^6b^5 + 12a^9b^{14} - 10a^8b\right) \div \left(12a^4b\right) = \dfrac{-32a^6b^5 + 12a^9b^{14} - 10a^8b}{12a^4b} = \dfrac{\overset{8}{\cancel{-32}}a^6b^5}{\underset{3}{\cancel{12}}a^4b} + \dfrac{12a^9b^{14}}{12a^4b} - \dfrac{\overset{5}{\cancel{10}}a^8b}{\underset{6}{\cancel{12}}a^4b}$

$$= -\dfrac{8}{3}a^2b^4 + a^5b^{13} - \dfrac{5}{6}a^4$$

Observe that all of the answers above are polynomials. As for the case of monomial ÷ monomial, the quotient does NOT have to be a polynomial. For example, observe that

$$\left(12a^2 + 5\right) \div (4a) = \dfrac{12a^2 + 5}{4a} = \dfrac{12a^2}{4a} + \dfrac{5}{4a} = 3a + \dfrac{5}{4a}$$

and the answer, $3a + \dfrac{5}{4a}$, is NOT a binomial since $\dfrac{5}{4a}$ is NOT a monomial. What does the expression $\dfrac{5}{4a}$ represent? Well, to understand this a little bit better, let's recall how we divide whole numbers. Suppose we want to divide $18 \div 7$. What we'll usually do is rewrite the example as either $7\overline{)\,18}$ (often seen when doing **long division**) or as $\dfrac{18}{7}$ (which is called an **improper fraction**). Let's look at the first case. To work out $7\overline{)\,18}$, we begin by figuring out the largest number, $q$, for which $7q$ is less than or equal to 18. Notice that $7(2) = 14$, but $7(3) = 21$ which is larger than 18. Therefore, our **quotient** is 2. Now, observe that $18 - 7(2) = 18 - 14 = 4$, so the **remainder** is 4. We usually write '2 R 4' to represent the fact that the quotient is 2 and the remainder is 4. In terms of long division, we have

$$
\begin{array}{r}
2 \text{ R } 4 \\
7\overline{)\,18} \\
-14 \\
\hline
4
\end{array}
$$

As for the second case, recall that we can evaluate $\dfrac{18}{7}$ by dividing the denominator into the numerator and express our improper fraction as a **mixed number.** We write the quotient as a whole number and the remainder as the numerator of a fraction whose denominator is the **divisor**, namely 7. We obtain the following:

$$\dfrac{18}{7} = 2 + \dfrac{4}{7} = 2\dfrac{4}{7}$$

No matter how it is written, the quotient and remainder are the same. Furthermore, we know that we can check our answer as follows:

$$18 = \underbrace{7(2) + 4}_{\text{divisor} \times \text{quotient} + \text{remainder}}$$

Now, let's return to our example $\dfrac{12a^2 + 5}{4a} = 3a + \dfrac{5}{4a}$. It turns out that in the expression $\dfrac{5}{4a}$, the numerator 5 is the remainder of our division problem and the term $3a$ is the quotient. We can also write this problem as

$$
\begin{array}{r}
3a \text{ R } 5 \\
4a\overline{)\,12a^2 + 5} \\
-\,12a^2 \\
\hline
5
\end{array}
$$

As above, we can check our answer by verifying that

$$12a^2 + 5 = 4a(3a) + 5,$$

which is true. **To summarize,** whenever you do a division problem (in fraction form) and end up with a fraction whose denominator (after simplifying) contains a variable, then the numerator of the fraction (before simplifying) is the remainder of the problem.

**Try These (Set 10):** Divide.

1) $(6x^2 + 12x) \div (3x)$                    4) $(36m^8 - 20m^6 + 7m^5) \div (-4m^6)$
2) $(25a^3 - 5a^2) \div (5a)$                   5) $(8y^2 + 14y^4 - y^5) \div (4y^3)$
3) $(-28x^6y^3 - 7x^5y^9 + 14x^{10}y^2) \div (-7x^5y)$

## 3.  Polynomial ÷ Polynomial

The method of dividing two polynomials is just like dividing two natural numbers. The first example below is done in detail.

**Examples.** Divide.

1) $(x^2 + 4x + 2) \div (x + 3)$

We begin by rewriting the example in long division format. If both polynomials are in one (and the same) variable, make sure that they are written in descending order. We obtain

$$x + 3 \overline{)\, x^2 + 4x + 2}$$

Now, divide the leading term of the dividend, $x^2 + 4x + 2$, by the leading term of the divisor, $x + 3$. We obtain $\dfrac{x^2}{x} = x$. Put this on top of the division symbol as follows:

$$\begin{array}{r} x \phantom{{}+ 4x + 2} \\ x + 3 \overline{)\, x^2 + 4x + 2} \end{array}$$

Next, we will multiply the divisor, $x + 3$, by $x$ and put the answer underneath the dividend, $x^2 + 4x + 2$. After doing so, we will subtract and obtain the following (remember to change the signs of the terms of the polynomial which is being subtracted):

$$\begin{array}{r} x \phantom{{}+ 4x + 2} \\ x + 3 \overline{)\, x^2 + 4x + 2} \\ -\ \underline{x^2 + 3x} \phantom{+ 2} \\ x \phantom{+ 2} \end{array}$$

As with division of natural numbers, you will carry down the term in the next column, namely $+2$, and repeat the process. Divide the leading term of $x + 2$ by the leading term of $x + 3$ and you will get $\dfrac{x}{x} = 1$. Put the $+1$ on top of the division symbol next to the $x$. You will have

$$\begin{array}{r} x + 1 \phantom{x + 2} \\ x + 3 \overline{)\, x^2 + 4x + 2} \\ -\ \underline{x^2 + 3x} \phantom{+ 2} \\ x + 2 \end{array}$$

Now multiply $x + 3$, by 1, put the answer underneath $x + 2$ and subtract. By doing so, you will get

$$
\begin{array}{r}
x + 1 \\
x + 3 \overline{)\ x^2 + 4x + 2} \\
-\ \underline{x^2 + 3x} \\
x + 2 \\
-\ \underline{\quad\quad x + 3} \\
-1
\end{array}
$$

Notice that there are no more terms to carry down and if you divide the leading term of $x + 3$ by the leading term of $-1$, you will have $\dfrac{-1}{x}$. Since this is not a monomial, we see that $-1$ is the remainder. Therefore, we write:

$$
\begin{array}{r}
x + 1\ \ \mathrm{R}\ \ -1 \\
x + 3 \overline{)\ x^2 + 4x + 2} \\
-\ \underline{x^2 + 3x} \\
x + 2 \\
-\ \underline{\quad\quad x + 3} \\
-1
\end{array}
$$

In order to check this answer, we need to verify that $\underbrace{x^2 + 4x + 2}_{\text{dividend}} = \underbrace{(x + 3)(x + 1) + (-1)}_{\text{divisor} \times \text{quotient} + \text{remainder}}$. Well, by applying the FOIL method, we obtain

$$(x + 3)(x + 1) + (-1) = x^2 + 3x + x + 3 + (-1) = x^2 + 4x + 2.$$

Notice that we can express the division problem in fractional form as

$$\frac{x^2 + 4x + 2}{x + 3} = x + 1 + \frac{-1}{x + 3} = x + 1 - \frac{1}{x + 3}.$$

2) $\left(2y^2 - y - 8\right) \div (y - 5)$

$$
\begin{array}{r}
2y + 9\ \ \mathrm{R}\ \ 37 \\
y - 5 \overline{)\ 2y^2 - y - 8} \\
-\ \underline{2y^2 - 10y} \\
9y -\ 8 \\
-\ \underline{\quad\quad 9y - 45} \\
37
\end{array}
$$

Once again, you can check this answer by verifying that

$$2y^2 - y - 8 = (y - 5)(2y + 9) + 37.$$

Notice that we can also write:

$$\frac{2y^2 - y - 8}{y - 5} = 2y + 9 + \frac{37}{y - 5}.$$

3) $\left(3x^2 + 5x - 1\right) \div \left(3x + 7\right)$

$$
\begin{array}{r}
x - \dfrac{2}{3} \ \ \text{R} \ \ \dfrac{11}{3} \\
\hline
3x + 7\overline{)\ 3x^2 + 5x - 1} \\
-\quad \underline{3x^2 + 7x} \\
-2x - \ 1 \\
-\quad \underline{-2x - \dfrac{14}{3}} \\
\dfrac{11}{3}
\end{array}
$$

4) $\left(14a^3 - 14a^2 - 2a + 8\right) \div \left(7a^2 - 7a\right)$

$$
\begin{array}{r}
2a \ \ \text{R} \ \ -2a + 8 \\
\hline
7a^2 - 7a\overline{)\ 14a^3 - 14a^2 - 2a + 8} \\
-\quad \underline{14a^3 - 14a^2} \\
-2a + 8
\end{array}
$$

Observe that $-2a + 8$ is the remainder since $\dfrac{-2a}{7a^2} = \dfrac{-2}{7a}$ contains a variable in the denominator. This means that we can't divide $-2a + 8$ by $7a^2 - 7a$ without a remainder. In fractional form, this division problem can be written as

$$\frac{14a^3 - 14a^2 - 2a + 8}{7a^2 - 7a} = 2a + \frac{-2a + 8}{7a^2 - 7a}.$$

5) $\left(5x^2 + 3\right) \div \left(x - 6\right)$

$$
\begin{array}{r}
5x + 30 \ \ \text{R} \ \ 183 \\
\hline
x - 6\overline{)\ 5x^2 + 0x + 3} \\
-\quad \underline{5x^2 - 30x} \\
30x + 3 \\
-\quad \underline{30x - 180} \\
183
\end{array}
$$

Notice that an '$x$-term' column was added into the binomial $5x^2 + 3$. This is done just in case an '$x$-term' appears as we work out the problem. Observe that this column was put in the middle of the terms $5x^2$ and 3 so that descending order is preserved. I usually call such a column a **ghost column**.

6) $\left(-2y^3 + 5y - 7\right) \div \left(2y + 3\right)$

Observe that there is no $y^2$ term in the dividend, $-2y^3 + 5y - 7$. Let's begin by creating a ghost column for the missing $y^2$. Then we will divide as before.

$$
\begin{array}{r}
-y^2 + \dfrac{3}{2}y + \dfrac{1}{4} \ \ \text{R} \ \ -\dfrac{31}{4} \\
\hline
2y + 3\overline{)\ -2y^3 + 0y^2 + 5y - 7} \\
-\quad \underline{-2y^3 - 3y^2} \\
3y^2 + 5y - 7 \\
-\quad \underline{3y^2 + \dfrac{9}{2}y} \\
\dfrac{1}{2}y - 7 \\
-\quad \underline{\dfrac{1}{2}y + \dfrac{3}{4}} \\
-\dfrac{31}{4}
\end{array}
$$

7) $\left(14x^4 - 10x^2 + x\right) \div \left(7x^2 - 3\right)$

This time, two ghost columns are needed, one for the '$x^3$-terms' and one for the constant terms.

$$
\begin{array}{r}
2x^2 - \dfrac{4}{7} \ \ \text{R} \ \ x - \dfrac{12}{7} \\[2pt]
\hline
7x^2 - 3\,) \ 14x^4 + 0x^3 - 10x^2 + x + 0 \\
\underline{-\,14x^4 \qquad\quad -\,6x^2 \qquad\qquad} \\
-\,4x^2 + x + 0 \\
\underline{- \qquad\qquad -\,4x^2 \qquad +\,\dfrac{12}{7} } \\[2pt]
x - \dfrac{12}{7}
\end{array}
$$

Notice that the '$x^3$-term' column was not needed here, but I put it there just in case I need it. It is better to be safe than sorry.

8) $\left(8x^3 - 27\right) \div (2x - 3)$

Insert two ghost columns, one for the '$x^2$-term' and one for the '$x$ term'.

$$
\begin{array}{r}
4x^2 + 6x + 9 \\
\hline
2x - 3\,) \ 8x^3 + \ 0x^2 + \ 0x - 27 \\
\underline{-\quad\ 8x^3 - 12x^2 \qquad\qquad} \\
12x^2 + \ 0x - 27 \\
\underline{-\qquad\ 12x^2 - 18x \qquad} \\
18x - 27 \\
\underline{-\qquad\qquad\quad 18x - 27} \\
0
\end{array}
$$

Here, both of the ghost columns were used. I'm glad we put them in there before getting ourselves into trouble. Notice that in fractional form, we have $\dfrac{8x^3 - 27}{2x - 3} = 4x^2 + 6x + 9$.

**Try These (Set 11):** Divide.

1) $\left(y^2 + 3y - 1\right) \div (y + 2)$  
2) $\left(4x^2 + 7x + 3\right) \div (4x - 1)$  
3) $\left(x^3 + 5x^2 - 6x + 3\right) \div (x + 3)$  

4) $\left(9x^2 + 8\right) \div (3x - 7)$  
5) $\left(a^4 + 2a^2 + 3a - 1\right) \div \left(a^2 + 3a - 1\right)$  

**Exercise 3.4**

Divide.

1. $\left(9x^6\right) \div \left(3x^3\right)$  2. $\left(4x^5\right) \div \left(2x^2\right)$   3. $\left(-16a^{14}\right) \div \left(4a^5\right)$   4. $\left(-20b^{10}\right) \div \left(2b^3\right)$

5. $\left(-25y^{18}\right) \div \left(-5y^{12}\right)$   6. $\left(-30y^{20}\right) \div \left(-3y^{11}\right)$   7. $\left(54x^9y^5\right) \div \left(9xy^4\right)$   8. $\left(42x^2y^8\right) \div \left(6xy^6\right)$

9. $\left(28s^5t^9\right) \div \left(-7s^3t^2\right)$   10. $\left(8m^{15}n^{18}\right) \div \left(-2m^4n^9\right)$   11. $\left(-7x^3y^7\right) \div \left(14x^3y^5\right)$

12. $\left(-2x^6y^{10}\right) \div \left(8x^2y^8\right)$    13. $\left(-6a^2b^3\right) \div \left(-16a^7b\right)$    14. $\left(-12x^4y^2\right) \div \left(-8x^2y\right)$

15. $\left(-25xy^6\right) \div \left(30x^7y^4\right)$    16. $\left(-32a^3b^4\right) \div \left(40a^2b^7\right)$    17. $(9x + 15) \div 3$

18. $(7x + 28) \div 7$    19. $\left(4x^2 - 12x\right) \div (4x)$    20. $\left(-6a^2 + 30a\right) \div (6a)$

21. $\left(-8x^3 + 24x^2\right) \div (-4x)$    22. $\left(12y^3 - 36y\right) \div (-6y)$    23. $\left(42x^3 + 18x^2 - 12x\right) \div (6x)$

24. $\left(28x^3 - 16x^2 + 20x\right) \div (4x)$    25. $\left(-9a^5 - 24a^4 + 3a^2\right) \div \left(-3a^2\right)$    26. $\left(-10b^7 + 14b^6 - 2b^3\right) \div \left(-2b^2\right)$

27. $\left(16x^2 + 15x\right) \div (8x)$    28. $\left(27x^3 - 10x\right) \div (9x)$    29. $\left(6x^3 - 8x^2 + 12x\right) \div (-6x)$

30. $\left(-5t^4 + 12t^3 - 25t^2\right) \div \left(-5t^2\right)$    31. $\left(-36x^6y^9 - 24x^4y^8 + 16x^{12}y^{10}\right) \div \left(-12x^3y^4\right)$

32. $\left(9a^4b^{13} + 24a^8b^4 - 30a^6b^7\right) \div \left(-6a^4b^3\right)$    33. $\left(16s^4t^5 - 18s^6t^{10} - 24s^4t^9\right) \div \left(8s^{12}t^9\right)$

34. $\left(-44x^6y^2 + 28xy^{14} - 6x^8y^{10}\right) \div \left(4x^{14}y\right)$    35. $\left(x^2 + 6x + 5\right) \div (x + 1)$

36. $\left(x^2 + 5x + 6\right) \div (x + 3)$    37. $\left(x^2 - x - 6\right) \div (x + 2)$

39. $\left(x^2 + 8x - 20\right) \div (x - 2)$    40. $\left(x^2 + 4x - 45\right) \div (x - 5)$    41. $\left(x^2 + 4x + 2\right) \div (x + 1)$

42. $\left(x^2 + 5x + 1\right) \div (x + 3)$    43. $\left(y^2 - 8y + 4\right) \div (y + 4)$    44. $\left(y^2 - 12y + 3\right) \div (y + 5)$

45. $\left(a^2 - 6a - 8\right) \div (a + 4)$    46. $\left(b^2 - 15b - 2\right) \div (b + 7)$    47. $\left(x^2 + 9x - 7\right) \div (x - 3)$

48. $\left(x^2 + 5x - 12\right) \div (x - 4)$    49. $\left(p^2 - 3p - 16\right) \div (p + 4)$    50. $\left(t^2 - 7t - 19\right) \div (t + 2)$

51. $\left(3x^2 + x + 2\right) \div (x + 5)$    52. $\left(4x^2 + 3x + 3\right) \div (x + 2)$    53. $\left(7y^2 - 3y + 1\right) \div (y + 3)$

54. $\left(4k^2 - k + 8\right) \div (k + 4)$    55. $\left(8m^2 - 2m - 5\right) \div (m - 2)$    56. $\left(12n^2 - 7n - 1\right) \div (n - 3)$

57. $\left(2x^2 + 3x - 4\right) \div (2x + 1)$    58. $\left(4x^2 + 7x - 2\right) \div (4x + 3)$    59. $\left(3a^2 - 6a + 5\right) \div (3a - 4)$

60. $\left(6a^2 - 7a - 2\right) \div (6a - 2)$    61. $\left(5t^2 - 10t - 3\right) \div (5t - 2)$    62. $\left(2y^2 - 3y - 8\right) \div (2y - 7)$

63. $\left(4y^2 + 2y + 3\right) \div (4y - 1)$    64. $\left(9x^2 - 2x + 2\right) \div (9x - 1)$    65. $\left(6n^2 - n + 4\right) \div (3n - 1)$

66. $\left(12p^2 + 2p - 4\right) \div (4p - 1)$    67. $\left(x^3 + 2x^2 - 3x + 1\right) \div (x + 4)$    68. $\left(x^3 + 5x^2 + 4x - 2\right) \div (x + 3)$

69. $\left(y^3 - 8y^2 - y + 2\right) \div (y + 3)$    70. $\left(y^3 - y^2 - 7y + 3\right) \div (y + 5)$    71. $\left(x^3 - 4x^2 - 3x + 2\right) \div (x - 2)$

72. $\left(x^3 - 8x^2 + x - 5\right) \div (x - 3)$    73. $\left(5a^3 + 3a^2 - a + 2\right) \div (a - 3)$    74. $\left(-3b^3 - 6b^2 + 4b - 1\right) \div (b - 3)$

75. $\left(y^2 - 5\right) \div (y + 3)$    76. $\left(x^2 + 12\right) \div (x + 7)$    77. $\left(8t^2 + 2t\right) \div (t - 4)$

78. $\left(-3m^2 + 4m\right) \div (m + 6)$    79. $\left(x^2 - 6x\right) \div \left(x^2 + 5\right)$    80. $\left(y^2 + 3y\right) \div \left(y^2 - 7\right)$

81. $\left(9p^2 + 2\right) \div \left(p^2 - 4p\right)$    82. $\left(2p^2 - 5\right) \div \left(p^2 - 6\right)$    83. $\left(4x^2 + 1\right) \div \left(x^2 - 6x\right)$

84. $\left(3x^2 - 2\right) \div \left(x^2 + 5x\right)$    85. $\left(x^3 - 3x + 4\right) \div (x - 2)$    86. $\left(y^3 - 4y^2 + 2\right) \div (y - 4)$

87. $\left(a^3 + 6a^2 + 2\right) \div (a + 5)$    88. $\left(a^3 + 4a - 9\right) \div (a - 3)$    89. $\left(4b^3 - b^2 + 3b\right) \div \left(b^2 + 3\right)$

90. $\left(7x^3 + x^2 - 2x\right) \div \left(x^2 - 2\right)$    91. $\left(x^4 + 5x^2 - 9\right) \div \left(x^2 - 1\right)$    92. $\left(t^4 - 6t^2 - 3\right) \div \left(t^2 + 4\right)$

93. $\left(8x^3 + 1\right) \div (2x + 1)$    94. $\left(27y^3 + 1\right) \div (3y + 1)$    95. $\left(64a^3 - 27\right) \div (4a - 3)$

96. $\left(125a^3 - 8\right) \div (5a - 2)$

# Section 3.5  Factoring Polynomials

In this section, we will learn how to factor a polynomial. Roughly speaking, to factor a polynomial means to express the polynomial as a product of polynomials other than 1 and itself. There are several techniques available for factoring a polynomial, depending on what the polynomial looks like. We will study a few such techniques in this section. To begin with, let's review some definitions which are used when factoring natural numbers.

**Definition:** The **factors** (or **divisors**) of a natural number, $n$, are those natural numbers which divide into $n$ without remainder.

For example, the set of factors of 6 is $\{1, 2, 3, 6\}$ and the set of factors of 32 is $\{1, 2, 4, 8, 16, 32\}$. Notice that every natural number has at least two factors. For example, 4 has three factors: 1, 2 and 4, while the number 17 has two factors: 1 and 17.

**Definition:** A natural number is called **factorable** (or **composite**) if it has factors other than 1 and itself. If a natural number has only the factors 1 and itself, it is called **prime**.

Notice that a factorable number can be written as a product of natural numbers other than 1 and itself, while a prime number can **only** be written as the product of 1 and itself. For example, $6 = 3 \times 2$, so 6 is factorable. The number 18 is also factorable, since it can be written as $18 = 2 \times 9 = 3 \times 6$. However, the number 23 is prime since $23 = 1 \times 23$ and this is the only way that 23 can be written as a product of two natural numbers. By convention, we consider the number 1 to be composite.

The definitions and examples given above should be familiar to you already. We would now like to generalize these definitions for polynomials. **Keep in mind that, when talking about factors, we are only considering natural numbers which are involved in the factoring process.**

**Definition:** The **factors** of a polynomial, $P$, are those polynomials which divide into $P$ without remainder. If $P$ has factors other than 1 and itself, it is called **factorable**. Otherwise, it is called **prime**.

For example, the polynomials $4x^2 + 2x$ and $x^2 + 6x + 5$ are factorable, since $4x^2 + 2x = 2x(2x + 1)$ and $x^2 + 6x + 5 = (x + 1)(x + 5)$. However, the polynomial $x^2 + 4$ is prime, which means that the only way to write it as a product is $1(x^2 + 4)$. If we allow rational numbers to be factors, then there will be infinitely many ways to factor this, but remember that we are only considering natural numbers as factors.

Our task is to learn how to factor a polynomial. Let's begin by recalling the definition of the greatest common factor of two or more natural numbers. Afterwards, we will generalize this definition for monomials and see how it helps us factor certain polynomials.

1. <u>**The Greatest Common Factor**</u>

**Definition:** The **greatest common factor** (**GCF**) of two or more natural numbers is the largest number which is a factor of each of the given numbers.

For example, let's find the GCF of 6 and 15. Well, the set of factors of 6 is $\{1, 2, 3, 6\}$ and the set of factors of 15 is $\{1, 3, 5, 15\}$. Notice that 1 and 3 are factors of both numbers, but 3 is the larger of the two. This means that the GCF is 3. An easier way to find the GCF of 6 and 15 is to take each factor of 6 and divide each into 15. The largest factor which doesn't give a remainder is the GCF. Observe that **any** two natural numbers have a GCF. For example, the GCF of 7 and 19 is 1, since the factors of 7 are 1 and 7 and the factors of 19 are 1 and 19.

We will define the GCF of two or more monomials.

**Definition:** The **greatest common factor (GCF)** of two or more monomials is the 'largest' monomial which is a factor of each of the given monomials.

We need to understand what it means to be the 'largest' monomial. Suppose we want the GCF of the monomials $5x^3$ and $10x^2$. Let's write down all of the factors of each monomial. Well, the set of factors of $5x^3$ is $\{1, 5, x, x^2, x^3, 5x, 5x^2, 5x^3\}$ and the set of factors of $10x^2$ is $\{1, 2, 5, 10, x, x^2, 2x, 5x, 10x, 2x^2, 5x^2, 10x^2\}$. The 'largest' monomial in common will be the monomial whose coefficient is the largest possible and whose variables are of the largest degree among all of the common factors. In our example, this monomial is $5x^2$.

There is a simple way to find the GCF of monomials. Rather than write down all of the factors of the monomials (which can take forever when the monomials have large degrees), all you have to do to find the GCF is to find the GCF of the coefficients and choose the **smallest** exponent of all of the exponents for each variable that appears in the monomials. For example, the GCF of $8x^4y^7$ and $20x^3y^{12}$ is $4x^3y^7$ since the GCF of 8 and 20 is 4, the smallest exponent of the $x$ variable ($x^4$ and $x^3$) is 3 and the smallest exponent of the $y$ variable ($y^{12}$ and $y^7$) is 7. Let's do some examples.

**Examples.** Find the GCF of the given monomials.

1) $4x^3$ and $6x^5$ is $2x^3$

2) $9y^4$ and $3y^8$ is $3y^4$

3) $16a^5b^2$ and $24ab^4$ is $8ab^2$

4) $25b^5$ and $15a^2b^6$ is $5b^5$

5) $7x^3y^6$ and $12x^8$ is $x^3$

6) $12x^5$, $9x^7$ and $21x^2$ is $3x^2$

So, why do we need GCF's? Well, suppose we want to factor the binomial $5x^3 + 10x^2$. Remember that to factor means expressing our polynomial as a product of other polynomials (with natural numbers as coefficients). Notice that the GCF of $5x^3$ and $10x^2$ is $5x^2$. This means that we can write our binomial as

$$5x^3 + 10x^2 = 5x^2 (x + 2).$$

Note that $x + 2$ is obtained by dividing the terms $5x^3$ and $10x^2$ by $5x^2$. Hence, $\dfrac{5x^3}{5x^2} = x$ and $\dfrac{10x^2}{5x^2} = 2$. Let's see some examples.

**Examples.** Factor.

1) $3x + 12 = 3 (x + 4)$, since the GCF of $3x$ and 12 is 3.

2) $6x^2 - 16x^3 = 2x^2 (3 - 8x)$, since the GCF of $6x^2$ and $16x^3$ is $2x^2$.

3) $7y^4 + 14y^2 = 7y^2 (y^2 + 2)$, since the GCF of $7y^4$ and $14y^2$ is $7y^2$.

4) $24a^2b^5 + 16a^5b^3 = 8a^2b^3 (3b^2 + 2a^3)$, since the GCF of $24a^2b^5$ and $16a^5b^3$ is $8a^2b^3$.

5) $9mn^4 - 15m^2 = 3m (3n^4 - 5m)$

6) $x^3 - 8x^2 + 10x = x\left(x^2 - 8x + 10\right)$

7) $4a^3 - 12a^5 - 18a^2 = 2a^2\left(2a - 6a^3 - 9\right)$

8) $20a^2b^4 + 15a^3b^3 - 25ab^5 = 5ab^3\left(4ab + 3a^2 - 5b^2\right)$

9) $\underbrace{x(x + 2) + 4(x + 2)}_{\text{Factors just like } xy+4y=y(x+4).} = (x + 2)(x + 4)$

10) $\underbrace{x^2(x - 3)^2 + 5(x - 3)}_{\text{Factors just like } x^2y^2+5y=y(x^2y+5).} = \underbrace{(x - 3)\left[x^2(x - 3) + 5\right]}_{\text{Simplify.}} = (x - 3)(x^3 - 3x^2 + 5)$

When you factor out a negative coefficient, the terms which appear in the parentheses will have different signs than in the original polynomial.

**Examples.** Factor out a negative coefficient.

1) $-6x + 12 = -6(x - 2)$   3) $-3a^3 + 9a^2 - 12 = -3(a^3 - 3a^2 + 4)$

2) $-8y - 24 = -8(y + 3)$   4) $-16t^2 + 32t + 64 = -16(t^2 - 2t - 4)$

**Try These (Set 12):** Factor.

1) $12x^4 + 20x^2$       3) $y^5 + 2y^2 - 6y$       5) $7st^8 - 21s^3t^2 + 7s^2t^2$       7) $x(x + 1) - 4(x + 1)$
2) $14a^3 - 9a$          4) $16x^4y^3 + 10xy^6$     6) $x^2y - xy^2 + xy$                 8) $3(x - 5) + (x - 5)^2$

2. **Difference of 2 Squares**

Whenever you have a polynomial which is a difference of two squares, you can factor it. The formula which tells us how to do this is already familiar to us from Section 3.3, namely:

$$A^2 - B^2 = (A + B)(A - B) \qquad \textbf{(Formula I)}$$

Before factoring such polynomials, it is good to have a list of perfect squares. Recall that a perfect square is a natural number which is the square of another natural number. The numbers on the left-hand side of each equals sign below are the perfect squares. I've only listed those which are seen frequently. You can find others if you'd like to.

## LIST OF SOME PERFECT SQUARES

| | |
|---|---|
| $1 = 1^2$ | $49 = 7^2$ |
| $4 = 2^2$ | $64 = 8^2$ |
| $9 = 3^2$ | $81 = 9^2$ |
| $16 = 4^2$ | $100 = 10^2$ |
| $25 = 5^2$ | $121 = 11^2$ |
| $36 = 6^2$ | $144 = 12^2$ |

Let's factor some differences of squares. In each of these examples, the GCF is 1, so we won't worry about looking for it.

**Examples.** Factor.

1) $x^2 - 1 = \underbrace{(x)^2 - (1)^2 = (x+1)(x-1)}_{\text{Let } A=x \text{ and } B=1 \text{ in Formula I.}}$

2) $y^2 - 9 = \underbrace{(y)^2 - (3)^2 = (y+3)(y-3)}_{\text{Let } A=y \text{ and } B=3 \text{ in Formula I.}}$

3) $49 - t^2 = \underbrace{(7)^2 - (t)^2 = (7+t)(7-t)}_{\text{Let } A=7 \text{ and } B=t \text{ in Formula I.}}$

4) $4x^2 - 25 = \underbrace{(2x)^2 - (5)^2 = (2x+5)(2x-5)}_{\text{Let } A=2x \text{ and } B=5 \text{ in Formula I.}}$

5) $100a^2 - 81b^2 = \underbrace{(10a)^2 - (9b)^2 = (10a+9b)(10a-9b)}_{\text{Let } A=10a \text{ and } B=9b \text{ in Formula I.}}$

6) $16x^2y^2 - 1 = \underbrace{(4xy)^2 - (1)^2 = (4xy+1)(4xy-1)}_{\text{Let } A=4xy \text{ and } B=1 \text{ in Formula I.}}$

7) $m^4 - 36 = \underbrace{(m^2)^2 - (6)^2 = (m^2+6)(m^2-6)}_{\text{Let } A=m^2 \text{ and } B=6 \text{ in Formula I.}}$

8) $\underbrace{(x+3)^2 - y^2 = [(x+3)+y][(x+3)-y]}_{\text{Let } A=x+3 \text{ and } B=y \text{ in Formula I.}} = (x+y+3)(x-y+3)$

9) $121x^2 - \dfrac{25}{4} = \underbrace{(11x)^2 - \left(\dfrac{5}{2}\right)^2 = \left(11x+\dfrac{5}{2}\right)\left(11x-\dfrac{5}{2}\right)}_{\text{Let } A=11x \text{ and } B=\frac{5}{2} \text{ in Formula I.}}$

Even though the difference of two squares always factors, the sum of two squares may not. In fact, we have the following theorem.

**Theorem:** If $A$ is a linear monomial whose coefficient is an integer, $B$ is a non-zero integer and the GCF of $A$ and $B$ is 1, then $A^2 + B^2$ is prime.

For example, the binomials $x^2 + 1$, $y^2 + 16$, $4a^2 + 9$, and $25x^2 + 36$ are all prime. However, the binomial $x^4 + 4$ is a sum of squares and **does** factor. In fact, we have $x^4 + 4 = (x^2 + 2x + 2)(x^2 - 2x + 2)$. Notice that in $x^4 + 4$, the term $x^4$ is **not** the square of a linear monomial, but rather the square of a quadratic monomial, $(x^2)^2$. Consequently, the above theorem does not apply to $x^4 + 4$.

**Try These (Set 13):** Factor. If any polynomial doesn't factor, state that it is prime.

1) $x^2 - 4$          4) $25 - 144y^2$          7) $x^2 + 100$

2) $a^2 - 16$          5) $s^2 - 9t^2$          8) $49m^2 + 9$

3) $121t^2 - 1$          6) $81x^2 - \dfrac{64}{169}y^2$

3. **Sum / Difference of 2 Cubes**

We will learn how to factor a sum of two cubes and a difference of two cubes. The formulas which tell us how to do this are already familiar to us from Section 3.3, namely:

$$\text{Formula II:} \quad A^3 + B^3 = (A + B)\left(A^2 - AB + B^2\right) \quad \text{and}$$
$$\text{Formula III:} \quad A^3 - B^3 = (A - B)\left(A^2 + AB + B^2\right)$$

Notice that the two formulas are pretty much identical, except the signs of the terms.

Let's write a list of perfect cubes which will often be seen. Recall that a perfect cube is a natural number which is the cube of another natural number.

### LIST OF SOME PERFECT CUBES

| | |
|---|---|
| $1 = 1^3$ | $216 = 6^3$ |
| $8 = 2^3$ | $343 = 7^3$ |
| $27 = 3^3$ | $512 = 8^3$ |
| $64 = 4^3$ | $729 = 9^3$ |
| $125 = 5^3$ | $1,000 = 10^3$ |

**Examples.** Factor.

1) $x^3 + 1 = \underbrace{(x)^3 + (1)^3 = (x + 1)\left(x^2 - (x)(1) + (1)^2\right)}_{\text{Let } A=x \text{ and } B=1 \text{ in Formula II.}} = (x + 1)\left(x^2 - x + 1\right)$

2) $y^3 - 27 = \underbrace{(y)^3 - (3)^3 = (y - 3)\left(y^2 + (y)(3) + (3)^2\right)}_{\text{Let } A=y \text{ and } B=3 \text{ in Formula III.}} = (y - 3)\left(y^2 + 3y + 9\right)$

3) $8 + t^3 = \underbrace{(2)^3 + (t)^3 = (2 + t)\left((2)^2 - (2)(t) + t^2\right)}_{\text{Let } A=2 \text{ and } B=t \text{ in Formula II.}} = (2 + t)\left(4 - 2t + t^2\right)$

4) $64a^3 - 27 = \underbrace{(4a)^3 - (3)^3 = (4a - 3)\left((4a)^2 + (4a)(3) + (3)^2\right)}_{\text{Let } A=4a \text{ and } B=3 \text{ in Formula III.}} = (4a - 3)\left(16a^2 + 12a + 9\right)$

5) $125m^3 + 8n^3 = \underbrace{(5m)^3 + (2n)^3 = (5m + 2n)\left((5m)^2 - (5m)(2n) + (2n)^2\right)}_{\text{Let } A=5m \text{ and } B=2n \text{ in Formula II.}}$

$$= (5m + 2n)\left(25m^2 - 10mn + 4n^2\right)$$

6) $27a^3 - \dfrac{1}{125} = (3a)^3 - \left(\dfrac{1}{5}\right)^3 = \left(3a - \dfrac{1}{5}\right)\left((3a)^2 + (3a)\left(\dfrac{1}{5}\right) + \left(\dfrac{1}{5}\right)^2\right) = \left(3a - \dfrac{1}{5}\right)\left(9a^2 + \dfrac{3a}{5} + \dfrac{1}{25}\right)$

**Try These (Set 14):** Factor.

1) $x^3 - 1$          3) $8y^3 + 1$          5) $216 - 125y^3$

2) $a^3 + 27$        4) $27x^3 - y^3$        6) $a^3 - \dfrac{125}{64}$

Let us now factor some polynomials which contain more than two factors in their factorizations. The key thing to remember is that whenever you want to factor a polynomial, **look for the GCF first**.

**Examples.** Factor completely.

1) $2x^2 - 8 = \underbrace{2(x^2 - 4)}_{\text{The GCF is 2.}} = \underbrace{2(x+2)(x-2)}_{x^2-4 \text{ factored}}$

2) $x^3 - x = \underbrace{x(x^2 - 1)}_{\text{The GCF is } x.} = \underbrace{x(x+1)(x-1)}_{x^2-1 \text{ factored}}$

3) $3xy^4 - 27xy^2 = \underbrace{3xy^2(y^2 - 9)}_{\text{The GCF is } 3xy^2.} = \underbrace{3xy^2(y+3)(y-3)}_{y^2-9 \text{ factored}}$

4) $32m^3n^3 + 4m^3 = \underbrace{4m^3(8n^3 + 1)}_{\text{The GCF is } 4m^3.} = \underbrace{4m^3(2n+1)(4n^2 - 2n + 1)}_{8n^3+1 \text{ factored}}$

5) $4x^2 - 64 = \underbrace{4(x^2 - 16)}_{\text{The GCF is 4.}} = \underbrace{4(x+4)(x-4)}_{x^2-16 \text{ factored}}$

Notice that if you don't factor out the GCF first, you will obtain

$$\underbrace{4x^2}_{(2x)^2} - \underbrace{64}_{(8)^2} = (2x+8)(2x-8),$$

which is **not** factored completely since both $2x + 8$ and $2x - 8$ can be factored further. By continuing this, we obtain:

$$4x^2 - 64 = (2x+8)(2x-8) = 2(x+4) \cdot 2(x-4) = 4(x+4)(x-4).$$

So we have now factored it completely. If you forget to factor out the GCF first, you may not realize that the polynomial is not factored completely. Be careful!

6) $\underbrace{t^4 - 81}_{\text{The GCF is 1.}} = \underbrace{(t^2)^2 - (9)^2 = (\overbrace{t^2 + 9}^{\text{prime}})(t^2 - 9)}_{\text{Use Formula I.}} = (t^2 + 9)\underbrace{(t+3)(t-3)}_{t^2-9 \text{ factored}}$

7) $x^6 - y^6 = \underbrace{(x^3)^2 - (y^3)^2}_{\text{Use Formula I.}} = (x^3 + y^3)(x^3 - y^3) = \underbrace{(x+y)(x^2 - xy + y^2)}_{x^3+y^3 \text{ factored}}\underbrace{(x-y)(x^2 + xy + y^2)}_{x^3-y^3 \text{ factored}}$

Observe that, if we factor $x^6 - y^6$ as a difference of two cubes rather than two squares, we obtain

$$x^6 - y^6 = \underbrace{(x^2)^3 - (y^2)^3}_{\text{Use Formula III.}} = (x^2 - y^2)(x^4 + x^2y^2 + y^4) = \underbrace{(x+y)(x-y)}_{x^2-y^2 \text{ factored}}(x^4 + x^2y^2 + y^4).$$

By comparing this factorization to the first one, we see that factoring $x^6 - y^6$ as a difference of two squares gives us a more complete factorization compared to factoring it as a difference of two cubes. This is good to keep in mind.

> If a binomial is both a difference of two squares and a difference of two cubes, factor it as a difference of two squares.

**Try These (Set 15):** Factor completely.

1) $5x^2 - 20$      3) $a^2x^3 + 27a^2$      5) $x^4 - 256$   (Hint: $256 = 16^2$)

2) $3y^3 - 48y$      4) $9st^4 - 72st$      6) $a^6 - 1$

## 4. <u>Quadratic Trinomials</u>

Recall that a quadratic polynomial (in one variable) is a polynomial of degree 2. We will now learn how to factor quadratic trinomials, which are polynomials of the form $ax^2 + bx + c$, where $a$, $b$, and $c$ are nonzero real numbers. To begin with, let us focus on those quadratic trinomials which have the leading coefficient of 1, namely: $x^2 + bx + c$. The first thing to observe is that any such trinomial comes from multiplying two binomials by the FOIL method. For example, recall that

$$(x+4)(x-7) \;=\; \overbrace{x^2}^{F} + \overbrace{(-7x)}^{O} + \overbrace{4x}^{I} + \overbrace{(-28)}^{L}$$

$$= \underbrace{x^2 \underset{O+I}{-3x} -28}_{F \qquad L}$$

and the trinomial $x^2 - 3x - 28$ is a quadratic trinomial. What's important to notice is that the last term, $-28$, comes from multiplying the numbers $+4$ and $-7$ in the factorization, whereas the coefficient of the term obtained by adding the outer and inner terms, $-3$, comes from adding the numbers $+4$ and $-7$. This provides us with a strategy for factoring a quadratic trinomial whose leading coefficient is 1. When factoring $x^2 + bx + c$, try to find two integers which multiply to $c$ and add up to $b$. If two such integers can be found (call them $p$ and $q$), then $x^2 + bx + c$ can be factored as

$$x^2 + bx + c = (x+p)(x+q), \text{ where } p+q = b \text{ and } pq = c.$$

If no such integers $p$ and $q$ can be found, then the trinomial $x^2 + bx + c$ is prime. This method of finding the numbers which yield the factorization is known as the **Reverse FOIL Method.** We will only look at polynomials for which $p$ and $q$ are integer valued. It is possible to have a quadratic trinomial which has factors whose coefficients are not integers. For example, notice that $(x+4)\left(x+\frac{1}{2}\right) = x^2 + \frac{9}{2}x + 2$. Going in the opposite direction, we have $x^2 + \frac{9}{2}x + 2 = (x+4)\left(x+\frac{1}{2}\right)$, and so the factor $x + \frac{1}{2}$ has a term with a rational coefficient, namely $\frac{1}{2}$. We will not be looking at polynomials which factor in this way. **We will only be concerned with factoring polynomials whose factors contain terms with integer coefficients.**

For example, let's factor the trinomial $x^2 + 7x + 12$. Observe that the leading coefficient is 1, so the Reverse FOIL Method requires us to find two numbers, say $p$ and $q$, such that $pq = +12$ and $p + q = +7$. What you should do is to think about all of the possible pairs of numbers which multiply to $+12$. For starters, notice that both numbers **must** be positive, since their product is positive and their sum is positive as well. Observe that

$$
\begin{aligned}
12 \;&=\; 12 \times 1 \quad \text{and} \quad 12 + 1 = 13, \quad \text{no good} \\
&=\; 6 \times 2 \quad \text{and} \quad 6 + 2 = 8, \quad \text{no good} \\
&=\; 4 \times 3 \quad \text{and} \quad 4 + 3 = 7, \quad \text{GOOD.}
\end{aligned}
$$

And so, $x^2 + 7x + 12 = (x+4)(x+3)$. Notice that the commutative property allows us to write the answer as $x^2 + 7x + 12 = (x+3)(x+4)$ as well.

**Examples.** Factor.

1) $x^2 + 3x + 2 = (x+2)(x+1)$, since $2 \times 1 = 2$ and $2 + 1 = 3$.

2) $y^2 - 7y + 12 = (y - 3)(y - 4)$, since $(-3)(-4) = 12$ and $(-3) + (-4) = -7$.

3) $x^2 + 2x - 35 = (x - 5)(x + 7)$, since $(-5)(7) = -35$ and $(-5) + 7 = 2$.

4) $a^2 + 9a + 18 = (a + 6)(a + 3)$, since $6 \times 3 = 18$ and $6 + 3 = 9$.

5) $t^2 + 10t - 24 = (t + 12)(t - 2)$, since $(12)(-2) = -24$ and $12 + (-2) = 10$.

6) $x^2 + 2x + 1 = (x + 1)(x + 1) = (x + 1)^2$

7) $y^2 + 10y + 25 = (y + 5)(y + 5) = (y + 5)^2$

8) $m^2 - 18m + 81 = (m - 9)(m - 9) = (m - 9)^2$

9) $k^2 - 6k + 9 = (k - 3)(k - 3) = (k - 3)^2$

10) $x^2 + 7x + 2$ is prime, since there are no two integers, $p$ and $q$, for which $pq = 2$ and $p + q = 7$.

11) $a^2 - 4a - 7$ is prime, since there are no two integers, $p$ and $q$, for which $pq = -7$ and $p + q = -4$.

12) $y^2 + 9 = y^2 + 0y + 9$ is prime, since there are no two integers, $p$ and $q$, for which $pq = 9$ and $p + q = 0$.

Notice that the trinomials $x^2 + 2x + 1$, $y^2 + 10y + 25$, $m^2 - 18m + 81$, and $k^2 - 6k + 9$ each factor into the square of another polynomial. These trinomials are special and will be useful later on.

**Definition: A trinomial square** is a trinomial which can be factored into the square of a polynomial.

There's a simple way of determining whether or not a trinomial is a trinomial square. If the first and last terms of the trinomial are squares of two monomials, say $A$ and $B$, look and see if the middle term is $2AB$. If it is, then the trinomial is a trinomial square. Otherwise, it isn't. This is a consequence of the formulas:

$$A^2 + 2AB + B^2 = (A + B)^2$$
$$A^2 - 2AB + B^2 = (A - B)^2$$

**Examples.** Factor.

1) $\underbrace{x^2}_{(x)^2} + \underbrace{2x}_{2(x)(1)} + \underbrace{1}_{(1)^2} = (x + 1)^2$

2) $\underbrace{y^2}_{(y)^2} - \underbrace{8y}_{2(y)(4)} + \underbrace{16}_{(4)^2} = (y - 4)^2$

3) $\underbrace{a^2}_{(a)^2} - \underbrace{20a}_{2(a)(10)} + \underbrace{100}_{(10)^2} = (a - 10)^2$

4) $\underbrace{t^2}_{(t)^2} + \underbrace{14t}_{2(t)(7)} + \underbrace{49}_{(7)^2} = (t + 7)^2$

**Try These (Set 16):** Factor. If a polynomial is not factorable, state that it is prime.

1) $x^2 + 7x + 10$

2) $k^2 + 16k + 64$

3) $y^2 - 13y + 30$

4) $x^2 - 3x + 12$

5) $y^2 + 16y + 20$

6) $m^2 - 24m + 144$

7) $a^2 - a - 56$

8) $p^2 + 11p - 42$

9) $b^2 - 18b + 81$

We will learn how to factor quadratic trinomials whose leading coefficient is positive and not equal to 1, namely $ax^2 + bx + c$ with $a \neq 1$ and $a > 0$. As before, notice that any trinomial of this form comes from multiplying two binomials by the FOIL method. For example, recall that

$$
\begin{aligned}
(2x + 7)(x - 3) &= \overbrace{2x^2}^{F} + \overbrace{(-6x)}^{O} + \overbrace{7x}^{I} + \overbrace{(-21)}^{L} \\
&= \underbrace{2x^2}_{F} \underbrace{+x}_{O+I} \underbrace{-21}_{L}
\end{aligned}
$$

and the trinomial $2x^2 + x - 21$ is a quadratic trinomial whose leading coefficient is 2. Notice that the first term, $2x^2$, comes from multiplying the first terms, $2x$ and $x$, whereas the last term, $-21$, comes from multiplying the numbers in the factorization, $+7$ and $-3$. Unlike the case where the leading coefficient is 1, the numbers $+7$ and $-3$ **do not** add up to the coefficient of the middle term, $+1$. This means that we cannot use the Reverse FOIL Method. There are two methods which we will learn about which will allow us to factor these types of polynomials. The first one is called the **Trial and Error Method** and the second is called the **Grouping Method.** Let me say a little bit about the Trial and Error Method. Roughly speaking, you choose two terms which multiply to first term of the trinomial and choose two numbers which multiply to the last term of the trinomial. Afterwards, check to see whether or not the outer and inner terms combine to the middle term in the trinomial. If so, you are done. If not, try out the other possible combinations.

To demonstrate how the Trial and Error Method works, let's factor $2x^2 + 5x - 3$. You begin by thinking of two monomials (each containing $x$) which multiply to $2x^2$. There is only one possibility, namely $2x$ and $x$. These will be the 'F' terms in FOIL. Now think of two numbers which multiply to $-3$. The possibilities are $\{-1, 3\}$ and $\{1, -3\}$. The numbers in one of these sets of possibilities will (hopefully) be the 'L' terms in FOIL. Now you try the different possibilities of factoring:

$$(2x + 3)(x - 1) \quad \text{fails, since } O + I = (2x)(-1) + 3(x) = +x \text{ and we want } +5x$$
$$(2x + 1)(x - 3) \quad \text{fails, since } O + I = (2x)(-3) + 1(x) = -5x \text{ and we want } +5x$$

but

$$(2x - 1)(x + 3) \quad \text{works, since } O + I = (2x)(3) + (-1)(x) = 5x, \text{ which is what we want.}$$

Notice that our second attempt, $(2x + 1)(x - 3)$, was close to what we wanted except the signs. When this happens, just change the signs of your numbers and it will work. Moreover, you should realize that it DOES matter where your numbers go.

Let's do another example in detail. Let's factor $4y^2 + 17y + 15$. As before, you begin by thinking of two monomials (each containing $y$) which multiply to $4y^2$. There are two possibilities, $\{2y, 2y\}$ and $\{4y, y\}$. Now think of two numbers which multiply to 15. Both numbers must be positive, since their product has to be $+15$ and the middle term of the trinomial is $+17y$. This means that we have $\{3, 5\}$ and $\{15, 1\}$. Let's try some different possibilities:

$$(2y + 3)(2y + 5) \quad \text{fails, since } O + I = (2y)(5) + 3(2y) = +16y \text{ and we want } +17y$$
$$(2y + 15)(2y + 1) \quad \text{fails, since } O + I = (2y)(1) + 15(2y) = +32y \text{ and we want } +17y$$
$$(4y + 3)(y + 5) \quad \text{fails, since } O + I = (4y)(5) + 3(y) = +23y \text{ and we want } +17y$$

but

$$(4y + 5)(y + 3) \quad \text{works, since } O + I = (4y)(3) + 5(y) = +17y.$$

If it has turned out that none of the possibilities work, then the polynomial is prime. It may get frustrating when there are lots of possibilities to check until you reach the right answer. As you do more examples, you will start to see patterns in the numbers which enable you to get the right answer quickly. Let me give you some examples. Try them out **without** looking at the answers. Afterwards, compare your results to mine.

**Examples.** Factor the following using the Trial and Error Method.

1) $2x^2 + 5x + 2 = \underbrace{(2x+1)\,(x+2)}_{O+I=(2x)(2)+1(x)=5x}$

5) $16x^2 - 14x - 15 = \underbrace{(8x+5)\,(2x-3)}_{O+I=(8x)(-3)+5(2x)=-14x}$

2) $3y^2 - 7y + 4 = \underbrace{(3y-4)\,(y-1)}_{O+I=(3y)(-1)+(-4)(y)=-7y}$

6) $20p^2 - 31p + 12 = \underbrace{(4p-3)\,(5p-4)}_{O+I=(4p)(-4)+(-3)(5p)=-31p}$

3) $5t^2 - 2t - 7 = \underbrace{(5t-7)\,(t+1)}_{O+I=(5t)(1)+(-7)(t)=-2t}$

7) $2y^2 + y + 8$ is prime, since none of the possibilities works.

4) $4a^2 + 16a + 15 = \underbrace{(2a+3)\,(2a+5)}_{O+I=(2a)(5)+3(2a)=16a}$

8) $13b^2 - 5b - 2$ is prime, since none of the possibilities works.

The other method of factoring a trinomial $ax^2 + bx + c$ is called the **Grouping Method**. Let me demonstrate how this works by factoring $2x^2 + 5x + 2$ (which we have already done in Example 1 above). The idea is to split up the monomial $5x$ into two monomials. The coefficients of these two monomials are obtained in the following way:

$$\text{find two numbers which multiply to } \overbrace{(2)(2)}^{\text{'F' and 'L'}} = 4 \text{ and add up to } \overbrace{5}^{\text{O+I}}.$$

Well, the numbers 4 and 1 do the trick, since $(4)(1) = 4$ and $4 + 1 = 5$. Now we rewrite our trinomial as

$$2x^2 + 5x + 2 = 2x^2 \underbrace{+ 4x + 1x}_{\text{split up } 5x} + 2.$$

Next, we factor the GCF from the first two and the last two terms and obtain:

$$2x^2 + 4x + 1x + 2 = 2x\underline{(x+2)} + 1\underline{(x+2)}.$$

The final step is to factor the polynomial in the parentheses and obtain:

$$2x^2 + 5x + 2 = 2x^2 + 4x + 1x + 2 = 2x\underline{(x+2)} + 1\underline{(x+2)} = (x+2)(2x+1).$$

If you have trouble with this, think of the $(x+2)$ as a letter, say $y$. Then $2x(x+2) + 1(x+2)$ is the same as $2xy + 1y$, which factors as $y(2x+1)$. By replacing $y$ with $(x+2)$, we obtain the factorization $(x+2)(2x+1)$ as before. Let's take a look at some examples. Try them out **without** looking at the answers. Afterwards, check your work.

**Examples.** Factor using the Grouping Method.

1) $2x^2 - x - 6$

Notice that the coefficients of the first term, last term and outer + inner term are 2, $-6$ and $-1$, respectively. We want to find two numbers which multiply to $(2)(-6) = -12$ and add up to $-1$. Observe that $(-4)(3) = -12$ and $-4 + 3 = -1$, so the numbers that we need are $-4$ and 3. We write the trinomial as

$$2x^2 - x - 6 = 2x^2 - 4x + 3x - 6$$

and now use the Grouping Method. We obtain:

$$\begin{aligned} 2x^2 - x - 6 &= 2x^2 - 4x + 3x - 6 \\ &= 2x(x-2) + 3(x-2) \\ &= (x-2)(2x+3) \end{aligned}$$

2) $5y^2 - 17y + 6 = \underbrace{5y^2 - 15y - 2y + 6}_{(-15)(-2)=30 \text{ and } -15+(-2)=-17} = 5y\underline{(y - 3)} - 2\underline{(y - 3)} = \underline{(y - 3)}(5y - 2)$

3) $6t^2 + 7t - 20 = \underbrace{6t^2 + 15t - 8t - 20}_{(15)(-8)=-120 \text{ and } 15+(-8)=7} = 3t\underline{(2t + 5)} - 4\underline{(2t + 5)} = \underline{(2t + 5)}(3t - 4)$

As Example 3 demonstrates, the process of finding the two numbers can be quite tedious, since there may be many possibilities for the two numbers to multiply to the one you want (here, it is $(6)(-20) = -120$). For this reason, I prefer to use the Trial and Error Method instead of the Grouping Method. You may use whichever method you like. Let's do some more.

4) $12a^2 + 29a + 15 = \underbrace{12a^2 + 9a + 20a + 15}_{(9)(20)=180 \text{ and } 9+20=29} = 3a\underline{(4a + 3)} + 5\underline{(4a + 3)} = \underline{(4a + 3)}(3a + 5)$

5) $6x^2 - 13x + 6 = \underbrace{6x^2 - 9x - 4x + 6}_{(-9)(-4)=36 \text{ and } (-9)+(-4)=-13} = 3x\underline{(2x - 3)} - 2\underline{(2x - 3)} = \underline{(2x - 3)}(3x - 2)$

6) $14n^2 + 43n + 20 = \underbrace{14n^2 + 35n + 8n + 20}_{(35)(8)=280 \text{ and } 35+8=43} = 7n\underline{(2n + 5)} + 4\underline{(2n + 5)} = \underline{(2n + 5)}(7n + 4)$

7) $25y^2 - 60y + 36 = \underbrace{25y^2 - 30y - 30y + 36}_{(-30)(-30)=900 \text{ and } (-30)+(-30)=-60} = 5y\underline{(5y - 6)} - 6\underline{(5y - 6)} = \underline{(5y - 6)}(5y - 6)$, which

can also be written as $(5y - 6)^2$.

Notice that the trinomial $25y^2 - 60y + 36$ is a trinomial square, since $25y^2 = (5y)^2$, $(6)^2 = 36$ and $60y = 2(5y)(6)$. Therefore, by using the formula $A^2 - 2AB + B^2 = (A - B)^2$ with $A = 5y$ and $B = 6$, we obtain the answer in a simpler way.

**Try These (Set 17):** Factor using any technique.

1) $3x^2 + 14x + 8$

2) $16y^2 + 24y + 9$

3) $10a^2 - 37a + 7$

4) $9t^2 - 30t + 16$

5) $14x^2 - 9x - 5$

6) $18p^2 + 37p - 20$

7) $100y^2 - 180y + 81$

## 5. Polynomials with Four Terms

In the previous examples, we factored quadratic trinomials using the Grouping Method. We will apply this method to factor polynomials containing 4 terms. Suppose we want to factor $x^3 + 2x^2 + 5x + 10$. As before, we group the first two and last two terms. Then we factor the GCF from each group. If the remaining polynomials in the parentheses are the same, we can factor it out and we are done. Following this routine, we have:

$$\begin{aligned} x^3 + 2x^2 + 5x + 10 &= \left(x^3 + 2x^2\right) + (5x + 10) \\ &= x^2(x + 2) + 5(x + 2) \\ &= (x + 2)\left(x^2 + 5\right). \end{aligned}$$

So, the polynomial is factored. Let's try some examples.

**Examples.** Factor.

1) $x^3 + 3x^2 + x + 3 = (x^3 + 3x^2) + (x + 3) = x^2\underline{(x + 3)} + 1\underline{(x + 3)} = \underline{(x + 3)}(x^2 + 1)$

2) $2y^3 + 8y^2 - y - 4 = (2y^3 + 8y^2) + (-y - 4) = 2y^2\underline{(y + 4)} - 1\underline{(y + 4)} = \underline{(y + 4)}(2y^2 - 1)$

3) $5n^3 - 30n^2 + 4n - 24 = 5n^2(n - 6) + 4(n - 6) = (n - 6)(5n^2 + 4)$

4) $a^5 - 3a^3 + 2a^2 - 6 = a^3(a^2 - 3) + 2(a^2 - 3) = (a^2 - 3)(a^3 + 2)$

5) $3p^6 + 12p^4 - 2p^2 - 8 = 3p^4(p^2 + 4) - 2(p^2 + 4) = (p^2 + 4)(3p^4 - 2)$

6) $7x^2y - 4x^2 + 14y - 8 = x^2(7y - 4) + 2(7y - 4) = (7y - 4)(x^2 + 2)$

There are polynomials which factor by grouping the first three terms rather than the first and last two terms. For example, notice that

$$x^2 + 2x + 1 - y^2 = (x^2 + 2x + 1) - y^2 = (x + 1)^2 - y^2 = (x + 1 + y)(x + 1 - y)$$

by applying the formula $A^2 - B^2 = (A + B)(A - B)$ with $A = x + 1$ and $B = y$.

7) $a^2 - 10a + 25 - b^2 = (a^2 - 10a + 25) - b^2 = (a - 5)^2 - b^2 = (a - 5 + b)(a - 5 - b)$

8) $4y^2 + 4y + 1 - 9x^2 = (4y^2 + 4y + 1) - 9x^2 = (2y + 1)^2 - (3x)^2 = (2y + 1 + 3x)(2y + 1 - 3x)$

Note that if a polynomial with four terms doesn't factor by the Grouping Method, that doesn't mean that it is prime. It just means that the method which we are using is not going to give us the factorization (if there is one). For example, if we try to factor $8x^4 - 3x^3 - 2x^2 - 3$ using the Grouping Method mentioned above, we will not succeed. However, $8x^4 - 3x^3 - 2x^2 - 3$ does factor into $(x - 1)(8x^3 + 5x^2 + 3x + 3)$ and so it is not prime.

**Try These (Set 18):** Factor.

1) $t^3 + 4t^2 + 2t + 8$
2) $x^4 + 7x^3 - 3x - 21$
3) $2y^3 - 10y^2 - y + 5$

4) $18a^4 + 27a^3 + 4a + 6$
5) $8p^5 + 18p^3 - 20p^2 - 45$
6) $a^2 - 14a + 49 - 9b^2$

6. **Putting it All Together**

**Examples.** Factor completely.

1) $2x^2 + 4x + 2 = \underbrace{2(x^2 + 2x + 1)}_{\text{GCF first}} = \underbrace{2(x + 1)(x + 1)}_{x^2+2x+1 \text{ factors}} = 2(x + 1)^2$

2) $5x^3 + 35x^2 + 30x = \underbrace{5x(x^2 + 7x + 6)}_{\text{GCF first}} = \underbrace{5x(x + 6)(x + 1)}_{x^2+7x+6 \text{ factors}}$

3) $6a^4b^2 - 6a^3b^2 - 120a^2b^2 = 6a^2b^2(a^2 - a - 20) = 6a^2b^2(a - 5)(a + 4)$

4) $10y^5 - 11y^4 - 6y^3 = y^3(10y^2 - 11y - 6) = y^3(5y + 2)(2y - 3)$

5) $36a^4b + 56a^3b - 32a^2b = 4a^2b(9a^2 + 14a - 8) = 4a^2b(9a - 4)(a + 2)$

6) $-24p^2 - 28p + 20 = \underbrace{-4(6p^2 + 7p - 5)}_{\text{Factor out a negative.}} = -4(3p + 5)(2p - 1)$

7) $48 - 2y - y^2 = \underbrace{-1(y^2 + 2y - 48)}_{\text{Factor out a negative.}} = -1(y + 8)(y - 6)$

8) $x^4 - 2x^2 + 1 = \underbrace{(x^2 - 1)(x^2 - 1)}_{\text{Use Reverse FOIL.}} = (x + 1)(x - 1)(x + 1)(x - 1) = (x + 1)^2(x - 1)^2$

9) $t^6 + 10t^3 + 16 = \underbrace{(t^3 + 2)(t^3 + 8)}_{\text{Use Reverse FOIL.}} = \overset{\text{prime}}{(t^3 + 2)}\underbrace{(t + 2)(t^2 - 2t + 4)}_{t^3 + 8 \text{ in factored form}}$

10) $12a^2 + 5ab - 2b^2 = \underbrace{(4a - b)(3a + 2b)}_{\text{Use Reverse FOIL.}}$

11) $6m^5n^3 + 14m^4n^4 + 4m^3n^5 = \underbrace{2m^3n^3(3m^2 + 7mn + 2n^2)}_{\text{The GCF first.}} = 2m^3n^3\underbrace{(3m + n)(m + 2n)}_{\text{Use Reverse FOIL.}}$

**Try These (Set 19):** Factor completely.

1) $3x^3 + 18x^2 + 24x$

2) $8y^4 - 8y^3 - 6y^2$

3) $-8t^5 + 11t^4 + 10t^3$

4) $-45m^3 - 120m^2 - 80m$

5) $x^4 - 18x^2 + 32$

6) $7y^7 + 14y^6 - 7y^4 - 14y^3$

7) $12a^2 + 23at + 10t^2$

**Exercise 3.5**

In Exercises 1-21, factor the GCF from each polynomial.

1. $3x + 12$        2. $5y + 35$        3. $2a^2 + 6$        4. $7b^2 + 7$

5. $5x^2 + 10x - 20$    6. $4t^2 + 12t - 28$    7. $12x^2 + 8x$    8. $24y^2 + 6y$

9. $3x^3 - 21x^2$    10. $11p^3 + 5p^2$    11. $8q^3 + 12q^2$    12. $18x^4 + 27x^3 - 9x^2$

13. $32y^4 - 16y^3 + 8y^2$    14. $12x^3y + 27x^2y^2$    15. $20a^2b^2 + 22ab^3$    16. $6s^3t - 5s^3t^2 + s^2t^2$

17. $27p^5q^3 + 3p^4q^6 - 6p^6q$    18. $15x^2y^3z^3 - 10xy^4z^3 + 35xy^3z^4$    19. $56a^5b^2c^3 - 14a^4b^3c^4 - 7a^5bc^7$

20. $8t^6 + 12st^5 + 20s^3t^4$    21. $36j^2k^5 - 27jk^6 + 18k^8$

In Exercises 22-31, factor out a negative coefficient from each polynomial.

22. $-2x + 4$        23. $-5x + 15$        24. $-6y - 30$        25. $-9t - 36$

26. $-4x^2 + 12x - 20$    27. $-8y^2 - 16y + 40$    28. $-9m^3 + 27m^2 + 81$

29. $-5n^4 - 25n^3 - 5$    30. $-12k^2 - 12k - 48$    31. $-16t^2 + 32t + 64$

In Exercises 32-53, factor the differences of two squares.

32. $x^2 - 1$      33. $y^2 - 4$      34. $u^2 - 16$      35. $v^2 - 9$

36. $a^2 - 49$      37. $b^2 - 25$      38. $9 - y^2$      39. $36 - x^2$

40. $81x^2 - 1$      41. $64t^2 - 9$      42. $25p^2 - 36$      43. $4q^2 - 121$

44. $x^2 - 64y^2$      45. $a^2 - 81b^2$      46. $144m^2 - 49n^2$    47. $36u^2 - 169v^2$

48. $x^2 - \dfrac{1}{16}$      49. $y^2 - \dfrac{1}{9}$      50. $64k^2 - \dfrac{25}{121}$      51. $\dfrac{36}{49} - 25d^2$

52. $\dfrac{1}{100}x^2 - 144y^2$      53. $\dfrac{4}{9}a^2 - 100b^2$

In Exercises 54-72, factor the sums or differences of two cubes.

54. $x^3 + 1$      55. $y^3 + 8$      56. $a^3 + 64$      57. $m^3 + 27$

58. $125 - x^3$      59. $64 - y^3$      60. $p^3 - 216$      61. $q^3 - 1,000$

62. $27a^3 + 1$      63. $8p^3 + 1$      64. $64p^3 - q^3$      65. $27x^3 - y^3$

66. $125a^3 + b^3$      67. $1,000m^3 + 27$      68. $8k^3 + 343$      69. $8x^3 + 125y^3$

70. $27m^3 - 8y^3$      71. $216a^3 - 125b^3$      72. $64p^3 + 125q^3$

In Exercises 73-88, factor the binomials completely.

73. $5x^2 - 20$      74. $7y^2 - 63$      75. $3m^5 - 48m^3$      76. $2n^4 - 72n^2$

77. $4a^2 - 16$      78. $9b^2 - 9$      79. $16x^2 - 64y^2$      80. $64x^2 - 4y^2$

81. $2p^3 + 16$      82. $4q^3 + 4$      83. $5u^3 - 5$      84. $3v^3 - 24$

85. $7x^5 + 56x^2$      86. $250k^7 - 2k^4$      87. $x^4y^2 - 1,000xy^2$      88. $mn^4 + 216mn$

In Exercises 89-146, factor the quadratic trinomials. If any trinomial isn't factorable, state that it is prime.

89. $x^2 + 3x + 2$      90. $x^2 + 6x + 8$      91. $y^2 + 11y + 24$      92. $y^2 + 12y + 35$

93. $x^2 + 5x - 6$      94. $x^2 + 7x - 18$      95. $y^2 + 8y - 48$      96. $y^2 + 8y - 20$

97. $a^2 - 9a + 20$      98. $a^2 - 10a + 16$      99. $b^2 - 18b + 45$      100. $b^2 - 13b + 36$

101. $p^2 - 4p - 21$      102. $p^2 + 16p + 55$      103. $q^2 + 16q + 39$      104. $q^2 - 15q + 54$

105. $x^2 + 2x + 1$      106. $y^2 + 6y + 9$      107. $m^2 - 16m + 64$      108. $k^2 - 14k + 49$

109. $t^2 + 24t + 144$      110. $s^2 + 20s + 100$      111. $x^2 - 10x + 25$      112. $y^2 - 18y + 81$

113. $x^2 + 3x + 7$      114. $x^2 + 4x + 12$      115. $y^2 - 9y + 3$      116. $a^2 - 8a + 13$

117. $2x^2 + 3x + 1$       118. $2x^2 + 5x + 2$       119. $3y^2 + y - 2$       120. $2y^2 + y - 3$

121. $5a^2 - a - 4$       122. $5b^2 + 19b - 4$       123. $14x^2 + 11x + 2$       124. $14y^2 + 13y + 3$

125. $4x^2 - 12x + 5$       126. $4x^2 - 20x + 21$       127. $4p^2 - 23p + 15$       128. $4q^2 - 15q + 14$

129. $6y^2 + 17y + 12$       130. $6y^2 + 31y + 35$       131. $8t^2 - 38t + 45$       132. $8s^2 - 42s + 27$

133. $12p^2 - 32p - 35$       134. $30p^2 + p - 3$       135. $9x^2 + 12x + 4$       136. $25y^2 + 40y + 16$

137. $49x^2 - 56x + 16$       138. $36m^2 - 132m + 121$       139. $16s^2 + 40s + 25$       140. $81t^2 + 36t + 4$

141. $2x^2 + 5x + 1$       142. $3y^2 + 7y + 3$       143. $5a^2 - 2a - 11$       144. $7a^2 - 7a - 2$

145. $6x^2 - x + 8$       146. $12p^2 - 2p + 3$

In Exercises 147-168, factor the polynomials by grouping.

147. $x^3 + x^2 + 2x + 2$       148. $x^3 + x^2 + 3x + 3$       149. $y^3 - 6y^2 + 4y - 24$       150. $y^3 - 7y^2 + 2y - 14$

151. $2a^3 + 8a^2 + 3a + 12$       152. $3b^3 + 15b^2 + 2b + 10$       153. $16m^3 - 40m^2 - 6m + 15$

154. $21n^3 - 14n^2 - 12n + 8$       155. $x^5 + x^3 + 9x^2 + 9$       156. $2y^4 + 7y^3 + 6y + 21$

157. $11a^5 + 99a^3 - 5a^2 - 45$       158. $8b^5 - 48b^3 + 3b^2 - 18$       159. $2p^3 + p + 6p^2q + 3q$

160. $27m^3 + 36m^2 + 3mn + 4n$       161. $80s^4 - 50s^2 - 24s^2y + 15y$       162. $36a^3 + 84a^2 - 33ab^2 - 77b^2$

163. $x^2 + 2x + 1 - y^2$       164. $x^2 + 6x + 9 - y^2$       165. $a^2 - 10a + 25 - 4b^2$

166. $a^2 - 14a + 49 - 9b^2$       167. $k^2 + 20k + 100 - 121l^2$       168. $u^2 - 18u + 81 - 100v^2$

In Exercises 169-216, factor the polynomials completely.

169. $2x^2 + 6x + 4$       170. $3x^2 + 15x + 18$       171. $4a^3 - 8a^2 - 60a$       172. $7a^4 + 21a^3 - 28a^2$

173. $5u^5 - 55u^4 + 150u^3$       174. $8v^4 - 40v^3 + 48v^2$       175. $2x^2y^3 - 6x^2y^2 - 56x^2y$

176. $4m^3n^3 - 12m^2n^3 - 40mn^3$       177. $27x^2 + 63x + 18$       178. $20t^2 + 32t + 12$

179. $24y^2 - 24y - 18$       180. $56y^2 + 14y - 21$       181. $42k^4 - 75k^3 + 18k^2$

182. $48b^5 - 58b^4 + 14b^3$       183. $8m^3 - 48m^2 + 72m$       184. $6n^3 + 48n^2 + 96n$

185. $18a^4 + 12a^3 + 2a^2$       186. $80x^4 - 120x^3 + 45x^2$       187. $6 + x - x^2$

188. $15 + 2x - x^2$       189. $-48 + 14t - t^2$       190. $-20 + 9s - s^2$       191. $36 + 15x - 6x^2$

192. $40 + 4x - 12x^2$       193. $x^4 + 4x^2 + 4$       194. $x^4 - 6x^2 + 9$       195. $y^6 + 14y^3 + 49$

196. $y^6 - 24y^3 + 144$       197. $t^4 - 8t^2 + 16$       198. $s^4 - 18s^2 + 81$       199. $x^4 - 81$

200. $81y^4 - 16$       201. $x^6 + 2x^3 + 1$       202. $y^6 - 16y^3 + 64$       203. $k^4 + 7k^2 - 8$

204. $l^4 - 13l^2 - 48$     205. $p^6 - 10p^3 + 16$     206. $q^6 + 29q^3 + 54$     207. $1 - x^6$

208. $a^6 - 1$     209. $b^6 - 64$     210. $1 - 64k^6$     211. $3a^2 - 13ab - 10b^2$

212. $28a^2 + 25ab + 3b^2$     213. $25p^2 - 40pq + 16q^2$     214. $9m^2 - 42mn + 49n^2$

215. $8x^4y + 42x^3y^2 + 54x^2y^3$     216. $60x^3y^4 + 25x^2y^5 - 15xy^6$

---

# END OF CHAPTER 3   QUIZ

1. The coefficient of the monomial $5x^2y^6$ is
   a) 5     b) 2     c) 6     d) 8     e) 12

2. The degree of the polynomial $-\frac{1}{2}x^3 + 5x^2 - x + 3$ is
   a) $-\frac{1}{2}$     b) 6     c) 3     d) $-\frac{1}{2}x^3$     e) 4

3. $\left(4a^2 + 3a - 7\right) + \left(-2a^2 + a - 15\right) =$
   a) $2a^2 + 3a + 8$     b) $2a^2 + 4a + 22$     c) $-2a^2 + 4a - 22$     d) $2a^2 + 4a - 8$     e) $2a^2 + 4a - 22$

4. $(-6a + 9b) - (7a - 12b) =$
   a) $a + 21b$     b) $-13a + 21b$     c) $-13a - 3b$     d) $13a - 21b$     e) $8ab$

5. $\left(6x^2 - 4y^2\right) - \left(3x^2 - xy + y^2\right) =$
   a) $3x^2 + xy - 5y^2$     b) $3x^2 - xy - 5y^2$     c) $3x^2 + xy - 3y^2$     d) $3x^2 + x^2y^2 + y^2$     e) $3x^2 - xy - 4y^2$

6. $(2m + 3n) + (5n - 7m) - (3m + 9n) =$
   a) $8m - n$     b) $-8m + n$     c) $-8m - n$     d) $5m - 13n$     e) $-9mn$

7. $5xy^2\left(3x^2 + 2xy - 4y^2\right) =$
   a) $15x^2y^2 + 10x^2y^3 - 20xy^4$     b) $15x^3y^3 + 5x^2y^3 - 4xy^4$     c) $15x^3y^2 + 10x^2y^3 - 20x^3y$
   d) $15x^3y^2 + 10x^2y^3 - 20xy^4$     e) $15x^3y^2 + 10x^2y^3 - 20x^2y^2$

8. $(8a + 3b)(7a - 2b) =$
   a) $56a^2 - 5ab - 6b^2$     b) $56a^2 + 5ab + 6b^2$     c) $56a^2 + 37ab - 6b^2$
   d) $56a^2 + 5ab - 6b^2$     e) $56a^2 - 16ab + 21b - 6b^2$

9. $(4x - 3)^2 =$
   a) $16x^2 + 9$     b) $16x^2 - 24x + 9$     c) $16x^2 - 24x - 9$     d) $16x^2 - 9$     e) $4x^2 - 9$

10. $(2x - 7)\left(x^2 + 3x - 5\right) =$
    a) $2x^3 + x^2 - 31x + 35$      b) $2x^3 - x^2 - 31x - 35$      c) $2x^3 - x^2 + 31x + 35$
    d) $2x^3 - 13x^2 - 31x + 35$      e) $2x^3 - x^2 - 31x + 35$

11. $\left(42x^8y^{11}\right) \div \left(-7x^6y^3\right) =$
    a) $-6x^2y^8$      b) $6x^2y^8$      c) $-6x^{14}y^{14}$      d) $6x^{14}y^{14}$      e) $-6xy^8$

12. $\dfrac{-18a^2b^5 + 8a^9b^7}{-2a^2b^3} =$
    a) $9b^2 + 8a^9b^7$      b) $9b^2 + 4a^7b^4$      c) $9b^2 - 4a^7b^4$      d) $9ab^2 - 4a^7b^4$      e) $9b^2 - 8a^9b^7$

13. $\left(3x^2 - 4x - 5\right) \div (x + 7) =$
    a) $3x - 25 \text{ R } -180$      b) $3x - 25 \text{ R } 170$      c) $3x - 4 \text{ R } 25$      d) $3x - \dfrac{7}{4} \text{ R } 7$      e) $3x + 17 \text{ R } -124$

14. Factor completely: $12x^8 - 8x^5 + 14x^3$
    a) $2\left(6x^8 - 4x^5 + 7x^3\right)$      b) $2x^3\left(6x^5 + 4x^2 + 7\right)$      c) $2x^2\left(6x^6 - 4x^3 + 7x\right)$
    d) $x^3\left(12x^5 - 8x^2 + 14\right)$      e) $2x^3\left(6x^5 - 4x^2 + 7\right)$

15. Factor completely: $64a^2 - 16b^2$
    a) $(8a - 4b)^2$      b) $16\left(4a^2 - b^2\right)$      c) $16(2a - b)^2$      d) $16(2a + b)(2a - b)$      e) $16(2a + b)^2$

16. Factor completely: $u^3 - 125$
    a) $(u - 5)\left(u^2 + 5u - 25\right)$      b) $(u - 5)^3$      c) $(u - 5)\left(u^2 + 5u + 25\right)$      d) $(u - 5)\left(u^2 + 5u + 10\right)$
    e) $(u + 5)\left(u^2 - 5u + 25\right)$

17. Factor completely: $x^2 + 3x - 54$
    a) $(x - 9)(x - 6)$      b) $(x + 9)(x - 6)$      c) $(x + 9)(x + 6)$      d) $(x - 9)(x + 6)$      e) it is prime

18. Factor completely: $12a^2 + 8a - 15$
    a) $(6a - 5)(2a + 3)$      b) $(6a + 5)(2a - 3)$      c) $(6a - 3)(2a + 5)$      d) $(12a - 5)(a + 3)$
    e) it is prime

19. Factor completely: $3p^2 - 3p - 60$
    a) $3\left(p^2 - p - 20\right)$      b) $3(p + 5)(p - 4)$      c) $(3p + 12)(p - 5)$      d) $(p - 5)(p + 4)$      e) $3(p - 5)(p + 4)$

20. Factor completely: $x^2(x + 3) - 25(x + 3)$
    a) $\left(x^2 - 25\right)(x + 3)$      b) $(x + 3)(x + 5)(x - 5)$      c) $x + 3\left(x^2 - 25\right)$      d) $(x + 3)^2(x + 5)(x - 5)$
    e) $x + 3(x + 5)(x - 5)$

ANSWERS FOR QUIZ 3      1. a      2. c      3. e      4. b      5. a
     6. c      7. d      8. d      9. b      10. e
     11. a      12. c      13. b      14. e      15. d
     16. c      17. b      18. a      19. e      20. b

# Chapter 4: Rational Expressions

In this chapter, we will study algebraic objects known as rational expressions. A **rational expression** is a fraction whose numerator and denominator consists of polynomials. As with rational numbers, we would like to know how to simplify, multiply, divide, add and subtract rational expressions. In Section 4.1, we will learn some definitions which will be used throughout the section, as well as the method for simplifying a rational expression into lowest terms. As we will see, factoring plays the key role in simplifying a rational expression. Section 4.2 will be devoted to multiplication and division of rational expressions. Addition and subtraction of rational expressions will be studied in Section 4.3. We will learn how to find the LCM of polynomials as well. The chapter concludes with the study of simplifying a mixed quotient. Roughly speaking, a mixed quotient is a fraction whose numerator and/or denominator contains rational expressions. In Section 4.4, we will study two methods for simplifying such an algebraic expression.

## Section 4.1 Definitions and Simplifying Rational Expressions

**Definition:** A **rational expression** is an expression of the form $\frac{p}{q}$, where both $p$ and $q$ are polynomials and $q \neq 0$.

Examples of rational expressions are $\frac{2}{5}$, $\frac{x+3}{2x-1}$, $\frac{9x^2 - 5x + 7}{4x^3 + x + 3}$, and $\frac{2x^2 + 3xy - y^2}{-8y^2 - 2yz + z^2}$.

Observe that any rational number is a rational expression, since both the numerator and denominator contain constant monomials, namely integers. Moreover, any polynomial, $P$, may be considered as a rational expression by simply writing $P = \frac{P}{1}$.

There are many rational expressions which may all be 'the same' in the sense that they simplify to the same expression. For example, observe that the fractions $\frac{3}{9}$, $\frac{6}{18}$ and $\frac{-12}{-36}$ all simplify to $\frac{1}{3}$. In fact, if $x$ represents **any** real number other than 0, then the fraction $\frac{x}{3x}$ will simplify to $\frac{1}{3}$.

**Definition:** Two or more rational expressions are called **equivalent** if they simplify to the same rational expression.

When we talk about rational expressions, we must always keep in mind that each of the variables in the expression has a domain (recall that the domain of a variable is the set of real numbers which can replace the variable to give a well-defined answer). When two rational expressions are equivalent, remember that they are equivalent provided that they are well-defined. We will see this in Examples 3 and 4 below.

**Examples.**

1) $\frac{5}{10}$ is equivalent to $\frac{20}{40}$, since $\frac{5}{10} = \frac{1}{2}$ and $\frac{20}{40} = \frac{1}{2}$.

2) $\frac{-12}{-16}$ is equivalent to $\frac{6}{8}$, since $\frac{-12}{-16} = \frac{3}{4}$ and $\frac{6}{8} = \frac{3}{4}$.

3) $\dfrac{6}{y}$ is equivalent to $\dfrac{6\,(y-2)}{y\,(y-2)}$, provided that $y \neq 0, 2$.

Notice that the numerator and denominator of $\dfrac{6\,(y-2)}{y\,(y-2)}$ are factored and there is an equal factor of $y-2$ in both. If you cancel out these factors, you'll get exactly the expression which is equivalent to it, $\dfrac{6}{y}$. In other words,

$$\frac{6\,(y-2)}{y\,(y-2)} = \frac{6}{y} \cdot \frac{\overset{1}{\cancel{y-2}}}{\underset{1}{\cancel{y-2}}} = \frac{6}{y}.$$

4) $\dfrac{-3t+1}{4t+11}$ is equivalent to $\dfrac{-t(-3t+1)}{-t(4t+11)}$, provided that $t \neq 0, \dfrac{-11}{4}$.

Once again, the numerator and denominator of $\dfrac{-t(-3t+1)}{-t(4t+11)}$ are factored and there is an equal factor of $-t$ in both  If you cancel out the $-t$, you get $\dfrac{-3t+1}{4t+11}$. In other words,

$$\frac{-t(-3t+1)}{-t(4t+11)} = \frac{\overset{1}{\cancel{-t}}}{\underset{1}{\cancel{-t}}} \cdot \frac{-3t+1}{4t+11} = \frac{-3t+1}{4t+11}.$$

This technique of canceling out equal factors can always be performed.

---

**Property of Simplifying a Rational Expression**

If $A$, $B$ and $C$ are polynomials and both $B, C \neq 0$, then $\dfrac{A\overset{1}{\cancel{C}}}{B\underset{1}{\cancel{C}}} = \dfrac{A}{B}$.

---

In particular, we have $\dfrac{A\overset{1}{\cancel{C}}}{\underset{1}{\cancel{C}}} = \dfrac{A}{1} = A$ and $\dfrac{\overset{1}{\cancel{C}}}{B\underset{1}{\cancel{C}}} = \dfrac{1}{B}$.

From this we see that in order to simplify a rational expression, we first need to factor the numerator and denominator. Afterwards, we'll see if any common factors can be cancelled out.

There is a similar property when division occurs in the numerator and denominator,

$$\frac{A \div \overset{1}{\cancel{C}}}{B \div \underset{1}{\cancel{C}}} = \frac{A}{B}, \text{ provided that } B, C \neq 0.$$

There are some very common mistakes which are often made with the simplifying property.

$$\textbf{BEWARE} \quad : \quad 1. \;\; \frac{A \pm \cancel{C}}{B \pm \cancel{C}} \neq \frac{A}{B}$$

$$2. \;\; \frac{A\cancel{C}}{B \pm \cancel{C}} \neq \frac{A}{B}$$

$$3. \;\; \frac{A \pm \cancel{C}}{B\cancel{C}} \neq \frac{A}{B}$$

**Examples.** Simplify.

1) $\dfrac{20}{32} = \dfrac{5 \times \overset{1}{\cancel{4}}}{8 \times \underset{1}{\cancel{4}}} = \dfrac{5}{8}$

Alternatively, we have $\dfrac{20}{32} = \dfrac{20 \div \overset{1}{\cancel{4}}}{32 \div \underset{1}{\cancel{4}}} = \dfrac{5}{8}$. This method of dividing is easy when we have numbers but not easy when we have polynomials.

2) $\dfrac{\overset{1}{\cancel{4}}x^2 y^9}{\underset{4}{\cancel{16}}x^7 y^3} = \dfrac{1y^6}{4x^5} = \dfrac{y^6}{4x^5}, \;\; x \neq 0 \text{ and } y \neq 0$

Notice that I canceled out 2 $x$'s and 3 $y$'s from both the numerator and denominator.

3) $\dfrac{3x + 9}{5x + 15} = \dfrac{3 \overset{1}{\cancel{(x + 3)}}}{5 \underset{1}{\cancel{(x + 3)}}} = \dfrac{3}{5}, \;\; x \neq -3$

4) $\dfrac{2a - 12}{2a + 12} = \dfrac{\overset{1}{\cancel{2}}(a - 6)}{\underset{1}{\cancel{2}}(a + 6)} = \dfrac{a - 6}{a + 6}, \;\; a \neq -6$

$$\textbf{BEWARE} \quad : \quad \frac{\overset{1}{\cancel{a}} - \overset{1}{\cancel{b}}}{\underset{1}{\cancel{a}} + \underset{1}{\cancel{b}}} \neq \frac{1 - 1}{1 + 1}$$

5) $\dfrac{7y - 4}{8 - 14y} = \underbrace{\dfrac{1(7y - 4)}{2(4 - 7y)} = \dfrac{1\overset{1}{\cancel{(7y - 4)}}}{-2\underset{1}{\cancel{(-4 + 7y)}}}}_{7y - 4 \text{ and } 4 - 7y \text{ are additive inverses.}} = -\dfrac{1}{2}, \;\; y \neq \dfrac{4}{7}$

6) $\dfrac{x^2 - 25}{x^2 + 10x + 25} = \dfrac{\overset{1}{\cancel{(x + 5)}}(x - 5)}{\underset{1}{\cancel{(x + 5)}}(x + 5)} = \dfrac{x - 5}{x + 5}, \;\; x \neq -5$

7) $\dfrac{t^3 - 7t^2 + 6t}{t^4 - t} = \underbrace{\dfrac{t(t^2 - 7t + 6)}{t(t^3 - 1)} = \dfrac{\overset{1}{\cancel{t}}(t - 6)\overset{1}{\cancel{(t-1)}}}{\underset{1}{\cancel{t}}\,\underset{1}{\cancel{(t-1)}}(t^2 + t + 1)}}_{\text{Factor the polynomials completely.}} = \dfrac{t - 6}{t^2 + t + 1},\quad t \neq 0, 1$

We will learn in Chapter 7 that $t^2 + t + 1 \neq 0$ when we replace $t$ by any real number. Therefore, the domain of $t$ in the expression $\dfrac{t^3 - 7t^2 + 6t}{t^4 - t}$ is all real numbers except 0 and 1.

8) $\dfrac{4x^4 - 10x^3 - 24x^2}{6x^5 - 24x^4} = \dfrac{2x^2(2x^2 - 5x - 12)}{6x^4(x - 4)} = \dfrac{\overset{1}{\cancel{2x^2}}(2x + 3)\overset{1}{\cancel{(x-4)}}}{\underset{3\;x^2}{\cancel{6x^4}}\underset{1}{\cancel{(x-4)}}} = \dfrac{2x + 3}{3x^2},\quad x \neq 0, 4$

9) $\dfrac{18x^2 + 23x - 6}{25x^2 - 1} = \dfrac{(9x - 2)(2x + 3)}{(5x + 1)(5x - 1)},\quad x \neq -\dfrac{1}{5}, \dfrac{1}{5}$

Notice that nothing cancels out since there are no common factors in the numerator and denominator. Therefore, this expression is already simplified.

10) $\dfrac{8a^4b + 27ab^4}{4a^2b - 6ab^2 + 9b^3} = \dfrac{ab(8a^3 + 27b^3)}{b(4a^2 - 6ab + 9b^2)} = \dfrac{a\overset{1}{\cancel{b}}(2a + 3b)\overset{1}{\cancel{(4a^2 - 6ab + 9b^2)}}}{\underset{1}{\cancel{b}}\underset{1}{\cancel{(4a^2 - 6ab + 9b^2)}}} = \dfrac{a(2a + 3b)}{1} = a(2a + 3b)$

As far as the domains of the variables $a$ and $b$ are concerned, we have that $b \neq 0$ and $4a^2 - 6ab + 9b^2 \neq 0$. Now, $4a^2 - 6ab + 9b^2 = 0$ **only if** both $a = 0$ and $b = 0$ (observe that $4a^2 - 6ab + 9b^2 = 4\,(0)^2 - 6\,(0)\,(0) + 9\,(0)^2 = 0$). Any value of $a$ besides 0 and any value of $b$ besides 0 that we simultaneously plug into $4a^2 - 6ab + 9b^2$ would **not** give us 0. Since we already know that $b \neq 0$, we have that $4a^2 - 6ab + 9b^2 \neq 0$ for any values of $a$ and $b \neq 0$. Hence, the domain of $a$ is the set of real numbers and the domain of $b$ is the set of all real numbers except 0. Don't worry too much about how to find the domain of a variable when the expression contains more than one variable. The key thing to understand is how to simplify these expressions.

**Exercise 4.1**   Simplify.

1. $\dfrac{3x^2}{4x}$       2. $\dfrac{6y^3}{11y}$       3. $\dfrac{4x^2}{8x^5}$       4. $\dfrac{3y^3}{9y^6}$

5. $\dfrac{24}{16x^7}$       6. $\dfrac{32}{12y^2}$       7. $\dfrac{5x^4}{x^{12}}$       8. $\dfrac{15y^8}{y^{17}}$

9. $\dfrac{x^8y^3}{x^2y^7}$       10. $\dfrac{x^3y^{15}}{x^{13}y^2}$       11. $\dfrac{-6a^3b^4}{16ab^2}$       12. $\dfrac{-10a^7b^8}{8a^3b}$

13. $\dfrac{15m^2n^3}{6m^5n^9}$       14. $\dfrac{22mn^4}{12m^6n^5}$       15. $\dfrac{14a^5b^4c^7}{21a^2b^6c^2}$       16. $\dfrac{8r^2s^8t^6}{20r^4st^9}$

17. $\dfrac{-18m^{12}n^{10}p^7}{-8m^3n^{10}}$       18. $\dfrac{-42m^2n^{16}p^{14}}{-22m^2p^{20}}$       19. $\dfrac{-56ab^7}{7a^8c^6}$       20. $\dfrac{48x^7z}{-8x^{18}y^2}$

21. $\dfrac{2x + 4}{3x + 6}$       22. $\dfrac{5x + 10}{15x + 30}$       23. $\dfrac{8y - 24}{6y - 18}$       24. $\dfrac{9y - 36}{3y - 12}$

25. $\dfrac{4t + 10}{4t - 10}$
  26. $\dfrac{6n - 14}{6n + 14}$
  27. $\dfrac{3x - 1}{2 - 6x}$
  28. $\dfrac{14 - 10x}{5x - 7}$

29. $\dfrac{6x^2 - 12}{6 - 3x^2}$
  30. $\dfrac{7y^2 - 21}{3 - y^2}$
  31. $\dfrac{4x^2 + 10}{-30 - 12x^2}$
  32. $\dfrac{-12x - 20}{50 + 30x}$

33. $\dfrac{3p^2 + 8p}{2p^2 - p}$
  34. $\dfrac{7q^2 - 2q}{4q^2 + q}$
  35. $\dfrac{10x^2 + 15x}{10x^2 + 10x}$
  36. $\dfrac{24y^2 - 32y}{32y^2 - 16y}$

37. $\dfrac{2x^3y^3 - 2x^2y^4}{12x^5y + 12x^4y^2}$
  38. $\dfrac{4x^2 - 8x}{6x - 3x^2}$
  39. $\dfrac{2t^3 + 6t^2}{-5t^4 - 15t^3}$
  40. $\dfrac{14s^4 + 7s^3}{-18s^5 - 9s^4}$

41. $\dfrac{x^2 + 3x + 2}{3x + 6}$
  42. $\dfrac{x^2 + 8x + 15}{4x + 20}$
  43. $\dfrac{2x^2 - 8x}{3x^3 - 48x}$
  44. $\dfrac{7x^2 - 63}{2x^2 - 6x}$

45. $\dfrac{x^3 + 1}{x^2 - 1}$
  46. $\dfrac{x^2 - 9}{x^3 - 27}$
  47. $\dfrac{4t^2 - 8t - 21}{4t^2 + 12t + 9}$
  48. $\dfrac{9t^2 - 30t + 25}{6t^2 - 7t - 5}$

49. $\dfrac{16x^3 - 8x^2}{4x^2 - 1}$
  50. $\dfrac{64s^2t^3 + 4t^3}{4s^3 - s}$
  51. $\dfrac{2x^4 - 8x^3 - 42x^2}{5x^6 - 45x^4}$
  52. $\dfrac{5x^2 + 22x + 21}{x^4 - 9x^2}$

# Section 4.2 Multiplication and Division of Rational Expressions

In this section, we will learn how to multiply and divide rational expressions. Let us recall how to multiply and divide rational numbers (see Section 1.2).

Suppose $A$, $B$, $C$, and $D$ are integers and both $B$, $D \neq 0$. Then $\dfrac{A}{B} \cdot \dfrac{C}{D} = \dfrac{AC}{BD}$. Moreover, if $C \neq 0$ as well, then $\dfrac{A}{B} \div \dfrac{C}{D} = \dfrac{A}{B} \cdot \dfrac{D}{C} = \dfrac{AD}{BC}$. When we multiply (or divide) two fractions, we can sometimes simplify the problem by cancelling out common factors and then multiply them together. For example,

$$\frac{2}{3} \times \frac{9}{8} \;=\; \frac{\overset{1}{\cancel{2}}}{\underset{1}{\cancel{3}}} \times \frac{\overset{3}{\cancel{9}}}{\underset{4}{\cancel{8}}} = \frac{3}{4}$$

and

$$\frac{15}{16} \div (-10) \;=\; \frac{15}{16} \div \left(\frac{-10}{1}\right) = \frac{\overset{3}{\cancel{15}}}{16} \times \left(\frac{1}{\underset{2}{\cancel{-10}}}\right) = -\frac{3}{32}.$$

As we have seen in the previous section, before we cancel out any common factors, we must factor the numerator and denominator in order to see what these common factors are. The same method applies to rational expressions whose numerator and denominator contain polynomials.

**In the examples below, we will not be concerned with the domain of each variable.**

**Examples.** Multiply and simplify.

1) $\dfrac{x^2}{8} \cdot \dfrac{xy^4}{2} = \dfrac{\left(x^2\right)\left(xy^4\right)}{(8)(2)} = \dfrac{x^3y^4}{16}$

2) $\dfrac{12a^3}{b^2} \cdot \dfrac{a^2b^7}{6} = \dfrac{\left(\overset{2}{\cancel{12}}a^3\right)\left(a^2b^7\right)}{(b^2)(\cancel{6})} = \dfrac{2a^5b^7}{b^2} = \dfrac{2a^5b^5}{1} = 2a^5b^5$

3) $\dfrac{5x^2}{3y^3} \cdot \dfrac{7x^4y^2}{12xy} = \dfrac{(5x^2)(7x^4y^2)}{(3y^3)(12xy)} = \dfrac{35x^6y^2}{36xy^4} = \dfrac{35x^5}{36y^2}$

4) $\dfrac{16a^3b}{9ab^2} \cdot \dfrac{3a^7b^6}{14a^3} = \dfrac{\overset{8}{\cancel{(16a^3b)}}\overset{1}{\cancel{(3a^7b^6)}}}{\underset{3}{\cancel{(9ab^2)}}\underset{7}{\cancel{(14a^3)}}} = \dfrac{8a^{10}b^7}{21a^4b^2} = \dfrac{8a^6b^5}{21}$

5) $\dfrac{x}{2x+4} \cdot \dfrac{6}{5x} = \dfrac{\overset{1}{\cancel{x}}}{\underset{1}{\cancel{2}(x+2)}} \cdot \dfrac{\overset{3}{\cancel{6}}}{\underset{1}{5\cancel{x}}} = \dfrac{3}{5(x+2)}$

Notice that I first factored $2x+4$ and then cancelled out any common factors. You can leave your answer with the numerator and denominator in factored form.

6) $\dfrac{8a^3}{4a^2-1} \cdot \dfrac{2a+1}{16a} = \dfrac{\overset{1}{\cancel{8}a^3}}{\cancel{(2a+1)}(2a-1)} \cdot \dfrac{\overset{}{\cancel{(2a+1)}}}{\underset{2}{\cancel{16}a}} = \dfrac{a^3}{2a(2a-1)} = \dfrac{a^2}{2(2a-1)}$

7) $\dfrac{5y+15}{y^3+27} \cdot \dfrac{y^4-2y}{5y^3} = \dfrac{\overset{1}{\cancel{5}}\overset{1}{\cancel{(y+3)}}}{\cancel{(y+3)}(y^2-3y+9)} \cdot \dfrac{y(y^3-2)}{\cancel{5}y^3} = \dfrac{\overset{1}{\cancel{y}}(y^3-2)}{\underset{y^2}{y^3}(y^2-3y+9)} = \dfrac{y^3-2}{y^2(y^2-3y+9)}$

8) $\dfrac{t^3-t^2-6t}{8t^2-24t} \cdot \dfrac{12t^2-12}{2t^3-2t} = \dfrac{\cancel{t}(t-3)(t+2)}{\underset{2}{8}t\cancel{(t-3)}} \cdot \dfrac{\overset{3}{\cancel{12}}\cancel{(t+1)}\cancel{(t-1)}}{\underset{1}{2}\cancel{t}\cancel{(t+1)}\cancel{(t-1)}} = \dfrac{3(t+2)}{4t}$

9) $\dfrac{x^2+14x+49}{2x^2+17x+21} \cdot \dfrac{4x-9}{18-8x} = \dfrac{(x+7)\cancel{(x+7)}}{(2x+3)\cancel{(x+7)}} \cdot \dfrac{1\cancel{(4x-9)}}{-2\cancel{(4x-9)}} = \dfrac{x+7}{-2(2x+3)}$ or $-\dfrac{x+7}{2(2x+3)}$

10) $\dfrac{9y^2+3y}{y^2+16} \cdot \dfrac{y^2-16y+64}{4y-12} = \underbrace{\dfrac{3y(3y+1)}{y^2+16} \cdot \dfrac{(y-8)(y-8)}{4(y-3)} = \dfrac{3y(3y+1)(y-8)^2}{4(y^2+16)(y-3)}}_{\text{Nothing cancels, so this is simplified.}}$

**Examples.** Divide and simplify.

1) $\dfrac{x^4}{3} \div \dfrac{x^3}{7} = \dfrac{x^4}{3} \cdot \dfrac{7}{x^3} = \dfrac{7x}{3}$

2) $\dfrac{20a^3b}{9ab^6} \div \left(-\dfrac{10b^7}{3a^2}\right) = \dfrac{\overset{2}{\cancel{20}}a^3b}{\cancel{9}ab^6} \cdot \left(-\dfrac{\overset{1}{\cancel{3}}a^2}{\cancel{10}b^7}\right) = -\dfrac{2a^5b}{3ab^{13}} = -\dfrac{2a^4}{3b^{12}}$

3) $\dfrac{9}{3x-6} \div \dfrac{18x^2-18x}{x^2-4} = \dfrac{9}{3x-6} \cdot \dfrac{x^2-4}{18x^2-18x} = \dfrac{\overset{1}{\cancel{9}}}{3\cancel{(x-2)}} \cdot \dfrac{(x+2)\overset{1}{\cancel{(x-2)}}}{\underset{2}{\cancel{18}}x(x-1)} = \dfrac{x+2}{6x(x-1)}$

4) $\dfrac{9a^2-4}{9a^2-4a} \div \dfrac{3a^2-2a}{3a^2+2} = \dfrac{9a^2-4}{9a^2-4a} \cdot \dfrac{3a^2+2}{3a^2-2a} = \dfrac{(3a+2)\cancel{(3a-2)}}{a(9a-4)} \cdot \dfrac{3a^2+2}{a\underset{1}{\cancel{(3a-2)}}} = \dfrac{(3a+2)(3a^2+2)}{a^2(9a-4)}$

5) $\dfrac{t^3 - 125}{t^3 + 125} \div \dfrac{t^2 - 5t}{t^2 + 5t} = \dfrac{t^3 - 125}{t^3 + 125} \cdot \dfrac{t^2 + 5t}{t^2 - 5t} = \dfrac{\overset{1}{(\cancel{t - 5})}\,(t^2 + 5t + 25)}{(\cancel{t + 5})\,(t^2 - 5t + 25)} \cdot \dfrac{\overset{1}{\cancel{t}}\,\overset{1}{(\cancel{t + 5})}}{\cancel{t}\,\cancel{(t - 5)}} = \dfrac{t^2 + 5t + 25}{t^2 - 5t + 25}$

6) $\dfrac{64 - 4x^2}{2x^2 - 32} \div \dfrac{24}{x^2 + 1} = \dfrac{64 - 4x^2}{2x^2 - 32} \cdot \dfrac{x^2 + 1}{24} = \dfrac{\overset{1}{\cancel{4}}\,\overset{1}{(\cancel{4 + x})}\,\overset{-1}{(\cancel{4 - x})}}{\underset{1}{2}\,\underset{1}{(\cancel{x + 4})}\,(\cancel{x - 4})} \cdot \dfrac{x^2 + 1}{\underset{6}{\cancel{24}}} = \dfrac{-1\,(x^2 + 1)}{12}$ or $-\dfrac{x^2 + 1}{12}$

As you can clearly see, division is just multiplication 'with a flip'. The name of the game for multiplication and division is factoring.

## Exercise 4.2

In Exercises 1-16, multiply and simplify.

1. $\dfrac{4x^2y^5}{12x^3y^2} \cdot \dfrac{6x^8y^2}{5xy^7}$

2. $\dfrac{8x^7y}{3x^2y^6} \cdot \dfrac{9x^4y^4}{2xy^{12}}$

3. $\dfrac{10a^3}{b^3c^7} \cdot \left(-\dfrac{2a^4b^6c^2}{5}\right)$

4. $\left(-\dfrac{24m^5}{n^2p^4}\right) \cdot \dfrac{7mn^{12}p}{8}$

5. $\dfrac{3x + 9}{8x - 16} \cdot \dfrac{4x - 8}{5x + 15}$

6. $\dfrac{9x + 9}{8x - 32} \cdot \dfrac{4x - 16}{3x + 3}$

7. $\dfrac{3u^3 + 18u^2}{9u^2 - 18u} \cdot \dfrac{8u + 8}{4u + 24}$

8. $\dfrac{12u^2 + 6u}{4u + 4} \cdot \dfrac{5u - 10}{3u^3 - 6u^2}$

9. $\dfrac{2a^2 - 2a - 12}{2a^2 + 10a + 12} \cdot \dfrac{3a - 9}{a + 1}$

10. $\dfrac{3b^2 + 24b + 48}{3b^2 + 6b - 24} \cdot \dfrac{2}{b + 4}$

11. $\dfrac{8y^3 - 8}{24y + 12} \cdot \dfrac{12y^2 + 12y + 3}{y^2 + y + 1}$

12. $\dfrac{7s^2 - 28s + 28}{14s + 28} \cdot \dfrac{18s + 24}{3s^2 - 2s - 8}$

13. $\dfrac{x^2 - 36}{x^2 - 16} \cdot \dfrac{x^2 - 9x + 20}{x^2 + 10x + 24}$

14. $\dfrac{3y^2 + 2y - 1}{9y^2 - 1} \cdot \dfrac{y^2 - 4}{y^2 - 1}$

15. $\dfrac{4t^2 + 5t - 6}{6 - 8t} \cdot \dfrac{5t}{t + 2}$

16. $\dfrac{9b^2 + 34b - 8}{9b - 2} \cdot \dfrac{4 - b}{b^2 - 16}$

In Exercises 17-38, divide and simplify.

17. $\dfrac{x^2}{4} \div \dfrac{x^4}{8}$

18. $\dfrac{y^3}{12} \div \dfrac{y^8}{3}$

19. $\left(\dfrac{-25}{3y^6}\right) \div \left(\dfrac{10}{-9y^2}\right)$

20. $\left(-\dfrac{16}{y^2}\right) \div \left(\dfrac{36}{5y^7}\right)$

21. $\left(\dfrac{a}{-15}\right) \div \dfrac{b^2}{6}$

22. $\left(\dfrac{m^3}{-18}\right) \div \dfrac{n^2}{14}$

23. $\dfrac{3x^6y^2}{5x^3y} \div \dfrac{15xy}{10x^4y^2}$

24. $\dfrac{9s^3t^5}{7st^6} \div \dfrac{9s^2t^3}{14st^7}$

25. $\left(\dfrac{-16u^3v}{15uv^3}\right) \div \left(\dfrac{8u^4v}{-10u^2v^5}\right)$

26. $\left(\dfrac{24u^6v^2}{-10u^3v^4}\right) \div \left(\dfrac{18uv}{-8u^5v^3}\right)$

27. $\dfrac{5x}{6} \div \dfrac{x^2 + x}{12x + 12}$

28. $\dfrac{3y}{8} \div \dfrac{16y - 32}{y^2 - 2y}$

29. $\dfrac{4t + 12}{5t + 15} \div \dfrac{9t - 54}{10t - 60}$

30. $\dfrac{2t - 14}{3t + 18} \div \dfrac{2t + 14}{6t + 36}$

31. $\dfrac{x^2 - 3x - 4}{3x + 3} \div \dfrac{x^2 - 6x + 8}{5x + 10}$

32. $\dfrac{x^2 - 7x + 12}{7x + 28} \div \dfrac{x^2 + x - 6}{2x + 6}$

33. $\dfrac{y^3 - 8}{4y^2 - 5y - 6} \div \dfrac{2y^2 + 4y + 8}{8y^2 - 22y - 21}$

34. $\dfrac{9p^2 + 9p - 10}{21p^2 - 14p} \div \dfrac{9p^2 - 25}{14p^4 + 56p^3}$

35. $\dfrac{7t^3 + 2t^2 - 21t - 6}{35t + 10} \div \dfrac{14t^3 + 4t^2 + 7t + 2}{6t^3 + 3t}$

36. $\dfrac{12y^3 + 18y^2 + 10y + 15}{6y^2 + 7y - 3} \div \dfrac{18y^3 - 6y^2 + 15y - 5}{9y^2 - 6y + 1}$

37. $\dfrac{9x^2 + 38xy + 8y^2}{3x^2y^3 + 12xy^4} \div \dfrac{x^2 - 2xy + y^2}{27x^3y + 6x^2y^2}$

38. $\dfrac{a^2 + 3ab - 18b^2}{a^2 - 9b^2} \div \dfrac{12a^2b + 72ab^2}{a^2 + 4ab + 3b^2}$

# Section 4.3  Addition and Subtraction of Rational Expressions

Now we will learn how to add and subtract rational expressions. As for real numbers, in order to add or subtract two rational expressions, the denominators of the rationals must be the same (or **common denominators**). Algebraically, we write

$$\frac{A}{C} + \frac{B}{C} = \frac{A + B}{C} \quad \text{and} \quad \frac{A}{C} - \frac{B}{C} = \frac{A - B}{C}, \text{ where } C \neq 0.$$

We will begin by doing some examples in which the rationals already have common denominators. If the rationals have denominators which are additive inverses of each other, it is easy to obtain the common denominator. Examples like these will be given as well. Following this, we will learn how to add and subtract rational expressions whose denominators are neither common nor additive inverses of each other. In this case, we need to find the least common denominator (LCD) of the expressions. The key to doing such examples involves factoring the denominators. Finding the least common denominator is the same as finding the LCM of the denominators. We will learn how to find the LCM of polynomials, starting with the case in which the polynomials are integers. After we've mastered this, we will be able to combine any two rational expressions.

**Examples.** Add or subtract and simplify.

1) $\dfrac{3}{x} + \dfrac{5}{x} = \dfrac{3 + 5}{x} = \dfrac{8}{x}$

Note that this makes sense as long as $x \neq 0$. **For the rest of these examples, we won't worry about the domain of the variables.**

2) $\dfrac{7}{y^2} - \dfrac{13}{y^2} = \dfrac{7 - 13}{y^2} = \dfrac{-6}{y^2} = -\dfrac{6}{y^2}$

3) $\dfrac{2x}{x - 4} + \dfrac{9x}{x - 4} = \dfrac{2x + 9x}{x - 4} = \dfrac{11x}{x - 4}$

4) $\dfrac{6a}{3a + 2} - \dfrac{3a}{3a + 2} = \dfrac{6a - 3a}{3a + 2} = \dfrac{3a}{3a + 2}$

Notice that the $3a$ in the numerator and denominator do not cancel, since the denominator is **not** factored. Remember that the only time you can cancel out terms is when both the numerator and denominator are **factored**.

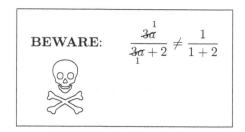

5) $\dfrac{4x+3}{2x-9}+\dfrac{2x-1}{2x-9}=\dfrac{(4x+3)+(2x-1)}{2x-9}=\dfrac{4x+3+2x-1}{2x-9}=\dfrac{6x+2}{2x-9}=\dfrac{2(3x+1)}{2x-9}$

The parentheses can be removed since the associative property holds for addition. Observe that I've factored the numerator in attempt to simplify my answer. No common factors appeared, so I left my answer as it is.

6) $\dfrac{4t^2-3}{t+5}-\dfrac{3t^2+22}{t+5}=\dfrac{(4t^2-3)-(3t^2+22)}{t+5}=\dfrac{4t^2-3-3t^2-22}{t+5}$

$$=\dfrac{t^2-25}{t+5}=\dfrac{\overset{1}{(\cancel{t+5})}(t-5)}{\underset{1}{\cancel{t+5}}}=\dfrac{t-5}{1}=t-5$$

This time, we cannot just remove the parentheses, since the associative property doesn't hold for subtraction. Instead, we need to distribute the negative sign (which is really just $-1$) into the second parentheses. This changes the signs of each of the terms in it. Notice that our answer **did** simplify this time.

7) $\dfrac{2x^2+3x-12}{x^2+4x-32}+\dfrac{-x^2+8x+36}{x^2+4x-32}=\dfrac{(2x^2+3x-12)+(-x^2+8x+36)}{x^2+4x-32}=\dfrac{x^2+11x+24}{x^2+4x-32}$

$$=\dfrac{(x+3)\overset{1}{(\cancel{x+8})}}{(x-4)\underset{1}{(\cancel{x+8})}}=\dfrac{x+3}{x-4}$$

8) $\dfrac{4y+3}{5y-6}-\dfrac{14y-9}{5y-6}=\underbrace{\dfrac{(4y+3)-(14y-9)}{5y-6}=\dfrac{4y+3-14y+9}{5y-6}}_{\text{Distributing the negative changes the signs.}}$

$$=\dfrac{-10y+12}{5y-6}=\underbrace{\dfrac{2\overset{-1}{(\cancel{-5y+6})}}{\underset{1}{\cancel{(5y-6)}}}=\dfrac{-2}{1}}_{-5y+6\text{ and }5y-6\text{ are additive inverses.}}=-2$$

9) $\dfrac{8}{x-11}+\dfrac{3}{11-x}$

The denominators are additive inverses of each other. To obtain common denominators, just multiply the numerator and denominator of either fraction by $-1$. I usually do this to the second fraction. We obtain:

$$\dfrac{8}{x-11}+\left(\dfrac{3}{11-x}\right)\left(\dfrac{-1}{-1}\right)=\underbrace{\dfrac{8}{x-11}+\dfrac{-3}{-11+x}=\dfrac{8-3}{x-11}}_{x-11=-11+x\text{ by the commutative property.}}=\dfrac{5}{x-11}$$

There is also a short-cut to doing this example. All that you have to do is to turn the second denominator into the first denominator and change the sign of the operation. In other words, we have

$$\underbrace{\frac{8}{x-11} + \frac{3}{11-x} = \frac{8}{x-11} - \frac{3}{x-11}}_{\text{Change addition to subtraction and } 11-x \text{ to } x-11.} = \frac{8-3}{x-11} = \frac{5}{x-11}$$

This short-cut will always work whenever the denominators are additive inverses of each other.

10) $$\underbrace{\frac{6b}{8-9b} - \frac{4b}{9b-8} = \frac{6b}{8-9b} + \frac{4b}{8-9b}}_{\text{The denominators are additive inverses, so use the short-cut.}} = \frac{6b+4b}{8-9b} = \frac{10b}{8-9b} \text{ or } -\frac{10b}{9b-8}$$

11) $$\underbrace{\frac{13y-12}{10y+7} - \frac{10-7y}{-10y-7} = \frac{13y-12}{10y+7} + \frac{10-7y}{10y+7}}_{\text{The denominators are additive inverses, so use the short-cut.}} = \frac{(13y-12)+(10-7y)}{10y+7} = \frac{6y-2}{10y+7} = \frac{2(3y-1)}{10y+7}$$

12) $$\underbrace{\frac{6t^2+t-4}{t-3} + \frac{5t^2+2t+2}{3-t} = \frac{6t^2+t-4}{t-3} - \frac{5t^2+2t+2}{t-3}}_{\text{The denominators are additive inverses, so use the short-cut.}} = \frac{(6t^2+t-4)-(5t^2+2t+2)}{t-3}$$

$$= \frac{6t^2+t-4-5t^2-2t-2}{t-3} = \frac{t^2-t-6}{t-3} = \frac{(t+2)\,(t-3)^{\,1}}{t-3_{\,1}} = \frac{t+2}{1} = t+2$$

**Try These (Set 1):** Add or subtract the following and simplify.

1) $\dfrac{5x}{2x+3} + \dfrac{3x-8}{2x+3}$

2) $\dfrac{y-6}{9y+1} - \dfrac{6y-2}{9y+1}$

3) $\dfrac{-2x+7}{x^2+10x+16} + \dfrac{4x+9}{x^2+10x+16}$

4) $\dfrac{14-2x}{3x^2-19x-14} - \dfrac{21-3x}{3x^2-19x-14}$

5) $\dfrac{8}{3x-5} - \dfrac{10}{5-3x}$

6) $\dfrac{7y+2}{y^2-36} + \dfrac{8y-4}{36-y^2}$

The previous set of examples dealt with combining rational expressions whose denominators were either common or additive inverses of each other. Before moving on to combining rational expressions whose denominators differ, we need to understand how to find the LCM of 2 or more polynomials.

**Definition:** The **least common multiple** (abbreviated as **LCM**) of 2 or more polynomials (with integer coefficients) is the 'smallest' polynomial (with integer coefficients) in which the original polynomials divide into without remainder.

By the 'smallest' polynomial, I mean the polynomial of smallest possible degree and smallest possible leading coefficient. For example, let's find the LCM of the monomials $6x^3$ and $8x^5$. We want the 'smallest' monomial for which $6x^3$ and $8x^5$ divide into without a remainder. First, notice that the LCM of 6 and 8 is 24, since both 6 and 8 divide into 24 without a remainder, and 24 is the smallest natural number for which this happens (we will recall how to find the LCM of two natural numbers shortly). Now, the LCM of $x^3$ and $x^5$ is $x^5$, since $x^5 \div x^3 = x^2$ and $x^5 \div x^5 = 1$, neither giving a remainder. Notice that $x^5$ is **the** 'smallest' monomial for which this happens (for example, if it were $x^4$ instead, then $x^4 \div x^5 = \dfrac{x^4}{x^5} = \dfrac{1}{x^1}$ which is a remainder term). Hence, the LCM is $24x^5$ since 5 is the smallest possible degree and 24 is the smallest possible coefficient.

Let's practice finding the LCM of polynomials. To find the LCM, we must first factor the given polynomials. The factors of the polynomials are the 'building blocks' of the LCM and we 'build' the LCM by multiplying these factors together. However, if a common prime factor occurs in more than one of the polynomials, we only put it into the LCM with the largest of the exponents. This will become clearer as we do some examples.

**Examples.** Find the LCM of the following:

1) The LCM of 2 and 3 is $2 \times 3 = 6$.

Notice that both 2 and 3 are prime. In general, whenever the given numbers (or polynomials) are prime and different from each other, the LCM is just their product.

2) The LCM of 7 and 11 is $7 \times 11 = 77$, since both numbers are prime.

3) The LCM of 5 and 9 is $5 \times 9 = 45$.

Notice that 9 factors into $3 \times 3 = 3^2$ and so the only prime factor of 9 is 3. The only prime factor of 5 is 5 itself (since 5 is prime). Now, note that there are no common prime factors of 5 (namely 5) and 9 (namely 3). Therefore, the LCM is their product which is 45. In general, whenever the given numbers (or polynomials) have no common **prime** factors, the LCM is just their product. Examples 1 and 2 are special cases of this.

4) The LCM of 8 and 15 is $8 \times 15 = 120$.

Observe that $8 = 2 \times 2 \times 2 = 2^3$, $15 = 5 \times 3$ and none of the prime factors of 8 (which is just 2) equal any of the prime factors of 15 (which are 5 and 3). Therefore, the LCM is the product of 8 and 15, which is 120.

5) The LCM of 12 and 14 is 84.

Observe that $12 = 2 \times 2 \times 3 = 2^2 \times 3$ and $14 = 2 \times 7$. Notice that 12 and 14 have a common prime factor of 2. When there is a common prime factor, the LCM is **not** the product of the numbers (in this case, of 12 and 14). To find the LCM in this case, you take all of the prime factors (with their **largest exponent**) of the numbers and build the LCM by multiplying these factors (with their largest exponent). Hence, our LCM must have as factors $2^2$, 3, 2, and 7. However, notice that the prime factor of 2 appears twice in our list, in $2^2$ and in $2 = 2^1$. **Only $2^2$ will be used in building the LCM,** since the exponent of $2^2$ (which is 2) is larger than the exponent of $2^1$ (which is 1). By multiplying these factors together, we obtain $2^2 \times 3 \times 7 = 84$.

6) The LCM of 100 and 48 is $1,200$.

To begin with, notice that $100 = 5 \times 5 \times 2 \times 2 = 5^2 \times 2^2$ and $48 = 2 \times 2 \times 2 \times 2 \times 3 = 2^4 \times 3$. The LCM is built up from $5^2$, $2^2$, $2^4$, and 3. Since the prime factor of 2 appears twice in the list (in $2^2$ and in $2^4$), we only put $2^4$ into the LCM since it has a larger exponent than $2^2$. Therefore, the LCM is $5^2 \times 2^4 \times 3 = 1,200$.

7) The LCM of 336 and 72 is $1,008$.

Observe that $336 = 7 \times 2 \times 2 \times 2 \times 2 \times 3 = 7 \times 2^4 \times 3$ and $72 = 3 \times 3 \times 2 \times 2 \times 2 = 3^2 \times 2^3$. The LCM is built up from 7, $2^4$, 3, $3^2$, and $2^3$. We will use **only 7, $2^4$, and $3^2$** to build the LCM, since $2^4$ has a larger exponent than $2^3$ and $3^2$ has a larger exponent than $3 = 3^1$. The LCM is $7 \times 2^4 \times 3^2 = 1,008$.

8) The LCM of 50 and 75 is 150.

Notice that $50 = 5 \times 5 \times 2 = 5^2 \times 2$ and $75 = 5 \times 5 \times 3 = 5^2 \times 3$. The LCM is built up from $5^2$, 2, $5^2$, and 3. We will use only $5^2$, 2, and 3 to build it, since the exponents of $5^2$ and $5^2$ are the same (whenever the exponents are equal, just use one of those terms as your 'building block'). The LCM, therefore, is $5^2 \times 2 \times 3 = 150$.

9) The LCM of $2^2 \times 5^3 \times 11^1$ and $2^5 \times 3^2 \times 11^1$ is $2^5 \times 5^3 \times 3^2 \times 11^1$.

10) The LCM of $3^3 \times 7^4 \times 13^4$ and $3^5 \times 7^2 \times 17^2$ is $3^5 \times 7^4 \times 13^4 \times 17^2$.

11) The LCM of $2x^3$ and $5x^6$ is $10x^6$.

Note that monomials are already in factored form. To find the LCM of two or more monomials, first find the LCM of their coefficients. Then multiply it by the product of the variables in the monomials with their corresponding exponents, choosing the largest one if the variable repeats itself. In this example, the LCM of 2 and 5 is $2 \times 5 = 10$. As for the variables, we will put $x^6$ into the LCM since it has a larger exponent than $x^3$. Therefore, the LCM is $10x^6$.

12) The LCM of $8x^2y^3$ and $12xy^5$ is $24x^2y^5$.

The LCM of 8 and 12 is 24. For the variable $x$, we use $x^2$ since it has a larger exponent than $x = x^1$. For the variable $y$, we use $y^5$ since it has a larger exponent than $y^3$. Therefore, the LCM is $24x^2y^5$.

13) The LCM of $7ab^8$ and $7a^3b^4$ is $7a^3b^8$.

The LCM of 7 and 7 is just 7. For the variable $a$, we use $a^3$ since it has a larger exponent than $a = a^1$. For the variable $b$, we use $b^8$ since it has a larger exponent than $b^4$. Therefore, the LCM is $7a^3b^8$.

14) The LCM of $x^5y^2$ and $20z^3$ is $20x^5y^2z^3$.

15) The LCM of $3x^2$ and $6y^3$ is $6x^2y^3$.

16) The LCM of $3x + 6$ and $2x + 4$ is $6(x + 2)$.

To obtain this LCM, first factor the polynomials. You proceed exactly as before (build the LCM by using the factors as the building blocks), keeping in mind that if a prime factor appears in more than one polynomial, use the largest exponent. Well, observe that $3x + 6 = 3(x + 2)$ and $2x + 4 = 2(x + 2)$. The LCM will contain 3, $x + 2$, 2, and $x + 2$. Since $x + 2 = (x + 2)^1$ has exponent 1 in both occurences, it will only appear once in the LCM. Hence, the LCM is $3(2)(x + 2) = 6(x + 2)$. Notice that 6 is just the LCM of 2 and 3.

17) The LCM of $6x^2 - 6$ and $4x^2 + 8x + 4$ is $12(x + 1)^2(x - 1)$.

Notice that $6x^2 - 6 = 6(x^2 - 1) = 6(x + 1)(x - 1)$ and $4x^2 + 8x + 4 = 4(x^2 + 2x + 1) = 4(x + 1)(x + 1) = 4(x + 1)^2$. The LCM of 6 and 4 is 12. We will use $(x + 1)^2$ in the LCM since it has a larger exponent than the factor $x + 1 = (x + 1)^1$ of the first polynomial. The LCM will also contain the factor $x - 1$. After multiplying these, we see that the LCM is $12(x + 1)^2(x - 1)$.

18) The LCM of $x$ and $x + 2$ is $x(x + 2)$, since both polynomials are prime.

19) The LCM of $x - 4$ and $7x + 2$ is $(x - 4)(7x + 2)$, since both polynomials are prime.

20) The LCM of $20x^3 (x-4)^2 (3x+5)^3$ and $10x^5 (x+2)(x-4)^3 (3x+5)^2$ is $20x^5 (x+2)(x-4)^3 (3x+5)^3$.

Observe that the LCM of 20 and 10 is 20, the factor $x^5$ has a larger exponent than the factor $x^3$, the factor $(x-4)^3$ has a larger exponent than the factor $(x-4)^2$ and the factor $(3x+5)^3$ has a larger exponent than the factor $(3x+5)^2$. Since the factor $x+2 = (x+2)^1$ only occurs in the second polynomial, it will only appear with exponent 1 in the LCM.

21) The LCM of $x^4 (2x-1)^2 (2x+3)^2$ and $x^4 (2x+1)^2 (2x+3)^5$ is $x^4 (2x-1)^2 (2x+1)^2 (2x+3)^5$ (why?).

**Try These (Set 2):** Find the LCM.

1) 60 and 24　　　3) $9x^3y^2$ and $15x^5y$　　　5) $x^2 + 5x + 4$ and $x^2 - 16$
2) 28 and 49　　　4) $10x^2 - 5x$ and $4x^3 - x^2$　　6) $6x^3 (x+1)^2 (x-3)^2$ and $2x^4 (x+1)(x-2)^2 (x-3)$

Now that we've practiced finding LCM's, let's go back to combining rational expressions. The name of the game is to find the LCM of the denominators (a.k.a. the least common denominator) and change the denominators of the fractions into the LCM. Let's give it a try.

**Examples.** Add or subtract the following and simplify.

1) $\dfrac{8}{x} + \dfrac{7}{y} = \underbrace{\left(\dfrac{y}{y}\right)\dfrac{8}{x} + \left(\dfrac{x}{x}\right)\dfrac{7}{y}}_{\text{The LCM of } x \text{ and } y \text{ is } xy.} = \dfrac{8y + 7x}{xy}$

2) $\dfrac{4x}{x+5} + \dfrac{3x}{x-2} = \underbrace{\left(\dfrac{x-2}{x-2}\right)\dfrac{4x}{x+5} + \left(\dfrac{x+5}{x+5}\right)\dfrac{3x}{x-2}}_{\text{The LCM of } x+5 \text{ and } x-2 \text{ is } (x+5)(x-2).} = \dfrac{4x(x-2) + 3x(x+5)}{(x+5)(x-2)}$

$= \dfrac{4x^2 - 8x + 3x^2 + 15x}{(x+5)(x-2)} = \dfrac{7x^2 + 7x}{(x+5)(x-2)} = \dfrac{7x(x+1)}{(x+5)(x-2)}$

3) $\dfrac{2}{5x} + \dfrac{3}{2y} = \underbrace{\left(\dfrac{2y}{2y}\right)\dfrac{2}{5x} + \left(\dfrac{5x}{5x}\right)\dfrac{3}{2y}}_{\text{The LCM of } 5x \text{ and } 2y \text{ is } 10xy.} = \dfrac{4y}{10xy} + \dfrac{15x}{10xy} = \dfrac{4y + 15x}{10xy}$

4) $\dfrac{1}{8x^2} - \dfrac{5}{6xy^2} = \underbrace{\left(\dfrac{3y^2}{3y^2}\right)\dfrac{1}{8x^2} - \left(\dfrac{4x}{4x}\right)\dfrac{5}{6xy^2}}_{\text{The LCM of } 8x^2 \text{ and } 6xy^2 \text{ is } 24x^2y^2.} = \dfrac{3y^2}{24x^2y^2} - \dfrac{20x}{24x^2y^2} = \dfrac{3y^2 - 20x}{24x^2y^2}$

5) $\dfrac{2t}{t^2-9} + \dfrac{5t}{t^2+6t+9} = \underbrace{\left(\dfrac{t+3}{t+3}\right)\dfrac{2t}{(t+3)(t-3)} + \left(\dfrac{t-3}{t-3}\right)\dfrac{5t}{(t+3)^2}}_{\text{The LCM of } (t+3)(t-3) \text{ and } (t+3)^2 \text{ is } (t+3)^2(t-3).} = \dfrac{2t(t+3) + 5t(t-3)}{(t+3)^2 (t-3)}$

$= \dfrac{2t^2 + 6t + 5t^2 - 15t}{(t+3)^2 (t-3)} = \dfrac{7t^2 - 9t}{(t+3)^2 (t-3)} = \dfrac{t(7t-9)}{(t+3)^2 (t-3)}$

6) $\underbrace{\dfrac{x+2}{4x^2+8x} - \dfrac{x-3}{x^2+9x+14} = \left(\dfrac{x+7}{x+7}\right)\dfrac{x+2}{4x\,(x+2)} - \left(\dfrac{4x}{4x}\right)\dfrac{x-3}{(x+7)\,(x+2)}}_{\text{The LCM of } 4x(x+2) \text{ and } (x+7)(x+2) \text{ is } 4x(x+7)(x+2).} = \dfrac{(x+7)\,(x+2) - 4x\,(x-3)}{4x\,(x+2)\,(x+7)}$

$= \dfrac{x^2+9x+14-4x^2+12x}{4x\,(x+2)\,(x+7)} = \dfrac{-3x^2+21x+14}{4x\,(x+2)\,(x+7)} = -\dfrac{3x^2-21x-14}{4x\,(x+2)\,(x+7)}$

Notice that $3x^2 - 21x - 14$ is prime, so our answer is in simplified form.

7) $\underbrace{\dfrac{2a}{a+4} + \dfrac{a-3}{a^3-64} = \left(\dfrac{a^2-4a+16}{a^2-4a+16}\right)\dfrac{2a}{a+4} + \dfrac{a-3}{(a+4)\,(a^2-4a+16)}}_{\text{The LCM of } a+4 \text{ and } (a+4)(a^2-4a+16) \text{ is } (a+4)(a^2-4a+16).} = \dfrac{2a\,(a^2-4a+16) + (a-3)}{(a^2-4a+16)\,(a+4)}$

$= \dfrac{2a^3-8a^2+32a+a-3}{(a^2-4a+16)\,(a+4)} = \dfrac{2a^3-8a^2+33a-3}{(a^2-4a+16)\,(a+4)}$

If we try to factor $2a^3 - 8a^2 + 33a - 3$ by using the Grouping Method (see Section 3.5), we'll see that it doesn't work. Therefore, we will leave our answer as it is. There is another method which can be used to show that this expression cannot be simplified, but we will not be concerned with it.

8) $\underbrace{\dfrac{1}{x^2+x} + \dfrac{1}{x^2+3x+2} = \left(\dfrac{x+2}{x+2}\right)\dfrac{1}{x\,(x+1)} + \left(\dfrac{x}{x}\right)\dfrac{1}{(x+2)\,(x+1)}}_{\text{The LCM of } x(x+1) \text{ and } (x+2)(x+1) \text{ is } x(x+2)(x+1).} = \dfrac{x+2+x}{x\,(x+2)\,(x+1)}$

$= \dfrac{2x+2}{x\,(x+2)\,(x+1)} = \dfrac{2\,\overset{1}{\cancel{(x+1)}}}{x\,(x+2)\,\underset{1}{\cancel{(x+1)}}} = \dfrac{2}{x\,(x+2)}$

9) $\underbrace{\dfrac{3}{x+4} - \dfrac{2}{x^2} + \dfrac{1}{x-1} = \left(\dfrac{x^2\,(x-1)}{x^2\,(x-1)}\right)\dfrac{3}{x+4} - \left(\dfrac{(x+4)\,(x-1)}{(x+4)\,(x-1)}\right)\dfrac{2}{x^2} + \left(\dfrac{x^2\,(x+4)}{x^2\,(x+4)}\right)\dfrac{1}{x-1}}_{\text{The LCM of } x+4,\ x^2 \text{ and } x-1 \text{ is } x^2(x+4)(x-1).}$

$= \dfrac{3x^2\,(x-1) - 2\,(x+4)\,(x-1) + x^2\,(x+4)}{x^2\,(x-1)\,(x+4)} = \dfrac{3x^3-3x^2-2\overset{(x+4)(x-1)}{\overbrace{(x^2+3x-4)}}+x^3+4x^2}{x^2\,(x-1)\,(x+4)}$

$= \dfrac{3x^3-3x^2-2x^2-6x+8+x^3+4x^2}{x^2\,(x-1)\,(x+4)} = \dfrac{4x^3-x^2-6x+8}{x^2\,(x-1)\,(x+4)}$

Once again, the Grouping Method does not help us in factoring $4x^3 - x^2 - 6x + 8$. Therefore, we will leave our answer as it is.

10) $\underbrace{\dfrac{1-6y}{3y+4} + 5 = \dfrac{1-6y}{3y+4} + \dfrac{5}{1} = \dfrac{1-6y}{3y+4} + \left(\dfrac{3y+4}{3y+4}\right)\dfrac{5}{1}}_{\text{The LCM of } 3y+4 \text{ and } 1 \text{ is } 3y+4.} = \dfrac{1-6y+5\,(3y+4)}{3y+4}$

$= \dfrac{1-6y+15y+20}{3y+4} = \dfrac{9y+21}{3y+4} = \dfrac{3\,(3y+7)}{3y+4}$

11) $1 + x - \dfrac{x^2 - x + 3}{5x - 2} = \underbrace{\dfrac{1 + x}{1} - \dfrac{x^2 - x + 3}{5x - 2} = \left(\dfrac{5x - 2}{5x - 2}\right)\dfrac{1 + x}{1} - \dfrac{x^2 - x + 3}{5x - 2}}_{\text{The LCM of } 5x-2 \text{ and } 1 \text{ is } 5x-2.}$

$= \underbrace{\dfrac{(5x - 2)(1 + x) - (x^2 - x + 3)}{5x - 2} = \dfrac{5x + 5x^2 - 2 - 2x - x^2 + x - 3}{5x - 2}}_{\text{FOIL and distribute the negative.}}$

$= \dfrac{4x^2 + 4x - 5}{5x - 2}$

**Try These (Set 3):** Add or subtract the following and simplify.

1) $\dfrac{7}{8} + \dfrac{2}{5y}$　　　3) $\dfrac{1}{x + 7} - \dfrac{1}{x + 1}$　　　5) $\dfrac{y - 2}{y^2 - 16} - \dfrac{2y - 5}{y^2 - 4y}$　　　7) $4u + \dfrac{u^2 + 9}{u + 7}$

2) $\dfrac{2}{3t} - \dfrac{4}{9t}$　　　4) $\dfrac{3}{a^2 - 5a} + \dfrac{4}{a^2 - 6a}$　　　6) $\dfrac{x}{x^2 + 12x + 36} + \dfrac{3x}{x^2 + 11x + 30}$

**Exercise 4.3**

In Exercises 1-28, perform the indicated operation and simplify.

1. $\dfrac{3}{x} + \dfrac{2}{x}$　　　　2. $\dfrac{5}{a} + \dfrac{7}{a}$　　　　3. $\dfrac{6}{7b} + \dfrac{9}{7b}$　　　　4. $\dfrac{12}{11t} + \dfrac{3}{11t}$

5. $\dfrac{8}{3y} - \dfrac{2}{3y}$　　　6. $\dfrac{9}{4p} - \dfrac{7}{4p}$　　　7. $\dfrac{1}{x + 3} + \dfrac{x + 4}{x + 3}$　　　8. $\dfrac{2x + 1}{x + 4} + \dfrac{8}{x + 4}$

9. $\dfrac{3t + 2}{7t - 1} + \dfrac{4t}{7t - 1}$　　10. $\dfrac{8s}{3s - 13} + \dfrac{2s + 5}{3s - 13}$　　11. $\dfrac{3a + 5}{2a - 6} + \dfrac{2a - 9}{2a - 6}$　　12. $\dfrac{m - 7}{8m + 5} + \dfrac{3m - 9}{8m + 5}$

13. $\dfrac{2x + 1}{x^2 - 4} - \dfrac{x - 1}{x^2 - 4}$　　14. $\dfrac{3y - 5}{y^2 - 9} - \dfrac{2y - 2}{y^2 - 9}$　　15. $\dfrac{6t - 7}{9t - 8} - \dfrac{t + 7}{9t - 8}$　　16. $\dfrac{12b + 9}{5b + 1} - \dfrac{3b + 1}{5b + 1}$

17. $\dfrac{18t^2 - 8}{4t + 1} - \dfrac{2t^2 - 7}{4t + 1}$　　18. $\dfrac{9u^2 - 10}{5u + 2} - \dfrac{4u^2 + 13u - 4}{5u + 2}$　　19. $\dfrac{10x^2 - x - 2}{2x^2 + 4x - 5} + \dfrac{-3x^2 - 3x + 7}{2x^2 + 4x - 5}$

20. $\dfrac{-2y^2 + 8y - 7}{3y^2 + y + 10} + \dfrac{4y^2 - 11y - 2}{3y^2 + y + 10}$　　21. $\dfrac{6x}{x - 3} + \dfrac{7}{3 - x}$　　22. $\dfrac{5}{y - 7} + \dfrac{8y}{7 - y}$

23. $\dfrac{5u + 3}{2u - 9} - \dfrac{2u}{9 - 2u}$　　24. $\dfrac{7v - 8}{3v - 7} - \dfrac{4}{7 - 3v}$　　25. $\dfrac{4x - 5}{6 - 8x} + \dfrac{3x - 4}{8x - 6}$

26. $\dfrac{12y - 1}{8 - 3y} + \dfrac{y - 6}{3y - 8}$　　27. $\dfrac{7a + 12}{3a - 13} - \dfrac{7 - 5a}{13 - 3a}$　　28. $\dfrac{2b + 4}{b - 9} - \dfrac{3b - 6}{9 - b}$

In Exercises 29-74, find the LCM of the given polynomials.

29. 3 and 7　　　30. 11 and 5　　　31. 36 and 24　　　32. 20 and 50

33. 6 and 14　　　34. 16 and 10　　　35. 90 and 75　　　36. 44 and 8

37. $2x^4$ and $5x^3$  38. $3y^2$ and $2y^5$  39. $12a^3b^2$ and $9ab^6$  40. $49ab^3$ and $28a^4b^2$

41. $10x^2y^5$ and $10x^2y^6$  42. $9a^3b^2$ and $9a^7b^2$  43. $2x$ and $11y$  44. $7a$ and $5b$

45. $8x^2$ and $6y^2$  46. $12a^3$ and $10b$  47. $18$ and $xy^2$  48. $27$ and $a^4b^2$

49. $x$ and $x-5$  50. $t$ and $t+4$  51. $x$ and $x+h$  52. $y$ and $y-9$

53. $7x^2$ and $8x+3$  54. $6y^3$ and $7y-1$  55. $x+3$ and $x-3$  56. $y-8$ and $y-2$

57. $3y+5$ and $y-1$  58. $5-2y$ and $2y+13$  59. $4x+8$ and $7x+14$  60. $3t-9$ and $4t-12$

61. $x^2-3x$ and $x^2+4x$  62. $y^2+5y$ and $y^2-y$  63. $y^3+6y^2$ and $y^2-36$

64. $x^3-7x$ and $x^2-49$  65. $x^2+5x+4$ and $x^2-3x-28$  66. $x^2-6x-7$ and $x^2+2x+1$

67. $3x^4-3x^3-18x^2$ and $6x^3+30x^2+36x$  68. $5y^5-20y^4+15y^3$ and $4y^3-28y^2-32y$

69. $18x^4(x-1)^2(x+1)$ and $12x^2(x-1)(x+1)^2$  70. $12y(y+2)(y+3)^2$ and $8y^4(y+2)^3(y+3)$

71. $5a^2(3a+4)^3(a-6)^2$ and $a^5(3a-4)^2(a-6)^2$  72. $9b(b-7)^4(8b-1)$ and $9b^2(b-7)^3(8b+1)$

73. $2(x-3)^2(x^2+4)^2$ and $2(x-3)^2(x^2-3)$  74. $11(8-y)^3(2y^2+3)^2$ and $11(8+y)(2y^2+3)^2$

In Exercises 75-120, perform the indicated operation and simplify.

75. $\dfrac{2x}{5}+\dfrac{7}{3}$  76. $\dfrac{10}{11}+\dfrac{6x}{5}$  77. $\dfrac{8y}{9}-\dfrac{5}{12}$

78. $\dfrac{14}{15}-\dfrac{7t}{25}$  79. $\dfrac{9}{4x}+\dfrac{5}{6}$  80. $\dfrac{12}{7}+\dfrac{1}{21y}$

81. $\dfrac{3}{x+7}+\dfrac{4}{x-2}$  82. $\dfrac{7}{y-8}+\dfrac{3}{y-2}$  83. $\dfrac{4a}{3a+1}-\dfrac{1}{5a-2}$

84. $\dfrac{b}{2b-1}-\dfrac{3}{3b+1}$  85. $\dfrac{t+2}{t-5}+\dfrac{t+1}{t-3}$  86. $\dfrac{s+6}{s+2}+\dfrac{s-3}{s+1}$

87. $\dfrac{1}{4+h}-\dfrac{1}{4}$  88. $\dfrac{1}{7+h}-\dfrac{1}{7}$  89. $\dfrac{1}{(3+h)^2}-\dfrac{1}{9}$

90. $\dfrac{1}{(x+h)^2}-\dfrac{1}{x^2}$  91. $\dfrac{2m-1}{3m+2}-\dfrac{m+2}{m-4}$  92. $\dfrac{2n+5}{3n-2}-\dfrac{4n-3}{6n+1}$

93. $\dfrac{1}{12xy}+\dfrac{6}{9y^2}$  94. $\dfrac{9}{20x^2}+\dfrac{3}{8y}$  95. $\dfrac{6}{11a^2b}-\dfrac{10}{3ab^2}$

96. $\dfrac{2}{15a^2b^2}-\dfrac{3}{25ab}$  97. $\dfrac{x}{18y^3}+\dfrac{5y}{6x^2}$  98. $\dfrac{3x}{7y^2}-\dfrac{2y}{21x^2}$

99. $\dfrac{1}{x+2}+\dfrac{4}{x^2-4}$  100. $\dfrac{1}{y+3}+\dfrac{1}{y^2+5y+6}$  101. $\dfrac{6}{a^2-a}-\dfrac{9}{a^2-1}$

102. $\dfrac{10}{b^2+4b}-\dfrac{2}{b^2+3b-4}$  103. $\dfrac{a+3}{a^2-4a-5}+\dfrac{a}{a^2-8a+15}$  104. $\dfrac{b-2}{b^2-4b-12}+\dfrac{b}{b^2-10b+24}$

105. $\dfrac{3x-10}{2x^2-11x+5} - \dfrac{7x+8}{2x^2-7x-15}$      106. $\dfrac{5y+12}{3y^2-5y-8} - \dfrac{6y-11}{12y^2-17y-40}$

107. $\dfrac{3m-1}{m^2+4m+4} + \dfrac{1}{m-3}$      108. $\dfrac{2n+9}{n^2-6n+5} + \dfrac{1}{n-4}$      109. $\dfrac{1}{x} + \dfrac{3x+2}{x+1} - \dfrac{2}{x-2}$

110. $\dfrac{3}{t} - \dfrac{5}{t+3} + \dfrac{2t+1}{t-2}$      111. $\dfrac{2}{x^2+4x} + \dfrac{3}{x^2-5x} + \dfrac{1}{x+3}$      112. $\dfrac{7}{y^2-6y} + \dfrac{4}{y^2+5y} + \dfrac{3}{y+1}$

113. $2 + \dfrac{3x-1}{2x+5}$      114. $3 + \dfrac{2a}{4a+7}$      115. $8b - \dfrac{3}{b+1}$      116. $4p - \dfrac{5}{p-6}$

117. $x^2 + 3x + \dfrac{2}{x}$      118. $t^2 - 2t + \dfrac{9}{t}$      119. $5u - 4 - \dfrac{10}{u-1}$      120. $-v + 3 - \dfrac{4v}{5v+1}$

# Section 4.4  Mixed Quotients (Complex Fractions)

Here we will learn how to simplify a mixed quotient. Roughly speaking, a mixed quotient is a fraction whose numerator and denominator contain fractions. There are two methods for simplifying a mixed quotient. One of them requires the usage of LCM's, while the other deals with converting the 'big' fraction into the quotient of two fractions. I prefer using the LCM Method and will use it throughout, although the other method will be demonstrated as well.

**Definition:** A **mixed quotient** (or **complex fraction**) is a fraction whose numerator and denominator contain rational expressions.

The expressions $\dfrac{\frac{1}{2}+\frac{3}{5}}{5}$, $\dfrac{6-\frac{2}{x^2}}{\frac{x}{7}-\frac{x}{2}}$, $\dfrac{2x+\frac{3x}{y}-\frac{2x}{7}}{y+\frac{x}{y}}$, and $\dfrac{a^2+3a+\frac{1}{a^2-4}}{a^2-7a+\frac{8}{a^2-4}}$ are examples of mixed quotients. Our goal is to simplify such an expression into a reduced, rational expression. In order to explain the LCM method, I will give names for the expressions in a mixed quotient. In the expression $\dfrac{\frac{1}{2}+\frac{3}{5}}{5}$, for instance, there are two fractions in the numerator (namely, $\frac{1}{2}$ and $\frac{3}{5}$) and one fraction in the denominator (namely, $5 = \frac{5}{1}$). I will refer to these as the 'little fractions' and to the expression $\dfrac{\frac{1}{2}+\frac{3}{5}}{5}$ as the 'big fraction'. In the mixed quotient $\dfrac{2x+\frac{3x}{y}-\frac{2x}{7}}{y+\frac{x}{y}}$, the 'big fraction' is $\dfrac{2x+\frac{3x}{y}-\frac{2x}{7}}{y+\frac{x}{y}}$ itself, and the 'little fractions' contained in it are $2x = \frac{2x}{1}$, $\frac{3x}{y}$, $\frac{2x}{7}$, $y = \frac{y}{1}$, and $\frac{x}{y}$. As we will see, the 'little fractions' which we are concerned with are those which have a denominator different from 1. Hence, $2x$ and $y$ will not play a role in the LCM Method (see Step I below).

We are now ready to simplify some mixed quotients. In the first example, I will explain the LCM Method step by step. After we simplify the expression, I will demonstrate the other method. You may use either.

**Examples.** Simplify the following.

1) $\dfrac{\frac{1}{6}+\frac{2}{3}}{\frac{3}{4}-2}$

The LCM Method goes as follows:

**Step I.** Find the LCM of the denominators of the 'little fractions'.

The denominators of our 'little fractions' are 6, 3, 4, and 1 (if we write $2 = \frac{2}{1}$). The LCM of these is 12. Notice that the denominator of 1 doesn't contribute any new factors toward the LCM. In other words, the LCM of 6, 3, 4, and 1 is the same as the LCM of 6, 3, and 4. The number 1 isn't needed in 'building' the LCM and can be left out. That is why I've mentioned earlier that any 'little fractions' whose denominator is 1 can be ignored.

**Step II.** Multiply the 'big fraction' by $\dfrac{\text{LCM}}{\text{LCM}}$.

We have

$$\frac{\frac{1}{6} + \frac{2}{3}}{\frac{3}{4} - 2} = \left( \frac{\frac{1}{6} + \frac{2}{3}}{\frac{3}{4} - 2} \right) \left( \frac{12}{12} \right) = \left( \frac{\frac{1}{6} + \frac{2}{3}}{\frac{3}{4} - 2} \right) \left( \frac{\frac{12}{1}}{\frac{12}{1}} \right)$$

$$= \frac{\frac{1}{6} \left( \frac{12}{1} \right) + \frac{2}{3} \left( \frac{12}{1} \right)}{\frac{3}{4} \left( \frac{12}{1} \right) - 2 \left( \frac{12}{1} \right)} = \frac{2 + 2(4)}{3(3) - 24}$$

Notice that after writing 12 as $\frac{12}{1}$ and distributing it in the numerator and denominator of the 'big fraction', all that I really did was multiply every expression in the 'big fraction' by $\frac{12}{1}$. Furthermore, observe that Step II allows us to kill off all of the denominators of the 'little fractions'. This is exactly what we wanted.

**Step III.** Simplify your answer.

$$\frac{2 + 2(4)}{3(3) - 24} = \frac{2 + 8}{9 - 24} = \frac{10}{-15} = -\frac{2}{3}$$

We now have a rational expression in simplified form.

Before doing more examples using this method, let me show you the other approach. We begin by combining the 'little fractions' in the numerator and denominator of the 'big fraction'. Then we will use the fact that

$$\frac{\frac{a}{b}}{\frac{c}{d}} = \frac{a}{b} \div \frac{c}{d} \text{ where } b, c, d \neq 0.$$

Following this method, we obtain

$$\frac{\frac{1}{6} + \frac{2}{3}}{\frac{3}{4} - \frac{2}{1}} = \frac{\frac{1}{6} + \frac{4}{6}}{\frac{3}{4} - \frac{8}{4}} = \frac{\frac{5}{6}}{\frac{-5}{4}} = \frac{5}{6} \div \left( \frac{-5}{4} \right) = \frac{5}{6} \left( -\frac{4}{5} \right) = -\frac{2}{3}$$

as before. If you like this method better than the LCM, use it. It's a matter of preference. As I've mentioned earlier, I prefer the LCM method.

2) $\dfrac{\frac{3}{4x} - \frac{4}{3x}}{\frac{1}{2} + \frac{5}{2x}} = \left( \dfrac{\frac{3}{4x} - \frac{4}{3x}}{\frac{1}{2} + \frac{5}{2x}} \right) \left( \dfrac{\frac{12x}{1}}{\frac{12x}{1}} \right) = \dfrac{\frac{3}{4x} \left( \frac{12x}{1} \right) - \frac{4}{3x} \left( \frac{12x}{1} \right)}{\frac{1}{2} \left( \frac{12x}{1} \right) + \frac{5}{2x} \left( \frac{12x}{1} \right)} = \dfrac{3(3) - 4(4)}{6x + 5(6)}$

The LCM of $4x$, $3x$, $2$ and $2x$ is $12x$

Cancel out the denominators of the 'little fractions'.

$$= \frac{9 - 16}{6x + 30} = \frac{-7}{6x + 30} = -\frac{7}{6(x + 5)}$$

If we use the other method, we have

$$\frac{\frac{3}{4x}-\frac{4}{3x}}{\frac{1}{2}+\frac{5}{2x}}=\frac{\frac{3}{4x}\left(\frac{3}{3}\right)-\frac{4}{3x}\left(\frac{4}{4}\right)}{\frac{1}{2}\left(\frac{x}{x}\right)+\frac{5}{2x}}=\frac{\frac{9}{12x}-\frac{16}{12x}}{\frac{x}{2x}+\frac{5}{2x}}=\frac{-\frac{7}{12x}}{\frac{x+5}{2x}}$$

$$=\left(-\frac{7}{12x}\right)\div\left(\frac{x+5}{2x}\right)=\left(-\frac{7}{12\overset{}{\underset{6}{x}}}\right)\left(\frac{\overset{1}{2x}}{x+5}\right)=-\frac{7}{6(x+5)}$$

3) $\underbrace{\dfrac{\frac{x}{5y}+2}{3x-\frac{7}{2xy}}=\left(\dfrac{\frac{x}{5y}+2}{3x-\frac{7}{2xy}}\right)\left(\dfrac{\frac{10xy}{1}}{\frac{10xy}{1}}\right)}_{\text{The LCM of }5y\text{ and }2xy\text{ is }10xy.}=\underbrace{\dfrac{\frac{x}{5y}\left(\overset{2x}{\frac{10xy}{1}}\right)+2\left(\frac{10xy}{1}\right)}{3x\left(\frac{10xy}{1}\right)-\frac{7}{2xy}\left(\overset{5}{\frac{10xy}{1}}\right)}}_{\text{Cancel out the denominators of the 'little fractions'.}}=\dfrac{x\,(2x)+20xy}{30x^2y-7\,(5)}$$

$$=\frac{2x^2+20xy}{30x^2y-35}=\frac{2x\,(x+10y)}{5\,(6x^2y-7)}$$

4) $\underbrace{\dfrac{\frac{a}{2b}-\frac{b}{2a}}{\frac{a-b}{4ab}}=\left(\dfrac{\frac{a}{2b}-\frac{b}{2a}}{\frac{a-b}{4ab}}\right)\left(\dfrac{\frac{4ab}{1}}{\frac{4ab}{1}}\right)}_{\text{The LCM of }2b,\ 2a\text{ and }4ab\text{ is }4ab.}=\underbrace{\dfrac{\frac{a}{2b}\left(\overset{2a}{\frac{4ab}{1}}\right)-\frac{b}{2a}\left(\overset{2b}{\frac{4ab}{1}}\right)}{\frac{a-b}{4ab}\left(\overset{1}{\frac{4ab}{1}}\right)}}_{\text{Cancel out the denominators of the 'little fractions'.}}=\dfrac{a\,(2a)-b(2b)}{a-b}$$

$$=\underbrace{\frac{2a^2-2b^2}{a-b}=\frac{2\,(a+b)\,\overset{1}{\cancel{(a-b)}}}{\underset{1}{\cancel{a-b}}}}_{\text{Factor the numerator completely.}}=\frac{2\,(a+b)}{1}=2\,(a+b)$$

5) $\underbrace{\dfrac{\frac{x}{x+1}+\frac{3}{x-4}}{1+\frac{1}{x^2-3x-4}}=\left(\dfrac{\frac{x}{x+1}+\frac{3}{x-4}}{1+\frac{1}{x^2-3x-4}}\right)\left(\dfrac{\frac{(x+1)(x-4)}{1}}{\frac{(x+1)(x-4)}{1}}\right)}_{\text{The LCM of }x+1,\ x-4\text{ and }x^2-3x-4=(x+1)(x-4)\text{ is }(x+1)(x-4).}=\dfrac{\frac{x}{\cancel{x+1}}\left(\frac{\cancel{(x+1)}(x-4)}{1}\right)+\frac{3}{\cancel{x-4}}\left(\frac{(x+1)\cancel{(x-4)}}{1}\right)}{1\left(\frac{(x+1)(x-4)}{1}\right)+\frac{1}{\cancel{(x+1)}\cancel{(x-4)}}\left(\overset{1}{\frac{\cancel{(x+1)}\cancel{(x-4)}}{1}}\right)}$$

$$=\underbrace{\frac{x\,(x-4)+3\,(x+1)}{(x+1)\,(x-4)+1}}_{\text{After cancelling out the denominators.}}=\frac{x^2-4x+3x+3}{x^2-3x-4+1}=\frac{x^2-x+3}{x^2-3x-3}$$

6) $\underbrace{\dfrac{\frac{1}{2+h}-\frac{1}{2}}{h}=\left(\dfrac{\frac{1}{2+h}-\frac{1}{2}}{h}\right)\left(\dfrac{\frac{2(2+h)}{1}}{\frac{2(2+h)}{1}}\right)}_{\text{The LCM of }2\text{ and }2+h\text{ is }2(2+h).}=\underbrace{\dfrac{\frac{1}{\cancel{2+h}}\left(\frac{2\cancel{(2+h)}}{1}\right)-\frac{1}{\cancel{2}}\left(\frac{\cancel{2}(2+h)}{1}\right)}{h\left(\frac{2(2+h)}{1}\right)}}_{\text{Cancel out the denominators of the 'little fractions'.}}=\dfrac{2-(2+h)}{2h(2+h)}$$

$$=\frac{2-2-h}{2h(2+h)}=\frac{\overset{1}{-\cancel{h}}}{2\cancel{h}(2+h)}=\frac{-1}{2(2+h)}\ \text{or}\ -\frac{1}{2(2+h)}$$

Here's an example which demonstrates why the 'flipping technique' for negative exponents works. Recall from Section 2.1 (Property IV) that if $a$ is any non-zero real number and $n$ is any whole number, then

$$a^{-n}=\frac{1}{a^n}.$$

Property VIII of Section 2.1 states that if $a$ and $b$ are any two non-zero real numbers and $n$ is any integer, then

$$\left(\frac{a}{b}\right)^{-n} = \left(\frac{b}{a}\right)^{n} = \frac{b^n}{a^n}.$$

We can now verify that Property VIII can be derived from Property IV. Notice that

$$\underbrace{\left(\frac{a}{b}\right)^{-n} = \frac{1}{\left(\frac{a}{b}\right)^n}}_{\text{by Property IV}} = \underbrace{\frac{1}{\frac{a^n}{b^n}} = \left(\frac{1}{\frac{a^n}{b^n}}\right)\left(\frac{\frac{b^n}{1}}{\frac{b^n}{1}}\right) = \frac{1\left(\frac{b^n}{1}\right)}{\frac{a^n}{b^n}\left(\frac{b^n}{1}\right)}}_{\text{the LCM of } b^n \text{ is just } b^n} = \frac{b^n}{a^n}.$$

And so Property VIII is verified.

Here's another example of the 'flipping technique'. Recall from Section 2.2 that $\dfrac{a^{-m}}{b^n} = \dfrac{1}{b^n a^m}$. Well, this works because

$$\underbrace{\frac{a^{-m}}{b^n} = \frac{\frac{1}{a^m}}{b^n}}_{\text{by Property IV}} = \frac{\frac{1}{a^m}}{b^n}\left(\frac{\frac{a^m}{1}}{\frac{a^m}{1}}\right) = \frac{\frac{1}{a^m}\left(\frac{a^m}{1}\right)}{b^n\left(\frac{a^m}{1}\right)} = \frac{1}{b^n a^m}.$$

Try to verify some of the others from Section 2.2 on your own.

### Exercise 4.4

In Exercises 1-26, simplify.

1. $\dfrac{\frac{2}{3} - \frac{1}{4}}{\frac{1}{6}}$

2. $\dfrac{\frac{7}{8} + \frac{3}{4}}{\frac{1}{2}}$

3. $\dfrac{2 - \frac{9}{10}}{3 + \frac{1}{5}}$

4. $\dfrac{4 + \frac{1}{6}}{1 - \frac{3}{8}}$

5. $\dfrac{3 + \frac{5}{8}}{3}$

6. $\dfrac{\frac{3}{10} - 6}{4}$

7. $\dfrac{2}{1 - \frac{7}{12}}$

8. $\dfrac{5}{2 + \frac{2}{3}}$

9. $\dfrac{\frac{1}{36} + \frac{5}{6}}{\frac{7}{18} - \frac{1}{6}}$

10. $\dfrac{\frac{7}{8} + \frac{1}{2}}{-\frac{5}{12} + \frac{1}{6}}$

11. $\dfrac{\frac{1}{3x} - 2}{\frac{4}{9x} + 1}$

12. $\dfrac{5 + \frac{1}{2a}}{\frac{7}{4a} - 3}$

13. $\dfrac{\frac{2}{y+1} - \frac{3}{y-2}}{\frac{5}{y^2 - y - 2}}$

14. $\dfrac{\frac{4}{x+3} + \frac{2}{x+2}}{\frac{9}{x^2 + 5x + 6}}$

15. $\dfrac{\frac{1}{12x^2} - \frac{5}{4x}}{\frac{2}{3x^2}}$

16. $\dfrac{\frac{2}{7x} - \frac{1}{14x^2}}{\frac{1}{4x}}$

17. $\dfrac{\frac{2}{y^2 + 3y} + \frac{3y}{y^2 - 9}}{\frac{4}{y^2 - 3y}}$

18. $\dfrac{\frac{4}{t^2 + 6t} - \frac{1}{t^2 - 4t}}{\frac{3}{t^2 + 2t - 24}}$

19. $\dfrac{-x + 3 + \frac{1}{x-6}}{x + 2}$

20. $\dfrac{\frac{3}{2x+1} - x + 6}{x - 7}$

21. $\dfrac{\frac{7}{2} + \frac{3}{x-9}}{4x - 12}$

22. $\dfrac{\frac{4}{5} + \frac{6}{x+8}}{3x + 5}$

23. $\dfrac{\frac{1}{5+h} - \frac{1}{5}}{h}$

24. $\dfrac{\frac{1}{x+h} - \frac{1}{x}}{h}$

25. $\dfrac{\frac{1}{(3+h)^2} - \frac{1}{9}}{h}$

26. $\dfrac{\frac{1}{(x+h)^2} - \frac{1}{x^2}}{h}$

In Exercises 27-44, perform the indicated operation and simplify.

27. $1 + \dfrac{1}{1 + \frac{1}{3}}$

28. $1 + \dfrac{2}{1 + \frac{3}{4}}$

29. $x - \dfrac{x}{1 + \frac{x}{x+3}}$

30. $t + \dfrac{3t}{1 - \frac{t}{t-4}}$

31. $\dfrac{a}{5 + \frac{1}{1+\frac{a}{3}}}$

32. $\dfrac{y}{\frac{2}{1+\frac{y}{2}} - 3}$

33. $1 + \dfrac{1}{1 + \frac{1}{x+1}}$

34. $1 + \dfrac{1}{1 - \frac{1}{x+1}}$

35. $\dfrac{2^{-1} + 5^{-1}}{10^{-1}}$

36. $\dfrac{3^{-1} + 6^{-1}}{6^{-1}}$

37. $\dfrac{-2 + 4^{-2}}{1 - 8^{-1}}$

38. $\dfrac{5 - 6^{-1}}{2 + 3^{-2}}$

39. $\dfrac{x + x^{-1}}{x^{-2}}$

40. $\dfrac{y^{-2} - y^2}{y^{-1}}$

41. $\dfrac{1 + 5a^{-1} + a^{-2}}{1 - 5a^{-1} - a^{-2}}$

42. $\dfrac{2 + 3a + a^{-1}}{2 - 3a - a^{-1}}$

43. $\dfrac{x^{-1} + x^{-1}}{x^{-1}}$

44. $\dfrac{y^{-1} + y^{-1} + y^{-1}}{y^{-1}}$

---

## END OF CHAPTER 4   QUIZ

1. Simplify: $\dfrac{7x^2 - 14x}{x^3 - 4x}$

   a) $\dfrac{7x}{x+2}$   b) $\dfrac{7x}{x-2}$   c) $\dfrac{7}{x+2}$   d) $\dfrac{7}{x} + 5$   e) $\dfrac{7(x-2)}{x^2 - 4}$

2. Simplify: $\dfrac{a^3 - 10a^2 + 25a}{2a^3 - 9a^2 - 5a}$

   a) $\dfrac{a^2 - 5}{2a + 1}$   b) $\dfrac{a^2 - 10a + 25}{2a^2 - 9a - 5}$   c) $6\frac{11}{18}$   d) $\dfrac{a - 5}{2a + 1}$   e) $\dfrac{a + 5}{2a - 1}$

3. Simplify: $\dfrac{27 - y^3}{y^2 - 7y + 12}$

   a) $\dfrac{y^2 + 3y + 9}{y - 4}$   b) $-\dfrac{y^2 + 3y + 9}{y - 4}$   c) $\dfrac{(3 - y)^2}{y - 4}$   d) $\dfrac{-(3 - y)^2}{y - 4}$   e) $\dfrac{27 - y}{-7y + 12}$

4. $\dfrac{2t^2}{t + 6} \cdot \dfrac{t^2 - 36}{10t^2} =$

   a) $\dfrac{t - 6}{5t^2}$   b) $\dfrac{1}{5(t - 6)}$   c) $5(t - 6)$   d) $\dfrac{t - 6}{5}$   e) $\dfrac{t - 36}{5}$

5. $\dfrac{4a^2 - 12ab}{6a^2b - 18ab^2} \cdot \dfrac{3a + 9b}{a + b} =$

   a) $\dfrac{2(a + 3b)}{ab(a + b)}$   b) $\dfrac{a + 3b}{a + b}$   c) $\dfrac{8}{b}$   d) $\dfrac{a + 3b}{b(a + b)}$   e) $\dfrac{2(a + 3b)}{b(a + b)}$

6. $\dfrac{2t^2 - t - 28}{4t^2 + 12t - 7} \cdot \dfrac{t^3 + 3t^2}{t^3 - 4t^2} =$

   a) $\dfrac{(t-4)(t+3)}{2t-1}$     b) $\dfrac{t+3}{t^2(2t-1)}$     c) $\dfrac{t+3}{2t-1}$     d) $\dfrac{t+3}{2t+1}$     e) $\dfrac{(2t-7)(t+3)}{2t-1}$

7. $\dfrac{4b^8}{9a^2b^3} \div \dfrac{8a^2}{5a^5b^9} =$

   a) $\dfrac{5b^{14}}{18a}$     b) $\dfrac{32}{45a^5b^4}$     c) $\dfrac{5ab^{14}}{18}$     d) $\dfrac{18}{5ab^{14}}$     e) $\dfrac{5ab^4}{18}$

8. $\dfrac{16x^2}{x^2-1} \div \dfrac{8x+8}{1-x} =$

   a) $-\dfrac{2x^2}{(x+1)^2}$     b) $\dfrac{2x^2}{(x+1)^2}$     c) $\dfrac{128x}{(x-1)(1-x)}$     d) $-\dfrac{2}{2x+1}$     e) $-\dfrac{16x^2}{(x+1)^2}$

9. $\dfrac{y^2+4y+16}{y^2-16} \div \dfrac{y^3-64}{y+4} =$

   a) $\dfrac{y-4}{y+4}$     b) $(y-4)^2$     c) $\dfrac{y+4}{y^2+4y+16}$     d) $\dfrac{1}{(y-4)^2}$     e) $\dfrac{1}{y^2-4}$

10. $\dfrac{7x+3}{4x-5} + \dfrac{8x-12}{4x-5} =$

   a) $\dfrac{101}{20}$     b) $\dfrac{3(5x-3)}{4x-5}$     c) $\dfrac{3(5x-3)}{2(4x-5)}$     d) $\dfrac{15(x-1)}{4x-5}$     e) $\dfrac{6x}{4x-5}$

11. $\dfrac{5a-9}{a^2-81} - \dfrac{4a-18}{a^2-81} =$

   a) $\dfrac{a-27}{(a+9)(a-9)}$     b) $\dfrac{a^2+9}{(a+9)(a-9)}$     c) $\dfrac{a}{a-9}$     d) $\dfrac{a-27}{a-9}$     e) $\dfrac{1}{a-9}$

12. $\dfrac{4b}{7b-2} - \dfrac{3b}{2-7b} =$

   a) $\dfrac{b}{7b-2}$     b) $\dfrac{b}{2(7b-2)}$     c) $\dfrac{7b}{2-7b}$     d) $\dfrac{7b}{7b-2}$     e) $\dfrac{1}{-2}$

13. $\dfrac{12}{x-8} - \dfrac{3}{x+1} =$

   a) $\dfrac{9(x+4)}{(x-8)(x+1)}$     b) $\dfrac{9x-12}{(x-8)(x+1)}$     c) $-1$     d) $\dfrac{9}{(x-8)(x+1)}$     e) $\dfrac{9(x+36)}{(x-8)(x+1)}$

14. $\dfrac{x+5}{x^2-2x} + \dfrac{4x-1}{x^2+x} =$

   a) $\dfrac{5x+4}{2x^2-x}$     b) $\dfrac{6x+5}{(x-2)(x+1)}$     c) $\dfrac{5x^2-3x+7}{x(x-2)(x+1)}$     d) $\dfrac{5x^2-3x+7}{x^2(x-2)(x+1)}$     e) $\dfrac{5x+4}{x}$

15. $y^2 - 3y + \dfrac{y-1}{y+6} =$

   a) $\dfrac{y^2 - 2y - 1}{y+6}$   b) $\dfrac{y^3 + 3y^2 + 17y + 1}{y+6}$   c) $\dfrac{y^3 - 3y^2 - 17y - 1}{y+6}$   d) $y^3 + 3y^2 - 17y - 1$

   e) $\dfrac{y^3 + 3y^2 - 17y - 1}{y+6}$

16. $\dfrac{5}{8x^4y^6} - \dfrac{3}{20x^5y^2} =$

   a) $\dfrac{19}{40x^4y^2}$   b) $\dfrac{25x - 6y^4}{40x^5y^6}$   c) $\dfrac{-1}{6x^{-1}y^4}$   d) $\dfrac{15xy^4}{4x^5y^6}$   e) $\dfrac{25x^2 - 6y^3}{40x^5y^6}$

17. The LCM of $16a^3b^2$ and $10ab^5$ is

   a) $80a^3b^5$   b) $80ab^2$   c) $160a^4b^7$   d) $2a^3b^5$   e) $80a^4b^7$

18. The LCM of $5x^3(x+2)^2(x-3)^4$ and $6x^5(x+2)(x-3)^5$ is

   a) $30x^8(x+2)^3(x-3)^9$   b) $30x^5(x+2)^2(x-3)^5$   c) $x^3(x+2)(x-3)^4$

   d) $30x^3(x+2)^2(x-3)^5$   e) $30x^5(x+2)(x-3)^4$

19. $\dfrac{\dfrac{4}{x} - \dfrac{3}{5x}}{1 + \dfrac{3}{5x}} =$

   a) $\dfrac{17}{8x}$   b) $\dfrac{17}{5x+3}$   c) $\dfrac{34}{5x+3}$   d) $\dfrac{23}{5x+3}$   e) $\dfrac{17}{5x+6}$

20. $\dfrac{\dfrac{1}{7+h} - \dfrac{1}{7}}{h} =$

   a) $-\dfrac{1}{7(7+h)}$   b) $\dfrac{1}{7(7+h)}$   c) $0$   d) $\dfrac{h^2}{7(7+h)}$   e) $\dfrac{-h^2}{7(7+h)}$

ANSWERS FOR QUIZ 4

| | | | | |
|---|---|---|---|---|
| 1. c | 2. d | 3. b | 4. d | 5. e |
| 6. c | 7. c | 8. a | 9. d | 10. b |
| 11. e | 12. d | 13. a | 14. c | 15. e |
| 16. b | 17. a | 18. b | 19. b | 20. a |

# Chapter 5:    Radical Expressions

In this chapter, we will study algebraic expressions known as **radicals**. We will primarily focus our attention on a specific type of radical called a **square root**. In our studies, we will learn how to do the usual arithmetic and algebraic operations, such as simplifying, multiplying, dividing and combining (that is, adding or subtracting). One important thing which we will observe is that such operations are related to those which were done for polynomials. For example, the distributive property, the FOIL method, combining like terms and factoring for square roots works the same way as for polynomials Another operation, called rationalizing, will be introduced as well. After we get a strong grasp on square roots, we will look at radical expressions in general.

## Section 5.1  Square Roots

## Section 5.1.1  Introduction to Square Roots

We begin by defining the square root of a real number.

**Definition:** Let $a$ and $b$ be two real numbers. If $b^2 = a$, then $b$ is called a **square root** of $a$.

For example, since $4^2 = 16$, the definition tells us that 4 is a square root of 16. Notice that $(-4)^2 = 16$ as well, so the definition tells us that $-4$ is also a square root of 16.

The example above shows us that 16 has two square roots, namely $-4$ and 4. In fact, **every** positive number has two square roots (one positive and the other negative). We would like to consider only one of these two answers. From this point on, we will recognize the **positive** square root as **the** square root of $a$ whenever $a$ is a positive number. We call this the **principal square root** of $a$ and denote it by $\sqrt{a}$. For example, $\sqrt{9} = 3$ ONLY and $\sqrt{25} = 5$ ONLY. Observe that $\sqrt{0} = 0$ ONLY, since $0^2 = 0$. The expression '$a$' underneath the **square root symbol** is referred to as the **radicand** of $\sqrt{a}$.

**Question:** Is $\sqrt{-1}$ a real number? Well, suppose that $b = \sqrt{-1}$ for some real number, $b$. Then, by the definition, we would have $b^2 = -1$. Let's think about the possible numbers for which $b$ can equal. If $b$ is a positive number, then $b^2$ is also positive, since $(+)^2 = +$. If $b$ is a negative number, then $b^2$ is a positive number, since $(-)^2 = +$. If $b = 0$, then $b^2 = 0$. In all three possible situations, observe that $b^2$ is either positive or zero. Therefore, $b^2$ cannot equal $-1$. This means that there is no real number for which $\sqrt{-1}$ can equal. In fact, $\sqrt{a}$ will never equal a real number when $a$ is a negative number.

To summarize the above,

$$\boxed{\sqrt{+} = +\ \text{(the principal square root)}, \ \sqrt{0} = 0 \text{ and } \sqrt{-} \text{ is not a real number.}}$$

Before getting into the algebra behind square roots, it is important to establish a list of square roots which often appear.

### LIST OF COMMONLY SEEN SQUARE ROOTS

| | |
|---|---|
| $\sqrt{1} = 1$ | $\sqrt{49} = 7$ |
| $\sqrt{4} = 2$ | $\sqrt{64} = 8$ |
| $\sqrt{9} = 3$ | $\sqrt{81} = 9$ |
| $\sqrt{16} = 4$ | $\sqrt{100} = 10$ |
| $\sqrt{25} = 5$ | $\sqrt{121} = 11$ |
| $\sqrt{36} = 6$ | $\sqrt{144} = 12$ |

You should notice that the list I've given contains the square roots of perfect squares (recall that a **perfect square** is a natural number which is the square of a natural number). As mentioned before, **every** positive number has a square root. For example, there are numbers like $\sqrt{3}$, $\sqrt{23}$, $\sqrt{501.41}$, and $\sqrt{\pi}$. However, the numbers which they equal are very strange looking. As a demonstration, let's look at $\sqrt{2}$. If we write $n = \sqrt{2}$, then we obtain $n^2 = 2$. It turns out that this $n$ is approximately 1.414. In order to figure out this value, you would need a calculator or computer. In fact, the actual value of $\sqrt{2}$ can be expressed as a decimal which is non-terminating and non-repeating (recall that we call such a number an **irrational number**). By writing $\sqrt{2}$ as 1.414, we are rounding off the actual answer to the nearest thousandth. There are many real numbers which have square roots that are irrational numbers. An enormous set of such numbers is described in the following:

**Theorem.** If $n$ is a natural number which is *not* a perfect square, then $\sqrt{n}$ is an irrational number. If $a > 0$, $b > 0$, neither are perfect squares and $\frac{a}{b}$ is in reduced form, then $\sqrt{\frac{a}{b}}$ is an irrational number.

So, now we have an idea of which numbers can and cannot be 'square rooted'. We also have a grasp on which positive numbers have 'nice looking' decimal forms and 'ugly looking' decimal forms. Let's begin doing some algebra. I would like to mention some properties which square roots satisfy.

## PROPERTIES OF SQUARE ROOTS

> **PROPERTY I.** If $a$ is any real number, then
> $$\sqrt{a^2} = |a|.$$

For example, if $a = 7$, then $\sqrt{7^2} = |7| = 7$. If $a = -7$, then $\sqrt{(-7)^2} = |-7| = 7$.

**Note:** Over the years, I've noticed that this property causes some confusion for students because of the presence of the absolute value. After doing some examples using this property, we will make things easier and assume that all variables represent either **positive numbers** or **nonnegative numbers** (a **nonnegative number** is a real number which is either positive or zero). By doing this, the property will simply become $\sqrt{a^2} = a$. Think of the square root and square as cancelling each other out when $a$ is a nonnegative number.

> **PROPERTY II.** Suppose that $a$ and $b$ are nonnegative numbers. Then
> $$\sqrt{a} \cdot \sqrt{b} = \sqrt{a \cdot b}.$$

**Examples.**

1) $\sqrt{(36)(25)} = \sqrt{36} \cdot \sqrt{25} = 6 \cdot 5 = 30$

2) $\sqrt{9x^2} = \sqrt{9} \cdot \sqrt{x^2} = 3\,|x|$

3) $\sqrt{49x^4} = \sqrt{49} \cdot \sqrt{x^4} = \sqrt{49} \cdot \sqrt{(x^2)^2} = 7\,|x^2| = 7x^2$, since $x^2 \geq 0$ for any real number, $x$.

>  **BEWARE:** $\sqrt{a+b} \neq \sqrt{a} + \sqrt{b}$ and $\sqrt{a-b} \neq \sqrt{a} - \sqrt{b}$.

For example, $\sqrt{1} + \sqrt{1} \neq \sqrt{2}$ and $\sqrt{25} - \sqrt{16} \neq \sqrt{9}$.

> **PROPERTY III.** Suppose that $a$ is a nonnegative number and $b$ is a positive number.
> Then $\sqrt{\dfrac{a}{b}} = \dfrac{\sqrt{a}}{\sqrt{b}}$.

**Examples.**

1) $\sqrt{\dfrac{81}{4}} = \dfrac{\sqrt{81}}{\sqrt{4}} = \dfrac{9}{2}$

2) $\sqrt{\dfrac{y^2}{64}} = \dfrac{\sqrt{y^2}}{\sqrt{64}} = \dfrac{|y|}{8}$

3) $\sqrt{\dfrac{a^4}{25}} = \dfrac{\sqrt{a^4}}{\sqrt{25}} = \dfrac{\sqrt{(a^2)^2}}{\sqrt{25}} = \dfrac{|a^2|}{5} = \dfrac{a^2}{5}$, since $a^2 \geq 0$ for any real number, $a$.

**Exercise 5.1.1**

In Exercises 1-30, evaluate (if possible).

1. $\sqrt{4}$          2. $-\sqrt{4}$          3. $\sqrt{0}$          4. $\sqrt{49}$          5. $-\sqrt{49}$

6. $\sqrt{-49}$      7. $\sqrt{7^2}$          8. $\sqrt{(-7)^2}$      9. $\sqrt{(-13)^2}$      10. $\sqrt{13^2}$

11. $-\sqrt{8^2}$    12. $-\sqrt{(-8)^2}$    13. $-\sqrt{-8^2}$      14. $\sqrt{(9)(36)}$    15. $\sqrt{(25)(25)}$

16. $\sqrt{(81)(100)}$          17. $\sqrt{(121)(4)}$          18. $\sqrt{(16)(-4)}$

19. $\sqrt{-16}\sqrt{121}$          20. $\sqrt{-49}\sqrt{-1}$          21. $\sqrt{\dfrac{1}{9}}$

22. $\sqrt{\dfrac{25}{81}}$          23. $\sqrt{\dfrac{64}{25}}$          24. $\sqrt{\dfrac{16}{9}}$

25. $\sqrt{\dfrac{100}{121}}$          26. $-\sqrt{\dfrac{1}{36}}$          27. $-\sqrt{\dfrac{144}{49}}$

28. $\sqrt{-\dfrac{144}{49}}$          29. $\sqrt{(16)\left(\dfrac{4}{81}\right)}$          30. $-\sqrt{\left(\dfrac{36}{25}\right)\left(\dfrac{144}{121}\right)}$

In Exercises 31-48, simplify. Assume that all variables represent positive numbers.

31. $\sqrt{4x^2}$          32. $\sqrt{36y^2}$          33. $\sqrt{64a^2}$          34. $\sqrt{(3x)^2}$          35. $\sqrt{(-3x)^2}$

36. $\sqrt{(-8y)^2}$      37. $\sqrt{(8y)^2}$          38. $-\sqrt{(8y)^2}$      39. $\sqrt{(14a^2b)^2}$      40. $\sqrt{(-5x^4)^2}$

41. $\sqrt{\dfrac{y^2}{36}}$          42. $\sqrt{\dfrac{4}{x^2}}$          43. $\sqrt{\dfrac{100}{t^2}}$          44. $\sqrt{\dfrac{81}{x^2}}$          45. $\sqrt{\dfrac{(7x)^2}{100}}$

46. $\sqrt{\dfrac{9x^2}{(7y)^2}}$  47. $\sqrt{\left(\dfrac{3}{16x^4}\right)^2}$  48. $\sqrt{\dfrac{(11a)^2}{(18b^2)^2}}$

In Exercises 49-61, determine whether or not the square root is a rational or an irrational number.

49. $\sqrt{1}$  50. $\sqrt{16}$  51. $\sqrt{15}$  52. $\sqrt{27}$

53. $\sqrt{\dfrac{25}{36}}$  54. $\sqrt{\dfrac{2}{3}}$  55. $-\sqrt{\dfrac{5}{8}}$  56. $-\sqrt{\dfrac{9}{4}}$

57. $\sqrt{0.09}$  58. $\sqrt{0.7}$  59. $\sqrt{0.3}$  60. $\sqrt{1.44}$

61. $\sqrt{1.21}$

## Section 5.1.2  Simplifying Square Roots

Now we will learn how to simplify a square root. Let's begin by simplifying square roots of natural numbers. Suppose we want to simplify $\sqrt{8}$. The first thing to do is to factor the number 8 so that one of the factors is a perfect square. Notice that $8 = 4 \times 2$ and 4 is a perfect square. Next, we apply Property II of Section 5.1.1 and factor the square root into a product of square roots. Once this is done, we'll simplify $\sqrt{4}$. In other words, we have

$$\sqrt{8} = \sqrt{4 \times 2} = \underbrace{\sqrt{4} \times \sqrt{2}}_{\text{by Property II}} = 2 \times \sqrt{2}, \text{ or just } 2\sqrt{2}.$$ Note that the '$\times$' symbol is omitted in the final answer.

**Examples.** Simplify.

1) $\sqrt{18} = \sqrt{9 \times 2} = \sqrt{9} \times \sqrt{2} = 3 \times \sqrt{2} = 3\sqrt{2}$

2) $\sqrt{27} = \sqrt{9 \times 3} = \sqrt{9} \times \sqrt{3} = 3 \times \sqrt{3} = 3\sqrt{3}$

3) $\sqrt{50} = \sqrt{25 \times 2} = \sqrt{25} \times \sqrt{2} = 5 \times \sqrt{2} = 5\sqrt{2}$

4) $\sqrt{40} = \sqrt{4 \times 10} = \sqrt{4} \times \sqrt{10} = 2 \times \sqrt{10} = 2\sqrt{10}$

5) $-\sqrt{98} = -\sqrt{49 \times 2} = -\sqrt{49} \times \sqrt{2} = -7 \times \sqrt{2} = -7\sqrt{2}$

6) $\sqrt{32} = \sqrt{16 \times 2} = \sqrt{16} \times \sqrt{2} = 4 \times \sqrt{2} = 4\sqrt{2}$

Notice that I used $32 = 16 \times 2$, not $32 = 4 \times 8$. If I use $32 = 4 \times 8$ instead, then

$$\sqrt{32} = \sqrt{4 \times 8} = \sqrt{4} \times \sqrt{8} = 2\sqrt{8}.$$

However, $\sqrt{8}$ can be further simplified to become $2\sqrt{2}$ by the example we've done before. Therefore, $\sqrt{32} = 2\sqrt{8} = 2(2\sqrt{2}) = 4\sqrt{2}$, giving the same answer as before but by doing twice the amount of work. The moral of the story is:

> When you have different possible ways of factoring your number, choose as one of your factors the largest possible perfect square in the factorization.

Another thing to notice is that not all square roots will simplify (in other words, they are already expressed in simplified form). For example, $\sqrt{22}$ doesn't simplify, since $22 = 11 \times 2$ and neither 11 nor 2 are perfect squares. Similarly, $\sqrt{7}$ doesn't simplify, since $7 = 7 \times 1$ and 7 is not a perfect square. Observe that $\sqrt{7} = \sqrt{7} \times \sqrt{1} = \sqrt{7} \times 1 = \sqrt{7}$ and we don't get anything new. In fact, if $n$ is **any** prime number, then $\sqrt{n}$ doesn't simplify (which is the same as saying that it is already in simplified form).

**Try These (Set 1):** Simplify the following (if possible).

1) $\sqrt{20}$        2) $\sqrt{54}$        3) $\sqrt{120}$        4) $\sqrt{39}$        5) $\sqrt{26}$

We will now simplify square roots whose radicand contains variables. For now, let's assume that the variables represent any real number for which the square root is well-defined. Suppose we want to simplify $\sqrt{x^7}$. We want to apply a method similar to the above and somehow incorporate some of our properties into the problem. First of all, notice that $x$ must represent a nonnegative number for this to make sense (if $x$ were allowed to be a negative number, then $x^7$ would also be negative and this would not have a square root). Now, the trick is to divide $7 \div 2 = 3\ R\ 1$. This means that we can now write $7 = 3(2) + 1$ (remember that this is how you check a division problem). We can rewrite our example as follows:

$$\sqrt{x^7} = \underbrace{\sqrt{x^{3(2)+1}} = \sqrt{(x^3)^2 \cdot x^1}}_{\text{by Properties I and V of exponents}} = \underbrace{\sqrt{(x^3)^2} \cdot \sqrt{x^1} = x^3\sqrt{x}}_{\text{by Properties I and II of square roots}}$$

and now it is simplified.

There is a much simpler way of handling this problem, but let's do one more example using this technique before doing it the easier way. Suppose we want to simplify $\sqrt{x^{10}}$. Notice that $x$ may be **any** real number, since $x^{10}$ will be either positive or zero and we can always take the square root of such a number. As before, we divide $10 \div 2 = 5\ R\ 0$. This means that we can write $10 = 5(2)$. Our example now simplifies to

$$\sqrt{x^{10}} = \underbrace{\sqrt{x^{5(2)}} = \sqrt{(x^5)^2}}_{\text{Property V of exponents}} = \left|x^5\right|.$$

Notice, however, that by our properties of absolute value (see Section 1.7), we obtain

$$\left|x^5\right| = \left|x^4 \cdot x^1\right| = \underbrace{\left|x^4\right| \cdot |x| = x^4\,|x|}_{\text{since } x^4 \geq 0,\ |x^4|=x^4}$$

and so $\sqrt{x^{10}} = x^4\,|x|$ is (finally) in simplified form. Now, this is all tedious stuff, especially the part with the absolute value. To make our lives a bit easier, we will assume that **all variables represent either positive or nonnegative numbers only.** By doing so, the absolute value becomes unnecessary and the examples we've done before become much simpler. For instance, to simplify $\sqrt{x^7}$, all we have to do is divide (as before) $7 \div 2 = 3\ R\ 1$. The quotient, 3, tells us 'how many $x$'s come out of the square root'. The remainder, 1, tells us 'how many $x$'s remain inside the square root'. Therefore, $\sqrt{x^7} = \underbrace{x^3\sqrt{x^1}}_{\text{3 out, 1 in}} = x^3\sqrt{x}$. Similarly, to

simplify $\sqrt{x^{10}}$, just divide $10 \div 2 = 5\ R\ 0$. Therefore, $\sqrt{x^{10}} = \underbrace{x^5}_{\text{5 out, 0 in}}$. Let's try some more examples using

this easier technique.

**Examples.** Simplify. Assume that all variables represent nonnegative numbers.

1) $\sqrt{x^5} = \underbrace{x^2\sqrt{x^1}}_{5\div 2\ =\ 2\ R\ 1} = x^2\sqrt{x}$        2) $\sqrt{x^{13}} = \underbrace{x^6\sqrt{x^1}}_{13\div 2\ =\ 6\ R\ 1} = x^6\sqrt{x}$

3) $\sqrt{x^8} = \underbrace{x^4}_{8 \div 2 \,=\, 4 \ R \ 0}$

5) $\sqrt{t^2} = \underbrace{t^1}_{2 \div 2 \,=\, 1 \ R \ 0} = t$

4) $\sqrt{y^{14}} = \underbrace{y^7}_{14 \div 2 \,=\, 7 \ R \ 0}$

6) $\sqrt{a} = \underbrace{\sqrt{a}}_{1 \div 2 \,=\, 0 \ R \ 1}$  (hence, $\sqrt{a}$ is **already simplified.**)

**Try These (Set 2):** Simplify the following. Assume that all variables represent nonnegative numbers.

1) $\sqrt{x^6}$    2) $\sqrt{y^{15}}$    3) $\sqrt{m^3}$    4) $\sqrt{x^{34}}$    5) $\sqrt{p^{19}}$

By using what we've learned, we can actually simplify the square root of **any** monomial. To do this, we simplify each 'piece' of the monomial separately and then 'put it all together'.

**Examples.** Simplify. Assume that all variables represent nonnegative numbers.

1) $\sqrt{25x^2} = 5x$, since $\sqrt{25} = 5$ and $\underbrace{\sqrt{x^2} = x^1 = x}_{2 \div 2 \,=\, 1 \ R \ 0}$.

2) $\sqrt{44a^3} = 2a\sqrt{11a}$, since $\sqrt{44} = \sqrt{4}\sqrt{11} = 2\sqrt{11}$ and $\underbrace{\sqrt{a^3} = a^1\sqrt{a^1} = a\sqrt{a}}_{3 \div 2 \,=\, 1 \ R \ 1}$.

3) $\sqrt{9x^2y^3} = 3xy\sqrt{y}$, since $\sqrt{9} = 3$, $\underbrace{\sqrt{x^2} = x^1 = x}_{2 \div 2 \,=\, 1 \ R \ 0}$ and $\underbrace{\sqrt{y^3} = y^1\sqrt{y^1} = y\sqrt{y}}_{3 \div 2 \,=\, 1 \ R \ 1}$.

4) $\sqrt{12x^9y^4} = 2x^4y^2\sqrt{3x}$, since $\sqrt{12} = \sqrt{4}\sqrt{3} = 2\sqrt{3}$, $\underbrace{\sqrt{x^9} = x^4\sqrt{x^1} = x^4\sqrt{x}}_{9 \div 2 \,=\, 4 \ R \ 1}$ and $\underbrace{\sqrt{y^4} = y^2}_{4 \div 2 \,=\, 2 \ R \ 0}$.

5) $\sqrt{300x^8t} = 10x^4\sqrt{3t}$, since $\sqrt{300} = \sqrt{100}\sqrt{3} = 10\sqrt{3}$, $\underbrace{\sqrt{x^8} = x^4}_{8 \div 2 \,=\, 4 \ R \ 0}$ and $\underbrace{\sqrt{t} = \sqrt{t}}_{1 \div 2 \,=\, 0 \ R \ 1}$.

**Try These (Set 3):** Simplify. Assume that all variables represent nonnegative numbers.

1) $\sqrt{8x^3y^5}$    2) $\sqrt{63x^6y^2}$    3) $\sqrt{400p^7q^4}$    4) $\sqrt{98a^4b^{17}c^2}$    5) $\sqrt{14x^2y}$

**Exercise 5.1.2**

In each of the following, simplify the square root. Assume that all variables represent nonnegative numbers.

1. $\sqrt{8}$    2. $\sqrt{12}$    3. $\sqrt{20}$    4. $\sqrt{27}$    5. $\sqrt{24}$

6. $\sqrt{44}$    7. $-\sqrt{50}$    8. $\sqrt{56}$    9. $\sqrt{32}$    10. $-\sqrt{72}$

11. $\sqrt{54}$    12. $\sqrt{48}$    13. $-\sqrt{300}$    14. $\sqrt{125}$    15. $-\sqrt{63}$

16. $\sqrt{x^2}$  17. $\sqrt{y^5}$  18. $\sqrt{t^9}$  19. $\sqrt{x^4}$  20. $\sqrt{a^{13}}$

21. $\sqrt{b^{11}}$  22. $\sqrt{4x}$  23. $\sqrt{25y}$  24. $\sqrt{121x^2}$  25. $\sqrt{49y^4}$

26. $\sqrt{24x^6y}$  27. $\sqrt{8a^2b^9}$  28. $\sqrt{20x^{13}y^4}$  29. $\sqrt{6m^8n^3}$

30. $-\sqrt{75x^7y}$  31. $-\sqrt{80xy^5}$  32. $\sqrt{56a^6b^{15}c^3}$  33. $\sqrt{68x^{14}y^{11}z}$

## Section 5.1.3    Multiplying and Dividing Square Roots

We will apply the properties mentioned in Section 5.1.1 to divide and multiply square roots. From this point on, we will **assume that all variables represent positive numbers.**

Recall Properties 1 and 2 from Section 5.1.1:

$$\sqrt{a} \cdot \sqrt{b} = \sqrt{a \cdot b} \quad \text{and} \quad \sqrt{\frac{a}{b}} = \frac{\sqrt{a}}{\sqrt{b}}, \ b \neq 0,$$

provided that these square roots are well-defined.

**Examples.** Multiply or Divide. Simplify your answers.

1) $\sqrt{5} \cdot \sqrt{5} = \sqrt{5 \cdot 5} = \sqrt{25} = 5$

2) $\sqrt{6} \cdot \sqrt{7} = \sqrt{6 \cdot 7} = \sqrt{42}$, which is in simplified form.

3) $\sqrt{2x^2} \cdot \sqrt{6x^4} = \sqrt{2x^2 \cdot 6x^4} = \underbrace{\sqrt{12x^6} = 2x^3\sqrt{3}}_{\sqrt{12}=2\sqrt{3}\ \text{and}\ \sqrt{x^6}=x^3.}$

4) $\sqrt{8xy^5} \cdot \sqrt{2x^6y} = \sqrt{8xy^5 \cdot 2x^6y} = \underbrace{\sqrt{16x^7y^6} = 4x^3y^3\sqrt{x}}_{\sqrt{16}=4,\ \sqrt{x^7}=x^3\sqrt{x}\ \text{and}\ \sqrt{y^6}=y^3.}$

5) $\underbrace{\sqrt{5a^2b}\left(\sqrt{2b^3}\right)\left(\sqrt{9a^2b^7}\right) = \sqrt{5a^2b(2b^3)(9a^2b^7)}}_{\text{Multiply the radicands together.}} = \underbrace{\sqrt{90a^4b^{11}} = 3a^2b^5\sqrt{10b}}_{\sqrt{90}=3\sqrt{10},\ \sqrt{a^4}=a^2\ \text{and}\ \sqrt{b^{11}}=b^5\sqrt{b}.}$

6) $\frac{\sqrt{72x^{14}}}{\sqrt{8x^9}} = \sqrt{\frac{72x^{14}}{8x^9}} = \underbrace{\sqrt{9x^5} = 3x^2\sqrt{x}}_{\sqrt{9}=3\ \text{and}\ \sqrt{x^5}=x^2\sqrt{x}.}$

7) $\frac{\sqrt{120a^{11}b^8}}{\sqrt{12a^9b^9}} = \sqrt{\frac{120a^{11}b^8}{12a^9b^9}} = \underbrace{\sqrt{\frac{10a^2}{b}} = \frac{a\sqrt{10}}{\sqrt{b}}}_{\sqrt{10}\ \text{and}\ \sqrt{b}\ \text{are simplified and}\ \sqrt{a^2}=a.} = \frac{a\sqrt{10}}{1\sqrt{b}} = \frac{a}{1}\left(\frac{\sqrt{10}}{\sqrt{b}}\right) = a\sqrt{\frac{10}{b}}$

**Try These (Set 4):** Multiply or Divide. Simplify your answers.

1) $\sqrt{7x^2y^5} \cdot \sqrt{7xy^3}$    2) $\frac{\sqrt{56x^8}}{\sqrt{7x^6}}$    3) $\frac{\left(\sqrt{15a^{10}}\right)\left(\sqrt{12a^9}\right)}{\sqrt{5a^6}}$

**Exercise 5.1.3**

In Exercises 1-23, multiply and simplify the square roots. Assume that all variables represent nonnegative numbers.

1. $\sqrt{3} \cdot \sqrt{2}$      2. $\sqrt{5} \cdot \sqrt{3}$      3. $\sqrt{7} \cdot \sqrt{6}$      4. $\sqrt{11} \cdot \sqrt{3}$      5. $\sqrt{5} \cdot \sqrt{10}$

6. $\sqrt{6} \cdot \sqrt{4}$      7. $\sqrt{8} \cdot \sqrt{8}$      8. $\sqrt{5} \cdot \sqrt{5}$      9. $\sqrt{12} \cdot \sqrt{5}$      10. $\sqrt{14} \cdot \sqrt{6}$

11. $\sqrt{10} \cdot \sqrt{2}$      12. $\sqrt{x^2} \cdot \sqrt{x^3}$      13. $\sqrt{y^5} \cdot \sqrt{y^4}$      14. $\sqrt{b} \cdot \sqrt{b}$      15. $\sqrt{xy^2} \cdot \sqrt{x^3y^2}$

16. $\sqrt{x^4y^5} \cdot \sqrt{3xy^3}$      17. $\sqrt{5a^3b^3} \cdot \sqrt{a^4b}$      18. $\sqrt{3x} \cdot \sqrt{3x^4}$      19. $\sqrt{8x^2y} \cdot \sqrt{5x^3y^2}$

20. $\sqrt{16x^5} \cdot \sqrt{3x^3y^7}$      21. $\sqrt{7a^6b^3} \cdot \sqrt{7a^2b}$      22. $\sqrt{12x^2y^5} \cdot \sqrt{6x^4y^4}$      23. $\sqrt{6s^3t} \cdot \sqrt{6s^2t}$

In Exercises 24-38, divide and simplify the square roots. Assume that all variables represent positive numbers.

24. $\dfrac{\sqrt{24}}{\sqrt{6}}$      25. $\dfrac{\sqrt{50}}{\sqrt{2}}$      26. $\dfrac{\sqrt{56}}{\sqrt{7}}$      27. $\dfrac{\sqrt{40}}{\sqrt{2}}$      28. $\dfrac{\sqrt{30x^2}}{\sqrt{5x}}$

29. $\dfrac{\sqrt{16x^5}}{\sqrt{8x^4}}$      30. $\dfrac{\sqrt{24x^9}}{\sqrt{8x^3}}$      31. $\dfrac{\sqrt{49y^{12}}}{\sqrt{7y^5}}$      32. $\dfrac{\sqrt{75m^6n^{10}}}{\sqrt{3m^2n^7}}$      33. $\dfrac{\sqrt{200x^{15}y^4}}{\sqrt{4x^8y^4}}$

34. $\dfrac{\sqrt{68x^9y^3}}{\sqrt{17x^4y^7}}$      35. $\dfrac{\sqrt{7a^3b^2}}{\sqrt{63a^2b^4}}$      36. $\dfrac{\sqrt{9a^5b^7c}}{\sqrt{45a^2b^{11}c^5}}$      37. $\dfrac{\sqrt{11x^6yz^9}}{\sqrt{5x^6y^2z^7}}$      38. $\dfrac{\sqrt{23xy^5z^7}}{\sqrt{14x^2y^3}}$

# Section 5.1.4   Combining (Adding and Subtracting) Square Roots

We will now learn how to combine square roots. Combining square roots is just like combining like terms when working with addition or subtraction of monomials. So, how does it work? Suppose we want to combine $7\sqrt{3}+2\sqrt{3}$. The first thing to notice is that both square roots have the same radicand, namely 3. If you think of $\sqrt{3}$ as '$x$', then the problem can be thought of as $7x + 2x$. Now, this we can handle. Since these are like terms, we combine them by adding their coefficients and keeping the same variable part, namely $x$. As we know, the answer is $9x$. The same technique works for square roots. We have $7\sqrt{3}+2\sqrt{3} = (7+2)\sqrt{3} = 9\sqrt{3}$. We can think of $7\sqrt{3}$ and $2\sqrt{3}$ as 'like-roots' and the numbers 7 and 2 as the 'coefficients' of the terms. Let's see some examples.

**Examples.** Combine and simplify.

1) $2\sqrt{5} + 8\sqrt{5} = (2+8)\sqrt{5} = 10\sqrt{5}$

2) $7\sqrt{11} - 3\sqrt{11} = (7-3)\sqrt{11} = 4\sqrt{11}$

3) $6\sqrt{7} + 13\sqrt{7} - 20\sqrt{7} = (6+13-20)\sqrt{7} = -1\sqrt{7} = -\sqrt{7}$

4) $\underbrace{5\sqrt{2} + 9\sqrt{8}}_{\text{not like-roots}} = 5\sqrt{2} + 9\underbrace{(2\sqrt{2})}_{\sqrt{8}=2\sqrt{2}} = \underbrace{5\sqrt{2} + 18\sqrt{2}}_{\text{like-roots}} = 23\sqrt{2}$

5) $\underbrace{11\sqrt{5} - 8\sqrt{20} + \sqrt{125}}_{\text{no like-roots}} = \underbrace{11\sqrt{5} - 8(2\sqrt{5}) + 5\sqrt{5}}_{\sqrt{20}=2\sqrt{5} \text{ and } \sqrt{125}=5\sqrt{5}.} = \underbrace{11\sqrt{5} - 16\sqrt{5} + 5\sqrt{5}}_{\text{all like-roots}} = 0\sqrt{5} = 0$

6) $\underbrace{3\sqrt{10} - 4\sqrt{18}}_{\text{not like-roots}} = 3\sqrt{10} - 4\underbrace{\left(3\sqrt{2}\right)}_{\sqrt{18}=3\sqrt{2}} = \underbrace{3\sqrt{10} - 12\sqrt{2}}_{\text{still not like-roots}}$    (These **DO NOT** combine.)

7) $\underbrace{\dfrac{\sqrt{12} + 3\sqrt{3}}{5}}_{\text{simplify }\sqrt{12}} = \dfrac{2\sqrt{3} + 3\sqrt{3}}{5} = \dfrac{\overset{1}{\cancel{5}}\sqrt{3}}{\underset{1}{\cancel{5}}} = \dfrac{\sqrt{3}}{1} = \sqrt{3}$

8) $\underbrace{\dfrac{2\sqrt{20} - 7\sqrt{45}}{34}}_{\text{simplify }\sqrt{20}\text{ and }\sqrt{45}} = \dfrac{2\left(2\sqrt{5}\right) - 7\left(3\sqrt{5}\right)}{34} = \dfrac{4\sqrt{5} - 21\sqrt{5}}{34} = \dfrac{\overset{1}{-\cancel{17}}\sqrt{5}}{\underset{2}{\cancel{34}}} = \dfrac{-\sqrt{5}}{2}$ or $-\dfrac{1}{2}\sqrt{5}$

9) $\underbrace{\dfrac{4 + 12\sqrt{40}}{16}}_{\text{simplify }\sqrt{40}} = \dfrac{4 + 12\left(2\sqrt{10}\right)}{16} = \underbrace{\dfrac{4 + 24\sqrt{10}}{16} = \dfrac{\overset{1}{\cancel{4}}\left(1 + 6\sqrt{10}\right)}{\underset{4}{\cancel{16}}}}_{\text{Factor the numerator the same way as }4+24x.} = \dfrac{1 + 6\sqrt{10}}{4}$ or $\dfrac{1}{4}\left(1 + 6\sqrt{10}\right)$

10) $\underbrace{\dfrac{-5 + \sqrt{200}}{-25}}_{\text{simplify }\sqrt{200}} = \dfrac{-5 + 10\sqrt{2}}{-25} = \dfrac{\overset{1}{\cancel{5}}\left(-1 + 2\sqrt{2}\right)}{\underset{5}{\cancel{-25}}} = \dfrac{-1 + 2\sqrt{2}}{-5}$ or $-\dfrac{1}{5}\left(-1 + 2\sqrt{2}\right)$

Notice that we can eliminate the negative sign in the denominator as follows:

$$\frac{-1 + 2\sqrt{2}}{-5} = \frac{\cancel{-}1\left(1 - 2\sqrt{2}\right)}{\cancel{-}5} = \frac{1 - 2\sqrt{2}}{5}$$

As you can see, all that I really did was to change the signs of EACH of the terms in the fraction.

**Try These (Set 5)**: Combine and simplify.

1) $3\sqrt{14} + 5\sqrt{14}$        3) $9\sqrt{27} - 2\sqrt{3}$        5) $15\sqrt{52} + 3\sqrt{13} - 8\sqrt{4}$

2) $\dfrac{\sqrt{2} + \sqrt{8}}{6}$        4) $\dfrac{\sqrt{18} - 9}{3}$        6) $\dfrac{2\sqrt{3} - 4\sqrt{75}}{10}$

**Exercise 5.1.4**

In each of the following, combine and simplify the square roots if possible.

1. $2\sqrt{3} + 6\sqrt{3}$        2. $8\sqrt{6} + 7\sqrt{6}$        3. $3\sqrt{10} - 8\sqrt{10}$

4. $17\sqrt{14} - 9\sqrt{14}$        5. $5\sqrt{5} + 9\sqrt{5} - 13\sqrt{5}$        6. $7\sqrt{2} - 14\sqrt{2} - 6\sqrt{2}$

7. $-3\sqrt{7} + 6\sqrt{7} - \sqrt{7}$        8. $5\sqrt{15} - 9\sqrt{15} - 2\sqrt{15}$        9. $\sqrt{3} + \sqrt{27}$

10. $2\sqrt{8} + \sqrt{2}$        11. $5\sqrt{6} - 3\sqrt{72}$        12. $-7\sqrt{12} + 9\sqrt{3}$

13. $-2\sqrt{18} - 8\sqrt{8}$

14. $7\sqrt{24} - 8\sqrt{54}$

15. $10\sqrt{5} + \sqrt{20} - 18\sqrt{45}$

16. $8\sqrt{6} - 3\sqrt{24} + \sqrt{54}$

17. $4\sqrt{5} + \sqrt{2}$

18. $6\sqrt{32} - \sqrt{7}$

19. $-4\sqrt{3} + 2\sqrt{40} + 9\sqrt{243}$

20. $3\sqrt{8} + 5\sqrt{20} - 2\sqrt{500}$

21. $8\sqrt{4} - \sqrt{7} + \sqrt{63} + 2\sqrt{121}$

22. $5\sqrt{49} + 3\sqrt{144} - 6\sqrt{7} + \sqrt{28}$

23. $\dfrac{2\sqrt{7} + 8\sqrt{28}}{9}$

24. $\dfrac{3\sqrt{18} - 2\sqrt{2}}{14}$

25. $\dfrac{6\sqrt{4} - 5\sqrt{25}}{23}$

26. $\dfrac{-\sqrt{9} + 4\sqrt{81}}{11}$

27. $\dfrac{10 + \sqrt{32}}{2}$

28. $\dfrac{12 - \sqrt{128}}{2}$

29. $\dfrac{8\sqrt{3} - 12\sqrt{2}}{4}$

30. $\dfrac{9\sqrt{5} + 12\sqrt{7}}{3}$

31. $\dfrac{2 + \sqrt{8}}{2}$

32. $\dfrac{-4 + \sqrt{32}}{2}$

33. $\dfrac{-12 - \sqrt{18}}{-6}$

34. $\dfrac{8 - \sqrt{24}}{-4}$

## Section 5.1.5    Multiplying Square Roots (Revisited)

In Section 5.1.2, we looked at how to multiply and divide square roots which contain monomials as radicands. We will continue our study of multiplication of square roots in this subsection. Once again, we will see a huge resemblance between square roots and polynomials. **Whenever you get stuck with a square root problem, think of the square roots as monomials and use your knowledge of polynomials to help solve the problem.** I will demonstrate how to do this as we continue.

**Examples.** Multiply and simplify.

1) $\underbrace{\left(4\sqrt{3}\right)\left(8\sqrt{3}\right) = 4(8)(\sqrt{3})(\sqrt{3})}_{\text{by the associative and commutative properties}} = 32\sqrt{9} = 32(3) = 96$

2) $\underbrace{\left(-3\sqrt{5}\right)\left(6\sqrt{10}\right)}_{\text{Compute -3(6), then } \sqrt{5}(\sqrt{10}).} = -18\sqrt{50} = -18(5\sqrt{2}) = -90\sqrt{2}$

3) $\underbrace{\left(2\sqrt{6}\right)\left(-4\sqrt{3}\right)\left(-\sqrt{6}\right)}_{\text{Compute } 2(-4)(-1), \text{ then } \sqrt{6}(\sqrt{3})(\sqrt{6}).} = 8\sqrt{108} = 8(6\sqrt{3}) = 48\sqrt{3}$

4) $7\sqrt{3}\underbrace{\left(2\sqrt{3} + 4\sqrt{2}\right)}_{\text{Do not combine them.}} = \underbrace{7\sqrt{3}(2\sqrt{3}) + 7\sqrt{3}(4\sqrt{2})}_{\text{by the distributive property}} = 14\sqrt{9} + 28\sqrt{6} = 14(3) + 28\sqrt{6}$

$$= 42 + 28\sqrt{6}$$

 **BEWARE:**  $42 + 28\sqrt{6} \neq 70\sqrt{6}$

If you think of $42 + 28\sqrt{6}$ as $42 + 28x$, you'll realize that this binomial can't be simplified into a monomial. The same is true for $42 + 28\sqrt{6}$.

Before moving on, I would like to mention a property which will be useful to us. It says that squares cancel out square roots.

**PROPERTY**: If $a$ is a nonnegative number, then $(\sqrt{a})^2 = a$.

5) $\underbrace{\left(\sqrt{3}+4\right)\left(\sqrt{3}-2\right)}_{\text{binomial} \times \text{binomial}} = \underbrace{\overbrace{\left(\sqrt{3}\right)^2}^{3} - 2\left(\sqrt{3}\right) + 4\left(\sqrt{3}\right) + 4(-2)}_{\text{FOIL method}} = 3 - 2\sqrt{3} + 4\sqrt{3} - 8 = -5 + 2\sqrt{3}$

**BEWARE**:  $-5 + 2\sqrt{3} \neq -3\sqrt{3}$

6) $\underbrace{\left(4\sqrt{2}-5\right)\left(2\sqrt{5}-1\right)}_{\text{binomial} \times \text{binomial}} = \underbrace{4\sqrt{2}\left(2\sqrt{5}\right) + 4\sqrt{2}(-1) - 5\left(2\sqrt{5}\right) - 5(-1)}_{\text{FOIL method}}$

$= \underbrace{8\sqrt{10} - 4\sqrt{2} - 10\sqrt{5} + 5}_{\text{Nothing combines.}}$

7) $\left(\sqrt{5}+6\right)^2 = \left(\sqrt{5}+6\right)\left(\sqrt{5}+6\right) = \left(\sqrt{5}\right)^2 + 6\sqrt{5} + 6\sqrt{5} + (6)^2$
$= 5 + \underbrace{6\sqrt{5} + 6\sqrt{5}}_{\text{Combine these.}} + 36 = 41 + 12\sqrt{5}$

Another way to do this is to use the '**Square of a Sum**' Formula from Chapter 3,

$$(A+B)^2 = A^2 + 2AB + B^2.$$

If we set $A = \sqrt{5}$ and $B = 6$, we obtain:

$$\left(\sqrt{5}+6\right)^2 = \left(\sqrt{5}\right)^2 + 2\left(\sqrt{5}\right)(6) + (6)^2$$
$$= 5 + 12\sqrt{5} + 36$$
$$= 41 + 12\sqrt{5}$$

A common mistake that is sometimes made in the previous problem goes as follows:

**BEWARE**:  $\left(\sqrt{5}+6\right)^2 \neq \left(\sqrt{5}\right)^2 + 6^2$

Be careful!!!

8) Assume that $x$ represents a nonnegative number. Then, by the FOIL method,

$$\left(6\sqrt{x}-1\right)\left(3\sqrt{x}+4\right) = 18\overbrace{\left(\sqrt{x}\right)^2}^{x} + \underbrace{24\sqrt{x} - 3\sqrt{x}}_{\text{combine}} - 4 = 18x + 21\sqrt{x} - 4$$

For the next example, I will use the formula

$$(A+B)(A-B) = A^2 - B^2.$$

9) 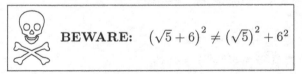 $\underbrace{\left(2\sqrt{7}+3\right)\left(2\sqrt{7}-3\right)}_{\text{Let A=}2\sqrt{7}\text{ and B=3.}} = \left(2\sqrt{7}\right)^2 - (3)^2 = \underbrace{2^2}_{4}\underbrace{\left(\sqrt{7}\right)^2}_{7} - 9 = 4(7) - 9 = 28 - 9 = 19$

**Try These (Set 6):** Multiply and simplify.

1) $\left(2\sqrt{5}\right)\left(3\sqrt{12}\right)$

2) $\left(5\sqrt{2}-\sqrt{3}\right)\left(\sqrt{3}+4\sqrt{2}\right)$

3) $5\sqrt{3}\left(-2\sqrt{3}+6\sqrt{27}\right)$

4) $\left(1+x\sqrt{7}\right)^2$

**Exercise 5.1.5**

In the following exercises, multiply and simplify. Assume that all variables represent nonnegative numbers.

1. $\sqrt{3}\left(5\sqrt{3}\right)$

2. $\sqrt{6}\left(2\sqrt{6}\right)$

3. $\left(7\sqrt{2}\right)\left(3\sqrt{2}\right)$

4. $\left(5\sqrt{3}\right)\left(4\sqrt{3}\right)$

5. $\left(-6\sqrt{5}\right)\left(2\sqrt{5}\right)$

6. $\left(-9\sqrt{2}\right)\left(-4\sqrt{2}\right)$

7. $\left(4\sqrt{8}\right)\left(3\sqrt{2}\right)$

8. $\left(8\sqrt{6}\right)\left(2\sqrt{2}\right)$

9. $\left(4\sqrt{12}\right)\left(3\sqrt{2}\right)$

10. $\left(6\sqrt{9}\right)\left(2\sqrt{5}\right)$

11. $\left(2\sqrt{25}\right)\left(-3\sqrt{2}\right)$

12. $\left(\sqrt{18}\right)\left(2\sqrt{3}\right)$

13. $\left(4\sqrt{7}\right)\left(\sqrt{20}\right)$

14. $\left(3\sqrt{10}\right)\left(-4\sqrt{5}\right)$

15. $\left(-10\sqrt{8}\right)\left(-3\sqrt{7}\right)$

16. $\left(2\sqrt{3}\right)^2$

17. $\left(3\sqrt{6}\right)^2$

18. $\left(-9\sqrt{2}\right)^2$

19. $\left(-5\sqrt{5}\right)^2$

20. $\sqrt{2}\left(3\sqrt{2}+4\right)$

21. $2\sqrt{3}\left(7\sqrt{3}-5\right)$

22. $6\sqrt{5}\left(\sqrt{5}-4\sqrt{20}\right)$

23. $3\sqrt{3}\left(4\sqrt{3}+5\sqrt{27}\right)$

24. $6\sqrt{8}\left(2\sqrt{3}+\sqrt{5}\right)$

25. $-2\sqrt{6}\left(5\sqrt{3}+4\sqrt{2}\right)$

26. $4\sqrt{2}\left(5+2\sqrt{6}-3\sqrt{12}\right)$

27. $2\sqrt{3}\left(7\sqrt{3}-\sqrt{6}+4\sqrt{10}\right)$

28. $\left(\sqrt{2}+\sqrt{3}\right)\left(\sqrt{2}+3\sqrt{2}\right)$

29. $\left(2\sqrt{3}-\sqrt{5}\right)\left(\sqrt{3}-\sqrt{5}\right)$

30. $\left(4\sqrt{6}-2\sqrt{3}\right)\left(\sqrt{6}+5\sqrt{3}\right)$

31. $\left(8\sqrt{3}+4\sqrt{7}\right)\left(2\sqrt{3}-2\sqrt{7}\right)$

32. $\left(\sqrt{6}+\sqrt{2}\right)^2$

33. $\left(\sqrt{5}+\sqrt{7}\right)^2$

34. $\left(5\sqrt{7}-\sqrt{2}\right)^2$

35. $\left(\sqrt{10}-4\sqrt{3}\right)^2$

36. $\left(\sqrt{a}+3\right)^2$

37. $\left(\sqrt{x}-4\right)^2$

38. $\left(\sqrt{x}+7\right)\left(\sqrt{x}-4\right)$

39. $\left(8+\sqrt{y}\right)\left(6-\sqrt{y}\right)$

40. $\left(5-2\sqrt{t}\right)\left(3+\sqrt{t}\right)$

41. $\left(\sqrt{6}-\sqrt{3}\right)\left(\sqrt{6}+\sqrt{3}\right)$

42. $\left(\sqrt{5}+7\right)\left(\sqrt{5}-7\right)$

43. $\left(2\sqrt{3}+4\right)\left(2\sqrt{3}-4\right)$

44. $\left(7-3\sqrt{2}\right)\left(7+3\sqrt{2}\right)$

45. $\left(-6\sqrt{2}+5\right)\left(-6\sqrt{2}-5\right)$

46. $\left(\sqrt{x}+8\right)\left(\sqrt{x}-8\right)$

47. $\left(\sqrt{x}-3\right)\left(\sqrt{x}+3\right)$

48. $\left(3\sqrt{x}+1\right)\left(3\sqrt{x}-1\right)$

49. $\left(2\sqrt{x}+7\right)\left(2\sqrt{x}-7\right)$

## Section 5.1.6   Rationalizing the Numerator or Denominator

Suppose we are given a fraction which contains a square root in the numerator (or denominator) and we wish to get rid of this square root. The process of rewriting the given fraction into an equivalent one which has a numerator (or denominator) **without** a square root is called **rationalizing the numerator (or denominator)**.

**Examples.** Rationalize the denominator

**NOTE:** Remember that the goal in these examples is to get rid of the square root in the denominator.

1) $\dfrac{1}{\sqrt{2}} = \dfrac{1}{\sqrt{2}} \left(\dfrac{\sqrt{2}}{\sqrt{2}}\right) = \dfrac{\sqrt{2}}{\left(\sqrt{2}\right)^2} = \dfrac{\sqrt{2}}{2}$ or $\dfrac{1}{2}\sqrt{2}$

2) $\dfrac{7}{\sqrt{7}} = \dfrac{7}{\sqrt{7}} \left(\dfrac{\sqrt{7}}{\sqrt{7}}\right) = \dfrac{7\sqrt{7}}{\left(\sqrt{7}\right)^2} = \underbrace{\dfrac{7\sqrt{7}}{7}}_{\text{Simplify.}} = \sqrt{7}$

(Notice that $\dfrac{7\sqrt{7}}{7}$ is just like $\dfrac{7x}{7}$ and the 7's cancel out.)

3) $\dfrac{6}{5\sqrt{3}} = \underbrace{\dfrac{6}{5\sqrt{3}} \left(\dfrac{\sqrt{3}}{\sqrt{3}}\right)}_{\text{We only need the } \sqrt{3}.} = \dfrac{6\sqrt{3}}{5\left(\sqrt{3}\right)^2} = \dfrac{6\sqrt{3}}{5\,(3)} = \dfrac{\overset{2}{\cancel{6}}\sqrt{3}}{\underset{5}{\cancel{15}}} = \dfrac{2\sqrt{3}}{5}$ or $\dfrac{2}{5}\sqrt{3}$

(Notice that $\dfrac{6\sqrt{3}}{15}$ is like $\dfrac{6x}{15}$ and the 3's cancel out.)

4) $\dfrac{4}{\sqrt{20}} = \dfrac{4}{\sqrt{20}} \left(\dfrac{\sqrt{20}}{\sqrt{20}}\right) = \dfrac{4\sqrt{20}}{\left(\sqrt{20}\right)^2} = \dfrac{4\sqrt{20}}{20} = \underbrace{\dfrac{4\left(2\sqrt{5}\right)}{20}}_{\text{Simplify the square root.}} = \dfrac{\overset{2}{\cancel{8}}\sqrt{5}}{\underset{5}{\cancel{20}}} = \dfrac{2\sqrt{5}}{5}$ or $\dfrac{2}{5}\sqrt{5}$

Observe that, in the above example, $\sqrt{20}$ could've been simplified in the very beginning. Let's do the problem again by simplifying first.

4) (again) $\underbrace{\dfrac{4}{\sqrt{20}} = \dfrac{\overset{2}{\cancel{4}}}{\underset{1}{\cancel{2}}\sqrt{5}} = \dfrac{2}{1\sqrt{5}}}_{\text{Simplify the square root.}} = \underbrace{\dfrac{2}{\sqrt{5}} \left(\dfrac{\sqrt{5}}{\sqrt{5}}\right)}_{\text{Rationalize the denominator.}} = \dfrac{2\sqrt{5}}{\left(\sqrt{5}\right)^2} = \dfrac{2\sqrt{5}}{5}$

In my opinion, it is easier to simplify the problem BEFORE doing the rationalizing. I will use the second method from now on.

5) $\underbrace{\dfrac{6\sqrt{3}}{\sqrt{18}} = \dfrac{\overset{2}{\cancel{6}}\sqrt{3}}{\underset{1}{\cancel{3}}\sqrt{2}} = \dfrac{2\sqrt{3}}{1\sqrt{2}}}_{\text{Simplify things first.}} = \dfrac{2\sqrt{3}}{\sqrt{2}} \left(\dfrac{\sqrt{2}}{\sqrt{2}}\right) = \dfrac{2\sqrt{6}}{\left(\sqrt{2}\right)^2} = \dfrac{\cancel{2}\sqrt{6}}{\cancel{2}} = \dfrac{\sqrt{6}}{1} = \sqrt{6}$

6) $\sqrt{\dfrac{7}{24}} = \underbrace{\dfrac{\sqrt{7}}{\sqrt{24}} = \dfrac{\sqrt{7}}{2\sqrt{6}}}_{\text{Simplify things first.}} = \left(\dfrac{\sqrt{7}}{2\sqrt{6}}\right)\left(\dfrac{\sqrt{6}}{\sqrt{6}}\right) = \dfrac{\sqrt{42}}{2\left(\sqrt{6}\right)^2} = \dfrac{\sqrt{42}}{2(6)} = \dfrac{\sqrt{42}}{12}$ or $\dfrac{1}{12}\sqrt{42}$

7) Assume that $x$ represents a positive number. Then

$$\dfrac{4}{7\sqrt{x}} = \left(\dfrac{4}{7\sqrt{x}}\right)\left(\dfrac{\sqrt{x}}{\sqrt{x}}\right) = \dfrac{4\sqrt{x}}{7\left(\sqrt{x}\right)^2} = \dfrac{4\sqrt{x}}{7x} \text{ or } \dfrac{4}{7x}\sqrt{x}.$$

Let's now do an example of rationalizing the numerator.

**Example.** Rationalize the numerator: $\dfrac{3\sqrt{5}}{\sqrt{2}} = \dfrac{3\sqrt{5}}{\sqrt{2}}\left(\dfrac{\sqrt{5}}{\sqrt{5}}\right) = \dfrac{3\left(\sqrt{5}\right)^2}{\sqrt{10}} = \dfrac{3(5)}{\sqrt{10}} = \dfrac{15}{\sqrt{10}}$

Let's move on to something slightly different. Suppose we want to rationalize the denominator of the expression $\dfrac{3}{2+\sqrt{2}}$. To begin with, notice that the denominator contains 2 terms which don't combine into a single square root. This reminds us of a binomial. The examples that we've looked at so far had only a single term in the denominator, which reminds us of a monomial. If we try to rationalize the denominator using the same method as before, let's see what happens:

$$\underbrace{\dfrac{3}{2+\sqrt{2}} = \left(\dfrac{3}{2+\sqrt{2}}\right)\left(\dfrac{\sqrt{2}}{\sqrt{2}}\right) = \dfrac{3\sqrt{2}}{2\sqrt{2}+\left(\sqrt{2}\right)^2}}_{\text{Distribute in the denominator.}} = \dfrac{3\sqrt{2}}{2\sqrt{2}+2}$$

Notice that we did **NOT** rationalize the denominator, since there is still a square root in it. This means that we need a different method than the one used before. To prepare for this new method, we have the next definition.

**Definition:** The **conjugate** of the binomial $A+B$ is $A-B$.

For example, the conjugate of $2+\sqrt{2}$ is $2-\sqrt{2}$ and the conjugate of $-5-8\sqrt{6}$ is $-5+8\sqrt{6}$. Observe that when you multiply the binomial $A+B$ by its conjugate, $A-B$, you obtain $A^2-B^2$. This is useful to us, since the squaring of the terms $A$ and $B$ would eliminate any square roots present in them. This is precisely what rationalizing is all about: **getting rid of the square roots**.

**Examples.** Rationalize the denominator.

1) $\dfrac{3}{2+\sqrt{2}} = \underbrace{\left(\dfrac{3}{2+\sqrt{2}}\right)\left(\dfrac{2-\sqrt{2}}{2-\sqrt{2}}\right) = \dfrac{3\left(2-\sqrt{2}\right)}{(2)^2-\left(\sqrt{2}\right)^2}}_{\text{Multiply the numerator and denominator by the conjugate.}} = \dfrac{3\left(2-\sqrt{2}\right)}{4-2} = \underbrace{\dfrac{3\left(2-\sqrt{2}\right)}{2}}_{\text{Nothing simplifies.}}$

Note that our answer can be written in several different ways:

$$\dfrac{3\left(2-\sqrt{2}\right)}{2} = \dfrac{3}{2}\left(2-\sqrt{2}\right) = \dfrac{6-3\sqrt{2}}{2} = \dfrac{-3\sqrt{2}+6}{2}$$

2) $\dfrac{4+\sqrt{6}}{4-\sqrt{6}} = \underbrace{\left(\dfrac{4+\sqrt{6}}{4-\sqrt{6}}\right)\left(\dfrac{4+\sqrt{6}}{4+\sqrt{6}}\right) = \dfrac{16+4\sqrt{6}+4\sqrt{6}+\left(\sqrt{6}\right)^2}{(4)^2-\left(\sqrt{6}\right)^2}}_{\text{Multiply the numerator and denominator by the conjugate and FOIL on top.}}$

$$= \dfrac{16+4\sqrt{6}+4\sqrt{6}+6}{16-6} = \dfrac{22+8\sqrt{6}}{10} = \dfrac{\overset{1}{\cancel{2}}\left(11+4\sqrt{6}\right)}{\underset{1}{\cancel{2}}(5)} = \dfrac{11+4\sqrt{6}}{5}$$

Note that the numerator could've been worked out by using the 'square of a sum' formula from Chapter 3. Give it a try.

3) Suppose that $x$ represents a nonnegative number other than 5. Then

$$\frac{\sqrt{x}-2\sqrt{5}}{\sqrt{x}-\sqrt{5}} = \left(\frac{\sqrt{x}-2\sqrt{5}}{\sqrt{x}-\sqrt{5}}\right)\left(\frac{\sqrt{x}+\sqrt{5}}{\sqrt{x}+\sqrt{5}}\right) = \frac{\overbrace{(\sqrt{x})^2}^{x}+\sqrt{5x}-2\sqrt{5x}-2\overbrace{(\sqrt{5})^2}^{2(5)}}{\underbrace{(\sqrt{x})^2}_{x}-\underbrace{(\sqrt{5})^2}_{5}}$$

$$= \frac{x+\overbrace{\sqrt{5x}-2\sqrt{5x}}^{\text{Combine.}}-10}{x-5} = \frac{x-\sqrt{5x}-10}{x-5}.$$

**Examples.** Rationalize the numerator.

**NOTE:** To rationalize the numerator, you now find the conjugate of the numerator and do the same as before.

1) $\dfrac{\sqrt{5}+4}{3} = \left(\dfrac{\sqrt{5}+4}{3}\right)\left(\dfrac{\sqrt{5}-4}{\sqrt{5}-4}\right) = \dfrac{(\sqrt{5})^2-(4)^2}{3(\sqrt{5}-4)} = \dfrac{5-16}{3(\sqrt{5}-4)}$

   $= \dfrac{-11}{3(\sqrt{5}-4)}\left(\text{or } \dfrac{-11}{3\sqrt{5}-12} = \dfrac{11}{-3\sqrt{5}+12}\right)$

2) $\dfrac{\sqrt{7}-1}{2\sqrt{5}} = \left(\dfrac{\sqrt{7}-1}{2\sqrt{5}}\right)\left(\dfrac{\sqrt{7}+1}{\sqrt{7}+1}\right) = \dfrac{(\sqrt{7})^2-(1)^2}{2\sqrt{5}(\sqrt{7}+1)} = \dfrac{7-1}{2\sqrt{5}(\sqrt{7}+1)}$

   $= \dfrac{\overset{3}{\cancel{6}}}{\underset{1}{\cancel{2}}\sqrt{5}(\sqrt{7}+1)} = \dfrac{3}{\sqrt{5}(\sqrt{7}+1)} \text{ or } \dfrac{3}{\sqrt{35}+\sqrt{5}}$

3) $\dfrac{\sqrt{5}+2\sqrt{3}}{\sqrt{5}-3\sqrt{2}} = \left(\dfrac{\sqrt{5}+2\sqrt{3}}{\sqrt{5}-3\sqrt{2}}\right)\left(\dfrac{\sqrt{5}-2\sqrt{3}}{\sqrt{5}-2\sqrt{3}}\right) = \dfrac{(\sqrt{5})^2-(2\sqrt{3})^2}{(\sqrt{5})^2-2\sqrt{15}-3\sqrt{10}+6\sqrt{6}}$

   $= \dfrac{5-4(3)}{5-2\sqrt{15}-3\sqrt{10}+6\sqrt{6}} = \dfrac{-7}{5-2\sqrt{15}-3\sqrt{10}+6\sqrt{6}}$

   $= -\dfrac{7}{5-2\sqrt{15}-3\sqrt{10}+6\sqrt{6}}$

**Try These (Set 7):** Rationalize the denominator.

1) $\dfrac{5}{6\sqrt{7}}$ 　　　　 2) $\dfrac{8\sqrt{3}}{\sqrt{18}}$ 　　　　 3) $\dfrac{5\sqrt{11}}{\sqrt{11}+\sqrt{6}}$ 　　　　 4) $\dfrac{3+\sqrt{6}}{2-\sqrt{6}}$

**Try These (Set 8):** Rationalize the numerator.

1) $\dfrac{\sqrt{5}}{2\sqrt{3}}$ 　　　　 2) $\dfrac{\sqrt{56}}{12}$ 　　　　 3) $\dfrac{\sqrt{7}-\sqrt{3}}{8}$ 　　　　 4) $\dfrac{3+\sqrt{6}}{2-\sqrt{6}}$

**Exercise 5.1.6**

In Exercises 1-38, rationalize the denominator. Assume that all variables represent positive numbers.

1. $\dfrac{1}{\sqrt{6}}$　　　　2. $\dfrac{3}{\sqrt{2}}$　　　　3. $\dfrac{8}{\sqrt{3}}$　　　　4. $\dfrac{4}{\sqrt{7}}$　　　　5. $\dfrac{13}{\sqrt{26}}$

6. $\dfrac{5}{\sqrt{10}}$　　　　7. $\dfrac{18}{\sqrt{10}}$　　　　8. $\dfrac{14}{\sqrt{7}}$　　　　9. $\dfrac{10}{\sqrt{8}}$　　　　10. $\dfrac{4}{\sqrt{12}}$

11. $\dfrac{8}{3\sqrt{20}}$　　　　12. $\dfrac{21}{4\sqrt{18}}$　　　　13. $\dfrac{-12}{5\sqrt{24}}$　　　　14. $\dfrac{-6}{7\sqrt{52}}$　　　　15. $\sqrt{\dfrac{1}{5}}$

16. $\sqrt{\dfrac{2}{3}}$　　　　17. $\sqrt{\dfrac{10}{7}}$　　　　18. $\sqrt{\dfrac{14}{5}}$　　　　19. $\sqrt{\dfrac{11}{12}}$　　　　20. $\sqrt{\dfrac{3}{8}}$

21. $\dfrac{3}{\sqrt{x}}$　　　　22. $\dfrac{8}{\sqrt{y}}$　　　　23. $\dfrac{2}{3\sqrt{2x}}$　　　　24. $\dfrac{5}{4\sqrt{5y}}$　　　　25. $\dfrac{1}{\sqrt{2}+1}$

26. $\dfrac{1}{\sqrt{3}+2}$　　　　27. $\dfrac{1}{\sqrt{5}-2}$　　　　28. $\dfrac{1}{\sqrt{6}+2}$　　　　29. $\dfrac{2}{\sqrt{5}-3}$　　　　30. $\dfrac{4}{\sqrt{3}-5}$

31. $\dfrac{1+\sqrt{2}}{2-\sqrt{2}}$　　　　32. $\dfrac{2-\sqrt{3}}{1+\sqrt{3}}$　　　　33. $\dfrac{\sqrt{5}-\sqrt{2}}{\sqrt{5}+\sqrt{2}}$　　　　34. $\dfrac{\sqrt{7}+\sqrt{10}}{\sqrt{7}-\sqrt{10}}$　　　　35. $\dfrac{-2\sqrt{6}+3}{3\sqrt{2}+\sqrt{6}}$

36. $\dfrac{-5-4\sqrt{3}}{2\sqrt{3}+\sqrt{5}}$　　　　37. $\dfrac{4+\sqrt{x}}{2-\sqrt{x}}$　　　　38. $\dfrac{\sqrt{x}-7}{\sqrt{x}+5}$

In Exercises 39-60, rationalize the numerator. Assume that all variables represent positive numbers.

39. $\dfrac{\sqrt{7}}{2}$　　　　40. $\dfrac{\sqrt{3}}{5}$　　　　41. $\dfrac{\sqrt{12}}{3}$　　　　42. $\dfrac{\sqrt{40}}{4}$　　　　43. $\dfrac{2\sqrt{3}}{\sqrt{5}}$

44. $\dfrac{6\sqrt{10}}{\sqrt{3}}$　　　　45. $\dfrac{\sqrt{8}}{\sqrt{7}}$　　　　46. $\dfrac{\sqrt{24}}{\sqrt{5}}$　　　　47. $\sqrt{\dfrac{5}{9}}$　　　　48. $\sqrt{\dfrac{7}{16}}$

49. $\dfrac{\sqrt{x}}{3}$　　　　50. $\dfrac{\sqrt{2x}}{5}$　　　　51. $\dfrac{2+\sqrt{6}}{4}$　　　　52. $\dfrac{-3+\sqrt{6}}{2}$　　　　53. $\dfrac{\sqrt{2}-\sqrt{5}}{\sqrt{3}}$

54. $\dfrac{\sqrt{3}+\sqrt{7}}{\sqrt{5}}$　　　　55. $\dfrac{\sqrt{6}+4}{\sqrt{6}-4}$　　　　56. $\dfrac{\sqrt{7}-2}{\sqrt{7}+2}$　　　　57. $\dfrac{\sqrt{x}+9}{\sqrt{x}-3}$

58. $\dfrac{\sqrt{x}+3}{\sqrt{x}+5}$　　　　59. $\dfrac{\sqrt{7+h}-\sqrt{7}}{h}$　　　　60. $\dfrac{\sqrt{x+h}-\sqrt{x}}{h}$

# Section 5.2　Cube Roots

In this section, we will learn about another type of radical called a **cube root**.

**Definition:** Let $a$ and $b$ be two real numbers. If $b^3 = a$, then $b$ is called a **cube root** of $a$.

**Examples.**

1) Since $2^3 = 8$, the definition tells us that 2 is a cube root of 8. In fact, 2 is the **only** real number which is a cube root of 8. It turns out that **every** positive number has one cube root which is a real number and it is positive.

2) Since $(-2)^3 = -8$, the definition tells us that $-2$ is a cube root of $-8$. As above, $-2$ is the **only** real number which is a cube root of $-8$. In fact, **every** negative number has one cube root which is a real number and it is negative.

3) Since $0^3 = 0$, we have that 0 is the unique cube root of 0.

In general, every real number has a unique (real) cube root. This root is sometimes called the **principal cube root.** We denote the phrase '$b$ is the (principal) **cube root** of $a$' by $b = \sqrt[3]{a}$. As for square roots, we call the term '$a$' under the **cube root symbol** the **radicand.** The '3' on the left of the symbol is there to tell us that this is a cube root. Notice that we do **not** put a '2' for square roots.

Here is a list of cube roots of perfect cubes. Recall that a perfect cube is an integer which is the cube of another integer.

## LIST OF COMMONLY SEEN CUBE ROOTS

$$\sqrt[3]{1} = 1 \qquad\qquad \sqrt[3]{-1} = -1$$
$$\sqrt[3]{8} = 2 \qquad\qquad \sqrt[3]{-8} = -2$$
$$\sqrt[3]{27} = 3 \qquad\qquad \sqrt[3]{-27} = -3$$
$$\sqrt[3]{64} = 4 \qquad\qquad \sqrt[3]{-64} = -4$$
$$\sqrt[3]{125} = 5 \qquad\qquad \sqrt[3]{-125} = -5$$
$$\sqrt[3]{216} = 6 \qquad\qquad \sqrt[3]{-216} = -6$$
$$\sqrt[3]{1,000} = 10 \qquad\qquad \sqrt[3]{-1,000} = -10$$

The numbers in the above list are the cube roots of perfect cubes. It turns out that **every** real number has a cube root. For example, there are numbers such as $\sqrt[3]{2}$, $\sqrt[3]{7.4456}$, and $\sqrt[3]{\pi}$. However, we will not be concerned with the exact values of these (in decimal form). We only need to know that they exist. If we **did** want to know $\sqrt[3]{2}$, for example, we would use a calculator to figure it out. If $n = \sqrt[3]{2}$, then we have $n^3 = 2$. You can imagine how strange the value of $n$ must be.

## PROPERTIES OF CUBE ROOTS

> **PROPERTY I.** Suppose that $a$ is a real number. Then
> $$\sqrt[3]{a^3} = a.$$

> **PROPERTY II.** Suppose that $a$ and $b$ are real numbers. Then
> $$\sqrt[3]{a} \cdot \sqrt[3]{b} = \sqrt[3]{a \cdot b}.$$

> **PROPERTY III.** Suppose that $a$ and $b$ are real numbers and $b \neq 0$. Then
> $$\frac{\sqrt[3]{a}}{\sqrt[3]{b}} = \sqrt[3]{\frac{a}{b}}.$$

> **PROPERTY IV.** Suppose that $a$ is a real number. Then
> $$\sqrt[3]{-a} = -\sqrt[3]{a}.$$

Notice that, in Property I, there is no need for absolute value (like for the square roots). Putting absolute value would, in fact, be incorrect. The reason for this is that we can get a negative answer when we take the cube root, but not when we take the square root. Also, Property IV isn't true for square roots unless $a = 0$. Property IV can be easily obtained from Property I as follows:

$$\sqrt[3]{-a} = \sqrt[3]{(-1)(a)} = \left(\sqrt[3]{-1}\right)\left(\sqrt[3]{a}\right) = (-1)\left(\sqrt[3]{a}\right) = -\sqrt[3]{a}$$

We will do a series of examples which are similar to those we did for square roots.

**Examples.** Simplify.

1) $\sqrt[3]{16} = \underbrace{\sqrt[3]{8 \times 2}}_{8 \text{ is a perfect cube.}} = \sqrt[3]{8} \times \sqrt[3]{2} = 2 \times \sqrt[3]{2} = 2\sqrt[3]{2}$

2) $\sqrt[3]{81} = \underbrace{\sqrt[3]{27 \times 3}}_{27 \text{ is a perfect cube.}} = \sqrt[3]{27} \times \sqrt[3]{3} = 3 \times \sqrt[3]{3} = 3\sqrt[3]{3}.$

3) $\underbrace{\sqrt[3]{x^{14}} = x^4 \sqrt[3]{x^2}}_{14 \div 3 = 4 \ R \ 2, \text{ so } 4 \text{ out, } 2 \text{ in.}}$

Note that for square roots, we divided the exponent by 2. For cube roots, we divide the exponent by 3.

4) $\underbrace{\sqrt[3]{y^{28}} = y^9 \sqrt[3]{y^1} = y^9 \sqrt[3]{y}}_{28 \div 3 = 9 \ R \ 1, \text{ so } 9 \text{ out and } 1 \text{ in.}}$

5) $\sqrt[3]{40m^7 n^2} = 2m^2 \sqrt[3]{5mn^2}$

Notice that $\sqrt[3]{40} = \sqrt[3]{8}\sqrt[3]{5} = 2\sqrt[3]{5}$, $\underbrace{\sqrt[3]{m^7} = m^2 \sqrt[3]{m}}_{7 \div 3 = 2 \ R \ 1}$ and $\sqrt[3]{n^2}$ is already simplified, since $2 \div 3 = 0 \ R \ 2$.

**Examples.** Perform the indicated operation and simplify all answers.

1) $\sqrt[3]{3x^4} \cdot \sqrt[3]{16x^5} = \sqrt[3]{3x^4 \cdot 16x^5} = \underbrace{\sqrt[3]{48x^9} = 2x^3 \sqrt[3]{6}}_{\sqrt[3]{48} = \sqrt[3]{8 \times 6} = 2\sqrt[3]{6} \text{ and } 9 \div 3 = 3 \ R \ 0.}$

2) $\dfrac{\sqrt[3]{55x^{19}}}{\sqrt[3]{5x^4}} = \sqrt[3]{\dfrac{55x^{19}}{5x^4}} = \sqrt[3]{11x^{15}} = \underbrace{x^5 \sqrt[3]{11}}_{15 \div 3 = 5 \ R \ 0}$

3) $\sqrt[3]{7} + 8\sqrt[3]{7} - 5\sqrt[3]{7} = (1 + 8 - 5)\sqrt[3]{7} = 4\sqrt[3]{7}$

4) $\underbrace{9\sqrt[3]{4} + \sqrt[3]{32}}_{\sqrt[3]{32} = \sqrt[3]{8}\sqrt[3]{4} = 2\sqrt[3]{4}} = 9\sqrt[3]{4} + 2\sqrt[3]{4} = (9 + 2)\sqrt[3]{4} = 11\sqrt[3]{4}$

5) $\underbrace{6x^2\sqrt[3]{3x} - 5\sqrt[3]{81x^7} = 6x^2\sqrt[3]{3x} - 5\left(3x^2\sqrt[3]{3x}\right)}_{\sqrt[3]{81} = \sqrt[3]{27}\sqrt[3]{3} = 3\sqrt[3]{3} \text{ and } \sqrt[3]{x^7} = x^2\sqrt[3]{x}.} = \underbrace{6x^2\sqrt[3]{3x} - 15x^2\sqrt[3]{3x} = \left(6x^2 - 15x^2\right)\sqrt[3]{3x} = -9x^2\sqrt[3]{3x}}_{\text{These are like-roots, so combine them.}}$

6) $\left(\sqrt[3]{9}\right)\left(-\sqrt[3]{12}\right) = -\sqrt[3]{9 \times 12} = -\underbrace{\sqrt[3]{108}}_{\sqrt[3]{27} \times \sqrt[3]{4}} = -3\sqrt[3]{4}$

7) $\sqrt[3]{5}\left(3\sqrt[3]{-2} + 6\sqrt[3]{25}\right) = \sqrt[3]{5}\left(3\sqrt[3]{-2}\right) + \sqrt[3]{5}\left(6\sqrt[3]{25}\right) = 3\sqrt[3]{-10} + 6\sqrt[3]{125}$

$= 3\sqrt[3]{-10} + 6(5) = \underbrace{3\sqrt[3]{-10} + 30 = -3\sqrt[3]{10} + 30}_{\text{by Property IV of cube roots}}$

8) $\left(\sqrt[3]{x^2} + 2\right)\left(\sqrt[3]{x^2} - 4\right) = \underbrace{\sqrt[3]{x^4} - 4\sqrt[3]{x^2} + 2\sqrt[3]{x^2} - 8}_{\text{by the FOIL method}} = x\sqrt[3]{x} - 2\sqrt[3]{x^2} - 8$

We will not be concerned with rationalizing numerators or denominators for cube roots.

**Try These (Set 9):**

1) Simplify: $\sqrt[3]{-16}$

2) Simplify: $\sqrt[3]{128x^5y^{12}}$

3) Multiply and Simplify: $\sqrt[3]{4}\left(6\sqrt[3]{2} + 8\right)$

4) Multiply and Simplify: $\left(\sqrt[3]{5} - 2\right)^2$

**Exercise 5.2**

In Exercises 1-20, evaluate.

1. $\sqrt[3]{8}$      2. $\sqrt[3]{-8}$      3. $-\sqrt[3]{-8}$      4. $\sqrt[3]{64}$      5. $\sqrt[3]{-64}$

6. $-\sqrt[3]{-64}$      7. $\sqrt[3]{\dfrac{1}{27}}$      8. $\sqrt[3]{-\dfrac{1}{27}}$      9. $-\sqrt[3]{-\dfrac{1}{27}}$      10. $\sqrt[3]{\dfrac{125}{8}}$

11. $\sqrt[3]{-\dfrac{216}{125}}$      12. $\sqrt[3]{\dfrac{0}{1,000}}$      13. $\sqrt[3]{(27)(125)}$      14. $\sqrt[3]{(8)(-216)}$      15. $\left(\sqrt[3]{9}\right)^3$

16. $\left(\sqrt[3]{15}\right)^3$      17. $\left(\sqrt[3]{-11}\right)^3$      18. $\left(\sqrt[3]{-20}\right)^3$      19. $\sqrt[3]{(9^3)(8)}$      20. $\sqrt[3]{(15^3)(-27)}$

In Exercises 21-40, simplify.

21. $\sqrt[3]{24}$      22. $\sqrt[3]{32}$      23. $\sqrt[3]{-24}$      24. $\sqrt[3]{-32}$      25. $\sqrt[3]{54}$

26. $\sqrt[3]{250}$      27. $\sqrt[3]{-54}$      28. $\sqrt[3]{-250}$      29. $\sqrt[3]{4,000}$      30. $\sqrt[3]{-4,000}$

31. $\sqrt[3]{x^3}$      32. $\sqrt[3]{x^5}$      33. $\sqrt[3]{y^7}$      34. $\sqrt[3]{y^9}$      35. $\sqrt[3]{t^{17}}$

36. $\sqrt[3]{x^{25}}$      37. $\sqrt[3]{9x^5y^6}$      38. $\sqrt[3]{16x^2y^{10}}$      39. $\sqrt[3]{-40x^8y^5}$      40. $\sqrt[3]{-27x^3y}$

In Exercises 41-50, combine and simplify.

41. $2\sqrt[3]{4} + 5\sqrt[3]{4}$      42. $3\sqrt[3]{6} + 9\sqrt[3]{6}$      43. $8\sqrt[3]{9} - 6\sqrt[3]{9}$      44. $-3\sqrt[3]{10} + 12\sqrt[3]{10}$

45. $\sqrt[3]{16} + 2\sqrt[3]{24}$

46. $3\sqrt[3]{54} - 7\sqrt[3]{81}$

47. $5\sqrt[3]{2} - 12\sqrt[3]{16} + 6\sqrt[3]{54}$

48. $3\sqrt[3]{2,000} + \sqrt[3]{3,000} - 4\sqrt[3]{4,000}$

49. $6x\sqrt[3]{5x} + \sqrt[3]{40x^4}$

50. $-3x\sqrt[3]{2x} - \sqrt[3]{250x^4}$

In Exercises 51-72, multiply and simplify.

51. $\left(\sqrt[3]{2}\right)\left(\sqrt[3]{4}\right)$

52. $\left(\sqrt[3]{5}\right)\left(\sqrt[3]{25}\right)$

53. $\left(-\sqrt[3]{3}\right)\left(\sqrt[3]{9}\right)$

54. $\left(\sqrt[3]{100}\right)\left(-\sqrt[3]{10}\right)$

55. $\left(\sqrt[3]{4}\right)\left(\sqrt[3]{10}\right)$

56. $\left(\sqrt[3]{6}\right)\left(\sqrt[3]{4}\right)$

57. $\left(\sqrt[3]{8}\right)^2$

58. $\left(-\sqrt[3]{64}\right)^2$

59. $\left(\sqrt[3]{4}\right)^2$

60. $\left(\sqrt[3]{12}\right)^2$

61. $\sqrt[3]{2}\left(\sqrt[3]{3} + 6\right)$

62. $\sqrt[3]{5}\left(\sqrt[3]{6} - 2\right)$

63. $\sqrt[3]{16}\left(\sqrt[3]{2} + 5\sqrt[3]{3}\right)$

64. $\sqrt[3]{12}\left(3\sqrt[3]{3} + 5\sqrt[3]{6}\right)$

65. $\left(\sqrt[3]{2} - 1\right)\left(\sqrt[3]{2} + 2\right)$

66. $\left(\sqrt[3]{3} + 2\right)\left(\sqrt[3]{3} - 4\right)$

67. $\left(\sqrt[3]{4} + 5\right)^2$

68. $\left(\sqrt[3]{12} - 2\right)^2$

69. $\left(\sqrt[3]{x} + 3\right)\left(\sqrt[3]{x} + 4\right)$

70. $\left(\sqrt[3]{x} - 5\right)\left(\sqrt[3]{x} - 7\right)$

71. $\left(\sqrt[3]{x^2} - 6\right)\left(\sqrt[3]{x^5} - 2\right)$

72. $\left(\sqrt[3]{x^4} + 7\right)\left(\sqrt[3]{x^2} - 3\right)$

# Section 5.3   Radicals

Up until this point, we have studied square roots and cube roots. In this section, we will examine radicals of any index. The square root and the cube root are special types of radicals. I will begin by defining a radical in general. Afterwards, we will look at some properties of radicals and examples which are analogous to the ones we've already seen.

**Definition:** Suppose that $a$ and $b$ are real numbers, and let $n$ be a natural number greater than 1 ($n$ can equal 2, 3, ...). If $b^n = a$, then we say that $b$ **is an** $n^{th}$ **root of** $a$.

We have already seen that if $n = 2$, then we deal with a square root. Recall that '$a$' must be a nonnegative number and $b = \sqrt{a}$ is the (principal) square root of '$a$'. If $n = 3$, then we deal with a cube root. In this case, $a$ can be any real number and $b = \sqrt[3]{a}$ has the same sign as '$a$'. It is called the principal cube root of '$a$'. In general, we have the following definition.

**Definition:** Suppose '$a$' is a real number which has an $n^{th}$ root. Then the **principal** $n^{th}$ **root of** '$a$', written as $\sqrt[n]{a}$, is the $n^{th}$ root that has the same sign as '$a$'. The natural number $n$ is called the **index** of the radical and the real number '$a$' is called the **radicand.** The symbol is often called the **radical symbol**.

For example, if the index is 2, then we have a square root. Note that the 2 is not written in the radical symbol. If the index is 3, then we have a cube root.

**Examples.** Evaluate.

1) $\sqrt{25} = 5$, since $5^2 = 25$.

2) $\sqrt[3]{\dfrac{8}{125}} = \dfrac{2}{5}$, since $\left(\dfrac{2}{5}\right)^3 = \dfrac{2^3}{5^3} = \dfrac{8}{125}$.

3) $\sqrt[4]{81} = 3$, since $3^4 = 81$.

4) $\sqrt[4]{-81}$ is not a real number. To see why not, suppose that $\sqrt[4]{-81} = b$ for some real number $b$. Then $b^4 = -81$, which doesn't make sense since any real number raised to the $4^{th}$ power must be either positive or zero. We have already seen something like this when we studied square roots.

5) $\sqrt[5]{32} = 2$, since $2^5 = 32$.

6) $\sqrt[5]{-32} = -2$, since $(-2)^5 = -32$.

Let's now list some properties of radicals. Keep in mind what you already know for square roots and cube roots.

## PROPERTIES OF RADICALS OF INDEX n

**PROPERTY I.** Suppose that $a$ is any real number.
If $n$ is an even number, then $\sqrt[n]{a^n} = |a|$.
If $n$ is an odd number, then $\sqrt[n]{a^n} = a$.

**PROPERTY II.** $\sqrt[n]{a} \cdot \sqrt[n]{b} = \sqrt[n]{a \cdot b}$, provided that these radicals are real numbers.

**PROPERTY III.** $\sqrt[n]{\dfrac{a}{b}} = \dfrac{\sqrt[n]{a}}{\sqrt[n]{b}}$, provided that these radicals are real numbers and $b \neq 0$.

As for square roots, if we assume that $a$ is a nonnegative number, then $\sqrt[n]{a^n} = a$ for any $n = 2, 3, \ldots$

**Examples.** Simplify. Assume that all variables represent nonnegative numbers.

1) $\sqrt[5]{64} = \sqrt[5]{32 \times 2} = \sqrt[5]{32} \times \sqrt[5]{2} = 2 \times \sqrt[5]{2} = 2\sqrt[5]{2}$

2) $\sqrt[4]{243} = \sqrt[4]{81 \times 3} = \sqrt[4]{81} \times \sqrt[4]{3} = 3 \times \sqrt[4]{3} = 3\sqrt[4]{3}$

3) $\sqrt[5]{-\dfrac{1}{128}} = \dfrac{\sqrt[5]{-1}}{\sqrt[5]{128}} = \dfrac{-1}{\sqrt[5]{32 \times 4}} = \dfrac{-1}{\sqrt[5]{32} \times \sqrt[5]{4}} = \dfrac{-1}{2\sqrt[5]{4}}$ or $-\dfrac{1}{2\sqrt[5]{4}}$

When simplifying a radical which contains variables (nonnegative valued), we can apply the 'division technique' discussed earlier. When working with square roots, we divided 'exponent ÷ 2'. When working with cube roots, we divided 'exponent ÷ 3'. In general, we divide 'exponent ÷ index'.

4) $\sqrt[4]{x^{31}} = \underbrace{x^7 \sqrt[4]{x^3}}_{31 \div 4 = 7 \; R \; 3}$

5) $\sqrt[6]{x^{17}} = \underbrace{x^2 \sqrt[6]{x^5}}_{17 \div 6 = 2 \; R \; 5}$

6) $\sqrt[7]{x^{22}y^{28}z^6} = x^3 y^4 \sqrt[7]{x z^6}$, since $22 \div 7 = 3 \; R \; 1$, $28 \div 7 = 4$ and $6 \div 7 = 0 \; R \; 6$.

Notice that I have not changed the index of any of the above examples when I simplified them. Remember to keep the index the same.

7) $\left(\sqrt[4]{8}\right)\left(\sqrt[4]{2}\right) = \sqrt[4]{8 \times 2} = \sqrt[4]{16} = 2$

8) $\left(\sqrt[5]{4}\right)\left(\sqrt[5]{-8}\right) = \sqrt[5]{4 \times (-8)} = \sqrt[5]{-32} = -2$

9) $\left(\sqrt[4]{6x^3y^7}\right)\left(\sqrt[4]{8x^2y}\right) = \sqrt[4]{(6x^3y^7)(8x^2y)} = \underbrace{\sqrt[4]{48x^5y^8} = 2x^1y^2\sqrt[4]{3x^1}}_{\sqrt[4]{48}=\sqrt[4]{16}\sqrt[4]{3}=2\sqrt[4]{3},\ 5\div4=1\ R\ 1\ \text{and}\ 8\div4=2\ R\ 0.} = 2xy^2\sqrt[4]{3x}$

10) $\dfrac{\sqrt[6]{128a^{25}b^3}}{\sqrt[6]{2a^8b^{16}}} = \sqrt[6]{\dfrac{128a^{25}b^3}{2a^8b^{16}}} = \underbrace{\sqrt[6]{\dfrac{64a^{17}}{b^{13}}} = \dfrac{2a^2}{b^2}\sqrt[6]{\dfrac{a^5}{b}}}_{\sqrt[6]{64}=2,\ 17\div6=2\ R\ 5\ \text{and}\ 13\div6=2\ R\ 1.} \quad \text{or} \quad \dfrac{2a^2\sqrt[6]{a^5}}{b^2\sqrt[6]{b}}$

11) $\sqrt[4]{9}\left(5\sqrt[4]{9} + 7\right) = \sqrt[4]{9}\left(5\sqrt[4]{9}\right) + \sqrt[4]{9}\,(7) = 5\underbrace{\sqrt[4]{81}}_{3} + 7\sqrt[4]{9} = 15 + 7\sqrt[4]{9}$

We will see in the next chapter that $\sqrt[4]{9}$ can be further simplified to $\sqrt{3}$.

12) $\underbrace{\left(\sqrt[6]{16} + 3\right)\left(\sqrt[6]{4} - 2\right) = \overset{2}{\overbrace{\sqrt[6]{64}}} - 2\sqrt[6]{16} + 3\sqrt[6]{4} - 6}_{\text{using the FOIL method}} = -4 - 2\sqrt[6]{16} + 3\sqrt[6]{4}$

In the next chapter, we will learn that $\sqrt[6]{16} = \sqrt[3]{4}$ and $\sqrt[6]{4} = \sqrt[3]{2}$. Hence, the answer can be simplified to $-4 - 2\sqrt[3]{4} + 3\sqrt[3]{2}$.

13) $\underbrace{\left(\sqrt[7]{5x^4} - 1\right)^2 = \left(\sqrt[7]{5x^4}\right)^2 - 2\left(\sqrt[7]{5x^4}\right)(1) + (1)^2}_{\text{Use the formula } (A-B)^2 = A^2 - 2AB + B^2.}$

$= \sqrt[7]{25x^8} - 2\sqrt[7]{5x^4} + 1 = \underbrace{x\sqrt[7]{25x}}_{8\div7=1\ R\ 1} - 2\sqrt[7]{5x^4} + 1$

14) $\underbrace{\left(\sqrt[5]{x^7} + 3\right)\left(\sqrt[5]{x^7} - 3\right) = \left(\sqrt[5]{x^7}\right)^2 - (3)^2}_{\text{use the formula } (A+B)(A-B)=A^2-B^2} = \underbrace{\sqrt[5]{x^{14}} - 9 = x^2\sqrt[5]{x^4} - 9}_{14\div5=2\ R\ 4}$

As you may have noticed, the examples on radicals are solved in the same way as for square roots and cube roots. The only difference is that things get quite messy once the index is larger than 3. Even though we will primarily focus on square roots and cube roots, I wanted you to be aware that these other radicals do exist. If you plan on taking more mathematics, such as precalculus or calculus, you will encounter such algebraic objects. I have supplied you with enough examples to get you through the basics. Have fun with it! In the next chapter, we will see all of this again when learning about rational exponents.

**Exercise 5.3**

In Exercises 1-10, evaluate.

1. $\sqrt[4]{16}$      2. $\sqrt[4]{81}$      3. $\sqrt[5]{32}$      4. $\sqrt[5]{243}$      5. $\sqrt[5]{-32}$

6. $\sqrt[5]{-243}$      7. $\sqrt[6]{64}$      8. $-\sqrt[6]{64}$      9. $\sqrt[4]{\dfrac{16}{81}}$      10. $\sqrt[5]{\dfrac{1}{32}}$

In Exercises 11-28, simplify. Assume that all variables represent nonnegative numbers.

11. $\sqrt[4]{48}$

12. $\sqrt[4]{162}$

13. $-\sqrt[4]{162}$

14. $\sqrt[4]{7^4}$

15. $\sqrt[5]{8^5}$

16. $\sqrt[5]{(-13)^5}$

17. $\sqrt[7]{(-20)^7}$

18. $\sqrt[5]{64}$

19. $\sqrt[5]{-64}$

20. $\sqrt[4]{x^{13}}$

21. $\sqrt[6]{x^{17}}$

22. $\sqrt[8]{a^{11}}$

23. $\sqrt[5]{a^8 b^{14}}$

24. $\sqrt[9]{m^{13}n^4}$

25. $\sqrt[7]{x^3 y^{20}}$

26. $\sqrt[4]{x^5 y^{11}}$

27. $\sqrt[4]{48x^7 y^8}$

28. $\sqrt[5]{-243x^{15}y^{10}}$

In Exercises 29-48, multiply and simplify. Assume that all variables represent nonnegative numbers.

29. $\sqrt[5]{3}\left(2\sqrt[5]{3}+8\right)$

30. $\sqrt[5]{2}\left(\sqrt[5]{2}-6\right)$

31. $\sqrt[7]{10}\left(3\sqrt[7]{10}-6\sqrt[7]{5}\right)$

32. $\sqrt[4]{5}\left(2\sqrt[4]{2}+9\sqrt[4]{8}\right)$

33. $\left(\sqrt[5]{3}+1\right)\left(\sqrt[5]{3}-2\right)$

34. $\left(\sqrt[5]{4}-8\right)\left(\sqrt[5]{4}-3\right)$

35. $\left(\sqrt[7]{6}+3\right)^2$

36. $\left(\sqrt[5]{4}-8\right)^2$

37. $\left(\sqrt[5]{2}+9\right)\left(\sqrt[5]{2}-9\right)$

38. $\left(\sqrt[5]{7}-6\right)\left(\sqrt[5]{7}+6\right)$

39. $\left(\sqrt[3]{x}+2\right)\left(\sqrt[3]{x}+3\right)$

40. $\left(\sqrt[7]{t}-3\right)\left(\sqrt[7]{t}+4\right)$

41. $\left(\sqrt[7]{x}+y\right)^2$

42. $\left(\sqrt[7]{x}-y\right)^2$

43. $\left(\sqrt[5]{a}-\sqrt[5]{b}\right)\left(\sqrt[5]{a}+\sqrt[5]{b}\right)$

44. $\left(\sqrt[3]{a}+\sqrt[3]{b}\right)\left(\sqrt[3]{a}-\sqrt[3]{b}\right)$

45. $\sqrt[5]{x^2}\left(\sqrt[5]{x^3}-3x\right)$

46. $\sqrt[4]{x^3}\left(5x^2+\sqrt[4]{x}\right)$

47. $3\sqrt[5]{x^3}\left(x+6\sqrt[5]{x^2}\right)$

48. $-7\sqrt[6]{x^5}\left(\sqrt[6]{x}-2x^2\right)$

---

## END OF CHAPTER 5   QUIZ

1. $\sqrt{25}+\sqrt[3]{64}=$

   a) 13     b) 9     c) $\dfrac{203}{6}$     d) $\sqrt[5]{89}$     e) 1

2. $\sqrt{\dfrac{81}{100}}-\sqrt[4]{\dfrac{1}{16}}=$

   a) $\dfrac{2}{5}$     b) $\dfrac{7}{5}$     c) $-\sqrt[3]{\dfrac{20}{21}}$     d) 0     e) $\dfrac{9}{5}$

3. $\sqrt{50}=$

   a) $5\sqrt{2}$     b) $2\sqrt{5}$     c) 25     d) $5\sqrt{5}$     e) $2\sqrt{2}$

4. If $x\geq 0$ and $y$ is any real number, then $\sqrt{44x^3 y^8}=$

   a) $4xy^4\sqrt{11x}$     b) $2x^2 y^4\sqrt{11x}$     c) $2xy^8\sqrt{11x}$     d) $4x^2 y^4\sqrt{11x}$     e) $2xy^4\sqrt{11x}$

5. $-\sqrt{6} + 8\sqrt{6} - 12\sqrt{6} =$
   a) $-5\sqrt{18}$    b) $0$    c) $-5\sqrt{6}$    d) $5\sqrt{6}$    e) $-4\sqrt{6}$

6. $9\sqrt{12} + 6\sqrt{27} =$
   a) $15\sqrt{39}$    b) $36\sqrt{6}$    c) $15\sqrt{6}$    d) $36\sqrt{3}$    e) $27\sqrt{2} + 18\sqrt{3}$

7. $-2\sqrt[3]{16} + 12\sqrt[3]{128} =$
   a) $10\sqrt[3]{144}$    b) $44\sqrt[3]{2}$    c) $44\sqrt[3]{3}$    d) $52\sqrt[3]{2}$    e) $-44\sqrt[3]{2}$

8. If $x \geq 0$, then $\sqrt{10x} \cdot \sqrt{10x^4} =$
   a) $10x^2$    b) $10x\sqrt{x}$    c) $50x^2\sqrt{x}$    d) $x^2\sqrt{10x}$    e) $10x^2\sqrt{x}$

9. If $a > 0$ and $b > 0$, then $\dfrac{\sqrt{148a^9b^4}}{\sqrt{4ab^3}} =$
   a) $\sqrt{37a^9b}$    b) $a^8\sqrt{37b}$    c) $a^4\sqrt{37b}$    d) $6a^4\sqrt{b}$    e) $a^5b^3\sqrt{37b}$

10. $4\sqrt{7}\left(2\sqrt{7} + 7\sqrt{2}\right) =$
    a) $56 + 28\sqrt{14}$    b) $8\sqrt{7} + 28\sqrt{14}$    c) $56 + 7\sqrt{2}$    d) $108\sqrt{7}$    e) $84\sqrt{14}$

11. $\left(\sqrt{5} - 2\right)\left(\sqrt{5} + 6\right) =$
    a) $-3\sqrt{5}$    b) $5\sqrt{5} - 12$    c) $4\sqrt{5} - 7$    d) $-7 - 4\sqrt{5}$    e) $-7$

12. $\left(2\sqrt{10} + 3\right)^2 =$
    a) $49$    b) $49 + 12\sqrt{10}$    c) $61\sqrt{10}$    d) $49 + 24\sqrt{5}$    e) $122\sqrt{5}$

13. Rationalize the denominator: $\dfrac{4}{3\sqrt{18}} =$
    a) $\dfrac{4}{3}$    b) $\dfrac{2\sqrt{2}}{9}$    c) $\dfrac{9\sqrt{2}}{2}$    d) $\dfrac{4}{9\sqrt{2}}$    e) $\dfrac{4\sqrt{2}}{9}$

14. Rationalize the denominator: $\dfrac{1 - \sqrt{3}}{3 + \sqrt{3}} =$
    a) $\dfrac{1}{3}$    b) $\dfrac{6 - 4\sqrt{3}}{9}$    c) $1 - 4\sqrt{3}$    d) $\dfrac{6 - 2\sqrt{3}}{3}$    e) $\dfrac{3 - 2\sqrt{3}}{3}$

15. Rationalize the numerator: $\dfrac{2\sqrt{2} + \sqrt{11}}{1 + \sqrt{10}} =$
    a) $\dfrac{4\sqrt{2} - 11}{2\sqrt{2} - \sqrt{11} + 4\sqrt{5} - \sqrt{110}}$    b) $\dfrac{-3}{4\sqrt{106}}$    c) $\dfrac{-3}{2\sqrt{2} - \sqrt{11} + 4\sqrt{5} - \sqrt{110}}$
    d) $\dfrac{2\sqrt{2} - 4\sqrt{5} + \sqrt{11} - \sqrt{110}}{-9}$    e) $\dfrac{-3}{2\sqrt{2} + \sqrt{11} + 4\sqrt{5} + \sqrt{110}}$

*College Algebra: A Narrative Approach*

16. $\dfrac{4\sqrt{32} - \sqrt{2}}{5} =$

    a) $3\sqrt{2}$     b) $\dfrac{3\sqrt{30}}{5}$     c) $\dfrac{16\sqrt{2}}{5}$     d) $\sqrt{2}$     e) $\dfrac{13\sqrt{2}}{8}$

17. $\dfrac{4\sqrt{20} + 2\sqrt{5}}{8} =$

    a) $\sqrt{5} + \dfrac{\sqrt{5}}{4}$     b) $\dfrac{15}{4}$     c) $\dfrac{5\sqrt{5}}{4}$     d) $\dfrac{5\sqrt{10}}{4}$     e) $\dfrac{\sqrt{5}}{4}$

18. If $x$ and $y$ are any real numbers, then $\sqrt[3]{-81x^{14}y} =$

    a) $-9x^4\sqrt[3]{3x^2y}$     b) $-3x^4\sqrt[3]{3x^2y}$     c) $-3x^{14}\sqrt[3]{3y}$     d) $-3x^4y^3\sqrt[3]{3x^2}$     e) $3x^4\sqrt[3]{3x^2y}$

19. If $x \geq 0$, then $\left(\sqrt[4]{x} - 5\right)\left(\sqrt[4]{x^3} + 3\right) =$

    a) $x - 15$     b) $x - 2\sqrt[4]{x^2} - 15$     c) $x + \sqrt[4]{3x} - \sqrt[4]{5x^3} - 15$     d) $x + 3\sqrt[4]{x} - 5\sqrt[4]{x^3} - 15$
    e) $x^2 + 3\sqrt[4]{x} - 5\sqrt[4]{x^3} - 15$

20. If $x$ is any real number, then $\sqrt[5]{x^{11}} - 3\sqrt[5]{32x} =$

    a) $\sqrt[5]{x} - 6x^2\sqrt[5]{x}$     b) $-2\sqrt[5]{32x}$     c) $-6x^2\sqrt[5]{x}$     d) $x^2 - 6\sqrt[5]{x}$     e) $\left(x^2 - 6\right)\sqrt[5]{x}$

ANSWERS FOR QUIZ 5

| | 1. b | 2. a | 3. a | 4. e | 5. c |
|---|---|---|---|---|---|
| | 6. d | 7. b | 8. e | 9. c | 10. a |
| | 11. c | 12. b | 13. b | 14. e | 15. c |
| | 16. a | 17. c | 18. b | 19. d | 20. e |

# Chapter 6:    Rational Exponents

In the previous chapter, we learned about radicals. The important thing to remember about a radical is that it is just the opposite of exponentiation. For example, $\sqrt{25} = 5$ comes from the fact that $25 = 5^2$. Similarly, $\sqrt[3]{-64} = -4$ because $-64 = (-4)^3$. Now, since we have this relationship between radicals and exponentiation, there should be a way of working with radicals by using only exponents. In this chapter, we will define a **rational exponent** to serve this purpose. Rational exponents will allow us to work with radicals by using our properties of exponents which were discussed in Chapter 2. In Section 6.1, the definition of a rational exponent will be given. After doing numerous examples, we will see how to use our exponent properties to work with radicals in an easy way (Section 6.2).

## Section 6.1  Definition and Examples of Rational Exponents

We want to somehow link a radical to an exponent. How should we do this? Well, remember that we have a list of properties which exponents satisfy when the exponent is an integer (see Chapter 2). If we define a new type of exponent, we would like all of these properties to work for the new exponent as well. In particular, recall that if $a$ is any real number and $m$ and $n$ are integers, then

$$(a^m)^n = a^{mn}$$

(the only exception is if $a = 0$ and either $m = 0$ or $n = 0$, in which case the above is undefined).

Suppose that we allow $m = \frac{1}{2}$ and let $n = 2$. If the property above is to be satisfied, we must have

$$\left(a^{\frac{1}{2}}\right)^2 = a^{\left(\frac{1}{2}\right)(2)} = a^{\left(\frac{1}{2}\right)\left(\frac{2}{1}\right)} = a^1 = a.$$

Therefore, $a^{\frac{1}{2}}$ has the property that when it is squared, the answer is $a$. For example, if $a = 16$, then

$$\left(16^{\frac{1}{2}}\right)^2 = 16^{\left(\frac{1}{2}\right)\left(\frac{2}{1}\right)} = 16^1 = 16.$$

Consequently, it makes sense to define $16^{\frac{1}{2}}$ to be equal to 4 since both $\left(16^{\frac{1}{2}}\right)^2$ and $(4)^2$ equal 16. Similarly, if $m = \frac{1}{3}$ and $n = 3$, then

$$\left(a^{\frac{1}{3}}\right)^3 = a^{\left(\frac{1}{3}\right)(3)} = a^{\left(\frac{1}{3}\right)\left(\frac{3}{1}\right)} = a^1 = a.$$

and so $a^{\frac{1}{3}}$ has the property that when it is cubed, the answer is $a$. For example, if $a = 8$, then

$$\left(8^{\frac{1}{3}}\right)^3 = 8^{\left(\frac{1}{3}\right)\left(\frac{3}{1}\right)} = 8^1 = 8.$$

Hence, it makes sense to define $8^{\frac{1}{3}}$ to be equal to 2 since both $\left(8^{\frac{1}{3}}\right)^3$ and $(2)^3$ equal 8. In general, if $n > 1$ is an integer, then

$$\left(a^{\frac{1}{n}}\right)^n = a^{\left(\frac{1}{n}\right)(n)} = a^{\left(\frac{1}{n}\right)\left(\frac{n}{1}\right)} = a^1 = a$$

and so $a^{\frac{1}{n}}$ has the property that when it is raised to the $n^{th}$ power, the answer is $a$. Now we know from our properties of radicals that

$$\left(\sqrt[n]{a}\right)^n = a,$$

where $\sqrt[n]{a}$ is the principal $n^{th}$ root of $a$. From what we've observed before, it makes sense to define this new exponent to be a radical. In other words, we should define $a^{\frac{1}{n}} = \sqrt[n]{a}$ since both equal $a$ when raised to the $n^{th}$ power. However, we need to make sure that all of the other properties of exponents are satisfied. Without verifying every one of them, I'll just say that they do work the way that we hope for. Hence, our definition is a valid one.

**Definition 1:** Let $a$ be a real number and suppose that $n > 1$ is an integer. Then $a^{\frac{1}{n}} = \sqrt[n]{a}$, provided that $\sqrt[n]{a}$ is well-defined.

Since $\frac{1}{n}$ is a rational number, we call it a **rational exponent**. Notice that the denominator of the exponent becomes the index of the radical. Hence, we have

$$a^{\frac{1}{2}} = \sqrt{a}, \ a^{\frac{1}{3}} = \sqrt[3]{a}, \ a^{\frac{1}{4}} = \sqrt[4]{a}, \text{ etc.}$$

**Examples.** Evaluate the following.

1) $4^{\frac{1}{2}} = \sqrt{4} = 2$

6) $\underbrace{(-9)^{\frac{1}{2}} = \sqrt{-9}}$ , which is not a real number (it is **undefined**)
   The $\frac{1}{2}$ applies to the $-9$.

2) $100^{\frac{1}{2}} = \sqrt{100} = 10$

7) $\underbrace{-125^{\frac{1}{3}} = -\sqrt[3]{125}} = -5$
   The $\frac{1}{3}$ only applies to the 125.

3) $8^{\frac{1}{3}} = \sqrt[3]{8} = 2$

8) $\underbrace{(-125)^{\frac{1}{3}} = \sqrt[3]{-125}} = -5$
   The $\frac{1}{3}$ applies to the $-125$.

4) $81^{\frac{1}{4}} = \sqrt[4]{81} = 3$

9) $\left( \dfrac{4}{81} \right)^{\frac{1}{2}} = \sqrt{\dfrac{4}{81}} = \dfrac{2}{9}$

5) $\underbrace{-9^{\frac{1}{2}} = -\sqrt{9}} = -3$
   The $\frac{1}{2}$ only applies to the 9.

10) $32^{\frac{1}{2}} = \sqrt{32} = 4\sqrt{2}$

Now, since $a^{\frac{1}{n}} = \sqrt[n]{a}$ if $n > 1$ is any integer and $\sqrt[n]{a}$ is well-defined, we have (for any integer, $m$)

$$\left( a^{\frac{1}{n}} \right)^m = \left( \sqrt[n]{a} \right)^m$$
$$a^{\left(\frac{1}{n}\right)\left(\frac{m}{1}\right)} = \left( \sqrt[n]{a} \right)^m$$
$$a^{\frac{m}{n}} = \left( \sqrt[n]{a} \right)^m = \sqrt[n]{a^m}.$$

**Definition 2:** Let $a$ be a real number and suppose that $n > 1$ is any integer. Then

$$a^{\frac{m}{n}} = \left( \sqrt[n]{a} \right)^m = \sqrt[n]{a^m}$$

for any natural number $m$, provided that $\sqrt[n]{a}$ is well-defined (or is a real number).

Since $\frac{m}{n}$ is a rational number, we call it a **rational exponent**. Notice that the numerator of the exponent becomes the exponent of the radical, whereas the denominator of the exponent becomes the index of the radical. Furthermore, notice that if $m = 1$, we get Definition 1.

**Definition 3:** Let $a \neq 0$ be a real number and suppose that $n > 1$ is any integer. Then

$$a^{-\frac{m}{n}} = \frac{1}{\left( \sqrt[n]{a} \right)^m} = \frac{1}{\sqrt[n]{a^m}},$$

provided that $\sqrt[n]{a}$ is well-defined and $m$ is an integer.

Observe that the negative exponent 'flips' the radical into the denominator of the fraction whose numerator equals 1. We've seen this before when learning about the properties of exponents (Chapter 2, Property IV). From this, it follows that all of the things that we learned with regards to the 'flipping technique' will now work for rational exponents as well.

When you do an example which requires you to evaluate an expression, the easiest way to do it is to use $a^{\frac{m}{n}} = (\sqrt[n]{a})^m$, leaving the exponent $m$ on the outside of the radical.

**Examples.** Evaluate.

1) $9^{\frac{3}{2}} = \left(\sqrt{9}\right)^3 = (3)^3 = 27$

2) $8^{\frac{2}{3}} = \left(\sqrt[3]{8}\right)^2 = (2)^2 = 4$

3) $27^{\frac{4}{3}} = \left(\sqrt[3]{27}\right)^4 = (3)^4 = 81$

4) $16^{\frac{7}{4}} = \left(\sqrt[4]{16}\right)^7 = (2)^7 = 128$

5) $\underbrace{-49^{\frac{3}{2}} = -\left(\sqrt{49}\right)^3}_{\frac{3}{2}\text{ only applies to 49.}} = \underbrace{-(7)^3 = -343}_{3\text{ only applies to 7.}}$

6) $\underbrace{(-49)^{\frac{3}{2}} = \left(\sqrt{-49}\right)^3}_{\frac{3}{2}\text{ applies to }-49.}$ is undefined, since $\sqrt{-49}$ is not a real number.

7) $\underbrace{-125^{\frac{4}{3}} = -\left(\sqrt[3]{125}\right)^4}_{\frac{4}{3}\text{ only applies to 125.}} = \underbrace{-(5)^4 = -625}_{4\text{ only applies to 5.}}$

8) $\underbrace{(-125)^{\frac{4}{3}} = \left(\sqrt[3]{-125}\right)^4}_{\frac{4}{3}\text{ applies to }-125.} = (-5)^4 = 625$

9) $16^{-\frac{1}{2}} = \dfrac{1}{16^{\frac{1}{2}}} = \dfrac{1}{\sqrt{16}} = \dfrac{1}{4}$

10) $216^{-\frac{2}{3}} = \dfrac{1}{216^{\frac{2}{3}}} = \dfrac{1}{\left(\sqrt[3]{216}\right)^2} = \dfrac{1}{(6)^2} = \dfrac{1}{36}$

11) $(-8)^{-\frac{4}{3}} = \dfrac{1}{(-8)^{\frac{4}{3}}} = \dfrac{1}{\left(\sqrt[3]{-8}\right)^4} = \dfrac{1}{(-2)^4} = \dfrac{1}{16}$

12) $\underbrace{-8^{-\frac{4}{3}} = -\left(8^{-\frac{4}{3}}\right)}_{-\frac{4}{3}\text{ only applies to 8.}} = -\dfrac{1}{8^{\frac{4}{3}}} = -\dfrac{1}{\left(\sqrt[3]{8}\right)^4} = -\dfrac{1}{(2)^4} = -\dfrac{1}{16}$

13) $\dfrac{4^{\frac{1}{2}}}{9^{-\frac{1}{2}}} = \dfrac{4^{\frac{1}{2}} \cdot 9^{\frac{1}{2}}}{1} = \dfrac{\sqrt{4} \cdot \sqrt{9}}{1} = \dfrac{2 \cdot 3}{1} = 6$

14) $\dfrac{64^{-\frac{2}{3}}}{49^{\frac{1}{2}}} = \dfrac{1}{49^{\frac{1}{2}} \cdot 64^{\frac{2}{3}}} = \dfrac{1}{\sqrt{49} \cdot \left(\sqrt[3]{64}\right)^2} = \dfrac{1}{7 \cdot (4)^2} = \dfrac{1}{112}$

15) $\dfrac{25^{-\frac{3}{2}} \cdot 16^{\frac{3}{4}}}{36^{-\frac{1}{2}}} = \dfrac{36^{\frac{1}{2}} \cdot 16^{\frac{3}{4}}}{25^{\frac{3}{2}}} = \dfrac{\sqrt{36} \cdot \left(\sqrt[4]{16}\right)^3}{\left(\sqrt{25}\right)^3} = \dfrac{6 \cdot (2)^3}{(5)^3} = \dfrac{48}{125}$

16) $\dfrac{(-1{,}000)^{-\frac{1}{3}} \cdot 4^{-\frac{3}{2}}}{27^{-\frac{1}{3}}} = \dfrac{27^{\frac{1}{3}}}{(-1{,}000)^{\frac{1}{3}} \cdot 4^{\frac{3}{2}}} = \dfrac{\sqrt[3]{27}}{\sqrt[3]{-1{,}000} \cdot \left(\sqrt{4}\right)^3} = \dfrac{3}{-10 \cdot (2)^3} = -\dfrac{3}{80}$

**Examples.** Rewrite each of the expressions in terms of radicals with positive integer exponents only and simplify. Assume that all variables represent positive numbers.

1) $a^{\frac{1}{2}} = \sqrt{a}$

6) $x^{\frac{2}{3}} y^{-\frac{5}{6}} = \dfrac{x^{\frac{2}{3}} y^{-\frac{5}{6}}}{1} = \dfrac{x^{\frac{2}{3}}}{y^{\frac{5}{6}}} = \dfrac{\sqrt[3]{x^2}}{\sqrt[6]{y^5}}$

2) $b^{\frac{2}{3}} = \sqrt[3]{b^2}$

7) $m^{-\frac{1}{4}} n^{-\frac{3}{7}} = \dfrac{m^{-\frac{1}{4}} n^{-\frac{3}{7}}}{1} = \dfrac{1}{m^{\frac{1}{4}} n^{\frac{3}{7}}} = \dfrac{1}{\sqrt[4]{m} \cdot \sqrt[7]{n^3}}$

3) $x^{-\frac{3}{5}} = \dfrac{1}{x^{\frac{3}{5}}} = \dfrac{1}{\sqrt[5]{x^3}}$

8) $x(x-2)^{\frac{1}{2}} = x\sqrt{x-2}$

4) $y^{-\frac{7}{9}} = \dfrac{1}{y^{\frac{7}{9}}} = \dfrac{1}{\sqrt[9]{y^7}}$

9) $[x(x-2)]^{\frac{1}{2}} = \sqrt{x(x-2)} = \sqrt{x^2 - 2x}$

5) $a^{\frac{1}{2}} b^{\frac{4}{5}} = \sqrt{a} \cdot \sqrt[5]{b^4}$

10) $3y^2(6y+1)^{-\frac{1}{3}} = \dfrac{3y^2(6y+1)^{-\frac{1}{3}}}{1} = \dfrac{3y^2}{(6y+1)^{\frac{1}{3}}} = \dfrac{3y^2}{\sqrt[3]{6y+1}}$

**Examples.** Rewrite each of the expressions using rational exponents.

1) $\sqrt{y} = y^{\frac{1}{2}}$

5) $\dfrac{\sqrt{x}}{6} = \dfrac{x^{\frac{1}{2}}}{6}$

9) $\sqrt[6]{t^7(t+2)^5} = \left[t^7(t+2)^5\right]^{\frac{1}{6}}$

2) $\sqrt[3]{x^2} = x^{\frac{2}{3}}$

6) $\sqrt{\dfrac{x}{6}} = \left(\dfrac{x}{6}\right)^{\frac{1}{2}}$

10) $\sqrt[3]{\dfrac{2x^2}{5} \cdot \dfrac{\sqrt[9]{4x}}{6}} = \left(\dfrac{2x^2}{5}\right)^{\frac{1}{3}} \cdot \dfrac{(4x)^{\frac{1}{9}}}{6}$

3) $\left(\sqrt[5]{a}\right)^8 = a^{\frac{8}{5}}$

7) $t^7 \sqrt[6]{(t+2)^5} = t^7(t+2)^{\frac{5}{6}}$

4) $\left(\sqrt[4]{b}\right)^3 = b^{\frac{3}{4}}$

8) $\sqrt[6]{[t^7(t+2)]^5} = \left[t^7(t+2)\right]^{\frac{5}{6}}$

**Try These (Set 1):**

I) Evaluate.

1) $49^{\frac{1}{2}}$     2) $8^{\frac{4}{3}}$     3) $32^{-\frac{2}{5}}$     4) $64^{\frac{1}{2}} \cdot 100^{-\frac{3}{2}}$     5) $\dfrac{(-64)^{-\frac{1}{3}}}{-49^{-\frac{1}{2}}}$

II) Rewrite each of the expressions with positive integer exponents only and simplify. Assume that all variables represent positive numbers.

1) $x^{\frac{1}{4}}$     2) $y^{-\frac{3}{4}}$     3) $5x^{\frac{2}{3}}$     4) $(5x)^{\frac{2}{3}}$     5) $\dfrac{(3a)^{\frac{2}{5}}}{4b^{-\frac{1}{3}}}$

III) Rewrite each of the expressions using rational exponents.

1) $\sqrt{y}$     2) $\sqrt[3]{\dfrac{4}{t}}$     3) $\dfrac{\sqrt[3]{4}}{t}$     4) $3x\sqrt{4x-1}$     5) $\sqrt{3x(4x-1)}$

# Section 6.2  Radical Problems Made Easy

In Section 6.1, we learned how to write expressions containing rational exponents as radicals and vice versa. For reference purposes, recall that if $a$ is a real number for which $\sqrt[n]{a}$ is well-defined, $n > 1$ is an integer and $m$ is an integer, then

$$1. \quad a^{\frac{1}{n}} = \sqrt[n]{a}$$
$$2. \quad a^{\frac{m}{n}} = \left(\sqrt[n]{a}\right)^m = \sqrt[n]{a^m}$$
$$3. \quad a^{-\frac{m}{n}} = \frac{1}{\left(\sqrt[n]{a}\right)^m} = \frac{1}{\sqrt[n]{a^m}}, \ a \neq 0$$

In this section, we will use the properties of exponents to work with radicals. Let's state the properties for **rational exponents:**

Let $a$ and $b$ be (non-zero) real numbers and let $m$ and $n$ be any **rational numbers.** Then

**Property I**    $a^m \cdot a^n = a^{m+n}$         **Property V**    $(a^m)^n = a^{mn}$

**Property II**   $\dfrac{a^m}{a^n} = a^{m-n}$       **Property VI**   $(ab)^n = a^n b^n$

**Property III**  $a^0 = 1$                          **Property VII**  $\left(\dfrac{a}{b}\right)^n = \dfrac{a^n}{b^n}$

**Property IV**   $a^{-n} = \dfrac{1}{a^n}$          **Property VIII** $\left(\dfrac{a}{b}\right)^{-n} = \dfrac{b^n}{a^n}$

**Examples.** Use the properties of exponents to simplify the following. Assume that all variables represent positive numbers.

1) $\underbrace{2^{\frac{1}{2}} \cdot 2^{\frac{1}{4}} = 2^{\frac{1}{2}+\frac{1}{4}} = 2^{\frac{2}{4}+\frac{1}{4}} = 2^{\frac{3}{4}}}_{\text{by Property I}}$

5) $\underbrace{\left(15^{\frac{2}{9}}\right)^6 = 15^{\left(\frac{2}{\cancel{9}_3}\right)\left(\frac{\cancel{6}^2}{1}\right)} = 15^{\frac{4}{3}}}_{\text{by Property V}}$

2) $\underbrace{x^{\frac{1}{6}} \cdot x^{-\frac{2}{3}} = x^{\frac{1}{6}+\left(-\frac{2}{3}\right)} = x^{\frac{1}{6}-\frac{4}{6}} = x^{-\frac{3}{6}} = x^{-\frac{1}{2}}}_{\text{by Property I}}$

6) $\underbrace{\left(a^{\frac{1}{2}}\right)^{\frac{1}{2}} = a^{\left(\frac{1}{2}\right)\left(\frac{1}{2}\right)} = a^{\frac{1}{4}}}_{\text{by Property V}}$

3) $\underbrace{\dfrac{7^{\frac{2}{5}}}{7^{\frac{1}{3}}} = 7^{\frac{2}{5}-\frac{1}{3}} = 7^{\frac{6}{15}-\frac{5}{15}} = 7^{\frac{1}{15}}}_{\text{by Property II}}$

7) $\underbrace{\left(b^{-\frac{2}{5}}\right)^{\frac{3}{4}} = b^{\left(-\frac{2}{5}\right)\left(\frac{3}{4}\right)} = b^{-\frac{3}{10}}}_{\text{by Property V}}$

4) $\underbrace{\dfrac{y^{-\frac{1}{4}}}{y^{\frac{1}{10}}} = y^{-\frac{1}{4}-\frac{1}{10}} = y^{-\frac{5}{20}-\frac{2}{20}} = y^{-\frac{7}{20}}}_{\text{by Property II}}$

8) $\underbrace{\left(3^{\frac{7}{8}} \cdot 4^{\frac{1}{3}}\right)^{\frac{1}{2}} = \left(3^{\frac{7}{8}}\right)^{\frac{1}{2}} \cdot \left(4^{\frac{1}{3}}\right)^{\frac{1}{2}} = 3^{\frac{7}{16}} \cdot 4^{\frac{1}{6}}}_{\text{by Properties VI and V}}$

9) $\underbrace{\left(x^{\frac{3}{4}}y^{-\frac{5}{6}}\right)^{\frac{4}{5}} = \left(x^{\frac{3}{4}}\right)^{\frac{4}{5}}\left(y^{-\frac{5}{6}}\right)^{\frac{4}{5}} = x^{\frac{3}{5}}y^{-\frac{2}{3}}}_{\text{by Properties VI and V}}$

11) $\underbrace{\left(\frac{m^{\frac{2}{3}}}{n^{\frac{1}{6}}}\right)^{\frac{3}{7}} = \frac{\left(m^{\frac{2}{3}}\right)^{\frac{3}{7}}}{\left(n^{\frac{1}{6}}\right)^{\frac{3}{7}}} = \frac{m^{\frac{2}{7}}}{n^{\frac{1}{14}}}}_{\text{by Properties VII and V}}$

10) $\underbrace{\left(\frac{11^{\frac{1}{3}}}{2^{\frac{3}{5}}}\right)^{\frac{2}{3}} = \frac{\left(11^{\frac{1}{3}}\right)^{\frac{2}{3}}}{\left(2^{\frac{3}{5}}\right)^{\frac{2}{3}}} = \frac{11^{\frac{2}{9}}}{2^{\frac{2}{5}}}}_{\text{by Properties VII and V}}$

12) $\underbrace{\left(\frac{x^3 y^{\frac{1}{5}}}{z^{\frac{9}{10}}}\right)^{\frac{10}{3}} = \frac{\left(x^{\frac{3}{1}}\right)^{\frac{10}{3}}\left(y^{\frac{1}{5}}\right)^{\frac{10}{3}}}{\left(z^{\frac{9}{10}}\right)^{\frac{10}{3}}} = \frac{x^{10}y^{\frac{2}{3}}}{z^3}}_{\text{by Properties VII, VI and V}}$

We are now prepared to do some examples with radicals. The first step is to convert the radicals to expressions containing rational exponents. The second step is to use the properties of exponents to perform whatever operation is being required. When you get your answer (in simplified form), you convert it back into a radical.

**Examples.** Perform the indicated operation and write the answer as a simplified, single radical. Assume that all variables represent positive numbers.

1) $\underbrace{\left(\sqrt{x}\right)\left(\sqrt[4]{x}\right) = \left(x^{\frac{1}{2}}\right)\left(x^{\frac{1}{4}}\right) = x^{\frac{1}{2}+\frac{1}{4}} = x^{\frac{2}{4}+\frac{1}{4}} =}_{\text{Go to exponents and use Property I.}} \underbrace{x^{\frac{3}{4}} = \sqrt[4]{x^3}}_{\text{Go back to radicals.}}$

2) $\underbrace{\frac{\sqrt[6]{x^5}}{\sqrt[4]{x^3}} = \frac{x^{\frac{5}{6}}}{x^{\frac{3}{4}}} = x^{\frac{5}{6}-\frac{3}{4}}}_{\text{Go to exponents and use Property II.}} = x^{\frac{10}{12}-\frac{9}{12}} = \underbrace{x^{\frac{1}{12}} = \sqrt[12]{x}}_{\text{Go back to radicals.}}$

3) $\underbrace{\left(\sqrt[3]{y^2}\right)^{15} = \left(y^{\frac{2}{3}}\right)^{15} = y^{\left(\frac{2}{3}\right)\left(\frac{15}{1}\right)} = y^{10}}_{\text{Go to exponents and use Property V.}}$

4) $\underbrace{\left(\sqrt[12]{t}\right)^6 = \left(t^{\frac{1}{12}}\right)^6 = t^{\left(\frac{1}{12}\right)\left(\frac{6}{1}\right)} =}_{\text{Go to exponents and use Property V.}} \underbrace{t^{\frac{1}{2}} = \sqrt{t}}_{\text{Go back to radicals.}}$

5) $\sqrt[4]{9} = 9^{\frac{1}{4}} = \left(3^2\right)^{\frac{1}{4}} = 3^{\left(\frac{2}{1}\right)\left(\frac{1}{4}\right)} = 3^{\frac{1}{2}} = \sqrt{3}$

6) $\sqrt[6]{8} = 8^{\frac{1}{6}} = \left(2^3\right)^{\frac{1}{6}} = 2^{\left(\frac{3}{1}\right)\left(\frac{1}{6}\right)} = 2^{\frac{1}{2}} = \sqrt{2}$

7) $\underbrace{\sqrt{\sqrt{b}} = \left(b^{\frac{1}{2}}\right)^{\frac{1}{2}} = b^{\left(\frac{1}{2}\right)\left(\frac{1}{2}\right)}}_{\text{Go to exponents and use Property V.}} = \underbrace{b^{\frac{1}{4}} = \sqrt[4]{b}}_{\text{Go back to radicals.}}$

8) $\sqrt[3]{\sqrt[4]{\sqrt[5]{x^{12}}}} = \left(\left(x^{\frac{12}{5}}\right)^{\frac{1}{4}}\right)^{\frac{1}{3}} = x^{\left(\frac{12}{5}\right)\left(\frac{1}{4}\right)\left(\frac{1}{3}\right)} = \underbrace{x^{\frac{1}{5}} = \sqrt[5]{x}}$

$\underbrace{\phantom{\sqrt[3]{\sqrt[4]{\sqrt[5]{x^{12}}}}}}$
Go to exponents and use Property V.                                    Go back to radicals.

9) $\underbrace{\left(\sqrt[8]{a^3} \cdot \sqrt[10]{a^3}\right)^{20} = \left(a^{\frac{3}{8}} \cdot a^{\frac{3}{10}}\right)^{20} = \left(a^{\frac{3}{8}+\frac{3}{10}}\right)^{20} = \left(a^{\frac{15}{40}+\frac{12}{40}}\right)^{20} = \left(a^{\frac{27}{40}}\right)^{20} = a^{\left(\frac{27}{40}\right)\left(\frac{20}{1}\right)}} = \underbrace{a^{\frac{27}{2}} = \sqrt{a^{27}}}$

Go to exponents and use Properties I and V.                                    Go back to radicals.

Notice that $\dfrac{27}{2} = 13 + \dfrac{1}{2}$, so we can write $a^{\frac{27}{2}} = \underbrace{a^{13+\frac{1}{2}} = a^{13} \cdot a^{\frac{1}{2}}}_{\text{Property I, going \textbf{backwards}.}} = a^{13} \cdot \sqrt{a}$. In other words,

$\sqrt{a^{27}} = a^{13}\sqrt{a}$. Do you remember when we used a division problem to simplify radicals? Well, it turns out that we were doing exactly what has just been done. Recall that to simplify $\sqrt{a^{27}}$, we divide $27 \div 2 = 13\ R\ 1$, so 13 of the $a$'s come out and 1 of the $a$'s stays in, giving us $a^{13}\sqrt{a}$ as above.

10) $\underbrace{\left(\dfrac{\sqrt[12]{x^5}}{\sqrt[16]{x^3}}\right)^4 = \left(\dfrac{x^{\frac{5}{12}}}{x^{\frac{3}{16}}}\right)^4 = \left(x^{\frac{5}{12}-\frac{3}{16}}\right)^4 = \left(x^{\frac{20}{48}-\frac{9}{48}}\right)^4 = \left(x^{\frac{11}{48}}\right)^4 = x^{\left(\frac{11}{48}\right)\left(\frac{4}{1}\right)}} = \underbrace{x^{\frac{11}{12}} = \sqrt[12]{x^{11}}}$

Go to exponents and use Properties II and V.                                    Go back to radicals.

11) $\underbrace{\left(\sqrt[4]{\sqrt[3]{b} \cdot \sqrt{b}}\right)^3 = \left(\left(b^{\frac{1}{3}} \cdot b^{\frac{1}{2}}\right)^{\frac{1}{4}}\right)^3 = \left(\left(b^{\frac{1}{3}+\frac{1}{2}}\right)^{\frac{1}{4}}\right)^3 = \left(\left(b^{\frac{2}{6}+\frac{3}{6}}\right)^{\frac{1}{4}}\right)^3 = \left(\left(b^{\frac{5}{6}}\right)^{\frac{1}{4}}\right)^3 = b^{\left(\frac{5}{6}\right)\left(\frac{1}{4}\right)\left(\frac{3}{1}\right)}} = \underbrace{b^{\frac{5}{8}} = \sqrt[8]{b^5}}$

Go to exponents and use Properties I and V.                                    Go back to radicals.

**Try These (Set 2):**

I) Use the properties of exponents to simplify.

1) $x^{\frac{2}{3}} \cdot x^{\frac{3}{4}}$       2) $\left(x^{-\frac{1}{8}}\right)\left(x^{\frac{1}{4}}\right)$       3) $\dfrac{y^{\frac{1}{2}}}{y^{\frac{5}{6}}}$       4) $\left(a^7 b^{-\frac{1}{3}}\right)^6$       5) $\left(\dfrac{m^{\frac{9}{10}}}{n^{-\frac{2}{5}}}\right)^{\frac{5}{3}}$

II) Perform the indicated operation and write the answer as a simplified, single radical. Assume that all variables represent positive numbers.

1) $\sqrt[4]{x} \cdot \sqrt{x}$       2) $\dfrac{\sqrt[6]{y}}{\sqrt{y}}$       3) $\sqrt{\sqrt[3]{t^2}}$       4) $\sqrt[100]{a^{50}}$       5) $\left(\sqrt[3]{x} \cdot \sqrt[6]{x^5}\right)^9$

**Exercise 6**

In Exercises 1-58, evaluate and simplify.

1. $9^{\frac{1}{2}}$          2. $16^{\frac{1}{2}}$          3. $49^{\frac{1}{2}}$          4. $121^{\frac{1}{2}}$

5. $25^{\frac{3}{2}}$         6. $100^{\frac{3}{2}}$        7. $64^{\frac{3}{2}}$         8. $121^{\frac{3}{2}}$

9. $8^{\frac{1}{3}}$          10. $27^{\frac{1}{3}}$        11. $64^{\frac{2}{3}}$        12. $27^{\frac{2}{3}}$

13. $1,000^{\frac{1}{3}}$      14. $1,000^{\frac{2}{3}}$      15. $16^{\frac{3}{4}}$       16. $81^{\frac{3}{4}}$

17. $-9^{\frac{1}{2}}$        18. $(-9)^{\frac{1}{2}}$      19. $(-8)^{\frac{1}{3}}$     20. $-8^{\frac{1}{3}}$

21. $-27^{\frac{2}{3}}$      22. $(-27)^{\frac{2}{3}}$      23. $(-4)^{\frac{3}{2}}$      24. $-4^{\frac{3}{2}}$

25. $16^{-\frac{1}{2}}$      26. $81^{-\frac{1}{2}}$      27. $27^{-\frac{1}{3}}$      28. $125^{-\frac{1}{3}}$

29. $1,000^{-\frac{2}{3}}$      30. $216^{-\frac{4}{3}}$      31. $81^{-\frac{3}{4}}$      32. $16^{-\frac{3}{4}}$

33. $\left(\dfrac{81}{4}\right)^{\frac{1}{2}}$      34. $\left(\dfrac{16}{25}\right)^{\frac{1}{2}}$      35. $\left(\dfrac{125}{216}\right)^{\frac{2}{3}}$      36. $\left(\dfrac{1}{81}\right)^{\frac{5}{4}}$

37. $\left(\dfrac{1}{8}\right)^{-\frac{1}{3}}$      38. $\left(\dfrac{8}{27}\right)^{-\frac{1}{3}}$      39. $\left(\dfrac{1,000}{27}\right)^{-\frac{2}{3}}$      40. $\left(\dfrac{27}{64}\right)^{-\frac{2}{3}}$

41. $-25^{-\frac{1}{2}}$      42. $(-25)^{-\frac{1}{2}}$      43. $-8^{-\frac{1}{3}}$      44. $(-8)^{-\frac{1}{3}}$

45. $(-64)^{-\frac{2}{3}}$      46. $-64^{-\frac{2}{3}}$      47. $4^{\frac{3}{2}} \cdot 9^{\frac{1}{2}}$      48. $64^{\frac{1}{3}} \cdot 16^{\frac{1}{2}}$

49. $81^{\frac{1}{4}} \cdot 36^{-\frac{1}{2}}$      50. $100^{\frac{1}{2}} \cdot 125^{-\frac{1}{3}}$      51. $\dfrac{36^{-\frac{1}{2}}}{27^{\frac{1}{3}}}$      52. $\dfrac{1,000^{-\frac{1}{3}}}{25^{\frac{1}{2}}}$

53. $\dfrac{25^{\frac{1}{2}}}{64^{-\frac{1}{3}}}$      54. $\dfrac{49^{\frac{1}{2}}}{16^{-\frac{1}{4}}}$      55. $\dfrac{16^{-\frac{3}{4}}}{100^{-\frac{1}{2}}}$      56. $\dfrac{81^{-\frac{1}{2}}}{8^{-\frac{2}{3}}}$

57. $\dfrac{4^{\frac{1}{2}} + 8^{-\frac{1}{3}}}{9^{-\frac{1}{2}} + 27^{\frac{1}{3}}}$      58. $\dfrac{64^{\frac{2}{3}} - 1^{\frac{4}{3}}}{25^{-\frac{1}{2}} + 16^{\frac{1}{2}}}$

In Exercises 59-100, rewrite each of the expressions in terms of radicals with positive integer exponents only and simplify. Assume that all variables represent positive numbers.

59. $x^{\frac{1}{2}}$    60. $x^{\frac{1}{3}}$    61. $y^{\frac{1}{6}}$    62. $y^{\frac{1}{13}}$    63. $a^{\frac{2}{3}}$

64. $a^{\frac{2}{5}}$    65. $b^{\frac{3}{5}}$    66. $b^{\frac{4}{7}}$    67. $t^{\frac{5}{9}}$    68. $t^{\frac{2}{9}}$

69. $x^{-\frac{1}{2}}$    70. $m^{-\frac{1}{4}}$    71. $m^{-\frac{2}{3}}$    72. $n^{-\frac{3}{5}}$    73. $y^{-\frac{2}{9}}$

74. $p^{-\frac{5}{6}}$    75. $x^{\frac{1}{2}}y^{\frac{1}{2}}$    76. $a^{\frac{1}{2}}b^{\frac{1}{2}}c^{\frac{1}{2}}$    77. $16^{\frac{1}{2}}m^{\frac{1}{2}}$

78. $8^{\frac{1}{3}}n^{\frac{1}{3}}$    79. $x^{\frac{1}{2}}y^{\frac{2}{3}}$    80. $a^{\frac{1}{5}}b^{\frac{2}{3}}$    81. $m^{\frac{3}{4}}n^{\frac{2}{5}}$

82. $p^{\frac{1}{3}}q^{\frac{3}{7}}$    83. $x(x+1)^{\frac{1}{2}}$    84. $y(y-3)^{\frac{1}{2}}$    85. $x^2(x-5)^{-\frac{1}{2}}$

86. $t^3(t+7)^{-\frac{1}{3}}$    87. $\dfrac{1}{2}x^{-\frac{1}{2}}$    88. $\dfrac{1}{3}x^{-\frac{2}{3}}$    89. $\dfrac{1}{5}(x^2 - 2x + 8)^{-\frac{4}{5}}$

90. $\dfrac{4}{9}(y^2 + 9)^{-\frac{5}{9}}$    91. $\left(\dfrac{x}{25}\right)^{\frac{1}{2}}$    92. $\left(\dfrac{144}{y}\right)^{\frac{1}{2}}$    93. $\dfrac{x^{\frac{1}{2}}}{25}$

94. $\dfrac{144^{\frac{1}{2}}}{y}$    95. $\left(\dfrac{a}{16}\right)^{-\frac{1}{2}}$    96. $\left(\dfrac{64}{b}\right)^{-\frac{1}{2}}$    97. $\left(\dfrac{x}{125}\right)^{-\frac{2}{3}}$

98. $\left(\dfrac{t}{64}\right)^{-\frac{2}{3}}$    99. $\dfrac{x^{-\frac{2}{3}}}{125}$    100. $\dfrac{t^{-\frac{2}{3}}}{164}$

In Exercises 101-120, rewrite each of the expressions using rational exponents.

101. $\sqrt{a}$      102. $\sqrt[3]{b}$      103. $\sqrt[3]{x^2}$      104. $\sqrt[4]{t^5}$

105. $\sqrt[4]{m}$      106. $\sqrt[8]{k}$      107. $\left(\sqrt[5]{n}\right)^3$      108. $\left(\sqrt[4]{y}\right)^3$

109. $\sqrt{a}\sqrt[3]{b}$      110. $\sqrt[4]{a^3}\sqrt{b}$      111. $\sqrt{\dfrac{x}{3}}$      112. $\sqrt[5]{\dfrac{y}{2}}$

113. $\dfrac{\sqrt{x}}{3}$      114. $\dfrac{\sqrt[5]{y}}{2}$      115. $\left(\sqrt[5]{u^2 v}\right)^2$      116. $\left(\sqrt[6]{uv^5}\right)^5$

117. $x\sqrt[6]{y}$      118. $m^4\sqrt[4]{n}$      119. $\left(\sqrt[3]{\dfrac{m}{9}}\right)^2$      120. $\dfrac{\left(\sqrt[3]{m}\right)^2}{9}$

In Exercises 121-148, perform the indicated operation and simplify. Leave your answer in terms of **positive rational exponents.** Assume that all variables represent positive numbers.

121. $x^{\frac{1}{2}} \cdot x^{\frac{2}{3}}$      122. $y^{\frac{1}{4}} \cdot y^{\frac{1}{6}}$      123. $a^{-\frac{4}{5}} \cdot a^{\frac{1}{5}}$      124. $b^{\frac{4}{3}} \cdot b^{-\frac{7}{3}}$

125. $y^{-\frac{5}{6}} \cdot y^{-\frac{1}{9}}$      126. $m^{-\frac{1}{8}} \cdot m^{-\frac{3}{4}}$      127. $\left(x^{\frac{2}{3}}\right)\left(x^{-\frac{1}{6}}\right)\left(x^{\frac{5}{3}}\right)$      128. $\left(t^{\frac{1}{10}}\right)\left(t^{\frac{2}{5}}\right)\left(t^{-\frac{3}{10}}\right)$

129. $\dfrac{u^{\frac{3}{8}}}{u^{\frac{1}{8}}}$      130. $\dfrac{v^{\frac{8}{9}}}{v^{\frac{2}{9}}}$      131. $\dfrac{n^{\frac{1}{2}}}{n^{-\frac{1}{4}}}$      132. $\dfrac{k^{\frac{1}{6}}}{k^{-\frac{5}{12}}}$

133. $\dfrac{p^{-\frac{4}{5}}}{p^{-\frac{2}{15}}}$      134. $\dfrac{q^{-\frac{3}{2}}}{q^{-\frac{7}{6}}}$      135. $\left(x^{\frac{1}{2}}\right)^2$      136. $\left(y^{\frac{2}{3}}\right)^3$

137. $\left(s^{\frac{6}{7}}\right)^{14}$      138. $\left(t^{\frac{4}{5}}\right)^{20}$      139. $\left(a^2 b^4\right)^{\frac{3}{2}}$      140. $\left(a^3 b^9\right)^{\frac{2}{3}}$

141. $\left(x^{\frac{6}{5}} y^{\frac{1}{3}}\right)^{\frac{10}{3}}$      142. $\left(x^{\frac{8}{11}} y^{\frac{2}{7}}\right)^{\frac{22}{3}}$      143. $\left(m^{-3} n^{10}\right)^{-\frac{4}{5}}$      144. $\left(p^8 q^{-2}\right)^{-\frac{3}{4}}$

145. $\left(\dfrac{p^{\frac{2}{5}}}{q^{-\frac{3}{5}}}\right)^{\frac{1}{4}}$      146. $\left(\dfrac{s^{-\frac{3}{10}}}{t^{\frac{1}{10}}}\right)^3$      147. $\left(\dfrac{x^2 y^{\frac{1}{3}}}{z^{-\frac{2}{5}}}\right)^{\frac{1}{6}}$      148. $\left(\dfrac{a^5 b^{-\frac{1}{6}}}{c^{\frac{2}{3}}}\right)^{\frac{1}{5}}$

In Exercises 149-176, perform the indicated operation and write your answer as a **simplified, single radical.** Assume that all variables represent positive numbers.

149. $(\sqrt{x})(\sqrt[3]{x})$      150. $(\sqrt[4]{y})(\sqrt[3]{y})$      151. $\left(\sqrt[3]{x^2}\right)\left(\sqrt[6]{x^5}\right)$      152. $\left(\sqrt[9]{t^2}\right)\left(\sqrt[3]{t^2}\right)$

153. $(\sqrt[4]{a})(\sqrt[4]{a})$      154. $\left(\sqrt[6]{b}\right)\left(\sqrt[6]{b}\right)$      155. $\dfrac{\sqrt[5]{m^2}}{\sqrt[10]{m}}$      156. $\dfrac{\sqrt[6]{n}}{\sqrt[4]{n^3}}$

157. $\left(\sqrt[7]{x^2}\right)^{14}$      158. $\left(\sqrt[4]{x^3}\right)^{12}$      159. $\sqrt[15]{a^5}$      160. $\sqrt[20]{b^{10}}$

161. $\sqrt[18]{t^6}$      162. $\sqrt[4]{s^2}$      163. $\sqrt{\sqrt{x}}$      164. $\sqrt{\sqrt[3]{x}}$

165. $\sqrt[3]{\sqrt[3]{b}}$      166. $\sqrt[4]{\sqrt{t}}$      167. $\sqrt[6]{\sqrt[4]{x^{12}}}$      168. $\sqrt[5]{\sqrt[4]{x^{10}}}$

169. $\left( \sqrt[7]{x^4} \cdot \sqrt[14]{x^3} \right)^7$    170. $\left( \sqrt[10]{x^3} \cdot \sqrt[5]{x^2} \right)^5$    171. $\left( \dfrac{\sqrt[3]{a}}{\sqrt[6]{a}} \right)^{12}$    172. $\left( \dfrac{\sqrt[8]{a}}{\sqrt[4]{a}} \right)^{16}$

173. $\left( \dfrac{\sqrt{m} \cdot \sqrt[3]{m}}{\sqrt[6]{m^5}} \right)^9$    174. $\left( \dfrac{\sqrt[4]{n^3} \cdot \sqrt[6]{n}}{\sqrt[12]{n^5}} \right)^4$    175. $\sqrt{\sqrt[3]{x^2} \cdot \sqrt[4]{x^3}}$    176. $\sqrt[3]{\sqrt{t} \cdot \sqrt[5]{t^2}}$

---

# END OF CHAPTER 6    QUIZ

1. $36^{\frac{1}{2}} =$

a) 6    b) 18    c) $\dfrac{1}{72}$    d) $1,276$    e) 12

2. $(-8)^{\frac{5}{3}} =$

a) $\dfrac{-40}{3}$    b) $\dfrac{40}{3}$    c) 32    d) $-32$    e) $-10$

3. $\left( \dfrac{16}{25} \right)^{\frac{3}{2}} =$

a) $\dfrac{64}{25}$    b) $\dfrac{64}{125}$    c) $\dfrac{48}{75}$    d) $\dfrac{16}{125}$    e) $\dfrac{4}{5}$

4. $216^{-\frac{2}{3}} =$

a) $-36$    b) $\dfrac{1}{36}$    c) $-\dfrac{1}{36}$    d) $-144$    e) $\dfrac{1}{216\sqrt{216}}$

5. $4^{-\frac{1}{2}} \cdot 27^{\frac{1}{3}} =$

a) $-18$    b) $\dfrac{1}{6}$    c) $\dfrac{3}{2}$    d) $108^{-\frac{1}{6}}$    e) $\dfrac{3}{\sqrt[3]{2}}$

6. $\dfrac{100^{-\frac{1}{2}} \cdot 8^{\frac{1}{3}}}{49^{-\frac{3}{2}}} =$

a) $\dfrac{343}{5}$    b) $\dfrac{343}{20}$    c) $\dfrac{7\sqrt{7}}{5}$    d) $\dfrac{\sqrt[3]{7}}{10}$    e) $\dfrac{5}{343}$

7. If $x \geq 0$ and $y \geq 0$, then $x^{\frac{1}{4}} y^{\frac{3}{4}} =$

a) $\sqrt[4]{x} + \sqrt[4]{y^3}$    b) $x^4 \sqrt[3]{y^4}$    c) $\left( \sqrt[4]{xy} \right)^3$    d) $\left( \sqrt[3]{xy} \right)^4$    e) $\sqrt[4]{xy^3}$

8. If $a > 0$ and $b > 0$, then $\left(\dfrac{a^2}{20b}\right)^{-\frac{1}{2}} =$

a) $\dfrac{a}{2\sqrt{5b}}$
b) $\dfrac{2b\sqrt{5}}{a}$
c) $\dfrac{a}{2\sqrt{10b}}$
d) $\dfrac{10\sqrt{b}}{a}$
e) $\dfrac{2\sqrt{5b}}{a}$

9. If $n \neq 0$ and $m$ is any real number, then $m^{\frac{2}{3}} n^{-\frac{1}{5}} =$

a) $-\sqrt[3]{m^2}\,\sqrt[5]{n}$
b) $\dfrac{\sqrt[3]{m^2}}{\sqrt[5]{n}}$
c) $\dfrac{\sqrt{m^3}}{\sqrt[5]{n}}$
d) $\dfrac{1}{\sqrt[5]{m^2 n}}$
e) $\dfrac{\sqrt[3]{m^2}}{n^5}$

10. $9^{\frac{1}{4}} \cdot 9^{\frac{5}{8}} =$

a) $729$
b) $9^{\frac{5}{8}}$
c) $81^{\frac{7}{8}}$
d) $9^{\frac{7}{8}}$
e) $9^{\frac{5}{32}}$

11. If $x > 0$, then $\dfrac{x^{\frac{5}{6}}}{x^{\frac{3}{8}}} =$

a) $x^{\frac{20}{9}}$
b) $1$
c) $x^{\frac{11}{24}}$
d) $x^{\frac{29}{24}}$
e) $x^{\frac{5}{12}}$

12. $\left(x^{\frac{16}{5}}\right)^{15} =$

a) $x^{\frac{91}{5}}$
b) $x^{\frac{16}{75}}$
c) $x^{48}$
d) $x^{28}$
e) $x^{\frac{31}{5}}$

13. If $b > 0$ and $a$ is any real number, then $\left(\dfrac{a^{\frac{6}{7}}}{b^{\frac{1}{4}}}\right)^8 =$

a) $\dfrac{a^{\frac{48}{7}}}{b^2}$
b) $\dfrac{a^{\frac{48}{7}}}{b^{\frac{1}{4}}}$
c) $\dfrac{a^{\frac{62}{7}}}{b^{\frac{33}{4}}}$
d) $a^8 b^8$
e) $\dfrac{a^{\frac{48}{7}}}{b^{\frac{1}{32}}}$

14. If $x > 0$ and $y > 0$, then $\left(25 x^{-\frac{1}{2}} y^{\frac{3}{2}}\right)^{\frac{1}{2}} =$

a) $5\sqrt[4]{xy^3}$
b) $25\sqrt[4]{\dfrac{y^3}{x}}$
c) $\dfrac{5}{\sqrt[4]{xy^3}}$
d) $5\sqrt[4]{\dfrac{y^3}{x}}$
e) $5\sqrt[4]{\dfrac{x}{y^3}}$

15. If $a > 0$, then $\left(\sqrt[3]{\sqrt[4]{a}}\right)^8 =$

a) $a\sqrt[7]{a}$
b) $\sqrt[3]{a^2}$
c) $\sqrt[7]{a^8}$
d) $\sqrt[8]{a^7}$
e) $a\sqrt{a}$

16. If $x \geq 0$, then $\sqrt{x} \cdot \sqrt[3]{x^2} =$

a) $\sqrt[6]{x^3}$
b) $\sqrt[5]{x^2}$
c) $\sqrt[7]{x^6}$
d) $\sqrt[3]{x}$
e) $x\sqrt[6]{x}$

17. If $y > 0$, then $\dfrac{\sqrt[10]{y^7}}{\sqrt[15]{y^2}} =$

a) $\sqrt[30]{y^{17}}$
b) $y\sqrt[17]{y^{13}}$
c) $\sqrt[6]{y^5}$
d) $\dfrac{1}{y}$
e) $\dfrac{1}{\sqrt[30]{y^{17}}}$

18. $\left(a^2 \sqrt[3]{a^2}\right)^{12} =$

a) $a^{30}$
b) $a^{16}$
c) $a^{32}$
d) $a^{24}\sqrt[3]{a^2}$
e) $a^{24}\sqrt[36]{a^2}$

19. If $x \geq 0$, then $\sqrt[7]{\sqrt[3]{x} \cdot \sqrt[4]{x}} =$

    a) $\sqrt[14]{x}$    b) $\sqrt[49]{x^2}$    c) $\sqrt[12]{x}$    d) $x^4 \sqrt[12]{x}$    e) $\sqrt[12]{x^5}$

20. If $x \geq 0$ and $y \geq 0$, then $\sqrt[24]{x^6 y^8} =$

    a) $\sqrt[4]{xy}$    b) $\sqrt[3]{xy}$    c) $\sqrt[3]{x} \cdot \sqrt[4]{y}$    d) $\sqrt[4]{x} \cdot \sqrt[3]{y}$    e) $\sqrt[12]{xy}$

| ANSWERS FOR QUIZ 6 | 1. a | 2. d | 3. b | 4. b | 5. c |
|---|---|---|---|---|---|
| | 6. a | 7. e | 8. e | 9. b | 10. d |
| | 11. c | 12. c | 13. a | 14. d | 15. b |
| | 16. e | 17. a | 18. c | 19. c | 20. d |

# Chapter 7:   Solving Equations

In this chapter, we will learn how to solve an equation for a specified variable. Our main concern is in solving linear equations (Section 7.2), literal equations (Section 7.3), and quadratic equations (Section 7.4). In passing, we will also encounter rational equations. We will begin with some preliminary definitions (Section 7.1).

## Section 7.1   Preliminary Definitions

**Definition 1:** An **equation in one variable** is a mathematical sentence containing a single variable and the equals symbol.

**Examples.** The mathematical sentences below are equations in one variable:

1) $5x + 3 = 1$ is an equation in $x$.

2) $-4y + 3y - 9 = -y + 6$ is an equation in $y$.

3) $p^2 + 5p = -3$ is an equation in $p$.

4) $\dfrac{12t^2 - t}{3t + 2} = t$ is an equation in $t$.

5) $\sqrt{6x - 12} = 4 + x$ is an equation in $x$.

**Definition 2:** A real number which yields a true mathematical sentence when the variable in the equation is replaced by the number is called a **solution** to the equation. The set of all solutions of an equation is called the **solution set** of the equation.

**Examples.**

1. $x = 4$ is a solution of the equation $-2x + 1 = -7$ since $-2(4) + 1 \overset{\checkmark}{=} -7$ is a true mathematical sentence. However, $x = -3$ is not a solution of the equation $-2x + 1 = -7$ since $-2(-3) + 1 = -7$ is not true. In fact, the **only** solution of the equation $-2x + 1 = -7$ is $x = 4$. Therefore, we write the solution set as $\{4\}$.

2. The equation $x^2 - 7x - 8 = 0$ has two solutions, $x = -1$ and $x = 8$. To verify this, we need to check that both of these values yield a true mathematical sentence. For $x = -1$, we have $(-1)^2 - 7(-1) - 8 = 1 + 7 - 8 = 0$, so $x = -1$ checks out. Now, for $x = 8$, we have $(8)^2 - 7(8) - 8 = 64 - 56 - 8 = 0$, so $x = 8$ checks out as well. These are, in fact, the only solutions to the equation. We write the solution set as $\{-1, \ 8\}$.

3. Not all equations have solutions. For example, the equation $x + 3 = x + 2$ has no solution. Notice that if $x$ is replaced by any real number, then the two sides of the equation will never be equal. Similarly, the equation $\sqrt{x - 9} = -4$ has no solutions, since a square root cannot yield a negative answer no matter what real number replaces the variable $x$. When an equation has no solution, we write the solution set as $\{ \ \}$ or $\varnothing$ and we refer to either of these as the **empty set**.

4. There are equations which have infinitely many solutions. For example, $x + 1 = x + 1$ is such an equation. If you replace the variable $x$ by any real number, the two sides will always be the same. Therefore, $x$ can be **any** real number. Since there are infinitely many real numbers to choose from, we say that there are **infinitely many solutions** to the equation.

**Definition 3:** Two or more equations are called **equivalent equations** if they have the same solution set.

For example, the equations $3x + 7 = -5$ and $3x = -12$ are equivalent equations, each having solution set $\{-4\}$.

**Definition 4:** An **identity** is an equation which is true for every choice of that variable for which both sides are defined.

**Examples.**

1) The equation

$$6(x + 4) = 6x + 24$$

is an identity. If we replace $x$ with any real number, then the equation is true. Notice, for example, that if $x = -3$, then

$$6(-3 + 4) \overset{?}{=} 6(-3) + 24$$
$$6(1) \overset{?}{=} -18 + 24$$
$$6 \overset{\checkmark}{=} 6$$

which is a true sentence.

2) The equation

$$\frac{x^2 - x - 6}{x - 3} = x + 2, \ x \neq 3$$

is an identity since the value of 3 for $x$ has been omitted. This value of $x$ would make the denominator of the fraction equal to zero, making the fraction undefined. This is the only value for which this would occur. All other values of x satisfy this equation, since

$$\frac{x^2 - x - 6}{x - 3} = \frac{\overset{1}{\cancel{(x - 3)}}(x + 2)}{\underset{1}{\cancel{x - 3}}} = x + 2.$$

3) The equation

$$8y - 5 = 27$$

is not an identity, since the **only** number for which the equation is true is $y = 4$. If it were an identity, then the equation would be true for **all** values of $y$.

4) The equation

$$\frac{5y + 10}{y + 2} = 5$$

is not an identity. The value of $-2$ for $y$ makes the denominator of the fraction equal to zero, creating an undefined expression. In fact, any value for $y$ **except** $-2$ would satisfy the equation, since

$$\frac{5y + 10}{y + 2} = \frac{5\overset{1}{\cancel{(y + 2)}}}{\underset{1}{\cancel{y + 2}}} = 5.$$

Notice that the difference the equation $\dfrac{5y + 10}{y + 2} = 5$ in Example 4 and the equation $\dfrac{x^2 - x - 6}{x - 3} = x + 2, x \neq 3$, in Example 2 is that we are not being told to omit the 'bad' value of $-2$ for $y$.

The equations in Examples 3 and 4 are examples of **conditional equations**.

**Definition 5: A conditional equation** is an equation which is true for (possibly) some choices of the variable for which both sides are defined, but not others.

Some examples of conditional equations are

$$-4x + 1 = -7, \quad y^2 + 17y + 16 = 0 \quad \text{and} \quad \frac{2}{t^2 - 1} = \frac{1}{t - 1}.$$

Notice that $-4x + 1 = -7$ is true when $x = -2$ **only**, $y^2 + 17y + 16 = 0$ is true when $y = 1$ or $y = 16$ **only** and $\frac{2}{t^2 - 1} = \frac{1}{t - 1}$ has no solution (it is never true). None of these equations are identities.

Our goal is to learn how to solve (that is, find the solution set of) an equation. To achieve this, we need to perform a successive number of operations to each side of the equation. After each operation is performed, we obtain an equation equivalent to the original equation. We continue this process until we have our variable by itself on one side of the equals symbol. The quantity/quantities (if they exist) on the other side of the equals symbol makes up the solution set of the equation. As mentioned in the beginning, we will focus primarily on linear equations and quadratic equations. Let's write down the primary operations which will be used for these types of equations in particular.

---

**Properties of Equations**

Suppose $a$, $b$ and $c$ are real numbers.

1. If $a = b$, then $a + c = b + c$.
2. If $a + c = b + c$, then $a = b$.

3. If $a = b$, then $a - c = b - c$.

4. If $a - c = b - c$, then $a = b$.

5. If $a = b$, then $ac = bc$.
6. If $ac = bc$ and $c \neq 0$, then $a = b$.

7. If $a = b$ and $c \neq 0$, then $\frac{a}{c} = \frac{b}{c}$.

8. If $\frac{a}{c} = \frac{b}{c}$, then $a = b$.

---

These properties will help us with solving equations. They are sometimes referred to as the **Properties of Equality**.

**Exercise 7.1** Determine whether or not the given number is a solution to the equation.

1. $6x - 8 = -14$; $x = -1$

2. $3x^2 + x - 3$; $x = 0$

3. $-y^3 + 7y + 5 = 11$; $y = 2$

4. $(a - 4)^2 = a(a + 5) - 3$; $a = -2$

5. $\sqrt{3x - 2} = 4$; $x = 6$

6. $\frac{4}{3t + 2} = \frac{1}{2}$; $t = -\frac{5}{3}$

## Section 7.2 Linear Equations in One Variable

**Definition:** A **linear equation in one variable** is an equation which is equivalent to the equation $ax + b = 0$, where $a$ and $b$ are real numbers and $a \neq 0$.

Notice that $ax + b = ax^1 + b$ is a polynomial of degree one. You may recall that a polynomial is called linear if it has degree one. That is why such an equation is called linear. The variable is raised to the first power. A linear equation in one equation is also referred to as a **first-degree equation. Every linear equation in one variable has a unique solution.**

Let's solve some linear equations. We will do each example in detail.

**Examples.** Solve each of the equations.

1) $x + 5 = 7$

What you need to do is to get $x$ by itself. In order to eliminate the $+5$ next to the $x$, you **subtract** 5 on both sides of the equation.

$$\begin{array}{rl} x + \cancel{5} &= 7 \\ -\cancel{5} & \underline{\phantom{x}-5} \\ x &= 2 \end{array}$$

Notice that we just subtracted 5 from 7 and obtained $x$. We could write this simply as

$$x + 5 = 7$$
$$x = 7 - 5$$

and so $x = 2$.

2) $x - 2 = -16$

Once again, you want to get $x$ by itself. In order to eliminate the $-2$ next to the $x$, you **add** 2 on both sides of the equation.

$$\begin{array}{rl} x - \cancel{2} &= -16 \\ +\cancel{2} & \underline{\phantom{x}+2} \\ x &= -14 \end{array}$$

Similarly, we can get $x$ by itself by just adding 2 to $-16$. We obtain

$$x - 2 = -16$$
$$x = -16 + 2$$

and so $x = -14$.

3) $2y = 6$

To get $y$ by itself, you must get rid of the 2 next to the $y$. To do this, you **divide** both sides of the equation by 2.

$$\frac{\cancel{2}y}{\cancel{2}} = \frac{6}{2}$$
$$y = 3$$

4) $-4p = 24$

Just as in Example 3, you **divide** both sides of the equation by $-4$ to get $p$ by itself.

$$\frac{\cancel{-4}p}{\cancel{-4}} = \frac{24}{-4}$$
$$p = -6$$

5) $\frac{4}{3}t = -6$

One way of solving this equation is to divide both sides by $\frac{4}{3}$. However, on the right side, you will obtain $\frac{-6}{\frac{4}{3}}$ and now you have to play around with this mixed quotient (try it). An easier approach is to multiply both sides of the equation by the reciprocal of $\frac{4}{3}$, namely $\frac{3}{4}$.

$$\frac{4}{3}t = -6$$

$$\frac{3}{4}\left(\frac{4}{3}t\right) = \frac{3}{4}\left(\frac{-6}{1}\right)$$

$$t = \frac{-18}{4} = -\frac{9}{2}$$

The strategy to keep in mind is whenever you have a fraction multiplying the variable, just multiply both sides by the reciprocal.

6) $-\dfrac{1}{7}x = -\dfrac{1}{5}$

As in Example 5, multiply both sides of the equation by the reciprocal of $-\dfrac{1}{7}$, which is $-\dfrac{7}{1}$.

$$-\frac{1}{7}x = -\frac{1}{5}$$

$$-\frac{7}{1}\left(-\frac{1}{7}x\right) = -\frac{1}{5}\left(\frac{-7}{1}\right)$$

$$x = \frac{7}{5}$$

7) $7y + 6 = 20$

In this equation, you need to get rid of both the 7 and the 6 in order to get $y$ by itself. It is easier to get rid of the 6 first, then the 7. If you do it the other way, you will end up creating fractions and the equation becomes ugly. The better method is as follows:

$$\begin{array}{rcl} 7y + 6 &=& 20 \\ -6 & & -6 \\ \hline \dfrac{7y}{7} &=& \dfrac{14}{7} \end{array}$$

$$y = 2$$

8) $9a - 2 = 5a + 18$

Notice that there are terms on both sides of the equation which contain the variable, $a$. The first thing to do is to get all of the terms containing the variable on one side of the equation. You can either subtract $9a$ or subtract $5a$ on both sides. I like to have positive terms, so I will subtract $5a$ on both sides. Afterwards, the problem is solved the same way as in Example 7.

$$\begin{array}{rcl} 9a - 2 &=& 5a + 18 \\ -5a & & -5a \\ \hline 4a - 2 &=& 18 \\ +2 & & +2 \\ \hline \dfrac{4a}{4} &=& \dfrac{20}{4} \\ a &=& 5 \end{array}$$

9) $1 + 8(x - 2) = 3 - 4(2x + 1)$

The first thing we need to do is remove the parentheses by distributing. Afterwards, we will combine any like terms. The resulting equation will then be solved like that in Example 8.

$$1 + 8(x - 2) = 3 - 4(2x + 1)$$
$$1 + 8x - 16 = 3 - 8x - 4$$
$$-15 + 8x = -1 - 8x$$
$$\underline{\phantom{-15 +}+8x \qquad\quad +8x}$$
$$-15 + 16x = -1$$
$$\underline{+15 \qquad\qquad +15}$$
$$\frac{16x}{16} = \frac{14}{16} = \frac{7}{8}$$

10) $-2r + 3(r - 5) = 2r - 7$

You solve this the same way as Example 9.

$$-2r + 3(r - 5) = 2r - 7$$
$$-2r + 3r - 15 = 2r - 7$$
$$r - 15 = 2r - 7$$
$$\underline{-r \qquad\quad -r}$$
$$-15 = r - 7$$
$$\underline{+7 \qquad +7}$$
$$-8 = r$$

11) $\frac{1}{2}m + 3 = \frac{5}{6}m$

When dealing with a linear equation which contains fractions, one approach in solving the equation is to eliminate the fractions. To do this, multiply both sides of the equation by the LCM of the denominators. This is called **clearing the fractions**. Another approach is to solve the equation with the fractions in it. I will clear the fractions. Notice that the LCM of 2 and 6 is 6.

$$\frac{1}{2}m + 3 = \frac{5}{6}m$$
$$\frac{6}{1}\left(\frac{1}{2}m + 3\right) = \frac{6}{1}\left(\frac{5}{6}m\right)$$
$$\overset{3}{\frac{6}{1}}\left(\frac{1}{2}m\right) + \frac{6}{1}(3) = \frac{6}{1}\left(\frac{5}{6}m\right)$$
$$3m + 18 = 5m$$
$$\underline{-3m \qquad\qquad -3m}$$
$$\frac{18}{2} = \frac{2m}{2}$$
$$9 = m$$

12) $-\frac{2}{3}t + \frac{5}{8} = \frac{3}{4}t - \frac{1}{24}$

Solve by first clearing the fractions as in Example 11. Notice that the LCM of 3, 8, 4, and 24 is 24.

$$-\frac{2}{3}t + \frac{5}{8} = \frac{3}{4}t - \frac{1}{24}$$

$$\frac{24}{1}\left(-\frac{2}{3}t + \frac{5}{8}\right) = \frac{24}{1}\left(\frac{3}{4}t - \frac{1}{24}\right)$$

$$\frac{\cancel{24}^{8}}{1}\left(-\frac{2}{\cancel{3}}t\right) + \frac{\cancel{24}^{3}}{1}\left(\frac{5}{\cancel{8}}\right) = \frac{\cancel{24}^{6}}{1}\left(\frac{3}{\cancel{4}}t\right) - \frac{\cancel{24}^{1}}{1}\left(\frac{1}{\cancel{24}}\right)$$

$$-16t + 15 = 18t - 1$$
$$\underline{+16t \qquad\qquad + 16t}$$
$$15 \;=\; 34t - 1$$
$$\underline{+1 \qquad\qquad\quad +1}$$
$$\frac{16}{34} = \frac{\cancel{34}t}{\cancel{34}}$$
$$\frac{8}{17} = t$$

Many equations which are not linear can be solved by using the same methods as before. We will now take a look at some examples of such equations.

13) $\dfrac{6}{x-2} + \dfrac{1}{x^2-4} = \dfrac{3}{x+2}$

This equation is an example of a rational equation. **A rational equation** is an equation whose expressions are rational expressions. Notice that the equations in Examples 11 and 12 are also rational equations. The difference between those equations and the given equation is that the denominators of the given equation contain the variable. Nevertheless, we can still solve it by clearing the fractions.

Observe that the LCM of $x-2$, $x^2-4 = (x+2)(x-2)$ and $x+2$ is $(x+2)(x-2)$. We will multiply both sides of the equations by the LCM as before. When we obtain our solution(s), we must check to make sure that they are valid. I will explain this further at the end of the example.

$$\frac{6}{x-2} + \frac{1}{x^2-4} = \frac{3}{x+2}$$

$$\frac{(x+2)(x-2)}{1}\left(\frac{6}{x-2} + \frac{1}{(x+2)(x-2)}\right) = \frac{(x+2)(x-2)}{1}\left(\frac{3}{x+2}\right)$$

$$\frac{(x+2)(x-2)}{1}\left(\frac{6}{x-2}\right) + \frac{(x+2)(x-2)}{1}\left(\frac{1}{(x+2)(x-2)}\right) = \frac{(x+2)(x-2)}{1}\left(\frac{3}{x+2}\right)$$

$$6(x+2) + 1 = 3(x-2)$$
$$6x + 12 + 1 = 3x - 6$$
$$6x + 13 = 3x - 6$$
$$\underline{-3x \qquad\qquad -3x}$$
$$3x + 13 = \quad -6$$
$$\underline{-13 \qquad\quad -13}$$
$$\frac{\cancel{3}x}{\cancel{3}} = \frac{-19}{3}$$

We now have to make sure that this answer is valid. One way to do this is to replace $x$ by $\frac{-19}{3}$ in the denominators of the fractions in the equation and see if they become zero. If at least one of them does, then the answer is not valid. If none of the denominators becomes zero, then it is valid. Observe that $\frac{-19}{3} + 2 \neq 0$ and $\frac{-19}{3} - 2 \neq 0$. Moreover, $\left(\frac{-19}{3}\right)^2 - 4 \neq 0$. Therefore, our solution is valid. In fact, all we need to check that is that the LCM doesn't equal 0 when we replace $x$ with the answer. Shortly, we will see an example in which the solution we obtain is invalid.

14) $\dfrac{7y-4}{9y} = \dfrac{7}{8}$

This is another example of a rational equation. When you have an equation in which two fractions are equal, you can use the following property:

**Cross Multiplication Property**

If $\dfrac{A}{B} = \dfrac{C}{D}$, then $AD = BC$.

After using this property, we solve the equation as before.

$$\frac{7y-4}{9y} = \frac{7}{8}$$
$$8(7y-4) = 7(9y)$$
$$56y - 32 = 63y$$
$$\underline{-56y \qquad\qquad -56y}$$
$$\frac{-32}{7} = \frac{7y}{7}$$

Again, we must make sure that this answer is valid. Observe that the only way that the denominator of $\dfrac{7y-4}{9y}$ can equal zero is if $y = 0$, which is definitely not the same as our solution. Therefore, $y = \frac{-32}{7}$ is valid.

15) $(p+5)^2 = (p-6)(p-2)$

We have an equation which does not appear to be linear but, in fact, it is. To solve this, go with your gut feeling. My gut feeling tells me to multiply things out first. Let's see what will happen:

$$(p+5)^2 = (p-6)(p-2)$$
$$(p+5)(p+5) = (p-6)(p-2)$$
$$p^2 + 10p + 25 = p^2 - 8p + 12$$
$$\underline{-p^2 \qquad\qquad\quad -p^2}$$
$$10p + 25 = -8p + 12$$
$$\underline{+8p \qquad\qquad +8p}$$
$$18p + 25 = 12$$
$$\underline{-25 \qquad\quad -25}$$
$$\frac{18p}{18} = \frac{-13}{18}$$

By going with my instincts, I was able to solve the equation. Keep this in mind.

16) $4x - 3 = 6 + 4x$

This equation is easy to solve, yet something weird will happen. Let's see.

$$4x - 3 = 6 + 4x$$
$$\underline{-4x \qquad\qquad -4x}$$
$$-3 = 6$$

What's strange about this equation is that not only did the variable totally drop out of the equation, but we obtain a mathematical sentence which is always invalid: $-3$ is never equal to $6$ no matter what real number $x$ is replaced by in our equation. Therefore, the solution set is empty. Recall that we may write $\varnothing$ in this situation. Observe that this equation is NOT linear, since it has no solution.

17) $\dfrac{2}{x^2 - 1} = \dfrac{1}{x - 1}$

We will not solve this rational equation by cross multiplying. Instead, we will clear the fractions. Note that the LCM of $x^2 - 1 = (x + 1)(x - 1)$ and $x - 1$ is $(x + 1)(x - 1)$.

$$\frac{2}{x^2 - 1} = \frac{1}{x - 1}$$

$$\frac{\cancel{(x + 1)}\cancel{(x - 1)}}{1} \left( \frac{2}{\cancel{(x + 1)}\cancel{(x - 1)}} \right) = \frac{(x + 1)\cancel{(x - 1)}}{1} \left( \frac{1}{\cancel{x - 1}} \right)$$

$$\begin{array}{r} 2 = x + \cancel{1} \\ -1 \quad -\cancel{1} \\ \hline 1 = x \end{array}$$

Let's check and see whether or not this answer is valid. Observe that the first denominator becomes $(1)^2 - 1 = 0$!!! Therefore, our solution is **invalid** because $\dfrac{2}{(1)^2 - 1} = \dfrac{2}{0}$ is undefined. The solution set is $\varnothing$.

18) $7(b - 3) = 4b + 3(b - 7)$

We use the same technique as Example 9. This time, something strange occurs.

$$\begin{array}{r} 7(b - 3) = 4b + 3(b - 7) \\ 7b - 21 = 4b + 3b - 21 \\ 7\!\!\!\!\diagup b - 21 = 7\!\!\!\!\diagup b - 21 \\ -7\!\!\!\!\diagup b \qquad\quad -7\!\!\!\!\diagup b \\ \hline -21 = \quad -21 \end{array}$$

The variable, $b$, drops out, and we end up with a mathematical sentence which is always true, since $-21 = -21$ no matter what real number replaces the variable $b$ in the equation. Therefore, there are infinitely many solutions in the solution set. In fact, $b$ can equal **any** real number. This equation is an identity.

Some equations which are not linear can be solved by using a property known as the **Zero-Product Property**.

---

**The Zero-Product Property**

1. If $a$ and $b$ are real numbers for which $ab = 0$, then either $a = 0$ or $b = 0$ or both.

2. If either $a = 0$ or $b = 0$ or both, then $ab = 0$.

---

19) $(x + 7)(x - 3) = 0$

The property shows us that in order for a product to equal zero, at least one of its factors must equal zero. To solve for $x$, we will set each of the factors equal to zero. By doing so, we will produce two linear equations.

$$(x + 7)(x - 3) = 0$$

$$\begin{array}{r|r} x + 7 = 0 & x - 3 = 0 \\ -7 \quad -7 & +3 \quad +3 \\ \hline x = -7 & x = 3 \end{array}$$

Therefore, the roots of the equations are $-7$ and $3$. The solution set is $\{-7, 3\}$.

20) $9x(x + 8)(3x - 5) = 0$

We will use the zero product property. This time, we produce three linear equations.

$$9x(x + 8)(3x - 5) = 0$$

| $9x = 0$ | $x + \cancel{8} = 0$ | $3x - \cancel{5} = 0$ |
|---|---|---|
| $x = 0$ | $-\cancel{8} \quad -8$ | $+\cancel{5} \quad +5$ |
| | $x = -8$ | $\dfrac{\cancel{3}x}{\cancel{3}} = \dfrac{5}{3}$ |

The roots of the equation are $0$, $-8$ and $\dfrac{5}{3}$. The solution set is $\{0, -8, \frac{5}{3}\}$.

**Try These (Set 1):** Solve the equations.

1) $x + 7 = -12$

2) $6a = -30$

3) $\dfrac{5}{8}y = -2$

4) $-2x + 3 = 11$

5) $4t - 9(t + 2) = -2t$

6) $\dfrac{6}{4s - 1} - \dfrac{5}{s + 2} = \dfrac{3}{4s^2 + 7s - 2}$

7) $(p - 6)^2 = (p + 6)^2$

8) $2x + 3(x + 7) = -x + 6(x - 9)$

9) $\dfrac{8}{4m + 3} = \dfrac{-1}{6 - m}$

10) $\dfrac{x}{x} = \dfrac{4}{3}$

11) $\dfrac{x}{x} = \dfrac{9}{9}$

**Exercise 7.2**

Solve the equations.

1. $x + 4 = 7$

2. $x + 8 = 13$

3. $y - 7 = 12$

4. $y - 2 = 6$

5. $p - 8 = -6$

6. $q - 3 = -14$

7. $x + 5 = -9$

8. $y + 16 = -10$

9. $2x = 6$

10. $4x = 24$

11. $-3y = 24$

12. $-5y = 45$

13. $-7k = -49$

14. $-8l = -72$

15. $\dfrac{4}{5}x = 6$

16. $\dfrac{2}{7}x = 3$

17. $\dfrac{5}{2}t = -10$

18. $\dfrac{8}{3}s = -16$

19. $-\dfrac{5}{6}y = -7$

20. $-\dfrac{4}{9}y = -9$

21. $2x + 3 = 9$

22. $5t + 2 = 12$

23. $4y - 7 = 11$

24. $8p - 12 = 16$

25. $-x + 17 = 25$

26. $-s + 3 = 15$

27. $-3q + 8 = -21$

28. $-9a + 14 = -19$

29. $2(3b+4) - 6 = 16$    30. $5(2c+7) + 3 = 40$    31. $1 + 9(d-3) = 13$    32. $2 + 3(x-7) = 8$

33. $8a - 9 = 5a + 3$    34. $5l + 3 = 18l + 29$    35. $-13a + 2 = -a - 22$    36. $-t + 16 = -19t + 4$

37. $5y - 6 = 12(2y+1) - 2$    38. $9y + 1 = 11(3y-2) + 3$    39. $\frac{1}{2}x + 5 = 3x - \frac{1}{2}$

40. $\frac{1}{3}x - \frac{2}{3} = x + 2$    41. $\frac{1}{4}p + \frac{2}{5} = \frac{3}{5}p - \frac{1}{5}$    42. $2q - \frac{4}{7} = \frac{1}{14}q + 2$

43. $\frac{5}{6}y - \frac{1}{8} = \frac{2}{3}y + \frac{1}{16}$    44. $-\frac{1}{9}s + \frac{5}{6} = \frac{2}{3}s - 1$    45. $\frac{4}{5}u + \frac{2}{5} = -\frac{9}{5}$

46. $\frac{7}{8}v + \frac{3}{8} = \frac{5}{8}$    47. $\frac{3}{x+1} + \frac{2}{x-1} = \frac{9}{x^2-1}$    48. $\frac{7}{x+3} + \frac{4}{x+2} = \frac{4}{x^2+5x+6}$

49. $\frac{2}{y-4} - \frac{3}{y+5} = \frac{6}{y^2+y-20}$    50. $\frac{8}{y+3} - \frac{5}{y-2} = \frac{2}{y^2+y-6}$

51. $\frac{1}{p^2+6p+9} + \frac{4}{p+3} = \frac{8}{p^2+6p+9}$    52. $\frac{12}{q^2-10q+25} + \frac{2}{q-5} = \frac{2}{q^2-10q+25}$

53. $\frac{7}{x^2-7x} - \frac{8}{x^2-9x+14} = \frac{3}{x^2-2x}$    54. $\frac{5}{x^2+8x} - \frac{6}{x^2-5x} = \frac{2}{x^2+3x-40}$

55. $\frac{4x}{x-2} + 1 = \frac{8}{x-2}$    56. $\frac{8t}{t+3} - 2 = \frac{7}{t+3}$    57. $\frac{6m}{m^2-4} + \frac{1}{m-2} = \frac{3}{m+2}$

58. $\frac{4}{n^2+7n+12} - \frac{3}{n+4} = \frac{4}{n+3}$    59. $\frac{2y-3}{y+1} = \frac{4}{5}$    60. $\frac{3y-7}{y+3} = \frac{2}{3}$

61. $\frac{5a+2}{4} = \frac{-a+3}{3}$    62. $\frac{-2b+1}{7} = \frac{2b+5}{2}$    63. $\frac{3k-8}{7k-2} = 3$

64. $\frac{6l-11}{2l-1} = 5$    65. $\frac{-2}{s+3} = \frac{12}{s^2-9}$    66. $\frac{8}{t^2-4} = \frac{-2}{t-2}$

67. $(x+3)(x-4) = (x+2)(x+1)$    68. $(x-5)(x+2) = (x+3)(x+6)$

69. $(a+7)^2 = (a+8)(a+2)$    70. $(b-6)^2 = (b+4)(b-9)$    71. $\frac{k-2}{k+3} = \frac{k+7}{k-1}$

72. $\frac{l+5}{l+1} = \frac{l-2}{l-4}$    73. $\frac{3p+11}{6p} = \frac{p+1}{2p}$    74. $4x - 2(x+5) = 3(x-6) - x$

75. $-8(y-2) = 4y + 3 - 3(4y+7)$    76. $2a + 5 = 2(a-8) + 21$    77. $7b - 12 = 6(b-2) + b$

# Section 7.3  Literal Equations

**Definition:** A **literal equation** is an equation containing more than one variable.

For example, the equations $x - 7y = 3$, $a + 3b - 5c = 4$, $\frac{m}{3} - \frac{n}{5} = mn$, and $e = mc^2$ are literal equations.

Often literal equations appear in mathematics and science as formulas. For example, the formula $P = 2l + 2w$ tells us the perimeter of a rectangle with length $l$ and width $w$. The formula $a = \dfrac{v}{t}$ tells us the acceleration of a moving object for a period of time $t$ whose velocity is $v$. Our goal is to solve for a specified variable in a literal equation. For now, we will only focus our attention on solving for a variable which is of degree one (equivalently, an equation which is linear in the variable for which we are solving).

**Examples.** Solve the literal equations for the specified variable in terms of the other variables.

1) $x + y = 5$, for $x$.

$$
\begin{array}{rl}
x + \cancel{y} &= 5 \\
-\cancel{y} & \phantom{=5}-y \\
\hline
x &= 5 - y
\end{array}
$$

2) $xy = -2$, for $y$.

$$
\frac{\cancel{x}y}{\cancel{x}} = \frac{-2}{x}
$$

Note that the above is valid only if $x \neq 0$ and $y \neq 0$.

3) $y = mx + b$, for $x$ ($m \neq 0$).

$$
\begin{array}{rl}
y &= mx + \cancel{b} \\
-b & \phantom{=mx}-\cancel{b} \\
\hline
\dfrac{y - b}{m} &= \dfrac{\cancel{m}x}{\cancel{m}}
\end{array}
$$

4) $3k - 7m = 2l$, for $k$.

$$
\begin{array}{rl}
3k - 7\cancel{m} &= 2l \\
+\cancel{7}m & \phantom{=2l}+ 7m \\
\hline
\dfrac{\cancel{3}k}{\cancel{3}} &= \dfrac{2l + 7m}{3}
\end{array}
$$

5) $4n - 3m + 2n = 5(m + 2n)$, for $n$.

$$
\begin{array}{rl}
4n - 3m + 2n &= 5(m + 2n) \\
6\cancel{n} - 3m &= 5m + 10n \\
-\cancel{6}n & \phantom{=5m+10n}- 6n \\
\hline
-3m &= 5\cancel{n} + 4n \\
-5m & -\cancel{5}m \\
\hline
\dfrac{-8m}{4} &= \dfrac{\cancel{4}n}{\cancel{4}} \\
-2m &= n
\end{array}
$$

6) $a(y + b) - 2 = 4 - ab$, for $y$ $(a \neq 0)$.

$$a(y + b) - 2 = 4 - ab$$
$$ay + \cancel{ab} - 2 = 4 - ab$$
$$\underline{\phantom{ay} - \cancel{ab} \qquad\qquad - ab}$$
$$ay \qquad \cancel{-2} = 4 - 2ab$$
$$\underline{\qquad\qquad \cancel{+2} + 2}$$
$$\frac{\cancel{a}y}{\cancel{a}} = \frac{6 - 2ab}{a}$$

Notice that if $a = 0$, then $a(y + b) - 2 = 4 - ab$ becomes $-2 = 4$, which is not true.

7) $mx - 7y = nx + 12y$, for $x$ $(m \neq n)$.

For this one, notice that two terms contain $x$. We must first group the $x$ terms together on one side of the equation. Afterwards, we factor out the $x$. Once this is done, we divide by the remaining factor. Let's see how this works:

$$mx - 7y = n\cancel{x} + 12y$$
$$\underline{\quad - nx \qquad - \cancel{n}x \quad}$$
$$mx - nx - \cancel{7}y = 12y$$
$$\underline{\qquad\quad + \cancel{7}y \qquad + 7y}$$
$$mx - nx \qquad = 19y \quad \text{(Now the } x \text{ terms are grouped.)}$$
$$x(m - n) \qquad = 19y \quad \text{(Factor out the } x.)$$
$$\frac{x\cancel{(m - n)}}{\cancel{m - n}} = \frac{19y}{m - n} \quad \text{(Divide by the stuff in the (—).)}$$

Note that if $m = n$, then $mx - 7y = nx + 12y$ becomes $-7y = 12y$ and there is no $x$ to solve for.

8) $at + bt + ct = 16$, for $t$ $(a + b + c \neq 0)$.

$$at + bt + ct = 16 \quad \text{(The } t\text{'s are grouped.)}$$
$$\frac{t\cancel{(a + b + c)}}{\cancel{a + b + c}} = \frac{16}{a + b + c} \quad \text{(Factor out the } t \text{ and divide.)}$$

9) $\dfrac{1}{x} + \dfrac{1}{y} = \dfrac{1}{z}$, for $x$ $(x \neq 0, \ y \neq 0, \ z \neq 0 \text{ and } y \neq z)$.

Let's begin by clearing the fractions. The LCM of $x$, $y$, and $z$ is $xyz$.

$$\frac{1}{x} + \frac{1}{y} = \frac{1}{z}$$

$$\frac{xyz}{1}\left(\frac{1}{x} + \frac{1}{y}\right) = \frac{xyz}{1}\left(\frac{1}{z}\right)$$

$$\frac{\cancel{x}yz}{1}\left(\frac{1}{\cancel{x}}\right) + \frac{x\cancel{y}z}{1}\left(\frac{1}{\cancel{y}}\right) = \frac{xy\cancel{z}}{1}\left(\frac{1}{\cancel{z}}\right)$$

$$yz + \cancel{y}z = xy$$
$$\underline{\quad - \cancel{x}z \qquad\quad - xz}$$
$$yz = xy - xz$$
$$\frac{yz}{y - z} = \frac{x\cancel{(y - z)}}{\cancel{y - z}}$$

Observe that if $y = z$, then $\dfrac{1}{x} + \dfrac{1}{y} = \dfrac{1}{z}$ becomes $\dfrac{1}{x} = 0$ which has no solution for $x$.

10) $\dfrac{Q}{4+Q} = 2R$, for $Q$ ($Q \neq -4$ and $R \neq \frac{1}{2}$).

$$\frac{Q}{4+Q} = \frac{2R}{1}$$

$$Q(1) = 2R(4+Q)$$
$$Q = 8R + 2RQ$$
$$\underline{-2RQ \qquad -2RQ}$$
$$Q - 2RQ = 8R$$

$$\frac{Q(1-2R)}{1-2R} = \frac{8R}{1-2R}$$

Notice that if $Q = -4$, then $\dfrac{Q}{4+Q}$ is undefined. Furthermore, if $R = \dfrac{1}{2}$, then $\dfrac{Q}{4+Q} = 2R$ becomes $\dfrac{Q}{4+Q} = 1$ which has no solution for $Q$.

**Try These (Set 2):** Solve the literal equations for the specified variable.

1) $y = 3x - 4$, for $x$

2) $2a - 3b = 4(a - 2b + 8c)$, for $c$

3) $C = \dfrac{5}{9}(F - 32)$, for $F$

4) $A = \dfrac{h}{2}(b_1 + b_2)$, for $b_1$ ($h \neq 0$, $b_1 \neq b_2$)

5) $8t + 7 = mt - 13$, for $t$ ($m \neq 8$)

6) $\dfrac{x}{4} - \dfrac{x}{6} = y$, for $x$

7) $\dfrac{a}{r^2 - r - 6} + \dfrac{b}{r+2} = \dfrac{3}{r^2 - r - 6}$, for $r$ ($r \neq -2$, $r \neq 3$, $b \neq 0$)

**Exercise 7.3**

Solve each literal equation for the specified variable.

1. $x + y = 4$, for $x$      2. $p + q = 9$, for $q$      3. $a - 3b = 7$, for $a$      4. $m - 6n = -2$, for $m$

5. $5p = q$, for $p$      6. $8a = b$, for $a$      7. $V = lwh$, for $w$      8. $I = prt$, for $t$

9. $7m + 5 = 4n$, for $m$   10. $y = 9x - 18$, for $x$   11. $y = -4x + 2$, for $x$   12. $12x + 1 = 3y$, for $x$

13. $10a + 2b = 1$, for $a$   14. $8l + 9m = 2$, for $m$   15. $-5j + k = 7$, for $j$   16. $-2p + 3q = 1$, for $p$

17. $4(a + 3b) - 2a = 7a + 1$, for $a$      18. $2(3a + 7b) - 4b = 3a - 2$, for $a$      19. $a(x + y) + 4 = y$, for $x$

20. $b(x - y) + 7 = x$, for $y$      21. $6j - 2k = 9j + 3k$, for $j$      22. $-j + 5k = 8j - 3k$, for $j$

23. $ax + 2x = 1$, for $x$      24. $bz - 3z = 6$, for $z$      25. $ay + by = cy + 2$, for $y$

26. $al = 7 + bl - cl$, for $l$      27. $\dfrac{3}{4}x - \dfrac{1}{2}y = \dfrac{7}{2}x + \dfrac{1}{4}y$, for $x$      28. $\dfrac{2}{9}a + \dfrac{1}{3}b = \dfrac{5}{3}a - \dfrac{1}{9}b$, for $b$

29. $\dfrac{1}{3x} + \dfrac{1}{2x} = \dfrac{4}{y}$, for $x$      30. $\dfrac{7}{2s} - \dfrac{3}{4s} = \dfrac{1}{t}$, for $s$      31. $\dfrac{2}{u} + \dfrac{3}{v} = \dfrac{6}{w}$, for $u$      32. $\dfrac{5}{p} = \dfrac{9}{q} + \dfrac{3}{t}$, for $q$

33. $3 = \dfrac{1}{m} - \dfrac{1}{n}$, for $m$      34. $\dfrac{1}{b} - \dfrac{1}{d} = 5c$, for $d$      35. $\dfrac{a}{x+2} + \dfrac{b}{x-2} = \dfrac{4}{x^2 - 4}$, for $x$

36. $\dfrac{m}{x^2 - x - 30} - \dfrac{n}{x - 6} = \dfrac{1}{x + 5}$, for $x$      37. $(x + p)(x + q) = x(x + p)$, for $x$

38. $x(x - t) = (x - s)(x - t)$, for $x$      39. $\dfrac{2Q}{5Q - 3} = P$, for $Q$      40. $\dfrac{4s + 3}{s + 7} = t$, for $s$

41. $A = \dfrac{bh}{2}$, for $h$      42. $v = \dfrac{d}{t}$, for $t$      43. $S = \dfrac{a}{1 - r}$, for $r$      44. $\dfrac{p_1 v_1}{t_1} = \dfrac{p_2 v_2}{t_2}$, for $v_2$

## Section 7.4  Quadratic Equations

**Definition 1:** A **quadratic equation** is an equation which is equivalent to the equation $ax^2 + bx + c = 0$, where $a$, $b$, and $c$ are real numbers and $a \neq 0$. A quadratic equation is also referred to as a **second-degree equation**.

**Definition 2:** A quadratic equation written in the form $ax^2 + bx + c = 0$ is in **standard form**.

Observe that $ax^2 + bx + c$ is a polynomial of degree two, which is why we call the equation a quadratic equation. Notice that, when the equation is in standard form, one side of the equation is zero, and the other side contains the quadratic is in descending order.

Our goal is to learn how to solve a quadratic equation. As we will see, a quadratic equation can have either two real solutions, one real solution or no real solutions. In the next section of this chapter, we will learn about quadratic equations which have **complex solutions**.

There are several methods which we will learn about to solve a quadratic equation based on its appearance. The first method, called the **Factoring Method**, deals with solving a quadratic equation (in standard form) in which the quadratic polynomial can be factored. The second method deals with the case where the quadratic polynomial of the quadratic equation (in standard form) is a binomial. Afterwards, we will learn how to solve quadratic equations (in standard form) which do not factor. The method used in this case will require a technique called **Completing the Square**. In fact, even if the equation can be solved by using the factoring method, completing the square can still be applied. Finally, we will see that there is a formula, called the **Quadratic Formula**, which is derived from completing the square. It's this formula that will allow us to solve any quadratic equation.

Let's learn the methods mentioned above.

1. **The Factoring Method**

To understand how the Factoring Method works, let's do our first example and write down the steps needed.

**Example.** Solve the equation: $x^2 - 9x + 20 = 0$

**Step I:** Write the equation in standard form.
Notice that we have this form already in our example.

**Step II:** Factor the quadratic.
We have $(x - 4)(x - 5) = 0$.

**Step III:** Apply the following property:

---

### The Zero-Product Property

If $a$ and $b$ are real numbers for which $ab = 0$, then either $a = 0$, or $b = 0$, or both.

---

Note that the zero-product property can be 'reversed' to become:

---

If either $a = 0$ or $b = 0$ or both, then $ab = 0$.

---

By applying the zero-product property, we obtain

$$(x - 4)(x - 5) = 0$$
$$x - 4 = 0 \mid x - 5 = 0$$

Notice that we now have two linear equations which we know how to solve.

**Step IV:** Solve each of the linear equations.

$$(x - 4)(x - 5) = 0$$

$$
\begin{array}{c|c}
x - 4 = 0 & x - 5 = 0 \\
+4 \quad +4 & +5 \quad +5 \\
\hline
x = 4 & x = 5
\end{array}
$$

Therefore, there are two solutions to the equation. We say that the **roots** of the equation are 4 and 5. Alternatively, we can say that the solution set (or the set of roots) is $\{4, \ 5\}$. Notice that both roots satisfy the equation, since

$$(4)^2 - 9(4) + 20 = 16 - 36 + 20 = 0 \ \ \checkmark$$

and

$$(5)^2 - 9(5) + 20 = 25 - 45 + 20 = 0 \ \ \checkmark$$

**Examples.** Solve the equations by using the factoring method.

1) $x^2 + 7x + 12 = 0$

$$(x + 4)(x + 3) = 0$$

$$
\begin{array}{c|c}
x + 4 = 0 & x + 3 = 0 \\
-4 \quad -4 & -3 \quad -3 \\
\hline
x = -4 & x = -3
\end{array}
$$

The set of roots is $\{-4, \ -3\}$.

2) $y^2 + 5y - 24 = 0$

$$(y + 8)(y - 3) = 0$$

| $y + 8 = 0$ | $y - 3 = 0$ |
|---|---|
| $-8 \quad -8$ | $+3 \quad +3$ |
| $y = -8$ | $y = 3$ |

and the set of roots is $\{-8,\ 3\}$.

3) $x^2 + 8x + 16 = 0$

$$(x + 4)(x + 4) = 0$$

| $x + 4 = 0$ | $x + 4 = 0$ |
|---|---|
| $-4 \quad -4$ | $-4 \quad -4$ |
| $x = -4$ | $x = -4$ |

Notice that we obtain two equal roots, $-4$ and $-4$. When this occurs, we say that $x = -4$ is a **double root**. Double roots occur precisely when we have a quadratic equation in standard form and the quadratic is a non-zero multiple of a trinomial square.

4) $10a^2 - 21a + 8 = 0$

$$(5a - 8)(2a - 1) = 0$$

| $5a - 8 = 0$ | $2a - 1 = 0$ |
|---|---|
| $+8 \quad +8$ | $+1 \quad +1$ |
| $\dfrac{5a}{5} = \dfrac{8}{5}$ | $\dfrac{2a}{2} = \dfrac{1}{2}$ |

5) $9t^2 + 5t = 0$

$$t(9t + 5) = 0$$

| $t = 0$ | $9t + 5 = 0$ |
|---|---|
| | $-5 \quad -5$ |
| | $\dfrac{9t}{9} = \dfrac{-5}{9}$ |

6) $64p^2 - 9 = 0$

$$(8p + 3)(8p - 3) = 0$$

| $8p + 3 = 0$ | $8p - 3 = 0$ |
|---|---|
| $-3 \quad -3$ | $+3 \quad +3$ |
| $\dfrac{8p}{8} = \dfrac{-3}{8}$ | $\dfrac{8p}{8} = \dfrac{3}{8}$ |

In all of the above examples, we were given a quadratic equation in standard form. Let's solve some equations which are not in standard form. Remember that standard form is the form in which one side of the equation is zero and the quadratic on the other side is in descending order.

7) $x(6x - 1) = 1$

To get standard form, first distribute the $x$ into the parentheses. Then subtract 1 on both sides:

$$x(6x - 1) = 1$$
$$6x^2 - x = 1$$
$$\underline{\phantom{6x^2 - x} -1 \quad -1}$$
$$6x^2 - x - 1 = 0$$

Now continue with the factoring method.

$$(3x+1)(2x-1)=0$$

$$\begin{array}{c|c} 3x + \cancel{1} = 0 & 2x \cancel{-1} = 0 \\ \underline{-\cancel{1} \;\; -1} & \underline{+\cancel{1} \;\; +1} \\ \dfrac{\cancel{3}x}{\cancel{3}} = \dfrac{-1}{3} & \dfrac{\cancel{2}x}{\cancel{2}} = \dfrac{1}{2} \end{array}$$

8) $1 + \dfrac{3m - 10}{m^2} = 0$

This is a rational equation. We can solve this equation by clearing the fractions by multiplying both sides of the equation by the LCM of the denominators, which is just $m^2$. Afterwards, we will apply the factoring method.

$$1 + \frac{3m - 10}{m^2} = 0$$

$$m^2 \left(1 + \frac{3m - 10}{m^2}\right) = m^2(0)$$

$$m^2(1) + \frac{\cancel{m^2}}{1}\left(\frac{3m - 10}{\cancel{m^2}}\right) = 0$$

$$m^2 + 3m - 10 = 0$$

and now we have

$$(m + 5)(m - 2) = 0$$

$$\begin{array}{c|c} m + \cancel{5} = 0 & m \cancel{-2} = 0 \\ \underline{-\cancel{5} \;\; -5} & \underline{+\cancel{2} \;\; +2} \\ m = -5 & m = 2 \end{array}$$

Notice that both of these solutions are valid, since they do not make the denominator of the fraction in the equation equal zero. In fact, the only number which does this is $m = 0$ (Right?).

**Try These (Set 3):** Solve the following quadratic equations by factoring.

1) $x^2 - 3x - 4 = 0$      3) $m^2 - 3m = 0$      5) $25t^2 - 10t + 1 = 0$

2) $y^2 + 15y + 56 = 0$      4) $16x^2 - 25 = 0$      6) $(2x + 1)(3x + 7) = 0$

2. **Special Cases of $ax^2 + bx + c = 0$, $a \neq 0$**

The special cases that I am referring to are when the quadratic is a binomial. More precisely, these are the cases when either $c = 0$ or $b = 0$. As we will now see, when one of these two situations arises, there is a method of solving the equation.

**Case 1.** When $c = 0$; $ax^2 + bx = 0$.

You may notice right away that when the equation takes this form, you can solve it by factoring (the GCF will **always** contain $x$, which can certainly be factored out). Consequently, it will always happen that one of the roots to the equation $ax^2 + bx = 0$ is $x = 0$, since $a(0)^2 + b(0) = 0$ checks out. What we need to do, however, is to find the other root. Let's do an example (check out Example 5 above as well).

**Example.** Solve: $18x^2 - 6x = 0$

By applying the factoring method, we have

$$\frac{6x\,(3x-1)}{\phantom{xx}} = 0$$

$$\frac{\cancel{6}x}{\cancel{6}} = \frac{0}{6} \quad \bigg| \quad 3x - \cancel{1} = 0$$

$$x = 0 \quad \bigg| \quad \underline{+\cancel{1} \quad +1}$$

$$\frac{\cancel{3}x}{\cancel{3}} = \frac{1}{3}$$

**Try These (Set 4):** Solve the following quadratic equations by factoring.

1) $x^2 + x = 0$

2) $3n^2 - 7n = 0$

3) $7y^2 - 28y = 0$

4) $-2a^2 = 18a$

5) $4x(x - 7) = 9x(x + 1)$

6) $\frac{2}{3}k^2 + 5k = 0$

**Case 2.** When $b = 0$; $ax^2 + c = 0$.

When the equation is in this form (the 'middle term' is missing), there is a property which helps us solve the equation. Let's do the first example step by step.

**Example.** Solve: $x^2 - 49 = 0$

Observe that this **can** be solved by factoring, since $x^2 - 49 = (x + 7)(x - 7)$. We will do it using a new method. Here's how it goes:

**Step I:** Solve for $x^2$ by itself first.

$$x^2 - \cancel{49} = 0$$

$$\underline{+\cancel{49} \quad + 49}$$

$$x^2 \phantom{xxx} = 49$$

**Step II:** Apply the following property:

---

**The Square Root Property**

If $X^2 = n$ and $n \geq 0$, then $X = -\sqrt{n}$ or $X = \sqrt{n}$.

---

Observe that both of these $X$-values are valid, since both $(-\sqrt{n})^2 = n$ and $(\sqrt{n})^2 = n$. Moreover, notice that we need $n$ to be positive valued or zero (that is, $n$ is nonnegative valued or $n \geq 0$) because if $n$ is a negative number (that is, $n < 0$), then we would have the square root of a negative number, which is not a real number.

We can abbreviate the square root property in the following way:

---

**The Square Root Property (abbreviated form)**

If $X^2 = n$ and $n \geq 0$, then $X = \pm\sqrt{n}$.

---

This way of writing it is more compact. Just remember that $\pm\sqrt{n}$ is the same as $\{-\sqrt{n},\ \sqrt{n}\}$.

Getting back to our example, we have

$$x^2 = 49$$
$$x = \pm\sqrt{49}$$

and we obtain

$$x = \pm 7 \text{ or, equivalently, the solution set is } \{-7, \ 7\}.$$

Notice that without the '$\pm$', we would've only obtained the solution $x = 7$.

---

**BEWARE:**    Don't forget the '$\pm$' when using the Square Root Property!!

---

**Examples.** Solve the following.

1) $x^2 - 6 = 0$

If you follow the steps I've given you before, you will be in good shape. First, solve for $x^2$, then apply the square root property.

$$
\begin{array}{rl}
x^2 - 6 & = 0 \\
+6 & +6 \\
\hline
x^2 & = 6
\end{array}
$$

By applying the Square Root Property, we obtain:

$$x = \pm\sqrt{6}$$

Since $\sqrt{6}$ doesn't simplify, we leave our answer as it is. The roots are $x = \pm\sqrt{6}$ or, equivalently, the solution set is $\left\{-\sqrt{6}, \ \sqrt{6}\right\}$.

2) $3x^2 - 9 = 0$

Again, first solve for $x^2$, then solve for $x$.

$$
\begin{array}{rl}
3x^2 - 9 & = 0 \\
+9 & +9 \\
\hline
\dfrac{3x^2}{3} & = \dfrac{9}{3} \\
x^2 & = 3
\end{array}
$$

and so

$$x = \pm\sqrt{3} \text{ or, equivalently, the solution set is } \left\{-\sqrt{3}, \ \sqrt{3}\right\}.$$

3) $5y^2 - 40 = 0$

$$5y^2 - \cancel{40} = 0$$
$$\underline{+40 \quad + 40}$$
$$\frac{\cancel{5}y^2}{\cancel{5}} = \frac{40}{5}$$
$$y^2 = 8$$

and so

$$y = \underbrace{\pm\sqrt{8} = \pm 2\sqrt{2}}_{\text{Simplify } \sqrt{8}.} \text{ or, equivalently, the solution set is } \{-2\sqrt{2},\ 2\sqrt{2}\}.$$

4) $-11n^2 + 44 = 0$

$$-11n^2 + \cancel{44} = 0$$
$$\underline{-44 \quad - 44}$$
$$\frac{-\cancel{11}n^2}{-\cancel{11}} = \frac{-44}{-11}$$
$$n^2 = 4$$

and so

$$n = \pm\sqrt{4} = \pm 2 \text{ or, equivalently, the solution set is } \{-2,\ 2\}.$$

5) $-8a^2 + 360 = 0$

$$-8a^2 + \cancel{360} = 0$$
$$\underline{-360 \quad - 360}$$
$$\frac{-\cancel{8}a^2}{-\cancel{8}} = \frac{-360}{-8}$$
$$a^2 = 45$$

and so

$$a = \pm\sqrt{45} = \pm 3\sqrt{5} \text{ or, equivalently, the solution set is } \{-3\sqrt{5},\ 3\sqrt{5}\}.$$

6) $7x^2 - 1 = 0$

$$7x^2 - \cancel{1} = 0$$
$$\underline{+\cancel{1} \quad + 1}$$
$$\frac{\cancel{7}x^2}{\cancel{7}} = \frac{1}{7}$$
$$x^2 = \frac{1}{7}$$

and so

$$x = \pm\sqrt{\frac{1}{7}} = \pm\frac{\sqrt{1}}{\sqrt{7}} = \underbrace{\pm\frac{1}{\sqrt{7}}\left(\frac{\sqrt{7}}{\sqrt{7}}\right) = \pm\frac{\sqrt{7}}{7}}_{\text{Rationalize the denominators.}} \text{ or, equivalently, the solution set is } \left\{-\frac{\sqrt{7}}{7},\ \frac{\sqrt{7}}{7}\right\}.$$

7) $25p^2 - 12 = 0$

$$\begin{array}{r} 25p^2 - \cancel{12} = 0 \\ +12 \quad + 12 \\ \hline \dfrac{\cancel{25}p^2}{\cancel{25}} = \dfrac{12}{25} \\ p^2 = \dfrac{12}{25} \end{array}$$

and so

$$p = \underbrace{\pm\sqrt{\frac{12}{25}} = \pm\frac{\sqrt{12}}{\sqrt{25}} = \pm\frac{2\sqrt{3}}{5}}_{\text{simplify this}} \quad \text{or, equivalently, the solution set is } \left\{-\frac{2\sqrt{3}}{5},\ \frac{2\sqrt{3}}{5}\right\}.$$

8) $125x^2 - 18 = 0$

$$\begin{array}{r} 125x^2 - \cancel{18} = 0 \\ +18 \quad + 18 \\ \hline \dfrac{125x^2}{125} = \dfrac{18}{125} \\ x^2 = \dfrac{18}{125} \end{array}$$

and so

$$x = \underbrace{\pm\sqrt{\frac{18}{125}} = \pm\frac{\sqrt{18}}{\sqrt{125}} = \pm\frac{3\sqrt{2}}{5\sqrt{5}}}_{\text{Simplify this.}} = \underbrace{\pm\frac{3\sqrt{2}}{5\sqrt{5}}\left(\frac{\sqrt{5}}{\sqrt{5}}\right) = \pm\frac{3\sqrt{10}}{5\left(\sqrt{5}\right)^2}}_{\text{Rationalize the denominator.}} = \pm\frac{3\sqrt{10}}{25}.$$

9) $y^2 + 4 = 0$

$$\begin{array}{r} y^2 + \cancel{4} = 0 \\ -4 \quad - 4 \\ \hline y^2 \quad = -4 \end{array}$$

The square root property **cannot** be applied here, since $-4$ is neither positive nor zero. Therefore, this equation has no real roots. In other words, no matter which real number you replace $y$ by in the equation, it will never be true that $y^2 + 4 = 0$. It makes sense: pick any real number and square it. Your answer will be either 0 (if the number you chose is 0) or positive (if the number you chose is positive or negative). Now, adding 4 to the square of it must give you a positive answer. This means that you will never get 0.

**Try These (Set 5):** Solve the quadratic equations.

1) $x^2 - 2 = 0$      4) $4x^2 - 100 = 0$      7) $-3n^2 + 150 = 0$

2) $y^2 - 44 = 0$      5) $6t^2 - 72 = 0$      8) $54y^2 - 49 = 0$

3) $-13a^2 + 65 = 0$      6) $-9s^2 + 28 = 0$      9) $2p^2 + 9 = 0$

## 3. Completing the Square

We will now learn how to solve a quadratic equation which cannot be solved by factoring. In fact, this method can even be used to solve **any** quadratic equation, factorable or not. The key technique used in the method that we will learn is called **completing the square**. To explain what this is all about, I will pose the problem as a question:

> **Question.**  What number do we need to add to the binomial $x^2 + bx$
> so that the resulting trinomial is a trinomial square?
>
> **Answer.**  If we add $\left(\dfrac{b}{2}\right)^2$ to $x^2 + bx$, we obtain $x^2 + bx + \underline{\left(\dfrac{b}{2}\right)^2} = \left(x + \dfrac{b}{2}\right)^2$.

To verify this, all we need to do is multiply $\left(x + \dfrac{b}{2}\right)^2$ by FOIL and check whether or not we obtain $x^2 + bx + \left(\dfrac{b}{2}\right)^2$:

$$
\begin{aligned}
\left(x + \frac{b}{2}\right)^2 &= \left(x + \frac{b}{2}\right)\left(x + \frac{b}{2}\right) = x^2 + \frac{b}{2}x + \frac{b}{2}x + \left(\frac{b}{2}\right)^2 \\
&= x^2 + \left(\frac{b}{2} + \frac{b}{2}\right)x + \left(\frac{b}{2}\right)^2 = x^2 + \frac{\cancel{2}b}{\cancel{2}}x + \left(\frac{b}{2}\right)^2 \\
&= x^2 + bx + \left(\frac{b}{2}\right)^2
\end{aligned}
$$

as we hoped for. The process of adding the number $\left(\dfrac{b}{2}\right)^2$ to the binomial $x^2 + bx$ is called **completing the square**.

**Examples.** Complete the square and factor.

1) $x^2 + 4x + \underline{?} = (x\underline{\phantom{?}?})^2$

Well, notice that $b = +4$ yields $\left(\dfrac{b}{2}\right)^2 = \left(\dfrac{+4}{2}\right)^2 = (2)^2 = 4$. This is the number that we need to add to $x^2 + 4x$ in order to complete the square. As far as the factorization goes, notice that $\dfrac{b}{2} = \dfrac{+4}{2} = +2$. Therefore, we have $x^2 + 4x + \underline{4} = (x\underline{+2})^2$.

2) $y^2 - 24y + \underline{?} = (y\underline{\phantom{?}?})^2$

Notice that $b = -24$ yields $\left(\dfrac{b}{2}\right)^2 = \left(\dfrac{-24}{2}\right)^2 = (-12)^2 = 144$. This is the number that we need to add to $y^2 - 24y$ in order to complete the square. As for the factorization, we have $\dfrac{b}{2} = \dfrac{-24}{2} = -12$. Therefore, we obtain $y^2 - 24y + \underline{144} = (y\underline{-12})^2$.

3) $p^2 + 5p + \underline{?} = (p\underline{\phantom{?}?})^2$

We have $b = 5$, giving us $\left(\dfrac{b}{2}\right)^2 = \left(\dfrac{5}{2}\right)^2 = \dfrac{25}{4}$. This number completes the square. Now, the number $\dfrac{b}{2} = \dfrac{5}{2}$ goes into the factorization. Therefore, we get $p^2 + 5p + \underline{\dfrac{25}{4}} = \left(p\underline{+\dfrac{5}{2}}\right)^2$.

4) $x^2 - x + \underline{?} = (x\underline{\ \ ?\ })^2$

We have $b = -1$, giving us $\left(\dfrac{b}{2}\right)^2 = \left(\dfrac{-1}{2}\right)^2 = \dfrac{1}{4}$. This number completes the square. Now, the number $\dfrac{b}{2} = -\dfrac{1}{2}$ goes into the factorization. We obtain $x^2 - x + \underline{\dfrac{1}{4}} = \left(x\underline{-\dfrac{1}{2}}\right)^2$.

5) $u^2 + \dfrac{3}{2}u + \underline{?} = (u\underline{\ \ ?\ })^2$

We know that $b = \dfrac{3}{2}$, giving us

$$\left(\frac{b}{2}\right)^2 = \left(\frac{\frac{3}{2}}{2}\right)^2 = \left(\frac{\frac{3}{2}\times\frac{2}{1}}{\frac{2}{1}\times\frac{2}{1}}\right)^2 = \left(\frac{3}{4}\right)^2 = \frac{9}{16}.$$

This number completes the square. The number $\dfrac{b}{2} = \dfrac{\frac{3}{2}}{2} = \dfrac{3}{4}$ will go into the factorization. We obtain $u^2 + \dfrac{3}{2}u + \underline{\dfrac{9}{16}} = \left(u+\underline{\dfrac{3}{4}}\right)^2$.

Now that we have learned how to complete the square, what does it help us with? Well, let's solve a quadratic equation which cannot be solved by factoring. I will include the steps needed for solving it as well.

**Example.** Solve: $x^2 + 2x - 6 = 0$

To begin with, notice that this equation is in standard form and the quadratic does not factor.

**Step I:** Solve for the binomial $x^2 + bx$ by itself.

By doing this in our example, we obtain

$$\begin{array}{r} x^2 + 2x - \cancel{6} = 0 \\ \underline{+6 \quad +6} \\ x^2 + 2x = 6 \end{array}$$

**Step II:** Complete the square of the binomial and factor.

For the binomial $x^2 + 2x$, we have $b = 2$. Therefore, the number which will complete the square is $\left(\dfrac{b}{2}\right)^2 = \left(\dfrac{2}{2}\right)^2 = 1$ and the number which goes into the factorization is $\dfrac{b}{2} = \dfrac{2}{2} = 1$. We obtain

$$x^2 + 2x + \underline{1} = 6 + \underline{1}$$
$$(x+1)^2 = 7$$

The next step shows the whole point behind why we care about completing the square.

**Step III:** Apply the Square Root Property, which states that if $X^2 = n$ and $n \geq 0$, then $X = \pm\sqrt{n}$.

$$(x+1)^2 = 7$$

and, by the Square Root Property, we have

$$x + 1 = \pm\sqrt{7}$$

**Step IV:** Solve for $x$

$$\begin{array}{rl} x + \cancel{1} & = \pm\sqrt{7} \\ \underline{-\cancel{1} \qquad -1} \\ x & = -1 \pm \sqrt{7} \end{array}$$

The solution set is $\left\{-1-\sqrt{7},\ -1+\sqrt{7}\right\}$.

Let's try some examples. Remember to follow the steps carefully.

**Examples.** Solve the following by completing the square.

1) $x^2 - 4x + 1 = 0$

$$\begin{array}{rl} x^2 - 4x + \cancel{1} & = 0 \\ \underline{-\cancel{1} \qquad -1} \\ x^2 - 4x & = -1 \end{array}$$

Now, $b = -4$ and so the number which will complete the square is $\left(\dfrac{b}{2}\right)^2 = \left(\dfrac{-4}{2}\right)^2 = (-2)^2 = 4$. The number which goes into the factorization is $\dfrac{b}{2} = \dfrac{-4}{2} = -2$. Therefore,

$$x^2 - 4x + \underline{4} = -1 + \underline{4}$$

$$(x-2)^2 = 3$$

and, by the Square Root Property, we'll obtain

$$\begin{array}{rl} x - \cancel{2} & = \pm\sqrt{3} \\ \underline{+\cancel{2} \qquad +2} \\ x & = 2 \pm \sqrt{3} \end{array}$$

The set of roots is $\left\{2-\sqrt{3},\ 2+\sqrt{3}\right\}$.

2) $x^2 + 6x - 15 = 0$

$$\begin{array}{rl} x^2 + 6x - \cancel{15} & = 0 \\ \underline{+\cancel{15} \quad + 15} \\ x^2 + 6x & = 15 \end{array}$$

Here, $b = 6$ and so the number which will complete the square is $\left(\dfrac{b}{2}\right)^2 = \left(\dfrac{6}{2}\right)^2 = (3)^2 = 9$ and the number which goes into the factorization is $\dfrac{b}{2} = \dfrac{6}{2} = 3$. Therefore,

$$x^2 + 6x + \underline{9} = 15 + \underline{9}$$

$$(x+3)^2 = 24$$

and, by the Square Root Property, we'll obtain

$$\begin{array}{rl} x + \cancel{3} & = \pm\sqrt{24} \\ \underline{-\cancel{3} \qquad -3} \\ x = -3 & \pm \sqrt{24} \end{array}$$

Notice that $\sqrt{24} = \sqrt{4}\sqrt{6} = 2\sqrt{6}$. Therefore, we can write our answer as $x = -3 \pm 2\sqrt{6}$. The solution set is $\left\{-3 - 2\sqrt{6}, -3 + 2\sqrt{6}\right\}$.

3) $y^2 - \dfrac{5}{2}y = \dfrac{3}{2}$

$$y^2 - \frac{5}{2}y = \frac{3}{2}$$

Here, $b = -\dfrac{5}{2}$, and so the number which will complete the square is

$$\left(\frac{b}{2}\right)^2 = \left(\frac{-\frac{5}{2}}{2}\right)^2 = \left(\frac{-\frac{5}{2} \times \frac{2}{1}}{\frac{2}{1} \times \frac{2}{1}}\right)^2 = \left(\frac{-5}{4}\right)^2 = \frac{25}{16}$$

and the number which goes into the factorization is $\dfrac{b}{2} = \dfrac{-\frac{5}{2}}{2} = \dfrac{-5}{4}$. Therefore,

$$y^2 - \frac{5}{2}y + \frac{25}{16} = \frac{3}{2} + \frac{25}{16}$$

$$\left(y - \frac{5}{4}\right)^2 = \frac{49}{16}$$

and, by the Square Root Property, we'll obtain

$$y - \frac{5}{4} = \pm\sqrt{\frac{49}{16}}$$

$$\begin{array}{r} y - \dfrac{5}{4} = \pm\dfrac{7}{4} \\ +\dfrac{5}{4} \qquad +\dfrac{5}{4} \\ \hline y = \dfrac{5}{4} \pm \dfrac{7}{4} \end{array}$$

Now, if we split up the '$\pm$' into two seperate expressions, we obtain

$$y = \frac{5}{4} - \frac{7}{4} = -\frac{2}{4} = -\frac{1}{2}$$

and

$$y = \frac{5}{4} + \frac{7}{4} = \frac{12}{4} = 3.$$

Therefore, the roots are $-\dfrac{1}{2}$ and 3.

4) $6t^2 - 6t - 3 = 0$

$$\frac{6t^2}{6} - \frac{6t}{6} - \frac{3}{6} = \frac{0}{6}$$

$$t^2 - t - \frac{1}{2} = 0$$

$$\begin{array}{r} t^2 - t \quad +\dfrac{1}{2} \quad +\dfrac{1}{2} \\ \hline t^2 - t = \dfrac{1}{2} \end{array}$$

Since $b = -1$, we have $\left(\dfrac{b}{2}\right)^2 = \left(\dfrac{-1}{2}\right)^2 = \dfrac{1}{4}$ and $\dfrac{b}{2} = \dfrac{-1}{2}$. Therefore,

$$t^2 - t + \frac{1}{4} = \frac{1}{2} + \frac{1}{4}$$

$$\left(t - \frac{1}{2}\right)^2 = \frac{3}{4}$$

and, by the Square Root Property, we'll obtain

$$
\begin{array}{c}
t - \frac{1}{2} = \pm\sqrt{\frac{3}{4}} \\
\frac{1}{2} \quad + \frac{1}{2} \\
\hline
t = \frac{1}{2} \pm \sqrt{\frac{3}{4}}
\end{array}
$$

Now, $\sqrt{\frac{3}{4}} = \frac{\sqrt{3}}{\sqrt{4}} = \frac{\sqrt{3}}{2}$ and so we can write our solutions as

$$
t = \frac{1}{2} \pm \frac{\sqrt{3}}{2} = \frac{1 \pm \sqrt{3}}{2}.
$$

The roots are $\dfrac{1 - \sqrt{3}}{2}$ and $\dfrac{1 + \sqrt{3}}{2}$.

5) $r^2 + 2r + 3 = 0$

$$
\begin{array}{c}
r^2 + 2r + 3 = 0 \\
-3 \quad - 3 \\
\hline
r^2 + 2r \quad\quad = -3
\end{array}
$$

Since $b = 2$, we have $\left(\dfrac{b}{2}\right)^2 = \left(\dfrac{2}{2}\right)^2 = 1$ and $\dfrac{b}{2} = \dfrac{1}{2} = 1$. Therefore,

$$
r^2 + 2r + \underline{1} = -3 + \underline{1}
$$

$$
(r + 1)^2 = -2
$$

Now, notice that the square root property cannot be applied here, since we have $-2$ on the right hand side. The property requires a real number which is either positive or zero. Consequently, this equation has **no real solutions**.

**Try These (Set 6):**

I) Complete the square and factor.

     1) $x^2 + 8x + \underline{\hspace{1cm}} = (x\underline{\hspace{0.8cm}})^2$         3) $p^2 - 11p + \underline{\hspace{1cm}} = (p\underline{\hspace{0.8cm}})^2$

     2) $y^2 - \dfrac{3}{2}y + \underline{\hspace{1cm}} = (y\underline{\hspace{0.8cm}})^2$         4) $k^2 + \dfrac{5}{6}k + \underline{\hspace{1cm}} = (k\underline{\hspace{0.8cm}})^2$

II) Solve by completing the square.

     1) $x^2 + 8x + 14 = 0$           3) $5n^2 + 25n + 45 = 0$

     2) $t^2 - 6t - 3 = 0$             4) $y^2 + \dfrac{1}{3}y - 1 = 0$

## 4. The Quadratic Formula

We will now see how completing the square can be used to derive a formula for solving a quadratic equation. Follow the steps from before to see how this works. Suppose we have an equation $ax^2 + bx + c = 0$ where $a \neq 0$. Then

$$ax^2 + bx + \cancel{c} = 0$$
$$\underline{\qquad -\cancel{c} \quad -c \qquad}$$
$$\frac{\cancel{a}x^2}{\cancel{a}} + \frac{bx}{a} = \frac{-c}{a}$$
$$x^2 + \frac{b}{a}x + \left(\frac{\frac{b}{a}}{2}\right)^2 = -\frac{c}{a} + \left(\frac{\frac{b}{a}}{2}\right)^2$$
$$x^2 + \frac{b}{a}x + \left(\frac{b}{2a}\right)^2 = -\frac{c}{a} + \left(\frac{b}{2a}\right)^2$$
$$x^2 + \frac{b}{a}x + \frac{b^2}{4a^2} = -\frac{c}{a} + \frac{b^2}{4a^2}$$

Observe that $-\dfrac{c}{a} + \dfrac{b^2}{4a^2} = -\dfrac{c}{a}\left(\dfrac{4a}{4a}\right) + \dfrac{b^2}{4a^2} = \dfrac{-4ac + b^2}{4a^2}$. Moreover, the factorization on the left hand side will contain $\dfrac{\frac{b}{a}}{2} = \dfrac{b}{2a}$. Hence,

$$\left(x + \frac{b}{2a}\right)^2 = \frac{b^2 - 4ac}{4a^2}$$ and by the Square Root Property (assuming that $b^2 - 4ac \geq 0$),

$$x + \frac{b}{2a} = \pm\sqrt{\frac{b^2 - 4ac}{4a^2}}.$$

Now,

$$\pm\sqrt{\frac{b^2 - 4ac}{4a^2}} = \pm\frac{\sqrt{b^2 - 4ac}}{\sqrt{4a^2}} = \pm\frac{\sqrt{b^2 - 4ac}}{\sqrt{(2a)^2}} = \pm\frac{\sqrt{b^2 - 4ac}}{|2a|} = \pm\frac{\sqrt{b^2 - 4ac}}{2\,|a|}.$$

If $a > 0$, then $2\,|a| = 2a$ and we have

$$\pm\sqrt{\frac{b^2 - 4ac}{4a^2}} = \pm\frac{\sqrt{b^2 - 4ac}}{2\,|a|} = \pm\frac{\sqrt{b^2 - 4ac}}{2a} = \frac{\pm\sqrt{b^2 - 4ac}}{2a}.$$

If $a < 0$, then $2\,|a| = -2a$ and we have

$$\pm\sqrt{\frac{b^2 - 4ac}{4a^2}} = \pm\frac{\sqrt{b^2 - 4ac}}{2\,|a|} = \pm\frac{\sqrt{b^2 - 4ac}}{-2a} = \pm\frac{\sqrt{b^2 - 4ac}}{2a} = \frac{\pm\sqrt{b^2 - 4ac}}{2a}.$$

In either case, we see that the '$\pm$' in the numerator will appear. Therefore, we have

$$x + \frac{\cancel{b}}{\cancel{2}a} = \frac{\pm\sqrt{b^2 - 4ac}}{2a}$$
$$\underline{\quad -\frac{\cancel{b}}{\cancel{2}a} \qquad\qquad -\frac{b}{2a} \quad}$$
$$x = -\frac{b}{2a} \pm \frac{\sqrt{b^2 - 4ac}}{2a}$$

$$x = \frac{-b \pm \sqrt{b^2 - 4ac}}{2a}$$

and so we now have our formula.

---

### The Quadratic Formula

If $ax^2 + bx + c = 0$ and $a \neq 0$, then $x = \dfrac{-b \pm \sqrt{b^2 - 4ac}}{2a}$ (provided that $b^2 - 4ac \geq 0$).

Observe that the numbers $a$, $b$ and $c$ which are used in the formula are just the coefficients of the terms of the equation when written in standard form. Moreover, the quantity $b^2 - 4ac$ underneath the square root symbol provides us with information about the roots of the equation.

**Definition 3:**  $b^2 - 4ac$ is called the **discriminant** of the quadratic equation $ax^2 + bx + c = 0$.

Let's see how the quadratic formula can be used to solve a quadratic equation. The first three equations we will solve will be equations which can be solved either by factoring or by the square root property. I want you to see that, even though the quadratic formula always gives us the solutions (when they exist), the other methods which we've learned shouldn't be forgotten. In fact, the other methods are easier to use (when possible, of course). After each of the equations is solved, we will see what is the relationship between the discriminant and the roots of the equation.

**Examples.** Solve the following by using the quadratic formula.

1) $x^2 + 5x + 4 = 0$

Notice that the equation is in standard form. We have $a = 1$, $b = 5$, and $c = 4$. First we plug the numbers into the formula. Afterwards, we simplify the discriminant and the denominator. Then we'll see if the radical in the numerator can be simplified. If it can, then we simplify it and try to simplify further (we will see this in this example, in fact). If not, we are finished.

$$x = \frac{-b \pm \sqrt{b^2 - 4ac}}{2a} = \frac{-5 \pm \sqrt{(5)^2 - 4(1)(4)}}{2(1)} = \frac{-5 \pm \sqrt{25 - 16}}{2}$$

$$= \frac{-5 \pm \sqrt{9}}{2} = \frac{-5 \pm 3}{2} = \left\{ \begin{array}{l} \dfrac{-5 + 3}{2} = \dfrac{-2}{2} = -1 \\[3mm] \dfrac{-5 - 3}{2} = \dfrac{-8}{2} = -4 \end{array} \right\}$$

Therefore, the set of roots is $\{-1, \ -4\}$.

Observe that we could've solved the equation by factoring:

$$x^2 + 5x + 4 = 0$$
$$(x + 4)(x + 1) = 0$$

$$\begin{array}{c|c} x + 4 = 0 & x + 1 = 0 \\ \ \ -4 \ \ -4 & \ \ -1 \ \ -4 \\ \hline x = -4 & x = -1 \end{array}$$

In my opinion, using the factoring method is easier. Another thing to observe is that the discriminant is $b^2 - 4ac = +9$, and the roots to the equation are real and unequal (or distinct). It turns out that the roots to a quadratic equation will always be **real and unequal** if the discriminant, $b^2 - 4ac$, is **positive**.

2) $x^2 - 14x + 49 = 0$

Notice that the equation is in standard form. We have $a = 1$, $b = -14$, and $c = 49$. Using the formula, we have:

$$x = \frac{-b \pm \sqrt{b^2 - 4ac}}{2a} = \frac{-(-14) \pm \sqrt{(-14)^2 - 4(1)(49)}}{2(1)} = \frac{14 \pm \sqrt{196 - 196}}{2}$$

$$= \frac{14 \pm \sqrt{0}}{2} = \frac{14 \pm 0}{2} = \left\{ \begin{array}{l} \dfrac{14 + 0}{2} = \dfrac{14}{2} = 7 \\[3mm] \dfrac{14 - 0}{2} = \dfrac{14}{2} = 7 \end{array} \right\}$$

Therefore, we have the double root $x = 7$.

Once again, observe that we could've solved the equation by factoring:

$$x^2 - 14x + 49 = 0$$
$$(x - 7)(x - 7) = 0$$

| $x - 7 = 0$ | $x - 7 = 0$ |
|---|---|
| $+7 \quad +7$ | $+7 \quad +7$ |
| $x = 7$ | $x = 7$ |

Using the factoring method seems easier to me. Observe that the discriminant is $b^2 - 4ac = 0$ and the equation has a real double root. It turns out that a quadratic equation will always have a real **double root** if the discriminant, $b^2 - 4ac$, is **zero**. Such a situation arises whenever the quadratic in the equation (in standard form) is a trinomial square.

3) $25x^2 + 9 = 0$

The equation is in standard form, $a = 25$, $b = 0$, and $c = 9$ ($b = 0$ since this equation is a special case in which there is no $x$ term present). Using the formula, we have:

$$x = \frac{-b \pm \sqrt{b^2 - 4ac}}{2a} = \frac{-(0) \pm \sqrt{(0)^2 - 4(25)(9)}}{2(25)}$$
$$= \frac{0 \pm \sqrt{0 - 900}}{50} = \frac{0 \pm \sqrt{-900}}{50}$$

Since $\sqrt{-900}$ is not a real number, there are no real roots for this equation.

Notice that this is a special case, as mentioned above. We could solve it without using the formula as follows:

$$25x^2 + 9 = 0$$
$$\underline{\qquad -9 \quad -9}$$
$$\frac{25x^2}{25} = \frac{-9}{25}$$
$$x^2 = -\frac{9}{25}$$

and so there are no real roots. This seems much simpler to me. The discriminant is $b^2 - 4ac = -900$ and the equation has no real roots. In general, if the discriminant, $b^2 - 4ac$, is a negative number, then the equation will not have any real roots. The reason for this is because the numerator of the formula contains the term $\sqrt{b^2 - 4ac}$. However, as we know, the square root of a negative number is not a real number.

Once again, the purpose of these three examples is to demonstrate that the formula should be your **last resort** to solving a quadratic equation. First, see if the equation can be solved by factoring. If not, see if it is the special case in which the linear term isn't present (in other words, $b = 0$). If that isn't the case either, you should use the quadratic formula or completing the square. Let's try some more:

4) $x^2 + 3x + 1 = 0$

Here, $a = 1$, $b = 3$, and $c = 1$.

$$x = \frac{-b \pm \sqrt{b^2 - 4ac}}{2a} = \frac{-3 \pm \sqrt{(3)^2 - 4(1)(1)}}{2(1)}$$
$$= \frac{-3 \pm \sqrt{9 - 4}}{2} = \frac{-3 \pm \sqrt{5}}{2}$$

Since $\sqrt{5}$ doesn't simplify, we are done. The set of roots is $\left\{ \dfrac{-3+\sqrt{5}}{2}, \ \dfrac{-3-\sqrt{5}}{2} \right\}$.

5) $y^2 + 4y - 1 = 0$

We have $a = 1$, $b = 4$, and $c = -1$.

$$
\begin{aligned}
y &= \frac{-b \pm \sqrt{b^2 - 4ac}}{2a} = \frac{-4 \pm \sqrt{(4)^2 - 4(1)(-1)}}{2(1)} \\
&= \frac{-4 \pm \sqrt{16 + 4}}{2} = \underbrace{\frac{-4 \pm \sqrt{20}}{2} = \frac{-4 \pm 2\sqrt{5}}{2}}_{\sqrt{20} = \sqrt{4}\sqrt{5} = 2\sqrt{5}} \\
&= -\frac{\overset{2}{\cancel{4}}}{\underset{1}{\cancel{2}}} \pm \frac{\overset{1}{\cancel{2}}\sqrt{5}}{\underset{1}{\cancel{2}}} = -2 \pm \sqrt{5}
\end{aligned}
$$

The set of roots is $\left\{ -2 - \sqrt{5}, \ -2 + \sqrt{5} \right\}$.

6) $3t^2 - t - 1 = 0$

We have $a = 3$, $b = -1$, and $c = -1$.

$$
\begin{aligned}
t &= \frac{-b \pm \sqrt{b^2 - 4ac}}{2a} = \frac{-(-1) \pm \sqrt{(-1)^2 - 4(3)(-1)}}{2(3)} \\
&= \frac{1 \pm \sqrt{1 + 12}}{6} = \frac{1 \pm \sqrt{13}}{6}
\end{aligned}
$$

The set of roots is $\left\{ \dfrac{1 + \sqrt{13}}{6}, \ \dfrac{1 - \sqrt{13}}{6} \right\}$.

7) $5p^2 - 2p - 4 = 0$

We have $a = 5$, $b = -2$, and $c = -4$.

$$
\begin{aligned}
p &= \frac{-b \pm \sqrt{b^2 - 4ac}}{2a} = \frac{-(-2) \pm \sqrt{(-2)^2 - 4(5)(-4)}}{2(5)} \\
&= \frac{2 \pm \sqrt{4 + 80}}{10} = \underbrace{\frac{2 \pm \sqrt{84}}{10} = \frac{2 \pm 2\sqrt{21}}{10}}_{\sqrt{84} = \sqrt{4}\sqrt{21} = 2\sqrt{21}} \\
&= \frac{\overset{1}{\cancel{2}}}{\underset{5}{\cancel{10}}} \pm \frac{\overset{1}{\cancel{2}}\sqrt{21}}{\underset{5}{\cancel{10}}} = \frac{1}{5} \pm \frac{\sqrt{21}}{5}
\end{aligned}
$$

The set of roots is $\left\{ \dfrac{1}{5} + \dfrac{\sqrt{21}}{5}, \ \dfrac{1}{5} - \dfrac{\sqrt{21}}{5} \right\}$ or, after combining, $\left\{ \dfrac{1 + \sqrt{21}}{5}, \ \dfrac{1 - \sqrt{21}}{5} \right\}$.

8) $9x^2 - 12x + 5 = 0$

We have $a = 9$, $b = -12$, and $c = 5$.

$$x = \frac{-b \pm \sqrt{b^2 - 4ac}}{2a} = \frac{-(-12) \pm \sqrt{(-12)^2 - 4(9)(5)}}{2(9)}$$

$$= \frac{12 \pm \sqrt{144 - 180}}{18} = \frac{12 \pm \sqrt{-36}}{18}$$

Since $\sqrt{-36}$ is not a real number, we conclude that there are no real roots for this equation.

9) $\frac{5}{7}y^2 + \frac{3}{14}y - \frac{1}{7} = 0$

Rather than playing around with fractions, let's clear them out. The LCM of 7 and 14 is 14. Therefore, we have the equivalent equation:

$$\frac{14}{1}\left(\frac{5}{7}y^2 + \frac{3}{14}y - \frac{1}{7}\right) = \frac{14}{1}(0)$$

$$\frac{\overset{2}{\cancel{14}}}{1}\left(\frac{5}{\underset{1}{7}}y^2\right) + \frac{\overset{1}{\cancel{14}}}{1}\left(\frac{3}{\underset{1}{\cancel{14}}}y\right) - \frac{\overset{2}{\cancel{14}}}{1}\left(\frac{1}{\underset{1}{7}}\right) = 0$$

$$10y^2 + 3y - 2 = 0$$

We have $a = 10$, $b = 3$, and $c = -2$.

$$y = \frac{-b \pm \sqrt{b^2 - 4ac}}{2a} = \frac{-3 \pm \sqrt{(3)^2 - 4(10)(-2)}}{2(10)}$$

$$= \frac{-3 \pm \sqrt{9 + 80}}{20} = \frac{-3 \pm \sqrt{89}}{20}$$

The set of roots is $\left\{\dfrac{-3 + \sqrt{89}}{20}, \dfrac{-3 - \sqrt{89}}{20}\right\}$.

10) $-7x - 8 = \dfrac{2}{x}$

To solve this rational equation, we will begin by clearing the fractions. To do this, we will multiply both sides of the equation by $x$. Once this is done, we'll get one side equal to 0.

$$x(-7x - 8) = x\left(\frac{2}{x}\right)$$

$$x(-7x) + x(-8) = \frac{\cancel{x}}{1}\left(\frac{2}{\cancel{x}}\right)$$

$$-7x^2 - 8x = 2$$

$$\underline{\qquad\qquad -2 \quad -2}$$

$$-7x^2 - 8x - 2 = 0$$

Now, $a = -7$, $b = -8$, and $c = -2$.

$$x = \frac{-b \pm \sqrt{b^2 - 4ac}}{2a} = \frac{-(-8) \pm \sqrt{(-8)^2 - 4(-7)(-2)}}{2(-7)}$$

$$= \frac{8 \pm \sqrt{64 - 56}}{-14} = \underbrace{\frac{8 \pm \sqrt{8}}{-14} = \frac{8 \pm 2\sqrt{2}}{-14}}_{\sqrt{8} = \sqrt{4}\sqrt{2} = 2\sqrt{2}}$$

$$= \frac{\overset{4}{\cancel{8}}}{\underset{7}{\cancel{-14}}} \pm \frac{\overset{1}{\cancel{2}}\sqrt{2}}{\underset{7}{\cancel{-14}}} = -\frac{4}{7} \pm \frac{\sqrt{2}}{-7} \text{ or just } -\frac{4}{7} \pm \frac{\sqrt{2}}{7}.$$

The set of roots is $\left\{ \dfrac{-4}{7} - \dfrac{\sqrt{2}}{7}, \dfrac{-4}{7} + \dfrac{\sqrt{2}}{7} \right\}$. Notice that both of these roots are valid since neither of them is 0 (why would $x = 0$ be invalid?). By the way, another approach to solving the equation $-7x^2 - 8x - 2 = 0$ is to multiply both sides by $-1$, thus eliminating the negative signs and obtaining $7x^2 + 8x + 2 = 0$. There will be fewer negative numbers to worry about. Try it.

**Try These (Set 7):**

I) Using the discriminant, determine whether or not the roots are real. If they are real, are they equal or unequal?

1) $x^2 + 8x + 3 = 0$      4) $3t^2 + 3t + 8 = 0$
2) $2y^2 - 4y + 2 = 0$      5) $25m^2 + 20m + 4 = 0$
3) $-5x^2 - x + 7 = 0$      6) $8x^2 - 6x + 3 = 0$

II) Solve using the quadratic formula.

1) $x^2 + 5x + 6 = 0$      4) $2k^2 - 6k + 3 = 0$
2) $x^2 - 10 = 0$      5) $7u^2 + 2u + 3 = 0$
3) $4y^2 + y - 2 = 0$      6) $\dfrac{1}{18}x^2 - \dfrac{1}{9}x - \dfrac{1}{2} = 0$

**Exercise 7.4**

In Exercises 1-26, solve each quadratic equation by factoring.

1. $x^2 - 7x + 12 = 0$    2. $x^2 + 7x + 6 = 0$    3. $y^2 - 9y + 14 = 0$    4. $y^2 - 12y + 32 = 0$

5. $t^2 + 5t - 36 = 0$    6. $t^2 + 8t - 33 = 0$    7. $2x^2 - 11x - 21 = 0$    8. $3x^2 - 25x - 18 = 0$

9. $4m^2 - 29m + 30 = 0$    10. $6m^2 - 19m + 14 = 0$    11. $x^2 + 5x = 0$    12. $x^2 + 16x = 0$

13. $3y^2 - 24y = 0$    14. $7y^2 - 21y = 0$    15. $a^2 - 9 = 0$    16. $b^2 - 25 = 0$

17. $4t^2 - 49 = 0$    18. $36s^2 - 121 = 0$    19. $p^2 = 5p$    20. $2q^2 = 16q$

21. $k(k + 15) = -36$    22. $l(l + 10) = -16$    23. $x(5x + 3) = 2$    24. $y(18y - 23) = 6$

25. $x - 10 = -\dfrac{21}{x}$    26. $a - 2 = \dfrac{48}{a}$

In Exercises 27-50, solve each quadratic equation by using the square root property.

27. $x^2 = 4$

28. $y^2 = 25$

29. $t^2 = 18$

30. $s^2 = 28$

31. $y^2 - 64 = 0$

32. $x^2 - 121 = 0$

33. $m^2 - 100 = 0$

34. $n^2 - 36 = 0$

35. $a^2 - 5 = 0$

36. $b^2 - 22 = 0$

37. $p^2 - 32 = 0$

38. $y^2 - 45 = 0$

39. $3k^2 - 48 = 0$

40. $5l^2 - 125 = 0$

41. $2x^2 - 150 = 0$

42. $7y^2 - 56 = 0$

43. $(x + 2)^2 = 3$

44. $(x + 5)^2 = 2$

45. $(a - 7)^2 = 4$

46. $(b - 12)^2 = 1$

47. $\left(m + \dfrac{1}{2}\right)^2 = \dfrac{1}{4}$

48. $\left(n + \dfrac{2}{3}\right)^2 = \dfrac{1}{9}$

49. $\left(x - \dfrac{1}{4}\right)^2 = \dfrac{3}{16}$

50. $\left(y - \dfrac{1}{5}\right)^2 = \dfrac{2}{25}$

In Exercises 51-62, complete the square of each binomial and factor the resulting trinomial square.

51. $x^2 + 4x$

52. $y^2 + 12y$

53. $t^2 - 6t$

54. $u^2 - 10u$

55. $p^2 + 3p$

56. $q^2 + q$

57. $m^2 - 9m$

58. $s^2 - 13s$

59. $y^2 + \dfrac{2}{3}y$

60. $x^2 + \dfrac{4}{5}x$

61. $k^2 - \dfrac{3}{7}k$

62. $l^2 - \dfrac{5}{9}l$

In Exercises 63-96, solve by using the quadratic formula.

63. $x^2 + 3x + 2 = 0$

64. $x^2 + 5x + 6 = 0$

65. $y^2 - 6y + 8 = 0$

66. $y^2 - 7y + 12 = 0$

67. $x^2 - x - 20 = 0$

68. $x^2 - 4x - 5 = 0$

69. $y^2 + 8y + 16 = 0$

70. $y^2 + 12y + 36 = 0$

71. $p^2 - 10p + 25 = 0$

72. $q^2 - 4q + 4 = 0$

73. $3y^2 + 10y + 8 = 0$

74. $4y^2 + 11y + 7 = 0$

75. $5t^2 + 4t = 0$

76. $2s^2 - 7s = 0$

77. $x^2 - 16 = 0$

78. $x^2 - 64 = 0$

79. $x^2 + 9 = 0$

80. $x^2 + 25 = 0$

81. $y^2 + 2y - 4 = 0$

82. $y^2 + 6y - 2 = 0$

83. $x^2 - 8x - 2 = 0$

84. $x^2 - 4x - 6 = 0$

85. $2t^2 + t - 2 = 0$

86. $5s^2 + 3s - 1 = 0$

87. $4m^2 - 2m - 3 = 0$

88. $6n^2 - 4n - 3 = 0$

89. $-2y^2 + 3y + 4 = 0$

90. $-7y^2 + 3y + 2 = 0$

91. $x^2 + 5x + 9 = 0$

92. $x^2 + 2x + 6 = 0$

93. $4m^2 - m + 6 = 0$

94. $12n^2 - 2n + 7 = 0$

95. $\dfrac{1}{4}x^2 + \dfrac{3}{2}x - 3 = 0$

96. $\dfrac{3}{10}x^2 - \dfrac{1}{5}x - 2 = 0$

In Exercises 97-105, use the discriminant to determine the nature of the roots of each quadratic equation.

97. $x^2 + 4x - 2 = 0$

98. $x^2 - 2x - 5 = 0$

99. $y^2 + y - 3 = 0$

100. $y^2 + 5y - 2 = 0$

101. $x^2 + 6x + 9 = 0$

102. $x^2 + 2x + 1 = 0$

103. $3x^2 - x - 4 = 0$

104. $6x^2 + 2x - 1 = 0$

105. $4t^2 - 20t + 25 = 0$

In Exercises 106-117, solve each quadratic equation by using the completing the square method.

106. $x^2 - 4x + 2 = 0$     107. $x^2 + 6x - 3 = 0$     108. $x^2 - 10x - 2 = 0$

109. $x^2 - 12x + 4 = 0$     110. $y^2 + 5y + 3 = 0$     111. $y^2 + 3y + 1 = 0$

112. $3x^2 + 3x - 14 = 0$     113. $4y^2 + 4y - 5 = 0$     114. $2m^2 - 4m + 1 = 0$

115. $3m^2 - 12m - 2 = 0$     116. $3k^2 + 5k + 2 = 0$     117. $5k^2 + k + 4 = 0$

## Section 7.5 Complex Numbers and Quadratic Equations with Negative Discriminant

In Section 7.3, we learned how to solve quadratic equations whose discriminant is either positive or zero. More precisely, if $ax^2 + bx + c = 0$ and $a \neq 0$, then we are guaranteed to obtain real solutions whenever $b^2 - 4ac > 0$ or $b^2 - 4ac = 0$. However, the quadratic equations for which $b^2 - 4ac < 0$ do not have real solutions. In this section, we will learn how to deal with such equations. We will look at a new number system which contains square roots of negative numbers in it. This number system is called the set of **complex numbers**. We begin by defining a complex number. We will then learn how to do arithmetic and algebra in this number system. After we get used to these new numbers, we will solve quadratic equations which have a negative discriminant.

Let's take a look at the equation $x^2 + 1 = 0$. Since this is the special case of a quadratic equation for which $b = 0$, we can solve it by first getting $x^2$ by itself, then applying the square root property. Doing so, we'll obtain:

$$\begin{array}{c} x^2 + \cancel{1} = 0 \\ \underline{-\cancel{1} \quad -1} \\ x^2 \quad = -1 \end{array}$$

Now we are stuck, since the square root property does not permit us to have $x^2$ equaling a negative number. Let's now imagine that there **is** such a thing as the square root of a negative number. We know that it is not a real number, but maybe some brand new number. Then our square root property can be reformulated to allow us to solve this equation. We would then obtain:

$$x^2 = -1$$
$$x = \pm\sqrt{-1}$$

Now all we need to do is to give a name to this new number, $\sqrt{-1}$. We write $i = \sqrt{-1}$ and call it the **imaginary unit**. Notice that $i$ has the property that $i^2 = -1$, since $i$ is a solution to the equation $x^2 = -1$.

Going back to our example, we know that the equation $x^2 + 1 = 0$ has no real roots (Observe that $b^2 - 4ac = -3$). However, in terms of this imaginary unit, $i$, we have $x = \pm\sqrt{-1} = \pm i$. Therefore, the roots to this equation can be expressed in terms of the imaginary unit. We can write the set of roots as $\{-i, \, i\}$.

Now, what we would like to do is figure out a way of writing the square root of **any** negative number in terms of the imaginary unit. To do so, we need a definition.

**Definition 4:** Suppose $n > 0$. Then the **principal square root** of $-n$, written as $\sqrt{-n}$, is $\sqrt{-n} = \sqrt{n}i$.

In other words, if $n > 0$, we can think of this as

$$\sqrt{-n} = \sqrt{n(-1)} = \sqrt{n}\sqrt{-1} = \sqrt{n}i.$$

Notice that the $i$ **does not** lie underneath the square root symbol. Using this definition, we can write the square root of **any** negative number in terms of the imaginary unit, $i$.

**Examples.** Express in terms of $i$.

1) $\sqrt{-4} = \sqrt{4}\, i = 2i$

2) $\sqrt{-36} = \sqrt{36}\, i = 6i$

3) $\sqrt{-81} = \sqrt{81}\, i = 9i$

4) $\sqrt{-\dfrac{9}{25}} = \sqrt{\dfrac{9}{25}}\, i = \dfrac{3}{5}i$

5) $\sqrt{-27} = \sqrt{27}\, i = 3\sqrt{3}\, i$

6) $\sqrt{-15} = \sqrt{15}\, i = \sqrt{15}\, i$

**Try These (Set 8):**  Express in terms of $i$.

1) $\sqrt{-16}$

2) $\sqrt{-121}$

3) $\sqrt{-54}$

4) $\sqrt{-\dfrac{1}{100}}$

5) $\sqrt{-125}$

6) $\sqrt{-19}$

By taking sums of real multiples of $i$, we develop a new number system, called the set of **complex numbers**.

**Definition 5:** The set of numbers of the form $a + bi$, where $a$ and $b$ are real numbers, is called the set of **complex numbers**. If $w = a + bi$ is a complex number, then we call $a$ the **real part of** $w$ and we call $b$ the **imaginary part** of $w$. We say that the complex number $a + bi$ is in **standard form**.

If a complex number $w = a + bi$ has imaginary part $b = 0$, then we can write $w = a + 0i = a$. Since $a$ is a real number, $w$ is also a real number and so the set of real numbers is contained in the set of complex numbers. In other words, every real number can be thought of as a complex number whose imaginary part is zero.

If the complex number $w = a + bi$ has imaginary part $b \neq 0$ then we call $w$ an **imaginary number**. Furthermore, if $a = 0$ and $b \neq 0$, then $w = bi$ is called a **pure imaginary number**.

**Examples.** Find the real and imaginary parts of the complex numbers.

1) $7 + 3i$ has real part 7 and imaginary part 3.

2) $-4 + 8i$ has real part $-4$ and imaginary part 8.

3) $1 = 1 + 0i$ has real part 1 and imaginary part 0.

4) $-\dfrac{2}{5}i = 0 + \left(-\dfrac{2}{5}\right)i$ has real part 0 and imaginary part $-\dfrac{2}{5}$ (hence, $-\dfrac{2}{5}i$ is an imaginary number).

5) $0 = 0 + 0i$ has real part 0 and imaginary part 0.

**Try These (Set 9):** Find the real and imaginary parts of the complex numbers.

1) $2 + 3i$            3) $-12$            5) $-i$

2) $4 - 8i$          4) $\dfrac{-15}{16} + \dfrac{25}{4}i$        6) $10$

Now that we have the set of complex numbers at our disposal, we would like to know how to do arithmetic with them. As we will see, working with complex numbers is just like working with polynomials if you think of $i$ as being a variable. Moreover, the commutative and associative properties of addition and multiplication hold for complex numbers the same way as they do for the real numbers. Let's begin our arithmetic by learning how to add and subtract complex numbers. We define these operations in the following way:

---

**Addition and Subtraction of Complex Numbers**

$$(a + bi) + (c + di) = (a + c) + (b + d)i$$
$$(a + bi) - (c + di) = (a - c) + (b - d)i$$

---

So, all you need to do is combine the real parts together, then combine the imaginary parts together. By using the definition of subtraction, the following can be proven:

**Theorem:** If $a$, $b$, $s$ and $t$ are real numbers and $a + bi = s + ti$, then $a = s$ and $b = t$.

In other words, two complex numbers are equal if and only if they have the same real parts and the same imaginary parts. From this, it follows that the commutative and associative properties for addition hold. If $u$, $v$ and $w$ are complex numbers, then we have:

---

**Commutativity:** $u + v = v + u$
**Associativity:** $(u + v) + w = u + (v + w)$

---

**Examples.** Combine.

1) $(7 + 2i) + (-4 + 3i) = (7 + (-4)) + (2 + 3)i = 3 + 5i$

2) $(-5 - 3i) + (2 - 7i) = (-5 + 2) + (-3 + -7)i = -3 - 10i$

3) $(9 - i) - (16 + 5i) = (9 - 16) + (-1 - 5)i = -7 - 6i$

4) $(-8 + 4i) - (-3 + 4i) = (-8 - (-3)) + (4 - 4)i = -5 + 0i = -5$

**Try These (Set 10):** Combine.

1) $(1 + 8i) + (4 - 5i)$        3) $(-3 + i) - (9 - 17i)$        5) $6i - (-1 + 4i)$

2) $(-12 - 16i) + (10 - 14i)$    4) $\left(\dfrac{4}{5} - 4i\right) - \left(-\dfrac{3}{5} + 2i\right)$    6) $\left(\dfrac{1}{3} + \dfrac{2}{7}i\right) + 3$

Let's take a look at multiplication of complex numbers. How should we multiply $(a + bi)(c + di)$? Well, if you think of $i$ as a variable, say $x$, then notice that this product becomes

$$(a + bx)(c + dx) = ac + adx + bxc + bdx^2$$
$$= ac + (ad + bc)x + bdx^2$$

by our friend, the FOIL method. The same thing will work for our complex numbers. Hence, remembering that $i^2 = -1$, we get:

$$
\boxed{
\begin{aligned}
&\textbf{Multiplication of Complex Numbers} \\[4pt]
(a + bi)(c + di) &= ac + adi + bic + bdi^2 \\
&= ac + (ad + bc)i + bd(-1) \\
&= (ac - bd) + (ad + bc)i
\end{aligned}
}
$$

This shows us how to multiply two complex numbers, but what is more important than the knowing formula is knowing the method (FOIL in this case). As for addition, the multiplication of complex numbers satisfies the commutative and associative properties. If $u$, $v$ and $w$ are complex numbers, then we have:

$$
\boxed{
\begin{aligned}
\textbf{Commutativity:} \quad & uv = vu \\
\textbf{Associativity:} \quad & (uv)w = u(vw)
\end{aligned}
}
$$

Let us look at a variety of examples which involve multiplication. Remember that if you get stuck, you should think of the techniques that you learned for polynomials.

**Examples.** Multiply.

1) $\underbrace{3i(5 + 2i) = 3i(5) + 3i(2i)}_{\text{Distribute.}} = 15i + 6i^2 = 15i + 6\underbrace{(-1)}_{i^2 = -1} = 15i - 6$ or $-6 + 15i$

2) $(4 + 6i)(-1 + 5i) = -4 + \underbrace{20i - 6i}_{\text{Combine.}} + 30i^2 = -4 + 14i + 30\underbrace{(-1)}_{i^2 = -1} = -4 + 14i - 30 = -34 + 14i$

3) $(-3 - 7i)^2 = (-3 - 7i)(-3 - 7i) = 9 + 21i + 21i + 49i^2 = 9 + 42i + 49(-1) = \underbrace{-40}_{9-49} + 42i$

4) $\sqrt{-9} \cdot \sqrt{-4} = \sqrt{9}i \cdot \sqrt{4}i = 3i \cdot 2i = 6i^2 = 6(-1) = -6$

Notice that I did **not** multiply it as $\sqrt{-9} \cdot \sqrt{-4} = \sqrt{(-9)(-4)} = \sqrt{36} = 6$, giving us a different answer. We don't have any property which says that we can multiply square roots when the radicand is negative. However, by our definition of the principal square root of a negative number, we can extract $\sqrt{-1}$ from a square root. That's why the first way that I worked it out **is** the correct way.

5) $\sqrt{-6} \cdot \sqrt{-5} = \sqrt{6}i \cdot \sqrt{5}i = \sqrt{30}i^2 = \sqrt{30}(-1) = -\sqrt{30}$

**Try These (Set 11):** Multiply.

1) $6i(-2 + 5i)$             3) $(-8 + i)^2$             5) $\sqrt{-3} \cdot \sqrt{-3}$

2) $(2 - 7i)(2 + 6i)$          4) $(9 - 4i)(9 + 4i)$        6) $\sqrt{-12} \cdot \sqrt{-5}$

## Nonnegative Integer Powers of $i$

An interesting phenomenon takes place when taking positive integer powers of $i$. Let's take a look. We know that $i^1 = i$ and $i^2 = -1$. Moreover, one can show just as for real numbers that $i^0 = 1$. Now, notice that $i^3 = i \cdot i^2 = i(-1) = -i$ and $i^4 = i^2 \cdot i^2 = (-1)(-1) = 1$. So far we have

$$i^0 = 1$$
$$i^1 = i$$
$$i^2 = -1$$
$$i^3 = -i$$
$$i^4 = 1$$

If $m$ is any whole number, then $i^{4m} = \left(i^4\right)^m = 1^m = 1$. This means that if we want to compute $i^n$ for some whole number, $n$, what we should do is divide $n$ by 4 and use the quotient and remainder to rewrite $n$. It is the remainder that will give us what we want, since the remainder will be either 0, 1, 2 or 3 and we know what $i^0$, $i^1$, $i^2$ and $i^3$ equal. Let me demonstrate.

**Examples.** Simplify.

1) $\underbrace{i^7 = \left(i^4\right)^1 \cdot i^3}_{7 \div 4 = 1 \ R3} = 1^1 \cdot i^3 = i^3 = -i$

2) $\underbrace{i^{25} = \left(i^4\right)^6 \cdot i^1}_{25 \div 4 = 6 \ R1} = 1^6 \cdot i^1 = i^1 = i$

3) $\underbrace{i^{22} = \left(i^4\right)^5 \cdot i^2}_{22 \div 4 = 5 \ R2} = 1^5 \cdot i^2 = i^2 = -1$

4) $\underbrace{i^{56} = \left(i^4\right)^{14} \cdot i^0}_{56 \div 4 = 14 \ R0} = 1^{14} \cdot i^0 = i^0 = 1$

**Try These (Set 12):** Simplify.

1) $i^7$
2) $i^{20}$
3) $i^{34}$
4) $i^{47}$
5) $i^5 \cdot \left(i^3\right)^9$
6) $\left(i^2\right)\left(i^4\right)\left(i^{15}\right)\left(i^{12}\right)$

We will now see how to divide two complex numbers. A tool which will help us with this is actually something we've seen before when learning how to rationalize the numerator (or denominator) of a fraction containing a square root. You may want to look back at Section 5.1.6 for a little review.

**Definition 6:** Let $w = a + bi$ be a complex number written in standard form. The **conjugate** of $w$, written as $\overline{w}$, is the complex number $\overline{w} = a - bi$.

In particular, if $a = 0$ and $b$ is any real number, then $\overline{bi} = -bi$.

Notice that $w \cdot \overline{w} = (a + bi)(a - bi) = a^2 + abi - bai - b^2 i^2 = a^2 - b^2(-1) = a^2 + b^2$. This shows that when you multiply a complex number by its conjugate, the product will be a real number (the $i$ disappears).

Observe that to get this product, all we need to do is square the real and imaginary parts of $w$ and add them up. This is a nice short cut!

To divide $a + bi$ by $c + di$, you write the division problem in fraction form. Next, you multiply the numerator and denominator of the fraction by the conjugate of the denominator. As mentioned above, this gets rid of the $i$ in the denominator, allowing us to write the quotient in standard form.

$$
\boxed{
\begin{aligned}
\textbf{Division of Complex Numbers} \\[4pt]
\frac{a+bi}{c+di} &= \left(\frac{a+bi}{c+di}\right)\left(\frac{c-di}{c-di}\right) = \frac{(a+bi)(c-di)}{(c+di)(c-di)} \\[6pt]
&= \frac{ac-adi+bci-bdi^2}{c^2-d^2i^2} = \frac{(ac+bd)+(bc-ad)i}{c^2+d^2} \\[6pt]
&= \frac{ac+bd}{c^2+d^2} + \frac{bc-ad}{c^2+d^2}\, i \quad \text{(standard form)}
\end{aligned}
}
$$

Don't drive yourself crazy memorizing this formula! Understand the technique involved. Let's try some.

**Examples.** Divide and write each answer in standard form.

1) $\dfrac{2+3i}{1-2i} = \left(\dfrac{2+3i}{1-2i}\right)\left(\dfrac{1+2i}{1+2i}\right) = \dfrac{(2+3i)(1+2i)}{(1-2i)(1+2i)} = \underbrace{\dfrac{2+4i+3i+\overbrace{6i^2}^{-6}}{(1)^2+(2)^2}}_{\text{I'm using the 'short cut'.}} = \dfrac{-4+7i}{5} = -\dfrac{4}{5}+\dfrac{7}{5}i$

2) $\dfrac{-5+i}{-4-i} = \left(\dfrac{-5+i}{-4-i}\right)\left(\dfrac{-4+i}{-4+i}\right) = \dfrac{(-5+i)(-4+i)}{(-4-i)(-4+i)} = \dfrac{20-5i-4i+\overbrace{i^2}^{-1}}{(-4)^2+(1)^2} = \dfrac{19-9i}{17} = \dfrac{19}{17}+\dfrac{-9}{17}i$

3) $\dfrac{4+5i}{-3i} = \left(\dfrac{4+5i}{-3i}\right)\left(\dfrac{3i}{3i}\right) = \dfrac{(4+5i)(3i)}{-9i^2} = \dfrac{12i+\overbrace{15i^2}^{-15}}{-9(-1)} = \dfrac{-15+12i}{9} = \dfrac{-15}{9}+\dfrac{12i}{9} = \dfrac{-5}{3}+\dfrac{4}{3}i$

Observe that we simplified our answer by canceling out a 3 in both fractions. This occured because we initially multiplied the numerator and denominator by $3i$, when all we really needed was the $i$. In other words, whenever the denominator is of the form $bi$, where $b \neq 0$ is any real number, then multiply the numerator and denominator by just $i$ rather than the conjugate, $-bi$. We could do this example in the following, simpler, way:

$$
\dfrac{4+5i}{-3i} = \left(\dfrac{4+5i}{-3i}\right)\left(\dfrac{i}{i}\right) = \dfrac{(4+5i)(i)}{-3i^2} = \dfrac{4i+\overbrace{5i^2}^{-5}}{(-3)(-1)} = \dfrac{-5+4i}{3} = \dfrac{-5}{3}+\dfrac{4i}{3}
$$

4) $\dfrac{1}{i} = \left(\dfrac{1}{i}\right)\left(\dfrac{-i}{-i}\right) = \dfrac{1(-i)}{-i^2} = \dfrac{-i}{-(-1)} = \dfrac{-i}{1} = -i$

**Try These (Set 13):** Divide and write each answer in standard form.

1) $\dfrac{4+i}{2+3i}$  2) $\dfrac{1-7i}{5+2i}$  3) $\dfrac{-8i}{-1+5i}$  4) $\dfrac{6-8i}{12i}$

## Solving Quadratic Equations with Negative Discriminant

We now come to the main attraction, solving quadratic equations which have a negative discriminant. For starters, let's restate the square root property in which squares of real numbers can be negative.

---

### The Square Root Property (In General)

If $X^2 = n$ for **any** real number, $n$, then $X = \pm\sqrt{n}$.

---

Recall that the completing the square technique for solving a quadratic equation, as well as the quadratic formula, uses the square root property. With this generalization, we can now solve **ANY** quadratic equation with real coefficients, regardless of its discriminant. As we learned in Section 7.4, a quadratic equation whose discriminant is negative will not have real roots. In fact, it has complex roots, since we will have the square root of a negative. To summarize, we have

---

### Notes on the Discriminant

If $ax^2 + bx + c = 0$, $a \neq 0$ and $a$, $b$ and $c$ are real numbers, then the roots will be
1. real and unequal if $b^2 - 4ac > 0$.
2. real and equal if $b^2 - 4ac = 0$.
3. both complex if $b^2 - 4ac < 0$.

---

When complex roots occur, they always come as **conjugate pairs,** that is, one is of the form $a + bi$ and the other is of the form $a - bi$ where $a$ and $b$ are real numbers and $b \neq 0$.

Let's solve some quadratic equations whose roots are complex.

**Examples.** Solve the following equations. Express the roots in standard form.

1) $36x^2 + 25 = 0$

Notice that the quadratic is not factorable. However, this is the special case where $b = 0$. Therefore, we will solve for $x^2$ first, then apply the Square Root Property.

$$36x^2 + 25 = 0$$
$$\underline{\phantom{36x^2}-25 \quad -25}$$
$$\frac{36x^2}{36} = \frac{-25}{36}$$
$$x^2 = -\frac{25}{36}$$
$$x = \pm\sqrt{-\frac{25}{36}} = \pm\frac{5}{6}i$$

Therefore, the set of roots is $\left\{-\dfrac{5}{6}i, \dfrac{5}{6}i\right\}$. Notice that the roots are conjugates of each other.

2) $y^2 + 2y + 2 = 0$ (by completing the square)

If you need to remind yourself of the steps, now's the time to do it (see Section 7.4).

$$y^2 + 2y + \cancel{2} = 0$$
$$\underline{\qquad -\cancel{2} \quad -2}$$
$$y^2 + 2y = -2$$

Now, $b = 2$ and so the number which will complete the square is $\left(\dfrac{b}{2}\right)^2 = \left(\dfrac{2}{2}\right)^2 = (1)^2 = 1$, while the number which goes into the factorization is $\dfrac{b}{2} = \dfrac{2}{2} = 1$. Therefore,

$$y^2 + 2y + \underline{1} = -2 + \underline{1}$$

$$(y+1)^2 = -1$$

and, by the Square Root Property, we obtain

$$y + \cancel{1} = \pm\sqrt{-1}$$
$$\underline{\quad -\cancel{1} \qquad\qquad -1}$$
$$y = -1 \pm \sqrt{-1}$$
$$= -1 \pm i$$

The set of roots is $\{-1 - i, \ -1 + i\}$. Notice, again, that the roots are conjugates of each other. By the way, you can verify that these roots really do check out. Let's try it. For the solution $y = -1 - i$, we have

$$(-1-i)^2 + 2(-1-i) + 2 =$$
$$(-1-i)(-1-i) + 2(-1-i) + 2 =$$
$$1 + i + i + i^2 - 2 - 2i + 2 =$$
$$1 + 2i - 1 - 2 - 2i + 2 = 0$$

and, for the solution $y = -1 + i$, we have

$$(-1+i)^2 + 2(-1+i) + 2 =$$
$$(-1+i)(-1+i) + 2(-1+i) + 2 =$$
$$1 - i - i + i^2 - 2 + 2i + 2 =$$
$$1 - 2i - 1 - 2 + 2i + 2 = 0$$

Therefore, they both check out.

3) $-t^2 + 3t - 9 = 0$ (using the quadratic formula)

We have $a = -1$, $b = 3$ and $c = -9$.

$$t = \frac{-b \pm \sqrt{b^2 - 4ac}}{2a} = \frac{-3 \pm \sqrt{(3)^2 - 4(-1)(-9)}}{2(-1)}$$

$$= \frac{-3 \pm \sqrt{9 - 36}}{-2} = \underbrace{\frac{-3 \pm \sqrt{-25}}{-2} = \frac{-3 \pm 5i}{-2}}_{\sqrt{-25}=\sqrt{25}i=5i}$$

$$= \frac{-3}{-2} \pm \frac{5}{-2}i = \frac{3}{2} \pm \frac{5}{2}i$$

The set of roots is $\left\{ \dfrac{3}{2} - \dfrac{5}{2}i, \ \dfrac{3}{2} + \dfrac{5}{2}i \right\}$.

4) $5x^2 + x + 5 = 0$ (using the quadratic formula)

We are given that $a = 5$, $b = 1$ and $c = 5$.

$$
\begin{aligned}
x &= \frac{-b \pm \sqrt{b^2 - 4ac}}{2a} = \frac{-1 \pm \sqrt{(1)^2 - 4(5)(5)}}{2(5)} \\[2mm]
&= \frac{-1 \pm \sqrt{1 - 100}}{10} = \underbrace{\frac{-1 \pm \sqrt{-99}}{10} = \frac{-1 \pm 3\sqrt{11}\,i}{10}}_{\sqrt{-99} = \sqrt{99}\,i = \sqrt{9}\sqrt{11}\,i = 3\sqrt{11}\,i} \\[2mm]
&= -\frac{1}{10} \pm \frac{3\sqrt{11}}{10}i
\end{aligned}
$$

The set of roots is $\left\{ -\dfrac{1}{10} - \dfrac{3\sqrt{11}}{10}i, \ -\dfrac{1}{10} + \dfrac{3\sqrt{11}}{10}i \right\}$.

5) $8x^2 - 7x + 3 = 0$ (using the quadratic formula)

We have $a = 8$, $b = -7$ and $c = 3$.

$$
\begin{aligned}
x &= \frac{-b \pm \sqrt{b^2 - 4ac}}{2a} = \frac{-(-7) \pm \sqrt{(-7)^2 - 4(8)(3)}}{2(8)} \\[2mm]
&= \frac{7 \pm \sqrt{49 - 96}}{16} = \underbrace{\frac{7 \pm \sqrt{-47}}{16} = \frac{7 \pm \sqrt{47}\,i}{16}}_{\sqrt{-47} = \sqrt{47}\,i} \\[2mm]
&= \frac{7}{16} \pm \frac{\sqrt{47}}{16}i
\end{aligned}
$$

The set of roots is $\left\{ \dfrac{7}{16} - \dfrac{\sqrt{47}}{16}i, \ \dfrac{7}{16} + \dfrac{\sqrt{47}}{16}i \right\}$.

**Try These (Set 14):** Solve the following using any method.

1) $6x^2 + 24 = 0$            3) $9p^2 + 72 = 0$            5) $t^2 + t + 1 = 0$
2) $-3y^2 - 21 = 0$           4) $2m^2 - 4m + 3 = 0$        6) $-7x^2 + 2x - 1 = 0$

### Exercise 7.5

In Exercises 1-16, express each radical in terms of $i$.

1. $\sqrt{-4}$            2. $\sqrt{-9}$            3. $\sqrt{-49}$            4. $\sqrt{-121}$

5. $\sqrt{-144}$          6. $\sqrt{-100}$          7. $\sqrt{-32}$            8. $\sqrt{-50}$

9. $\sqrt{-45}$           10. $\sqrt{-28}$          11. $\sqrt{-30}$           12. $\sqrt{-70}$

13. $\sqrt{-55}$          14. $\sqrt{-21}$          15. $\sqrt{-200}$          16. $\sqrt{-90}$

In Exercises 17-34, combine and write the answer in standard form.

17. $(1 + 4i) + (2 + 3i)$    18. $(5 + 5i) + (6 + i)$    19. $(3 - 7i) + (8 + 9i)$    20. $(9 + 12i) + (18 - 16i)$

21. $(-12 - 15i) + (4 - i)$    22. $(-6 + 11i) + (-9 - 27i)$    23. $(5 + 10i) - (3 + 6i)$    24. $(2 + 8i) - (8 + 3i)$

25. $(-4 + 6i) - (2 - 7i)$    26. $(8 - 12i) - (-5 + 14i)$    27. $(-1 - 7i) - (-17 - 3i)$

28. $(-13 - i) - (-16 - 19i)$    29. $(9 + 5i) + (3 - 18i) + (7 - 12i)$    30. $(2 - 9i) + (11 - 14i) + (8 + 10i)$

31. $(4 - 3i) + (-6 + 5i) - (7 - 4i)$    32. $(-1 - 8i) + (10 + 2i) - (-6 + 16i)$

33. $(2 + 2i) - (-1 + 5i) - (9 - 3i)$    34. $(1 - 7i) - (3 - 6i) - (-1 + i)$

In Exercises 35-62, multiply and write the answer in standard form.

35. $(3i)(7i)$    36. $(5i)(6i)$    37. $(-2i)(9i)$    38. $(-8i)(8i)$

39. $(-4i)(-11i)$    40. $(-3i)(-12i)$    41. $4(-1 + 2i)$    42. $7(-2 + 6i)$

43. $-8(3 - 6i)$    44. $-10(4 - 12i)$    45. $2i(1 + 6i)$    46. $9i(2 + 4i)$

47. $8i(7 - 5i)$    48. $10i(3 - 2i)$    49. $-i(12 - 13i)$    50. $-i(8 - 15i)$

51. $(1 + 5i)(2 + 3i)$    52. $(1 + 4i)(6 + i)$    53. $(7 - 2i)(4 + 5i)$    54. $(14 + 4i)(2 - i)$

55. $(6 - 8i)(3 - i)$    56. $(4 - i)(9 - 10i)$    57. $(2 + 6i)^2$    58. $(3 + 7i)^2$

59. $(1 - 5i)^2$    60. $(9 - 3i)^2$    61. $(4 + 9i)(4 - 9i)$    62. $(3 - 11i)(3 + 11i)$

In Exercises 63-70, compute the power of $i$.

63. $i^2$    64. $i^3$    65. $i^4$    66. $i^8$

67. $i^{15}$    68. $i^{21}$    69. $i^{39}$    70. $i^{34}$

In Exercises 71-82, divide and write the answer in standard form.

71. $\dfrac{1 + 2i}{3 + i}$    72. $\dfrac{2 + 5i}{2 + i}$    73. $\dfrac{3 - 7i}{3 + 2i}$    74. $\dfrac{5 - 4i}{5 + 2i}$

75. $\dfrac{10 + 3i}{2 - 3i}$    76. $\dfrac{12 + 2i}{8 - i}$    77. $\dfrac{-5 - 6i}{4 - i}$    78. $\dfrac{-2 + 9i}{1 - i}$

79. $\dfrac{-8 + i}{-7 + 4i}$    80. $\dfrac{-6 + 3i}{-5 + 2i}$    81. $\dfrac{i}{11 + i}$    82. $\dfrac{3i}{5 - i}$

In Exercises 83-110, solve the quadratic equations and express the roots in standard form.

83. $x^2 + 4 = 0$    84. $y^2 + 25 = 0$    85. $a^2 + 121 = 0$    86. $b^2 + 49 = 0$

87. $9y^2 + 25 = 0$    88. $100x^2 + 1 = 0$    89. $p^2 + 12 = 0$    90. $q^2 + 32 = 0$

91. $m^2 + 27 = 0$    92. $n^2 + 75 = 0$    93. $x^2 + 300 = 0$    94. $y^2 + 40 = 0$

95. $4p^2 + 28 = 0$      96. $5q^2 + 50 = 0$      97. $3s^2 + 24 = 0$      98. $6t^2 + 120 = 0$

99. $x^2 + x + 1 = 0$      100. $x^2 - x + 1 = 0$      101. $y^2 + 3y + 9 = 0$      102. $y^2 - 4y + 16 = 0$

103. $3t^2 - 2t + 1 = 0$      104. $4t^2 - 2t + 1 = 0$      105. $5m^2 - 2m + 2 = 0$      106. $2n^2 + 2n + 5 = 0$

107. $-2x^2 + 2x - 3 = 0$    108. $-x^2 + 5x - 1 = 0$    109. $-4y^2 + 4y - 5 = 0$    110. $-3z^2 + 2z - 7 = 0$

---

## END OF CHAPTER 7   QUIZ

1. Solve for $x$:   $2x + 7 = 13$
   a) $x = 3$    b) $x = 10$    c) $x = -3$    d) $x = \dfrac{5}{2}$    e) $x = \dfrac{10}{3}$

2. Solve for $x$:   $-4x + 15 = 8x - 9$
   a) $x = 4$    b) $x = -2$    c) $x = 2$    d) $x = -3$    e) $x = 6$

3. Solve for $y$:   $-y + 3(2y - 6) = 27$
   a) $y = \dfrac{45}{7}$    b) $y = -9$    c) $y = 9$    d) $y = \dfrac{33}{5}$    e) $y = \dfrac{10}{9}$

4. Solve for $k$:   $\dfrac{7}{2k - 5} = \dfrac{8}{k + 7}$
   a) $k = \dfrac{4}{3}$    b) $k = \dfrac{80}{9}$    c) $k = -\dfrac{89}{9}$    d) $k = \dfrac{89}{9}$    e) no solution

5. Solve for $x$:   $\dfrac{4}{5}x - 2 = \dfrac{3}{10}x + 3$
   a) $x = \dfrac{25}{2}$    b) $x = 10$    c) $x = -10$    d) $x = \dfrac{25}{7}$    e) $x = 5$

6. Solve for $a$:   $\dfrac{7}{4a} + \dfrac{9}{8} = \dfrac{11}{12a}$
   a) $a = -\dfrac{20}{9}$    b) $a = \dfrac{20}{27}$    c) $a = -\dfrac{20}{21}$    d) $a = -\dfrac{20}{27}$    e) $a = 8$

7. Solve for $t$:   $\dfrac{2}{t + 4} - \dfrac{4}{t + 3} = \dfrac{1}{t^2 + 7t + 12}$
   a) $t = \dfrac{11}{2}$    b) $t = -11$    c) $t = -5$    d) $t = -\dfrac{11}{2}$    e) no solution

8. Solve for $x$:   $\dfrac{3}{x - 4} + \dfrac{3}{x} = \dfrac{12}{x^2 - 4x}$
   a) $x = 4$    b) $x = -4$    c) $x = -3$    d) $x = 2$    e) no solution

9. Solve for $x$:  $8x - 3y = 2$

a) $x = \dfrac{3y + 2}{8}$     b) $x = \dfrac{2 - 3y}{8}$     c) $x = \dfrac{8}{2 + 3y}$     d) $x = -3y + \dfrac{1}{8}$     e) $x = 24y + 16$

10. Solve for $y$:  $2y - 7(3y - x) = 6x + 2$

a) $y = \dfrac{-x + 2}{23}$     b) $y = \dfrac{1}{19}x - \dfrac{2}{19}$     c) $y = 19x - 38$     d) $y = -\dfrac{13}{19}x - \dfrac{2}{19}$     e) $y = -x + 21$

11. Solve for $p$:  $mp + 3p = 9$

a) $p = \dfrac{m + 3}{9}$     b) $p = \dfrac{m}{3}$     c) $p = \dfrac{9}{m + 3}$     d) $p = \dfrac{3}{m}$     e) $p = \dfrac{9 - mp}{3}$

12. Solve for $k$:  $\dfrac{10}{k} + \dfrac{n}{3} = \dfrac{5}{6}$

a) $k = \dfrac{n}{20}$     b) $k = \dfrac{5 - 2n}{60}$     c) $k = 12 + \dfrac{2kn}{5}$     d) $k = \dfrac{60}{5 + 2n}$     e) $k = \dfrac{60}{5 - 2n}$

13. Solve for $x$:  $x^2 + 4x - 32 = 0$

a) $x = -4, x = 8$     b) $x = 4, x = 8$     c) $x = -4, x = -8$     d) $x = 4, x = -8$     e) no real roots

14. Solve for $y$:  $10y^2 + 11y - 6 = 0$

a) $y = -\dfrac{2}{5}, y = -\dfrac{3}{2}$     b) $y = \dfrac{2}{5}, y = -\dfrac{3}{2}$     c) $y = \dfrac{2}{5}, y = \dfrac{3}{2}$     d) $y = -\dfrac{2}{5}, y = \dfrac{3}{2}$     e) no real roots

15. The solution set of $8x^2 - 40x = 0$ is

a) $\{0, 5\}$     b) $\{0, -5\}$     c) $\{-\sqrt{5}, \sqrt{5}\}$     d) $\{5\}$     e) $\left\{0, \dfrac{1}{5}\right\}$

16. The roots of $9t^2 - 72 = 0$ are

a) $-8$ and $8$     b) $-6$ and $6$     c) $-4\sqrt{5}$ and $4\sqrt{5}$     d) $2\sqrt{2}$ only   e) $-2\sqrt{2}$ and $2\sqrt{2}$

17. The solution set of $2x^2 - x - 7 = 0$ is

a) $\left\{\dfrac{-1 - \sqrt{57}}{4}, \dfrac{-1 + \sqrt{57}}{4}\right\}$     b) $\left\{\dfrac{1 - \sqrt{57}}{2}, \dfrac{1 + \sqrt{57}}{2}\right\}$     c) $\left\{\dfrac{1 - \sqrt{57}}{4}, \dfrac{1 + \sqrt{57}}{4}\right\}$

d) $\left\{\dfrac{1 - 2\sqrt{14}}{4}, \dfrac{1 + 2\sqrt{14}}{4}\right\}$     e) $\{\ \}$

18. Solve for $x$:  $x^2 - 12x - 4 = 0$

a) $x = 4\sqrt{10}, x = 8\sqrt{10}$     b) $x = 6 - 4\sqrt{10}, x = 6 + 4\sqrt{10}$     c) $x = 2\sqrt{10}, x = 10\sqrt{10}$
d) $x = 6 - 2\sqrt{10}, x = 6 + 2\sqrt{10}$     e) $x = 12 - 2\sqrt{10}, x = 12 + 2\sqrt{10}$

19. Solve for $p$:  $p + \dfrac{7}{p} = 3$

    a) $p = \dfrac{3 - \sqrt{37}}{2}, p = \dfrac{3 + \sqrt{37}}{2}$    b) $p = \dfrac{1 - \sqrt{37}}{4}, p = \dfrac{1 + \sqrt{37}}{4}$    c) $p = -1, p = 5$

    d) $p = \dfrac{-3 - \sqrt{37}}{2}, p = \dfrac{-3 + \sqrt{37}}{2}$    e) no real solutions

20. Solve for $x$:  $\dfrac{x - 3}{x + 1} = \dfrac{x - 2}{x - 4}$

    a) $x = \dfrac{3}{7}$    b) $x = \dfrac{7}{3}$    c) $x = 0$    d) $x = -\dfrac{7}{3}$    e) no real solutions

ANSWERS FOR QUIZ 7    1. a      2. c      3. c      4. d      5. b

                            6. d      7. d      8. e      9. a    10. b

                          11. c    12. e    13. d    14. b    15. a

                          16. e    17. c    18. d    19. e    20. b

# Chapter 8:    Geometry Formulas

Algebra appears in many areas of study. In particular, solving problems in geometry often requires algebra. In this chapter, we will take a look at some of the commonly seen formulas which appear in geometry. In Section 8.1, we will study the Pythagorean Theorem. This theorem tells us how the lengths of the sides of a right triangle are related. Section 8.2 contains the formulas for the perimeter and area of certain plane figures such as squares, rectangles, etc. In Section 8.3, we will study some formulas which pertain to solid figures such as cubes, spheres, etc.

## Section 8.1  The Pythagorean Theorem

Let $\triangle ABC$ be a right triangle (see diagram below). We call sides $\overline{AC}$ and $\overline{BC}$ the **legs** of $\triangle ABC$ and $\overline{AB}$ the **hypotenuse** of $\triangle ABC$.

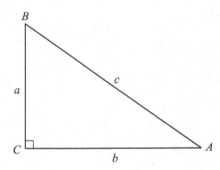

The hypotenuse of any right triangle is the side of the triangle with the largest length. In our triangle above, we have $c > a$ and $c > b$. However, the sum of the lengths of the legs is larger than the length of the hypotenuse. In our triangle above, we have $a + b > c$. These are just a couple of basic facts about right triangles.

Referring to $\triangle ABC$ above, we have

---

**The Pythagorean Theorem**

$$a^2 + b^2 = c^2$$

---

**Examples.**

1) Find $x$.

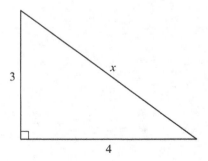

Let $a = 3$ and $b = 4$. By the Pythagorean theorem, we have

$$a^2 + b^2 = c^2$$
$$3^2 + 4^2 = x^2$$
$$9 + 16 = x^2$$
$$25 = x^2$$
$$x = \sqrt{25} = 5$$

Notice that I did not write $x = \pm\sqrt{25}$ since the length of a line segment cannot be negative. This right triangle is often called the **3−4−5 right triangle.**

2)  Find $a$.

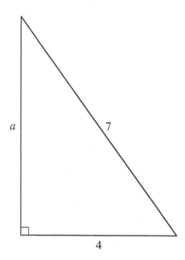

Let $b = 4$ and $c = 7$. By the Pythagorean theorem, we have

$$a^2 + b^2 = c^2$$
$$a^2 + 4^2 = 7^2$$
$$a^2 + 16 = 49$$
$$\underline{\phantom{a^2+}-16 \quad -16}$$
$$a^2 = 33$$
$$a = \sqrt{33}$$

3) Find the length of the hypotenuse of a right triangle whose legs measure $2\sqrt{2}$ inches and $5\sqrt{3}$ inches.

The given measurements correspond to the lengths of the legs. Let $a = 2\sqrt{2}$ and $b = 5\sqrt{3}$. We need to find the length of the hypotenuse, $c$.

$$a^2 + b^2 = c^2$$
$$\left(2\sqrt{2}\right)^2 + \left(5\sqrt{3}\right)^2 = c^2$$
$$8 + 75 = c^2$$
$$83 = c^2$$
$$c = \sqrt{83}$$

The hypotenuse has length $\sqrt{83}$ inches.

4) Find the length of the leg of a right triangle whose hypotenuse measures 5 feet and whose other leg measures $\sqrt{7}$ feet.

Let $a = \sqrt{7}$ and $c = 5$. We need to solve for $b$.

$$a^2 + b^2 = c^2$$
$$\left(\sqrt{7}\right)^2 + b^2 = 5^2$$
$$7 + b^2 = 25$$
$$\underline{-7 \qquad\qquad -7}$$
$$b^2 = 18$$
$$b = \sqrt{18} = 3\sqrt{2}$$

The leg has length $3\sqrt{2}$ feet.

5) Find $x$.

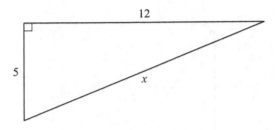

Let $a = 5$ and $b = 12$.

$$a^2 + b^2 = c^2$$
$$5^2 + 12^2 = x^2$$
$$25 + 144 = x^2$$
$$169 = x^2$$
$$x = \sqrt{169} = 13$$

In examples 1 and 5 above, notice that the lengths of the sides of each triangle are natural numbers. In the other examples, however, there is at least one side whose length contains a square root in it, making it an irrational number.

**Definition:** A set of natural numbers $\{a,\ b,\ c\}$ is called a **Pythagorean triple** if $a^2 + b^2 = c^2$.

If the set $\{a,\ b,\ c\}$ is a Pythagorean triple, then a right triangle can be constructed whose sides measure $a$, $b$, and $c$ (provided that the units for each measure are all the same). For example, the set $\{3,\ 4,\ 5\}$ is a Pythagorean triple since $3^2 + 4^2 = 5^2$ (see example 1). This means that if we wanted to make a triangle whose sides measure 3 inches, 4 inches and 5 inches, then this triangle **must** contain a right angle, making it a right triangle. Let's look at some examples.

**Examples.** Is the given set a Pythagorean triple?

1) $\{6,\ 8,\ 10\}$ is a Pythagorean triple since $6^2 + 8^2 = 10^2$. Notice that the numbers in this set can be obtained from the numbers in the set $\{3,\ 4,\ 5\}$ by multiplying each of them by 2.

2) $\{15,\ 20,\ 25\}$ is a Pythagorean triple since $15^2 + 20^2 = 25^2$. Once again, notice that the numbers in this set can be obtained from the numbers in the set $\{3,\ 4,\ 5\}$ by multiplying each of them by 5. In general, we have the following:

> If $\{a,\ b,\ c\}$ is a Pythagorean triple and $n$ is a natural
> number, then $\{na,\ nb,\ nc\}$ is also a Pythagorean triple.

3) $\{30,\ 72,\ 78\}$ is a Pythagorean triple. Once way to see this is to check that $30^2 + 72^2 = 78^2$. Another way is to observe that

$$
\begin{aligned}
30 &= 5 \times 6 \\
72 &= 12 \times 6 \\
78 &= 13 \times 6
\end{aligned}
$$

and we know that $\{5,\ 12,\ 13\}$ is a Pythagorean triple. Hence, $\{30,\ 72,\ 78\}$ is a Pythagorean triple as well.

4) $\{5,\ 9,\ 12\}$ is not a Pythagorean triple, since $5^2 + 9^2 \neq 12^2$. Geometrically, this means that if we construct a triangle whose sides measure 5 units, 9 units and 12 units (all units being the same), then the triangle will not contain a right angle. It will **not** be a right triangle.

5) {40, 72, 96} is not a Pythagorean triple. Observe that

$$40 = 8 \times 5$$
$$72 = 8 \times 9$$
$$96 = 8 \times 12$$

and we already know by example 4 that {5, 9, 12} is not a Pythagorean triple. Therefore, {40, 72, 96} is not a Pythagorean triple.

**Try These (Set 1):**

1) Find $x$.

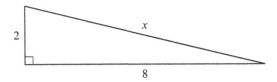

2) Find the length of the leg of a right triangle whose hypotenuse measures 5 meters and whose other leg measures $\sqrt{13}$ meters.

3) Is the set {8, 15, 17} a Pythagorean triple?

# Section 8.2  Formulas for Plane Figures

In this section, we will look at the **perimeter** and **area** formulas for a square, a rectangle and a triangle. We will also study the **circumference** and **area** formulas for a circle.

1.  **Squares**

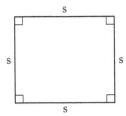

A square is a four sided figure whose sides have equal length and whose angles are right angles.

The perimeter of the square is   $P = 4s$.
The area of the square is        $A = s^2$.

**Examples.** Find the perimeter and area of each square.

1)

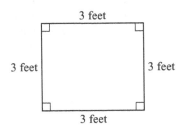

The length of each side is $s = 3$ feet. The perimeter is $P = 4s = 4(3 \text{ feet}) = 12$ feet. The area is $A = s^2 = (3 \text{ feet})^2 = 9$ square feet or 9 ft$^2$.

2)

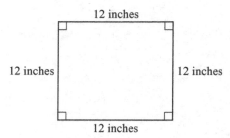

The length of each side is $s = 12$ inches. The perimeter is $P = 4s = 4(12 \text{ inches}) = 48$ inches. The area is $A = s^2 = (12 \text{ inches})^2 = 144$ square inches or 144 in$^2$.

**Examples.**

1) Find the perimeter and area of a square whose sides each measure $7\sqrt{2}$ meters.

The length of each side is $s = 7\sqrt{2}$ meters. The perimeter is $P = 4s = 4(7\sqrt{2} \text{ meters}) = 28\sqrt{2}$ meters and the area is $A = s^2 = \left(7\sqrt{2} \text{ meters}\right)^2 = 98$ square meters or 98 m$^2$.

2) Find the length of a side of a square whose perimeter is 36 inches.

We are given $P = 36$ inches and we want to find $s$. Well, we know that $P = 4s$. Replacing $P$ by 36 inches in the formula gives us

$$\frac{36 \text{ inches}}{4} = \frac{\cancel{4}s}{\cancel{4}}$$
$$s = 9 \text{ inches}$$

The length of each side is 9 inches.

2.  **Rectangles**

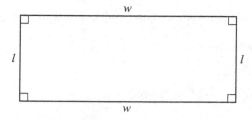

A rectangle is a four sided figure whose opposite sides have equal length and whose angles are right angles. Notice that every square is a rectangle, but not every rectangle is a square. In the figure above, the length of the rectangle is $l$ and the width is $w$. Any side of a rectangle may be called the **base** of the rectangle and a side adjacent to the base is called the **altitude**. If we call the bottom segment of our rectangle the base, then either side labeled $l$ is altitude.

The perimeter of the rectangle is   $P = 2l + 2w$.
The area of the rectangle is         $A = lw$.

**Examples.** Find the perimeter and area of each rectangle.

1)

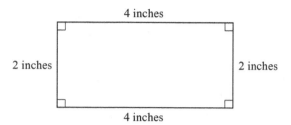

The length is $l = 2$ inches and the width is $w = 4$ inches. The perimeter is $P = 2l + 2w = 2(2 \text{ inches}) + 2(4 \text{ inches}) = 12$ inches. The area is $A = lw = (2 \text{ inches})(4 \text{ inches}) = 8$ square inches or 8 in$^2$.

2)

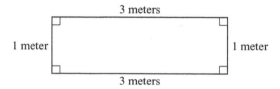

The length is $l = 1$ meter and the width is $w = 3$ meter. The perimeter is $P = 2l + 2w = 2(1 \text{ meter}) + 2(3 \text{ meters}) = 8$ meters. The area is $A = lw = (1 \text{ meter})(3 \text{ meters}) = 3$ square meters or 3 m$^2$.

**Examples.**

1) Find the perimeter and area of a rectangle whose base measures 10 yards and whose altitude measures $3\sqrt{3}$ yards.

Let $w = 10$ yards and $l = 3\sqrt{3}$ yards. The perimeter is $P = 2l + 2w = 2(10 \text{ yards}) + 2(3\sqrt{3} \text{ yards}) = (20 + 6\sqrt{3})$ yards. The area is $A = lw = (3\sqrt{3} \text{ yards})(10 \text{ yards}) = 30\sqrt{3}$ square yards or $30\sqrt{3}$ yd$^2$.

2) Find the width of a rectangle whose perimeter is 28 inches and whose length is 10 inches.

We are given $P = 28$ inches and $l = 10$ inches. We want to find $w$. Well, we know that $P = 2l + 2w$. Replacing $P$ by 28 inches and $l$ by 10 inches in the formula gives us

$$28 \text{ inches} = 2(10 \text{ inches}) + 2w$$
$$28 \text{ inches} = 20 \text{ inches} + 2w$$
$$\underline{-20 \text{ inches} \quad -20 \text{ inches}}$$
$$\frac{8 \text{ inches}}{2} = \frac{\cancel{2}w}{\cancel{2}}$$
$$w = 4 \text{ inches}$$

The width of the rectangle is 4 inches.

3.  **Triangles**

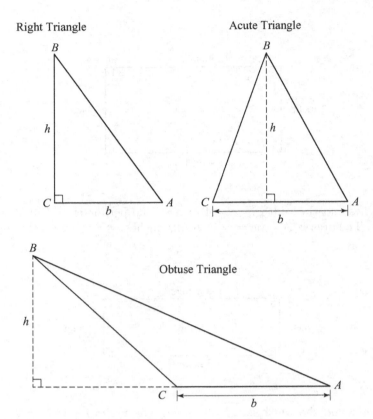

In the triangles above, the **base** of each triangle is labeled $b$ and the **height** is labeled $h$. The height of a triangle is also called its **altitude**. An **acute triangle** is a triangle whose angles each measure less than 90°. An **obtuse triangle** is a triangle which has an angle whose measurement is more than 90°. Irrespective of what type of triangle we are dealing with, the area and perimeter formulas are the same.

The perimeter of a triangle is the sum of the lengths of its sides.

The area of the triangle is $$A = \frac{1}{2}bh = \frac{bh}{2}.$$

**Examples.** Find the area of each triangle.

1)

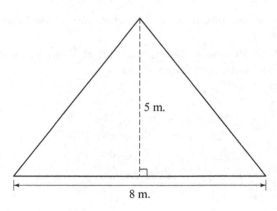

The base is $b = 8$ m. and the height is $h = 5$ m. The area is $A = \frac{1}{2}bh = \frac{1}{2}(8 \text{ m.})(5 \text{ m.}) = 20 \text{ m}^2$.

2)

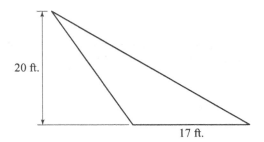

20 ft.

17 ft.

The base is $b = 17$ ft. and the height is $h = 20$ ft. The area is $A = \frac{1}{2}bh = \frac{1}{2}(17 \text{ ft.})(20 \text{ ft.}) = 170 \text{ ft}^2$.

3) Find the area of a triangle whose base measures $(\sqrt{7} + 1)$ yards and whose height measures $(3\sqrt{7} - 2)$ yards.

Let $b = (\sqrt{7} + 1)$ yds and $h = (3\sqrt{7} - 2)$ yds. The area is

$$
\begin{aligned}
A &= \frac{1}{2}bh = \frac{1}{2}\left[\left(\sqrt{7} + 1\right) \text{ yds}\right]\left[\left(3\sqrt{7} - 2\right) \text{ yds}\right] \\
&= \frac{1}{2}\left(3\left(\sqrt{7}\right)^2 - 2\sqrt{7} + 3\sqrt{7} - 2\right) \text{ yd}^2 \\
&= \frac{1}{2}\left(3(7) - 2\sqrt{7} + 3\sqrt{7} - 2\right) \text{ yd}^2 \\
&= \frac{1}{2}\left(19 + \sqrt{7}\right) \text{ yd}^2 = \frac{19 + \sqrt{7}}{2} \text{ yd}^2
\end{aligned}
$$

**Example.** Two sides of a triangle with perimeter 23 miles measure $(2\sqrt{3} - 1)$ miles and $(5\sqrt{3} + 8)$ miles. Find the dimensions of the third side.

Let's call the third side $x$. Since the perimeter is the sum of the measurements of the three sides, we have

$$(2\sqrt{3} - 1) \text{ miles} + (5\sqrt{3} + 8) \text{ miles} + x = 23 \text{ miles}.$$

We have to solve for $x$.

$$
\begin{aligned}
(2\sqrt{3} - 1) \text{ miles} + (5\sqrt{3} + 8) \text{ miles} + x &= 23 \text{ miles} \\
(7\sqrt{3} + 7) \text{ miles} + x &= 23 \text{ miles} \\
\underline{-7 \text{ miles} \qquad\qquad -7 \text{ miles}} & \\
7\sqrt{3} \text{ miles} + x &= 16 \text{ miles} \\
\underline{-7\sqrt{3} \text{ miles} \qquad -7\sqrt{3} \text{ miles}} & \\
x &= \left(16 - 7\sqrt{3}\right) \text{ miles}
\end{aligned}
$$

Therefore, the third side has a measurement of $\left(16 - 7\sqrt{3}\right)$ miles.

4.  **Circles**

A circle of radius $r$. The point O is called the center of
the circle. The diameter is the length of the horizontal line segment.

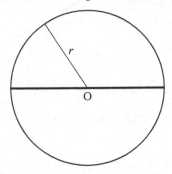

A circle is the collection of points, all of whose distance from a fixed point (called the **center** of the circle) is constant. Any line segment connecting the center of the circle to a point on the circle is called a **radius**. There are infinitely many radii which can be drawn in our figure. Since they all have the same length, we usually refer to the length of a radius as simply **the radius of the circle** (denoted by $r$ in the picture above). Any line segment connecting two points of the circle and going through the center of the circle is called a **diameter**. There are infinitely many diameters which can be drawn in our figure. Since they all have the same length, we usually refer to the length of a diameter as simply **the diameter of the circle** (often represented by $d$). Since a diameter is formed by connecting two radii, we have $d = 2r$.

The circumference of a circle is      $C = 2\pi r = \pi d$.
The area of a circle is      $A = \pi r^2$.

Note that the circumference of a circle is just the length of the circle. Imagine making a circle out of a piece of string. The length of the string needed to make the circle is the circumference of the circle.

**Examples.** Find the circumference and area of each circle. Leave your answer in terms of $\pi$.

1)

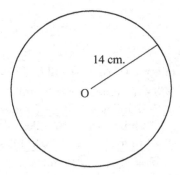

The radius of the circle is $r = 14$ cm. The circumference is $C = 2\pi r = 2\pi(14 \text{ cm.}) = 28\pi$ cm. and the area is $A = \pi r^2 = \pi(14 \text{ cm.})^2 = 196\pi \text{ cm}^2$.

2)

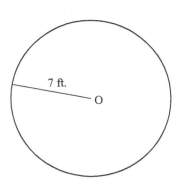

The radius of the circle is $r = 7$ ft. The circumference is $C = 2\pi r = 2\pi(7 \text{ ft.}) = 14\pi$ ft. and the area is $A = \pi r^2 = \pi(7 \text{ ft.})^2 = 49\pi$ ft$^2$.

3) Find the circumference and area of a circle whose radius is $\left(8 - \sqrt{3}\right)$ kilometers.

We are given that $r = \left(8 - \sqrt{3}\right)$ km. The circumference is

$$
\begin{aligned}
C &= 2\pi r \\
&= 2\pi \left(8 - \sqrt{3}\right) \text{ km.} \\
&= \left(16\pi - 2\pi\sqrt{3}\right) \text{ km.}
\end{aligned}
$$

The area is

$$
\begin{aligned}
A &= \pi r^2 = \pi \left[\left(8 - \sqrt{3}\right) \text{ km.}\right]^2 \\
&= \pi \left[\left(8 - \sqrt{3}\right) \text{ km.}\right]\left[\left(8 - \sqrt{3}\right) \text{ km.}\right] \\
&= \pi \left(64 - 8\sqrt{3} - 8\sqrt{3} + \left(\sqrt{3}\right)^2\right) \text{ km}^2 \\
&= \pi \left(64 - 8\sqrt{3} - 8\sqrt{3} + 3\right) \text{ km}^2 \\
&= \pi \left(67 - 16\sqrt{3}\right) \text{ km}^2 \\
&= \left(67\pi - 16\sqrt{3}\pi\right) \text{ km}^2.
\end{aligned}
$$

**Example.** The area of a circle is $28\pi$ in$^2$. Find its radius and diameter.

We are given $A = 28\pi$ in$^2$ and we want to find $r$ and $d$. Using the fact that $A = \pi r^2$, we obtain

$$
\begin{aligned}
28\pi \text{ in}^2 &= \pi r^2 \\
\frac{28\cancel{\pi} \text{ in}^2}{\cancel{\pi}} &= \frac{\cancel{\pi} r^2}{\cancel{\pi}} \\
28 \text{ in}^2 &= r^2 \\
r &= \sqrt{28 \text{ in}^2} = 2\sqrt{7} \text{ in.}
\end{aligned}
$$

Therefore, the radius is $2\sqrt{7}$ in. and the diameter is $d = 2r = 2\left(2\sqrt{7} \text{ in.}\right) = 4\sqrt{7}$ in.

**Try These (Set 2):**

1) Find the area of a square whose sides measure 8 feet each.
2) Find the perimeter of a rectangle whose length is $2\sqrt{5}$ yards and whose width is $6\sqrt{5}$ yards.
3) The area of a triangle whose base measures 9 meters is 15 square meters. Find its height.
4) The radius of a circle is $4\sqrt{11}$ feet. Find its area.
5) Find the area of a rectangle whose length is $\left(5 - \sqrt{2}\right)$ inches and whose width is $\left(2 + 3\sqrt{2}\right)$ inches.

# Section 8.3  Formulas for Solid Figures

The formulas which arise when studying solid figures are the **volume** and the **surface area** formulas. The volume of a solid figure measures the 'inside' of the solid and the surface area of a solid figure measures the 'outside' of the solid. For example, a metal can filled with water is a solid figure whose volume measures the amount of water in the can and whose surface area measures the amount of metal used to make the can itself. The volume of a solid figure is measured in cubic units, whereas the surface area is measured in square units. We will look at the formulas for spheres, rectangular solids, cubes, and right circular cylinders. The definition of each of these figures is somewhat abstract and will not be given here. I'll let the pictures speak for themselves.

1.  **Spheres**

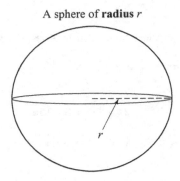

A sphere of **radius** $r$

A sphere, like a circle, has a **center** and any line segment connecting the center to a point on the sphere is called a **radius**. Since every radius has the same length, we usually refer to the length of a radius as simply **the radius of the sphere** (labeled $r$ in the diagram above). Any line segment connecting two points of the sphere and going through the center of the sphere is called a **diameter**. Since they all have the same length, we usually refer to the length of a diameter as simply **the diameter of the sphere.** Observe that $d = 2r$.

The volume of a sphere is    $V = \dfrac{4}{3}\pi r^3$.

The surface area of a sphere is    $A = 4\pi r^2$.

**Examples.** Find the volume and surface area of each sphere. Leave your answer in terms of $\pi$.

1)

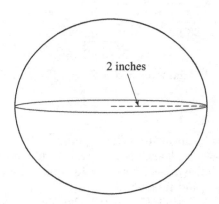

2 inches

The radius is $r = 2$ inches. The volume is $V = \frac{4}{3}\pi r^3 = \frac{4}{3}\pi(2 \text{ inches})^3 = \frac{32}{3}\pi$ cubic inches or $\frac{32}{3}\pi$ in³. The surface area is $A = 4\pi r^2 = 4\pi(2 \text{ inches})^2 = 16\pi$ square inches or $16\pi$ in².

2)

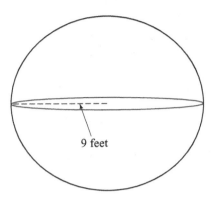

9 feet

The radius is $r = 9$ feet. The volume is $V = \frac{4}{3}\pi r^3 = \frac{4}{3}\pi(9 \text{ feet})^3 = 972\pi$ cubic feet and the surface area is $A = 4\pi r^2 = 4\pi(9 \text{ feet})^2 = 324\pi$ square feet.

3) Find the volume of a sphere whose radius is $(1 + 2\sqrt{5})$ miles.

Let $r = (1 + 2\sqrt{5})$ mi. Then

$$
\begin{aligned}
V &= \frac{4}{3}\pi r^3 = \frac{4}{3}\pi \left[\left(1 + 2\sqrt{5}\right) \text{ mi.}\right]^3 \\
&= \frac{4}{3}\pi \left[\left(1 + 2\sqrt{5}\right) \text{ mi.}\right] \underbrace{\left[\left(1 + 2\sqrt{5}\right) \text{ mi.}\right]\left[\left(1 + 2\sqrt{5}\right) \text{ mi.}\right]}_{\left(21 + 4\sqrt{5}\right) \text{ mi}^2} \\
&= \frac{4}{3}\pi \underbrace{\left[\left(1 + 2\sqrt{5}\right) \text{ mi.}\right]\left[\left(21 + 4\sqrt{5}\right) \text{ mi}^2\right]}_{\left(61 + 46\sqrt{5}\right) \text{ mi}^3} \\
&= \frac{4}{3}\pi \left(61 + 46\sqrt{5}\right) \text{ mi}^3 \\
&= \frac{4\pi \left(61 + 46\sqrt{5}\right)}{3} \text{ mi}^3.
\end{aligned}
$$

**Example.** The surface area of a sphere is $8\pi$ in². Find its radius.

We are given $A = 8\pi$ in² and we want to find $r$. Using the fact that $A = 4\pi r^2$, we obtain

$$
\begin{aligned}
8\pi \text{ in}^2 &= 4\pi r^2 \\
\frac{\overset{2}{\cancel{8\pi}} \text{ in}^2}{\underset{1}{\cancel{4\pi}}} &= \frac{\overset{1}{\cancel{4\pi}} r^2}{\underset{1}{\cancel{4\pi}}} \\
2 \text{ in}^2 &= r^2 \\
r &= \sqrt{2} \text{ in.}
\end{aligned}
$$

Therefore, the radius is $\sqrt{2}$ inches.

2. **Rectangular Solids**

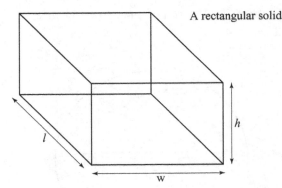

A rectangular solid

In the rectangular solid above, $h$ represents the height, $w$ represents the width and $l$ represents the length of the solid.

The volume of a rectangular solid is    $V = lwh$.
The surface area of a rectangular solid is    $A = 2lw + 2wh + 2lh$.

Notice that the surface area of a rectangular is obtained by adding the areas of the rectangles which make up the **faces** of the solid:

$$A = \underbrace{lw + lw}_{\text{top and bottom}} + \underbrace{wh + wh}_{\text{front and back}} + \underbrace{lh + lh}_{\text{left and right}}$$
$$= 2lw + 2wh + 2lh$$

**Examples.**

1) Find the volume and surface area of the rectangular solid.

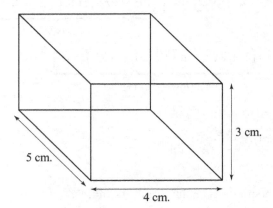

3 cm.

5 cm.

4 cm.

Set $h = 3$ cm., $w = 4$ cm. and $l = 5$ cm. The volume is $V = lwh = (5 \text{ cm.}) (4 \text{ cm.}) (3 \text{ cm.}) = 60 \text{ cm}^3$. The surface area is

$$\begin{aligned} A &= 2lw + 2wh + 2lh \\ &= 2(5 \text{ cm.})(4 \text{ cm.}) + 2(4 \text{ cm.})(3 \text{ cm.}) + 2(5 \text{ cm.})(3 \text{ cm.}) \\ &= 40 \text{ cm}^2 + 24 \text{ cm}^2 + 30 \text{ cm}^2 = 94 \text{ cm}^2. \end{aligned}$$

2) Find the volume and surface area of a rectangular solid which has length 1 foot, width 2 feet and height $\sqrt{3}$ feet.

Set $h = \sqrt{3}$ ft., $w = 2$ ft. and $l = 1$ ft. The volume is $V = lwh = (1 \text{ ft.}) (2 \text{ ft.}) (\sqrt{3} \text{ ft.}) = 2\sqrt{3} \text{ ft}^3$. The surface area is

$$
\begin{aligned}
A &= 2lw + 2wh + 2lh \\
&= 2(1 \text{ ft.})(2 \text{ ft.}) + 2(2 \text{ ft.})(\sqrt{3} \text{ ft.}) + 2(1 \text{ ft.})(\sqrt{3} \text{ ft.}) \\
&= 4 \text{ ft}^2 + 4\sqrt{3} \text{ ft}^2 + 2\sqrt{3} \text{ ft}^2 = (4 + 6\sqrt{3}) \text{ ft}^2.
\end{aligned}
$$

3) A rectangular solid of length 9 meters and height 22 meters has a volume of 116 cubic meters. What is its width?

We are given that $l = 9$ m., $h = 22$ m. and $V = 116 \text{ m}^3$. We want to find $w$. Well, since we know that $V = lwh$, we have

$$
\begin{aligned}
V &= lwh \\
116 \text{ m}^3 &= (9 \text{ m.})\, w\, (22 \text{ m.}) \\
116 \text{ m}^3 &= (198 \text{ m}^2)\, w \\
\frac{\overset{58}{\cancel{116 \text{ m}^3}} \text{ m}}{\underset{99}{\cancel{198 \text{ m}^2}}} &= \frac{(\cancel{198 \text{ m}^2})\, w}{\cancel{198 \text{ m}^2}} \\
\frac{58}{99} \text{ m.} &= w
\end{aligned}
$$

Therefore, the width is $\dfrac{58}{99}$ meters.

## 3.  **Cubes**

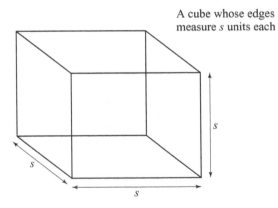

A cube whose edges measure $s$ units each

A cube is a rectangular solid whose length, width and height are all equal. As the diagram above shows, if $s$ represents the length of one of the edges, then all of the edges have length $s$. We can use the formulas for the rectangular solid to obtain the volume and surface area formulas for a cube by setting $l$, $w$ and $h$ each equal to $s$.

The volume of a cube is     $V = s^3$.
The surface area of a cube is     $A = 6s^2$.

**Examples.**

1) Find the volume and surface area of a cube whose height measures 5 feet.

Let $s = 5$ feet. Then the volume is $V = s^3 = (5 \text{ feet})^3 = 125$ cubic feet and the surface area is $A = 6s^2 = 6(5 \text{ feet})^2 = 150$ square feet.

2) Find the volume and surface area of a cube whose edges measure $\frac{2}{3}$ kilometers each.

Let $s = \frac{2}{3}$ km. Then the volume is $V = s^3 = \left(\frac{2}{3} \text{ km.}\right)^3 = \frac{8}{27}$ km$^3$ and the surface area is $A = 6s^2 = 6\left(\frac{2}{3} \text{ km.}\right)^2 = \frac{8}{3}$ km$^2$.

3) Find the length of an edge of a cube whose surface area is 72 yd$^2$.

We are given that $A = 72$ yd$^2$ and we want to find $s$. Using the formula $A = 6s^2$, we obtain

$$A = 6s^2$$
$$72 \text{ yd}^2 = 6s^2$$
$$\frac{72 \text{ yd}^2}{6} = \frac{\cancel{6}s^2}{\cancel{6}}$$
$$12 \text{ yd}^2 = s^2$$
$$s = \sqrt{12 \text{ yd}^2} = 2\sqrt{3} \text{ yd.}$$

Therefore, the length of each edge is $2\sqrt{3}$ yards.

4. **Right Circular Cylinders**

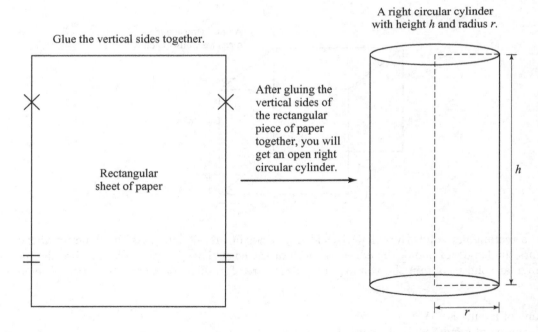

Glue the vertical sides together.

Rectangular sheet of paper

After gluing the vertical sides of the rectangular piece of paper together, you will get an open right circular cylinder.

A right circular cylinder with height $h$ and radius $r$.

As the figure shows, a right circular cylinder is like a can. You can make a cylinder by taking a rectangular sheet of paper and gluing one pair of opposite edges together. Every right circular cylinder has a radius and a height. We will only be concerned with the volume formula for such a cylinder. There are several surface area formulas for a right circular cylinder, each one depending on whether or not the cylinder has an open top, an open bottom, both or neither. We will not study these formulas here.

The volume of a right circular cylinder is $V = \pi r^2 h$.

**Examples.**

1) Find the volume of the right circular cylinder.

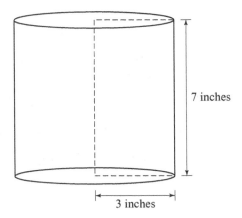

We are given that $r = 3$ in. and $h = 7$ in. The volume is $V = \pi r^2 h = \pi \left(3 \text{ in.}\right)^2 \left(7 \text{ in.}\right) = 63\pi \text{ in}^3$.

2) Find the volume of the right circular cylinder.

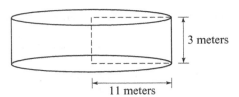

We have $r = 11$ m. and $h = 3$ m. The volume is $V = \pi r^2 h = \pi \left(11 \text{ m.}\right)^2 \left(3 \text{ m.}\right) = 363\pi \text{ m}^3$.

3) Find the volume of the right circular cylinder whose radius is $5\sqrt{6}$ miles and whose height is $\sqrt{10}$ miles.

We have $r = 5\sqrt{6}$ miles and $h = \sqrt{10}$ miles. The volume is $V = \pi r^2 h = \pi \underbrace{\left(5\sqrt{6} \text{ miles}\right)^2}_{150 \text{ square miles}} \left(\sqrt{10} \text{ miles}\right) =$

$150\sqrt{10}\pi$ cubic miles.

4) The volume of a right circular cylinder of height 9 centimeters is 13 cubic centimeters. What is the radius of the cylinder?

We are given $h = 9$ cm. and $V = 13$ cm$^3$. We want to find $r$. Using the volume formula, we have

$$V = \pi r^2 h$$
$$13 \text{ cm}^3 = \pi r^2 \left(9 \text{ cm.}\right)$$
$$\frac{13 \text{ cm}^3}{9\pi \text{ cm}} = \frac{\pi r^2 \left(9 \text{ cm.}\right)}{9\pi \text{ cm.}}$$
$$\frac{13}{9\pi} \text{ cm}^2 = r^2$$
$$r = \sqrt{\frac{13}{9\pi} \text{ cm}^2} = \frac{\sqrt{13}}{3\sqrt{\pi}} \text{ cm.} = \frac{\sqrt{13}}{3\sqrt{\pi}} \left(\frac{\sqrt{\pi}}{\sqrt{\pi}}\right) \text{ cm.} = \frac{\sqrt{13\pi}}{3\pi} \text{ cm.}$$

The radius is $\dfrac{\sqrt{13\pi}}{3\pi}$ centimeters.

**Try These (Set 3):**

1) Find the surface area of a cube whose edges measure 3 feet each.
2) Find the volume of a sphere whose radius is 8 meters.
3) The volume of a right circular cylinder whose radius measures $\dfrac{2}{5}$ centimeters is 8 cubic centimeters. Find its height.
4) The length and width of a rectangular solid are 4 feet each and its surface area is 100 ft². Find its height.
5) Find the surface area of a sphere whose radius is $\left(-1 + 6\sqrt{5}\right)$ inches.

**Exercise 8**

1. Find the length of the hypotenuse of the right triangle whose legs measure 4 inches and 3 inches.

2. Find the length of the hypotenuse of the right triangle whose legs measure 12 inches and 5 inches.

3. Find the length of the hypotenuse of the right triangle whose legs measure $5\sqrt{2}$ feet and 1 foot.

4. Find the length of the hypotenuse of the right triangle whose legs measure 2 feet and $3\sqrt{7}$ feet.

5. Find the length of the leg of a right triangle whose hypotenuse measures 8 yards and whose other leg measures 2 yards.

6. Find the length of the leg of a right triangle whose hypotenuse measures 6 yards and whose other leg measures 4 yards.

7. Find the length of the leg of a right triangle whose hypotenuse measures $6\sqrt{3}$ meters and whose other leg measures $2\sqrt{2}$ meters.

8. Find the length of the leg of a right triangle whose hypotenuse measures $3\sqrt{5}$ meters and whose other leg measures $\sqrt{6}$ meters.

9. Find the length of the hypotenuse of the right triangle whose legs measure 9 feet each.

10. Find the length of the hypotenuse of the right triangle whose legs measure 12 feet each.

11. Is the set $\{6,\ 8,\ 10\}$ a Pythagorean triple?

12. Is the set $\{12,\ 16,\ 20\}$ a Pythagorean triple?

13. Is the set $\{7,\ 24,\ 25\}$ a Pythagorean triple?

14. Is the set $\{10,\ 24,\ 26\}$ a Pythagorean triple?

15. Is the set $\{2,\ 7,\ 12\}$ a Pythagorean triple?

16. Is the set $\{9,\ 10,\ 14\}$ a Pythagorean triple?

17. Can a right triangle have sides measuring 6 inches, 3 inches, and 8 inches?

18. Can a right triangle have sides measuring 4 feet, 4 feet, and 1 foot?

19. Can a right triangle have sides measuring 30 meters, 40 meters, and 50 meters?

20. Can a right triangle have sides measuring 14 yards, 48 yards, and 50 yards?

21. Find the perimeter of a square whose sides measure 7 inches each.

22. Find the area of a square whose sides measure 13 inches each.

23. Find the area of a rectangle whose length is 2 yards and width is 5 yards.

24. Find the perimeter of a rectangle whose length is 2 yards and width is 5 yards.

25. Find the area of a triangle whose base measures $5\sqrt{5}$ inches and height is $4\sqrt{5}$ inches.

26. Find the area of a triangle whose base measures $\sqrt{7}$ inches and height is $3\sqrt{7}$ inches.

27. Find the area of a circle whose radius is 14 feet.

28. Find the area of a circle whose radius is 10 meters.

29. Find the circumference of a circle whose radius is $8\sqrt{10}$ feet.

30. Find the circumference of a circle whose radius is $2\sqrt{2}$ yards.

31. Find the length of a side of a square whose perimeter is 16 inches.

32. Find the length of a side of a square whose area is 36 in$^2$.

33. Find the length of a rectangle whose perimeter is 46 inches and width is 8 inches.

34. Find the width of a rectangle whose area is 28 square inches and length is 3 inches.

35. Find the area of a triangle whose base measures 7 yards and height measures 8 yards.

36. Find the area of a triangle whose base measures 9 feet and height measures 2 feet.

37. Find the area of a triangle whose base measures $\sqrt{11}$ miles and height measures $5\sqrt{11}$ miles.

38. Find the area of a triangle whose base measures $2\sqrt{3}$ kilometers and height measures $3\sqrt{15}$ kilometers.

39. The area of a circle is $36\pi$ ft$^2$. Find its radius and diameter.

40. The area of a circle is $144\pi$ m$^2$. Find its radius and diameter.

41. The area of a circle is $54\pi$ yd$^2$. Find its radius and diameter.

42. The area of a circle is $32\pi$ ft$^2$. Find its radius and diameter.

43. Find the volume and surface area of a cube whose edges measure 5 feet each.

44. Find the volume and surface area of a cube whose edges measure 7 centimeters each.

45. Find the volume and surface area of a sphere whose radius is 2 yards.

46. Find the volume and surface area of a sphere whose radius is 6 centimeters.

47. Find the volume and surface area of a rectangular solid which has length 3 feet, width 1 foot, and height 3 feet.

48. Find the volume and surface area of a rectangular solid which has length 4 feet, width 9 feet, and height 2 feet.

49. The length and width of a rectangular solid are 2 inches each and its surface area is 90 in². Find its height.

50. The length and height of a rectangular solid are 6 yards each and its surface area is 126 yd². Find its width.

51. Find the volume of the right circular cylinder whose radius is 3 miles and whose height is 18 miles.

52. Find the volume of the right circular cylinder whose radius is 11 feet and whose height is 10 feet.

53. Find the volume of the right circular cylinder whose radius is $9\sqrt{2}$ meters and whose height is 4 meters.

54. Find the volume of the right circular cylinder whose radius is $11\sqrt{3}$ inches and whose height is 1 inch.

---

## END OF CHAPTER 8    QUIZ

1. The perimeter of a square whose sides measure 8 centimeters each is
   a) 8 cm.    b) 16 cm.    c) 32 cm²    d) 32 cm.    e) 64 cm²

2. The area of a rectangle whose length measures 7 feet is 42 ft². The width of the rectangle is
   a) 298 ft²    b) 35 feet    c) 6 feet    d) 14 feet    e) 6 ft²

3. The circumference of a circle whose radius is 12 inches is
   a) $24\pi$ inches    b) $12\pi$ inches    c) $24\pi$ square inches    d) $144\pi$ inches    e) $144\pi$ square inches

4. The length of the hypotenuse of a right triangle whose legs measure 2 meters and 3 meters is
   a) $\sqrt{5}$ meters    b) 13 meters    c) $\sqrt{13}$ meters    d) 5 meters    e) 169 meters

5. Find $x$.
   a) $x = 8$ in.    b) $x = 11$ in.    c) $x = \sqrt{194}$ in.    d) $x = 12$ in.    e) $x = 4$ in.

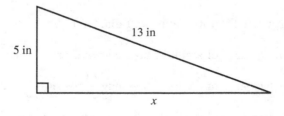

6. The area of a triangle whose base is 17 yards is 51 square yards. What is its height?
   a) 34 yards     b) 6 yards     c) 19 yards     d) 12 yards     e) 6 square yards

7. The surface area of a cube whose edges measure 6 feet each is
   a) 18 ft$^2$     b) 216 ft$^3$     c) 36 ft$^2$     d) 216 ft$^2$     e) 108 ft$^3$

8. The volume of a right circular cylinder whose radius measures 2 cm. and whose height is 5 cm. is
   a) 20$\pi$ cm$^3$     b) 10$\pi$ cm$^3$     c) 20$\pi$ cm$^2$     d) 28$\pi$ cm$^3$     e) 40$\pi$ cm$^3$

9. A right triangle has hypotenuse measuring $8\sqrt{2}$ inches and one of its legs measuring $2\sqrt{6}$ inches. The other leg measures
   a) $(64\sqrt{2} - 4\sqrt{6})$ inches     b) $2\sqrt{38}$ inches     c) $2\sqrt{26}$ inches     d) $26\sqrt{2}$ inches     e) $16\sqrt{6}$ inches

10. Which of the following is a Pythagorean triple?
    a) {1, 1, 4}     b) {1, 3, 7}     c) {6, 8, 10}     d) {9, 10, 19}     e) {5, 12, 14}

11. The volume of a sphere whose radius measures 3 feet is
    a) $9\pi$ ft$^3$     b) 36 ft$^3$     c) $27\pi$ ft$^3$     d) $36\pi$ ft$^3$     e) $36\pi$ ft$^2$

12. Two sides of a triangle measure 17 meters and 24 meters. If the perimeter of the triangle is 73 meters, then the third side must measure
    a) 41 meters     b) 42 meters     c) 31 meters     d) 32 meters     e) 51 meters

13. The area of a rectangle whose base measures $(\sqrt{5} + 2)$ inches and whose height is $(\sqrt{5} + 12)$ inches is
    a) $(2\sqrt{5} + 14)$ inches     b) 29 square inches     c) $(24 + 14\sqrt{5})$ square inches
    d) $(4\sqrt{5} + 28)$ inches     e) $(29 + 14\sqrt{5})$ square inches

14. Which of the following sets contains numbers which **cannot** represent the lengths (in feet) of the sides of a right triangle?
    a) {6, 8, 10}     b) {10, 24, 26}     c) {3, 4, 5}     d) {7, 8, 12}     e) {50, 120, 130}

15. The radius of a circle whose area is $243\pi$ m$^2$ is
    a) $9\sqrt{3}$ m.     b) $9\sqrt{3}\pi$ m.     c) $\dfrac{243}{2}$ m.     d) 9 m.     e) $9\sqrt{3}$ m$^2$

16. The perimeter of a rectangle whose length measures 12 feet is 93 feet. What is the width of the rectangle?
    a) 81 feet     a) 69 feet     c) $34\dfrac{1}{2}$ feet     d) $40\dfrac{1}{2}$ feet     e) $7\dfrac{3}{4}$ feet

17. The volume of a cube, each of whose edges measure $(\sqrt{10}+3)$ yards, is

   a) $(10\sqrt{10}+27)$ yd$^3$   b) $(19+6\sqrt{3})$ yd$^3$   c) $(3\sqrt{10}+9)$ yd$^3$

   d) $(19\sqrt{10}+6\sqrt{30})$ yd$^3$   e) $(19\sqrt{10}+6\sqrt{30}+18\sqrt{3}+57)$ yd$^3$

18. If a right triangle has a base measuring $3\sqrt{3}$ cm. and hypotenuse measuring 9 cm., then its area is

   a) $3\sqrt{6}$ cm$^2$   b) $\dfrac{27\sqrt{2}}{2}$ cm$^2$   c) $\dfrac{27}{2}$ cm$^2$   d) $27\sqrt{2}$ cm$^2$   e) $\dfrac{3\sqrt{3}}{2}$ cm$^2$

19. Find $x$.

   a) $x=\sqrt{58}$   b) $x=7\sqrt{3}$   c) $x=\sqrt{46}$   d) $x=2\sqrt{13}$   e) $x=13\sqrt{2}$

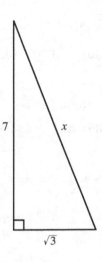

20. The radius of a sphere whose surface area is 25 in$^2$ is

   a) $\dfrac{5\sqrt{\pi}}{2\pi}$ inches   b) $\dfrac{5\sqrt{\pi}}{2}$ inches   c) $\sqrt[3]{\dfrac{75}{4\pi}}$ inches   d) $\dfrac{5}{4\sqrt{\pi}}$ inches   e) $\dfrac{5}{2\pi}$ inches

ANSWERS FOR QUIZ 8   1. d      2. c      3. a      4. c      5. d
                        6. b      7. d      8. a      9. c     10. c
                     11. d     12. d     13. e     14. d     15. a
                     16. c     17. e     18. b     19. d     20. a

# Chapter 9:    Solving Linear Inequalities

In this chapter, we will learn how to solve linear inequalities. Recall from Chapter 1 that the inequality symbol is used to compare two real numbers. Another use of the inequality symbol is to describe a collection, or set, of elements. For example, when we write $\{x \mid x > 1\}$, we are describing the set of all real numbers which are greater than 1. Clearly, we could not possibly write down this list of numbers since there are infinitely many of them. Therefore, the inequality symbol is used to give us a way of describing this set.

In Section 9.1, we will learn some basic set theory. We will be using inequalities to describe sets and you should be familiar with some of the basic notions and symbols used. We will not learn all of set theory, but just enough to get through solving linear inequalities. Section 9.2 contains some notations which will be used to write inequalities in different ways. We will then learn some properties which inequalities satisfy in Section 9.3. Several of these properties will enable us to solve linear inequalities. This will be studied in Section 9.4. In particular, we will learn how to solve one-sided linear inequalities, compound linear inequalities and disjoint linear inequalities.

## Section 9.1    Basic Set Theory

We've already seen sets being used for describing the different collections of numbers (Chapter 1) and solution set of equations (Chapter 7). Let's begin by recalling the definition of a set and take a look at some examples. Following this, we will learn about subsets, intersections and unions of sets. These notions will be enough for us to describe sets using inequalities.

**Definition 1:** A **set** is a collection of objects, called **elements** or **members**.

Recall from Chapter 1 that we use the braces '{   }' to denote the set of elements. The elements are those things which appear in the braces.

**Examples.** The following are sets:

1) The set of whole numbers less than 5 is $\{0, 1, 2, 3, 4\}$.

We can also write this as $\{x \mid x$ is a whole number and $x < 5\}$. We read this as 'the set of all $x$-values such that $x$ is a whole number and $x < 5$'.

2) The set of negative integers greater than or equal to $-6$ is $\{-6, \ -5, \ -4, \ -3, \ -2, \ -1\}$.

This can be written as $\{y \mid y$ is a negative integer and $y \geq -6\}$. We read this as 'the set of all $y$-values such that $y$ is a negative integer and $y \geq -6$'. Notice that I used the variable $y$ this time, not $x$. The name of the variable is up to you. As long as you use it consistently, you will be safe.

3) The set of even numbers between 1 and 13 is $\{2, 4, 6, 8, 10, 12\}$.

4) The set of parents of a baby is {father, mother}.

This cannot be written with inequalities, of course, but it still is a set. The members of the set are 'father' and 'mother'.

5) The set of elements which comprise water is {hydrogen, oxygen}.

When we want to describe a collection of real numbers which satisfy a certain condition, the **set notation** '$\{x \mid ?????\}$' is used, where $x$ is the name of the variable which represents any real number and '?????' is the condition for which the real numbers in our set must satisfy. For example, to write the collection of all positive numbers in set notation, we write (using the variable $x$ to denote a real number)

$$\{x \mid x > 0\}.$$

This is read as 'the set of all $x$-values such that $x > 0$' which is the same as the set of all real numbers which are greater than 0, hence positive. The set $\{t \mid t \leq -2\}$, for example, is the set of all real numbers (each being represented by the variable $t$ this time) which are less than or equal to $-2$.

Sometimes this notation arises when the elements in the set are not real numbers. For example, the set $\{y \mid y = \text{apple}\}$ is the set consisting of the element called 'apple'. **Whenever the elements of the set are not specified, we will assume that they are real numbers.**

There are situations where the set in question does not contain elements. For example, the set of positive numbers which are less than 0 does not contain any elements, since there are no positive numbers which are less than 0. Recall from Chapter 7 that a set which contains no elements is called the **empty set** and is denoted by either $\{\quad\}$ or $\varnothing$.

Let's now practice writing down and describing sets which are given to us in terms of variables.

**Examples.** Describe each set.

1) Let $X = \{x \mid x < 3\}$. Then $X$ is the set of all real numbers which are less than 3.

2) Let $Y = \{y \mid y \geq -4\}$. Then $Y$ is the set of all real numbers which are greater than or equal to $-4$.

3) Let $O = \{t \mid t \text{ is an odd number}\}$. Then $O$ is the set of all odd numbers.

4) Let $S = \{k \mid k + 7 = -2\}$. Then $S$ is the set of all numbers which solve the equation $k + 7 = -2$, that is, $S = \{-9\}$.

5) $\{x \mid x \text{ is an integer}, x = 9 \text{ or } x > 12\}$ is the set of integers $\{9, 13, 14, 15, ...\}$. Recall that the ellipsis, ..., is used to represent that the list continues forever. In other words, there are infinitely many elements in this set and we can't possibly write all of them down. A set which contains an infinite number of elements is called an **infinite set**.

6) $\{B \mid B \text{ is the name of a base in baseball}\}$ is the set {first base, second base, third base, home plate}. There are only 4 elements in this set. In other words, there is a **finite** number (we can write them all down and the list eventually stops) of elements in the set. A set which contains a finite number of elements is called a **finite set**.

7) Let $U = \{u \mid u > 7 \text{ and } u < -2\}$. Then $U = \varnothing$ (that is, $U$ is the empty set), since there is no real number which is both greater than 7 **and** less than $-2$.

**Try These (Set 1):** Describe each set.

1) $Y = \{y \mid y \leq 6\}$              4) $M = \{m \mid m \text{ is an odd number and } 8m + 3 = 6\}$
2) $X = \{x \mid 3x - 5 = 16\}$          5) $P = \{x \mid x \text{ is a prime number and } x < 14\}$
3) $T = \{t \mid t^2 - 9 = 0 \text{ or } -t + 4 = 0\}$     6) $V = \{v \mid v \text{ is a vowel of the alphabet}\}$

**Definition 2:** A **subset** of a set, $S$, is a collection of elements which are also elements of $S$.

By definition, $S$ is a subset of itself. We will consider the empty set to be a subset of every set.

**Notation:** 1. If $S$ is a set and $T$ is a subset of $S$ other than $S$ itself, then we write $T \subset S$.
2. If $S$ is a set and $T$ is not a subset of $S$, then we write $T \not\subseteq S$.
3. If $x$ is an element of $S$, then we write $x \in S$.

Using the notations above, we say that $T$ is a subset of $S$ if $x \in T$ implies that $x \in S$.

**Examples.** Which of the following are subsets of $X = \{x \mid x$ is a positive number and $x$ is an even number$\}$?

1) $S = \{2, 6, 18\}$ is a subset of $X$, since 2, 6 and 18 are all positive numbers and even. We write $S \subset X$.

2) $T = \{4,\ 3,\ 28\}$ is not a subset of $X$, since 3 is not an even number. We write $T \not\subseteq X$.

3) $W = \{12,\ 20,\ 42,\ 0\}$ is not a subset of $X$, since 0 is not a positive number. Therefore, $W \not\subseteq X$.

4) $T = \{100\}$ is a subset of $X$, since 100 is a positive, even number. Hence $T \subset X$.

If it happens that $T$ is a subset of $S$ **and** $S$ is a subset of $T$, then the sets are identical to one another. In this situation, the two sets have the same elements.

**Definition 3:** Two sets, $S$ and $T$, are called **equal** if $S$ has the same elements as $T$. We write $S = T$ when this occurs.

**Examples.** Which of the following sets are equal?

1) $A = \{1,\ 2,\ 3\}$ and $B = \{3,\ 1,\ 2\}$ are equal, since they have the same elements. Notice that the order in which the elements are written in each set is irrelevant.

2) $X = \{x \mid x \geq 0\}$ and $Y = \{y \mid y$ is a nonnegative number$\}$ are equal, since every nonnegative number is either positive or zero.

3) $M = \{m \mid 4m - 2 = 8\}$ and $N = \{n \mid n$ is a rational number$\}$ are not equal sets, since $M$ consists of the solution to $4m - 2 = 8$ (which is just $\frac{5}{2}$), whereas $N$ contains ALL of the rational numbers.

4) $S = \{s \mid s$ is a prime number and $s = 6\}$ and $T = \{t \mid t$ is a perfect square$\}$ are not equal, since $S = \varnothing$ (if $s$ is prime, it cannot equal 6 as well) and $T$ is not the empty set (there are infinitely many perfect squares).

**Try These (Set 2):** Which of the following are subsets of $X = \{x \mid x$ is a negative odd number and $x < -3\}$?

1) $Y = \{-5,\ -19,\ -31\}$        3) $S = \{-3\}$
2) $T = \{t \mid 5t + 4 = 15\}$        4) $K = \{k \mid k^2 - k - 30 = 0$ and $k \leq 0\}$

## The Intersection of Sets

**Definition 4:** The **intersection** of two sets, $S$ and $T$, (written as $S \cap T$) is the set of all elements which are elements of both $S$ and $T$.

Symbolically, we have $S \cap T = \{x \mid x \in S$ and $x \in T\}$.

**Examples.** Find the intersection of the given sets.

1) Let $A = \{-1,\ -2,\ -3,\ -4\}$ and $B = \{-2,\ -4,\ -6,\ -8\}$. Then $A \cap B = \{-2,\ -4\}$, since $-2$ and $-4$ are elements of both $A$ and $B$.

2) Let $X = \{\text{John, Joe, Pat}\}$ and $Y = \{\text{Mary, John, Pete}\}$. Then $X \cap Y = \{\text{John}\}$.

3) Let $P = \{p \mid p \text{ is a positive, odd number}\}$ and $Q = \{q \mid q \leq 7\}$. Then $P \cap Q = \{1,\ 3, 5,\ 7\}$.

4) Let $A = \{x \mid x \text{ is a prime number}\}$ and $B = \{y \mid y \text{ is even and } y > 2\}$. Then $A \cap B = \varnothing$ since there is no prime number which is larger than 2 **and** even.

Note that if $A$ is any set and $B = \varnothing$, then $A \cap B = \varnothing$.

**Try These (Set 3):** Find the intersection of the given sets.

1) $M = \{0,\ 1, 3,\ 5\}$ and $N = \{-1,\ 0, 2,\ 5\}$
2) $X = \{x \mid x \text{ is an odd number}\}$ and $Y = \{q \mid 1 \leq q \leq 12\}$
3) $S = \left\{s \mid s < -\frac{1}{2}\right\}$ and $T = \{t \mid t^2 - 1 = 0\}$
4) $A = \{\text{Kate, Jim, Danielle}\}$ and $B = \{\text{Mary, Bill, Fred}\}$

## The Union of Sets

**Definition 4:** The **union** of two sets, $S$ and $T$, (written as $S \cup T$) is the set of all elements which are elements of $S$ or $T$ or both.

Symbolically, we have $S \cup T = \{x \mid x \in S \text{ or } x \in T \text{ or both}\}$.

**Examples.** Find the union of the given sets.

1) Let $A = \{3,\ 6, 9,\ 12\}$ and $B = \{-5,\ -10\}$. Then $A \cup B = \{3,\ 6, 9,\ 12,\ -5,\ -10\}$, since each of these elements is an element of either $A$ or $B$.

2) Let $X = \{\text{Jack, Jill}\}$ and $Y = \{\text{Tom, Jerry}\}$. Then $X \cup Y = \{\text{Jack, Jill, Tom, Jerry}\}$.

3) Let $M = \{m \mid 7m + 2 = 23\}$ and $N = \{n \mid n^2 = 81\}$. Then $M \cup N = \{3,\ -9, 9\}$.

4) Let $S = \{-2,\ -1, 0,\ 1\}$ and $T = \{-1, 1,\ 2,\ 0\}$. Then $S \cup T = \{-2,\ -1, 0, 1,\ 2\}$.

5) Let $U = \{u \mid u \geq 0\}$ and $V = \{v \mid v < 0\}$. Then $U \cup V$ is the set of all real numbers.

Note that if $A$ is any set and $B = \varnothing$, then $A \cup B = A$.

**Try These (Set 4):** Find the union of the given sets.

1) $P = \{1,\ 4, 9,\ 16\}$ and $Q = \{2, 3, 5,\ 7\}$
2) $S = \{4,\ 7, 12\}$ and $T = \{-3,\ 3, 7\}$
3) $X = \{x \mid -9x + 2 = 4\}$ and $Y = \{y \mid y^2 + 8y + 16 = 0\}$
4) $A = \{a \mid a \geq 8\}$ and $B = \varnothing$

**Exercise 9.1**

In Exercises 1-12, describe the given sets.

1. $X = \{x \mid x > 5\}$   2. $T = \{t \mid t \leq 1\}$   3. $Y = \{y \mid y < 0\}$   4. $S = \{s \mid s \geq 0\}$

5. $E = \{k \mid k \text{ is an even number}\}$   6. $P = \{p \mid p \text{ is a prime number}\}$   7. $A = \{a \mid a - 4 = 11\}$

8. $B = \{b \mid b + 5 = 4\}$   9. $\{x \mid x \text{ is an integer and } x > 1\}$   10. $\{y \mid y \text{ is an integer and } y \geq 2\}$

11. $\{p \mid p \text{ is a natural number and } p \leq 6\}$   12. $\{q \mid q \text{ is a whole number and } q < 9\}$

In Exercises 13-20, determine whether or not the given set is a subset of $N = \{n \mid n \text{ is a negative integer and } n > -8\}$.

13. $A = \{-2, \ -5, \ -1\}$   14. $B = \{-3, \ 7, \ 1\}$   15. $C = \{-4, \ -6, \ -5\}$

16. $D = \{-3, \ -2, \ 0, \ -7\}$   17. $E = \{-1, \ -2, \ -8\}$   18. $F = \{-2, \ -4, \ -\frac{1}{2}\}$

19. $X = \{x \mid x + 4 = -2\}$   20. $Y = \{y \mid \ -7y = 21\}$

In Exercises 21-28, determine which pairs of sets are equal.

21. $A = \{2, \ 0, \ 6\}$ and $B = \{0, \ 6, \ 2\}$

22. $C = \{-3, \ 5, \ -8\}$ and $D = \{-8, \ 5, \ -3\}$

23. $M = \{0.5, \ -0.9, \ 1.45, \ -8.2\}$ and $N = \{1.45, -8.2, \ 0.9, \ 0.5\}$

24. $M = \{3, \ -\pi\}$ and $N = \{-\pi, \ -3\}$

25. $X = \{x \mid x < 0\}$ and $Y = \{y \mid y \text{ is a negative real number}\}$

26. $P = \{p \mid p \geq 0\}$ and $Q = \{q \mid q \text{ is a positive number or } q = 0\}$

27. $S = \{s \mid 3s + 5 = 9\}$ and $T = \{t \mid t \text{ is an irrational number}\}$

28. $U = \{u \mid \ -9u - 1 = 8\}$ and $V = \{v \mid v = -1\}$

In Exercises 29-36, find the intersection of the given sets.

29. $A = \{2, \ 3, \ 5\}$ and $B = \{2, \ 4, \ 5\}$

30. $C = \{-1, \ -4, \ -9\}$ and $B = \{-2, \ -4, \ -6\}$

31. $X = \{\text{Nick, Mike, Bill, Tim, Steve}\}$ and $Y = \{\text{Steve, Bill, Anthony}\}$

32. $U = \{\text{Annemarie, Maggie, Danielle, Ashley}\}$ and $V = \{\text{Nancy, Annemarie, Maggie, Mary}\}$

33. $M = \{m \mid m \text{ is an even number}\}$ and $N = \{n \mid n \text{ is a prime number}\}$

34. $X = \{x \mid x \text{ is a negative odd number}\}$ and $Y = \{y \mid y > -7\}$

35. $P = \{p \mid p \text{ is a prime number}\}$ and $Q = \{q \mid q \text{ is an irrational number}\}$

36. $F = \{f \mid f^2 = 36\}$ and $G = \{g \mid g \leq -12\}$

In Exercises 37-44, find the union of the given sets.

37. $A = \{1,\ 2,\ 4,\ 8\}$ and $B = \{3,\ 2,\ 7\}$        38. $C = \{0,\ -1,\ +1\}$ and $D = \{2,\ 0,\ -2\}$

39. $X = \{\text{Frank, Ned, Vinny, Tony}\}$ and $Y = \{\text{Tom, Avram, Vinny}\}$

40. $M = \{\text{Kaitlyn, Annie, Angelina}\}$ and $N = \{\text{Angelina, Eliana, Lauren, }\}$

41. $P = \{p \mid 5p - 12 = 2\}$ and $Q = \{q \mid q \text{ is an even, prime number}\}$

42. $U = \{u \mid u^2 - 9 = 0\}$ and $V = \{v \mid v^2 - v - 6 = 0\}$

43. $S = \{s \mid s^2 + 10s + 24 = 0\}$ and $T = \{t \mid 3t + 7 = 0\}$

44. $X = \{x \mid x > 0\}$ and $Y = \varnothing$

## Section 9.2   Notations Used with Inequalities and Their Interpretations

In this section, we will learn different ways of expressing an inequality. There are two notations that you should become familiar with. They are the **set notation** (sometimes called the **set-builder notation**) and the **interval notation**. We can also represent a set described by an inequality geometrically by graphing the set on the real number line.

What I have done is constructed a chart below which consists of four columns. The first column contains the inequality, the second contains the set notation, the third contains the interval notation and the fourth contains the graph. As you will see, once you know how the notations look for a specific inequality, the others look the same except for the number being used. After studying the chart for a little while, look at the examples which follow. These will get you used to converting from one notation to another. In the chart below, suppose that $a$ and $b$ represent real numbers and $x$ is a variable.

| Inequality | Set Notation | Interval Notation | Graph |
|---|---|---|---|
| $x > a$ | $\{x \mid x > a\}$ | $(a, \infty)$ | |
| $x \geq a$ | $\{x \mid x \geq a\}$ | $[a, \infty)$ | |
| $x < a$ | $\{x \mid x < a\}$ | $(-\infty, a)$ | |
| $x \leq a$ | $\{x \mid x \leq a\}$ | $(-\infty, a]$ | |
| $a < x < b$ | $\{x \mid a < x < b\}$ | $(a, b)$ | |
| $a \leq x \leq b$ | $\{x \mid a \leq x \leq b\}$ | $[a, b]$ | |
| $a < x \leq b$ | $\{x \mid a < x \leq b\}$ | $(a, b]$ | |
| $a \leq x < b$ | $\{x \mid a \leq x < b\}$ | $[a, b)$ | |

**Examples.** Write each inequality in both set notation and interval notation. Graph each set.

1) $x > 2$

In set notation, we have $\{x \mid x > 2\}$. In interval notation, we have $(2, \infty)$. The graph is

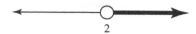

2) $x \leq -4$

In set notation, we have $\{x \mid x \leq -4\}$. In interval notation, we have $(-\infty, -4]$. The graph is

3) $y < 0$

The set notation is $\{y \mid y < 0\}$ and the interval notation is $(-\infty, 0)$. The graph is

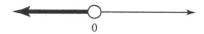

4) $m \geq 9$

The set notation is $\{m \mid m \geq 9\}$ and the interval notation is $[9, \infty)$. The graph is

5) $t \leq 12$

The set notation is $\{t \mid t \leq 12\}$ and the interval notation is $(-\infty, 12]$. The graph is

6) $-2 < x < 5$

The set notation is $\{x \mid -2 < x < 5\}$ and interval notation is $(-2, 5)$. Note that neither $-2$ nor $5$ is included in the set. For this reason, we say that $(-2, 5)$ is an **open interval**. The graph is

7) $0 \leq y \leq 7$

In set notation, we have $\{y \mid 0 \leq y \leq 7\}$ and, in interval notation, we have $[0, 7]$. This time, both $0$ and $7$ are included in the set. We call $[0, 7]$ a **closed interval**. The graph is

8) $-8 < t \leq -4$

In set notation, we have $\{t \mid -8 < t \leq -4\}$ and, in interval notation, we have $(-8, -4]$. Observe that only one of the two numbers, namely $-4$, is included in the set. We call $(-8, -4]$ a **half-open** (or **half-closed**) **interval**. The graph is

9) $6 \leq x < 11$

The set notation is $\{x \mid 6 \leq x < 11\}$ and the interval notation is $[6 , 11)$. We call $[6 , 11)$ a **half-open** (or **half-closed**) **interval**. The graph is

$$\underset{6 \qquad\qquad 11}{\phantom{x}}$$

**Exercise 9.2**

In Exercises 1-24, write each inequality in both set notation and interval notation. Graph the inequality.

1. $x < 2$       2. $y \geq -3$       3. $t > 7$       4. $t \leq 0$       5. $a \leq 5$

6. $b < -8$       7. $x \geq -1$       8. $y > 8$       9. $p < \dfrac{1}{3}$       10. $q \geq \dfrac{5}{7}$

11. $x > \sqrt{2}$       12. $y \leq \sqrt[3]{7}$       13. $a \leq 5.927$       14. $b > -2.116$       15. $-4 \leq x \leq 0$

16. $1 < y < 5$       17. $0 \leq x < 3$       18. $-9 \leq p \leq -7$       19. $0 < q < 2$       20. $3 < t \leq 11$

21. $-4 < x \leq 4$       22. $-6 \leq y < -2$       23. $-\pi \leq x \leq \pi$       24. $0 < x < 2\pi$

In Exercises 25-42, write each interval as an inequality using $x$ as the variable.

25. $(4 , \infty)$       26. $(-\infty , -1]$       27. $[-3 , \infty)$       28. $(7 , \infty)$       29. $(-\infty , 6)$

30. $(-\infty , 1]$       31. $(10, \infty)$       32. $[14 , \infty)$       33. $(-\infty , 3]$       34. $(2 , \infty)$

35. $(-1 , 1)$       36. $(-4 , -2)$       37. $[2 , 8]$       38. $[-3 , 0]$       39. $(0 , 5]$

40. $[-12 , -11)$       41. $[-2\pi , 0)$       42. $(-\pi , \pi)$

## Section 9.3   Properties of Inequalities

In this section, we will take a look at some properties which inequalities satisfy.

**Property I:   The Transitive Property**

Suppose $a$, $b$ and $c$ are any real numbers. Then

$$a < b \text{ and } b < c \text{ implies that } a < c.$$

For example, $-2 < 5$ and $5 < 7$ implies that $-2 < 7$.

**Property II:   The Nonnegative Property**

$$\text{If } a \text{ is any real number, then } a^2 \geq 0.$$

In other words, whenever you square a real number, your answer is guarenteed to be either positive or zero.

**Property III:   The Addition (and Subtraction) Property of Inequalities**

Suppose $a$, $b$ and $c$ are any real numbers.
1. If $a < b$, then $a + c < b + c$.       3. If $a > b$, then $a + c > b + c$.
2. If $a \leq b$, then $a + c \leq b + c$.       4. If $a \geq b$, then $a + c \geq b + c$.

For example, let's pick any two numbers, say $-3$ and $4$. We know that $-3 < 4$. Now, if we add (or subtract) any real number on both sides, then the inequality will remain unchanged. If we choose the number $6$, then observe that $\underbrace{-3 + 6}_{3} < \underbrace{4 + 6}_{10}$. If we choose the number $-13$ instead, then $\underbrace{-3 - 13}_{-16} < \underbrace{4 - 13}_{-9}$. In both cases, the inequality remains unchanged.

**Property IV:   The Multiplication (and Division) Property of Inequalities**

Suppose $a$ and $b$ are any real numbers. There are two cases to consider.

**Case i.** Suppose $c > 0$ (so $c$ is a positive number).

1. If $a < b$, then $ac < bc$.       3. If $a > b$, then $ac > bc$.
2. If $a \leq b$, then $ac \leq bc$.       4. If $a \geq b$, then $ac \geq bc$.

For example, we know that $-4 < 6$. If we multiply (or divide) any positive number on both sides, then the inequality will remain unchanged. If we choose the number $2$, then observe that $\underbrace{-4(2)}_{-8} < \underbrace{6(2)}_{12}$. If we divide both sides by $12$ instead, then $\underbrace{-\frac{4}{12}}_{-\frac{1}{3}} < \underbrace{\frac{6}{12}}_{\frac{1}{2}}$. In both cases, the inequality remains unchanged.

**Case ii.** Suppose $c < 0$ (so $c$ is a negative number).

1. If $a < b$, then $ac > bc$.       3. If $a > b$, then $ac < bc$.
2. If $a \leq b$, then $ac \geq bc$.       4. If $a \geq b$, then $ac \leq bc$.

Notice that the inequality symbol **reverses**. For example, we know that $-1 < 7$. If we multiply (or divide) by any **negative** number on both sides, then the **inequality reverses** and 'points' in the other direction. If we choose the number $-4$, say, then observe that $\underbrace{-1(-4)}_{4} > \underbrace{7(-4)}_{-28}$ and the inequality reversed. If we divide both sides by the number $-7$ instead, then $\underbrace{\frac{-1}{-7}}_{\frac{1}{7}} > \underbrace{\frac{7}{-7}}_{-1}$ and the inequality reversed once again.

The next property follows from Properties II and IV.

**Property V:  The Reciprocal Property of Inequalities**

1. If $a > 0$, then $\dfrac{1}{a} > 0$.

2. If $a < 0$, then $\dfrac{1}{a} < 0$.

For example, since $6 > 0$, we have $\dfrac{1}{6} > 0$. Since $-9 < 0$, we have $\dfrac{1}{-9} < 0$.

Of the properties mentioned above, the important ones for us will be Properties III and IV. By using these, we will be able to solve linear inequalities.

**Exercise 9.3**

Fill in the blanks with either $<$, $>$, $\leq$ or $\geq$ .

1. If $x < y$ and $y < 4$, then $x$___4.     2. If $a < 7$ and $7 < b$, then $a$___$b$.

3. If $p > q$ and $q > 1$, then $p$___1.     4. If $0 > s$ and $s > t$, then $0$___$t$.

5. If $x > y$ and $z < y$, then $z$___$x$.     6. If $7 > m$ and $7 < k$, then $k$___$m$.

7. $6^2$___0     8. $0$___$4^2$     9. $0$___$(-4)^2$     10. $(-7)^2$___$0$     11. $6^2$___$-6^2$     12. $-2^2$___$(-2)^2$

13. If $x > 1$, then $x + 5$___6.          14. If $y \geq 3$, then $y + 2$___5.     15. If $a \leq 4$, then $a + 7$___11.

16. If $b < 7$, then $b + 2$___9.     17. If $p \geq -6$, then $p - 4$___$-10$.     18. If $q > 0$, then $q - 12$___$-12$.

19. If $x > 3$, then $x - 9$___$-6$.     20. If $y \leq -10$, then $y - 13$___$-23$.     21. If $x \leq 5$, then $3x$___15.

22. If $y > -4$, then $7y$___$-28$.     23. If $a \geq -8$, then $\dfrac{a}{4}$___$-2$ .     24. If $m \leq -32$, then $\dfrac{m}{16}$___$-2$.

25. If $n < 16$, then $-2n$___$-32$.     26. If $k \geq -3$, then $-7k$___21.     27. If $x \leq -\dfrac{2}{3}$, then $-9x$___6.

28. If $t > -\dfrac{5}{7}$, then $-14t$___10.

# Section 9.4   Solving Linear Inequalities

We are ready to solve linear inequalities. By using Properties III and IV mentioned in the previous section, we can solve for a variable in a linear inequality. To do this, you take the same steps as if you are solving a linear equation. You can add and subtract on both sides of an inequality without reversing the inequality symbol. You can also multiply or divide both sides of an inequality by a positive number without reversing the inequality symbol. However, if you multiply or divide both sides of an inequality by a negative number, then the inequality symbol will reverse. This is really the only catch to solving a linear inequality. Let's try some examples of solving linear inequalities which contain one inequality symbol (**one-sided inequalities**). Afterwards, we will solve compound (or two-sided) linear inequalities.

**Examples.** Solve each linear inequality. Write the solution set in both set notation and interval notation.

1) $x + 5 > 9$

Subtracting 5 from both sides doesn't reverse the inequality.

$$x + \cancel{5} > 9$$
$$\underline{-\cancel{5} \quad - 5}$$
$$x \quad\quad > 4$$

In set notation, we write $\{x \mid x > 4\}$. In interval notation, we write $(4, \infty)$.

2) $y - 3 \leq 8$

Adding 3 on both sides doesn't reverse the inequality.

$$y - \cancel{3} \leq 8$$
$$\underline{+\cancel{3} \quad + 3}$$
$$y \quad\quad \leq 11$$

In set notation, we write $\{y \mid y \leq 11\}$. In interval notation, we write $(-\infty, 11]$.

3) $6x \geq 42$

Dividing by 6 on both sides doesn't reverse the inequality, since 6 is positive.

$$\frac{\cancel{6}x}{\cancel{6}} \geq \frac{42}{6}$$
$$x \geq 7$$

In set notation, we write $\{x \mid x \geq 7\}$. In interval notation, we write $[7, \infty)$.

4) $\dfrac{7}{8}t < -14$

Multiplying by $\dfrac{8}{7}$ on both sides doesn't reverse the inequality, since $\dfrac{8}{7}$ is positive.

$$\frac{7}{8}t \quad < \quad -14$$
$$\frac{\cancel{8}}{7}\left(\frac{7}{\cancel{8}}t\right) \quad < \quad \frac{\overset{2}{\cancel{-14}}}{1}\left(\frac{8}{7}\right)$$
$$t \quad < \quad -16$$

In set notation, we write $\{t \mid t < -16\}$. In interval notation, we write $(-\infty, -16)$.

5) $-2x < -18$

Dividing by $-2$ on both sides **does** reverse the inequality, since $-2$ is **negative**.

$$-2x \quad < \quad -18$$
$$\frac{\cancel{-2x}}{\cancel{-2}} \quad > \quad \frac{-18}{-2}$$
$$x \quad > \quad 9$$

In set notation, we write $\{x \mid x > 9\}$. In interval notation, we write $(9, \infty)$.

6) $-\frac{2}{3}y \geq 8$

Multiplying by $-\frac{3}{2}$ on both sides **does** reverse the inequality, since $-\frac{3}{2}$ is **negative**.

$$-\frac{2}{3}y \;\geq\; 8$$

$$-\frac{3}{2}\left(-\frac{2}{3}y\right) \;\leq\; -\frac{3}{2}\left(\frac{\overset{4}{8}}{1}\right)$$

$$y \;\leq\; -12$$

In set notation, we write $\{y \mid y \leq -12\}$. In interval notation, we write $(-\infty, -12]$.

7) $6x + 3 < x - 17$

Solve this by applying the same steps as for solving an equation.

$$
\begin{array}{r}
6x + 3 < x - 17 \\
\underline{-x \qquad\quad -x} \\
5x + 3 < \quad -17 \\
\underline{-3 \qquad -3} \\
\dfrac{5x}{5} < \dfrac{-20}{5} \\
\end{array}
$$

$$x < -4$$

In set notation, we write $\{x \mid x < -4\}$. In interval notation, we write $(-\infty, -4)$.

8) $-5(x + 2) - 1 \leq 2x + 4(2x + 1)$

First remove the parentheses by distributing, then combine like terms. Afterwards, the rest is the same as in example 7.

$$
\begin{array}{c}
-5(x + 2) - 1 \leq 2x + 4(2x + 1) \\
-5x - 10 - 1 \leq 2x + 8x + 4 \\
-5x - 11 \leq 10x + 4 \\
\underline{+5x \qquad\qquad +5x} \\
-11 \leq 15x + 4 \\
\underline{-4 \qquad\qquad -4} \\
\dfrac{-15}{15} \leq \dfrac{15x}{15} \\
-1 \leq x
\end{array}
$$

In set notation, we write $\{x \mid -1 \leq x\}$. In interval notation, we write $[-1, \infty)$.

9) $\frac{3}{7}t - 2 \geq \frac{1}{2}t + \frac{2}{7}$

First, clear the fractions by multiplying both sides by the LCM of 2 and 7, which is 14. Then procede as before.

$$\frac{3}{7}t - 2 \geq \frac{1}{2}t + \frac{2}{7}$$

$$\frac{14}{1}\left(\frac{3}{7}t - 2\right) \geq \frac{14}{1}\left(\frac{1}{2}t + \frac{2}{7}\right)$$

$$\overset{2}{\frac{14}{1}}\left(\frac{3}{7}t\right) - \frac{14}{1}(2) \geq \overset{7}{\frac{14}{1}}\left(\frac{1}{2}t\right) + \overset{2}{\frac{14}{1}}\left(\frac{2}{7}\right)$$

$$6t - 28 \geq 7t + 4$$
$$\underline{-6t \qquad\qquad -6t}$$
$$-28 \geq t + 4$$
$$\underline{-4 \qquad -4}$$
$$-32 \geq t$$

In set notation, we write $\{t \mid -32 \geq t\}$. In interval notation, we write $(-\infty, -32]$.

10) $\dfrac{-8x + 9}{3} < 12$

As in example 9, let's first clear the fraction by multiplying both sides by 3. In the last step, we will divide by $-8$, causing the inequality symbol to reverse.

$$\frac{-8x + 9}{3} < 12$$

$$\frac{3}{1}\left(\frac{-8x + 9}{3}\right) < \frac{3}{1}(12)$$

$$\frac{3}{1}\left(\frac{-8x + 9}{3}\right) < 36$$

$$-8x + 9 < 36$$
$$\underline{\qquad -9 \quad -9}$$
$$-8x < 27$$
$$\frac{-8x}{-8} > \frac{27}{-8}$$
$$x > \frac{27}{-8}$$

In set notation, we write $\left\{x \mid x > -\dfrac{27}{8}\right\}$. In interval notation, we write $\left(-\dfrac{27}{8}, \infty\right)$.

**Try These (Set 5):** Solve each linear inequality. Write the solution set in interval notation.

1) $4x - 2 > 18$

2) $-3y + 7 \geq 16$

3) $5t - 6(2t - 3) \leq 16$

4) $\dfrac{2}{5}x + 3 < -\dfrac{1}{6}x - 1$

5) $\dfrac{2x + 1}{9} \leq -3$

6) $\dfrac{-1}{12}y > \dfrac{5}{6}$

Let's solve some compound inequalities. There are two types of compound inequalities which we will be concerned with. The first type deals with two inequalities which are joined by the word 'and'. The solution to such an inequality is obtained by taking the **intersection** of two sets. The second type deals with two inequalities which are joined by the word 'or'. The solution to this type of inequality is found by taking the **union** of two sets in this case.

# The Word 'AND'

Suppose we want to solve the compound inequality $-1 < 5x + 4 < 1$. Observe that this inequality can be broken up in the following way:

$$-1 < 5x + 4 \quad \text{and} \quad 5x + 4 < 1$$

Now all we need to do is solve each of these inequalities individually. Notice that the values of $x$ which we are looking for MUST satisfy both inequalities in order to be a solution to the original compound inequality. In other words, the solution set of $-1 < 5x + 4 < 1$ is the intersection of the solution sets of $-1 < 5x + 4$ and $5x + 4 < 1$. Let's find each solution set.

$$
\begin{array}{ccc}
-1 < 5x + \cancel{4} & & 5x + \cancel{4} < 1 \\
\underline{-4 \qquad -\cancel{4}} & \text{and} & \underline{\qquad -\cancel{4} \ -4} \\
\dfrac{-5}{5} < \dfrac{\cancel{5}x}{\cancel{5}} & & \dfrac{\cancel{5}x}{\cancel{5}} < \dfrac{-3}{5} \\
-1 < x & \text{and} & x < -\dfrac{3}{5}
\end{array}
$$

Therefore, the set of numbers which satisfy the original inequality is $\left\{ x \mid -1 < x < -\dfrac{3}{5} \right\}$. In interval notation, we have $\left( -1, -\dfrac{3}{5} \right)$. The graph is obtained by taking the graphs of each inequality, $-1 < x$ and $x < -\dfrac{3}{5}$, and putting them on the same number line. The place where they overlap each other is the graph of the inequality $-1 < x < -\dfrac{3}{5}$. The reason for this is because the set $\left\{ x \mid -1 < x < -\dfrac{3}{5} \right\}$ represents the intersection of the two sets $\{ x \mid -1 < x \}$ and $\left\{ x \mid x < -\dfrac{3}{5} \right\}$:

$$\left\{ x \mid -1 < x < -\frac{3}{5} \right\} = \{ x \mid -1 < x \} \cap \left\{ x \mid x < -\frac{3}{5} \right\}$$

We can solve the above compound inequality without splitting it up into two seperate problems. Roughly speaking, whatever you do to the middle expression of the inequality, you do to both 'ends' as well. Let's see how this works.

$$
\begin{array}{c}
-1 < 5x + \cancel{4} < 1 \\
\underline{-4 \qquad -\cancel{4} \quad -4} \\
\dfrac{-5}{5} < \dfrac{\cancel{5}x}{\cancel{5}} < \dfrac{-3}{5} \\
-1 < x < -\dfrac{3}{5}
\end{array}
$$

As you can see, it is simpler to solve it in this way. Let's try some examples using this shorter method.

**Examples.** Solve each of the following inequalities. Write the solution set in both set notation and interval notation.

1) $-2 \le 8x - 9 \le 7$

$$-2 \le 8x - 9 \le 7$$
$$\underline{+9 \qquad\quad +9 \quad +9}$$
$$\frac{7}{8} \le \frac{8x}{8} \le \frac{16}{8}$$
$$\frac{7}{8} \le x \le 2$$

The set notation is $\left\{ x \mid \frac{7}{8} \le x \le 2 \right\}$. The interval notation is $\left[ \frac{7}{8}, 2 \right]$.

2) $0 < 6x + 5 < 11$

$$0 < 6x + 5 < 11$$
$$\underline{-5 \qquad\quad -5 \quad -5}$$
$$\frac{-5}{6} < \frac{6x}{6} < \frac{6}{6}$$
$$-\frac{5}{6} < x < 1$$

The set notation is $\left\{ x \mid -\frac{5}{6} < x < 1 \right\}$. The interval notation is $\left( -\frac{5}{6}, 1 \right)$.

3) $-\frac{1}{3} < -x + 2 \le 3$

In this example, notice that **both** inequality symbols reverse when multiplying by $-1$.

$$-\frac{1}{3} < -x + 2 \le 3$$
$$\underline{-2 \qquad\quad -2 \quad -2}$$
$$\frac{-7}{3} < -x \le 1$$
$$-1\left(\frac{-7}{3}\right) > -1(-x) \ge -1(1)$$
$$\frac{7}{3} > x \ge -1$$

The set notation is $\left\{ x \mid \frac{7}{3} > x \ge -1 \right\}$. The interval notation is $\left[ -1, \frac{7}{3} \right)$.

4) $4 \le \frac{5y - 6}{-2} \le 5$

Once again, **both** inequality symbols reverse when multiplying by $-2$.

$$4 \le \frac{5y - 6}{-2} \le 5$$

$$-2(4) \ge -2\left(\frac{5y - 6}{-2}\right) \ge -2(5)$$

$$-8 \ge 5y - 6 \ge -10$$
$$\underline{+6 \qquad +6 \qquad +6}$$
$$\frac{-2}{5} \ge \frac{5y}{5} \ge \frac{-4}{5}$$

$$-\frac{2}{5} \ge y \ge -\frac{4}{5}$$

The set notation is $\left\{y \mid -\frac{2}{5} \ge y \ge -\frac{4}{5}\right\}$. The interval notation is $\left[-\frac{4}{5}, \ -\frac{2}{5}\right]$.

5) $-7 \le \dfrac{-2t + 5}{-3} < -5$

In this example, two inequality reversals take place, one from multiplying by $-3$ and the other from dividing by $-2$.

$$-7 \le \frac{-2t + 5}{-3} < -5$$

$$-3(-7) \ge -3\left(\frac{-2t + 5}{-3}\right) > -3(-5)$$
$$21 \ge -2t + 5 > 15$$
$$\underline{-5 \qquad -5 \qquad -5}$$
$$16 \ge -2t > 10$$
$$\frac{16}{-2} \le \frac{-2t}{-2} < \frac{10}{-2}$$

$$-8 \le t < -5$$

The set notation is $\{t \mid -8 \le t < -5\}$. The interval notation is $[-8, -5)$.

**Try These (Set 6):** Solve each of the following inequalities. Write the solution set in interval notation.

1) $-1 < 7x + 9 < 3$      3) $-6 < -t + 12 \le -3$

2) $0 \le -\frac{2}{7}y - 5 \le 1$      4) $4 \le \dfrac{9x + 2}{5} < 5$

# The Word 'OR'

Let's solve the compound inequality

$$3x + 2 < -1 \text{ or } 3x + 2 \ge 8$$

The word 'or' in this problem is used to represent the fact that we are looking for those $x-$values which satisfy either the first inequality $3x + 2 < -1$, the second inequality $3x + 2 \geq 8$ or both of them. Notice the difference between the word 'or' and the word 'and'. If $x = n$ is a solution to a compound inequality containing the word 'and', then **both** inequalities to be satisfied by $x = n$ in order to be a solution (see the examples above). The word 'or', however, only requires that **at least one** of the two inequalities be satisfied by $x = n$, say, in order to be a solution. Now, how do we solve the problem? Well, it's very simple. Just solve each inequality individually and join the solution sets of each by the word 'or'. In other words, the solution set of the compound inequality will be the union of the solution sets of each individual inequality. Let's solve this problem.

$$
\begin{array}{ccc}
3x + 2 < -1 & \text{or} & 3x + 2 \geq 8 \\
\underline{\phantom{3x} - 2 \quad -2} & & \underline{\phantom{3x} - 2 \quad -2} \\
\dfrac{3x}{3} < \dfrac{-3}{3} & & \dfrac{3x}{3} \geq \dfrac{6}{3} \\
x < -1 & \text{or} & x \geq 2
\end{array}
$$

The set notation for this solution is $\{x \mid x < -1 \text{ or } x \geq 2\}$. The interval notation is $(-\infty, -1) \cup [2, \infty)$. Since we are taking the union of the two sets, the graph of $\{x \mid x < -1\} \cup \{x \mid x \geq 2\}$ will just be the graph of each set on the **same** number line. Hence, our graph is

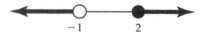

Observe that the sets $\{x \mid x < -1\}$ and $\{x \mid x \geq 2\}$ have no elements in common, so we have

$$\{x \mid x < -1\} \cap \{x \mid x \geq 2\} = \varnothing.$$

In this case, we say that the sets are **disjoint** and we call $(-\infty, -1) \cup [2, \infty)$ the **disjoint union** of the sets $(-\infty, -1)$ and $[2, \infty)$.

**Examples.** Solve each of the following inequalities. Write the solution set in both set notation and interval notation.

1) $2x - 1 \leq -5$ or $2x - 1 \geq 5$

$$
\begin{array}{ccc}
2x - 1 \leq -5 & \text{or} & 2x - 1 \geq 5 \\
\underline{+1 \quad +1} & & \underline{+1 \quad +1} \\
\dfrac{2x}{2} \leq \dfrac{-4}{2} & & \dfrac{2x}{2} \geq \dfrac{6}{2} \\
x \leq -2 & \text{or} & x \geq 3
\end{array}
$$

The set notation for this solution is $\{x \mid x \leq -2 \text{ or } x \geq 3\}$. The interval notation is $(-\infty, -2] \cup [3, \infty)$.

2) $\frac{4}{5}x + 6 \le 2$ or $\frac{4}{5}x + 6 > 5$

$$
\begin{array}{ccc}
\frac{4}{5}x + \cancel{6} \le 2 & \text{or} & \frac{4}{5}x + \cancel{6} > 5 \\
\underline{-\cancel{6} \quad -6} & & \underline{-\cancel{6} \quad -6} \\
\frac{4}{5}x \le -4 & & \frac{4}{5}x > -1 \\
\frac{\cancel{5}}{4}\left(\frac{\cancel{4}x}{\cancel{5}}\right) \le \frac{5}{4}\left(\frac{-\cancel{4}}{1}\right) & & \frac{\cancel{5}}{4}\left(\frac{\cancel{4}x}{\cancel{5}}\right) > \frac{5}{4}(-1) \\
x \le -5 & \text{or} & x > -\frac{5}{4}
\end{array}
$$

The set notation for this solution is $\left\{ x \mid x \le -5 \text{ or } x > -\frac{5}{4} \right\}$. The interval notation is $(-\infty, -5] \cup \left(-\frac{5}{4}, \infty\right)$.

3) $-9y + 3 < -12$ or $-9y + 3 \ge -10$

Notice that **both** inequalities reverse when dividing by $-9$.

$$
\begin{array}{ccc}
-9y + \cancel{3} < -12 & \text{or} & -9y + \cancel{3} \ge -10 \\
\underline{-\cancel{3} \quad -3} & & \underline{-\cancel{3} \quad -3} \\
-9y < -15 & & -9y \ge -13 \\
\frac{\cancel{-9}y}{\cancel{-9}} > \frac{-15}{-9} & & \frac{\cancel{-9}y}{\cancel{-9}} \le \frac{-13}{-9} \\
y > \frac{5}{3} & \text{or} & y \le \frac{13}{9}
\end{array}
$$

The set notation for this solution is $\left\{ y \mid y > \frac{5}{3} \text{ or } y \le \frac{13}{9} \right\}$. The interval notation is $\left(\frac{5}{3}, \infty\right) \cup \left(-\infty, \frac{13}{9}\right]$.

   As you may observe, solving the compound inequalities containing the word 'or' isn't so bad. You just have to solve two seperate inequalities and put the word 'or' in between their solution sets. As we will soon see, you can sometimes get a compound inequality containing the word 'or' in which the seperate inequalities have solution sets that are not disjoint. Before doing these, try the next examples on your own.

**Try These (Set 7):** Solve each of the following inequalities. Write the solution set in interval notation.

1) $4x - 1 \le -2$ or $4x - 1 \ge 2$

2) $-y - 6 < 7$ or $-y - 6 \ge 10$

3) $\frac{2x+3}{-5} < -1$ or $\frac{2x+3}{-5} > 0$

4) $\frac{6}{7}t + 2 \le 2$ or $\frac{6}{7}t + 2 > 6$

   When solving a compound inequality, you must be careful. Sometimes, when the given example contains the word 'and' or 'or', the intersection or union of the set described by the inequalities may not be as we learned above. For example, suppose we want to write the set $\{y \mid y < 1 \text{ and } y > 6\}$ in a more simplified form. If you read this carefully, you will notice that the set being described is the **empty set**. There is no real number which is less than 1 and, at the same time, greater than 6. Therefore, $\{y \mid y < 1 \text{ and } y > 6\} = \{y \mid y < 1\} \cap \{y \mid y > 6\} = \varnothing$. Graphically, you will notice that if both sets are graphed on the same number line, no overlapping occurs. Let's now simplify $\{x \mid x < 4 \text{ or } x > 0\}$. This set is just the set of **all** of the real numbers. To see this, notice that if you pick any real number, then the number must be either less than 4 or greater than 0 or possibly both (remember that the word 'or' means than at least one of the two inequalities must be satisfied). Therefore, $\{x \mid x < 4 \text{ or } x > 0\} = (-\infty, \infty)$. Once again, if you graph both of these inequalities on the real number line, then, together, they cover the whole line. However, the whole line represents the set of all of the real numbers. Let's now do some examples.

**Examples.** Solve each inequality. Write the solution set in both set notation and interval notation.

1) $x + 3 > 7$ and $2x - 5 \leq -1$

Well, we just need to solve each inequality individually and then simplify our answer.

$$
\begin{array}{ccc}
x \cancel{+ 3} > 7 & \text{and} & 2x \cancel{- 5} \leq -1 \\
\underline{-3 \quad - 3} & & \underline{+5 \quad + 5} \\
x > 4 & & \dfrac{\cancel{2}x}{\cancel{2}} \leq \dfrac{4}{2} \\
x > 4 & \text{and} & x \leq 2
\end{array}
$$

Now, there is **no** real number which is both greater than 4 and less than or equal to 2. Therefore, the solution set is $\varnothing$.

2) $x - 5 > -8$ or $3x + 1 < 10$

As above, we will solve each inequality individually and then simplify our answer.

$$
\begin{array}{ccc}
x \cancel{- 5} > -8 & \text{or} & 3x + \cancel{1} < 10 \\
\underline{+ 5 \quad + 5} & & \underline{-1 \quad - 1} \\
x > -3 & & \dfrac{\cancel{3}x}{\cancel{3}} < \dfrac{9}{3} \\
x > -3 & \text{or} & x < 3
\end{array}
$$

Now, if you choose **any** real number, isn't it true that the number must be either greater than $-3$ or less than 3 or possibly both? Pick any number and see for yourself. You can even graph both of these sets on the same number line and notice that you cover the whole line. The solution set, therefore, is $\{x \mid -\infty < x < \infty\}$. In interval form, we write $(-\infty, \infty)$.

3) $8t - 1 < 9$ and $-\dfrac{t}{3} \geq \dfrac{1}{6}$

$$
\begin{array}{ccc}
8t - \cancel{1} < 9 & \text{and} & -\dfrac{t}{3} \geq \dfrac{1}{6} \\
& & \dfrac{-\cancel{3}}{1}\left(-\dfrac{t}{\cancel{3}}\right) \leq -\dfrac{\cancel{3}}{1}\left(\dfrac{1}{\cancel{6}}\right) \\
\underline{+1 \qquad +1} & & \\
\dfrac{\cancel{8}t}{\cancel{8}} < \dfrac{10}{8} & & t \leq -\dfrac{1}{2} \\
t < \dfrac{5}{4} & \text{and} & t \leq -\dfrac{1}{2}
\end{array}
$$

To simplify this set, the easiest way is to graph each on the same number line and see where they overlap (remember that the word 'and' corresponds to the intersection of sets). If you do it in this way, you will see that

$$\left\{ t \mid t < \frac{5}{4} \right\} \cap \left\{ t \mid t \leq -\frac{1}{2} \right\} = \left\{ t \mid t \leq -\frac{1}{2} \right\}.$$

Hence, the solution is $\left( -\infty, \, -\frac{1}{2} \right]$.

4) $8t - 1 < 9$ or $-\dfrac{t}{3} \geq \dfrac{1}{6}$

YES, the inequalities are the same as above. However, the word 'or' is now in the problem. To solve this, you do exactly the same thing as above. We get

$$t < \frac{5}{4} \quad \text{or} \quad t \leq -\frac{1}{2}.$$

To simplify this set, once again I recommend that you graph each of the sets on the same number line. The graph containing both sets is the graph of the solution set (remember that the word 'or' corresponds to the union of sets). If you do it in this way, you will see that

$$\left\{ t \mid t < \frac{5}{4} \right\} \cup \left\{ t \mid t \leq -\frac{1}{2} \right\} = \left\{ t \mid t < \frac{5}{4} \right\}.$$

Hence, the solution is $\left( -\infty, \dfrac{5}{4} \right)$.

**Try These (Set 8):** Solve each inequality.

1) $4x - 3 < 17$ and $\dfrac{1}{3}x \geq 6$

2) $-2y + 4 \leq 9$ and $\dfrac{1}{5}(y + 5) > 2$

3) $\dfrac{-3t + 1}{-8} \leq -2$ or $t \geq -16$

4) $12x - 1 > 3$ or $x + 15 \geq 23$

**Exercise 9.4**

In Exercises 1-37, solve each of the linear inequalities. Write your answer in both set and interval notation.

1. $x + 2 > 9$

2. $x + 5 \geq -1$

3. $y - 6 \leq 2$

4. $y - 7 < 12$

5. $3t \geq 15$

6. $5s < 35$

7. $-2a > 8$

8. $-9b < 27$

9. $\frac{2}{5}x \geq 13$

10. $\frac{3}{7}x < 9$

11. $-\frac{1}{3}p > 14$

12. $-\frac{2}{5}q \leq 8$

13. $3a + 7 \geq 16$

14. $8a - 4 \leq 12$

15. $-2y + 1 < 7$

16. $-3y + 4 \geq 19$

17. $5y - 1 < 9y + 3$

18. $2y + 7 > y - 6$

19. $8b + 10 \leq b$

20. $12b \geq 6b + 20$

21. $-3a + 7 > -10a - 2$

22. $-a + 6 < 8a + 12$

23. $6m + 2(m - 9) < 26m$

24. $4(n + 3) - 12 \leq -14$

25. $\frac{1}{2}x \leq \frac{1}{6}x - \frac{7}{6}$

26. $\frac{2}{5}x - \frac{1}{2} < \frac{1}{10}x$

27. $2 + \frac{1}{8}x \geq \frac{3}{4}x - 9$

28. $4 - \frac{5}{12}x > \frac{5}{6}x + \frac{1}{2}$

29. $\dfrac{6x+3}{4} > 7$  30. $\dfrac{12y-1}{5} \le 3$  31. $\dfrac{-2a+3}{5} < 6$  32. $\dfrac{-11b+3}{10} > 3$

33. $\dfrac{-x+2}{-6} \le 5$  34. $\dfrac{-x+14}{-2} \ge 8$  35. $\dfrac{-9y+2}{-12} > 4$  36. $\dfrac{-10y+8}{-5} \ge 11$

In Exercises 37-70, solve each of the compound inequalities. Write your answer in both set and interval notation.

37. $5 < 2x+1 < 7$  38. $12 < 5x+2 < 27$  39. $-3 < 4y+9 \le 5$  40. $-7 \le 3y+5 \le 2$

41. $0 \le 7y-3 < 11$  42. $-8 < 2y+4 \le 3$  43. $-2 \le 6a+1 \le 12$  44. $-9 \le 4a-1 < -1$

45. $3 < -2x+3 < 9$  46. $1 \le -5x+6 \le 11$  47. $-4 \le -m+7 \le 0$  48. $0 < -n-3 \le 2$

49. $2 < \dfrac{4y-1}{6} \le 4$  50. $-3 \le \dfrac{2y+3}{5} < 5$  51. $7 \le \dfrac{-4a+5}{2} < 8$  52. $-12 < \dfrac{-2b+1}{3} < -10$

53. $-2 < \frac{3}{2}x - \frac{1}{2} < 0$  54. $4 \le \frac{2}{5}x + \frac{1}{10} \le 5$  55. $-6 \le \dfrac{t+3}{-4} \le 1$  56. $-3 \le \dfrac{t-1}{-6} \le 1$

57. $2x+5 < -1$ or $2x+5 > 1$  58. $3y-1 < -2$ or $3y-1 > 2$  59. $\frac{1}{4}a - 1 < 0$ or $\frac{1}{4}a - 1 \ge 5$

60. $\frac{4}{5}b + 2 \le -3$ or $\frac{4}{5}b + 2 > -1$  61. $-x-5 \le 8$ or $-x-5 \ge 12$  62. $-y+1 \le 4$ or $-y+1 \ge 6$

63. $-7p+2 \le -12$ or $-7p+2 > 7$  64. $-5q-8 \le 7$ or $-5q-8 \ge 8$

65. $\dfrac{-3x+2}{5} < 0$ or $\dfrac{-3x+2}{5} > 2$  66. $\dfrac{-5y+1}{6} < 2$ or $\dfrac{-5y+1}{6} \ge 6$

67. $\dfrac{x}{7} - \dfrac{6}{5} \le -3$ or $\dfrac{x}{7} - \dfrac{6}{5} > 3$  68. $\dfrac{t}{3} + \dfrac{4}{7} < -2$ or $\dfrac{t}{3} + \dfrac{4}{7} > 2$

69. $\frac{-1}{6}y + \frac{1}{8} < 0$ or $\frac{-1}{6}y + \frac{1}{8} \ge 2$  70. $\frac{-3}{4}b + \frac{1}{6} \le 4$ or $\frac{-3}{4}b + \frac{1}{6} \ge 5$

In Exercises 71-86, write each set in simplified form.

71. $x < 4$ and $x \le 5$  72. $x \le 2$ and $x \le -3$  73. $x \ge 6$ and $x \le 12$  74. $x > -1$ and $x < 3$

75. $y > -3$ and $y \le 0$  76. $y \le 6$ and $y \ge 8$  77. $y \le -1$ and $y \ge 5$  78. $y > 9$ and $y < 9$

79. $t \le 0$ or $t \le -4$  80. $t < -6$ or $t \le 2$  81. $u > 1$ or $u > -9$  82. $u \ge 2$ or $u \ge 1$

83. $x \ge -8$ or $x \le 0$  84. $x < 10$ or $x > 1$  85. $m \le 0$ or $m > 0$  86. $n \ge 7$ or $n \le 7$

---

# END OF CHAPTER 9   QUIZ

1. In interval notation, the set $\{x \mid x > 3\}$ is
   a) $(\infty, 3)$  b) $(3, \infty)$  c) $(-\infty, 3)$  d) $[3, \infty)$  e) $(3, \infty]$

2. In interval notation, the set $\{y \mid y \le -4\}$ is
   a) $(-\infty, -4)$  b) $[-4, \infty)$  c) $(-4, \infty)$  d) $(-\infty, -4]$  e) $[-\infty, -4]$

3. In interval notation, the set $\{p \mid -1 \leq p < 10\}$ is

    a) $[-1, 10)$    b) $[-1, 10]$    c) $(-1, 10]$    d) $(-1, 10)$    e) $(10, -1]$

4. In interval notation, the set $\{x \mid x < 0 \text{ or } x \geq 6\}$ is

    a) $(-\infty, 0) \cup (6, \infty)$    b) $(-\infty, 0] \cup [6, \infty)$    c) $(-\infty, 0) \cup [6, \infty)$    d) $(0, 6]$
    e) $(-\infty, 0] \cap [6, \infty)$

5. The graph of the set $[2, \infty)$ is

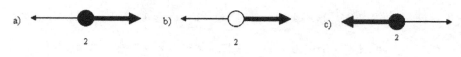

6. The graph of the set $\{t \mid 4 \leq t < 9\}$ is

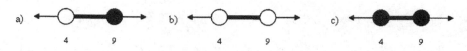

7. Solve for $x$:  $4x - 3 > 9$

    a) $x < 3$    b) $x > 3$    c) $x > \dfrac{3}{2}$    d) $x < \dfrac{3}{2}$    e) $x > 12$

8. Solve for $y$:  $12y - 6 \geq 3y + 6$

    a) $y \geq \dfrac{3}{4}$    b) $y \geq 9$    c) $y \leq \dfrac{4}{3}$    d) $y \geq -\dfrac{4}{3}$    e) $y \geq \dfrac{4}{3}$

9. Solve for $t$:  $-4t - 3(t + 6) < 1$

    a) $t < -\dfrac{19}{7}$    b) $t > \dfrac{19}{7}$    c) $t > -\dfrac{19}{7}$    d) $t > \dfrac{17}{7}$    e) $t < -\dfrac{17}{7}$

10. Solve for $x$:  $\dfrac{x + 2}{3} \leq 10$

    a) $[28, \infty)$    b) $(-\infty, 28]$    c) $\left(\dfrac{4}{3}, \infty\right)$    d) $\left(-\infty, \dfrac{4}{3}\right]$    e) $(-\infty, 28)$

11. Solve for $y$:  $-\dfrac{4}{9}y < 16$

    a) $(36, \infty)$    b) $(-\infty, 36)$    c) $(-\infty, -36)$    d) $(-36, \infty)$    e) $[-36, \infty)$

12. Solve for $m$:  $\dfrac{1}{4}m - \dfrac{1}{2} > \dfrac{2}{3}m + \dfrac{1}{6}$

    a) $\left(-\infty, -\dfrac{8}{5}\right)$    b) $\left(-\dfrac{8}{5}, \infty\right)$    c) $\left(-\infty, -\dfrac{1}{2}\right)$    d) $\left(-\dfrac{7}{5}, \infty\right)$    e) $\left(-\infty, -\dfrac{5}{8}\right)$

13. Solve for $x$: $-5 \le 6x + 1 < 12$

 a) $\left\{ x \mid 1 \le x < \dfrac{11}{6} \right\}$     b) $\left\{ x \mid -1 \le x < \dfrac{13}{6} \right\}$     c) $\left\{ x \mid -1 \le x < \dfrac{11}{6} \right\}$

 d) $\left\{ x \mid -1 \ge x > \dfrac{11}{6} \right\}$     e) $\left\{ x \mid x < \dfrac{11}{6} \right\}$

14. Solve for $x$: $0 < -x + 8 < 16$
 a) $\{ x \mid 8 < x < -8 \}$     b) $\{ x \mid -8 < x < 8 \}$     c) $\{ x \mid x < 8 \}$     d) $\{ x \mid x > -8 \}$
 e) $\{ x \mid -24 < x < 8 \}$

15. Solve for $n$: $-7 \le \dfrac{3n - 2}{-4} \le 6$

 a) $\left[ 10, \ -\dfrac{22}{3} \right]$     b) $\left[ -10, \ \dfrac{22}{3} \right]$     c) $\left( -\dfrac{22}{3}, \ 10 \right)$     d) $\left( -10, \ \dfrac{22}{3} \right)$     e) $\left[ -\dfrac{22}{3}, \ 10 \right]$

16. Solve for $p$: $9p + 2 < -7$ or $9p + 2 > 7$

 a) $\left\{ p \mid p < 1 \text{ or } p > \dfrac{5}{9} \right\}$     b) $\left\{ p \mid p < -1 \text{ or } p > -\dfrac{5}{9} \right\}$     c) $\left\{ p \mid p < -1 \text{ or } p > \dfrac{5}{9} \right\}$

 d) $\left\{ p \mid \dfrac{5}{9} < p < -1 \right\}$     e) $\{ p \mid p < -1 \}$

17. Solve for $k$: $\dfrac{-k + 2}{5} \le -1$ or $\dfrac{-k + 2}{5} > 2$

 a) $\{ k \mid k \le 7 \text{ or } k > -8 \}$     b) $\{ k \mid k < -8 \text{ or } k \ge 7 \}$     c) $\{ k \mid k \le -7 \text{ or } k > 8 \}$
 d) $\{ k \mid 7 \le k < -8 \}$     e) $\{ k \mid k \ge 3 \text{ or } k < -12 \}$

18. Solve for $m$: $\dfrac{-6}{5}m \le 12$ or $\dfrac{-6}{5}m > 13$

 a) $(-\infty, \ -10] \cup \left( -\dfrac{65}{6}, \ \infty \right)$     b) $(-\infty, \ -10) \cup \left[ -\dfrac{65}{6}, \ \infty \right)$     c) $(-10, \ \infty) \cup \left( -\infty, \ -\dfrac{65}{6} \right]$

 d) $[-10, \ \infty) \cup \left( -\infty, \ -\dfrac{65}{6} \right)$     e) $\left[ -\dfrac{72}{5}, \ \infty \right) \cup \left( -\infty, \ -\dfrac{78}{5} \right)$

19. In simplified form, the set $\{ x \mid x \le 5 \text{ or } x < 4 \}$ is
 a) $\{ x \mid x \le 5 \}$     b) $\{ x \mid x < 4 \}$     c) $\{ x \mid 4 < x \le 5 \}$     d) $\{ x \mid x \le 4 \}$     e) $\{ x \mid x < 5 \}$

20. Solve for $y$: $-2y > 16$ and $3y + 2 \le 35$
 a) $(-\infty, \ -8)$     b) $(-\infty, \ 11)$     c) $(-\infty, \ 11]$     d) $(-8, \ 11]$     e) $(-\infty, \ 11] \cup (-8, \ \infty)$

ANSWERS FOR QUIZ 9    1. b        2. d        3. a        4. c        5. a

                    6. d        7. b        8. e        9. c        10. b

                    11. d       12. a       13. c       14. b       15. e

                    16. c       17. b       18. d       19. a       20. a

# Chapter 10:    Equations of Lines and Circles

In Chapter 1, we learned how to locate a number on the real number line. Recall that the point is the geometrical representation of the number and the coordinates for the point is the number itself. One use of the real number line is to graph the solution(s) to an equation in one variable. For example, the solutions to the quadratic equation $x^2 - 8x + 15 = 0$ are $x = 3$ and $x = 5$. We can graph these numbers on the real number line to get a 'picture' of the solution set $\{3, \ 5\}$ as follows:

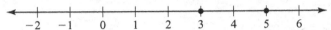

In this chapter, we will learn how to graph the solutions to an equation in two variables, $x$ and $y$. We will be primarily concerned with linear equations in two variables and equations whose graph is a circle. Later on in precalculus, you will learn about other types of equations and their graphs.

In Section 10.1, we will learn about the **Cartesian Plane** (or the **Rectangular Coordinate System**). Roughly speaking, the Cartesian plane is the object on which we will draw things. Besides being used to graph the solutions to an equation in two variables, the Cartesian plane (named after the famous philosopher and mathematician Rene Decartes) is used to prove theorems in geometry. The study of geometric proofs and the techniques being applied in carrying out such proofs is an area of mathematics called **analytic geometry**. Although we will not study this subject in detail, I will discuss the formulas which are used and touch on one or two specific examples which are of interest. Section 10.2 will be devoted to the study of linear equations in two variables and their graphs. In Section 10.3, we will learn about parallel and perpendicular lines. The definition of two lines being parallel or perpendicular has nothing to do with the Cartesian Plane. However, once we understand how to link the graph of a line to an algebraic equation representing the line, we will have an algebraic description of what it means for two lines to be parallel or perpendicular. These notions are important in the study of analytic geometry. The chapter will conclude with Section 10.4, the study of circles and their equations.

## Section 10.1   The Cartesian Plane and Analytic Geometry

Let's begin with the construction of the Cartesian plane. On a piece of paper (which, geometrically speaking, is a two-dimensional object), draw two real number lines, one vertical and the other horizontal. These real number lines are called the **coordinate axes** for our plane. The **vertical axis** will be labeled the $y$-**axis** and the **horizontal axis** will be labeled the $x$-**axis**. The place where both axes intersect is where both the $x$-axis and the $y$-axis have the point 0. Label the $x$-axis in such a way that the numbers are increasing from left to right. Label the $y$-axis in such a way that the numbers are increasing as you go upward. You will obtain the following picture:

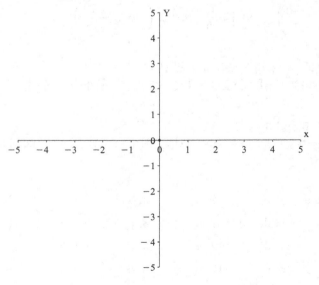

Notice that I only labeled some of the integers on each axis. Of course, I could locate **any** real number on each axis since an axis is just a real number line. The object drawn above is called the **Cartesian Plane** (or **Rectangular Coordinate System** or the $xy$**-plane**).

We want to develop a way of drawing (or graphing) on the Cartesian plane. The first thing we need to do is understand what it is that we want to graph.

**Definition 1:** An **ordered pair** is a pair of real numbers, written as $(x, y)$, where $x$ is the $x$**-coordinate** (or **abscissa**) and $y$ is the $y$**-coordinate** (or **ordinate**).

For example, $(1, -3)$ is an ordered pair with $x$-coordinate 1 and $y$-coordinate $-3$. To draw a picture of this ordered pair, you begin at the place where the axes meet and go 1 unit to the right (along the positive $x$-axis, since 1 is the $x$-coordinate and is positive). You then go down by 3 units (since $-3$ is the $y$-coordinate and is negative). After you do this, you draw a dot. This is the **graph** of the ordered pair $(1, -3)$. Before we graph this, we have some definitions.

**Definition 2:** The graph of an ordered pair is called a **point** in the Cartesian plane. The process of graphing an ordered pair is called **point plotting**.

**Definition 3:** The point with ordered pair $(0, 0)$ is called the **origin**.

We will now plot the point whose ordered pair is $(1, -3)$. In other words, we will plot the point whose coordinates are $x = 1$ and $y = -3$. We will identify a point in the Cartesian plane with its ordered pair. For example, if I say 'the point $(-5, 0)$', I'm referring to the point whose ordered pair is $(-5, 0)$. Below, I plotted several points for you to look at, including $(1, -3)$ and $(-5, 0)$.

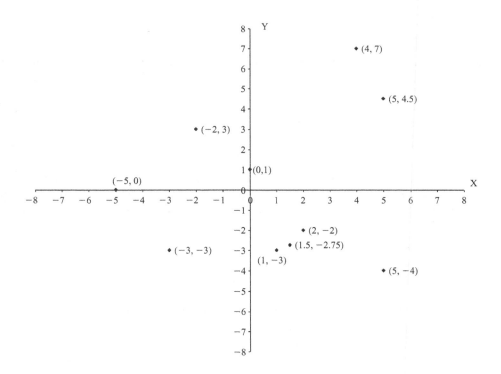

Notice that the coordinate axes divide the $xy$−plane into four pieces. We call these the **quadrants** of the Cartesian plane. On the next page, I have labeled the quadrants using roman numerals. I also mentioned the sign of each variable in each quadrant. Notice that points which lie on the $x$- or $y$-axis do not lie in a quadrant.

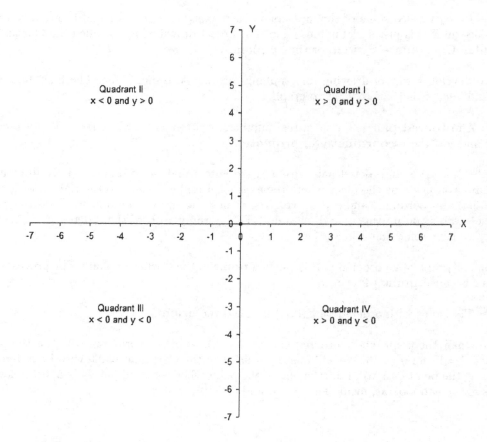

**Try These (Set 1):** Plot the points whose ordered pairs are given and state the quadrant it lies in (if any).

1) $(2, 1)$      3) $\left(\frac{1}{2}, 3\right)$      5) $(0, \pi)$      7) $(-1.75, 0)$

2) $(-6, 4)$      4) $\left(-\frac{4}{3}, -5\right)$      6) $(1.7, -2.6)$      8) $(0, 0)$

    Let's take a look at some formulas which arise in the study of analytic geometry. There are several of them, but in this section, we will be concerned with only two of them. They are the distance formula and the midpoint formula. In the next section, we will learn about the slope formula.

---

### The Distance Formula

The **distance** between the two points $(x_1, \ y_1)$ and $(x_2, \ y_2)$ is given by

$$d = \sqrt{(x_2 - x_1)^2 + (y_2 - y_1)^2}.$$

---

    It is good to know where this formula comes from, just in case you ever forget what it is. Take a look at the picture on page 253.

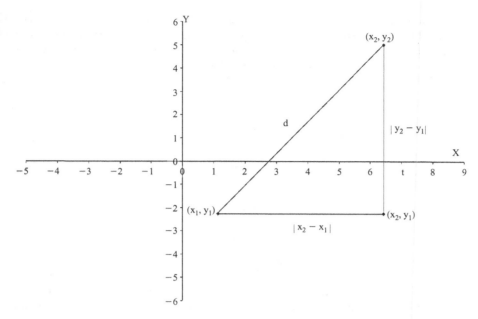

Notice that the distance between $(x_1, y_1)$ and $(x_2, y_2)$ is the same as the length of the line segment whose endpoints are $(x_1, y_1)$ and $(x_2, y_2)$. Now, what I've done is constructed a right triangle whose legs are parallel to the coordinate axes and whose hypotenuse is the line segment that we want the length of. Well, by Pythagoreans theorem, we have

$$|x_2 - x_1|^2 + |y_2 - y_1|^2 = d^2$$

and, by a property of absolute value (see Section 1.7, Property 2), we have

$$(x_2 - x_1)^2 + (y_2 - y_1)^2 = d^2.$$

By applying the square root property (see Section 7.4), we obtain

$$\pm\sqrt{(x_2 - x_1)^2 + (y_2 - y_1)^2} = d$$

However, the distance between two points cannot be negative. After getting rid of the negative sign, we obtain

$$\sqrt{(x_2 - x_1)^2 + (y_2 - y_1)^2} = d$$

and here's our formula.

**Examples.** Find the distance between the given points.

1) $(1, 0)$ and $(1, 5)$

We begin by labeling our numbers by variable names. It doesn't matter which ordered pair you call $(x_1, y_1)$ or $(x_2, y_2)$ when using the formula, since the distance from $(x_1, y_1)$ to $(x_2, y_2)$ is the same as the distance from $(x_2, y_2)$ to $(x_1, y_1)$. Therefore, let $(x_1, y_1) = (1, 0)$ and $(x_2, y_2) = (1, 5)$. Then

$$\begin{aligned}
d &= \sqrt{(x_2 - x_1)^2 + (y_2 - y_1)^2} \\
&= \sqrt{(1 - 1)^2 + (5 - 0)^2} \\
&= \sqrt{(0)^2 + (5)^2} \\
&= \sqrt{0 + 25} = \sqrt{25} = 5
\end{aligned}$$

Note: If you plot these two points and connect them with a line segment, you will notice that the line segment is vertical. A vertical line segment will always occur when the $x$-values of the two points are equal (in other words, whenever $x_1 = x_2$). When such a situation arises, you only need to figure out $|y_2 - y_1|$ to get the distance. This is often referred to as a **vertical distance**.

2) $(-2, \ 3)$ and $(4, \ 3)$

Let $(x_1, \ y_1) = (-2, \ 3)$ and $(x_2, \ y_2) = (4, \ 3)$. Then

$$
\begin{aligned}
d &= \sqrt{(x_2 - x_1)^2 + (y_2 - y_1)^2} \\
&= \sqrt{(4 - (-2))^2 + (3 - 3)^2} \\
&= \sqrt{(6)^2 + (0)^2} \\
&= \sqrt{36 + 0} = \sqrt{36} = 6
\end{aligned}
$$

If you plot these two points and connect them with a line segment, the line segment that you obtain is horizontal. A horizontal line segment will always occur when the $y$-values of the two points are equal (in other words, whenever $y_1 = y_2$). When such a situation arises, you only need to figure out $|x_2 - x_1|$ to get the distance. This is referred to as a **horizontal distance**.

3) $(1, \ -2)$ and $(-3, \ 6)$

Let $(x_1, \ y_1) = (1, \ -2)$ and $(x_2, \ y_2) = (-3, \ 6)$. Then

$$
\begin{aligned}
d &= \sqrt{(x_2 - x_1)^2 + (y_2 - y_1)^2} \\
&= \sqrt{(-3 - 1)^2 + (6 - (-2))^2} \\
&= \sqrt{(-3 - 1)^2 + (6 + 2)^2} \\
&= \sqrt{(-4)^2 + (8)^2} \\
&= \sqrt{16 + 64} \\
&= \sqrt{80} = \sqrt{16}\sqrt{5} = 4\sqrt{5}
\end{aligned}
$$

You should always simplify your answer. Be careful when working out the problem. It is very easy to slip on the arithmetic and make a mistake with the signs. You should also be careful with the algebra. For example, notice that I did **NOT** do $\sqrt{16 + 64} \overset{??}{=} \sqrt{16} + \sqrt{64}$. Instead, I simply followed the order of operations, evaluating what is underneath the square root symbol first.

4) $(0, \ 4)$ and $(3, \ 0)$

Let $(x_1, \ y_1) = (0, \ 4)$ and $(x_2, \ y_2) = (3, \ 0)$. Then

$$
\begin{aligned}
d &= \sqrt{(x_2 - x_1)^2 + (y_2 - y_1)^2} \\
&= \sqrt{(3 - 0)^2 + (0 - 4)^2} \\
&= \sqrt{(3)^2 + (-4)^2} \\
&= \sqrt{9 + 16} = \sqrt{25} = 5
\end{aligned}
$$

5) $(-2, \ -5)$ and $(-1, \ -7)$

   Let $(x_1, \ y_1) = (-2, \ -5)$ and $(x_2, \ y_2) = (-1, \ -7)$. Then

$$
\begin{aligned}
d &= \sqrt{(x_2 - x_1)^2 + (y_2 - y_1)^2} \\
&= \sqrt{(-1 - (-2))^2 + (-7 - (-5))^2} \\
&= \sqrt{(-1 + 2)^2 + (-7 + 5)^2} \\
&= \sqrt{(1)^2 + (-2)^2} \\
&= \sqrt{1 + 4} = \sqrt{5}
\end{aligned}
$$

Here's an example from analytic geometry.

**Example.** By connecting the points $(3, \ -1)$, $(2, 4)$ and $(0, 1)$ with line segments, we obtain a triangle. Is this a right triangle?

One way to do this is by plotting the given points, construct the triangle and measure each angle with a protractor. If one of the angles has a measurement of $90°$, then it is a right triangle. This is the geometric approach. Another way is to use the distance formula. This is the algebraic approach. Remember that if a triangle is a right triangle, then the lengths of the sides must satisfy the Pythagorean theorem and vice-versa. What we need to do is find the length of each side of the triangle and see if the theorem is satisfied. To begin with, let's name our given points $A = (3, \ -1)$, $B = (2, 4)$ and $C = (0, 1)$. Now, let's find the lengths of line segments $\overline{AB}$, $\overline{AC}$ and $\overline{BC}$.

The length of $\overline{AB}$ is (letting $(x_1, \ y_1) = A = (3, \ -1)$ and $(x_2, \ y_2) = B = (2, \ 4)$):

$$
\begin{aligned}
\text{length of } \overline{AB} &= \sqrt{(x_2 - x_1)^2 + (y_2 - y_1)^2} \\
&= \sqrt{(2 - 3)^2 + (4 - (-1))^2} \\
&= \sqrt{(-1)^2 + (5)^2} \\
&= \sqrt{1 + 25} = \sqrt{26}
\end{aligned}
$$

The length of $\overline{AC}$ is (letting $(x_1, \ y_1) = A = (3, \ -1)$ and $(x_2, \ y_2) = C = (0, \ 1)$):

$$
\begin{aligned}
\text{length of } \overline{AC} &= \sqrt{(x_2 - x_1)^2 + (y_2 - y_1)^2} \\
&= \sqrt{(0 - 3)^2 + (1 - (-1))^2} \\
&= \sqrt{(-3)^2 + (2)^2} \\
&= \sqrt{9 + 4} = \sqrt{13}
\end{aligned}
$$

The length of $\overline{BC}$ is (letting $(x_1, \ y_1) = B = (2, \ 4)$ and $(x_2, \ y_2) = C = (0, \ 1)$):

$$
\begin{aligned}
\text{length of } \overline{BC} &= \sqrt{(x_2 - x_1)^2 + (y_2 - y_1)^2} \\
&= \sqrt{(0 - 2)^2 + (1 - 4)^2} \\
&= \sqrt{(-2)^2 + (-3)^2} \\
&= \sqrt{4 + 9} = \sqrt{13}
\end{aligned}
$$

The sides of this triangle measure $\sqrt{26}$, $\sqrt{13}$ and $\sqrt{13}$. Observe that $\left(\sqrt{13}\right)^2 + \left(\sqrt{13}\right)^2 = \left(\sqrt{26}\right)^2$. Therefore, it is a right triangle. In fact, since two of the sides have equal measurement of $\sqrt{13}$, this is an **isosceles right triangle** (a triangle is called **isosceles** if it has two sides of equal length).

**Try These (Set 2):** Find the distance between the given points.

1) $(1, \ 0)$ and $(4, \ 4)$                 3) $(-2, \ -1)$ and $(8, \ -1)$
2) $(6, \ -5)$ and $(-3, \ 1)$                 4) $(0, \ 0)$ and $(-12, \ 5)$

---

### The Midpoint Formula

The **midpoint**, $M$, of the line segment with endpoints $A = (x_1, \ y_1)$ and $B = (x_2, \ y_2)$ is

$$\text{midpoint of } \overline{AB} = M = \left( \frac{x_1 + x_2}{2}, \ \frac{y_1 + y_2}{2} \right).$$

---

The midpoint of a line segment is the point on the segment which divides it into two equal segments (hence, it lies in the **middle** of the segment). A simple way to remember this formula is to notice that $\frac{x_1 + x_2}{2}$ is just the average of $x_1$ and $x_2$ and $\frac{y_1 + y_2}{2}$ is the average of $y_1$ and $y_2$. Hence, to find the midpoint, just find the average of the $x$'s and the average of the $y$'s and pair them up. Notice that the distance from point $A$ to point $M$ is **equal to** the distance from point $M$ to point $B$.

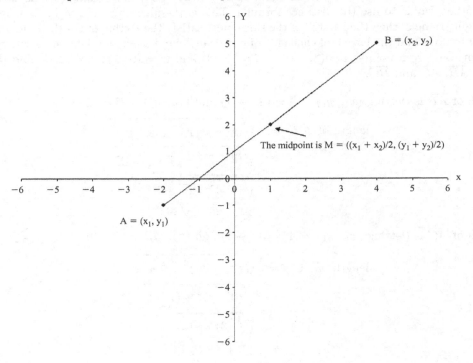

**Examples.** Find the midpoint of line segment $\overline{AB}$, where $A$ and $B$ are given.

1) $A = (4, \ 3)$ and $B = (2, \ 9)$

Let $(x_1, \ y_1) = (4, \ 3)$ and $(x_2, \ y_2) = (2, \ 9)$. Then

$$
\begin{aligned}
\text{midpoint of } \overline{AB} \ &= \ \left( \frac{x_1 + x_2}{2}, \ \frac{y_1 + y_2}{2} \right) \\
&= \ \left( \frac{4 + 2}{2}, \ \frac{3 + 9}{2} \right) \\
&= \ \left( \frac{6}{2}, \ \frac{12}{2} \right) = (3, \ 6)
\end{aligned}
$$

Note that we could've chosen $(x_1, \ y_1) = (2, \ 9)$ and $(x_2, \ y_2) = (4, \ 3)$ instead and the answer would've been the same (why?).

2) $A = (-3, \ 8)$ and $B = (1, \ -13)$

Let $(x_1, \ y_1) = (-3, \ 8)$ and $(x_2, \ y_2) = (1, \ -13)$. Then

$$
\begin{aligned}
\text{midpoint of } \overline{AB} &= \left(\frac{x_1 + x_2}{2}, \ \frac{y_1 + y_2}{2}\right) \\
&= \left(\frac{-3 + 1}{2}, \ \frac{8 + (-13)}{2}\right) \\
&= \left(\frac{-2}{2}, \ \frac{-5}{2}\right) = \left(-1, \ -\frac{5}{2}\right)
\end{aligned}
$$

3) $A = \left(0, \ \dfrac{2}{5}\right)$ and $B = \left(-\dfrac{3}{4}, \ -\dfrac{1}{10}\right)$

Let $(x_1, \ y_1) = \left(0, \ \dfrac{2}{5}\right)$ and $(x_2, \ y_2) = \left(-\dfrac{3}{4}, \ -\dfrac{1}{10}\right)$. Then

$$
\begin{aligned}
\text{midpoint of } \overline{AB} &= \left(\frac{x_1 + x_2}{2}, \ \frac{y_1 + y_2}{2}\right) \\
&= \left(\frac{0 + \left(-\dfrac{3}{4}\right)}{2}, \ \frac{\dfrac{2}{5} + \left(-\dfrac{1}{10}\right)}{2}\right) \\
&= \left(\frac{-\dfrac{3}{4} \times 4}{2 \times 4}, \ \frac{\left(\dfrac{2}{5} - \dfrac{1}{10}\right) \times 10}{2 \times 10}\right) \\
&= \left(\frac{-3}{8}, \ \frac{4 - 1}{20}\right) = \left(-\frac{3}{8}, \ \frac{3}{20}\right)
\end{aligned}
$$

**Try These (Set 3):** Find the midpoint of line segment $\overline{MN}$, where $M$ and $N$ are given.

1) $M = (0, \ 2)$ and $N = (6, \ -2)$           3) $M = (8, \ 3)$ and $N = (-9, \ -2)$

2) $M = (-3, \ -1)$ and $N = (-12, \ 4)$          4) $M = \left(-\dfrac{1}{6}, \ 5\right)$ and $N = \left(-\dfrac{5}{4}, \ 0\right)$

**Exercise 10.1**

In Exercises 1-20, plot each point in the Cartesian plane. State the quadrant (if any) for which each point lies in.

1. $(x, \ y) = (2, \ 1)$          2. $(x, \ y) = (3, \ 4)$          3. $(x, \ y) = (-5, \ 2)$     4. $(x, \ y) = (-1, \ 1)$

5. $(x, \ y) = (-4, \ -3)$      6. $(x, \ y) = (-7, \ -2)$      7. $(x, \ y) = (4, \ -8)$     8. $(x, \ y) = (7, \ -3)$

9. $(x, \ y) = (3, \ 0)$          10. $(x, \ y) = (0, \ -9)$      11. $(x, \ y) = (0, \ 2)$     12. $(x, \ y) = (1, \ 0)$

13. $(x, y) = (0, 0)$     14. $(x, y) = (0, 6)$     15. $(x, y) = \left(5, \ -\dfrac{32}{7}\right)$     16. $(x, y) = \left(-\dfrac{1}{6}, \dfrac{8}{5}\right)$

17. $(x, y) = (2, \ -\sqrt{2})$     18. $(x, y) = (-3, 4\sqrt{5})$     19. $(x, y) = (\pi, \pi)$     20. $(x, y) = (-\pi, \ -\pi)$

In Exercises 21-32, find the distance between the given points.

21. $(1, 0)$ and $(4, 4)$     22. $(3, 7)$ and $(11, 13)$     23. $(-2, 1)$ and $(4, 9)$

24. $(8, \ -3)$ and $(5, 1)$     25. $(2, \ -6)$ and $(1, \ -1)$     26. $(5, \ -3)$ and $(1, \ -2)$

27. $(0, \ -6)$ and $(4, 2)$     28. $(1, \ -5)$ and $(7, 1)$     29. $(7, \ -2)$ and $(-3, \ -2)$

30. $(-4, 12)$ and $(1, 12)$     31. $(-6, 5)$ and $(-6, \ -7)$     32. $(8, \ -2)$ and $(8, \ -7)$

In Exercises 33-44, find the midpoint of the line segment whose endpoints are given.

33. $A = (3, 4)$ and $B = (1, 10)$     34. $A = (7, 8)$ and $B = (5, 0)$

35. $P = (-4, 6)$ and $Q = (8, \ -6)$     36. $P = (2, \ -1)$ and $Q = (-2, 3)$

37. $S = (-11, \ -6)$ and $T = (-3, \ -1)$     38. $G = (8, 3)$ and $H = (-8, \ -3)$

39. $P = (-6, \ -6)$ and $Q = (5, 6)$     40. $G = (-2, 2)$ and $H = (2, \ -2)$

41. $A_1 = \left(\dfrac{1}{2}, \ -\dfrac{1}{3}\right)$ and $A_2 = \left(\dfrac{1}{4}, \dfrac{1}{6}\right)$     42. $S_1 = \left(\dfrac{3}{4}, \dfrac{2}{3}\right)$ and $S_2 = \left(\dfrac{1}{8}, \ -\dfrac{2}{3}\right)$

43. $T_1 = \left(-5, \dfrac{1}{10}\right)$ and $T_2 = \left(\dfrac{1}{6}, \ -3\right)$     44. $M = \left(8, \ -\dfrac{2}{7}\right)$ and $N = \left(\dfrac{1}{3}, \ -5\right)$

In Exercises 45-50, determine whether or not the triangle determined by the given points is a right triangle.

45. $(3, 0), (0, 0)$ and $(0, 4)$     46. $(0, 0), (-4, 0)$ and $(0, 3)$

47. $(2, \ -1), (3, 1)$ and $(0, \ -2)$     48. $(-6, 0), (2, 3)$ and $(4, \ -1)$

49. $(6, 3), (-2, \ -3)$ and $(-5, 1)$     50. $(2, 9), (-1, \ -1)$ and $(4, 1)$

## Section 10.2  Linear Equations in Two Variables and Their Graphs

In this section, we will learn how to graph the solutions to a linear equation in two variables. It turns out that such a graph will always be a straight line. We will also see that if we know some information about the graph of a line, then we can find an equation for it. Consequently, there is a relationship between a linear equation in two variables (an algebraic object) and the graph of a line (a geometric object).

To begin with, we need to understand what a linear equation in two variables looks like algebraically. A technique for graphing the solutions to such an equation will then be needed. For example, let's graph the solutions to the equation $y = 2x + 1$. This is called a **linear equation** in $x$ and $y$. Recall from Section 3.1 that a polynomial is called **linear** if it is **degree one**. The equation $y = 2x + 1$ is called linear because both $x$ and $y$ have degree one. In other words, we have $y^1 = 2x^1 + 1$. This is an algebraic equation, since it contains variables and an equals sign. We now want to relate this equation to a geometric object, namely the graph of its solutions.

**Definition:** A **solution** to an equation in two variables, $x$ and $y$, is an ordered pair $(m, n)$ which satisfies the equation when we replace $x$ by $m$ and $y$ by $n$.

For example, the ordered pair $(0, 1)$ is a solution to $y = 2x + 1$ since $1 \overset{\checkmark}{=} 2(0) + 1$. However, the ordered pair $(-3, 2)$ is not a solution to $y = 2x + 1$ since $2 \neq 2(-3) + 1$. We are interested in finding the solutions to our equation and plotting them in the Cartesian plane. To find solutions, we will choose different numbers for our $x$-value and then find the $y$-value which corresponds to each. The reason we pick the $x$-value is because the $y$-variable is alone on one side of the equation, hence it is easier to figure out when $x$ is replaced by the chosen number. For this reason, we call $x$ the **independent variable** and $y$ the **dependent variable**. The value of $y$ **depends** on the chosen value of $x$. Below is a table of $x$-values and $y$-values which make up solutions to the equation.

| $x$ | $y = 2x + 1$ | Solution |
|---|---|---|
| 0 | $2(0) + 1 = 1$ | $(0, 1)$ |
| 1 | $2(1) + 1 = 3$ | $(1, 3)$ |
| $-1$ | $2(-1) + 1 = -1$ | $(-1, -1)$ |
| 2 | $2(2) + 1 = 5$ | $(2, 5)$ |

Observe that I chose numbers for $x$ which are easy to compute $2x + 1$ with. I could've chosen any real number for $x$, in fact, and I would've obtained the corresponding $y$-value by following the rule $y = 2x + 1$. For example, if I choose $x = 5.13$, then $y = 2(5.13) + 1 = 11.26$. This gives us a solution $(5.13, 11.26)$. Unfortunately, this pair would not be easy to graph, since it has decimals in its coordinates. That is why I used nice integers for my $x$−values. By doing so, I obtained ordered pairs with coordinates that are integers. Now, since there are infinitely many real numbers to choose from, there are infinitely many numbers which $x$ can equal. This means that there are infinitely many solutions to this equation. I found only four of them in the table above. If I did find **all** of the solutions, however, and plotted them in the Cartesian plane, what kind of graph would emerge? Well, it turns out that you get the graph of a straight line (see graph below).

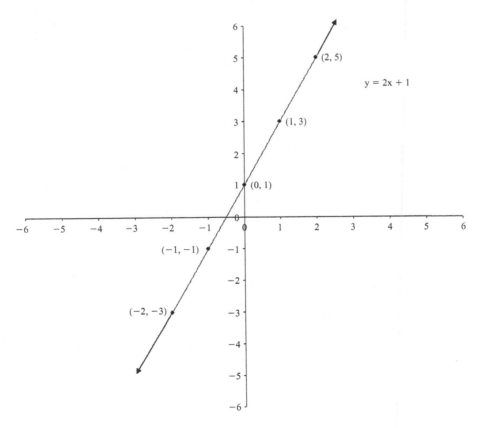

Keep in mind that the picture of the line above is a graphical representation of all of the solutions to the equation $y = 2x + 1$. In other words, if a point lies on the line, then it must satisfy the equation and vice-versa. For example, the point $(-2, 0)$ is not on the line (the geometric object) and $0 \neq 2(-2) + 1$ (the algebraic object). However, the point $(-2, -3)$ is on the line and $-3 = 2(-2) + 1$. We name the line according to its equation, $y = 2x + 1$ in this case. Whenever you encounter a question which asks to graph an equation, it is really asking you to graph the points representing the solutions to the equation.

**Try These (Set 4):**

I) Graph.

    1) $y = 3x - 1$          3) $y = x + 4$

    2) $y = -2x + 2$        4) $y = -x$

II) Which points are on the line $y = -5x + 1$?

    1) $(0, 1)$        3) $\left(\dfrac{1}{5}, 0\right)$        5) $(4, -2)$

    2) $(-2, 3)$      4) $(3, -14)$      6) $\left(-\dfrac{2}{3}, -6\right)$

What we want to do now is find any relationships between linear equations in two variables and lines. The key formula which tells the story is the slope formula. From this formula, everything you need to know about lines and linear equations will emerge.

---

**The Slope Formula**

The **slope** of the line containing the points $(x_1, y_1)$ and $(x_2, y_2)$ is

$$m = \frac{y_2 - y_1}{x_2 - x_1} = \frac{\Delta y}{\Delta x} = \frac{\text{rise}}{\text{run}}.$$

---

Notice that $\Delta y$ tells you how many units you need to go up (or down) and $\Delta x$ tells you how many units you need to go to the right (or left). In this picture, we have $\Delta y = +2$ and $\Delta x = +2$.

$\Delta x = +2$

$\Delta y = +2$

The '$\Delta$' symbol is the greek letter 'delta' and means 'the change in'. When we write $\Delta y$ (read as 'delta $y$'), we are saying 'the change in the $y$-value. Similarly, $\Delta x$ (read as 'delta $x$') means 'the change in the $x$-value. To compute the change in a variables value, you subtract its initial value from its final value. For example, let $T$ be the variable representing temperature. If the initial temperature is $T_1 = 60°C$ and the final temperature is $T_2 = 45°C$, then the change in the temperature is $\Delta T = T_2 - T_1 = 45°C - 60°C = -15°C$. In other words, the temperature decreased by $15°C$ (the fact that it decreased comes from the negative sign).

As the previous graph shows, $\Delta y$ and $\Delta x$ are values which are used in getting from $(x_1,\ y_1)$ to $(x_2,\ y_2)$ on the line. We will see that the slope not only tells us how to 'walk on the line' from $(x_1,\ y_1)$ to $(x_2,\ y_2)$, but from any point on the line to any other point on the line. Usually, I refer to the formula $\frac{y_2 - y_1}{x_2 - x_1}$ as the algebraic version of the formula (since it is an algebraic object) and $\frac{\Delta y}{\Delta x}$ as the geometric version of the formula (since the $\Delta y$ and $\Delta x$ tell us how to get from one point to the next on the line, a geometric object). Let's do some examples with finding slopes and see how the $\Delta y$ and $\Delta x$ are used for 'walking on the line'. The first example is done in plenty of detail for you to follow.

**Examples.** Find the slope of the line containing the given points. Graph the line and use the slope to find two additional points on the line.

1) $(1,\ 0)$ and $(2,\ 3)$

Let $(x_1,\ y_1) = (1,\ 0)$ and $(x_2,\ y_2) = (2,\ 3)$. Then

$$m = \frac{y_2 - y_1}{x_2 - x_1} = \frac{3 - 0}{2 - 1} = \frac{+3}{+1} = 3.$$

The slope of the line containing the given points is 3. What is it good for? Well, observe that $\Delta y = y_2 - y_1 = +3$ and $\Delta x = x_2 - x_1 = +1$. These values tell us how to travel along the line from one point to another. Before we go for a walk on the line, let me summarize which way we travel when the $\Delta y$ and $\Delta x$ have certain signs.

---

### The Story of $\Delta y$ and $\Delta x$

If $\Delta y$ is **positive**, then you go **up**.

If $\Delta y$ is **negative**, then you go **down**.

If $\Delta x$ is **positive**, then you go **to the right**.

If $\Delta x$ is **negative**, then you go **to the left**.

---

Let me explain why $\Delta y$ and $\Delta x$ work the way I've summarized above. Suppose that we are given a point on a line and we want to 'walk to' another point on the line. If $\Delta y$ is **positive**, then the $y-$value changes by a positive amount, therefore increasing in value. This means that $\Delta y$ tells us how many units we need to go **upward**. However, if $\Delta y$ is **negative**, then the $y-$value changes by a negative amount, therefore decreasing in value. In this case, $\Delta y$ tells us how many units we need to go **downward**. Now, if $\Delta x$ is **positive**, then then $x-$value changes by a positive amount, therefore increasing in value. This means that $\Delta x$ tells us how many units we need to go **to the right**. However, if $\Delta x$ is negative, then the $x-$value changes by a negative amount, therefore decreasing in value. In this case, $\Delta x$ tells you how many units we need to go **to the left**. If we start at the given point on our line and use $\Delta y$ and $\Delta x$ to tell us which direction to walk in and by how many units, we are guarenteed to 'walk to' another point on the line. Note that I didn't mention what happens if either $\Delta x = 0$ or $\Delta y = 0$. We will worry about these two cases later.

Now, using the fact that $\Delta y = +3$ and $\Delta x = +1$, we begin at the point $(x_1, y_1) = (1, 0)$ and go up by 3 units, then to the right by 1 unit. After doing this, notice that you end up at $(x_2, y_2) = (2, 3)$. Let's now use $\Delta y$ and $\Delta x$ to obtain another point. To do this, starting at $(2, 3)$, go up by 3 units, then to the right by 1 unit again. You will end up at the point $(3, 6)$, which is on the line. Now, if you keep using the slope to walk up by 3 and to the right by 1, you will always end up at a point on the line (see the graph below).

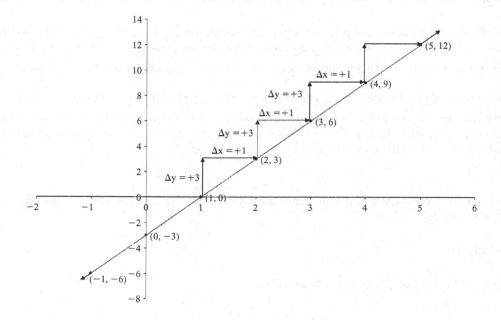

Observe that if we set $(x_1, y_1) = (2, 3)$ and $(x_2, y_2) = (1, 0)$ instead, then

$$m = \frac{y_2 - y_1}{x_2 - x_1} = \frac{0 - 3}{1 - 2} = \frac{-3}{-1} = 3.$$

The slope is still 3. However, the $\Delta y$ and $\Delta x$ are now different ($\Delta y = -3$ and $\Delta x = -1$). Consequently, we will take a different walk from one point on the line to another point on the line, namely 3 down and 1 to the left. This will take us to different points than before, but they are all on the line again! (see the picture below).

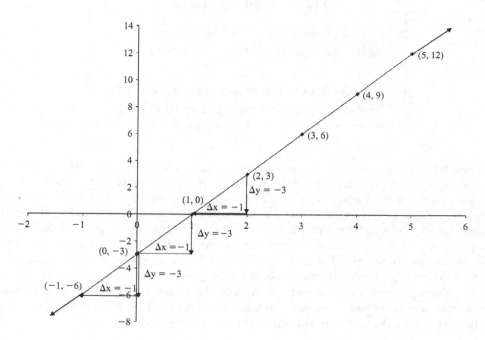

It turns out that if you start at **any** point on a line, the $\Delta y$ and $\Delta x$ which you are using will **always** walk you to a point on the **same line**. As we see in the example, $m = \dfrac{-3}{-1} = 3$ and $m = \dfrac{+3}{+1} = 3$ give different $\Delta y$'s and $\Delta x$'s, but we always walk to a point on the line regardless of which pair of $\Delta y$ and $\Delta x$ we use. In fact, we can write the slope in many different ways. For example, $m = 3 = \dfrac{-3}{-1} = \dfrac{+3}{+1} = \dfrac{+6}{+2} = \dfrac{-9}{-3} = \dfrac{+1}{+\frac{1}{3}} = ....$ are all equal to 3, but the $\Delta y$'s and $\Delta x$'s are all different. Nevertheless, each pair of $\Delta y$ and $\Delta x$ will walk us to a point on the line.

2) $(4, \ -1)$ and $(1, \ 3)$

Let $(x_1, \ y_1) = (4, \ -1)$ and $(x_2, \ y_2) = (1, \ 3)$. Then

$$m = \frac{y_2 - y_1}{x_2 - x_1} = \frac{3 - (-1)}{1 - 4} = \frac{+4}{-3} = -\frac{4}{3}.$$

Now, to find two additional points on the line, let $\Delta y = +4$ and $\Delta x = -3$. Then, starting at the point $(1, \ 3)$, we need to go up by 4 units and to the left by 3 units. After doing this two times, we will obtain the points $(-2, \ 7)$ and $(-5, \ 11)$ (see graph below). Note that I didn't start the 'walk' at $(4, \ -1)$, since I would 'walk' to $(1, \ 3)$ which I know is already on the line.

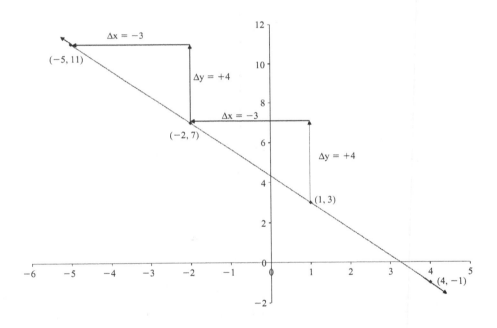

3) $(-2, \ 5)$ and $(-3, \ 0)$

Let $(x_1, \ y_1) = (-2, \ 5)$ and $(x_2, \ y_2) = (-3, \ 0)$. Then

$$m = \frac{y_2 - y_1}{x_2 - x_1} = \frac{0 - 5}{-3 - (-2)} = \frac{-5}{-1} = 5.$$

To find two additional points on the line, let $\Delta y = -5$ and $\Delta x = -1$. Then, starting at the point $(-3, \ 0)$, we need to go down by 5 units and to the left by 1 unit. After doing this two times, we will obtain the points $(-4,\ -5)$ and $(-5,\ -10)$ (see graph below).

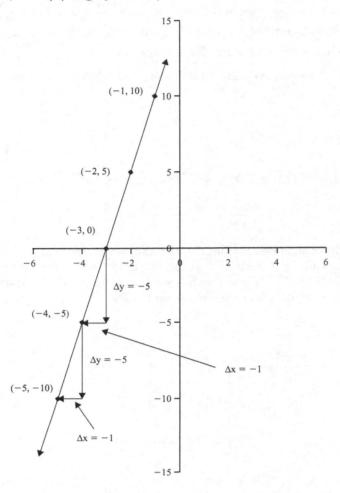

4) $(0,\ -1)$ and $(4,\ -7)$

Let $(x_1,\ y_1) = (0,\ -1)$ and $(x_2,\ y_2) = (4,\ -7)$. Then

$$m = \frac{y_2 - y_1}{x_2 - x_1} = \frac{-7 - (-1)}{4 - 0} = \frac{-6}{+4} = -\frac{3}{2}.$$

To find two additional points on the line, let $\Delta y = -3$ and $\Delta x = +2$ (I could've chosen $\Delta y = -6$ and $\Delta x = +4$). Then, starting at the point $(4,\ -7)$, we need to go down by 3 units and to the right by 2 units. After doing this two times, we will obtain the points $(6,\ -10)$ and $(8,\ -13)$ (try this one on your own).

5) $(4,\ 2)$ and $(-1,\ 2)$

Let $(x_1,\ y_1) = (4,\ 2)$ and $(x_2,\ y_2) = (-1,\ 2)$. Then

$$m = \frac{y_2 - y_1}{x_2 - x_1} = \frac{2 - 2}{-1 - 4} = \frac{0}{-5} = 0.$$

In this case, we have $\Delta y = 0$ and $\Delta x = -5$. Starting at the point $(-1,\ 2)$, we need to go to the left by 5 units and we **don't** go up or down (since $\Delta y = 0$). If you do this twice, you will obtain the points $(-6,\ 2)$ and $(-11,\ 2)$. Notice that the graph of this line is a horizontal line which crosses the $y$-axis at $(0,\ 2)$. In general, if a line has a slope equal to 0, then it must be a horizontal line.

6) $(-4, 3)$ and $(-4, 5)$

Let $(x_1, y_1) = (-4, 3)$ and $(x_2, y_2) = (-4, 5)$. Then

$$m = \frac{y_2 - y_1}{x_2 - x_1} = \frac{5 - 3}{-4 - (-4)} = \frac{+2}{0}, \text{ which is undefined.}$$

In this case, we have $\Delta y = +2$ and $\Delta x = 0$. Starting at the point $(-4, 5)$, we need to go up by 2 units and we **don't** go to the left or to the right (since $\Delta x = 0$). If you do this, you will obtain the points $(-4, 7)$ and $(-4, 9)$. Notice that the graph of this line is a vertical line which crosses the $x$-axis at $(-4, 0)$. In general, if a line has an undefined slope, then it must be a vertical line. We say that a vertical line has no slope.

**Try These (Set 5):** Find the slope of the line containing the given points. Graph the line and find two additional points on it.

1) $(0, 1)$ and $(3, 5)$     3) $(4, 1)$ and $(0, 6)$     5) $(-1, 7)$ and $(-1, 3)$
2) $(-2, 4)$ and $(-1, 2)$     4) $(-3, -3)$ and $(0, 0)$     6) $(8, -5)$ and $(5, -5)$

Suppose that we are given the slope of a line and a point on the line. We already know that we can graph a line if we are given two points which lie on it. By using our knowledge of slopes, we know that we can walk to a point on a line if we are given a 'starting point' for our walk. This means that we can graph a line if we know its slope and a point on it. Furthermore, there is only one line containing the given point and having the given slope.

**Examples.** Graph the line containing the point $(x_1, y_1)$ and whose slope is $m$.

1) $(x_1, y_1) = (1, -2)$ and $m = \dfrac{3}{2}$

As we have seen, we can write our slope in many different ways as long as it equals $\dfrac{3}{2}$. For example, we can write

$$m = \frac{+3}{+2} = \frac{-3}{-2} = \frac{+6}{+4} = \frac{-30}{-20} = \frac{3\pi}{2\pi} = \ldots$$

and each of these can be used for walking on the line. The simplest one to use is obviously $m = \dfrac{+3}{+2}$. In this case, we have $\Delta y = +3$ and $\Delta x = +2$. Now, starting at $(x_1, y_1) = (1, -2)$, we go up by 3 units and to the right by 2 units. We obtain the point $(3, 1)$. Now that we have two points, we can graph the line (see graph below).

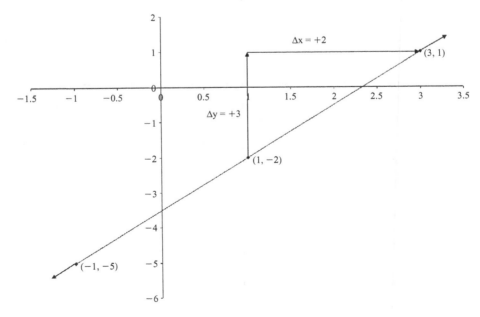

2) $(x_1, \ y_1) = (4, \ 0)$ and $m = -\dfrac{6}{5}$

    I will write the slope as $m = -\dfrac{6}{5} = \dfrac{-6}{+5}$, so that $\Delta y = -6$ and $\Delta x = +5$ (I could've written $m = \dfrac{+6}{-5}$ and used $\Delta y = +6, \Delta x = -5$ instead, but I would still walk to a point on the line). Starting at $(x_1, y_1) = (4, 0)$, I go down by 6 units and to the right by 5 units and obtain $(9, \ -6)$. I can now graph the line (see graph below).

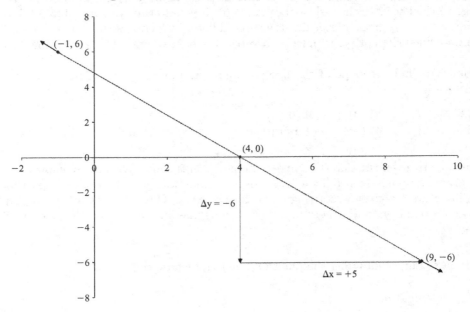

3) $(x_1, \ y_1) = (-3, \ -5)$ and $m = 8$

    I will write the slope as $m = 8 = \dfrac{+8}{+1}$, so that $\Delta y = +8$ and $\Delta x = +1$. Starting at $(x_1, \ y_1) = (-3, \ -5)$, I go up by 8 units and to the right by 1 unit and obtain $(-2, \ 3)$. I can now graph the line (see graph below).

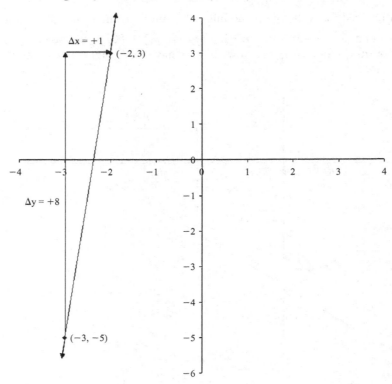

**Try These (Set 6):** Graph the line containing the point $(x_1, y_1)$ and whose slope is $m$.

1) $(x_1, y_1) = (-1, 4)$ and $m = 2$

2) $(x_1, y_1) = (3, -5)$ and $m = -\dfrac{4}{3}$

3) $(x_1, y_1) = (2, 1)$ and $m = -1$

4) $(x_1, y_1) = (0, 0)$ and $m = \dfrac{2}{7}$

If we are given the slope, $m$, of a line and a point, $(x_1, y_1)$, on the line, we've just seen that we can graph the line. It turns out that we can also obtain an equation for this line. Suppose that $(x, y)$ represents **any** point on the line other that $(x_1, y_1)$. Then, by the slope formula, we have

$$m = \frac{y - y_1}{x - x_1} \text{ which becomes } y - y_1 = m\,(x - x_1).$$

---

**The Point-Slope Form**

The equation of the line whose slope is $m$ and contains the point $(x_1, y_1)$ is

$$y - y_1 = m\,(x - x_1).$$

---

This is known as the **point-slope form** for the equation of the line. It is extremely useful in working with linear equations. Notice that the equation of a vertical line does not take this form, since such a line has no slope. We will learn about such equations later.

**Examples.**

1) Find an equation of the line whose slope is 4 and contains the point $(1, 2)$.

Whenever you want to find an equation of a line, you should think of the point-slope form. We are given $m = 4$, $x_1 = 1$ and $y_1 = 2$. We plug these numbers into the point-slope form and obtain:

$$
\begin{aligned}
y - y_1 &= m\,(x - x_1) \\
y - 2 &= 4\,(x - 1) \\
y - 2 &= 4x - 4 \\
\underline{+2 \qquad\quad +2} & \\
y &= 4x - 2
\end{aligned}
$$

You should get into the habit of simplifying the equation. Notice that the $y$-variable is by itself and the other side of the equal sign is in descending order.

2) Find an equation of the line whose slope is $\dfrac{3}{7}$ and contains the point $(-3, 5)$.

We are given $m = \dfrac{3}{7}$, $x_1 = -3$ and $y_1 = 5$. Using the point-slope form, we get:

$$
\begin{aligned}
y - y_1 &= m\,(x - x_1) \\
y - 5 &= \frac{3}{7}\,(x - (-3)) \\
y - 5 &= \frac{3}{7}\left(x + \frac{3}{1}\right) \\
y - 5 &= \frac{3}{7}x + \frac{9}{7} \\
\underline{+5 \qquad\qquad +5} & \\
y &= \frac{3}{7}x + \frac{44}{7}
\end{aligned}
$$

Note that $\frac{9}{7} + 5 = \frac{9}{7} + \frac{5}{1}\left(\frac{7}{7}\right) = \frac{9}{7} + \frac{35}{7} = \frac{44}{7}$, giving us the number on the right-hand side. Don't be afraid of working with fractions!

3) Find an equation of the line whose slope is $-\frac{10}{3}$ and contains the point $(1,\ -6)$.

We are given $m = -\frac{10}{3}$, $x_1 = 1$ and $y_1 = -6$. As before, we obtain:

$$y - y_1 = m\,(x - x_1)$$
$$y - (-6) = -\frac{10}{3}\,(x - 1)$$
$$y + 6 = -\frac{10}{3}x + \frac{10}{3}$$
$$\underline{\quad -6 \qquad\qquad\quad -6\quad}$$
$$y = -\frac{10}{3}x - \frac{8}{3}$$

Again, note that $\frac{10}{3} - 6 = \frac{10}{3} - \frac{6}{1}\left(\frac{3}{3}\right) = \frac{10}{3} - \frac{18}{3} = -\frac{8}{3}$.

4) Find an equation of the line containing the points $(4,\ -2)$ and $(5,\ 1)$.

We would like to use the point-slope form. However, we are not given a slope this time. We **do** know that we can find the slope, since we are given two points on the line. First, we will find the slope using our slope formula. Then, we will use the point-slope form to get our equation. Let $(x_1,\ y_1) = (4,\ -2)$ and $(x_2,\ y_2) = (5,\ 1)$. Then

$$m = \frac{y_2 - y_1}{x_2 - x_1} = \frac{1 - (-2)}{5 - 4} = \frac{3}{1} = 3.$$

Therefore, our equation is:

$$y - y_1 = m\,(x - x_1)$$
$$y - (-2) = 3\,(x - 4)$$
$$y + 2 = 3x - 12$$
$$\underline{\quad -2 \qquad\qquad -2\quad}$$
$$y = 3x - 14$$

One thing to notice is that I could've used the other point, $(5,\ 1)$, to find the equation instead of $(4,\ -2)$. Observe that

$$y - y_1 = m\,(x - x_1)$$
$$y - 1 = 3\,(x - 5)$$
$$y - 1 = 3x - 15$$
$$\underline{\quad +1 \qquad\qquad +1\quad}$$
$$y = 3x - 14$$

and we obtain the same answer. The moral of the story is that it doesn't matter which point you choose as your $(x_1,\ y_1)$ in the point-slope form. You will always end up with the same equation.

5) Find an equation of the line containing the points $(-3, 8)$ and $(9,\ 4)$.

Follow the same method as in the previous example. First let's find the slope, then use the point-slope form to get our equation. Let $(x_1,\ y_1) = (-3,\ 8)$ and $(x_2,\ y_2) = (9,\ 4)$. Then

$$m = \frac{y_2 - y_1}{x_2 - x_1} = \frac{4 - 8}{9 - (-3)} = \frac{-4}{12} = -\frac{1}{3}.$$

Therefore, our equation is (using $x_1 = -3$, $y_1 = 8$ in the point-slope form)

$$y - y_1 = m\,(x - x_1)$$
$$y - 8 = -\frac{1}{3}\,(x - (-3))$$
$$y - 8 = -\frac{1}{3}\left(x + \frac{3}{1}\right)$$
$$y - \cancel{8} = -\frac{1}{3}x - 1$$
$$\underline{+\cancel{8} \qquad\qquad +8}$$
$$y = -\frac{1}{3}x + 7$$

**Try These (Set 7):** Find an equation of the line with the given information.

1) slope is $\dfrac{1}{2}$ and contains $(0,\ -2)$      3) contains $(4,\ -5)$ and $(-1,\ 3)$

2) slope is $-6$ and contains $(-3,\ -12)$      4) contains $(2,\ 0)$ and $(0,\ 7)$

After we found our equations above using the point-slope form, we simplified our equation to get the $y$-variable on one side by itself and the other side in descending order. This form for the equation is called the **slope-intercept form**. Before discussing this form, we need a definition.

**Definition:** The **$y$-intercept** of a line is the point where the line crosses the $y$-axis.

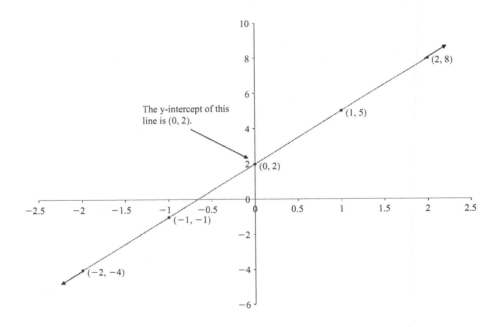

Notice that a $y$-intercept must be of the form $(0,\ b)$, where $b$ is a real number. Observe that not every line has a $y$-intecept (for example, any line which is parallel to the $y$-axis). Knowing about the $y$-intercept of a line is valuable information if we are interested in graphing the line. As we will see, the $y$-intercept is easy to figure out when the equation is given.

---

### The Slope-Intercept Form

The equation of the line whose slope is $m$ and whose $y$-intercept is $(0,\ b)$ is

$$y = mx + b.$$

---

This can be obtained by using the point-slope form by letting $x_1 = 0$, $y_1 = b$ and $m$ remaining the same. Notice that, the equation is in simplified form. Furthermore, we can easy read off the slope and $y$-intercept:

$$y = \underbrace{m}_{\text{slope}} x + \underbrace{b}_{y\text{-intercept}}$$

Sometimes, we say that the $y$-intercept is $b$. However, keep in mind that it is really the ordered pair $(0,\ b)$. I will usually write it as $(0,\ b)$. Another thing worth noting is that, in the form $y = mx + b$, you can really see why the equation is called linear: both $x$ and $y$ are of degree one.

**Examples.**

1) Find an equation of the line whose slope is 1 and whose $y$-intercept is $(0,\ 6)$.

We could use the point-slope form as before. However, notice that the given point is the $y$-intercept. This means that you could simply use the slope-intercept form to obtain the equation. We are given $m = 1$ and $b = 6$. Therefore, the equation is

$$y = mx + b$$
$$y = 1x + 6 \text{ or just } y = x + 6.$$

2) Find an equation of the line whose slope is $\dfrac{11}{12}$ and whose $y$-intercept is $(0,\ -3)$.

We are given $m = \dfrac{11}{12}$ and $b = -3$. Therefore, the equation is

$$y = mx + b$$
$$y = \frac{11}{12}x + (-3) \text{ or just } y = \frac{11}{12}x - 3.$$

3) Find an equation of the line whose slope is $-9$ and whose $y$-intercept is the origin.

Recall that the origin is $(0,\ 0)$. Hence, $m = -9$ and $b = 0$. Therefore, the equation is

$$y = mx + b$$
$$y = -9x + 0 \text{ or just } y = -9x.$$

4) Find the slope and $y$-intercept of the line whose equation is $y = 4x + 5$.

The given equation is of the form $y = mx + b$. By comparing $y = 4x + 5$ to $y = mx + b$, you should see that $m = 4$ and $b = 5$. Therefore, the slope is 4 and the $y$-intercept is $(0,\ 5)$. Notice that this information can now be used to graph the line whose equation is $y = 4x + 5$.

5) Find the slope and $y$-intercept of the line whose equation is $y = -x - 12$.

The given equation is of the form $y = mx + b$. By comparing the given equation to $y = mx + b$, you will see that $m = -1$ and $b = -12$. Therefore, the slope is $-1$ and the $y$-intercept is $(0, \ -12)$.

6) Find the slope and $y$-intercept of the line whose equation is $6x - 7y + 4 = 0$.

We first need to get the equation in the form $y = mx + b$. To do this, we have to solve for $y$ by itself. We can then read off $m$ and $b$ as before.

$$
\begin{array}{r}
6x - 7y + 4 = 0 \\
+7y \qquad\quad +7y \\
\hline
\dfrac{6x}{7} + \dfrac{4}{7} = \dfrac{7y}{7}
\end{array}
$$

Hence, $y = \dfrac{6}{7}x + \dfrac{4}{7}$ and so the slope is $\dfrac{6}{7}$ and the $y$-intercept is $\left(0, \ \dfrac{4}{7}\right)$.

7) Find an equation of the line whose slope is $-2$ and contains the point $(3, \ -5)$.

We know how to do this by using the point-slope form. Let's look at another technique. We would like to use the equation $y = mx + b$. Notice that we are given $m = -2$. All that we need is the value of $b$. Since $(3, \ -5)$ lies on the line, we know that when $x = 3$, $y = -5$ in our equation. Hence, substituting $m = -2$, $x = 3$ and $y = -5$ into the equation $y = mx + b$, we have

$$
\begin{array}{r}
-5 = (-2)(3) + b \\
-5 = -6 + b \\
+6 \qquad +6 \\
\hline
1 = b
\end{array}
$$

Now we know that $b = 1$. Since $m = -2$, the equation of the line is $y = -2x + 1$.

This method is an alternative method for finding the equation of a line. If you prefer to use this rather than the method which requires the point-slope form, be my guest. Both of them provide the same answer.

**Try These (Set 8):**

1) Find an equation of the line whose slope is $4$ and whose $y$-intercept is $(0, \ 1)$.
2) Find an equation of the line whose slope is $-\dfrac{2}{11}$ and whose $y$-intercept is $(0, \ 0)$.
3) Find the slope and $y$-intercept of the line whose equation is $y = x - 10$.
4) Find the slope and $y$-intercept of the line whose equation is $-8x + 2y - 9 = 0$.

Another form for which a linear equation can be written in is called the **general form**.

---

### The General Form

Every linear equation can be written in the form

$Ax + By + C = 0$, where $A$, $B$ and $C$ are real numbers.

---

In this form, you have one side of the equation equalling zero and the other side is written with the $x$−term, the $y$−term and the constant term in that order. It's like descending order, but alphabetically.

For example, suppose we have the linear equation $y - 8 = -4(x - (-7))$. You might notice that this equation is in point-slope form, with $m = -4$ and $(x_1, \, y_1) = (-7, \, 8)$. Now, to write this in slope-intercept form, you need to get $y$ by itself as follows:

$$
\begin{aligned}
y - 8 &= -4(x - (-7)) \\
y - 8 &= -4(x + 7) \\
y - 8 &= -4x - 28 \\
+8 \qquad & \qquad + 8 \\
\hline
y &= -4x - 20
\end{aligned}
$$

To get this equation into general form, all that we have to do is get the $y$-variable to the other side and write the polynomial as described above. That is, we first put the $x$-term, then the $y$-term and then the constant term. We obtain:

$$
\begin{aligned}
y &= -4x - 20 \\
-y \qquad & \quad - y \\
\hline
0 &= -4x - y - 20
\end{aligned}
$$

The equation is now in general form.

## More on Intercepts

We defined the $y$-intercept of a line to be the point where the line crosses the $y$-axis. There is also a point where a line can cross the x-axis, called the **$x$-intercept**. Let's now look at intercepts some more and learn an easy way of obtaining these points when we are given an equation of a line.

**Definition:** The **$x$-intercept** of a line is the point where the line crosses the $x$-axis.

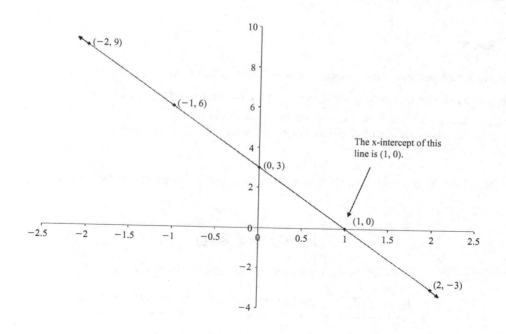

Notice that an $x$-intercept must be of the form $(a,\ 0)$, where $a$ is a real number. Also note that not every line has a $x$-intecept (for example, any line which is parallel to the $x$-axis).

Suppose we are given an equation of a line and we want to graph it. One way of doing this is by finding the intercepts for the line and using them to obtain our graph. How do we find these intercepts? Well, we looked at one way of finding the $y$-intercept. We get our equation in slope-intercept form and figure out $b$ (which is the $y$-coordinate of the $y$-intercept). However, this method tells us nothing about the $x$-intercept. It turns out that we can find the intercepts in a simple way by using a little bit of algebra.

> To find the $y$-intercept, you set $x = 0$ and solve for $y$.
> To find the $x$-intercept, you set $y = 0$ and solve for $x$.

**Examples.** Find the intercept(s) of the line whose equation is given.

1) $2x - 3y + 6 = 0$

To find the $y$-intercept, we set $x = 0$ and solve for $y$. We obtain:

$$2(0) - 3y + 6 = 0$$
$$-3y + 6 = 0$$
$$\underline{\phantom{-3y}-6 \quad -6}$$
$$\frac{-3y}{-3} = \frac{-6}{-3}$$
$$y = 2$$

Hence, the $y$-intercept is $(0,\ 2)$. To find the $x$-intercept, we set $y = 0$ and solve for $x$. We obtain:

$$2x - 3(0) + 6 = 0$$
$$2x + 6 = 0$$
$$\underline{\phantom{2x}-6 \quad -6}$$
$$\frac{2x}{2} = \frac{-6}{2}$$
$$x = -3$$

Therefore, the $x$-intercept is $(-3,\ 0)$. If we wanted to graph this line, we can now use these intercepts to do so.

2) $-x + 5y + 9 = 0$

To find the $y$-intercept, we set $x = 0$ and solve for $y$. We obtain:

$$-(0) + 5y + 9 = 0$$
$$5y + 9 = 0$$
$$\underline{\phantom{5y}-9 \quad -9}$$
$$\frac{5y}{5} = \frac{-9}{5}$$
$$y = \frac{-9}{5}$$

Hence, the $y$-intercept is $\left(0, -\dfrac{9}{5}\right)$. To find the $x$-intercept, set $y = 0$ and solve for $x$. We obtain:

$$-x + 5\,(0) + 9 = 0$$
$$-x + 9 = 0$$
$$\phantom{-x} \quad -9 \quad -9$$
$$\frac{-x}{-1} = \frac{-9}{-1}$$
$$x = 9$$

Therefore, the $x$-intercept is $(9,\ 0)$.

3) $7x - 3y = 0$

To find the $y$-intercept, you set $x = 0$ and solve for $y$. We obtain:

$$7\,(0) - 3y = 0$$
$$-3y = 0$$
$$\frac{-3y}{-3} = \frac{0}{-3}$$
$$y = 0$$

Hence, the $y$-intercept is $(0,\ 0)$. To find the $x$-intercept, set $y = 0$ and solve for $x$. We obtain:

$$7x - 3\,(0) = 0$$
$$7x = 0$$
$$\frac{7x}{7} = \frac{0}{7}$$
$$x = 0$$

Therefore, the $x$-intercept is $(0,\ 0)$. Notice that the x-intercept and y-intercept are the same. This makes sense, since the origin lies on both axes. If you wanted to graph this line, you couldn't do it by using only intercepts, since you didn't obtain two points. What you would need to do is find the slope of this line (do you remember how to do this?) and use the slope to 'walk' from $(0,\ 0)$ to another point on the line.

**Try These (Set 9):** Find the intercept(s) of the line whose equation is given. Graph the line.

1) $3x + y - 6 = 0$        3) $y = 9x + 8$           5) $8y - 10 = 4x$
2) $-2x - 7y + 3 = 0$      4) $-5x = -10y$

## Vertical and Horizontal Lines

We will now focus our attention on linear equations whose graph is either a vertical line or a horizontal line. To understand these, we will use the general form for a linear equation. Recall that the general form for a linear equation is $Ax + By + C = 0$, where $A$, $B$ and $C$ are real numbers. There are two cases that we will consider.

**Case I.** Suppose $A = 0$ and $B \neq 0$. Then we have $0x + By + C = 0$ which can be expressed as $y = b$, where $b = \dfrac{-C}{B}$ is a real number. Let's graph such an equation and see what happens.

**Example.** Graph: $y = 4$

We will use a table to come up with solutions for this equation. What's different about this example compared to the ones that we've seen is that the equation doesn't have the $x$-variable in it. The truth of the matter is that it really is there. We just don't see it (it's like a ghost). We can think of the equation $y = 4$ as $y = 0x + 4$. Notice that, whatever number we choose for $x$, the 0 will multiply by it and cancel it out. Hence, the $y$-value will always be equal to 4.

| $x$ | $y = 4$ | Solution |
|-----|---------|----------|
| 0   | 4       | (0, 4)   |
| 1   | 4       | (1, 4)   |
| $-1$ | 4      | $(-1, 4)$ |

The graph that we've obtained is a horizontal line whose $y$-intercept is (0, 4) (see graph below).

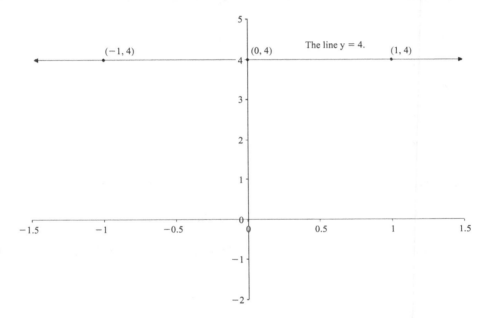

Observe that, since the $y$-value is 4 and never changes as the $x$-value changes, we have

$$m = \frac{\Delta y}{\Delta x} = \frac{0}{\Delta x} = 0.$$

In general, the graph of the equation $y = b$ is a horizontal line whose $y$-intercept is (0, $b$) and whose slope equals 0.

**Case II.** Suppose $B = 0$ and $A \neq 0$. Then we have $Ax + 0y + C = 0$ which can be expressed as $x = a$, where $a = \dfrac{-C}{A}$ is a real number. Let's graph such an equation and see what happens.

**Example.** Graph: $x = -2$

This time, the equation doesn't have the $y$-variable in it, though it really is there. We can think of the equation $x = -2$ as $x = -2 + 0y$. For any real number we choose for $y$, the 0 multiplies it and cancels it out. Hence, the $x$-value will always be equal to $-2$.

| $x = -2$ | $y$ | Solution |
|----------|-----|----------|
| $-2$     | $-1$ | $(-2, -1)$ |
| $-2$     | 0   | $(-2, 0)$ |
| $-2$     | 1   | $(-2, 1)$ |

The graph is a vertical line whose $x$-intercept is $(-2, 0)$ (see graph below).

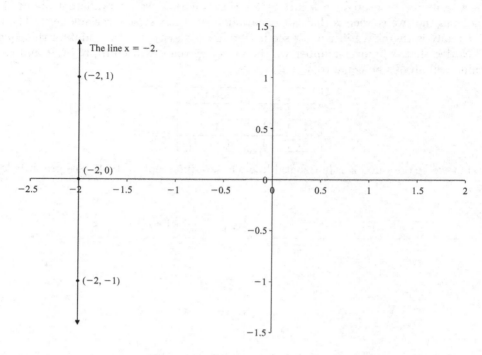

Notice that, since the $x$-value is $-2$ and never changes as the $y$-value changes, we have

$$m = \frac{\Delta y}{\Delta x} = \frac{\Delta y}{0}, \text{ which is undefined.}$$

In general, the graph of the equation $x = a$ is a vertical line whose $x$-intercept is $(a, 0)$. Such a line has **no** slope.

**Try These (Set 10):** Graph and find the slope.

1) $y = 2$       3) $x = -5$       5) $y = 0$

2) $x = 4$       4) $y = -8$       6) $x = 0$

**Exercise 10.2**

In Exercises 1-10, determine whether or not the given point is on the line whose equation is given.

1. $(1, 1)$; $y = 2x - 1$       2. $(2, -1)$; $y = 3x - 7$       3. $(-4, 3)$; $y = -2x - 5$

4. $(5, 9)$; $y = 3x - 6$       5. $(-2, 0)$; $y = \frac{2}{3}x + 4$       6. $(-5, 2)$; $y = -\frac{2}{5}x + 1$

7. $(3, 3)$; $5x - 4y - 3 = 0$       8. $(0, 0)$; $-7x + y = 0$       9. $(-12, 10)$; $-\frac{5}{6}x + \frac{1}{10}y - 11 = 0$

10. $(16, -5)$; $\frac{9}{8}x - \frac{3}{5}y - 21 = 0$

In Exercises 11-26, find the slope of the line containing the given points.

11. (1, 6) and (2, 9)

12. (1, 4) and (3, 8)

13. (9, $-2$) and (3, $-10$)

14. (6, $-5$) and (8, $-1$)

15. ($-1$, $-12$) and (0, $-2$)

16. (3, 0) and ($-12$, 3)

17. (4, 2) and ($-6$, $-5$)

18. ($-7$, $-4$) and (8, $-9$)

19. (4, 9) and ($-3$, 9)

20. ($-8$, 1) and ($-6$, 1)

21. (5, 7) and (5, $-3$)

22. ($-6$, 1) and ($-6$, 4)

23. $\left(\frac{1}{2}, -\frac{1}{3}\right)$ and $\left(\frac{3}{4}, \frac{2}{3}\right)$

24. $\left(-\frac{1}{6}, \frac{2}{3}\right)$ and $\left(\frac{1}{6}, -\frac{1}{3}\right)$

25. $\left(-\frac{2}{5}, -\frac{1}{9}\right)$ and $\left(\frac{3}{10}, -\frac{5}{6}\right)$

26. $\left(-\frac{3}{8}, \frac{2}{7}\right)$ and $\left(\frac{3}{4}, -\frac{1}{14}\right)$

In Exercises 27-44, graph and find the equation of the line (in slope-intercept form) whose slope is $m$ and contains the given point $(x_1, y_1)$.

27. $m = 1$; $(x_1, y_1) = (4, 2)$

28. $m = 1$; $(x_1, y_1) = (3, 5)$

29. $m = 4$; $(x_1, y_1) = (-1, 3)$

30. $m = 6$; $(x_1, y_1) = (-4, 1)$

31. $m = 7$; $(x_1, y_1) = (-2, -7)$

32. $m = 3$; $(x_1, y_1) = (-4, -6)$

33. $m = \frac{1}{2}$; $(x_1, y_1) = (0, 4)$

34. $m = \frac{1}{3}$; $(x_1, y_1) = (0, -2)$

35. $m = -\frac{1}{8}$; $(x_1, y_1) = (-3, 0)$

36. $m = -\frac{1}{7}$; $(x_1, y_1) = (1, 0)$

37. $m = -\frac{4}{5}$; $(x_1, y_1) = (-8, 2)$

38. $m = -\frac{3}{4}$; $(x_1, y_1) = (-4, 3)$

39. $m = \frac{3}{14}$; $(x_1, y_1) = (-9, -1)$

40. $m = \frac{2}{9}$; $(x_1, y_1) = (-5, 3)$

41. $m = 0$; $(x_1, y_1) = (2, -6)$

42. $m = 0$; $(x_1, y_1) = (-1, 5)$

43. no slope; $(x_1, y_1) = (-3, -10)$

44. no slope; $(x_1, y_1) = (-7, 1)$

In Exercises 45-64, find the slope and $y$-intercept of the line whose equation is given.

45. $y = 2x + 5$

46. $y = 3x + 1$

47. $y = -4x + 8$

48. $y = -7x + 12$

49. $y = \frac{1}{5}x - 3$

50. $y = \frac{1}{6}x - 4$

51. $3x + 4y - 6 = 0$

52. $9x - 2y + 18 = 0$

53. $y - 2 = 5(x - 3)$

54. $y - (-1) = 2(x - 2)$

55. $-8x + y - 3 = 0$

56. $x + 3y - 1 = 0$

57. $x + y = 8$

58. $x + y = -4$

59. $x - y - 2 = 0$

60. $-x - y + 7 = 0$

61. $y = 5$

62. $y = -11$

63. $x = 3$

64. $x = -8$

In Exercises 65-80, find the intercept(s) of the line whose equation is given.

65. $4x + y - 12 = 0$

66. $x + 3y - 9 = 0$

67. $-x - 2y + 6 = 0$

68. $12x - y - 4 = 0$

69. $8x - 5y - 7 = 0$

70. $-7x + 9y - 2 = 0$

71. $2x - y = 0$

72. $3x - y = 0$

73. $y = -\frac{1}{2}x + 7$

74. $y = -\frac{3}{5}x + 12$

75. $y = -3x - 17$

76. $y = -x + 6$

77. $x = -4$

78. $x = 13$

79. $y = 10$

80. $y = -9$

In Exercises 81-92, find the equation of the line (in slope-intercept form) containing the given points.

81. $(1, 1)$ and $(2, 3)$       82. $(2, 5)$ and $(3, 7)$       83. $(-2, 4)$ and $(2, 8)$

84. $(3, 1)$ and $(-5, 9)$       85. $(0, 6)$ and $(1, 0)$       86. $(4, 0)$ and $(0, -3)$

87. $(-1, -7)$ and $(-5, -6)$       88. $(-5, -1)$ and $(-8, -8)$       89. $(3, -4)$ and $(-2, -4)$

90. $(-4, 12)$ and $(0, 12)$       91. $(9, 1)$ and $(9, 14)$       92. $(-2, 8)$ and $(-2, 6)$

In Exercises 93-112, graph the line whose equation is given.

93. $y = 2x + 3$       94. $y = 4x + 1$       95. $y = \dfrac{1}{5}x - 2$       96. $y = \dfrac{2}{3}x - 1$

97. $y = -\dfrac{3}{7}x + 2$       98. $y = -\dfrac{5}{6}x + 7$       99. $y = x - 6$       100. $y = x + 8$

101. $y = -x + 7$       102. $y = -x - 5$       103. $2x + 5y - 5 = 0$       104. $-3x + 4y + 6 = 0$

105. $x - 2y + 1 = 0$       106. $6x - y + 12 = 0$       107. $5x + 9y = 0$       108. $3x - 7y = 0$

109. $x = 3$       110. $x = -1$       111. $y = -4$       112. $y = 5$

# Section 10.3  Parallel Lines and Perpendicular Lines

## Parallel Lines

**Definition:** Two distinct lines are **parallel** if they never intersect.

If you draw two lines on a piece of paper, they will be parallel if they are drawn in such a way that they don't intersect (or cross) each other.

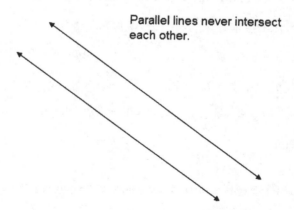

Parallel lines never intersect each other.

We use the symbol '//' to denote that two lines are parallel. Notice that this definition has absolutely nothing to do with the Cartesian plane. What we would like to do is come up with a way of describing two parallel lines in the Cartesian plane. After all, if we graph two lines in the Cartesian plane, we learned that these lines have equations. If they are parallel, is there any relationship between these equations? The answer is yes!

Suppose we are given two non-vertical, distinct lines in the Cartesian plane, say $L_1$ and $L_2$ (we will look at vertical lines later in this section). Then we can write the equation of each of these lines in slope-intercept form as

$$L_1 : y = m_1 x + b_1$$
$$L_2 : y = m_2 x + b_2$$

where $b_1 \neq b_2$. Then $L_1 // L_2$ if and only if $m_1 = m_2$.

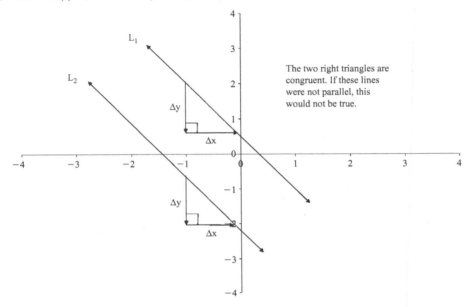

The two right triangles are congruent. If these lines were not parallel, this would not be true.

Note that this condition is **not** true for vertical lines, since a vertical line has no slope.

**Examples.** Are the given lines parallel?

1) $L_1 : y = 3x + 1$ and $L_2 : y = 3x - 5$

To show that these are parallel lines, we need to show that they have the same slopes and different $y$-intercepts. Recall that we can find the slope of a line when we are given its equation by writing it in slope-intercept form (a.k.a. $y = mx + b$ form). Well, observe that both $L_1$ and $L_2$ are already in slope-intercept form. As you can see, the slope of $L_1$ is $m_1 = 3$ and the slope of $L_2$ is $m_2 = 3$. Furthermore, the $y$-intercepts are different (since $b_1 = 1$ and $b_2 = -5$). Therefore, the lines $L_1$ and $L_2$ are parallel (see graph below).

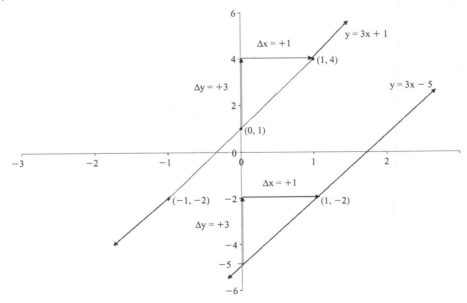

2) $L_1 : y = x - 4$ and $L_2 : y = -2x$

Both of the equations are in slope-intercept form. Notice that $L_1$ has slope $m_1 = 1$ (since $y = x - 4$ is the same as $y = 1x - 4$) and $L_2$ has slope $m_2 = -2$. Therefore, the lines $L_1$ and $L_2$ are not parallel (see graph below).

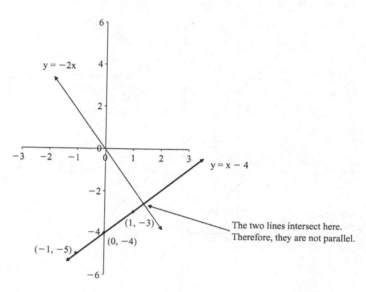

3) $L_1 : 2x + 5y - 1 = 0$ and $L_2 : -2x - 5y + 7 = 0$

We need to get both of the equations in slope-intercept form.

$$L_1 : 2x + 5y - 1 = 0$$
$$\frac{-5y \qquad\quad -5y}{\phantom{xx}}$$
$$\frac{2x}{-5} - \frac{1}{-5} = \frac{-5y}{-5}$$
$$-\frac{2}{5}x + \frac{1}{5} = y$$

$$L_2 : -2x - 5y + 7 = 0$$
$$\frac{+5y \qquad\quad +5y}{\phantom{xx}}$$
$$\frac{-2x}{5} + \frac{7}{5} = \frac{5y}{5}$$
$$-\frac{2}{5}x + \frac{7}{5} = y$$

Since $m_1 = m_2 = -\dfrac{2}{5}$ and the $y$-intercepts are different, the lines are parallel.

4) $L_1 : 3x - 2y = 8$ and $L_2 : -2x + 3y = 8$

We need to get the equations in slope-intercept form.

$$L_1 : 3x - 2y = 8$$
$$\frac{-3x \qquad\quad -3x}{\phantom{xx}}$$
$$\frac{-2y}{-2} = \frac{-3x}{-2} + \frac{8}{-2}$$
$$y = \frac{3}{2}x - 4$$

$$L_2 : -2x + 3y = 8$$
$$\frac{+2x \qquad\quad +2x}{\phantom{xx}}$$
$$\frac{3y}{3} = \frac{2x}{3} + \frac{8}{3}$$
$$y = \frac{2}{3}x + \frac{8}{3}$$

Therefore, $m_1 = \dfrac{3}{2}$ and $m_2 = \dfrac{2}{3}$ and so the lines are not parallel.

5) $L_1 : y = 5$ and $L_2 : y = -2$

Both of these lines are horizontal lines and with different $y$-intercepts, namely $(0, 5)$ and $(0, -2)$. Consequently, they are parallel. Recall that every horizontal line has slope 0, so they do have equal slopes.

**Examples.**

1) Find an equation of the line containing the point $(2,\ 1)$ and is parallel to the line $y = -6x + 5$.

Since we want to find an equation of a line, we will use the point-slope form $y - y_1 = m\,(x - x_1)$. We are given a point which our line must contain, $(x_1,\ y_1) = (2,\ 1)$. We need to find the slope of the line whose equation we are looking for. To find this slope, which I will call $m_{want}$, we will use the fact that parallel lines must have equal slopes. Notice that the slope of the given line, which I will call $m_{given}$, is $m_{given} = -6$ (why?). Therefore, $\underbrace{m_{want} = m_{given}}_{\text{parallel lines have equal slopes}} = -6$. We can now find our equation:

$$y - y_1 = m\,(x - x_1)$$
$$y - 1 = -6\,(x - 2)$$
$$y - \cancel{1} = -6x + 12$$
$$\underline{+\cancel{1} \qquad\qquad +1}$$
$$y = -6x + 13$$

Notice that the $y$-intercept of the line we've just found is different from the $y$-intercept of the given line. This guarentees that the lines are parallel (graph them and see for yourself).

2) Find an equation of the line containing the point $(-3,\ 4)$ and is parallel to the line $-x + 6y - 1 = 0$.

We follow the same technique as in the previous example. We will use the point-slope form $y - y_1 = m\,(x - x_1)$. We are given that $(x_1,\ y_1) = (-3,\ 4)$. We need to find the slope of the line whose equation whose equation we are looking for. To find $m_{want}$, we will use the fact that $m_{want} = m_{given}$. We must the first find $m_{given}$.

$$-x + \cancel{6}y - 1 = 0$$
$$\underline{\quad -\cancel{6}y \qquad\quad - 6y}$$
$$\frac{-x}{-6} - \frac{1}{-6} = \frac{-\cancel{6}y}{-\cancel{6}}$$
$$\frac{1}{6}x + \frac{1}{6} = y$$

and so $m_{given} = \dfrac{1}{6}$. Therefore, $m_{want} = \dfrac{1}{6}$ as well. Our equation is

$$y - y_1 = m\,(x - x_1)$$
$$y - 4 = \frac{1}{6}\,(x - (-3))$$
$$y - 4 = \frac{1}{6}\left(x + \frac{3}{1}\right)$$
$$y - \cancel{4} = \frac{1}{6}x + \frac{1}{2}$$
$$\underline{+\cancel{4} \qquad\qquad\quad +4}$$
$$y = \frac{1}{6}x + \frac{9}{2}$$

**Try These (Set 11):**

I) Are the lines parallel?

1) $L_1 : y = -3x + 7$ and $L_2 : y = -3x + 2$    2) $L_1 : 2x - 5y + 18 = 0$ and $L_2 : -y + \dfrac{7}{8}x = 2$

II) Find an equation of the line containing the given point which is parallel to the given line.

    1) $(6,\ 0)$; $y = -2x + 3$      2) $(-3,\ -10)$; $9x + 2y - 1 = 0$

## Perpendicular Lines

**Definition:** Two lines are **perpendicular** if they intersect and form right angles.

Recall that a right angle is an angle whose measurement is 90°. Notice that four right angles are formed when two lines intersect and are perpendicular to one other.

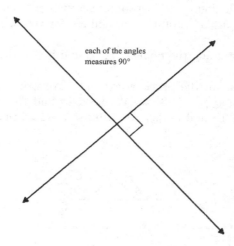

each of the angles
measures 90°

We use the symbol '$\perp$' to denote that two lines are perpendicular. The definition of two lines being perpendicular does not involve the Cartesian plane. As for parallel lines, we would like to come up with a way of describing two perpendicular lines in the Cartesian plane. Once again, there is a relationship between the slopes of two perpendicular lines.

Suppose that we are given two lines in the Cartesian plane, say $L_1$ and $L_2$ and that these lines are neither vertical nor horizontal. Let the equations of each of these lines be

$$L_1 : y = m_1 x + b_1$$
$$L_2 : y = m_2 x + b_2$$

Then $L_1 \perp L_2$ if and only if $m_1 m_2 = -1$. One way to remember this relationship is by observing that it can be written as $m_2 = -\dfrac{1}{m_1}$, which is the same as saying that '$m_2$ is the **negative reciprocal** of $m_1$' (recall that if $x$ is a non-zero real number, then $\dfrac{1}{x}$ is the reciprocal of $x$). In other words, perpendicular lines (which are non-vertical and non-horizontal) have slopes which are negative reciprocals of each other.

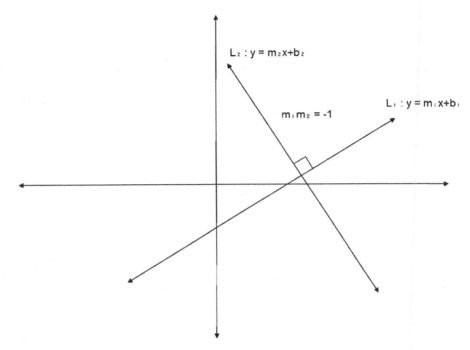

Note that this condition is **not** true for vertical and horizontal lines, since vertical lines have no slope and horizontal lines have zero slope, making the equation $m_1 m_2 = -1$ impossible.

**Examples.** Are the given lines perpendicular?

1) $L_1 : y = 4x - 2$ and $L_2 : y = -\dfrac{1}{4}x + 1$

To show that these are perpendicular lines, we need to show that their slopes multiply to $-1$. Observe that both $L_1$ and $L_2$ are already in slope-intercept form. The slope of $L_1$ is $m_1 = 4$ and the slope of $L_2$ is $m_2 = -\dfrac{1}{4}$. Notice that $m_1 m_2 = 4\left(-\dfrac{1}{4}\right) = -1$ and so the lines $L_1$ and $L_2$ are perpendicular (see graph below).

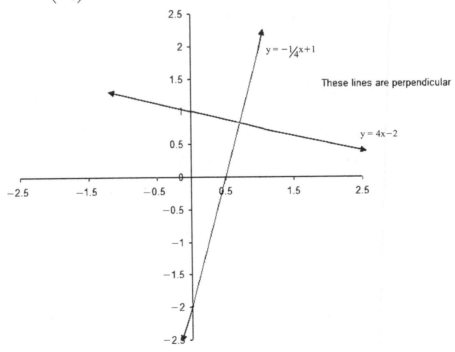

2) $L_1 : y = \dfrac{2}{5}x - 1$ and $L_2 : y = -\dfrac{1}{3}x + 3$

Both of the equations are in slope-intercept form. Line $L_1$ has slope $m_1 = \dfrac{2}{5}$ and line $L_2$ has slope $m_2 = -\dfrac{1}{3}$. Observe that $m_1 m_2 = \dfrac{2}{5}\left(-\dfrac{1}{3}\right) = -\dfrac{2}{15} \neq -1$. Therefore, the lines $L_1$ and $L_2$ are not perpendicular (see graph below).

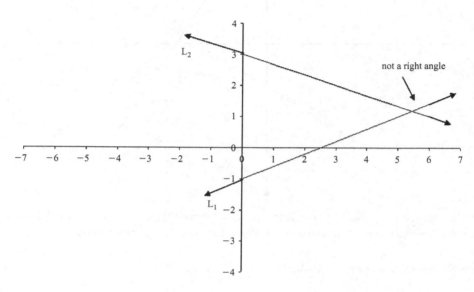

3) $L_1 : x - 3y - 8 = 0$ and $L_2 : -3x - y + 5 = 0$

We need to get both of the equations in slope-intercept form.

$$
\begin{array}{ll}
L_1 : x - 3y - 8 = 0 & \qquad L_2 : -3x - y + 5 = 0 \\
\underline{\phantom{x}+3y\phantom{--8}+3y} & \qquad \underline{\phantom{-3x}+y\phantom{+5}+y} \\
\dfrac{x}{3} - \dfrac{8}{3} = \dfrac{3y}{3} & \qquad -3x + 5 = y \\
\dfrac{1}{3}x - \dfrac{8}{3} = y &
\end{array}
$$

So, $m_1 = \dfrac{1}{3}$, $m_2 = -3$ and $m_1 m_2 = \dfrac{1}{3}(-3) = -1$. Hence, the lines are perpendicular.

4) $L_1 : 11x - 4y + 1 = 0$ and $L_2 : 4x - 9y = 0$

We need to get both of the equations in slope-intercept form.

$$
\begin{array}{ll}
L_1 : 11x - 4y + 1 = 0 & \qquad L_2 : 4x + 9y = 0 \\
\underline{\phantom{11x}+4y\phantom{+1}+4y} & \qquad \underline{\phantom{4x}-9y\phantom{=0}-9y} \\
\dfrac{11x}{4} + \dfrac{1}{4} = \dfrac{4y}{4} & \qquad \dfrac{4x}{-9} = \dfrac{-9y}{-9} \\
\dfrac{11}{4}x + \dfrac{1}{4} = y & \qquad -\dfrac{4}{9}x = y
\end{array}
$$

Now, $m_1 = \dfrac{11}{4}$ and $m_2 = -\dfrac{4}{9}$ yields $m_1 m_2 = \dfrac{11}{4}\left(-\dfrac{4}{9}\right) = \dfrac{-11}{9} \neq -1$. Therefore, the lines are not perpendicular.

**Examples.**

1) Find an equation of the line containing the point $(-7,\ 2)$ and is perpendicular to the line $y = \frac{1}{4}x + 3$.

We can use the same method as we used for parallel lines, except that the slopes are related in a different way now. We will use the point-slope form $y - y_1 = m\,(x - x_1)$ to obtain our equation. We are given a point which our line must contain, $(x_1,\ y_1) = (-7,\ 2)$. We need to find the slope of the line whose equation we are looking for. To find this slope, $m_{want}$, we will use the fact that perpendicular lines must have slopes which are negative reciprocals of one another. Notice that the slope of the given line is $m_{given} = \frac{1}{4}$ (why?). Therefore, $m_{want} = -\frac{4}{1} = -4$. We now find our equation:

$$y - y_1 = m\,(x - x_1)$$
$$y - 2 = -4\,(x - (-7))$$
$$y - 2 = -4\,(x + 7)$$
$$y - 2 = -4x - 28$$
$$\underline{\quad +2 \qquad\qquad +2\quad}$$
$$y = -4x - 26$$

2) Find an equation of the line which is perpendicular to the line $\frac{1}{2}x + \frac{5}{6}y - 1 = 0$ and contains the point $(-8,\ -5)$.

As before, we will use the point-slope form $y - y_1 = m\,(x - x_1)$. We are given that $(x_1,\ y_1) = (-8,\ -5)$ and we need to find the slope of the line whose equation we are looking for, $m_{want}$. Let's first find $m_{given}$:

$$\frac{1}{2}x + \frac{5}{6}y - 1 = 0$$
$$\underline{\qquad -\frac{5}{6}y \qquad\qquad -\frac{5}{6}y \qquad}$$
$$\frac{1}{2}x - 1 = -\frac{5}{6}y$$
$$-\frac{6}{5}\left(\frac{1}{2}x - 1\right) = -\frac{6}{5}\left(-\frac{5}{6}y\right)$$
$$-\frac{3}{5}x + \frac{6}{5} = y$$

and so $m_{given} = -\frac{3}{5}$. Therefore, $m_{want} = \frac{5}{3}$ and our equation is:

$$y - y_1 = m\,(x - x_1)$$
$$y - (-5) = \frac{5}{3}\,(x - (-8))$$
$$y + 5 = \frac{5}{3}\left(x + \frac{8}{1}\right)$$
$$y + 5 = \frac{5}{3}x + \frac{40}{3}$$
$$\underline{\quad -5 \qquad\qquad\qquad -5\quad}$$
$$y = \frac{5}{3}x + \frac{25}{3}$$

**Try These (Set 12):**

I) Are the lines perpendicular?

   1) $L_1 : y = -\frac{3}{10}x + 2$ and $L_2 : y = \frac{7}{3}x - 4$

   2) $L_1 : -5x + 2y + 15 = 0$ and $L_2 : -\frac{2}{5}x - y + 6 = 0$

II) Find an equation of the line containing the given point which is perpendicular to the given line.

1) $(0, \ -1); \ y = 6x - 8$        2) $(2, \ -9); \ 4x + 8y + 3 = 0$

## Parallel and Perpendicular Lines (The Case of Vertical and Horizontal Lines)

To solve a problem for parallel or perpendicular lines involving vertical or horizontal lines, the best approach is by using graphs.

**Examples.**

1) Find an equation of the line containing $(1, \ 3)$ and parallel to the line $y = -2$.

We want an equation of a line which is parallel to $y = -2$. What you need to remember is that the line $y = -2$ is a horizontal line with $y$-intercept $(0, -2)$ (see graph below). The only type of line which is parallel to a horizontal line is another horizontal line. Now, there are many different horizontal lines, but the one that we want must go through the point $(1, \ 3)$. Therefore, the equation of our line is $y = 3$.

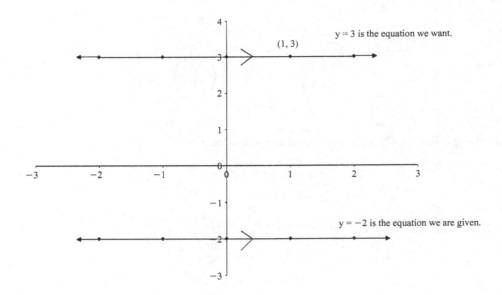

2) Find an equation of the line containing $(2, \ -2)$ and parallel to the line $x = -1$.

We want an equation of a line which is parallel to $x = -1$. Recall that the line $x = -1$ is a vertical line with $x$-intercept $(-1, 0)$ (see the graph that follows). The only type of line which is parallel to a vertical line is another vertical line. Our vertical line must pass through the point $(2, \ -2)$. Therefore, the equation of our line is $x = 2$.

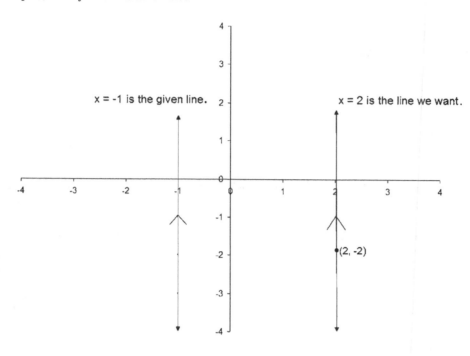

3) Find an equation of the line containing $(-4,\ 1)$ and perpendicular to the line $y = 4$.

    We will begin by graphing the line $y = 4$, which is a horizontal line with $y$-intercept $(0,\ 4)$ (see graph below). The only type of line which is perpendicular to a horizontal line is a vertical line. Our vertical line must pass through the point $(-4,\ 1)$. Therefore, the equation of our line is $x = -4$.

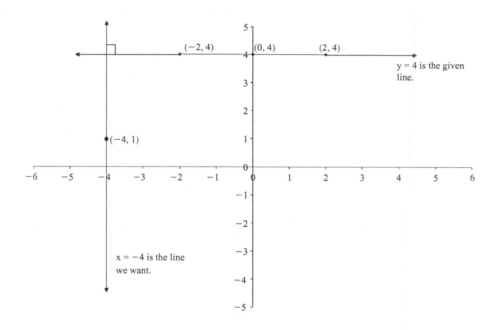

**Try These (Set 13):**

I) Find an equation of the line containing the given point which is parallel to the given line.
    1) $(-4,\ 0);\ x = 5$     2) $(3,\ -1);\ y = -6$

II) Find an equation of the line containing the given point which is perpendicular to the given line.

1) $(0,\ 6)$; $x = 3$        2) $(-2,\ 1)$; $y = -3$

### Exercise 10.3

In Exercises 1-25, determine whether the given pair of equations represent parallel lines, perpendicular lines or neither.

1. $L_1 : y = 2x + 1$ and $L_2 : y = 2x - 3$

2. $L_1 : y = 8x$ and $L_2 : y = 8x - 7$

3. $L_1 : y = \dfrac{4}{5}x - 4$ and $L_2 : y = -\dfrac{5}{4}x - 9$

4. $L_1 : y = -\dfrac{3}{8}x + 1$ and $L_2 : y = \dfrac{8}{3}x + 1$

5. $L_1 : y = -4x + 3$ and $L_2 : y = 4x + 6$

6. $L_1 : y = \dfrac{2}{9}x + 12$ and $L_2 : y = \dfrac{9}{2}x$

7. $L_1 : y = 7x + 3$ and $L_2 : y = 7x - 2$

8. $L_1 : y = -\dfrac{1}{12}x - 3$ and $L_2 : y = 12x + 9$

9. $L_1 : y = \dfrac{1}{6}x + 1$ and $L_2 : y = -6x - 7$

10. $L_1 : y = \dfrac{3}{8}x - 2$ and $L_2 : y = \dfrac{3}{8}x + 5$

11. $L_1 : 2x - y + 4 = 0$ and $L_2 : -6x + 3y - 1 = 0$

12. $L_1 : -x + y - 10 = 0$ and $L_2 : -2x + 2y - 3 = 0$

13. $L_1 : 7x - 3y + 15 = 0$ and $L_2 : -3x - 7y + 2 = 0$

14. $L_1 : -9x + 5y + 6 = 0$ and $L_2 : 5x + 9y - 7 = 0$

15. $L_1 : 4x + 16y - 13 = 0$ and $L_2 : 8x - 2y - 3 = 0$

16. $L_1 : 6x - y = 12$ and $L_2 : x - 6y = 12$

17. $L_1 : y = 7$ and $L_2 : y = -5$

18. $L_1 : x = 2$ and $L_2 : x = 6$

19. $L_1 : x = -9$ and $L_2 : x = 1$

20. $L_1 : y = -3$ and $L_2 : y = 0$

21. $L_1 : x = -4$ and $L_2 : x = 3$

22. $L_1 : x = 8$ and $L_2 : y = -2$

23. $L_1 : y = 1$ and $L_2 : x = 2$

24. $L_1 : x = 6$ and $L_2 : y = 10x$

25. $L_1 : y = -11$ and $L_2 : y = -11x + 1$

In Exercises 26-38, find an equation of the line containing the given point which is parallel to the given line.

26. $(-2,\ 0)$; $y = 3x - 4$

27. $(1,\ 0)$; $y = 2x + 1$

28. $(-5,\ 3)$; $-4x + y - 5 = 0$

29. $(6,\ -4)$; $5x - 10y + 1 = 0$

30. $(2,\ -3)$; $7x + 14y + 6 = 0$

31. $(0,\ -4)$; $-3x + y - 8 = 0$

32. $(0,\ 9)$; $-4x - y + 6 = 0$

33. $(-4,\ -2)$; $y + 6x = 0$

34. $(-5,\ -5)$; $-y + 8x = 0$

35. $(0,\ 4)$; $y = -8$

36. $(-2,\ 1)$; $x = 7$

37. $(6,\ -8)$; $x = 1$

38. $(7,\ 0)$; $y = -1$

In Exercises 39-51, find an equation of the line containing the given point which is perpendicular to the given line.

39. $(0,\ 3)$; $y = 2x + 2$ 40. $(0,\ -4)$; $y = -x + 3$ 41. $(-5,\ 4)$; $y = x + 3$

42. $(1,\ -1)$; $y = -5x - 1$ 43. $(9,\ -2)$; $3x - 2y + 12 = 0$ 44. $(-7,\ 1)$; $-5x + 3y + 3 = 0$

45. $(-1,\ -10)$; $-12x - 2y + 5 = 0$ 46. $(-3,\ -3)$; $-14x + 7y - 2 = 0$

47. $(7,\ -4)$; $y + 10x = 0$ 48. $(0,\ -2)$; $y = 4$ 49. $(2,\ 6)$; $x = -4$

50. $(5,\ -9)$; $x = 0$ 51. $(-4,\ -8)$; $y = 0$

## Section 10.4   Equations of Circles

We learn about graphing equations in order to relate an algebraic object (an equation) to a geometric object (the graph of solutions to the equation). As the old saying goes, 'a picture tells a thousand words'. It is nice to have a picture in front of you when trying to work with an equation. We have learned that any equation of the form $y = mx + b$ (that is, a linear equation in $x$ and $y$), as well as any equation of the form $x = a$, has a graph which is a straight line. Conversely, every graph which is a straight line has an equation which can be written in the form $Ax + By + C = 0$ which, when $B \neq 0$, can be expressed in the form $y = mx + b$ where $m = -\frac{A}{B}$ and $b = -\frac{C}{B}$. In this section, we are interested in finding the equation of a circle with a given center and radius. In other words, if we are given the center and radius of a circle, can we find an equation whose solutions are the points on the circle when graphed in the Cartesian plane? As we will now see, this can be done. First, let's understand the definition of a circle without making any use of the Cartesian plane. Afterwards, we will see how to obtain the equation for a circle.

**Definition:** A **circle** is a collection of points, all of whose distance from a fixed point (called the **center**) is constant.

In Chapter 8, we looked at examples pertaining to circles. The circle below has the property that the distance from the center to any point on the circle is 2 inches. Recall that any line segment connecting the center to any point on the circle is called a **radius** and we say that the **radius of the circle** is 2 inches. Hence, the term 'radius' means either any line segment connecting the center of a circle to a point on the circle or the length of any such line segment. Any line segment connecting two points on a circle and going through the center is called a **diameter** and a diameter is just two radii joined together to form a line segment. This means that the length of a diameter is twice the length of the radius. The length of any diameter of a circle is called the **diameter of the circle** (which is $2 \times 2 = 4$ inches in our picture below).

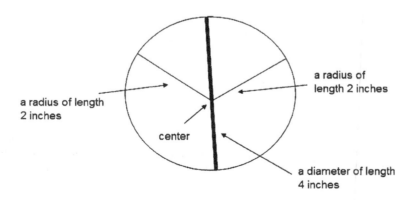

Now let's look at the graph of a circle in the Cartesian plane. Let the center of a circle be $(h, k)$ and let the radius be $r$ (see graph below). If we choose any point on the circle and call it $(x, y)$, then we know that the distance from the center, $(h, k)$, to the point on the circle, $(x, y)$, equals the radius, $r$. By the distance formula, we have

$$\sqrt{(x - h)^2 + (y - k)^2} = r$$

and, after squaring each side of the equation, we obtain

$$\boxed{(x - h)^2 + (y - k)^2 = r^2}$$

This is an equation of the circle with center $(h, k)$ and radius $r$ and is called the **standard form** for the equation. Notice how this resembles the Pythagorean theorem, $a^2 + b^2 = c^2$. This makes sense, since the distance formula comes from the Pythagorean theorem. If you ever have trouble remembering the standard form for a circle, think of the Pythagorean theorem.

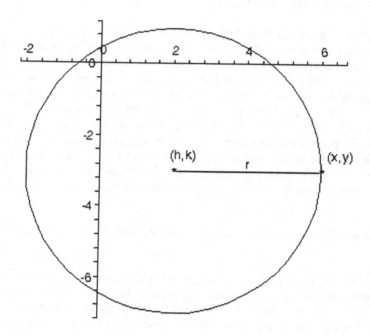

**Examples.** Find an equation of the circle whose center is $C$ and radius is $r$. Graph the circle.

1) $C = (1, 3)$ and $r = 2$

We are given $(h, k) = (1, 3)$ and $r = 2$. All that we need to do is plug these values into the standard form. By doing so, we obtain the equation:

$$\begin{aligned}
(x - 1)^2 + (y - 3)^2 &= 2^2 \text{ or} \\
(x - 1)^2 + (y - 3)^2 &= 4
\end{aligned}$$

We could expand this equation out further, but we won't for now. To graph this circle, we need to first plot the center and then use the radius to locate at least three points (since three points determine a unique circle). We can easily obtain four points, in fact, by going up, down, left and right by 2 units from the center (see graph on next page).

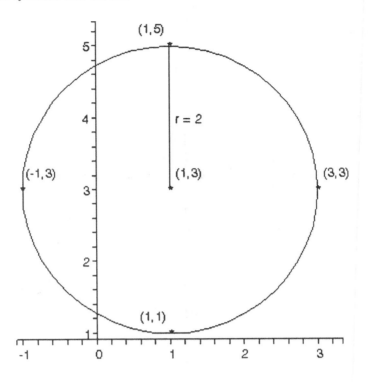

2) $C = (-2, 4)$ and $r = 4$

We are given $(h, k) = (-2, 4)$ and $r = 4$. By putting these values into the form, we obtain the equation:

$$(x - (-2))^2 + (y - 4)^2 \;=\; 4^2 \;\; \text{or}$$
$$(x + 2)^2 + (y - 4)^2 \;=\; 16$$

The graph is given below.

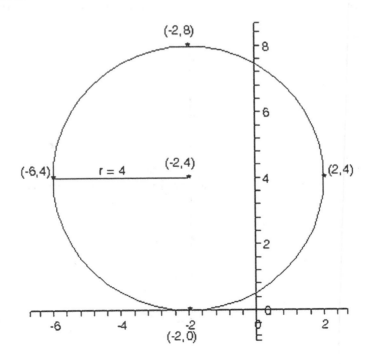

3) $C = (0, -5)$ and $r = 6$

We are given $(h, k) = (0, -5)$ and $r = 6$. By repeating the above method, we obtain the equation:
$$(x - 0)^2 + (y - (-5))^2 = 6^2 \text{ or}$$
$$x^2 + (y + 5)^2 = 36$$

The graph is given below.

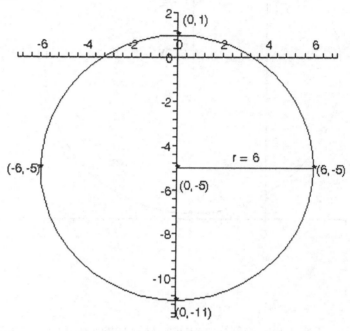

4) $C = (0, 0)$ and $r = 1$

We are given $(h, k) = (0, 0)$ and $r = 1$. The equation is
$$(x - 0)^2 + (y - 0)^2 = 1^2 \text{ or}$$
$$x^2 + y^2 = 1$$

The graph is given below. It is the circle whose center is $(0, 0)$ and whose radius is 1. This is called the **unit circle**. Notice that any circle whose center is the origin and radius is $r$ has the equation $x^2 + y^2 = r^2$.

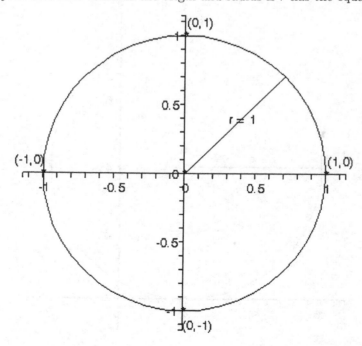

5) $C = (-3, -8)$ and $r = 2\sqrt{5}$

We are given $(h, k) = (-3, -8)$ and $r = 2\sqrt{5}$. The equation is

$$(x - (-3))^2 + (y - (-8))^2 = \left(2\sqrt{5}\right)^2 \quad \text{or}$$
$$(x + 3)^2 + (y + 8)^2 = 20$$

This circle isn't easy to graph without using a calculator to approximate the radius, $2\sqrt{5}$. We will not graph it.

**Examples.** Find the center and radius of the circle whose equation is given.

1) $(x - 4)^2 + (y - 7)^2 = 49$

To find the center and radius, you compare the given equation to the standard form with $h$, $k$ and $r$ in it. By doing this, you can read off the values of $h$, $k$ and $r$. Once this is done, you have that the center is $(h, k)$ and the radius is $r$. Let's see how all of this is done.

$$(x - h)^2 + (y - k)^2 = r^2 \text{ compared to}$$
$$(x - 4)^2 + (y - 7)^2 = 49$$

yields $h = 4$, $k = 7$ and $r^2 = 49$ (which means that $r = \sqrt{49} = 7$). Therefore, we have that the center is $(4, 7)$ and the radius is 7. If we wanted to, we can now graph this circle.

2) $(x - 8)^2 + (y + 5)^2 = 64$

We will compare the equation to $(x - h)^2 + (y - k)^2 = r^2$.

$$(x - h)^2 + (y - k)^2 = r^2 \text{ compared to}$$
$$(x - 8)^2 + (y + 5)^2 = 64$$

gives us $h = 8$, $k = -5$ (notice that $(y + 5)^2 = (y - (-5))^2$ and so $k = -5$) and $r^2 = 64$ (which means that $r = \sqrt{64} = 8$). Therefore, we have that the center is $(8, -5)$ and the radius is 8.

3) $(x - 12)^2 + y^2 = 25$

Let's repeat the method above.

$$(x - h)^2 + (y - k)^2 = r^2 \text{ compared to}$$
$$(x - 12)^2 + y^2 = 25$$

gives us $h = 12$, $k = 0$ (notice that $y^2 = (y - 0)^2$ and so $k = 0$) and $r^2 = 25$ (which means that $r = \sqrt{25} = 5$). Therefore, we have that the center is $(12, 0)$ and the radius is 5.

4) $x^2 + (y + 2)^2 = 54$

Repeating the method, we have

$$(x - h)^2 + (y - k)^2 = r^2 \text{ compared to}$$
$$x^2 + (y + 2)^2 = 54$$

gives us $h = 0$, $k = -2$ and $r^2 = 54$ (which means that $r = \sqrt{54} = \sqrt{9}\sqrt{6} = 3\sqrt{6}$). Therefore, we have that the center is $(0, -2)$ and the radius is $3\sqrt{6}$.

By taking the equation of a circle in standard form and simplifying it, we obtain another form for the equation (after grouping some terms). To demonstrate, let's write the equation $(x+2)^2 + (y-4)^2 = 16$ in a more simplified way. First, we will need to eliminate the parentheses by using the FOIL method. Afterwards, will commute some terms in order to 'group' the terms of common degrees. Here's how it looks:

$$(x+2)^2 + (y-4)^2 = 16$$

$$x^2 + 4x + 4 + y^2 - 8y + 16 = 16 \qquad \text{by FOIL}$$

$$x^2 + 4x + y^2 - 8y + 20 = 16 \qquad \text{combining 4 and 16}$$

$$x^2 + y^2 + 4x - 8y + 20 = 16 \qquad \text{grouping terms of the same degree}$$

$$x^2 + y^2 + 4x - 8y + 4 = 0 \qquad \text{subtract 16 from both sides}$$

Notice that the right-hand side of the equation is 0, whereas the left-hand side is 'descending alphabetically'. When an equation of a circle is written in this way, we say that it is in **general form**. In general, any equation of a circle can be written in the form

$$\boxed{x^2 + y^2 + Ax + By + C = 0.}$$

This is the **general form** for the equation of a circle.

**Examples.** Find the center and radius of the circle whose equation is given.

1) $x^2 + y^2 - 2x - 4y - 11 = 0$

The first thing we need to do is write this equation in standard form. We know how to get the center and radius when the equation is in this form. Well, to get the equation in standard form, we begin by grouping the $x$−terms and $y$−terms, as well as carry over the constant term to the other side. Afterwards, we complete the square of each group (see Section 7.4 if you forgot how to complete the square) and we will have standard form. Let's give it a try:

$$x^2 + y^2 - 2x - 4y - 11 = 0$$
$$\underline{\qquad\qquad\qquad\quad +11 \quad +11}$$
$$x^2 + y^2 - 2x - 4y = 11$$
$$x^2 - 2x + \underline{?} + y^2 - 4y + \underline{?} = 11 + \underline{?} + \underline{?}$$
$$\underbrace{x^2 - 2x + \underline{1}} + \underbrace{y^2 - 4y + \underline{4}} = 11 + \underline{1} + \underline{4}$$
$$(x-1)^2 \quad + \quad (y-2)^2 = 16$$

and we have the standard form. By comparison, we obtain

$$(x-h)^2 + (y-k)^2 \;=\; r^2 \text{ compared to}$$
$$(x-1)^2 + (y-2)^2 \;=\; 16$$

and so $h = 1$, $k = 2$ and $r^2 = 16$ (implying that $r = \sqrt{16} = 4$). The circle has center $(1, 2)$ and radius 4.

2) $x^2 + y^2 + 10x - 14y + 10 = 0$

We will carry out the same procedure as in the above example.

$$x^2 + y^2 + 10x - 14y + 10 = 0$$
$$\underline{\qquad\qquad\qquad\quad -10 \quad -10}$$
$$x^2 + y^2 + 10x - 14y = -10$$
$$x^2 + 10x + \underline{?} + y^2 - 14y + \underline{?} = -10 + \underline{?} + \underline{?}$$
$$\underbrace{x^2 + 10x + \underline{25}} + \underbrace{y^2 - 14y + \underline{49}} = -10 + \underline{25} + \underline{49}$$
$$(x+5)^2 \qquad + \qquad (y-7)^2 = 64$$

and we have the standard form. By comparison, we get

$$(x - h)^2 + (y - k)^2 \;=\; r^2 \text{ compared to}$$
$$(x + 5)^2 + (y - 7)^2 \;=\; 64$$

and so $h = -5$, $k = 7$ and $r^2 = 64$ (so $r = 8$). The circle has center $(-5, 7)$ and radius 8.

3) $x^2 + y^2 - 3x - 4 = 0$

Notice that there is no $y$-term in the equation. This means that we don't have to complete the square of the $y$-group (it is already completed).

$$x^2 + y^2 - 3x - 4 = 0$$
$$\underline{+4 \quad +4}$$
$$x^2 + y^2 - 3x = 4$$

$$x^2 - 3x + \underline{?} + y^2 = 4 + \underline{?}$$

$$x^2 - 3x + \frac{9}{4} + y^2 = 4 + \frac{9}{4}$$

$$\left(x - \frac{3}{2}\right)^2 + y^2 = \frac{25}{4}$$

and we have the standard form. By comparison, we get

$$(x - h)^2 + (y - k)^2 \;=\; r^2 \text{ compared to}$$
$$\left(x - \frac{3}{2}\right)^2 + y^2 \;=\; \frac{25}{4}$$

and so $h = \frac{3}{2}$, $k = 0$ and $r^2 = \frac{25}{4}$, giving us $r = \frac{5}{2}$. The circle has center $\left(\frac{3}{2}, 0\right)$ and radius $\frac{5}{2}$.

4) $5x^2 + 5y^2 - 10x + 2y = 0$

Be careful! This equation is **not** in general form. Notice that the first two terms have coefficient 5, whereas the general form requires coefficient 1. The first thing we need to do is divide both sides of the equation by 5. Only then can we proceed with the method we've been using. Notice, also, that the constant term is 0, which is nothing to worry about.

$$\frac{5x^2}{5} + \frac{5y^2}{5} - \frac{10x}{5} + \frac{2y}{5} = \frac{0}{5}$$

$$x^2 + y^2 - 2x + \frac{2}{5}y \;=\; 0$$

$$x^2 - 2x + \underline{?} + y^2 + \frac{2}{5}y + \underline{?} \;=\; 0 + \underline{?} + \underline{?}$$

$$x^2 - 2x + 1 + y^2 + \frac{2}{5}y + \frac{1}{25} \;=\; 0 + 1 + \frac{1}{25}$$

$$(x - 1)^2 \quad + \quad \left(y + \frac{1}{5}\right)^2 \;=\; \frac{26}{25}$$

and we have the standard form. Comparing this to $(x - h)^2 + (y - k)^2 = r^2$, we obtain $h = 1$, $k = -\frac{1}{5}$ and $r^2 = \frac{26}{25}$, yielding $r = \sqrt{\frac{26}{25}} = \frac{\sqrt{26}}{5}$. The circle has center $\left(1, -\frac{1}{5}\right)$ and radius $\frac{\sqrt{26}}{5}$.

Here are some examples which are often seen when studying analytic geometry.

**Examples.**

1) A diameter of a circle has endpoints (2, 5) and (−6, 2). Find the center of the circle.

Well, remember that any diameter of a circle goes through the center in such a way that the center is the **midpoint** of the diameter. This means that we can use the midpoint formula to find the center. Let $(x_1, y_1) = (2, 5)$ and $(x_2, y_2) = (-6, 2)$  Then the center is

$$
\begin{aligned}
\left(\frac{x_1 + x_2}{2}, \frac{y_1 + y_2}{2}\right) &= \left(\frac{2 + (-6)}{2}, \frac{5 + 2}{2}\right) \\
&= \left(\frac{-4}{2}, \frac{7}{2}\right) \\
&= \left(-2, \frac{7}{2}\right)
\end{aligned}
$$

2) The center of a circle is (−4, 3) and the point (2, −3) lies on the circle. Find the radius of the circle.

By definition, the radius of a circle is the length of a line segment connecting the center of the circle to any point on the circle. In other words, the radius is the **distance** from the center to any point on the circle. Hence, we can use the distance formula. Let $(x_1, y_1) = (-4, 3)$ and $(x_2, y_2) = (2, -3)$. The radius is

$$
\begin{aligned}
\sqrt{(x_2 - x_1)^2 + (y_2 - y_1)^2} &= \sqrt{(2 - (-4))^2 + (-3 - 3)^2} \\
&= \sqrt{6^2 + (-6)^2} \\
&= \sqrt{36 + 36} \\
&= \sqrt{72} \text{ or } 6\sqrt{2}
\end{aligned}
$$

3) Find an equation of the circle whose center is $(3, \ -1)$ and contains the point $(4, 6)$.

To find an equation of a circle, we need to know the center and radius. We are given that the center is $(h, \ k) = (3, \ -1)$. As the previous example shows, we can find the radius by finding the distance from the center to the given point on the circle. Let $(x_1, y_1) = (3, \ -1)$ and $(x_2, y_2) = (4, 6)$. Then the radius is

$$
\begin{aligned}
\sqrt{(x_2 - x_1)^2 + (y_2 - y_1)^2} &= \sqrt{(4 - 3)^2 + (6 - (-1))^2} \\
&= \sqrt{1^2 + 7^2} \\
&= \sqrt{1 + 49} = \sqrt{50}
\end{aligned}
$$

The equation of the circle is

$$
\begin{aligned}
(x - 3)^2 + (y - (-1))^2 &= \left(\sqrt{50}\right)^2 \text{ or} \\
(x - 3)^2 + (y + 1)^2 &= 50
\end{aligned}
$$

**Exercise 10.4**

In Exercises 1-14, write an equation of the circle whose center is $(h, k)$ and radius is $r$.

1. $(h, k) = (2, 3)$ ; $r = 2$  2. $(h, k) = (1, 4)$ ; $r = 2$  3. $(h, k) = (5, -1)$ ; $r = 3$

4. $(h, k) = (7, -6)$ ; $r = 5$  5. $(h, k) = (-2, 7)$ ; $r = \sqrt{7}$  6. $(h, k) = (-3, 8)$ ; $r = \sqrt{6}$

7. $(h, k) = (-8, -9)$ ; $r = 1$  8. $(h, k) = (-10, -6)$ ; $r = 12$  9. $(h, k) = (0, 1)$ ; $r = 2\sqrt{3}$

10. $(h, k) = (0, 5)$ ; $r = 4\sqrt{5}$  11. $(h, k) = (10, 0)$ ; $r = 8$  12. $(h, k) = (4, 0)$ ; $r = 3$

13. $(h, k) = (0, 0)$ ; $r = 9$  14. $(h, k) = (0, 0)$ ; $r = 3\sqrt{10}$

In Exercises 15-26, find the center and radius of the circle whose equation is given.

15. $(x - 1)^2 + (y - 3)^2 = 4$  16. $(x - 3)^2 + (y - 8)^2 = 25$  17. $(x + 2)^2 + (y - 7)^2 = 16$

18. $(x + 6)^2 + (y - 1)^2 = 81$  19. $(x + 12)^2 + (y + 10)^2 = 121$  20. $(x + 2)^2 + (y + 11)^2 = 64$

21. $(x - 3)^2 + y^2 = 8$  22. $x^2 + (y - 5)^2 = 24$  23. $x^2 + (y + 8)^2 = 80$

24. $(x + 12)^2 + y^2 = 63$  25. $x^2 + y^2 = 3$  26. $x^2 + y^2 = 10$

In Exercises 27-36, write the equation of the circle in general form.

27. $(x - 2)^2 + (y - 1)^2 = 9$  28. $(x - 4)^2 + (y + 3)^2 = 16$  29. $(x + 1)^2 + (y + 7)^2 = 5$

30. $(x + 3)^2 + (y + 5)^2 = 18$  31. $x^2 + (y - 12)^2 = 6$  32. $(x + 14)^2 + y^2 = 14$

33. $x^2 + y^2 = 16$  34. $x^2 + y^2 = 64$  35. $\left(x - \dfrac{1}{2}\right)^2 + \left(y + \dfrac{1}{2}\right)^2 = 16$

36. $\left(x + \dfrac{2}{3}\right)^2 + \left(y - \dfrac{1}{3}\right)^2 = 2$

In Exercises 37-42, write the equation of the circle in standard form.

37. $x^2 + y^2 - 4x - 6y + 12 = 0$  38. $x^2 + y^2 - 2x - 12y + 13 = 0$  39. $x^2 + y^2 + 10x - 2y - 10 = 0$

40. $x^2 + y^2 - 10x + 14y - 3 = 0$  41. $x^2 + y^2 + 8x - 16 = 0$  42. $x^2 + y^2 + 14y + 25 = 0$

In Exercises 43-50, find the center and radius of the circle whose equation is given.

43. $x^2 + y^2 - 4x + 6y + 12 = 0$  44. $x^2 + y^2 - 8x + 2y + 2 = 0$  45. $x^2 + y^2 - 8x - 4y - 4 = 0$

46. $x^2 + y^2 + 6x - 12y - 4 = 0$  47. $x^2 + y^2 + 3y - 1 = 0$  48. $x^2 + y^2 - 15x + 8 = 0$

49. $x^2 + y^2 - 169 = 0$  50. $x^2 + y^2 - 100 = 0$

# END OF CHAPTER 10   QUIZ

1. The point $(-4,\ 6)$ is in which quadrant?

   a) I     b) II     c) III     d) IV     e) none

2. The distance between the points $(-1,\ -7)$ and $(3,\ -5)$ is

   a) 6     b) $\sqrt{6}$     c) $2\sqrt{3}$     d) $\sqrt{22}$     e) $2\sqrt{5}$

3. The midpoint of $\overline{AB}$, where $A = (-4,\ 6)$ and $B = (0,\ 8)$, is

   a) $(-4,\ 14)$     b) $(-2,\ 2)$     c) $(2,\ 7)$     d) $(-2,\ 7)$     e) $(2,\ -7)$

4. The slope of the line containing the points $(10,\ 5)$ and $(3,\ -6)$ is

   a) $\dfrac{11}{7}$     b) $\dfrac{7}{11}$     c) $\dfrac{-11}{7}$     d) $\dfrac{1}{7}$     e) $\dfrac{-11}{13}$

5. An equation of the line whose slope is $\dfrac{3}{7}$ and contains $(-14,\ 1)$ is

   a) $y = \dfrac{3}{7}x - 7$     b) $y = \dfrac{3}{7}x + 43$     c) $y = \dfrac{3}{7}x + 7$     d) $y = \dfrac{3}{7}x$     e) $y = \dfrac{3}{7}x - \dfrac{101}{7}$

6. An equation of the line containing the points $(1,\ -5)$ and $(-3,\ 0)$ is

   a) $y = \dfrac{5}{4}x + \dfrac{15}{4}$     b) $y = \dfrac{4}{5}x - \dfrac{15}{4}$     c) $y = -\dfrac{5}{4}x - \dfrac{15}{4}$     d) $y = -\dfrac{5}{4}x + \dfrac{15}{4}$     e) $y = -\dfrac{4}{5}x - \dfrac{4}{15}$

7. The $x$-intercept of the line whose equation is $-7x + 12y - 3 = 0$ is

   a) $\left(0,\ -\dfrac{3}{7}\right)$     b) $\left(-\dfrac{3}{7},\ 0\right)$     c) $\left(\dfrac{3}{7},\ 0\right)$     d) $\left(0,\ \dfrac{1}{4}\right)$     e) $\left(\dfrac{1}{4},\ 0\right)$

8. The slope of the line whose equation is $\dfrac{1}{9}x + \dfrac{1}{2}y - 1 = 0$ is

   a) $-\dfrac{2}{9}$     b) $\dfrac{2}{9}$     c) $-\dfrac{9}{2}$     d) $\dfrac{9}{2}$     e) $\dfrac{1}{9}$

9. The slope of the line whose equation is $y = -6$ is

   a) $-6$     b) $\dfrac{1}{6}$     c) undefined     d) 0     e) 6

10. Which of the following points is on the line whose equation is $y = -7x + 13$?

    a) $(0,\ -13)$     b) $(-2,\ 27)$     c) $(1,\ 20)$     d) $(-8,\ 70)$     e) $\left(\dfrac{13}{-7},\ 0\right)$

11. Which of the following is a pair of equations representing parallel lines?

    a) $y = 2x + 6$ and $y = -\dfrac{1}{2}x + 2$     b) $y = -\dfrac{1}{5}x$ and $y = \dfrac{1}{5}x - 3$     c) $y = -9$ and $x = 2$

    d) $2x + y = 7$ and $-3x + 4y - 12 = 0$     e) $4x - 5y = 0$ and $y = \dfrac{4}{5}x - 3$

12. An equation of the line containing the point $(-3, \ -2)$ and parallel to the line whose equation is $y = \dfrac{1}{5}x - 1$ is

a) $y = \dfrac{1}{5}x + \dfrac{7}{5}$    b) $y = -5x + 13$    c) $y = \dfrac{1}{5}x - \dfrac{7}{5}$    d) $y = \dfrac{1}{5}x - \dfrac{13}{5}$    e) $y = -\dfrac{1}{5}x - \dfrac{7}{5}$

13. An equation of the line containing the point $(0, 8)$ and perpendicular to the line whose equation is $6x + 2y - 1 = 0$ is

a) $y = -3x + 8$    b) $y = -\dfrac{1}{6}x + 8$    c) $y = \dfrac{1}{3}x + 8$    d) $y = -\dfrac{1}{3}x + 8$    e) $y = \dfrac{1}{3}x - \dfrac{8}{3}$

14. The slope of a line parallel to the line whose equation is $-11x - 43y + 22 = 0$ is

a) $-\dfrac{11}{43}$    b) $\dfrac{11}{43}$    c) $-11$    d) $-\dfrac{43}{11}$    e) $-43$

15. An equation of the line containing the point $(6, \ -2)$ and perpendicular to the line whose equation is $y = 9$ is

a) $y = -2$    b) $y = 6x - 2$    c) $y = -\dfrac{1}{6}x$    d) $x = 6$    e) $x = -\dfrac{1}{6}$

16. Which of the following is an equation of a line perpendicular to the line whose equation is $3x - 17y + 12 = 0$?

a) $y = -\dfrac{1}{3}x - 1$    b) $y = -\dfrac{17}{3}x + 1$    c) $y = \dfrac{17}{3}x + \dfrac{4}{5}$    d) $y = -\dfrac{3}{17}x - 14$    e) $3x - 17y - 4 = 0$

17. An equation of a circle with center $(4, \ -3)$ and radius 6 is

a) $(x - 4) + (y + 3) = 6$    b) $(x - 4)^2 + (y + 3)^2 = 6$    c) $(x + 4)^2 + (y - 3)^2 = 36$

d) $(x - 4)^2 + (y + 3)^2 = 36$    e) $(x - 4)^2 + (y + 3)^2 = \sqrt{6}$

18. The center of the circle whose equation is $(x - 12)^2 + y^2 = 9$ is

a) $(12, 0)$    b) $(-12, 0)$    c) $(12, 1)$    d) $(0, 12)$    e) $3$

19. The radius of the circle whose equation is $x^2 + y^2 - 16x + 22y - 10 = 0$ is

a) $5\sqrt{7}$    b) $4\sqrt{3}$    c) $\sqrt{195}$    d) $(195)^2$    e) $\sqrt{29}$

20. The center of the circle whose equation is $x^2 + y^2 - 13x - 47 = 0$ is

a) $\left(\dfrac{13}{2}, 0\right)$    b) $\left(-\dfrac{169}{4}, 0\right)$    c) $\left(-\dfrac{13}{2}, 0\right)$    d) $\left(\dfrac{169}{4}, 0\right)$    e) $\left(0, \dfrac{13}{2}\right)$

ANSWERS FOR QUIZ 10

| | | | | |
|---|---|---|---|---|
| 1. b | 2. e | 3. d | 4. a | 5. c |
| 6. c | 7. b | 8. a | 9. d | 10. b |
| 11. e | 12. c | 13. c | 14. a | 15. d |
| 16. b | 17. d | 18. a | 19. c | 20. a |

# Chapter 11:    Introduction to Functions

In this chapter, the notion of a function is introduced. We begin with the definition of a relation between two sets, followed by the definition of a functional relation between two sets  When working with functions, some notations are used which allow us to write down these relations. Such notations will be discussed in Section 11.1. After understanding the definition of a function and the notations used, we will link functions to equations in two variables. Several examples of functions will be given to help us understand how these mathematical objects work. We will also learn how to find the value of a function when given a specified value to 'plug into the function'. This will be seen in Section 11.2. The final section, Section 11.3, deals with finding the 'domain' of a function. The functions which we will find the domains of are polynomial functions, rational functions and square root functions. If you plan on taking a course in precalculus, you will learn about many different types of functions and their properties. You will also learn how to obtain their domains. We will only focus on the three functions just mentioned.

## Section 11.1  Definition of a Function and Notations

We begin with the definition of a relation between two sets. Recall from Section 9.1 that if $X$ is a set, then '$x \in X$' means that $x$ is an element of $X$.

**Definition 1:** Suppose that $X$ and $Y$ are two nonempty sets. A **relation** between sets $X$ and $Y$ is a correspondence (or rule) between them. If $x \in X$ and $y \in Y$ and a relation exists between $x$ and $y$, then we say that $x$ **corresponds to** $y$.

A relation between two sets is usually given a name to describe the correspondence. When an element, $x$, corresponds to an element, $y$, we can write $x \rightarrow y$ or $(x, y)$ to denote the correspondence. For example, consider the two sets $X = \{$John, Bill, Pete$\}$ and $Y = \{$algebra, physics, chemistry, calculus$\}$. Suppose the relation between the two sets is named 'has taken the course'. Then the correspondence

$$\text{John} \longrightarrow \text{chemistry}$$
$$\text{Bill} \longrightarrow \text{algebra}$$
$$\text{Bill} \longrightarrow \text{calculus}$$
$$\text{Pete} \longrightarrow \text{algebra}$$
$$\text{Pete} \longrightarrow \text{physics}$$

describes the relation which states that John has taken the course chemistry, Bill has taken the course algebra, Bill has taken the course calculus, Pete has taken the course algebra and Pete has taken the course physics. Notice that the arrow symbol '$\longrightarrow$' represents the phrase 'has taken the course'. If we write down this relation as pairs, we obtain the set of pairs

$$\{(\text{John, chemistry}), (\text{Bill, algebra}), (\text{Bill, calculus}), (\text{Pete, algebra}), (\text{Pete, physics})\}.$$

Let's look at another example, something more mathematical. Suppose that both $X$ and $Y$ are the set of all real numbers and let the relation between the two sets be 'multiplied by 2 equals'. Here are a few correspondences which follow from this relation:

$$1 \longrightarrow 2$$
$$2 \longrightarrow 4$$
$$3 \longrightarrow 6$$
$$-4 \longrightarrow -8$$
$$\tfrac{1}{3} \longrightarrow \tfrac{2}{3}$$
$$\pi \longrightarrow 2\pi$$

To get these correspondences, I chose some real numbers randomly and found the corresponding value by multiplying by 2 (since this is the relation). Notice that there are infinitely many correspondences between elements, so I couldn't possibly write the full list obtained from this relation. However, if you give me an element $x \in X$, I know that it will correspond to the element $y \in Y$ which satisfies $y = 2x$. In the midst of discussing this example, notice that the equation $y = 2x$ shows up. We now see that correspondences between elements of sets are related to equations in two variables (one variable representing the domain elements and the other variable representing the range elements).

**Definition 2:** A **function** between two nonempty sets, $X$ and $Y$, is a relation between the sets in which **each** element of $X$ corresponds to **EXACTLY ONE** element of $Y$. We call the first set, $X$, the **domain** of the function. The elements of the second set, $Y$, which are corresponded to by elements of $X$ is called the **range** (or the **image set**) of the function.

If an element $x \in X$ corresponds to $y \in Y$, then we say that $y$ is the **image** of $x$. Hence, the range of a function is just the set of all images of elements of $X$. In general, the range of $Y$ may be a subset of $Y$ and not all of $Y$. In other words, not every element of $Y$ may be the image of some element $x \in X$. For the functions that we will be studying, however, the range will be the whole set $Y$. In such a case, we say that the function is **onto**.

**Examples.** Which of the following relations are functions? State the domain and range of those relations which are functions.

1)
$$\begin{aligned}
\text{Bill} &\longrightarrow 21 \\
\text{Danielle} &\longrightarrow 25 \\
\text{Sam} &\longrightarrow 31 \\
\text{Jason} &\longrightarrow 16
\end{aligned}$$

This is a function, since each element on the left hand side corresponds to exactly one element on the right hand side. The domain is the set {Bill, Danielle, Sam, Jason} and the range is the set {21, 25, 31, 16}.

2)
$$\begin{aligned}
\text{Steve} &\longrightarrow \text{blue} \\
\text{Pat} &\longrightarrow \text{green} \\
\text{Anne} &\longrightarrow \text{yellow} \\
\text{Mary} &\longrightarrow \text{orange} \\
\text{Pete} &\longrightarrow \text{green}
\end{aligned}$$

This is a function, since each element on the left hand side corresponds to exactly one element on the right hand side. The domain is the set {Steve, Pat, Anne, Mary, Pete} and the range is the set {blue, green, yellow, orange}. Notice that both 'Pat' and 'Pete' correspond to the range member 'green'. Two or more domain elements can certainly correspond to the same range element in a function.

3)
$$\begin{aligned}
-5 &\longrightarrow 3 \\
-2 &\longrightarrow -3 \\
0 &\longrightarrow 6 \\
-5 &\longrightarrow 2 \\
1 &\longrightarrow -6
\end{aligned}$$

This is a not a function, since the element '$-5$' corresponds to two elements, '3' and '2'.

$$-2 \longrightarrow 4$$
$$-1 \longrightarrow 1$$
4)   $\quad 0 \longrightarrow 0$
$$1 \longrightarrow 1$$
$$2 \longrightarrow 4$$

This is a function. The domain is the set $\{-2, -1, 0, 1, 2\}$ and the range is the set $\{4, 1, 0\}$. Notice that if we represent the domain elements by $x$ and the range elements by $y$, then the equation $y = x^2$ describes the correspondence.

5) $\{(\text{pizza, soda}), (\text{cereal, milk}), (\text{fish, water}), (\text{pasta, wine})\}$

Notice that this correspondence can be written as

$$\text{pizza} \longrightarrow \text{soda}$$
$$\text{cereal} \longrightarrow \text{milk}$$
$$\text{fish} \longrightarrow \text{water}$$
$$\text{pasta} \longrightarrow \text{wine}$$

This is a function whose domain is $\{\text{pizza, cereal, fish, pasta}\}$ and whose range is $\{\text{soda, milk, water, wine}\}$. In order to verify that this corresondence is a function by looking at the given set of pairs, all that we need to do is check that the first entries of the pairs appear exactly once in all of the pairs. If the first entry in a pair appears **more than once,** then the relation is **not** a function.

6) $\{(3, -1), (-5, 0), (2, 0), (-1, 6), (0, 4)\}$

This is a function, since the first entries of the pairs (which are 3, −5, 2, −1, 0) appear exactly once in all of the pairs. The domain is $\{3, -5, 2, -1, 0\}$ and range $\{-1, 0, 6, 4\}$.

7) $\{(0, -2), (1, 1), (0, 7), (-1, 5)\}$

This is not a function, since '0' appears in two pairs, namely $(0, -2)$ and $(0, 7)$. This means that '0' corresponds to both '−2' and '7', which cannot occur for a function.

**Try These (Set 1):** Which of the following relations are functions? Find the domain and range of those which are functions.

1)
$$4 \longrightarrow -2$$
$$8 \longrightarrow -1$$
$$12 \longrightarrow 0$$
$$16 \longrightarrow 1$$

2)
$$5 \longrightarrow 0$$
$$3 \longrightarrow 1$$
$$1 \longrightarrow 0$$

3)
$$8 \longrightarrow 3$$
$$7 \longrightarrow 2$$
$$8 \longrightarrow 7$$
$$8 \longrightarrow 6$$

4) $\{(1, 1), (2, 3), (3, 5), (4, 7)\}$

5) $\{(0, 0), (-1, -4), (-2, -5)\}$

6) $\{(-3, 10), (-2, 9), (-2, 8), (-1, 7)\}$

# Section 11.2 Functional Equations and Evaluating Functions

In the last section, we saw that a function whose domain and range consists of real numbers may be represented as an equation in two variables. For example, if both $X$ and $Y$ are the set of all real numbers, then for any $x \in X$, the correspondence

$$\underbrace{x}_{\text{domain element}} \longrightarrow \underbrace{2x}_{\text{range element}} = y$$

is a function. Why is it a function? Well, if you take any real number (which we are representing by $x$), then multiplying it by 2 can only give one possible answer (which we are representing by $y$). Hence, if $X$ is the domain and $Y$ is the range, then each $x \in X$ corresponds to EXACTLY ONE $y \in Y$. If we view the equation $y = 2x$ as the correspondence which takes us from an $x$-value to a $y$-value, then this correspondence is a function. Let us put this in a mathematical setting now:

> The **domain** is a set of real numbers whose elements represent the $x$-**values.**
> The **range** is a set of real numbers whose elements represent the $y$-**values.**
> The **correspondence** between the domain and range is an **equation in $x$ and $y$.**

Notice that the domain and range may not be the whole set of real numbers, but just a subset. For example, for our function $y = 2x$, we could've defined the domain to be the set of real numbers $X = \{x \mid -2 \leq x \leq 3\}$. In this case, the range would be $Y = \{y \mid -4 \leq y \leq 6\}$ (why?). If we chose the domain to be $X = \{0,\ 5,\ 9\}$, then the range would be $Y = \{0,\ 10,\ 18\}$ (why?).

When we have an equation which describes a functional relation, there is a special notation which is used. It is called the **functional notation** of the equation. A function is denoted by an alphabetical letter, like $f$ or $g$ or whatever you would like to name it. For example, the function $y = 2x$ can be given the name $f$ by renaming the $y$-variable as $f(x)$. By doing so, we obtain

$$\underbrace{y = 2x}_{\text{equation in } x \text{ and } y} \implies \underbrace{f(x) = 2x}_{\text{functional notation}}.$$

We read '$f(x)$' as '$f$ of $x$' and call $f(x)$ the **value** of $f$ at $x$. Notice that $f(x)$ is just another name for the $y$-variable. The reason why we bother renaming the $y$-variable is that we are stressing the fact that, for each $x$-value in the domain, there corresponds **exactly one** $y$-value in the range. We write $y = f(x)$ to represent the fact that $y$ equals a function of $x$ and read it as '$y$ is a function of $x$'.

It is helpful to think of a function as a machine. In the figure below, the machine is named $f$. If you input a number from the domain into the machine, the function $f$ computes the output according to its rule. The output is called $f(x)$. In this setting, we call $x$ (the input variable) the **independent variable** and $y$ (or $f(x)$, the output variable) the **dependent variable.**

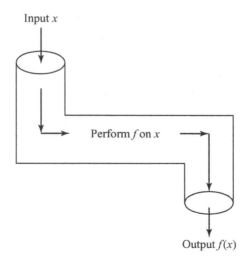

Let's look at some equations which are functions. We will rewrite each equation in functional notation and practice finding the values of a function.

**Examples.** The following equations are functions:

1) $y = -3x + 1$

This is a linear equation in $x$ and $y$. Notice that, for any real number that we choose for $x$, there corresponds **exactly one** value for $y$. Hence, this linear equation is a function. We can, therefore, write

$$\underbrace{y = -3x + 1}_{\text{linear equation}} \Longrightarrow \underbrace{f(x) = -3x + 1}_{\text{linear function}}$$

and obtain a **linear function.** Once again, I chose the name of the function to be $f$. You can choose any name you'd like. Let's practice doing computations with functions. Below, I've given a table with three columns. The first column contains some values for $x$ which I have chosen at random. The second column is the linear equation and the third column is the linear function. Keep an eye on how the answers are related for each column.

| | $y = -3x + 1$ | $f(x) = -3x + 1$ |
|---|---|---|
| $x = 0$ | $y = -3(0) + 1 = 1$ | $f(0) = -3(0) + 1 = 1$ |
| $x = 2$ | $y = -3(2) + 1 = -5$ | $f(2) = -3(2) + 1 = -5$ |
| $x = -\frac{1}{3}$ | $y = -3\left(-\frac{1}{3}\right) + 1 = 2$ | $f\left(-\frac{1}{3}\right) = -3\left(-\frac{1}{3}\right) + 1 = 2$ |
| $x = -6$ | $y = -3(-6) + 1 = 19$ | $f(-6) = -3(-6) + 1 = 19$ |

Notice how the $y$-value that we obtained for each of the chosen $x$-values is just equal to $f(x)$. For example, $f(0) = 1$ is the same as saying that when $x = 0$, $y = 1$ and $f\left(-\frac{1}{3}\right) = 2$ is the same as saying that when $x = -\frac{1}{3}$, $y = 2$.

2) $y = mx + b$, where $m$ and $b$ are real numbers.

It turns out that every linear equation (except those of the form $x = a$) is a function. It is not hard to see that, for any real number that we choose for $x$, there corresponds exactly one value for $y$. In functional notation, we have

$$\underbrace{y = mx + b}_{\text{linear equation}} \Longrightarrow \underbrace{f(x) = mx + b}_{\text{linear function}}.$$

3) $y = 4x^2 - x + 3$

This is a **quadratic equation** in $x$ and $y$. Observe that, for any real number that we choose for $x$, there corresponds **exactly one** value for $y$. Hence, this is a function. We can, therefore, write

$$\underbrace{y = 4x^2 - x + 3}_{\text{quadratic equation}} \Longrightarrow \underbrace{q(x) = 4x^2 - x + 3}_{\text{quadratic function}}$$

and obtain a **quadratic function.** Let's practice plugging numbers into this function. Let's compute $q(0)$, $q(-2)$ and $q(3)$. To begin with, I will put parentheses around my $x$'s in the function and write $q(x) = 4(x)^2 - (x) + 3$. This way, I won't make any mistakes with my signs when I put the $x$-values in. Now, I will plug the numbers into the function as we did in the table in example 1.

$$
\begin{aligned}
q(0) &= 4(0)^2 - (0) + 3 = 3
\end{aligned}
$$

$$
\begin{aligned}
q(-2) &= 4(-2)^2 - (-2) + 3 \\
&= 16 + 2 + 3 = 21
\end{aligned}
$$

$$
\begin{aligned}
q(3) &= 4(3)^2 - (3) + 3 \\
&= 36 - 3 + 3 = 36
\end{aligned}
$$

As you can see, computing the value of a function for a specified $x$-value is not so difficult.

4) $y = ax^2 + bx + c$, where $a$, $b$ and $c$ are real numbers and $a \neq 0$.

This, again, is a quadratic equation in $x$ and $y$. Every such equation is a function (you can verify that for each $x$-value, there corresponds exactly one $y$-value). We can write

$$\underbrace{y = ax^2 + bx + c}_{\text{quadratic equation}} \Longrightarrow \underbrace{q(x) = ax^2 + bx + c}_{\text{quadratic function}}.$$

5) $y =$ polynomial in $x$.

If you have an equation where $y$ is on one side of the equals sign and a polynomial in $x$ is on the other side, then this equation is a functional relation. The reason for this is a polynomial is a sum of monomials and monomials are just products of numbers and variables. If you take any real number and multiply it by other numbers, then add these results together, you can only obtain one answer. For example, if you replace $x$ by **any** number into the equation $y = -4x^6 + 9x^5 + 2x^4 - \frac{2}{7}x^2 + \pi$, you are guarenteed to get exactly one $y$-value. This will be the case no matter what the polynomial is. Consequently, we may write

$$\underbrace{y = \text{polynomial in } x}_{\text{polynomial equation}} \Longrightarrow \underbrace{P(x) = \text{polynomial in } x}_{\text{polynomial function}}.$$

6) $y = \dfrac{6x}{x^2 - 4}$

If $y = P(x)$ and $y = Q(x)$ are two functions, then the quotient $y = \dfrac{P(x)}{Q(x)}$ is also a function. In our example, both the numerator and the denominator are linear functions, making the quotient a function as well. We write

$$\underbrace{y = \frac{6x}{x^2 - 4}}_{\text{rational equation}} \Longrightarrow \underbrace{R(x) = \frac{6x}{x^2 - 4}}_{\text{rational function}}.$$

Let's compute $R(0)$, $R(1)$, $R(6)$ and $R(-2)$. First, put parentheses around the $x$'s. Then plug in the numbers.

$$R(0) = \frac{6\,(0)}{(0)^2 - 4} = \frac{0}{-4} = 0$$

$$R(1) = \frac{6\,(1)}{(1)^2 - 4} = \frac{6}{-3} = -2$$

$$R(6) = \frac{6\,(6)}{(6)^2 - 4} = \frac{36}{32} = \frac{9}{8}$$

$$R(-2) = \frac{6\,(-2)}{(-2)^2 - 4} = \frac{-12}{0} \text{ which is undefined}$$

Now we have a problem! When we plug $-2$ into the function $R$, we get an undefined answer. This is not good, since we need to obtain a real number for our answer. If we think of the function as a machine, then putting $-2$ into our machine will make the machine explode! What this tells us is that $-2$ cannot be in the domain of our function, since it doesn't correspond to a real number. In the next section, we will learn how to find the domain of a function like this one. When working with a function, it is important to know **what** numbers can be plugged into it. By the way, notice that 2 is also a bad number for this function since

$$R(2) = \frac{6\,(2)}{(2)^2 - 4} = \frac{12}{0} \text{ which is undefined.}$$

Thus, $-2$ and $2$ are not in the domain of this function. These turn out to be the **only** two numbers which make the function undefined.

7) $y = \dfrac{P(x)}{Q(x)}$, where $y = P(x)$ and $y = Q(x)$ are polynomial functions.

As mentioned in the previous example, such a quotient is a function. We can write

$$\underbrace{y = \frac{P(x)}{Q(x)}}_{\text{rational equation}} \implies \underbrace{R(x) = \frac{P(x)}{Q(x)}}_{\text{rational function}}.$$

8) $y = \sqrt{4x - 12}$

If $y = f(x)$ is a function, then $y = \sqrt{f(x)}$ is also a function. Since $y = 4x - 12$ is a linear function, we can write

$$\underbrace{y = \sqrt{4x - 12}}_{\text{square root equation}} \implies \underbrace{S(x) = \sqrt{4x - 12}}_{\text{square root function}}.$$

Let's compute $S(4)$, $S(3)$, $S(8)$ and $S(-1)$.

$$\begin{aligned}
S(4) &= \sqrt{4(4) - 12} = \sqrt{4} = 2 \\
S(3) &= \sqrt{4(3) - 12} = \sqrt{0} = 0 \\
S(8) &= \sqrt{4(8) - 12} = \sqrt{20} = 2\sqrt{5} \\
S(-1) &= \sqrt{4(-1) - 12} = \sqrt{-16}, \text{ which is not a real number}
\end{aligned}$$

Once again, we have a problem! When we plug $-1$ into the function $S$, we don't get a real number. Remember that the functions which we are concerned with have domain and range containing real numbers only. It is true that $\sqrt{-16} = 4i$ is an imaginary number, but these numbers cannot 'live' in our range. Therefore, if we put $-1$ into our machine, the machine will explode! This means that $-1$ cannot be in the domain of our function. In fact, if you plug any real number which is less than 3 into the function $S$, it will yield an imaginary number. Consequently, any real number less than 3 will not be in the domain. We will see how to obtain this information in the next section.

**Try These (Set 2):** For each of the given functions, find (if it exists) $f(-1)$, $f(5)$, and $f(-4)$.

1) $f(x) = -2x + 3$                     3) $f(x) = \sqrt{3 - 6x}$

2) $f(x) = x^2 - 7x + 1$                 4) $f(x) = \dfrac{5x - 1}{x + 4}$

# Section 11.3   Finding the Domain of a Function

In this section, we will learn how to find the domain of a polynomial function, a rational function and a square root function.

## I. Polynomial Functions

A polynomial function is of the form $P(x) = $ polynomial in $x$. The domain of $P$ is the set of all real numbers. To see this, recall that a polynomial is just a sum of products of numbers and variables. Isn't it true that if you multiply real numbers and add real numbers, you are guaranteed to get a real number for an answer?. For example, in the quadratic function $P(x) = -7x^2 + 9x + 2$, if you replace the variable $x$ by **any** real number, say $n$, then you will obtain the value of $P(n)$ by working out each of the monomials $-7(n)^2$ and $9(n)$. You will then have to add up the numbers $-7n^2$, $9n$ and $2$, which is definitely going to be a real number. Hence,

$$\boxed{\text{the domain of P is the set of all real numbers.}}$$

In interval notation, we write the domain as $(-\infty, \infty)$.

**Examples.** The domain of each of the functions below is the set of all real numbers.

1) $f(x) = mx + b$, where $m$ and $b$ are real numbers.

2) $g(x) = ax^2 + bx + c$, where $a$, $b$ and $c$ are real numbers.

3) $h(x) = 6x^3 + 11x^2 - \frac{1}{8}$

4) $f(x) = -x^4 - 6x^3 + 3x + 1$

5) $g(x) = 12x^5 + \frac{3}{5}x^4 - \frac{2}{9}x^3 + \pi x - \sqrt{5}$

## II. **Rational Functions**

A rational function is of the form $R(x) = \dfrac{P(x)}{Q(x)}$, where $y = P(x)$ and $y = Q(x)$ are polynomial functions polynomial in $x$.

$$\boxed{\text{The domain of } R \text{ is } \{x \mid Q(x) \neq 0\}.}$$

**Examples.** Find the domain of each function.

1) $R(x) = \dfrac{x - 4}{6x + 12}$

To find the domain of a rational function, you set the denominator equal to 0 and solve. Any solutions that you get are bad values, since they make the denominator equal 0. Hence, the domain is the set of all real numbers except for the bad values. Following this routine, we have

$$
\begin{array}{r}
6x + \cancel{12} = 0 \\
\underline{-\cancel{12} \quad - 12} \\
\dfrac{\cancel{6}x}{\cancel{6}} = \dfrac{-12}{6} \\
x = -2
\end{array}
$$

So, $x = -2$ is a bad value for the function. This means that the domain of $R$ is $\{x \mid x \neq -2\}$. Notice that I did **not** set $x - 4 = 0$ and solve. **It is only a zero denominator which makes a fraction undefined.**

2) $f(x) = \dfrac{5x}{x^2 - x - 42}$

We will first find the bad values.

$$x^2 - x - 42 = 0$$
$$(x + 6)(x - 7) = 0$$

$$
\begin{array}{c|c}
x + \cancel{6} = 0 & x - \cancel{7} = 0 \\
\underline{\phantom{x}-\cancel{6}\ -6} & \underline{+\cancel{7}\ +7} \\
x = -6 & x = 7
\end{array}
$$

Since $x = -6$ and $x = 7$ are bad values for $f$, the domain of $f$ is $\{x \mid x \neq -6 \text{ and } x \neq 7\}$.

3) $f(x) = \dfrac{2x^2 + x - 1}{4x^2 - 3}$

Let's find the bad values.

$$4x^2 - \cancel{3} = 0$$
$$\underline{+\cancel{3}\ +3}$$
$$\frac{\cancel{4}x^2}{\cancel{4}} = \frac{3}{4}$$
$$x^2 = \frac{3}{4}$$
$$x = \pm\sqrt{\frac{3}{4}} = \pm\frac{\sqrt{3}}{2}$$

So, $x = -\dfrac{\sqrt{3}}{2}$ and $x = \dfrac{\sqrt{3}}{2}$ are bad values for $f$. Therefore, the domain of $f$ is $\left\{x \mid x \neq -\dfrac{\sqrt{3}}{2} \text{ and } x \neq \dfrac{\sqrt{3}}{2}\right\}$.

4) $g(x) = \dfrac{2}{x^2 + 25}$

Let's find the bad values.

$$x^2 + \cancel{25} = 0$$
$$\underline{-\cancel{25}\ -25}$$
$$x^2 \phantom{+25} = -25$$

and so

$$x = \pm\sqrt{-25}$$

which are imaginary numbers. However, we were looking for **real numbers** which satisfy $x^2 + 25 = 0$. Since there are no real numbers which satisfy this equation, there are no bad values. Therefore, the domain of $g$ is the set of all real numbers.

## III. Square Root Functions

A square root function is of the form $S(x) = \sqrt{f(x)}$, where $y = f(x)$ is a function of $x$. Recall that the only real numbers that we can take the square root of which give a real number are those which are either positive or 0. In other words, the numbers which can replace the variable $x$ in $S$ are those which make $f(x)$ either positive or 0. Therefore, we have

$$\boxed{\text{the domain of } S \text{ is } \{x \mid f(x) \geq 0\}.}$$

**Examples.** Find the domain of each function.

1) $S(x) = \sqrt{2x - 8}$

Unlike the situation for rational functions where we had to first find the bad values, we look for the good values right away. All that we have to do is set the radicand (the expression under the square root symbol) greater than or equal to 0 and solve. The solution set is the domain. By doing so, we get

$$
\begin{array}{r}
2x - \cancel{8} \geq 0 \\
\underline{+8 \quad +8} \\
\dfrac{\cancel{2}x}{\cancel{2}} \geq \dfrac{8}{2} \\
x \geq 4
\end{array}
$$

The domain of S is $\{x \mid x \geq 4\}$. In interval notation, we write $[4, \infty)$.

2) $f(x) = \sqrt{3x + 7}$

Following the method above, we have

$$
\begin{array}{r}
3x + \cancel{7} \geq 0 \\
\underline{-7 \quad -7} \\
\dfrac{\cancel{3}x}{\cancel{3}} \geq \dfrac{-7}{3} \\
x \geq -\dfrac{7}{3}
\end{array}
$$

The domain of $f$ is $\{x \mid x \geq -\frac{7}{3}\}$. In interval notation, we write $[-\frac{7}{3}, \infty)$.

3) $f(x) = \sqrt{6 - 24x}$

Same method, different function. Observe that the inequality symbol reverses (why?).

$$
\begin{array}{r}
\cancel{6} - 24x \geq 0 \\
\underline{-6 \qquad\qquad -6} \\
\dfrac{-24x}{-24} \geq \dfrac{-6}{-24} \\
x \leq \dfrac{1}{4}
\end{array}
$$

The domain of $f$ is $\{x \mid x \leq \frac{1}{4}\}$. In interval notation, we write $(-\infty, \frac{1}{4}]$.

Notice that the examples above each have a radicand which was linear. Later on in precalculus, you will learn how to find domains of square root functions whose radicand is non-linear. For example, you will learn how to find the domains of functions like $f(x) = \sqrt{x^2 - 9}$, $g(x) = \sqrt{\dfrac{5x + 5}{3x - 6}}$ and $h(x) = \sqrt{4x^3 - 4x}$.

**Try These (Set 3):** Find the domain of each function.

1) $f(x) = 5x + 7$

2) $g(x) = 6x^2 - 9$

3) $f(x) = \dfrac{3 + 7x}{5 - 4x}$

4) $h(x) = \sqrt{6x - 15}$

5) $f(x) = \sqrt{19 - 3x}$

6) $f(x) = \dfrac{12}{x^2 - 175}$

As the title of this chapter says, this is merely an introduction to functions. There are many more things to learn about, but we will not pursue this study any further. In precalculus, you will learn how to graph various types of functions and learn about both their algebraic and geometric properties. Functions are important to understand if you plan on taking calculus in the future.

## Exercise 11

In Exercises 1-16, determine which relation is a function. State the domain and range of those which are functions.

1.
$$\text{Kaitlyn} \longrightarrow 4$$
$$\text{Ashley} \longrightarrow 7$$
$$\text{Tim} \longrightarrow 5$$

2.
$$\text{Tom} \longrightarrow \text{medium}$$
$$\text{Matt} \longrightarrow \text{large}$$
$$\text{Lisa} \longrightarrow \text{small}$$

3.
$$\text{Steve} \longrightarrow \text{diet cola}$$
$$\text{Anne} \longrightarrow \text{seltzer}$$
$$\text{Tony} \longrightarrow \text{root beer}$$
$$\text{Anne} \longrightarrow \text{lemonade}$$

4.
$$\text{Nancy} \longrightarrow \text{nurse}$$
$$\text{John} \longrightarrow \text{police officer}$$
$$\text{Simona} \longrightarrow \text{police officer}$$
$$\text{Vinny} \longrightarrow \text{electrician}$$
$$\text{John} \longrightarrow \text{fisherman}$$

5.
$$3 \longrightarrow -6$$
$$0 \longrightarrow 2$$
$$-8 \longrightarrow 4$$

6.
$$-7 \longrightarrow 3$$
$$6 \longrightarrow 3$$
$$-7 \longrightarrow 1$$

7. $\{(0,\ 1),\ (1,\ 3),\ (2,\ 5),\ (3,\ 7)\}$

8. $\{(-3,\ 0),\ (-6,\ 2),\ (-9,\ 4),\ (-12,\ 6)\}$

9. $\{(2,\ -2),\ (-4,\ 0),\ (0,\ -2),\ (1,\ 1)\}$

10. $\{(4,\ 9),\ (-3,\ 3),\ (0,\ 0),\ (-7,\ 9)\}$

11. $\{(5,\ 3),\ (8,\ 3),\ (-12,\ 3)\}$

12. $\{(0,\ 1),\ (-5,\ 1),\ (19,\ 2),\ (-14,\ 2)\}$

13. $\{(a,\ 3),\ (b,\ 1),\ (c,\ 5),\ (b,\ 2)\}$

14. $\{(a,\ 0),\ (b,\ -3),\ (b,\ 6),\ (c,\ -6)\}$

15. $\{(x,\ -4),\ (y,\ -4),\ (z,\ 0),\ (x,\ -5)\}$

16. $\{(m,\ 3),\ (n,\ 7),\ (p,\ -1),\ (n,\ 0)\}$

In Exercises 17-36, find the values of the given function when $x = 1$, $x = -3$ and $x = 6$.

17. $f(x) = 5x - 2$

18. $f(x) = -3x + 9$

19. $g(x) = 6x + 1$

20. $g(x) = 5x - 6$

21. $f(x) = x^2 - 7x + 2$

22. $f(x) = 2x^2 + x - 15$

23. $h(x) = -x^2 + 24$

24. $h(x) = 2x - x^2$

25. $f(x) = \dfrac{5}{2x - 1}$

26. $f(x) = \dfrac{-2}{7x - 21}$

27. $R(x) = \dfrac{2}{x^2 - 4x + 2}$

28. $R(x) = \dfrac{4}{x^2 - 4x - 20}$

29. $S(x) = \sqrt{2x + 7}$

30. $S(x) = \sqrt{8x + 25}$

31. $f(x) = \sqrt{14 - 2x}$

32. $f(x) = \sqrt{8 - x}$

33. $h(x) = \dfrac{6 - x}{\sqrt{x + 6}}$

34. $h(x) = \dfrac{-x + 9}{\sqrt{x + 11}}$

35. $p(x) = \dfrac{x^2}{\sqrt{x^2 + 3}}$

36. $q(x) = \dfrac{x^2 - 2}{\sqrt{x^2 + 1}}$

In Exercises 37-64, find the domain of each function.

37. $f(x) = 6x + 7$

38. $f(x) = x + 2$

39. $h(x) = \dfrac{1}{9}x - 9$

40. $h(x) = \dfrac{2}{7}x - \dfrac{7}{9}$

41. $g(x) = 8x^2 + x - 5$

42. $g(x) = -x^2 - x + 12$

43. $P(x) = 6x^4 - 4x^2 + \dfrac{2}{3}x + 1$

44. $P(x) = 3x^5 + x^3 - \frac{1}{8}x^2 - \sqrt{2}$

45. $g(x) = \dfrac{1}{x}$

46. $g(x) = \dfrac{2}{x + 8}$

47. $R(x) = \dfrac{x + 2}{4x - 16}$

48. $R(x) = \dfrac{3x - 8}{6x + 30}$

49. $g(x) = \dfrac{9}{x^2 + 9x + 20}$

50. $h(x) = \dfrac{-6x}{4x^2 - 25}$

51. $g(x) = \dfrac{10x^2 + 8x - 15}{3x^2 - 27}$

52. $f(x) = \dfrac{11x^2 - 20}{2x^2 - 7x + 5}$

53. $g(x) = \dfrac{-15}{x^2 + 4}$

54. $g(x) = \dfrac{-9}{9 + x^2}$

55. $f(x) = \dfrac{x - 2}{x^2 + 2x + 4}$

56. $f(x) = \dfrac{4x + 1}{x^2 - x + 1}$

57. $S(x) = \sqrt{x + 3}$

58. $S(x) = \sqrt{x - 7}$

59. $g(x) = \sqrt{5x - 40}$

60. $h(x) = \sqrt{8x - 32}$

61. $f(x) = \sqrt{18 - 22x}$

62. $f(x) = \sqrt{36 - 14x}$

63. $f(x) = \sqrt{\dfrac{2}{5}x - \dfrac{1}{10}}$

64. $S(x) = \sqrt{\dfrac{1}{9}x + \dfrac{7}{3}}$

---

# END OF CHAPTER 11    QUIZ

1. Which of the following relations is a function?

a) $4 \to 3$    b) $-1 \to 6$    c)  John $\to$ fish    d) Steve $\to$ teach    e)  blue $\to$ sky
   $2 \to 2$       $-2 \to 0$       Maggie $\to$ salad       Bill $\to$ sports       green $\to$ grass
   $4 \to 1$       $-2 \to 8$       Tony $\to$ pasta         Bill $\to$ cook        yellow $\to$ sun
                                    Annie $\to$ pasta                               blue $\to$ ocean

2. Which of the following sets of ordered pairs represents a functional relation?
a) $\{(1, 3), (2, -3), (2, 0)\}$    b) $\{(6, 3), (-4, -2)\}$    c) $\{(9, -3), (4, -2), (9, 3), (4, 2)\}$
d) $\{(0, 0), (0, 1), (0, 2)\}$    e) $\{(-8, -1), (-8, 12)\}$

3. Which of the following relations is not a function?

a) $1 \to 1$    b)  Bugs $\to$ Daffy    c) $8 \to -3$    d) $-3 \to 8$    e)  algebra$\to$ math
   $2 \to 2$        Tom $\to$ Jerry        $7 \to -3$       $-3 \to 7$       mechanics$\to$ physics
   $3 \to 3$        Homer $\to$ Barney     $6 \to -3$       $-3 \to 6$       genetics$\to$ biology

4. The domain of the function defined by the ordered pairs $\{(-2, 5), (-1, 6), (4, -8), (5, -12)\}$ is
a) $\{-2, 5, -1, 6, 4, -8 -12\}$    b) $\{-2, 5\}$    c) $\{-2, -1, 4, 5\}$
d) $\{5, 6, -8, -12\}$    e) $\emptyset$

5. If $f(x) = 3x - 2$, then $f(7) =$
a) 23    b) 21    c) 3    d) 18    e) 19

6. If $h(x) = -5x^2 + 4x - 1$, then $h(-2) =$

    a) $-29$    b) $11$    c) $-13$    d) $27$    e) $-22$

7. If $g(x) = \dfrac{4x^2 - 6x - 5}{2x + 3}$, then $g(4) =$

    a) $-\dfrac{13}{11}$    b) $\dfrac{3}{11}$    c) $\dfrac{35}{9}$    d) $\dfrac{35}{11}$    e) $\dfrac{83}{9}$

8. If $f(x) = \sqrt{11 - 15x}$, then $f(-3) =$

    a) $\sqrt{34}$    b) $2\sqrt{14}$    c) $\sqrt{55}$    d) $14\sqrt{2}$    e) $\sqrt{51}$

9. Which of the following is an ordered pair of the function $g(x) = -8x + 3$?

    a) $(0,\ 6)$    b) $(-3,\ -21)$    c) $(5,\ -4)$    d) $(1,\ -8)$    e) $(3,\ -21)$

10. Which of the following is not an ordered pair of the function $g(x) = \dfrac{x - 2}{2x + 6}$?

    a) $\left(0,\ -\dfrac{1}{3}\right)$    b) $\left(4,\ \dfrac{1}{7}\right)$    c) $\left(-6,\ -\dfrac{4}{3}\right)$    d) $(2,\ 0)$    e) $\left(-9,\ \dfrac{11}{12}\right)$

11. The domain of $f(x) = \dfrac{1}{2}x + 9$ is

    a) $\{x \mid x \neq 18\}$    b) $\{x \mid x \geq -18\}$    c) $\{x \mid x = 9\}$    d) $\{x \mid x \text{ is any real number}\}$

    e) $\left\{x \mid \dfrac{1}{2} \leq x \leq 9\right\}$

12. The domain of $g(x) = \sqrt{6x - 30}$ is

    a) $\{x \mid x \geq 5\}$    b) $\{x \mid x > 5\}$    c) $\{x \mid x \neq 5\}$    d) $\{x \mid x \text{ is any real number}\}$
    e) $\{x \mid x \leq 5\}$

13. The domain of $f(x) = \dfrac{7x - 12}{x^2 - x - 42}$ is

    a) $\left\{x \mid x \neq \dfrac{12}{7}\right\}$    b) $\left\{x \mid x \neq \dfrac{12}{7}, -6, 7\right\}$    c) $\{x \mid -6 \leq x \leq 7\}$    d) $\{x \mid x \neq -6, 7\}$

    e) $\{x \mid x \neq 6, -7\}$

14. Which of the following is not in the domain of $g(x) = \sqrt{11x - 27}$?

    a) $6$    b) $-6$    c) $3$    d) $10$    e) $8$

15. Which of the following is not in the domain of $h(x) = \dfrac{3x}{6x - 5}$?

    a) $0$    b) $-\dfrac{5}{6}$    c) $\dfrac{5}{6}$    d) $-1$    e) $3$

16. The domain of $f(x) = 5x^3 - x^2 + 14$ is

   a) $(-\infty,\ 14)$    b) $(14,\ \infty)$    c) $(-\infty,\ 5) \cup (14,\ \infty)$    d) $[5,\ 14]$    e) $(-\infty,\ \infty)$

17. Which of the following is not in the domain of $g(x) = \dfrac{-4x + 3}{x^2 - 6x}$?

   a) 6    b) $\dfrac{3}{4}$    c) $-2$    d) 5    e) $\dfrac{4}{7}$

18. The domain of $f(x) = \sqrt{9 - 2x}$ is

   a) $\left[\dfrac{9}{2},\ \infty\right)$    b) $\left[-\dfrac{9}{2},\ \infty\right)$    c) $\left(-\infty,\ \dfrac{9}{2}\right]$    d) $\left(-\infty, \dfrac{9}{2}\right)$    e) $\left(-\infty,\ \dfrac{2}{9}\right]$

19. The domain of $h(x) = \dfrac{10x - 10}{3x^2 - 9}$ is

   a) $\{x \mid x \neq 1\}$    b) $\{x \mid x \neq -3, 3\}$    c) $\{x \mid x \neq 1, -\sqrt{3}, \sqrt{3}\}$    d) $\{x \mid x \neq \sqrt{3}\}$    e) $\{x \mid x \neq -\sqrt{3}, \sqrt{3}\}$

20. If $f(x) = 9x - 5$ and $f(a) = 49$, then $a =$

   a) 9    b) $\dfrac{44}{9}$    c) $-6$    d) 6    e) 436

ANSWERS FOR QUIZ 11

| | | | | |
|---|---|---|---|---|
| 1. c | 2. b | 3. d | 4. c | 5. e |
| 6. a | 7. d | 8. b | 9. e | 10. c |
| 11. d | 12. a | 13. d | 14. b | 15. c |
| 16. e | 17. a | 18. c | 19. e | 20. d |

# Chapter 12:    Systems of Linear Equations

In this chapter, we will learn how to find the solution(s) of a system of linear equations which contain two linear equations and two variables. We begin by defining a system of linear equations and discuss what is meant by a solution to a system (Section 12.1). In Sections 12.2 - 12.4, we will learn how to solve a system of linear equations. The techniques for solving a system of linear equations that we will study are the graphing method (Section 12.2), the substitution method (Section 12.3) and the elimination method (Section 12.4).

## Section 12.1    Definition of a System of Linear Equations

**Definition:** A **system of linear equations** (or **linear system**) is a set of two or more linear equations, each containing one or more variables.

We will focus our attention on linear systems which contain two linear equations and two variables. Such a system is called a $2 \times 2$ **linear system**. Note that '$2 \times 2$' represents the fact that there are two equations and two variables. In general, an $m \times n$ system of linear equations is a system with $m$ linear equations and $n$ variables.

For example, the following pair of equations is a $2 \times 2$ linear system:

$$\begin{aligned} x - y &= 5 \\ x + y &= -3 \end{aligned}$$

Notice that there are two linear equations, each containing two variables, $x$ and $y$.

**Definition:** A **solution** of a $2 \times 2$ system of linear equations in $x$ and $y$ is a pair of numbers which can replace $x$ and $y$ and solve **both equations** in the system (we say that the equations are solved **simultaneously**).

For example, a solution of the system

$$\begin{aligned} x - y &= 5 \\ x + y &= -3 \end{aligned}$$

is $x = 1$ and $y = -4$. To check this, all that we need to do is plug these numbers into **both** equations and see if they are **both** satisfied. Well, we have

$$\begin{aligned} (1) - (-4) &= 5 \ \checkmark \\ (1) + (-4) &= -3 \ \checkmark \end{aligned}$$

Since both equations are satisfied, $x = 1$ and $y = -4$ is a solution of the system. We usually write the solution as an ordered pair. In this case, we have $(1, \ -4)$. As we will see, $(1, \ -4)$ is the **only** solution to this system.

There are $2 \times 2$ systems which have infinitely many solutions. For example, any solution of the first equation in the system

$$\begin{aligned} 2x + 3y &= 6 \\ -4x - 6y &= -12 \end{aligned}$$

will also be a solution of the second equation and, hence, for the system. The pairs $(6, \ -2)$ and $(3, 0)$, for example, are solutions to both equations. Since there are infinitely many solutions for the first equation (why?), there are infinitely many solutions of the system. When a $2 \times 2$ linear system has at least one solution, we call it **consistent**. In the case where there are infinitely many solutions, we say that the equations are **dependent**.

There are also $2 \times 2$ linear systems which have no solution. For example, the system

$$x = 3 + y$$
$$x = 5 + y$$

has no solution (we will learn why later). In other words, any solution of the first equation will not be a solution of the second equation and any solution of the second equation will not be a solution of the first equation (try it for yourself!). A $2 \times 2$ linear system with no solution is called **inconsistent** and the equations are **independent**.

**Examples.** Decide whether or not the ordered pair $(-2, 3)$ is a solution of the given system.

1)    $x - y = -5$
      $2x + y = -1$

Replace $x$ by $-2$ and $y$ by 3 in both of the equations. Since $(-2) - (3) \overset{\checkmark}{=} -5$ and $2(-2) + (3) \overset{\checkmark}{=} -1$, $(-2, 3)$ is a solution of the system.

2)   $-x = y + 5$
     $6x + y = 0$

If we replace $x$ by $-2$ and $y$ by 3 in the first equation, we obtain $-(-2) \neq (3) + 5$. Therefore, $(-2, 3)$ is not a solution of the system. There is no need to check the second equation.

3)   $4y = 3x + 18$
     $x - 7y = 12$

Notice that $4(3) \overset{\checkmark}{=} 3(-2) + 18$, but $(-2) - 7(3) \neq 12$. Therefore, it is not a solution.

4)   $-3x + 2y - 12 = 0$
         $y = 5x + 13$

Since $-3(-2) + 2(3) - 12 \overset{\checkmark}{=} 0$ and $(3) \overset{\checkmark}{=} 5(-2) + 13$, it is a solution.

Now that we know what it means for an ordered pair to be a solution to a $2 \times 2$ linear system, how do we find such a solution? Well, since the solutions to a linear equation in two variables can be graphed, it makes sense to try to solve a system graphically. A solution to a $2 \times 2$ linear system turns out to be precisely where their graphs (which are two lines) intersect each other. The next section deals with this technique.

**Try These (Set 1):** Decide whether or not the ordered pair (4, 2) is a solution of the given system.

1) $x + 5y - 14 = 0$
   $2x - 8y + 8 = 0$

2) $y = -x + 6$
   $y = -3x + 1$

3) $x - 2y = 0$
   $x + y = 6$

4) $5x - 4y = 12$
   $x = 10 - 3y$

5) $\frac{1}{2}x - \frac{1}{2}y + 1 = 0$
   $y = -\frac{3}{8}x + \frac{7}{2}$

## Section 12.2   The Graphing Technique

To solve a $2 \times 2$ linear system, we can graph the solutions to each of the equations in the Cartesian plane. By doing so, we will obtain two lines. The point(s) where the lines intersect (**if they intersect**) is the solution of the system. If you need to review linear equations and graphing lines, read over Section 10.2 before continuing.

**Examples.** Solve each system by graphing.

1) $x - y = 5$
   $x + y = -3$

To graph each of these, I will use the intercept method. Notice that the first line has intercepts $(0, -5)$ and $(5, 0)$. The second line has intercepts $(0, -3)$ and $(-3, 0)$. After plotting these points and graphing the lines containing them, we obtain the following:

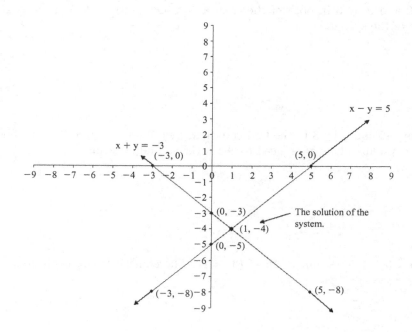

Observe that the lines intersect at $(1, -4)$. This is the solution of the system.

2) $y = 2x - 1$
   $y = -\frac{1}{3}x + 6$

Since each of these equations are in slope-intercept form, I will use the slope-intercept method to graph each of them. For the first line, the $y$-intercept is $(0, -1)$ and the slope, $m = \frac{+2}{+1}$, takes us up by 2 units and to the right by 1 unit, giving us $(1, 1)$. As for the second line, the $y$-intercept is $(0, 6)$ and the slope,

$m = \dfrac{-1}{+3}$, takes us down by 1 unit and to the right by 3 units, giving us $(3,\ 5)$. After plotting these points and graphing the lines going through them, respectively, we obtain:

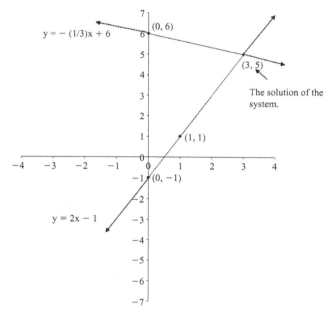

The solution of the system is $(3,\ 5)$.

3)     $y = -x + 3$
       $y = -x - 2$

Notice that both of these lines have slope equaling $-1$ and they have different $y$-intercepts, namely $(0,\ 3)$ and $(0,\ -2)$. Therefore, these lines are parallel (see graph below). Since parallel lines never intersect, this system has no solution. The system is inconsistent and the equations are independent.

4)     $y = \dfrac{2}{5}x - 3$
       $5y = 2x - 15$

For the first line, we have a $y$-intercept $(0, \; -3)$ and the slope, $m = \dfrac{+2}{+5}$, takes us up by 2 units and to the right by 5 units, giving us the point $(5, \; -1)$. Notice that the second equation, after dividing both sides by 5, gives us the first equation. Geometrically, this means that the second line is going to overlap the first line at every point (see graph below). Hence, there are infinitely many solutions. The system is consistent and the equations are dependent.

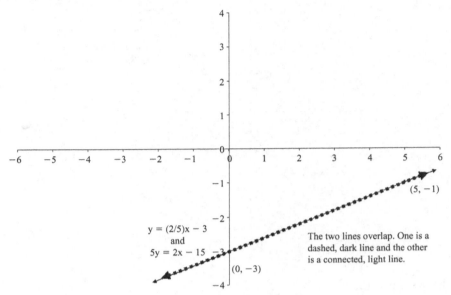

$y = (2/5)x - 3$
and
$5y = 2x - 15$

$(0, -3)$

$(5, -1)$

The two lines overlap. One is a dashed, dark line and the other is a connected, light line.

We have now exhibited each of the three possible solution sets that a $2 \times 2$ linear system can have.

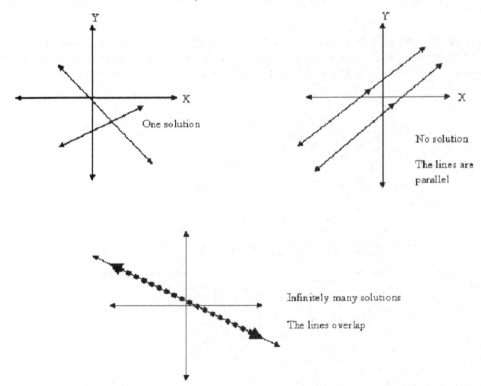

One solution

No solution

The lines are parallel

Infinitely many solutions

The lines overlap

Let's look at an example in which the graphing technique is not very useful in obtaining the solution.

5)    $x + 2y - 3 = 0$
      $y = \dfrac{1}{7}x + 2$

For the first line, I will use the intercept method. We have a $y$-intercept $\left(0, \dfrac{3}{2}\right)$ and an $x$-intercept (3, 0). For the second line, we have a $y$-intercept (0, 2) and the slope, $m = \dfrac{+1}{+7}$, taking us up by 1 unit and to the right by 7 units, giving us the point (7, 3). The graph of the system is given below. Observe that the $x$-value of the solution is between $-1$ and 0 and the $y$-value of the solution is between 1 and 2. Unfortunately, we can not read off their exact values from the graph. This shows us that the graphing method will not always give us the **exact** solution. In fact, the exact solution for this system is $x = -\dfrac{7}{9}$, $y = \dfrac{17}{9}$. How could we have possibly found this on our graph? In the next section, we will learn an algebraic method which will give us this solution.

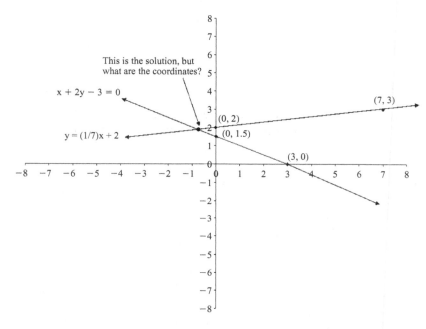

**Try These (Set 2):** Solve each system by graphing.

1) $y = 3x - 1$
   $x + y = 3$

2) $3x + 4y = 12$
   $y = x - 4$

3) $-4x + y + 4 = 0$
   $y = 2x - 6$

4) $y = 5x - 2$
   $y = 5x + 3$

## Section 12.3    The Substitution Method

The substitution method of solving a $2 \times 2$ linear system is an algebraic method which is used when one of the equations in the system has one of the variables solved for by itself. The method requires you to insert (or substitute) one equation into the other, obtaining one equation in one variable. This equation can be solved, since only one variable is present. If a solution for this variable exists (two special cases can arise, which I will discuss at the end of the section), you will then need to find the value of the other variable. To do this, you just plug the value of the known variable into one of the two equations and solve. This will yield the solution of the system. Let's see how this works.

**Examples.** Solve the system by using the substitution method.

1) $y = 3x - 1$
   $x + y = 3$

The first thing to look for is a variable by itself in one of the two equations. In the first equation, the variable $y$ is by itself (the other side of the equation only contains the variable $x$). We will replace the $y$-variable in the **second equation** by $3x - 1$ (we say that we're **substituting** the first equation into the second equation for $y$). By doing so, the second equation becomes

$$x + \overbrace{(3x - 1)}^{y} = 3$$

and now we can solve for $x$ :

$$
\begin{aligned}
x + (3x - 1) &= 3 \\
4x - 1 &= 3 \\
+1 \quad &+ 1 \\
\hline
\frac{4x}{4} &= \frac{4}{4} \\
x &= 1
\end{aligned}
$$

To find $y$, we replace $x$ by 1 in either one of the equations in the system. I'll choose the first equation, since it is easier to find the y-value for this equation than for the other equation.

$$
\begin{aligned}
y &= 3x - 1 \\
&= 3(1) - 1 \\
&= 3 - 1 = 2
\end{aligned}
$$

The solution of the system is $x = 1$, $y = 2$ or $(1, \ 2)$.

2) $2x - 7y = 2$
   $x = 3y + 4$

In the second equation, the variable $x$ is by itself. Therefore, we will substitute the second equation into the first equation for $x$, obtaining

$$
\begin{aligned}
2\overbrace{(3y + 4)}^{x} - 7y &= 2 \\
6y + 8 - 7y &= 2 \\
-y + 8 &= 2 \\
-8 \quad &- 8 \\
\hline
\frac{-y}{-1} &= \frac{-6}{-1} \\
y &= 6
\end{aligned}
$$

To find $x$, we replace $y$ by 6 in either one of the equations in the system. The second one is easier to work with.

$$
\begin{aligned}
x &= 3y + 4 \\
&= 3(6) + 4 \\
&= 18 + 4 = 22
\end{aligned}
$$

The solution of the system is $x = 22$, $y = 6$ or $(22, \ 6)$.

3) $-8x + 3y - 2 = 0$
   $y = 4x - 1$

Since the variable $y$ is by itself in the second equation, we will substitute the second equation into the first equation for $y$, obtaining

$$-8x + 3\overbrace{(4x - 1)}^{y} - 2 = 0$$
$$-8x + 12x - 3 - 2 = 0$$
$$4x - 5 = 0$$
$$\underline{\phantom{4x} +5 \quad +5}$$
$$\frac{4x}{4} = \frac{5}{4}$$
$$x = \frac{5}{4}$$

We'll find $y$ by replacing $x$ by $\dfrac{5}{4}$ in the second equation.

$$y = 4x - 1$$
$$= \frac{4}{1}\left(\frac{5}{4}\right) - 1$$
$$= 5 - 1 = 4$$

The solution is $\left(\dfrac{5}{4},\ 4\right)$.

4) $y = 10 - 6x$
   $y = -3 - 6x$

Since the variable $y$ is by itself in **both** equations, all that we need to do is set the right hand side of each equation equal to one another. We obtain

$$\overbrace{10 - 6x}^{y} = -3 - 6x$$
$$\underline{\phantom{10} +6x \qquad +6x}$$
$$10 \qquad = -3 \quad ??$$

Two strange things just occurred. First of all, the variable $x$ dropped out. Secondly, we have two unequal numbers equal to one another, which is absurd. What is going on here? Well, notice that each of the graphs of the linear equations has a slope of $-6$. They also have different $y$-intercepts, namely $(0, 10)$ and $(0, -3)$. This means that the two lines are parallel. Since parallel lines never intersect, this system has no solution.

**Remember:** Whenever you solve a system and a variable drops out, leaving two unequal numbers, the system has no solution. The system is inconsistent and the equations are independent.

5) $9y - 7 = x$
   $5x = 45y - 35$

Since the variable $x$ is by itself in the first equation, we will substitute the first equation into the second equation for $x$, obtaining

$$5\overbrace{(9y - 7)}^{x} = 45y - 35$$
$$45y - 35 = 45y - 35$$
$$\underline{-45y \qquad\quad -45y}$$
$$-35 = \qquad -35 \ ??$$

Once again, something weird occurs. The variable $y$ dropped out and we obtained two numbers equal to one another which **really are** equal. What does this mean? Well, observe that if you multiply the first equation by 5, you obtain the second equation. This means that the equations are equivalent and if you graph each of these lines, you will see that they overlap each other. Consequently, this system has infinitely many solutions.

**Remember:** Whenever you solve a system and a variable drops out, leaving two equal numbers, the system has infinitely many solutions. The system is consistent and the equations are dependent.

The substitution method may not be this easy to use sometimes. For example, let's solve the following system by using the substitution method:

$$5x - 13y = 4$$
$$-8x + 13y = 2$$

The first step is to solve for one of the variables in one of the equations. Suppose that we solve for $x$ in the first equation. Then we obtain

$$5x - 13y = 4$$
$$\underline{+13y \qquad + 13y}$$
$$\frac{5x}{5} = \frac{4 + 13y}{5}$$

If we now substitute $\dfrac{4 + 13y}{5}$ in the second equation for $x$, we obtain:

$$-8\left(\frac{4 + 13y}{5}\right) + 13y = 2$$
$$\frac{-32 - 104y}{5} + 13y = 2$$
$$5\left(\frac{-32 - 104y}{5} + 13y\right) = 5\,(2)$$
$$-32 - 104y + 65y = 10$$
$$-32 - 39y = 10$$
$$\underline{+32 \qquad\qquad + 32}$$
$$\frac{-39y}{-39} = \frac{42}{-39}$$
$$y = -\frac{14}{13}$$

We now have to solve for $x$. By replacing $y$ by $-\dfrac{14}{13}$ in the equation $x = \dfrac{4 + 13y}{5}$, we obtain

$$x = \frac{4 + 13\left(-\dfrac{14}{13}\right)}{5} = \frac{4 - 14}{5} = \frac{-10}{5} = -2.$$

Therefore, the solution is $x = 2$, $y = -\dfrac{14}{13}$. I think that we can agree that this took quite a bit of work. The difficulties came from the fact that we first had to solve for a variable in one of the equations. This produced fractions which created more work than we would've liked. In the next section, we will learn another algebraic method of solving a system which does not require us to have a variable solved for in one of the equations. By applying this method, the above system can be easily solved.

**Try These (Set 3):** Solve each system by using the substitution method.

1) $x = 4y - 7$
   $x + 2y = 5$

2) $-6x + 4y = 1$
   $y = 2x + 3$

3) $-x = y$
   $y = -x + 8$

4) $y = 3x - 11$
   $-3y = -9x + 33$

# Section 12.4    The Elimination Method

The elimination method of solving a $2 \times 2$ linear system is an algebraic method which is used when the columns of the system contain like terms and at least one such column contains additive inverse variable terms. When a system has these two features, all that we need to do is add up the two equations to **eliminate** the column(s) containing the additive inverse(s), thus eliminating (at least) one of the variables. After doing this, you will obtain one equation with one (or no) variable. This equation can (possibly) be solved, since only one variable is (possibly) present. As with the substitution method, you can obtain the value of the other variable by replacing the value of the known variable into one of the two equations and solve. This will yield the solution of the system.

**Examples.** Solve the system by using the elimination method.

1) $x + y = 5$
   $x - y = -7$

Notice that the columns of the system contain like terms. The first column contains the $x$-terms, the second contains the $y$-terms and the third contains the constant terms. Furthermore, notice that the $y$-terms are additive inverses of each other ($+y$ and $-y$). We can eliminate the $y$'s by adding the two equations together. This allows us to solve for $x$.

$$
\begin{array}{r}
x + \cancel{y} = 5 \\
+ \quad x - \cancel{y} = -7 \\
\hline
\dfrac{\cancel{2}x}{\cancel{2}} = \dfrac{-2}{2} \\
x = -1
\end{array}
$$

To find $y$, we will replace $x$ by $-1$ in the first equation (it doesn't matter which equation you choose).

$$
\begin{array}{r}
x + y = 5 \\
-1 + y = 5 \\
+1 \qquad +1 \\
\hline
y = 6
\end{array}
$$

The solution of the system is $x = -1$, $y = 6$ or $(-1, 6)$.

2) $-6x + 5y = -1$
   $6x + \ y = 13$

The columns of the system contain like terms and the $x$-terms are additive inverses of each other ($-6x$ and $+6x$). We can eliminate the $x$'s by adding the two equations together. This gives us an equation with just $y$ in it.

$$
\begin{array}{r}
-\cancel{6}x + 5y = -1 \\
+ \quad \cancel{6}x + \ y = 13 \\
\hline
\dfrac{\cancel{6}y}{\cancel{6}} = \dfrac{12}{6} \\
y = 2
\end{array}
$$

To find $x$, we will replace $y$ by 2 in the first equation.

$$-6x + 5y = -1$$
$$-6x + 5(2) = -1$$
$$-6x + 10 = -1$$
$$\underline{\phantom{-6x+} -10 \quad -10}$$
$$\frac{-6x}{-6} = \frac{-11}{-6}$$
$$x = \frac{11}{6}$$

The solution of the system is $\left( \dfrac{11}{6}, 2 \right)$.

3)  $7x + 2y = -2$
    $-x + 3y = 3$

The columns contain like terms, but we do not have additive inverses. However, we could make the $x$-terms additive inverses by multiplying the second equation by 7. We will obtain an equivalent system (a system whose solutions coincide with the original system) which can be solved by eliminating the $x$'s.

$$7x + 2y = -2 \qquad \text{becomes} \qquad 7x + 2y = -2$$
$$7(-x + 3y) = 7(3) \qquad\qquad +\ \underline{-7x + 21y = 21}$$
$$\frac{23y}{23} = \frac{19}{23}$$

To find $x$, we will replace $y$ by $\dfrac{19}{23}$ in the first equation.

$$7x + 2y = -2$$
$$7x + \frac{2}{1}\left( \frac{19}{23} \right) = -2$$
$$7x + \frac{38}{23} = -2$$
$$\frac{23}{1}\left( 7x + \frac{38}{23} \right) = \frac{23}{1}(-2)$$
$$161x + 38 = -46$$
$$\underline{\phantom{161x} -38 \quad -38}$$
$$\frac{161x}{161} = \frac{-84}{161}$$
$$x = -\frac{84}{161} = -\frac{12}{23}$$

The solution of the system is $\left( -\dfrac{12}{23}, \dfrac{19}{23} \right)$.

4)  $6x + 5y = 1$
    $-8x + 2y = -3$

The columns contain like terms, but we do not have additive inverses. Suppose that you want to eliminate the $x$'s. What you need to do is make the $x$-terms additive inverses of each other. To do this, you find the LCM of the coefficients 6 and 8, which is 24. This is the coefficient that you would like each of your $x$-terms to have. To obtain it, you multiply the first equation by 4 (creating the 24 that you want) and the second equation by 3 (again, creating the 24 that you want). Notice that one of the terms will be positive, while the other will be negative.

$$4(6x+5y)=4(1) \qquad \text{becomes} \qquad \begin{array}{r} 24x+20y=4 \\ + \ -24x+6y=-9 \\ \hline \dfrac{26y}{26}=\dfrac{-5}{26} \end{array}$$
$$3(-8x+2y)=3(-3)$$

Now you can find the value of $x$ in one of two ways. One way is to plug $y=-\dfrac{5}{26}$ into the either equation as we did before. Another approach is to solve for $x$ by eliminating the $y$'s. Let's do it by eliminating the $y$'s. You can try it the other way on your own. Observe that the LCM of 5 and 2 is 10, so we need to multiply the first equation by 2 and the second equation by $-5$ (notice that we need a negative sign in order to obtain additive inverses).

$$2(6x+5y)=2(1) \qquad \text{becomes} \qquad \begin{array}{r} 12x+10y=2 \\ + \ 40x-10y=15 \\ \hline \dfrac{52x}{52}=\dfrac{17}{52} \end{array}$$
$$-5(-8x+2y)=-5(-3)$$

The solution of the system is $\left(\dfrac{17}{52}, \ -\dfrac{5}{26}\right)$.

5) $\dfrac{1}{2}x+\dfrac{2}{3}y=4$

$-\dfrac{1}{4}x+\dfrac{5}{8}y=-1$

The first thing that we will do is clear out the fractions. For the first equation, the LCM of 2 and 3 is 6. For the second equation, the LCM of 4 and 8 is 8. Let's multiply each equation by its respective LCM.

$$\dfrac{6}{1}\left(\dfrac{1}{2}x+\dfrac{2}{3}y\right)=\dfrac{6}{1}(4) \qquad \text{becomes} \qquad 3x+4y=24$$
$$\dfrac{8}{1}\left(-\dfrac{1}{4}x+\dfrac{5}{8}y\right)=\dfrac{8}{1}(-1) \qquad\qquad\qquad -2x+5y=-8$$

Now we continue as before. To eliminate the $x$'s, observe that the LCM of 3 and 2 is 6. Thus, we need to multiply the first equation by 2 and the second equation by 3.

$$2(3x+4y)=2(24) \qquad \text{becomes} \qquad \begin{array}{r} 6x+\ 8y=\ \ 48 \\ + \ -6x+15y=-24 \\ \hline \dfrac{23y}{23}=\dfrac{24}{23} \end{array}$$
$$3(-2x+5y)=3(-8)$$

To find $x$, let's replace $y$ in the first equation by $\dfrac{24}{23}$ (alternatively, we could find $x$ by eliminating the $y$'s as in example 4). We obtain

$$3x+4y=24$$
$$3x+\dfrac{4}{1}\left(\dfrac{24}{23}\right)=24$$
$$3x+\dfrac{96}{23}=24$$
$$\dfrac{23}{1}\left(3x+\dfrac{96}{23}\right)=\dfrac{23}{1}(24)$$
$$69x+96=552$$
$$\underline{\quad -96 \ - \ 96\quad}$$
$$\dfrac{69x}{69}=\dfrac{456}{69}$$
$$x=\dfrac{152}{23}$$

The solution of the system is $\left(\dfrac{152}{23}, \dfrac{24}{23}\right)$.

6) $1.5x + 2y = 3$
   $1.25x + 1.2y = 1$

When a system contains decimals, the easiest approach to solving the system is to get rid of the decimals. In the first equation, notice that the term $1.5x$ has a coefficient whose decimal point has 1 digit proceeding it. To get rid of the decimal, all we need to do is multiply the equation by 10. Similarly, the terms $1.25x$ and $1.2y$ in the second equation each contain decimals. Since 1.25 has 2 digits proceeding its decimal point (which is more than the number of digits proceeding the decimal point in 1.2), we will multiply the second equation by 100. This will knock out the decimal points of each term in the second equation. Let's try it.

$$10\,(1.5x + 2y) = 10\,(3) \quad \text{becomes} \quad 15x + 20y = 30$$
$$100\,(1.25x + 1.2y) = 100\,(1) \qquad\qquad 125x + 120y = 100$$

The new system is now free of decimals. We solve it as before. Let's eliminate the $y$'s by multiplying the first equation by $-6$ (observe that the LCM of 20 and 120 is 120).

$$-6\,(15x + 20y) = -6\,(30) \quad \text{becomes} \quad -90x - 120y = -180$$
$$125x + 120y = 100 \qquad\qquad\qquad +\ \underline{\ 125x + 120y = \ \ \ 100\ }$$
$$\dfrac{35x}{35} = \dfrac{-80}{35}$$
$$x = -\dfrac{16}{7}$$

To find $y$, I will replace $x$ by $-\dfrac{16}{7}$ in the first equation (this is easier than doing another elimination in my opinion).

$$15x + 20y = 30$$
$$15\left(-\dfrac{16}{7}\right) + 20y = 30$$
$$-\dfrac{240}{7} + 20y = 30$$
$$7\left(-\dfrac{240}{7} + 20y\right) = 7\,(30)$$
$$-240 + 140y = 210$$
$$\underline{+240 \qquad\qquad + 240\ }$$
$$\dfrac{140y}{140} = \dfrac{450}{140}$$
$$y = \dfrac{45}{14}$$

The solution of the system is $\left(-\dfrac{16}{7}, \dfrac{45}{14}\right)$.

7) $y = -7x + 12$
   $y = -7x + 4$

To eliminate the $y$'s, you only need to multiply the second equation by $-1$ to get additive inverses.

$$y = -7x + 12 \quad \text{becomes} \quad y = -7x + 12$$
$$-1\,(y) = -1\,(-7x + 4) \qquad\qquad +\ \underline{\ -y = \ 7x - 4\ }$$
$$0 = \qquad 8 \ ??$$

Recall from the previous section that if you solve a system and a variable drops out, leaving two unequal numbers, the system has **no solution**.

8) $2x - 5y + 12 = 0$
$-4x + 10y - 24 = 0$

Notice that if you multiply the first equation by 2, the $x$-terms (and the $y$-terms) will be additive inverses of each other. We can, therefore, eliminate them.

$$2(2x - 5y + 12) = 2(0) \qquad \text{becomes} \qquad \cancel{4x} - \cancel{10y} + \cancel{24} = 0$$
$$-4x + 10y - 24 = 0 \qquad\qquad\qquad + \quad \underline{-\cancel{4x} + \cancel{10y} - \cancel{24} = 0}$$
$$0 \qquad = 0 \text{ ??}$$

Recall from the previous section that if you solve a system and a variable drops out, leaving two equal numbers, the system has **infinitely many solutions**.

**Try These (Set 4):** Solve each system by using the elimination method.

1)  $x - 2y = 9$
    $4x + 2y = 11$

2) $-3x + 5y = -2$
    $3x + 2y = 9$

3)  $7x - 3y = 6$
    $2x + 9y = -3$

4)  $4x - 11 = 2y$
    $-2x + 9 = -y$

**Exercise 12**

In Exercises 1-12, determine whether or not the ordered pair $(-3, \ -1)$ is a solution of the given system.

1. $y = x + 2$
   $y = 4x + 11$

2. $y = -4x - 13$
   $y = 2x + 5$

3. $y = 3x + 8$
   $y = -7x + 2$

4. $y = 6x$
   $y = -x - 4$

5. $2x - y + 5 = 0$
   $3x - 3y + 6 = 0$

6. $-4x + 3y - 9 = 0$
   $-7x + 8y - 13 = 0$

7. $x + y = -4$
   $x - 5y = 0$

8. $9x + 2y = -30$
   $4x - 3y = 12$

9. $\frac{1}{2}x + \frac{3}{2}y + 3 = 0$
   $\frac{4}{5}x - 2y + \frac{2}{5} = 0$

10. $4x - \frac{1}{3}y = \frac{35}{3}$
    $-x + \frac{3}{7}y = \frac{1}{7}$

11. $y = -x - 4$
    $x = -3$

12. $y = -1$
    $5y = 4x + 7$

In Exercises 13-20, solve the system by graphing.

13. $y = 2x - 1$
    $y = x + 2$

14. $y = x - 3$
    $y = -2x$

15. $x + 2y = 5$
    $y = 3 - x$

16. $y = x + 4$
    $y = -x - 6$

17. $x + y = 5$
    $x - y = -1$

18. $y = -\frac{1}{2}x$
    $y = \frac{1}{2}x + 4$

19. $3y + x = 0$
    $y = \frac{2}{3}x + 3$

20. $y = -5$
    $y = \frac{5}{7}x$

In Exercises 21-32, solve the system by using the substitution method.

21. $y = 3x + 5$
    $x + 2y = 17$

22. $-x + 2y = -5$
    $y = -3x + 1$

23. $x = 7 + 4y$
    $x + 3y - 4 = 0$

24. $y = -9x - 1$
    $6x + y + 12 = 0$

25. $y = -4x + 4$
    $y = 2x - 8$

26. $x = 11 - 10y$
    $x = 13 + 2y$

27. $\frac{2}{3}x + \frac{4}{3}y + 1 = 0$
    $x = 6y - 1$

28. $y = -5x + 12$
    $\frac{2}{5}x - \frac{1}{5}y - 2 = 0$

29. $4x + 7 = y$
    $-8x + 2y + 9 = 0$

30. $8x + 8y = 9$
    $x + y = -1$

31. $y = \frac{7}{8}x - 2$
    $16y = 14x - 32$

32. $x - y = 7$
    $5x - 13 = 5y$

In Exercises 33-50, solve the system by using the elimination method.

33. $x + y = 6$
$\quad x - y = -2$

34. $x - y = 8$
$\quad x + y = 2$

35. $x - 2y = 10$
$\quad 5x + 2y = 8$

36. $3x + 2y = 0$
$\quad -3x - y = 11$

37. $4x + 6y = 8$
$\quad -2x - 5y = 0$

38. $-7x + 10y = 1$
$\quad 3x - 5y = 6$

39. $-6x + 9y = 4$
$\quad -4x - 2y = 3$

40. $12x - 5y = -1$
$\quad -8x + 3y = 7$

41. $\frac{2}{3}x - \frac{5}{6}y = -4$
$\quad x + 3y = 7$

42. $9x - 3y + 10 = 0$
$\quad \frac{1}{4}x + \frac{3}{8}y - 1 = 0$

43. $1.5x + 3.5y = 2$
$\quad 2x + 0.5y = 4$

44. $0.5x + 0.25y = 5$
$\quad 0.75x + y = 8$

45. $3x + y = 13$
$\quad -3x - y = -17$

46. $6y - 5x = 2$
$\quad 12y - 10x = 3$

47. $8x - 2 = 6y$
$\quad -4x + 5 = -3y$

48. $y = 10x - 5$
$\quad y = 10x + 2$

49. $-6x - 9y + 12 = 0$
$\quad -2x - 3y + 4 = 0$

50. $\frac{4}{5}x - 9 = y$
$\quad 4x - 45 = 5y$

---

## END OF CHAPTER 12   QUIZ

1. The solution of the system $x - y = 7$ is
$\qquad\qquad\qquad\qquad x + y = 9$

a) $(8, \ -1)$    b) $(-8, \ 1)$    c) $(8, \ 1)$    d) $(1, \ 8)$    e) $(-1, \ -8)$

2. The solution of the system $y = 7x - 1$ is
$\qquad\qquad\qquad\qquad 3x + 2y = 15$

a) $(6, \ 1)$    b) $(1, \ 6)$    c) $(-1, \ 6)$    d) $\left(\frac{13}{17}, \frac{74}{17}\right)$    e) $\left(\frac{16}{17}, \frac{95}{17}\right)$

3. Which of the following is not a solution of the system $\quad x - 3y = 12$ ?
$\qquad\qquad\qquad\qquad\qquad\qquad\qquad\qquad\qquad -2x + 6y = -24$

a) $(0, \ -4)$    b) $\left(-2, \ -\dfrac{14}{3}\right)$    c) $(12, \ 0)$    d) $(3, \ -3)$    e) $(5, \ -4)$

4. What is the solution of the system $7x + 2y = 19$ ?
$\qquad\qquad\qquad\qquad\qquad\qquad\quad 7x + 2y = -12$

a) There is no solution.    b) 7    c) $(-3, \ 7)$    d) $(-1, \ 4)$    e) $(19, \ -12)$

5. The solution of the system $y = 3x + 6$ has an $x$-value of
$\qquad\qquad\qquad\qquad\qquad\quad -x - 2y = 7$

a) $\dfrac{19}{7}$    b) $-\dfrac{19}{7}$    c) $\dfrac{5}{7}$    d) $-\dfrac{19}{5}$    e) $-\dfrac{19}{3}$

6. The solution of the system $19x + 6y = 5$ has a $y$-value of
$\qquad\qquad\qquad\qquad\qquad\quad -19x - 9y = 7$

a) 4    b) $\dfrac{2}{3}$    c) 0    d) $-4$    e) $-\dfrac{1}{4}$

7. The solution of the system  $3x + 2y = 5$  is
$$-x + 5y = 2$$

a) $\left(\dfrac{11}{17}, \dfrac{21}{17}\right)$   b) $\left(\dfrac{21}{17}, -\dfrac{11}{17}\right)$   c) $\left(\dfrac{21}{17}, \dfrac{11}{17}\right)$   d) $\left(-\dfrac{89}{17}, \dfrac{11}{17}\right)$   e) There is no solution.

8. The solution of the system  $x - 3y = 0$  is
$$x = 5y - 11$$

a) $\left(\dfrac{33}{2}, \dfrac{11}{2}\right)$   b) $\left(-\dfrac{11}{2}, \dfrac{33}{2}\right)$   c) $\left(-\dfrac{33}{2}, -\dfrac{11}{2}\right)$   d) $\left(\dfrac{33}{2}, -\dfrac{11}{2}\right)$   e) There is no solution.

9. The solution of the system  $5x - 12y + 3 = 0$  is
$$-15x + 36y - 9 = 0$$

a) $(1,\ 6)$   b) $(-3,\ 2)$   c) $(0,\ 0)$   d) There are infinitely many solutions.   e) There is no solution.

10. The solution of the system  $y = 3x - 12$  is
$$y = 3x + 18$$

a) $(0,\ 6)$   b) There is no solution.   c) $(3,\ -6)$   d) There are infinitely many solutions.
e) $(1,\ -9)$

11. Which system has the solution $(-2,\ 2)$?

a) $x + y = 0$   b) $3x - 4y + 10 = 0$   c) $y = 4x + 10$   d) $y = \dfrac{2}{5}x - \dfrac{3}{5}$   e) $x - 3y + 8 = 0$

   $x - y = 4$      $-3x + 4y - 9 = 0$      $y = \dfrac{1}{2}x + 3$      $y = x + 6$      $y = 8x + 17$

12. The solution of the system  $y = x$  is
$$y = -x$$

a) $(1,\ 1)$   b) There is no solution.   c) $(-3,\ 3)$   d) There are infinitely many solutions.   e) $(0,\ 0)$

13. The solution of the system  $y = \dfrac{1}{3}x - \dfrac{2}{3}$  is
$$x = 5y + 2$$

a) $\left(-3,\ -\dfrac{5}{3}\right)$   b) $(2,\ 0)$   c) $(-1,\ -1)$   d) There is no solution.   e) $(0,\ -2)$

14. The solution of the system  $1.5x + 2y = 9$  is
$$0.25x + 3y = 9.5$$

a) $(-2,\ -3)$   b) $(1,\ 7)$   c) $(2,\ 3)$   d) $(3,\ 2)$   e) $(-8,\ 4)$

15. Which system has the solution $(4,\ -8)$?

a) $y = -2x$   b) $6x + 9y - 11 = 0$   c) $y = 8x - 1$   d) $y = 2x - 16$   e) $x - y = 12$

   $x = y + 12$      $3x - y - 28 = 0$      $y = \dfrac{1}{2}x - 10$      $y = 3x + 1$      $y = -7x + 2$

| ANSWERS FOR QUIZ 12 | 1. c | 2. b | 3. e | 4. a | 5. b |
|---|---|---|---|---|---|
| | 6. d | 7. c | 8. a | 9. d | 10. b |
| | 11. c | 12. e | 13. b | 14. c | 15. a |

# SOLUTIONS TO 'TRY THESE' EXAMPLES

### Chapter 1, Set 1

1a) 0.75 is a terminating decimal.
1b) 0.375 is a terminating decimal.
1c) $0.\overline{7}$ is a non-terminating, repeating.
1d) 0 is a terminating decimal.

2) a and e
3) a, b, d, and e
4) b and c

### Chapter 1, Set 2

1) 3
2) −24
3) −12
4) −4
5) −12
6) −11
7) −32
8) 21
9) 20
10) −5
11) 4
12) −7

### Chapter 1, Set 3

1) $\dfrac{7}{15}$

2) $\dfrac{5}{9}$

3) $-\dfrac{10}{7}$

4) $-\dfrac{7}{24}$

5) $-\dfrac{3}{4}$

6) $-\dfrac{21}{8}$

7) $-\dfrac{5}{12}$

8) $-\dfrac{189}{10}$

9) $\dfrac{9}{8}$

### Chapter 1, Set 4

1) 3.241 (both)
2) 7.905 truncated, 7.906 rounded off
3) 24.600 (both)
4) 9.222 truncated, 9.223 rounded off
5) 60.101 truncated, 60.102 rounded off
6) 0.149 (both)

### Chapter 1, Set 5

1) −1
2) −10
3) 10
4) 20
5) −18
6) 20
7) 8
8) −128
9) −2
10) −24
11) 0
12) 90

### Chapter 1, Set 6

I 1) commutative property    3) commutative property

2) associative property    4) distributive property

II The additive inverse of 9 is −9 and the reciprocal of 9 is $\dfrac{1}{9}$.

The additive inverse of $-\dfrac{3}{16}$ is $\dfrac{3}{16}$ and the reciprocal of $-\dfrac{3}{16}$ is $-\dfrac{16}{3}$.

III False

IV 1) $4x + 16$    3) $ab - 2a$
  2) $-8a - 40$    4) $-12 + x$

## Chapter 1, Set 7

I

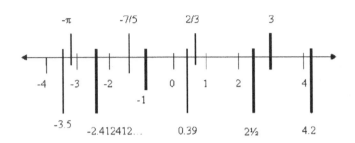

II 1) $5 > 2$          4) $-3.022 > -3.0225$     7) $-1.5656 > -\frac{155}{99}$
   2) $-7 > -20$        5) $-8.\overline{5} < 8.\overline{5}$
   3) $\frac{1}{6} < \frac{1}{5}$        6) $\pi < 3.16$

## Chapter 1, Set 8

I 1) 6          5) $\frac{9}{10}$
  2) 9          6) $4.217\overline{3}$
  3) 12         7) $-14$
  4) 25         8) $-12$

II 1) 11        3) 7
   2) 13        4) $\frac{29}{12}$

III 1) $y^2$          4) $\dfrac{5}{|x|}$

    2) $14\,|x|$       5) $\dfrac{|y|}{8}$

    3) $3a^2\,|b|$     6) $\dfrac{a^2 b^2\,|b|}{2}$

## Chapter 1, Set 9

I 1) 5       3) 2       5) $-\dfrac{3}{4}$

  2) 56      4) $-18$     6) $-23$

II 1) All real numbers except 1.
   2) All real numbers except $-8$.
   3) All real numbers except 12.

---

## Chapter 2, Set 1

1) 49        5) $\dfrac{16}{9}$        9) $-\dfrac{216}{125}$

2) 125       6) $\dfrac{1}{81}$        10) 165

3) 4         7) $-\dfrac{1}{81}$       11) 0.1681

4) $-4$      8) $-\dfrac{216}{125}$     12) $-0.000027$

## Chapter 2, Set 2

I 1) $x^6$          4) $27x^{15}y^{14}$

  2) $y^{17}$        5) $-12a^7b^9$

  3) $-30a^{15}$      6) $27x^{18}$

II 1) $x^4$          4) $-2x^5y^2$

  2) $a$          5) $\dfrac{5a^3b^{17}c^6}{3} = \dfrac{5}{3}a^3b^{17}c^6$

  3) $6m^6n^8$        6) $9^2 = 81$

## Chapter 2, Set 3

1) 1        3) 1        5) 1        7) 1

2) 8        4) 1        6) $-4a^2$      8) $-1$

## Chapter 2, Set 4

1) $\dfrac{1}{64}$      5) $\dfrac{1}{16}$      9) $-\dfrac{1}{27}$

2) $\dfrac{1}{64}$      6) $-\dfrac{1}{16}$     10) $-\dfrac{1}{27}$

3) $\dfrac{1}{6}$       7) $\dfrac{1}{x^6}$

4) $\dfrac{1}{81}$      8) $\dfrac{1}{y^4}$

## Chapter 2, Set 5

1) $x^6$        4) $a^4$

2) $t^{20}$      5) 1

3) $y^7$        6) $x^{36}$

## Chapter 2, Set 6

1) $a^3b^3$          4) $81x^{20}y^4z^{12}$

2) $25x^2y^2$        5) $-\dfrac{64}{343}a^{12}b^{21}$

3) $16x^4y^{12}$      6) $32x^5y^{25}z^{10}$

## Chapter 2, Set 7

1) $\dfrac{4}{49}$        4) $\dfrac{64a^{30}}{b^9}$

2) $-\dfrac{1}{216}$      5) $\dfrac{x^{14}}{121y^4}$

3) $\dfrac{x^6}{81}$      6) $\dfrac{8}{125n^{12}}$

## Chapter 2, Set 8

1) $40a^5$

2) $9x^{10}$

3) $-25x^{22}y^{38}$

4) $\dfrac{27x^6}{64y^{18}}$

5) $\dfrac{5s^{11}t^{10}}{9}$

6) $\dfrac{96a^{11}}{125}$

## Chapter 2, Set 9

1) 9

2) $\dfrac{729}{64}$

3) 11

4) 180

5) $\dfrac{1}{108}$

6) $\dfrac{1}{64}$

7) $\dfrac{27}{4}$

8) $\dfrac{8}{3}$

9) $-\dfrac{2}{45}$

## Chapter 2, Set 10

1) $\dfrac{81}{y^2}$

2) $\dfrac{8}{49x^9}$

3) $\dfrac{8a^4}{b^3}$

4) $\dfrac{x^{10}y^6}{64}$

5) $\dfrac{a^{18}}{125b^{12}}$

6) $\dfrac{9x^3y^3}{16}$

7) $-\dfrac{s^2t^5}{6}$

8) $\dfrac{9x^8y^8}{256}$

## Chapter 2, Set 11

I 1) $4.103 \times 10^3$

  2) $5.09334 \times 10^2$

  3) $2.00078 \times 10^{-1}$

  4) $1.2890028 \times 10^4$

  5) $6.992103 \times 10^{-2}$

  6) $1.0 \times 10^0$

II 1) 240

  2) $90,034$

  3) 18.7

  4) 0.00643

  5) 0.7005

  6) 0.00000001

## Chapter 2, Set 12

1) $6 \times 10^8$

2) $2.5 \times 10^6$

3) $7.29 \times 10^{14}$

4) $1 \times 10^{-27}$

5) $2.1 \times 10^1$

6) $1 \times 10^{-6}$

## Chapter 3, Set 1

1) $2y + 20$

2) $11x^2 + 6x + 22$

3) $2x^2 - 25xy + 12y^2$

4) $5a - 6ab - 1 + a^2$

5) $-16x^2 - 15 + 7x = -16x^2 + 7x - 15$

6) $-\dfrac{1}{6}t^2 - \dfrac{6}{5}t - \dfrac{1}{6}$

## Chapter 3, Set 2

1) $-6x$                              4) $-x^2 + y^2$
2) $-5x^2 + x - 3$                    5) $\dfrac{x}{6} - \dfrac{2x^2}{7}$
3) $7a^2 + 9ab^2$

## Chapter 3, Set 3

1) $5x - 8y$                          4) $-m^2 - 20mn + 3$
2) $5ab - 11b^2$                      5) $-14a^2 + a + 10$
3) $-2s^2 - 5st - t^2$                6) $y - x$

## Chapter 3, Set 4

1) $15a^7$                            3) $\dfrac{3}{4}x^2 y^9$
2) $-28x^9 y^8$                       4) $-12m^6 n^{10}$

## Chapter 3, Set 5

1) $4x^2 - 12x$                       3) $24a^3 - 40a^2 b - 8ab^2$
2) $-5y^4 - 20y^3 + 45y^2$            4) $14p^4 q^8 - 49p^6 q^7 - 56p^4 q^6$

## Chapter 3, Set 6

1) $54x^2 + 15x$
2) $19a^3 - 38a^2 - 66a$
3) $16y^3 + 10xy^2 - 18y^2 + 15x^2 y - 5x^3 + 10x^2$
4) $-39x^2 - 29x$
5) $6a^2 - 39ab + 10b^2 - a^2 b^2$
6) $-7 + 58x + 62y$

## Chapter 3, Set 7

1) $x^2 + 5x - 14$                    4) $24 - 22x + 5x^2$
2) $10a^2 - 26a + 12$                 5) $16y^2 - 49$
3) $2y^3 - 3y^2 - 27y$                6) $25a^2 + 110a + 121$

## Chapter 3, Set 8

1) $x^3 + 5x^2 + 7x + 2$              4) $x^3 - 4x^2 - 16x + 64$
2) $3y^3 - 22y^2 + 13y - 2$           5) $27t^3 - 54t^2 + 36t - 8$
3) $15a^3 - 7a^2 b - 12ab^2 - 2b^3$   6) $a^4 - 4a^3 + 2a^2 + 4a + 1$

## Chapter 3, Set 9

1) $4x^2$                3) $2y^{14}$              5) $\dfrac{7}{m^2 n}$

2) $-6a^3 b$             4) $\dfrac{-5t^2}{s}$     6) $\dfrac{-6}{z^6}$

## Chapter 3, Set 10

1) $2x + 4$

2) $5a^2 - a$

3) $4xy^2 + y^8 - 2x^5y$

4) $-9m^2 + 5 - \dfrac{7}{4m}$

5) $\dfrac{2}{y} + \dfrac{7}{2}y - \dfrac{y^2}{4}$

## Chapter 3, Set 11

1) $y + 1$ R $-3$

2) $x + 2$ R $5$

3) $x^2 + 2x - 12$ R $39$

4) $3x + 7$ R $57$

5) $a^2 - 3a + 12$ R $-36a + 11$

## Chapter 3, Set 12

1) $4x^2\left(3x^2 + 5\right)$

2) $a\left(14a^2 - 9\right)$

3) $y\left(y^4 + 2y - 6\right)$

4) $2xy^3\left(8x^3 + 5y^3\right)$

5) $7st^2\left(t^6 - 3s^2 + s\right)$

6) $xy\left(x - y + 1\right)$

7) $(x + 1)(x - 4)$

8) $(x - 5)(x - 2)$

## Chapter 3, Set 13

1) $(x + 2)(x - 2)$

2) $(a + 4)(a - 4)$

3) $(11t + 1)(11t - 1)$

4) $(5 + 12y)(5 - 12y)$

5) $(s + 3t)(s - 3t)$

6) $\left(9x + \frac{8}{13}y\right)\left(9x - \frac{8}{13}y\right)$

7) prime

8) prime

## Chapter 3, Set 14

1) $(x - 1)\left(x^2 + x + 1\right)$

2) $(a + 3)\left(a^2 - 3a + 9\right)$

3) $(2y + 1)\left(4y^2 - 2y + 1\right)$

4) $(3x - y)\left(9x^2 + 3xy + y^2\right)$

5) $(6 - 5y)\left(36 + 30y + 25y^2\right)$

6) $\left(a - \dfrac{5}{4}\right)\left(a^2 + \dfrac{5}{4}a + \dfrac{25}{16}\right)$

## Chapter 3, Set 15

1) $5(x + 2)(x - 2)$

2) $3y(y + 4)(y - 4)$

3) $a^2(x + 3)\left(x^2 - 3x + 9\right)$

4) $9st(t - 2)\left(t^2 + 2t + 4\right)$

5) $\left(x^2 + 16\right)(x + 4)(x - 4)$

6) $(a + 1)\left(a^2 - a + 1\right)(a - 1)\left(a^2 + a + 1\right)$

## Chapter 3, Set 16

1) $(x + 5)(x + 2)$

2) $(k + 8)^2$

3) $(y - 10)(y - 3)$

4) prime

5) prime

6) $(m - 12)^2$

7) $(a + 7)(a - 8)$

8) prime

9) $(b - 9)^2$

### Chapter 3, Set 17

1) $(3x + 2)(x + 4)$                5) $(14x + 5)(x - 1)$
2) $(4y + 3)^2$                       6) $(9p - 4)(2p + 5)$
3) $(5a - 1)(2a - 7)$              7) $(10y - 9)^2$
4) $(3t - 8)(3t - 2)$

### Chapter 3, Set 18

1) $(t^2 + 2)(t + 4)$              4) $(9a^3 + 2)(2a + 3)$
2) $(x^3 - 3)(x + 7)$              5) $(4p^2 + 9)(2p^3 - 5)$
3) $(2y^2 - 1)(y - 5)$            6) $(a - 7 + 3b)(a - 7 - 3b)$

### Chapter 3, Set 19

1) $3x(x + 4)(x + 2)$                    5) $(x^2 - 2)(x + 4)(x - 4)$
2) $2y^2(2y - 3)(2y + 1)$             6) $7y^3(y - 1)(y^2 + y + 1)(y + 2)$
3) $-t^3(8t + 5)(t - 2)$                7) $(4a + 5t)(3a + 2t)$
4) $-5m(3m + 4)^2$

---

### Chapter 4, Set 1

1) $\dfrac{8(x - 1)}{2x + 3}$        3) $\dfrac{2}{x + 2}$        5) $\dfrac{18}{3x - 5}$

2) $\dfrac{-5y - 4}{9y + 1}$        4) $\dfrac{1}{3x + 2}$        6) $-\dfrac{1}{y + 6}$

### Chapter 4, Set 2

1) 120          3) $45x^5y^2$                    5) $(x + 4)(x - 4)(x + 1)$
2) 196          4) $5x^2(2x - 1)(4x - 1)$    6) $6x^4(x + 1)^2(x - 2)^2(x - 3)^2$

### Chapter 4, Set 3

1) $\dfrac{35y + 16}{40y}$      3) $\dfrac{-6}{(x + 7)(x + 1)}$      5) $\dfrac{-y^2 - 5y + 20}{y(y + 4)(y - 4)}$      7) $\dfrac{5u^2 + 28u + 9}{u + 7}$

2) $\dfrac{2}{9t}$      4) $\dfrac{7a - 38}{a(a - 5)(a - 6)}$      6) $\dfrac{x(4x + 23)}{(x + 5)(x + 6)^2}$

---

### Chapter 5, Set 1

1) $2\sqrt{5}$          2) $3\sqrt{6}$          3) $2\sqrt{30}$          4) $\sqrt{39}$          5) $\sqrt{26}$

### Chapter 5, Set 2

1) $x^3$          2) $y^7\sqrt{y}$          3) $m\sqrt{m}$          4) $x^{17}$          5) $p^9\sqrt{p}$

## Chapter 5, Set 3

1) $2xy^2\sqrt{2xy}$      2) $3x^3y\sqrt{7}$      3) $20p^3q^2\sqrt{p}$      4) $7a^2b^8c\sqrt{2b}$      5) $x\sqrt{14y}$

## Chapter 5, Set 4

1) $7xy^4\sqrt{x}$      2) $2x\sqrt{2}$      3) $6a^6\sqrt{a}$

## Chapter 5, Set 5

1) $8\sqrt{14}$      3) $25\sqrt{3}$      5) $33\sqrt{13}-16$

2) $\dfrac{\sqrt{2}}{2}$      4) $\sqrt{2}-3$      6) $\dfrac{-9\sqrt{3}}{5}$

## Chapter 5, Set 6

1) $12\sqrt{15}$      3) $240$

2) $\sqrt{6}+37$      4) $1+2x\sqrt{7}+7x^2$

## Chapter 5, Set 7

1) $\dfrac{5\sqrt{7}}{42}$      2) $\dfrac{4\sqrt{6}}{3}$      3) $11-\sqrt{66}$      4) $\dfrac{12+5\sqrt{6}}{-2}$

## Chapter 5, Set 8

1) $\dfrac{5}{2\sqrt{15}}$      2) $\dfrac{7}{3\sqrt{14}}$      3) $\dfrac{1}{2\left(\sqrt{7}+\sqrt{3}\right)}$      4) $\dfrac{3}{12-5\sqrt{6}}$

## Chapter 5, Set 9

1) $-2\sqrt[3]{2}$      3) $12+8\sqrt[3]{4}$

2) $4xy^4\sqrt[3]{2x^2}$      4) $\sqrt[3]{25}-4\sqrt[3]{5}+4$

---

## Chapter 6, Set 1

I   1) $7$      2) $16$      3) $\dfrac{1}{4}$      4) $\dfrac{1}{125}$      5) $\dfrac{7}{4}$

II   1) $\sqrt[4]{x}$      2) $\dfrac{1}{\sqrt[4]{y^3}}$      3) $5\sqrt[3]{x^2}$      4) $\sqrt[3]{25x^2}$      5) $\dfrac{\sqrt[5]{9a^2}\cdot\sqrt[3]{b}}{4}$

III   1) $y^{\frac{1}{2}}$      2) $\left(\dfrac{4}{t}\right)^{\frac{1}{3}}$      3) $\dfrac{4^{\frac{1}{3}}}{t}$      4) $3x\left(4x-1\right)^{\frac{1}{2}}$      5) $\left[3x\left(4x-1\right)\right]^{\frac{1}{2}}$

## Chapter 6, Set 2

I 1) $x^{\frac{17}{12}}$    2) $x^{\frac{1}{8}}$    3) $y^{-\frac{1}{3}}$    4) $a^{42}b^{-2}$    5) $\dfrac{m^{\frac{3}{2}}}{n^{-\frac{2}{3}}}$

II 1) $\sqrt[4]{x^3}$    2) $\dfrac{1}{\sqrt[3]{y}}$    3) $\sqrt[3]{t}$    4) $\sqrt{a}$    5) $x^{10}\sqrt{x}$

---

## Chapter 7, Set 1

1) $x = -19$      5) $t = -6$       9) $m = \dfrac{51}{4}$

2) $a = -5$       6) $s = 1$        10) No solution, $\varnothing$.

3) $y = -\dfrac{16}{5}$   7) $p = 0$        11) $x$ can equal any real number except 0.

4) $x = -4$       8) No solution, $\varnothing$.

## Chapter 7, Set 2

1) $x = \dfrac{y+4}{3}$          5) $t = \dfrac{20}{m-8}$

2) $c = \dfrac{-2a+5b}{32}$       6) $x = 12y$

3) $F = \dfrac{9}{5}C + 32$       7) $r = \dfrac{-a+3b+3}{b}$

4) $b_1 = \dfrac{2}{h}A - b_2$

## Chapter 7, Set 3

1) $\{4, \ -1\}$          4) $\left\{-\dfrac{5}{4}, \ \dfrac{5}{4}\right\}$

2) $\{-8, \ -7\}$         5) $\left\{\dfrac{1}{5}\right\}$ (double root)

3) $\{0, \ 3\}$           6) $\left\{-\dfrac{1}{2}, \ -\dfrac{7}{3}\right\}$

## Chapter 7, Set 4

1) $\{0, \ -1\}$          4) $\{0, \ -9\}$

2) $\left\{0, \ \dfrac{7}{3}\right\}$        5) $\left\{0, \ -\dfrac{37}{5}\right\}$

3) $\{0, \ 4\}$           6) $\left\{0, \ -\dfrac{15}{2}\right\}$

## Chapter 7, Set 5

1) $\{-\sqrt{2}, \ \sqrt{2}\}$     4) $\{-5, \ 5\}$         7) $\{-5\sqrt{2}, \ 5\sqrt{2}\}$

2) $\{-2\sqrt{11}, \ 2\sqrt{11}\}$  5) $\{-2\sqrt{3}, \ 2\sqrt{3}\}$   8) $\left\{-\dfrac{7\sqrt{6}}{18}, \ \dfrac{7\sqrt{6}}{18}\right\}$

3) $\{-\sqrt{5}, \ \sqrt{5}\}$     6) $\left\{-\dfrac{2\sqrt{7}}{3}, \ \dfrac{2\sqrt{7}}{3}\right\}$   9) No real roots.

## Chapter 7, Set 6

I 1) $x^2 + 8x + \underline{16} = (x\underline{+4})^2$     3) $p^2 - 11p + \dfrac{121}{4} = \left(p - \dfrac{11}{2}\right)^2$

   2) $y^2 - \dfrac{3}{2}y + \dfrac{9}{16} = \left(y - \dfrac{3}{4}\right)^2$     4) $k^2 + \dfrac{5}{6}k + \dfrac{25}{\underline{144}} = \left(k + \dfrac{5}{12}\right)^2$

II 1) $\{-4 - \sqrt{2}, \ -4 + \sqrt{2}\}$     3) No real roots.

   2) $\{3 - 2\sqrt{3}, \ 3 + 2\sqrt{3}\}$     4) $\left\{-\dfrac{1}{6} - \dfrac{\sqrt{37}}{6}, \ -\dfrac{1}{6} + \dfrac{\sqrt{37}}{6}\right\}$

## Chapter 7, Set 7

I 1) Real and unequal     4) No real roots.
   2) Real and equal     5) Real and equal
   3) Real and unequal     6) No real roots.

II 1) $\{-3, \ -2\}$     4) $\left\{\dfrac{3 - \sqrt{3}}{2}, \ \dfrac{3 + \sqrt{3}}{2}\right\}$

   2) $\{-\sqrt{10}, \ \sqrt{10}\}$     5) No real roots.

   3) $\left\{\dfrac{-1 - \sqrt{33}}{8}, \ \dfrac{-1 + \sqrt{33}}{8}\right\}$     6) $\{1 - \sqrt{10}, \ 1 + \sqrt{10}\}$

## Chapter 7, Set 8

1) $4i$     3) $3\sqrt{6}i$     5) $5\sqrt{5}i$
2) $11i$     4) $\dfrac{1}{10}i$     6) $\sqrt{19}i$

## Chapter 7, Set 9

1) real part is 2, imaginary part is 3     4) real part is $\dfrac{-15}{16}$, imaginary part is $\dfrac{25}{4}$

2) real part is 4, imaginary part is $-8$     5) real part is 0, imaginary part is $-1$

3) real part is $-12$, imaginary part is 0     6) real part is 10, imaginary part is 0

## Chapter 7, Set 10

1) $5 + 3i$     3) $-12 + 18i$     5) $1 + 2i$
2) $-2 - 30i$     4) $\dfrac{7}{5} - 6i$     6) $\dfrac{10}{3} + \dfrac{2}{7}i$

## Chapter 7, Set 11

1) $-30 - 12i$     4) $97$
2) $46 - 2i$     5) $-3$
3) $63 - 16i$     6) $-2\sqrt{15}$

## Chapter 7, Set 12

1) $-i$        3) $-1$        5) $1$
2) $1$         4) $-i$        6) $i$

## Chapter 7, Set 13

1) $\dfrac{11}{13} - \dfrac{10}{13}i$        3) $-\dfrac{20}{13} + \dfrac{4}{13}i$

2) $-\dfrac{9}{29} - \dfrac{37}{29}i$        4) $-\dfrac{2}{3} - \dfrac{1}{2}i$

## Chapter 7, Set 14

1) $\{-2i,\ 2i\}$

2) $\{-\sqrt{7}i,\ \sqrt{7}i\}$

3) $\{-2\sqrt{2}i,\ 2\sqrt{2}i\}$

4) $\left\{\dfrac{2-\sqrt{2}i}{2},\ \dfrac{2+\sqrt{2}i}{2}\right\} = \left\{1 - \dfrac{\sqrt{2}}{2}i,\ 1 + \dfrac{\sqrt{2}}{2}i\right\}$

5) $\left\{\dfrac{-1-\sqrt{3}i}{2},\ \dfrac{-1+\sqrt{3}i}{2}\right\} = \left\{-\dfrac{1}{2} - \dfrac{\sqrt{3}}{2}i,\ -\dfrac{1}{2} + \dfrac{\sqrt{3}}{2}i\right\}$

6) $\left\{\dfrac{1-\sqrt{6}i}{7},\ \dfrac{1+\sqrt{6}i}{7}\right\} = \left\{\dfrac{1}{7} - \dfrac{\sqrt{6}}{7}i,\ \dfrac{1}{7} + \dfrac{\sqrt{6}}{7}i\right\}$

---

## Chapter 8, Set 1

1) $2\sqrt{17}$
2) $2\sqrt{3}$
3) Yes, since $8^2 + 15^2 \overset{\checkmark}{=} 17^2$

## Chapter 8, Set 2

1) $64$ ft$^2$              3) $\dfrac{10}{3}$ meters              5) $(4 + 13\sqrt{2})$ in$^2$
2) $16\sqrt{5}$ yards       4) $176\pi$ ft$^2$

## Chapter 8, Set 3

1) $64$ ft$^2$                    3) $\dfrac{50}{\pi}$ cm              5) $(724 - 48\sqrt{5})$ in$^2$
2) $\dfrac{2{,}048\pi}{3}$ m$^3$   4) $\dfrac{17}{4}$ ft

---

## Chapter 9, Set 1

1) The set of all real numbers less than or equal to 6.
2) The set $X = \{7\}$.
3) The set $T = \{-3,\ 3,\ 4\}$.
4) The set is empty, $M = \varnothing$.
5) The set $P = \{2,\ 3,\ 5,\ 7,\ 11,\ 13\}$.
6) The set $V = \{a,\ e,\ i,\ o,\ u\}$.

## Chapter 9, Set 2

1) Yes
2) No

3) No
4) Yes

## Chapter 9, Set 3

1) $M \cap N = \{0, 5\}$

2) $X \cap Y = \{1, 3, 5, 7, 9, 11\}$

3) $S \cap T = \{-1\}$

4) $A \cap B = \varnothing$

## Chapter 9, Set 4

1) $P \cup Q = \{1, 4, 9, 16, 2, 3, 5, 7\}$

2) $S \cup T = \{4, 7, 12, -3, 3\}$

3) $X \cup Y = \{-\frac{2}{9}, -4\}$

4) $A \cup B = A$

## Chapter 9, Set 5

1) $x > 5$    $(5, \infty)$      4) $x < -\frac{120}{17}$    $\left(-\infty, -\frac{120}{17}\right)$

2) $y \le -3$   $(-\infty, -3]$     5) $x \le -14$    $(-\infty, -14]$

3) $t \ge \frac{2}{7}$    $[\frac{2}{7}, \infty)$      6) $y < -10$    $(-\infty, -10)$

## Chapter 9, Set 6

1) $-\frac{10}{7} < x < -\frac{6}{7}$    $\left(-\frac{10}{7}, -\frac{6}{7}\right)$

2) $-\frac{35}{2} \ge y \ge -21$    $\left[-21, -\frac{35}{2}\right]$

3) $18 > t \ge 15$    $[15, 18)$

4) $2 \le x < \frac{23}{9}$    $[2, \frac{23}{9})$

## Chapter 9, Set 7

1) $x \le -\frac{1}{4}$ or $x \ge \frac{3}{4}$    $\left(-\infty, -\frac{1}{4}\right] \cup [\frac{3}{4}, \infty)$        3) $x > 1$ or $x < -\frac{3}{2}$    $(1, \infty) \cup \left(-\infty, -\frac{3}{2}\right)$

2) $y > -13$ or $y \le -16$    $(-13, \infty) \cup (-\infty, -16]$     4) $t \le 0$ or $t > \frac{14}{3}$    $(-\infty, 0] \cup \left(\frac{14}{3}, \infty\right)$

## Chapter 9, Set 8

1) No solution
2) $(5, \infty)$

3) all real numbers
4) $\left(\frac{1}{3}, \infty\right)$

**Chapter 10, Set 1**

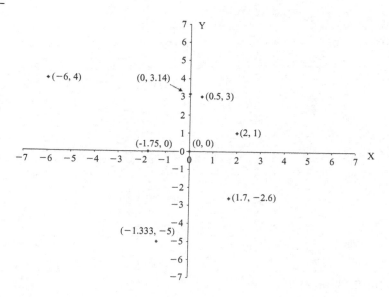

**Chapter 10, Set 2**

1) 5

2) $\sqrt{117}$

3) 10

4) 13

**Chapter 10, Set 3**

1) (3, 0)

2) $\left(-\dfrac{15}{2}, \dfrac{3}{2}\right)$

3) $\left(-\dfrac{1}{2}, \dfrac{1}{2}\right)$

4) $\left(-\dfrac{17}{24}, \dfrac{5}{2}\right)$

**Chapter 10, Set 4**

I 1)

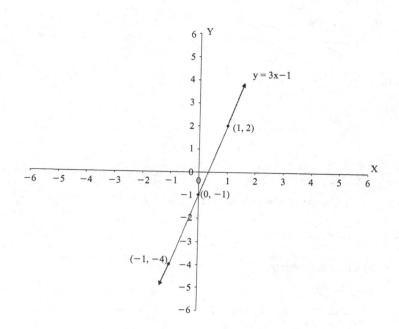

2)

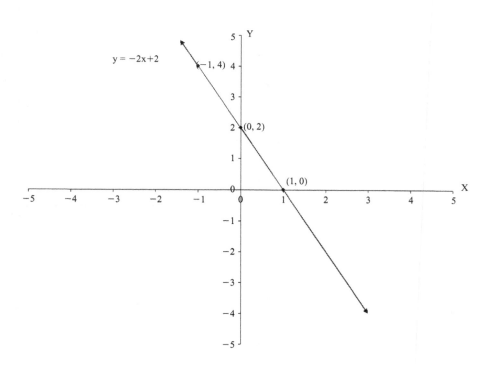

3)

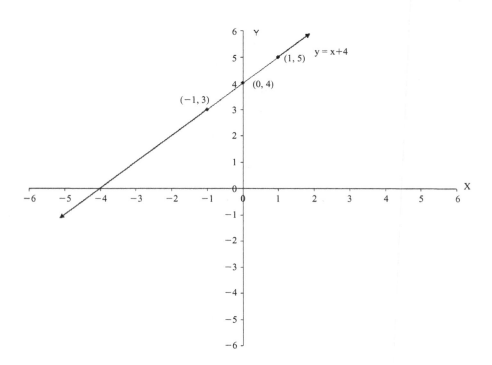

4)

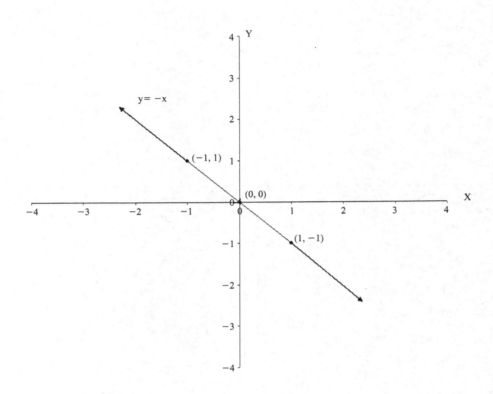

II 1) Yes          3) Yes          5) No
   2) No           4) Yes          6) No


## Chapter 10, Set 5

1) $\dfrac{4}{3}$

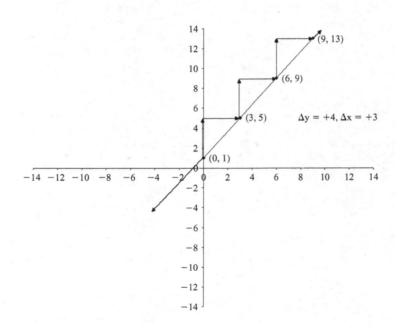

2) $-2$

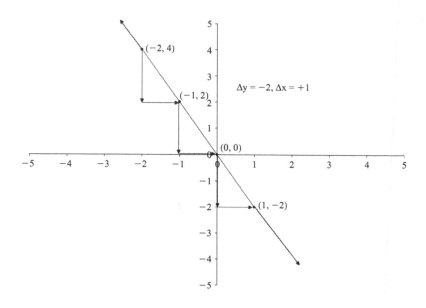

3) $-\dfrac{5}{4}$

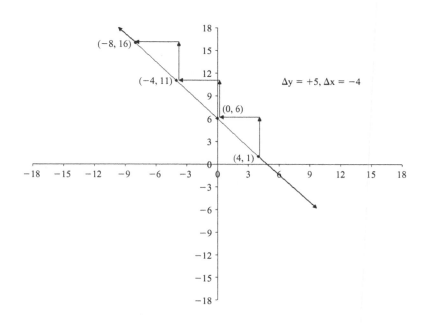

4) 1

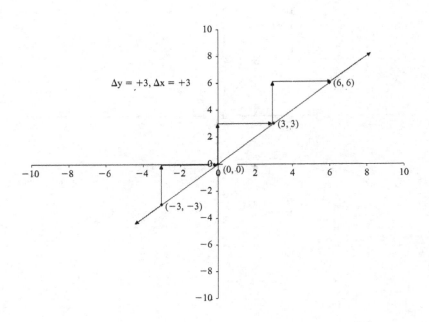

5) No slope (undefined)

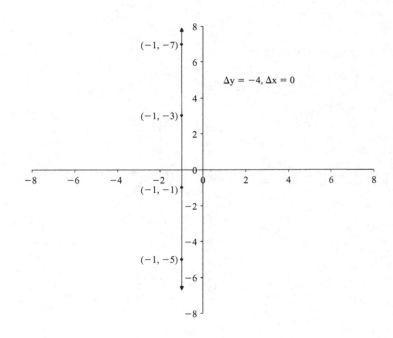

6) 0

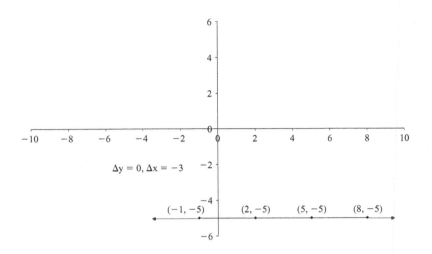

## Chapter 10, Set 6

1)

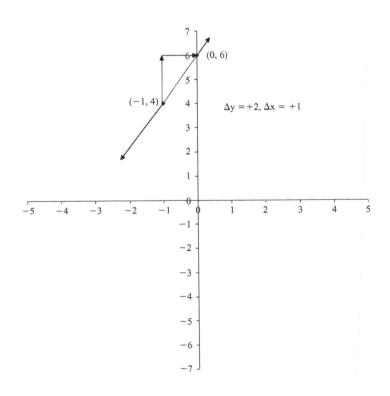

2)

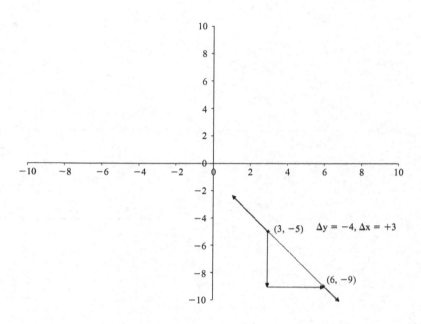

3)

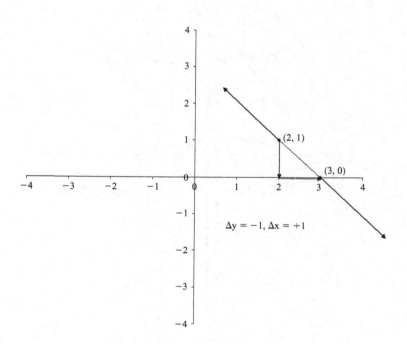

4)

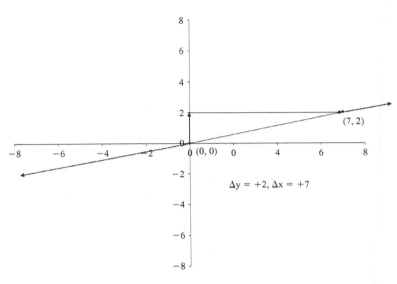

$\Delta y = +2, \Delta x = +7$

**Chapter 10, Set 7**

1) $y = \dfrac{1}{2}x - 2$     3) $y = -\dfrac{8}{5}x + \dfrac{7}{5}$

2) $y = -6x - 30$     4) $y = -\dfrac{7}{2}x + 7$

**Chapter 10, Set 8**

1) $y = 4x + 1$     3) slope is 1, $y-$intercept is $(0, \ -10)$

2) $y = -\dfrac{2}{11}x$     4) slope is 4, $y-$intercept is $\left(0, \ \dfrac{9}{2}\right)$

**Chapter 10, Set 9**

1) $x-$intercept is $(2, \ 0)$, $y-$intercept is $(0, \ 6)$

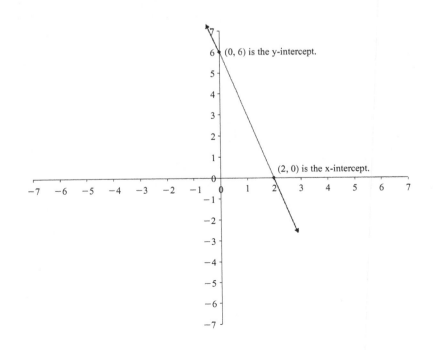

$(0, 6)$ is the y-intercept.

$(2, 0)$ is the x-intercept.

2) $x$–intercept is $\left(\dfrac{3}{2},\, 0\right)$, $y$–intercept is $\left(0,\, \dfrac{3}{7}\right)$

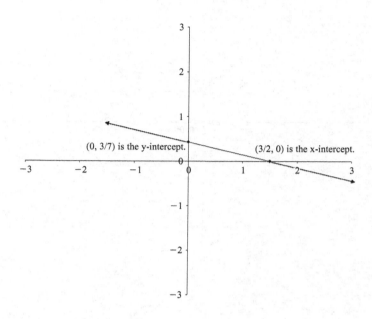

3) $x$–intercept is $\left(-\dfrac{8}{9},\, 0\right)$, $y$–intercept is $(0,\, 8)$

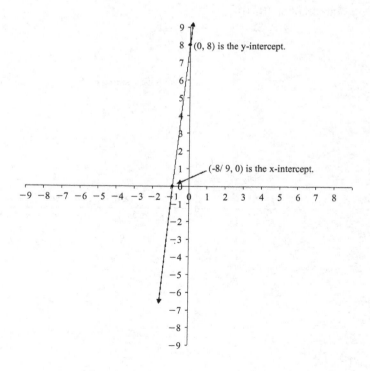

4) Both the $x$−intercept and the $y$−intercept are $(0,\ 0)$

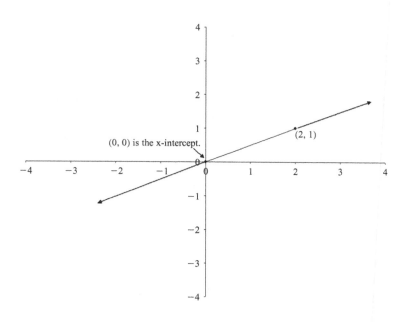

5) $x$−intercept is $\left(-\dfrac{5}{2},\ 0\right)$, $y$−intercept is $\left(0,\ \dfrac{5}{4}\right)$

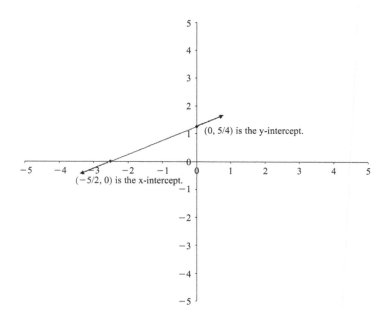

## Chapter 10, Set 10

1) slope is 0

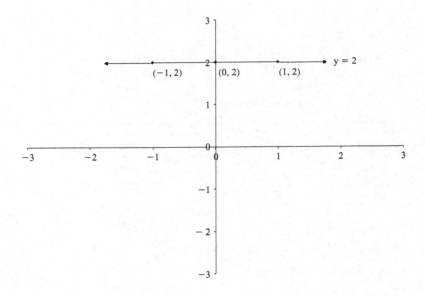

2) No slope

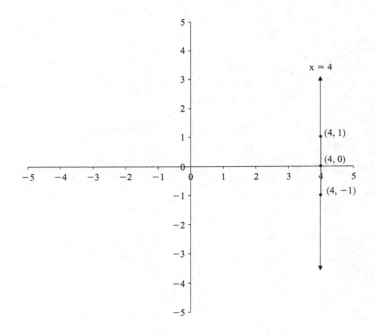

3) No slope

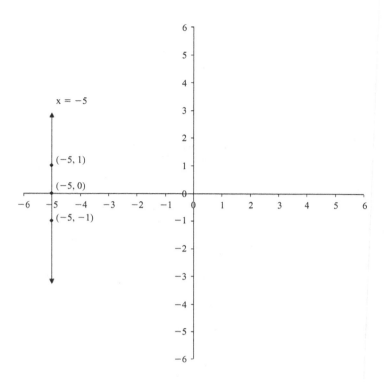

4) slope is 0

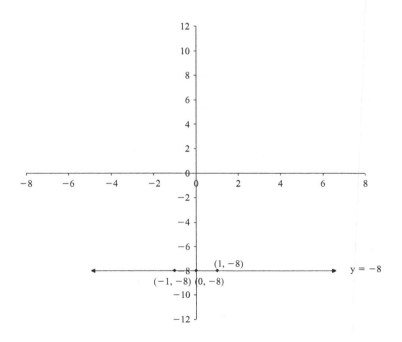

5) slope is 0

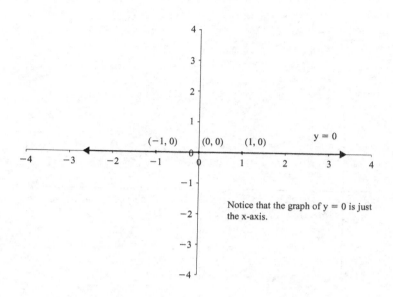

Notice that the graph of y = 0 is just the x-axis.

6) No slope

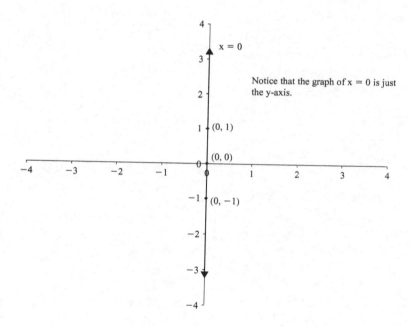

Notice that the graph of x = 0 is just the y-axis.

## Chapter 10, Set 11

I 1) Yes          2) No, since $m_1 = \dfrac{2}{5}$ and $m_2 = \dfrac{7}{8}$ are not equal.

II 1) $y = -2x + 12$

  2) $y = -\dfrac{9}{2}x - \dfrac{47}{2}$

## Chapter 10, Set 12

I 1) No, since $m_1 = -\dfrac{3}{10}$, $m_2 = \dfrac{7}{3}$ and $\left(-\dfrac{3}{10}\right)\left(\dfrac{7}{3}\right) \neq -1$.    2) Yes

II 1) $y = -\dfrac{1}{6}x - 1$
  2) $y = 2x - 13$

## Chapter 10, Set 13

I 1) $x = -4$
  2) $y = -1$

II 1) $y = 6$
  2) $x = -2$

## Chapter 11, Set 1

1) Is a function with domain $\{4, 8, 12, 16\}$ and range $\{-2, -1, 0, 1\}$.
2) Is a function with domain $\{5, 3, 1\}$ and range $\{0, 1\}$.
3) Is not a function.
4) Is a function with domain $\{1, 2, 3, 4\}$ and range $\{1, 3, 5, 7\}$.
5) Is a function with domain $\{0, -1, -2\}$ and range $\{0, -4, -5\}$.
6) Is not a function.

## Chapter 11, Set 2

1) $f(-1) = 5$, $f(5) = -7$ and $f(-4) = 11$.
2) $f(-1) = 9$, $f(5) = -9$ and $f(-4) = 45$.
3) $f(-1) = 3$, $f(5)$ does not exist and $f(-4) = 3\sqrt{3}$.
4) $f(-1) = -2$, $f(5) = \dfrac{8}{3}$ and $f(-4)$ does not exist.

## Chapter 11, Set 3

1) $(-\infty, \infty)$

2) $(-\infty, \infty)$

3) $\left\{x \mid x \neq \dfrac{5}{4}\right\}$

4) $[\dfrac{5}{2}, \infty)$

5) $(-\infty, \dfrac{19}{3}]$

6) $\{x \mid x \neq \pm 5\sqrt{7}\}$

## Chapter 12, Set 1

1) Yes        2) No        3) Yes        4) Yes        5) No

## Chapter 12, Set 2

1)

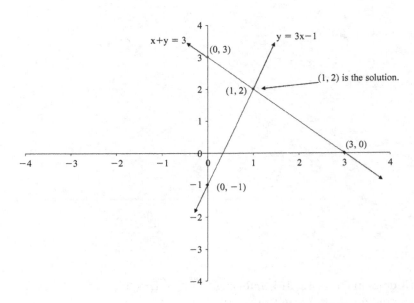

2)

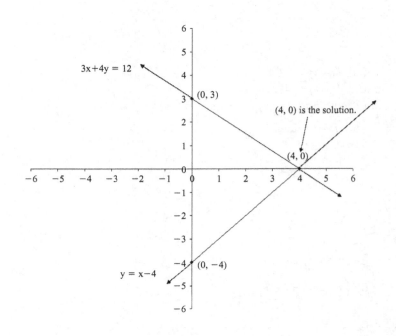

3)

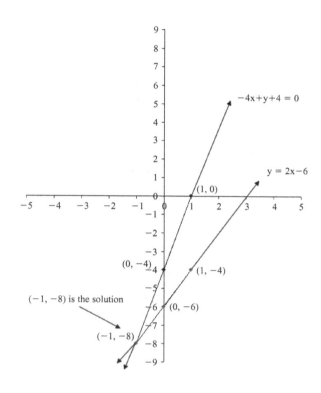

4)

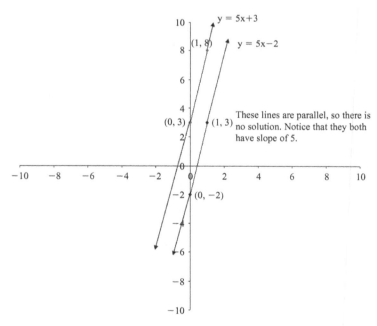

## Chapter 12, Set 3

1) $(2, 1)$    2) $\left(-\dfrac{11}{2}, -8\right)$    3) No solution    4) Infinitely many solutions

## Chapter 12, Set 4

1) $\left(4, -\dfrac{5}{2}\right)$    2) $\left(\dfrac{7}{3}, 1\right)$    3) $\left(\dfrac{15}{23}, -\dfrac{11}{23}\right)$    4) No solution

# SOLUTIONS TO ODD NUMBERED EXERCISES

**Chapter 1 Exercises**

1. 6 is a natural number, an integer and a rational number.

3. 10 is a natural number, an integer and a rational number.

5. $-4.18\overline{6}$ is a rational number.

7. 12.1963 is a rational number.

9. 18.131331333... is an irrational number.

11. 23.0 is a natural number, an integer and a rational number.

13. $\dfrac{1}{4} = 0.25$

$$
\begin{array}{r}
0.25 \\
4)\overline{1.00} \\
\underline{-8\phantom{0}} \\
20 \\
\underline{-20} \\
0
\end{array}
$$

15. $\dfrac{3}{2} = 1.5$

$$
\begin{array}{r}
1.5 \\
2)\overline{3.0} \\
\underline{-2\phantom{0}} \\
10 \\
\underline{-10} \\
0
\end{array}
$$

17. $\dfrac{1}{8} = 0.125$

$$
\begin{array}{r}
0.125 \\
8)\overline{1.000} \\
\underline{-8\phantom{00}} \\
20 \\
\underline{-16\phantom{0}} \\
40 \\
\underline{-40} \\
0
\end{array}
$$

19. $-\dfrac{1}{10} = -0.1$

$$
\begin{array}{r}
0.1 \\
10)\overline{1.0} \\
\underline{-1\,0} \\
0
\end{array}
$$

21. $\dfrac{17}{3} = 5.\overline{6}$

$$
\begin{array}{r}
5.66... \\
3\overline{)\,17.00...} \\
-15 \\
\hline
2\,0 \\
-1\,8 \\
\hline
20 \\
-\,18 \\
\hline
2 \\
\vdots
\end{array}
$$

23. $-\dfrac{1}{9} = -0.\overline{1}$

$$
\begin{array}{r}
0.11... \\
9\overline{)\,1.00...} \\
-\,9 \\
\hline
10 \\
-\,9 \\
\hline
1 \\
\vdots
\end{array}
$$

25. $\dfrac{18}{5} = 3.6$

$$
\begin{array}{r}
3.6 \\
5\overline{)\,18.00} \\
-15 \\
\hline
3\,0 \\
-\,3\,0 \\
\hline
0
\end{array}
$$

27. $\dfrac{16}{99} = 0.\overline{16}$

$$
\begin{array}{r}
0.1616... \\
99\overline{)\,16.000...} \\
-9\,9 \\
\hline
6\,10 \\
-\,5\,94 \\
\hline
160 \\
-\,99 \\
\hline
610 \\
-\,594 \\
\hline
16 \\
\vdots
\end{array}
$$

29. $\dfrac{100}{999} = 0.\overline{100}$

```
          0.100100...
   999) 100.000000...
        − 99 9
           1000
        −   999
           1000
        −   999
              1
              ⋮
```

31. $\dfrac{209}{990} = 0.2\overline{1}$

```
          0.211...
   990) 209.000...
        −198 0
          11 00
        −  9 90
           1 100
        −    990
            110
             ⋮
```

33. $-\dfrac{7}{15} = -0.4\overline{6}$

```
         0.466...
   15) 7.0000...
       − 6 0
         1 00
       −  90
          100
       −   90
           10
            ⋮
```

35. $\dfrac{35}{6} = 5.8\overline{3}$

$$
\begin{array}{r}
5.833... \\
6)\overline{35.0000...} \\
-30 \\ \hline
5\ 0 \\
-4\ 8 \\ \hline
20 \\
-\ 18 \\ \hline
20 \\
-\ 18 \\ \hline
2 \\
\vdots
\end{array}
$$

37. $\dfrac{18}{3} = 6$  39. $\dfrac{0}{14} = 0$  41. $\dfrac{59}{59} = 1$

43. $5 + (+8) = 13$  45. $(-7) + (-8) = -15$  47. $(-25) + (+9) = -16$

49. $(-2) + (+16) = 14$  51. $31 + (-16) = 15$  53. $-9 + 17 = 8$

55. $-21 + 6 = -15$  57. $-12 - 3 = (-12) + (-3) = -15$  59. $-5 - 15 = (-5) + (-15) = -20$

61. $7 - 15 = 7 + (-15) = -8$  63. $16 + (-16) = 0$  65. $-26 + 26 = 0$

67. $(+7)(-4) = -28$  69. $(-8)(+6) = -48$  71. $(3)(-16) = -48$

73. $(-9)(5) = -45$  75. $(-5)(-6) = 30$  77. $(-3)(-2) = 6$

79. $(+36) \div (-9) = -4$  81. $(-64) \div 4 = -16$  83. $45 \div (-5) = -9$

85. $(-35) \div (-5) = 7$  87. $(-60) \div (-10) = 6$  89. $\dfrac{-63}{+9} = -7$

91. $\dfrac{-14}{+7} = -2$  93. $\dfrac{-26}{2} = -13$  95. $\dfrac{-28}{-7} = 4$  97. $\dfrac{-64}{-16} = 4$

99. $\dfrac{4}{7} + \dfrac{3}{7} = \dfrac{7}{7} = 1$  101. $\dfrac{9}{13} - \dfrac{6}{13} = \dfrac{3}{13}$  103. $\dfrac{2}{9} + \dfrac{1}{9} = \dfrac{\cancel{3}^{1}}{\cancel{9}_{3}} = \dfrac{1}{3}$

105. $\dfrac{21}{10} - \dfrac{17}{10} = \dfrac{\cancel{4}^{2}}{\cancel{10}_{5}} = \dfrac{2}{5}$  107. $\dfrac{1}{2} + \dfrac{1}{4} = \dfrac{1(2)}{2(2)} + \dfrac{1}{4} = \dfrac{2}{4} + \dfrac{1}{4} = \dfrac{3}{4}$

109. $\dfrac{1}{3} + \dfrac{1}{6} = \dfrac{1(2)}{3(2)} + \dfrac{1}{6} = \dfrac{2}{6} + \dfrac{1}{6} = \dfrac{\cancel{3}^{1}}{\cancel{6}_{2}} = \dfrac{1}{2}$  111. $\dfrac{1}{4} - \dfrac{1}{12} = \dfrac{1(3)}{4(3)} - \dfrac{1}{12} = \dfrac{3}{12} - \dfrac{1}{12} = \dfrac{\cancel{2}^{1}}{\cancel{12}_{6}} = \dfrac{1}{6}$

113. $\dfrac{1}{8} - \dfrac{1}{16} = \dfrac{1(2)}{8(2)} - \dfrac{1}{16} = \dfrac{2}{16} - \dfrac{1}{16} = \dfrac{1}{16}$  115. $\dfrac{2}{7} + \dfrac{1}{3} = \dfrac{2(3)}{7(3)} + \dfrac{1(7)}{3(7)} = \dfrac{6}{21} + \dfrac{7}{21} = \dfrac{13}{21}$

117. $\dfrac{5}{6} + \dfrac{3}{8} = \dfrac{5(4)}{6(4)} + \dfrac{3(3)}{8(3)} = \dfrac{20}{24} + \dfrac{9}{24} = \dfrac{29}{24}$  119. $\dfrac{2}{3} - \dfrac{3}{5} = \dfrac{2(5)}{3(5)} - \dfrac{3(3)}{5(3)} = \dfrac{10}{15} - \dfrac{9}{15} = \dfrac{1}{15}$

121. $\dfrac{7}{10} - \dfrac{1}{4} = \dfrac{7(2)}{10(2)} - \dfrac{1(5)}{4(5)} = \dfrac{14}{20} - \dfrac{5}{20} = \dfrac{9}{20}$    123. $\left(-\dfrac{4}{5}\right) + \dfrac{1}{5} = -\dfrac{3}{5}$

125. $\dfrac{8}{13} + \left(-\dfrac{3}{13}\right) = \dfrac{5}{13}$    127. $\left(-\dfrac{1}{4}\right) + \left(-\dfrac{3}{4}\right) = \dfrac{-4}{4} = -1$

129. $\left(-\dfrac{2}{5}\right) + \left(-\dfrac{3}{10}\right) = \dfrac{-2(2)}{5(2)} + \left(\dfrac{-3}{10}\right) = \dfrac{-4}{10} + \left(\dfrac{-3}{10}\right) = \dfrac{-7}{15} = -\dfrac{7}{15}$

131. $-\dfrac{1}{8} - \dfrac{1}{8} = \dfrac{-1}{8} + \left(\dfrac{-1}{8}\right) = \dfrac{-\cancel{2}^{1}}{\cancel{8}_{4}} = -\dfrac{1}{4}$    133. $-\dfrac{2}{21} - \dfrac{5}{14} = \dfrac{-2(2)}{21(2)} + \left(\dfrac{-5(3)}{14(3)}\right) = \dfrac{-4}{42} + \left(\dfrac{-15}{42}\right) = -\dfrac{19}{42}$

135. $-\dfrac{1}{6} - \dfrac{1}{12} = \dfrac{-1(2)}{6(2)} - \dfrac{1}{12} = \dfrac{-2}{12} + \left(\dfrac{-1}{12}\right) = \dfrac{-\cancel{3}^{1}}{\cancel{12}_{4}} = \dfrac{-1}{4} = -\dfrac{1}{4}$

137. $-\dfrac{6}{7} + \dfrac{6}{7} = \dfrac{0}{7} = 0$    139. $\left(\dfrac{2}{5}\right)\left(\dfrac{1}{3}\right) = \dfrac{2}{15}$    141. $\left(\dfrac{7}{10}\right)\left(\dfrac{3}{4}\right) = \dfrac{21}{40}$

143. $\left(\dfrac{\cancel{4}^{1}}{1\cancel{7}}\right)\left(\dfrac{\cancel{21}^{3}}{\cancel{8}_{2}}\right) = \dfrac{3}{2}$    145. $\left(\dfrac{\overset{1}{\cancel{8}}}{\underset{1}{\cancel{15}}}\right)\left(\dfrac{\overset{2}{\cancel{30}}}{\underset{3}{\cancel{24}}}\right) = \dfrac{2}{3}$    147. $\left(-\dfrac{1}{6}\right)\left(\dfrac{1}{7}\right) = -\dfrac{1}{42}$

149. $\left(\dfrac{2}{3}\right)\left(-\dfrac{2}{5}\right) = -\dfrac{4}{15}$    151. $\left(-\dfrac{9}{\underset{2}{\cancel{10}}}\right)\left(\dfrac{\overset{3}{\cancel{15}}}{8}\right) = -\dfrac{27}{16}$    153. $\left(\dfrac{\overset{5}{\cancel{10}}}{11}\right)\left(-\dfrac{7}{\underset{4}{\cancel{8}}}\right) = -\dfrac{35}{44}$

155. $(15)\left(\dfrac{2}{3}\right) = \left(\dfrac{\overset{5}{\cancel{15}}}{1}\right)\left(\dfrac{2}{\cancel{3}_{1}}\right) = 10$    157. $(-6)\left(\dfrac{4}{9}\right) = \left(\dfrac{-\overset{2}{\cancel{6}}}{1}\right)\left(\dfrac{4}{\cancel{9}_{3}}\right) = -\dfrac{8}{3}$

159. $\left(-\dfrac{\overset{1}{\cancel{7}}}{\underset{2}{\cancel{12}}}\right)\left(-\dfrac{\overset{1}{\cancel{6}}}{\cancel{7}_{1}}\right) = \dfrac{1}{2}$    161. $\left(-\dfrac{5}{9}\right)(-21) = \left(-\dfrac{5}{\underset{3}{\cancel{9}}}\right)\left(\dfrac{-\overset{7}{\cancel{21}}}{1}\right) = \dfrac{35}{3}$

163. $\left(-\dfrac{\overset{1}{\cancel{3}}}{\underset{4}{\cancel{2}}}\right)\left(-\dfrac{\overset{5}{\cancel{10}}}{\underset{7}{\cancel{21}}}\right) = \dfrac{5}{14}$    165. $\dfrac{1}{3} \div \dfrac{2}{3} = \dfrac{1}{1\cancel{3}} \times \dfrac{\overset{1}{\cancel{3}}}{2} = \dfrac{1}{2}$

167. $\dfrac{2}{7} \div \dfrac{4}{5} = \dfrac{\overset{1}{\cancel{2}}}{7} \times \dfrac{5}{\cancel{4}_{2}} = \dfrac{5}{14}$    169. $\dfrac{9}{10} \div \dfrac{3}{4} = \dfrac{\overset{3}{\cancel{9}}}{\underset{5}{\cancel{10}}} \times \dfrac{\overset{2}{\cancel{4}}}{\cancel{3}_{1}} = \dfrac{6}{5}$

171. $\dfrac{1}{2} \div 8 = \dfrac{1}{2} \div \dfrac{8}{1} = \dfrac{1}{2} \times \dfrac{1}{8} = \dfrac{1}{16}$    173. $6 \div \dfrac{2}{3} = \dfrac{6}{1} \div \dfrac{2}{3} = \dfrac{\overset{3}{\cancel{6}}}{1} \times \dfrac{3}{\cancel{2}_{1}} = 9$

175. $\left(-\dfrac{3}{4}\right) \div \dfrac{1}{8} = \left(-\dfrac{3}{\cancel{4}_{1}}\right) \times \dfrac{\overset{2}{\cancel{8}}}{1} = -6$    177. $\left(-\dfrac{1}{2}\right) \div \dfrac{1}{2} = \left(-\dfrac{1}{2}\right) \times \dfrac{2}{1} = -1$

179. $\dfrac{5}{6} \div \left(-\dfrac{1}{3}\right) = \dfrac{5}{\cancel{6}_{2}} \times \left(-\dfrac{\overset{1}{\cancel{3}}}{1}\right) = -\dfrac{5}{2}$    181. $\dfrac{4}{5} \div (-5) = \dfrac{4}{5} \div \left(\dfrac{-5}{1}\right) = \dfrac{4}{5} \times \left(\dfrac{1}{-5}\right) = -\dfrac{4}{25}$

183. $\left(-\dfrac{4}{7}\right) \div \left(-\dfrac{1}{7}\right) = \left(-\dfrac{4}{\cancel{7}_{1}}\right) \times \left(-\dfrac{\overset{1}{\cancel{7}}}{1}\right) = 4$    185. $\left(-\dfrac{1}{6}\right) \div \left(-\dfrac{2}{9}\right) = \left(-\dfrac{1}{\underset{2}{\cancel{6}}}\right) \times \left(-\dfrac{\overset{3}{\cancel{9}}}{2}\right) = \dfrac{3}{4}$

187. $(-2) \div \left(-\dfrac{1}{2}\right) = (-2) \times \left(-\dfrac{2}{1}\right) = 4$    189. $\left(-\dfrac{5}{7}\right) \div (-5) = \left(-\dfrac{5}{7}\right) \div \left(\dfrac{-5}{1}\right) = \left(-\dfrac{\overset{1}{\cancel{5}}}{7}\right) \times \left(\dfrac{1}{-\cancel{5}_{1}}\right) = \dfrac{1}{7}$

191. $\left(-\dfrac{1}{2}\right) \div (-1) = \left(-\dfrac{1}{2}\right) \times (-1) = \dfrac{1}{2}$     193. $1 \div \left(-\dfrac{7}{16}\right) = 1 \times \left(-\dfrac{16}{7}\right) = -\dfrac{16}{7}$

195. $0 \div \left(-\dfrac{3}{20}\right) = 0$     197. $\underbrace{5(2)} + 6 = 10 + 6 = 16$     199. $\underbrace{9(-3)} + 16 = -27 + 16 = -9$

201. $\underbrace{3(-7)} - 2 = -21 - 2 = -23$     203. $6 - \underbrace{5 \times 7} = 6 - 35 = -29$     205. $6\underbrace{(2+8)} = 6(10) = 60$

207. $\underbrace{(7-12)} \times 3 = (-5) \times 3 = -15$     209. $\underbrace{(10+6)} \times (-4) = (16) \times (-4) = -64$

211. $(-1) + \underbrace{24 \div 8} = (-1) + 3 = 2$     213. $-11 - \underbrace{8 \div 4} = -11 - 2 = -13$

215. $\underbrace{(-11-9)} \div 4 = (-20) \div 4 = -5$   217. $\underbrace{7-12} - 3 + 4 = \underbrace{-5-3} + 4 = -8 + 4 = -4$

219. $\underbrace{12 \times 4} \div 2 \times 3 = \underbrace{48 \div 2} \times 3 = 24 \times 3 = 72$     221. $\underbrace{(7-12)} - \underbrace{(3+4)} = (-5) - (7) = -12$

223. $\underbrace{(12 \times 4)} \div \underbrace{(2 \times 3)} = (48) \div (6) = 8$     225. $\underbrace{5^2} + 4 = 25 + 4 = 29$

227. $(5+4)^2 = (9)^2 = 81$     229. $7 + \underbrace{6 \times 3} - \underbrace{5 \times 2} = \underbrace{7 + 18} - 10 = 25 - 10 = 15$

231. $\underbrace{(7+6)} \times \underbrace{(3-5)} \div 2 = \underbrace{(13) \times (-2)} \div 2 = (-26) \div 2 = -13$

233. $(4+2)^2 (5-7) = \underbrace{(6)^2} (-2) = (36)(-2) = -72$

235. $-10 - \underbrace{(-5)^2} \times 2 = -10 - \underbrace{25 \times 2} = -10 - 50 = -60$

237. $\dfrac{1 + 2 \overbrace{(4-15)}}{\underbrace{2^2} + 3} = \dfrac{1 + \overbrace{2(-11)}}{\underbrace{4+3}} = \dfrac{1 + (-22)}{7} = \dfrac{-21}{7} = -3$

239. $-1 + 5 \left\{ 2 - 8 \underbrace{(9-7)} \right\} = -1 + 5 \left\{ 2 - \underbrace{8(2)} \right\} = -1 + 5 \underbrace{\{2 - 16\}} = -1 + \underbrace{5\{-14\}} = -1 + (-70) = -71$

241. $12 + \underbrace{(4+1)^2} (-2) = 12 + \underbrace{(5)^2} (-2) = 12 + \underbrace{25(-2)} = 12 + (-50) = -38$

243. $(-4) \left(\dfrac{1}{6}\right) \left(-\dfrac{9}{10}\right) = \left(\dfrac{-4}{1}\right) \left(\dfrac{1}{6}\right) \left(-\dfrac{9}{10}\right) = \dfrac{3}{5}$

245. $5 + 3 \left(-\dfrac{1}{12}\right) = 5 + \dfrac{3}{1} \left(-\dfrac{1}{12}\right) = 5 + \left(-\dfrac{\overset{1}{\cancel{3}}}{\underset{4}{\cancel{12}}}\right) = \dfrac{5}{1} + \left(-\dfrac{1}{4}\right) = \dfrac{20}{4} + \left(-\dfrac{1}{4}\right) = \dfrac{19}{4}$

247. $\underbrace{(5+3)} \left(-\dfrac{1}{12}\right) = (8) \left(-\dfrac{1}{12}\right) = \left(\dfrac{\overset{2}{\cancel{8}}}{1}\right) \left(-\dfrac{1}{\underset{3}{\cancel{12}}}\right) = -\dfrac{2}{3}$

249. $\dfrac{4}{5} - \dfrac{1}{30} - \dfrac{2}{3} = \dfrac{4(6)}{5(6)} - \dfrac{1}{30} - \dfrac{2(10)}{3(10)} = \dfrac{24}{30} - \dfrac{1}{30} - \dfrac{20}{30} = \dfrac{23}{30} - \dfrac{20}{30} = \dfrac{\overset{1}{\cancel{3}}}{\underset{10}{\cancel{30}}} = \dfrac{1}{10}$

251. $\dfrac{4}{5} - \underbrace{\left(\dfrac{1}{30} - \dfrac{2}{3}\right)}_{} = \dfrac{4}{5} - \left(\dfrac{1}{30} - \dfrac{2(10)}{3(10)}\right) = \dfrac{4}{5} - \left(\dfrac{1}{30} - \dfrac{20}{30}\right) = \dfrac{4}{5} - \left(-\dfrac{19}{30}\right)$

$\qquad = \dfrac{4}{5} + \dfrac{19}{30} = \dfrac{4(6)}{5(6)} + \dfrac{19}{30} = \dfrac{24}{30} + \dfrac{19}{30} = \dfrac{43}{30}$

253. $\dfrac{1}{2} + 10 \div \underbrace{\dfrac{5}{7}}_{} = \dfrac{1}{2} + \dfrac{10}{1} \times \dfrac{7}{5} = \dfrac{1}{2} + \dfrac{14}{1} = \dfrac{1}{2} + \dfrac{14(2)}{1(2)} = \dfrac{1}{2} + \dfrac{28}{2} = \dfrac{29}{2}$

255. $\underbrace{\left(\dfrac{1}{2} + 10\right)}_{} \div \dfrac{5}{7} = \left(\dfrac{1}{2} + \dfrac{10(2)}{1(2)}\right) \div \dfrac{5}{7} = \underbrace{\left(\dfrac{1}{2} + \dfrac{20}{2}\right)}_{} \div \dfrac{5}{7} = \left(\dfrac{21}{2}\right) \div \dfrac{5}{7} = \left(\dfrac{21}{2}\right) \times \dfrac{7}{5} = \dfrac{147}{10}$

257. $\dfrac{2}{5} + \dfrac{2}{5} - \underbrace{\dfrac{2}{5} \times \dfrac{2}{5}}_{} = \underbrace{\dfrac{2}{5} + \dfrac{2}{5}}_{} - \dfrac{4}{25} = \dfrac{4}{5} - \dfrac{4}{25} = \dfrac{4(5)}{5(5)} - \dfrac{4}{25} = \dfrac{20}{25} - \dfrac{4}{25} = \dfrac{16}{25}$

259. $\dfrac{2}{5} + \underbrace{\left(\dfrac{2}{5} - \dfrac{2}{5}\right)}_{} \times \dfrac{2}{5} = \dfrac{2}{5} + \underbrace{(0) \times \dfrac{2}{5}}_{} = \dfrac{2}{5} + 0 = \dfrac{2}{5}$

261. 0.273 : rounded off **and** truncated to two decimals is 0.27.

263. 6.1129 : rounded off **and** truncated to two decimals is 6.11.

265. 14.3186 : rounded off to two decimals is 14.32 and truncated to two decimals is 14.31.

267. 123.65523 : rounded off to two decimals is 123.66 and truncated to two decimals is 123.65.

269. 1.19923 : rounded off to two decimals is 1.20 and truncated to two decimals is 1.19.

271. 0.0005 : rounded off **and** truncated to two decimals is 0.00.

273. 19.9992 : rounded off to two decimals is 20.00 and truncated to two decimals is 19.99.

275. 100.50505 : rounded off to two decimals is 100.51 and truncated to two decimals is 100.50.

277. $x + 5 = \underline{5} + x$ is the commutative property (for addition).

279. $4(7 + 2) = 4(7) + 4(\underline{2})$ is the distributive property.

281. $2 \times (\underline{6} \times 7) = (2 \times 6) \times 7$ is the associative property (for multiplication).

283. $(-4)[(2)(\underline{-12})] = [(-4)(2)](-12)$ is the associative property (for multiplication).

285. $(\underline{6} + 5)y = 6(y) + 5(y)$ is the distributive property.

287. $6 + (\underline{-6}) = 0$ is the additive inverse property.

289. $(-7)\left(\dfrac{1}{\underline{-7}}\right) = 1$ is the multiplicative inverse (or reciprocal) property.

291. $a + \underline{0} = a$ is the additive identity property.

293. $\left(\dfrac{7}{9}\right)(-5) = (\underline{-5})\left(\dfrac{7}{9}\right)$ is the commutative property (for multiplication).

295. $7 < 16$

297. $\dfrac{1}{3} > \dfrac{1}{6}$

299. $-6 < 13$

301. $-15 < -4$

303. $0 > -13$

305. $\dfrac{1}{9} > 0.11$

307. $0.333 < \dfrac{1}{3}$

309. $0.17 < \dfrac{17}{99}$

311. $-12.0115 < -12.011$

313. $-\dfrac{5}{9} < -0.05$

315. $\pi > 3.1$

317. $|9| = 9$

319. $|-7| = 7$

321. $|+25| = 25$

323. $|-30| = 30$

325. $\left|-\dfrac{5}{6}\right| = \dfrac{5}{6}$

327. $|0.754| = 0.754$

329. $|16 - 7| = |9| = 9$

331. $|6 - 23| = |-17| = 17$

333. $|-5 - 5| = |-10| = 10$

335. $|0 - 12 + 5| = |-7| = 7$

337. $\underbrace{|3|}_{} - \underbrace{|-4|}_{} = 3 - 4 = -1$

339. $\underbrace{|-10|}_{} + \underbrace{|-18|}_{} = 10 + 18 = 28$

341. $\left|-\dfrac{1}{2} - \dfrac{2}{7}\right| = \left|-\dfrac{1(7)}{2(7)} - \dfrac{2(2)}{7(2)}\right| = \left|-\dfrac{7}{14} - \dfrac{4}{14}\right| = \left|-\dfrac{11}{14}\right| = \dfrac{11}{14}$

343. $\left|-\dfrac{1}{2}\right| - \left|\dfrac{2}{7}\right| = \dfrac{1}{2} - \dfrac{2}{7} = \dfrac{1(7)}{2(7)} - \dfrac{2(2)}{7(2)} = \dfrac{7}{14} - \dfrac{4}{14} = \dfrac{3}{14}$

345. The distance between $\underbrace{9}_{a}$ and $\underbrace{2}_{b}$ is $|b - a| = |2 - 9| = |-7| = 7$.

347. The distance between $\underbrace{-3}_{a}$ and $\underbrace{0}_{b}$ is $|b - a| = |0 - (-3)| = |3| = 3$.

349. The distance between $\underbrace{-15}_{a}$ and $\underbrace{17}_{b}$ is $|b - a| = |17 - (-15)| = |32| = 32$.

351. The distance between $\underbrace{-\dfrac{5}{6}}_{a}$ and $\underbrace{\dfrac{3}{8}}_{b}$ is $|b - a| = \left|\dfrac{3}{8} - \left(-\dfrac{5}{6}\right)\right| = \left|\dfrac{3(3)}{8(3)} + \dfrac{5(4)}{6(4)}\right|$

$$= \left|\dfrac{9}{24} + \dfrac{20}{24}\right| = \left|\dfrac{29}{24}\right| = \dfrac{29}{24}.$$

353. The distance between $\underbrace{-6}_{a}$ and $\underbrace{-28}_{b}$ is $|b - a| = |-28 - (-6)| = |-28 + 6| = |-22| = 22$.

355. The distance between $\underbrace{-\dfrac{3}{16}}_{a}$ and $\underbrace{-\dfrac{7}{6}}_{b}$ is $|b - a| = \left|-\dfrac{7}{6} - \left(-\dfrac{3}{16}\right)\right| = \left|-\dfrac{7(8)}{6(8)} + \dfrac{3(3)}{16(3)}\right|$

$$= \left|-\dfrac{56}{48} + \dfrac{9}{48}\right| = \left|\dfrac{-47}{48}\right| = \dfrac{47}{48}.$$

357. $|4x| = |4| \cdot |x| = 4|x|$

359. $|-14a| = |-14| \cdot |a| = 14|a|$

361. $|5x^2| = |5| \cdot |x^2| = 5x^2$

363. $|-27a^2| = |-27| \cdot |a^2| = 27a^2$

365. $\left|\dfrac{6}{x}\right| = \dfrac{|6|}{|x|} = \dfrac{6}{|x|}$

367. $\left|\dfrac{-16}{x^2}\right| = \dfrac{|-16|}{|x^2|} = \dfrac{16}{x^2}$

369. $3(4) - 2(-3) + (0) = 12 + 6 + 0 = 18$

371. $2(4)^2 + (-3) + 3(0) = 2(16) - 3 + 0 = 32 - 3 + 0 = 29$

373. $3(4)(-3) + 2(-3)(0) - 7(4)(0) = -36 + 0 - 0 = -36$

375. $\dfrac{-2(4) + 3(-3)}{-2(-3) + 5(0)} = \dfrac{-8 + (-9)}{6 + 0} = \dfrac{-17}{6}$          377. $(4)^2 + 3(4) - 12 = 16 + 12 - 12 = 16$

379. $(0)^2 + (0) + 18 = 0 + 0 + 18 = 18$          381. $\dfrac{1}{4} + \dfrac{1}{-3} = \dfrac{3}{12} + \dfrac{-4}{12} = \dfrac{-1}{12} = -\dfrac{1}{12}$

383. $|5(4) + 7(-3)| = |20 + (-21)| = |-1| = 1$          385. $|5(4)| + |7(-3)| = |20| + |-21| = 20 + 21 = 41$

387. The domain of the variable $x$ for the expression $\dfrac{4}{x - 1}$ is the set of all real numbers except 1, since

$$\begin{aligned} x - \cancel{1} &= 0 \qquad \text{(which is bad)} \\ \underline{+\cancel{1} \ +1} & \\ x \ &= 1 \end{aligned}$$

389. The domain of the variable $x$ for the expression $\dfrac{-8}{x + 7}$ is the set of all real numbers except $-7$, since

$$\begin{aligned} x + \cancel{7} &= 0 \qquad \text{(which is bad)} \\ \underline{-\cancel{7} \ - 7} & \\ x \ &= -7 \end{aligned}$$

391. The domain of the variable $x$ for the expression $\dfrac{1}{5 - x}$ is the set of all real numbers except 5, since

$$\begin{aligned} 5 - \cancel{x} &= 0 \qquad \text{(which is bad)} \\ \underline{+\cancel{x} \ + x} & \\ 5 \ &= x \end{aligned}$$

393. The domain of the variable $x$ for the expression $\dfrac{15}{3 + x}$ is the set of all real numbers except $-3$, since

$$\begin{aligned} \cancel{3} + x &= 0 \qquad \text{(which is bad)} \\ \underline{-\cancel{3} \qquad - 3} & \\ x &= -3 \end{aligned}$$

395. The area is $A = \dfrac{1}{2}bh = \dfrac{1}{2}(8)(4) = \dfrac{1}{2}(32) = 16 \text{ in}^2$.

397. The volume is $V = s^3 = 4^3 = 64 \text{ ft}^3$.

399. $C = \dfrac{5}{9}(F - 32) = \dfrac{5}{9}(212 - 32) = \dfrac{5}{9}(180) = \dfrac{5}{\cancel{9}}\left(\dfrac{\overset{20}{\cancel{180}}}{1}\right) = 100° \ C.$

## Chapter 2 Exercise 2.1

1. $5^2 = (5)(5) = 25$     3. $\left(\dfrac{3}{4}\right)^3 = \left(\dfrac{3}{4}\right)\left(\dfrac{3}{4}\right)\left(\dfrac{3}{4}\right) = \dfrac{27}{64}$     5. $\left(-\dfrac{2}{11}\right)^2 = \left(-\dfrac{2}{11}\right)\left(-\dfrac{2}{11}\right) = \dfrac{4}{121}$

7. $-6^2 = -(6)(6) = -36$     9. $\left(-\dfrac{1}{3}\right)^5 = \left(-\dfrac{1}{3}\right)\left(-\dfrac{1}{3}\right)\left(-\dfrac{1}{3}\right)\left(-\dfrac{1}{3}\right)\left(-\dfrac{1}{3}\right) = -\dfrac{1}{243}$

11. $-4^3 = -(4)(4)(4) = -64$     13. $7^0 = 1$     15. $(-10)^0 = 1$

17. $\dfrac{5^6}{5^5} = 5^{6-5} = 5^1 = 5$     19. $\dfrac{(-3)^8}{(-3)^5} = (-3)^{8-5} = (-3)^3 = (-3)(-3)(-3) = -27$

21. $\dfrac{4^6}{4^8} = 4^{6-8} = 4^{-2} = \dfrac{1}{4^2} = \dfrac{1}{(4)(4)} = \dfrac{1}{16}$     23. $\dfrac{(-5)^5}{(-5)^6} = (-5)^{5-6} = (-5)^{-1} = \dfrac{1}{(-5)^1} = \dfrac{1}{-5} = -\dfrac{1}{5}$

25. $6^{-1} = \dfrac{1}{6^1} = \dfrac{1}{6}$     27. $9^{-2} = \dfrac{1}{9^2} = \dfrac{1}{(9)(9)} = \dfrac{1}{81}$     29. $5^{-3} = \dfrac{1}{5^3} = \dfrac{1}{(5)(5)(5)} = \dfrac{1}{125}$

31. $-8^{-2} = -\dfrac{1}{8^2} = -\dfrac{1}{(8)(8)} = -\dfrac{1}{64}$     33. $(-7)^{-3} = \dfrac{1}{(-7)^3} = \dfrac{1}{(-7)(-7)(-7)} = \dfrac{1}{-343} = -\dfrac{1}{343}$

35. $(-6)^{-2} = \dfrac{1}{(-6)^2} = \dfrac{1}{(-6)(-6)} = \dfrac{1}{36}$     37. $\left(3^2\right)^2 = 3^{2(2)} = 3^4 = (3)(3)(3)(3) = 81$

39. $\left(4^3\right)^{-1} = 4^{3(-1)} = 4^{-3} = \dfrac{1}{4^3} = \dfrac{1}{(4)(4)(4)} = \dfrac{1}{64}$ or $\left(4^3\right)^{-1} = (64)^{-1} = \dfrac{1}{(64)^1} = \dfrac{1}{64}$

41. $\dfrac{555^2}{111^2} = \left(\dfrac{\overset{5}{\cancel{555}}}{\underset{1}{\cancel{111}}}\right)^2 = 5^2 = (5)(5) = 25$     43. $\dfrac{1,000^5}{(-1,000)^5} = \left(\dfrac{\overset{1}{\cancel{1,000}}}{\underset{}{\cancel{-1,000}}}\right)^5 = (-1)^5 = -1$

45. $y^2 \cdot y^6 = y^{2+6} = y^8$     47. $t \cdot t^8 = t^{1+8} = t^9$     49. $\left(a^3\right)\left(a^7\right)\left(a^2\right) = a^{3+7+2} = a^{12}$

51. $\left(-5x^2\right)\left(8x^3\right) = -40x^{2+3} = -40x^5$     53. $\left(6x^7 y\right)\left(x^3 y^2\right) = 6x^{7+3}y^{1+2} = 6x^{10}y^3$

55. $\left(4a^4 b^3\right)\left(5a^2 b^5\right) = 20a^{4+2}b^{3+5} = 20a^6 b^8$     57. $\dfrac{x^9}{x^4} = x^{9-4} = x^5$     59. $\dfrac{\overset{7}{\cancel{-35}}s^7 t^4}{\underset{1}{\cancel{-5}}s^4 t} = 7s^{7-4}t^{4-1} = 7s^3 t^3$

61. $\dfrac{\overset{8}{\cancel{-24}}x^{15}y^{13}}{\underset{3}{\cancel{9}}x^{11}y^2} = -\dfrac{8}{3}x^{15-11}y^{13-2} = -\dfrac{8}{3}x^4 y^{11}$     63. $7x^0 = 7(1) = 7$

65. $-2t^3\left(5s^6 t^3\right)^0 = -2t^3(1) = -2t^3$     67. $x^{-3} = \dfrac{1}{x^3}$     69. $-y^{-8} = -\dfrac{1}{y^8}$

71. $x^{-3} \cdot x^{-4} = x^{-3+(-4)} = x^{-7} = \dfrac{1}{x^7}$     73. $t^{-6} \cdot t^{10} = t^{-6+10} = t^4$

75. $\dfrac{y^4}{y^{-6}} = y^{4-(-6)} = y^{10}$

77. $\underbrace{\dfrac{-15x^0y^{-1}}{-3x^5y^{-7}} = \dfrac{5y^{-1-(-7)}}{x^5}}_{\frac{-15}{-3}=5,\ x^0=1\ \text{and}\ \frac{y^{-1}}{y^{-7}}=y^{-1-(-7)}} = \dfrac{5y^6}{x^5}$

79. $\left(x^5\right)^3 = x^{5(3)} = x^{15}$

81. $\left(t^{-4}\right)^4 = t^{-4(4)} = t^{-16} = \dfrac{1}{t^{16}}$

83. $\left(x^0\right)^{-2} = (1)^{-2} = \dfrac{1}{1^2} = \dfrac{1}{1} = 1$

85. $(2x)^4 = 2^4x^4 = 16x^4$

87. $\left(-4x^2y^9\right)^3 = (-4)^3\left(x^2\right)^3\left(y^9\right)^3 = -64x^{2(3)}y^{9(3)} = -64x^6y^{27}$

89. $(5t)^{-3} = \dfrac{1}{(5t)^3} = \dfrac{1}{5^3t^3} = \dfrac{1}{125t^3}$

91. $\left(8x^3y\right)^{-1} = \dfrac{1}{\left(8x^3y\right)^1} = \dfrac{1}{8x^3y}$

93. $\left(\dfrac{3}{7}a^2b^7\right)^2 = \left(\dfrac{3}{7}\right)^2\left(a^2\right)^2\left(b^7\right)^2 = \dfrac{9}{49}a^{2(2)}b^{7(2)} = \dfrac{9}{49}a^4b^{14}$

95. $\left(\dfrac{x}{y}\right)^8 = \dfrac{x^8}{y^8}$

97. $\left(-\dfrac{5}{a^8}\right)^2 = \dfrac{(-5)^2}{\left(a^8\right)^2} = \dfrac{25}{a^{8(2)}} = \dfrac{25}{a^{16}}$

99. $\left(\dfrac{10x^4}{y^3}\right)^4 = \dfrac{10^4\left(x^4\right)^4}{\left(y^3\right)^4} = \dfrac{10,000x^{4(4)}}{y^{3(4)}} = \dfrac{10,000x^{16}}{y^{12}}$

101. $\left(-\dfrac{3m^7}{8n^{12}}\right)^2 = \dfrac{(-3)^2\left(m^7\right)^2}{8^2\left(n^{12}\right)^2} = \dfrac{9m^{7(2)}}{64n^{12(2)}} = \dfrac{9m^{14}}{64n^{24}}$

103. $-3a^4\left(4a^2\right)^2 = -3a^4\left(4^2\left(a^2\right)^2\right) = -3a^4\left(16a^{2(2)}\right) = -3a^4\left(16a^4\right) = -48a^{4+4} = -48a^8$

105. $\left(9x^4\right)^2\left(8x^5\right)^0 = 9^2\left(x^4\right)^2(1) = 81x^{4(2)} = 81x^8$

107. $\left(m^3n^9\right)^3\left(-5mn^{14}\right)^3 = \left(m^3\right)^3\left(n^9\right)^3(-5)^3m^3\left(n^{14}\right)^3 = -125m^{3(3)}n^{9(3)}m^3n^{14(3)}$

$$= -125m^9n^{27}m^3n^{42} = -125m^{9+3}n^{27+42} = -125m^{12}n^{69}$$

109. $\left(\dfrac{-11a^5}{4b^2}\right)^2 \cdot \dfrac{(-9a)^0}{2b^6} = \dfrac{(-11)^2\left(a^5\right)^2}{4^2\left(b^2\right)^2} \cdot \dfrac{1}{2b^6} = \dfrac{121a^{5(2)}}{16b^{2(2)}} \cdot \dfrac{1}{2b^6}$

$$= \dfrac{121a^{10}}{16b^4} \cdot \dfrac{1}{2b^6} = \dfrac{121a^{10}}{32b^{4+6}} = \dfrac{121a^{10}}{32b^{10}}$$

111. $\dfrac{\left(-3x^0y^{12}\right)^2}{-2\left(9x^5y\right)^2} \cdot \dfrac{\left(-3x^0y^{12}\right)^0}{(-4x)^3} = \dfrac{(-3)^2\left(y^{12}\right)^2}{-2\left(9^2\left(x^5\right)^2y^2\right)} \cdot \dfrac{1}{(-4)^3x^3} = \dfrac{9y^{12(2)}}{-2\left(81x^{5(2)}y^2\right)} \cdot \dfrac{1}{-64x^3}$

$$= \dfrac{\overset{1}{\cancel{9}}y^{24}}{-2(\underset{9}{\cancel{81}}x^{10}y^2)} \cdot \dfrac{1}{-64x^3} = \dfrac{y^{24}}{-2\left(9x^{10}y^2\right)} \cdot \dfrac{1}{-64x^3}$$

$$= \dfrac{y^{24}}{-18x^{10}y^2} \cdot \dfrac{1}{-64x^3} = \dfrac{y^{24}}{1,152x^{10}y^2x^3} = \dfrac{y^{24-2}}{1,152x^{10+3}}$$

$$= \dfrac{y^{22}}{1,152x^{13}}$$

## Chapter 2 Exercise 2.2

1. $\left(\dfrac{1}{2}\right)^{-1} = \left(\dfrac{2}{1}\right)^{1} = 2^1 = 2$

3. $\left(\dfrac{2}{3}\right)^{-1} = \left(\dfrac{3}{2}\right)^{1} = \dfrac{3}{2}$

5. $\left(\dfrac{3}{7}\right)^{-2} = \left(\dfrac{7}{3}\right)^{2} = \dfrac{49}{9}$

7. $\left(\dfrac{4}{7}\right)^{-3} = \left(\dfrac{7}{4}\right)^{3} = \dfrac{343}{64}$

9. $\dfrac{4^2}{3^{-1}} = \dfrac{4^2 \cdot 3^1}{1} = \dfrac{16 \cdot 3}{1} = \dfrac{48}{1} = 48$

11. $\dfrac{2^{-3}}{4^2} = \dfrac{1}{2^3 \cdot 4^2} = \dfrac{1}{8 \cdot 16} = \dfrac{1}{128}$

13. $\dfrac{(-9)^{-2}}{(-2)^1} = \dfrac{1}{(-9)^2(-2)^1} = \dfrac{1}{81(-2)} = -\dfrac{1}{162}$

15. $\dfrac{5^{-2}}{3^{-4}} = \dfrac{3^4}{5^2} = \dfrac{81}{25}$

17. $\dfrac{(-9)^{-2}}{-4^{-3}} = -\dfrac{4^3}{(-9)^2} = -\dfrac{64}{81}$

19. $\dfrac{7^1 \cdot 3^{-2}}{7^{-1} \cdot 3^2} = \dfrac{7^1 \cdot 7^1}{3^2 \cdot 3^2} = \dfrac{7 \cdot 7}{9 \cdot 9} = \dfrac{49}{81}$

21. $\dfrac{9^{-3} \cdot 7^0}{9^{-2} \cdot 7^{-2}} = \dfrac{9^2 \cdot 7^2}{9^3} = \dfrac{1 \cdot 49}{9^1} = \dfrac{49}{9}$

23. $2^4 \cdot 3^0 \cdot 6^{-1} = \dfrac{2^4 \cdot 3^0 \cdot 6^{-1}}{1} = \dfrac{2^4 \cdot 1}{6^1} = \dfrac{\overset{8}{\cancel{16}}}{\underset{3}{\cancel{6}}} = \dfrac{8}{3}$

25. $\dfrac{5^0}{6^{-3}} = \dfrac{1}{6^{-3}} = \dfrac{6^3}{1} = \dfrac{216}{1} = 216$

27. $\dfrac{5^{-2}}{4^0} = \dfrac{5^{-2}}{1} = \dfrac{1}{5^2} = \dfrac{1}{25}$

29. $\dfrac{(-4)^{-2} \cdot 2^{-1}}{3^2 \cdot (-5)^{-1}} = \dfrac{(-5)^1}{(-4)^2 \cdot 3^2 \cdot 2^1} = \dfrac{-5}{16 \cdot 9 \cdot 2} = -\dfrac{5}{288}$

31. $\left(\dfrac{2}{3}\right)^{-2} + \left(\dfrac{4}{7}\right)^{-1} = \left(\dfrac{3}{2}\right)^{2} + \left(\dfrac{7}{4}\right)^{1} = \dfrac{9}{4} + \dfrac{7}{4} = \dfrac{16}{4} = 4$

33. $\left(\dfrac{3}{4}\right)^{-3} - 2\left(\dfrac{9}{2}\right)^{-1} = \left(\dfrac{4}{3}\right)^{3} - 2\left(\dfrac{2}{9}\right)^{1} = \dfrac{64}{27} - \dfrac{2}{1}\left(\dfrac{2}{9}\right) = \dfrac{64}{27} - \dfrac{4}{9} = \dfrac{64}{27} - \dfrac{12}{27} = \dfrac{52}{27}$

35. $\left(\dfrac{1}{9}\right)^{0} - \dfrac{7}{4}\left(\dfrac{3}{2}\right)^{-2} = 1 - \dfrac{7}{4}\left(\dfrac{2}{3}\right)^{2} = 1 - \dfrac{7}{4}\left(\dfrac{4}{9}\right) = 1 - \dfrac{7}{9} = \dfrac{9}{9} - \dfrac{7}{9} = \dfrac{2}{9}$

37. $\left(\dfrac{x}{9}\right)^{-1} = \left(\dfrac{9}{x}\right)^{1} = \dfrac{9}{x}$

39. $\left(\dfrac{a}{8}\right)^{-2} = \left(\dfrac{8}{a}\right)^{2} = \dfrac{64}{a^2}$

41. $\left(\dfrac{4a}{7}\right)^{-2} = \left(\dfrac{7}{4a}\right)^{2} = \dfrac{49}{16a^2}$

43. $\left(\dfrac{6}{5x^3}\right)^{-3} = \left(\dfrac{5x^3}{6}\right)^{3} = \dfrac{125x^9}{216}$

45. $\left(\dfrac{10m^2}{3n^{12}}\right)^{-2} = \left(\dfrac{3n^{12}}{10m^2}\right)^{2} = \dfrac{9n^{24}}{100m^4}$

47. $5x^{-4}y^6z^0 = \dfrac{5x^{-4}y^6z^0}{1} = \dfrac{5y^6}{x^4}$

49. $\left(6a^6b^{-1}\right)^{-2} = \dfrac{\left(6a^6b^{-1}\right)^{-2}}{1} = \dfrac{1}{\left(6a^6b^{-1}\right)^2} = \dfrac{1}{36a^{12}b^{-2}} = \dfrac{b^2}{36a^{12}}$

51. $\left(\dfrac{x^{-3}}{y^7}\right)^{-2} = \left(\dfrac{y^7}{x^{-3}}\right)^{2} = \dfrac{y^{14}}{x^{-6}} = \dfrac{x^6 y^{14}}{1} = x^6 y^{14}$

53. $\left(\dfrac{a^0}{b^{-5}}\right)^{-3} = \left(\dfrac{1}{b^{-5}}\right)^{-3} = \left(\dfrac{b^{-5}}{1}\right)^{3} = b^{-15} = \dfrac{1}{b^{15}}$

55. $\left(\dfrac{3x^{-1}}{4x^0}\right)^{-1} = \left(\dfrac{4x^0}{3x^{-1}}\right)^{1} = \dfrac{4x^0}{3x^{-1}} = \dfrac{4}{3x^{-1}} = \dfrac{4x}{3}$

57. $\left(\dfrac{x^2}{6}\right)^{-2} \cdot \left(\dfrac{x^4}{2}\right)^{-1} = \left(\dfrac{6}{x^2}\right)^2 \cdot \left(\dfrac{2}{x^4}\right)^1 = \dfrac{36}{x^4} \cdot \dfrac{2}{x^4} = \dfrac{72}{x^8}$

59. $\left(\dfrac{12}{t^7}\right)^{-2} \cdot \left(\dfrac{t^5}{12}\right)^{-1} = \left(\dfrac{t^7}{12}\right)^2 \cdot \left(\dfrac{12}{t^5}\right)^1 = \dfrac{t^{14}}{\underset{12}{\cancel{144}}} \cdot \dfrac{\overset{1}{\cancel{12}}}{t^5} = \dfrac{t^9}{12}$

61. $\dfrac{\left(x^3 y^5\right)^{-1}}{2} \cdot \dfrac{x^4 y^9}{3} = \dfrac{1}{2 \left(x^3 y^5\right)^1} \cdot \dfrac{x^4 y^9}{3} = \dfrac{1}{2x^3 y^5} \cdot \dfrac{x^4 y^9}{3} = \dfrac{x^4 y^9}{6x^3 y^5} = \dfrac{xy^4}{6}$

63. $\dfrac{\left(s^6 t^{-1}\right)^{-1}}{s^3 t^4} = \dfrac{1}{s^3 t^4 \left(s^6 t^{-1}\right)^1} = \dfrac{1}{s^3 t^4 s^6 t^{-1}} = \dfrac{1}{s^9 t^3}$

65. $\dfrac{x^6 y^{-2}}{\left(x^{-3} y^5\right)^{-1}} = \dfrac{x^6 y^{-2} \left(x^{-3} y^5\right)^1}{1} = x^6 y^{-2} x^{-3} y^5 = x^3 y^3$

67. $\dfrac{x^{-7} y^3}{\left(x^2 y^{-4}\right)^{-1}} = \dfrac{x^{-7} y^3 \left(x^2 y^{-4}\right)^1}{1} = x^{-7} y^3 x^2 y^{-4} = x^{-5} y^{-1} = \dfrac{x^{-5} y^{-1}}{1} = \dfrac{1}{x^5 y}$

69. $5x^6 y^{-4} (2xy^2)^2 = 5x^6 y^{-4} (4x^2 y^4) = 20x^8 y^0 = 20x^8$

71. $(8x^4 y^{-4})^0 (-7x^2 y^{-6})^2 = 1(49x^4 y^{-12}) = 49x^4 y^{-12} = \dfrac{49x^4}{y^{12}}$

73. $(12a^5 b^{-2} c)^0 (-2a^{-1} b^0 c^2)^{-3} = 1(-2a^{-1} c^2)^{-3} = \dfrac{(-2a^{-1} c^2)^{-3}}{1} = \dfrac{1}{(-2a^{-1} c^2)^3} = \dfrac{1}{-8a^{-3} c^6} = -\dfrac{a^3}{8c^6}$

75. $\dfrac{\left(9x^{-13} y\right) \left(2x^5\right)^2}{(x^3 y^5)^0 (2x^2 y)} = \dfrac{\left(9x^{-13} y\right) \left(4x^{10}\right)}{1 \left(2x^2 y\right)} = \dfrac{\overset{18}{\cancel{36}} x^{-3} y}{\underset{1}{\cancel{2}} x^2 y} = \dfrac{18}{x^2 x^3} = \dfrac{18}{x^5}$

77. $\dfrac{\left(s^4 t^{-2}\right)^{-2}}{2s^5 t^{-1}} \cdot \dfrac{4t^3}{(8s^3 t^{-10})^0} = \dfrac{1}{2s^5 t^{-1} \left(s^4 t^{-2}\right)^2} \cdot \dfrac{4t^3}{1} = \dfrac{4t^3}{2s^5 t^{-1} \left(s^8 t^{-4}\right)} = \dfrac{\overset{2}{\cancel{4}} t^3}{\underset{1}{\cancel{2}} s^{13} t^{-5}} = \dfrac{2t^3 t^5}{s^{13}} = \dfrac{2t^8}{s^{13}}$

79. $\left[\left(25x^3 y^{-2}\right)^{-1} \left(5x^0 y^{-5}\right)^3\right]^{-2} = \left[\dfrac{\left(25x^3 y^{-2}\right)^{-1} \left(5x^0 y^{-5}\right)^3}{1}\right]^{-2} = \left[\dfrac{\left(5x^0 y^{-5}\right)^3}{\left(25x^3 y^{-2}\right)^1}\right]^{-2} = \left[\dfrac{\overset{5}{\cancel{125}} y^{-15}}{\underset{1}{\cancel{25}} x^3 y^{-2}}\right]^{-2}$

$= \left[\dfrac{5y^2}{x^3 y^{15}}\right]^{-2} = \left[\dfrac{5}{x^3 y^{13}}\right]^{-2} = \left[\dfrac{x^3 y^{13}}{5}\right]^2 = \dfrac{x^6 y^{26}}{25}$

## Chapter 2 Exercise 2.3

1. $0.3 = 3 \times 10^{-1}$      3. $0.00734 = 7.34 \times 10^{-3}$      5. $0.0001000101 = 1.000101 \times 10^{-4}$

7. $8 = 8 \times 10^0$      9. $4.18 = 4.18 \times 10^0$      11. $3.14 = 3.14 \times 10^0$

13. $50 = 5.0 \times 10^1$      15. $94.16 = 9.416 \times 10^1$      17. $452.935 = 4.52935 \times 10^2$

19. $1,726 = 1.726 \times 10^3$      21. $77,829.003 = 7.7829003 \times 10^4$

23. $20,437,441.86 = 2.043744186 \times 10^7$      25. $2 \times 10^1 = 20.0$      27. $9.1 \times 10^2 = 910.0$

29. $7.56 \times 10^1 = 75.6$       31. $6.914 \times 10^4 = 69,140.0$       33. $5.62093 \times 10^4 = 56,209.3$

35. $4.0 \times 10^5 = 400,000.0$       37. $3 \times 10^8 = 300,000,000.0$       39. $2.61694 \times 10^8 = 261,694,000.0$

41. $7.42902 \times 10^1 = 74.2902$       43. $5 \times 10^{-1} = 0.5$       45. $1.903 \times 10^{-2} = 0.01903$

47. $3.55562 \times 10^{-3} = 0.00355562$       49. $1 \times 10^{-5} = 0.00001$       51. $\left(2 \times 10^1\right)\left(3 \times 10^2\right) = 6 \times 10^3$

53. $\left(2.5 \times 10^4\right)\left(5 \times 10^3\right) = 12.5 \times 10^7 = 1.25 \times 10^8$       55. $\left(1 \times 10^{-5}\right)\left(2 \times 10^{-1}\right) = 2 \times 10^{-6}$

57. $\left(9 \times 10^{-5}\right)\left(8 \times 10^6\right) = 72 \times 10^1 = 7.2 \times 10^2$       59. $\left(7 \times 10^{-6}\right)\left(9 \times 10^2\right) = 63 \times 10^{-4} = 6.3 \times 10^{-3}$

61. $\dfrac{4 \times 10^5}{2 \times 10^3} = 2 \times 10^2$       63. $\dfrac{120 \times 10^9}{2 \times 10^4} = 60 \times 10^5 = 6.0 \times 10^6$       65. $\dfrac{65 \times 10^{-4}}{5 \times 10^3} = 13 \times 10^{-7} = 1.3 \times 10^{-6}$

67. $\dfrac{144 \times 10^{-2}}{6 \times 10^{-7}} = 24 \times 10^5 = 2.4 \times 10^6$       69. $\left(3 \times 10^2\right)^2 = 9 \times 10^4$

71. $\left(6 \times 10^5\right)^3 = 216 \times 10^{15} = 2.16 \times 10^{17}$       73. $\left(8 \times 10^{-4}\right)^2 = 64 \times 10^{-8} = 6.4 \times 10^{-7}$

75. $\left(2 \times 10^{-2}\right)^{-2} = 2^{-2} \times 10^4 = \dfrac{1}{4} \times 10^4 = 0.25 \times 10^4 = 2.5 \times 10^3$

77. $\left(3 \times 10^5\right)\left(2 \times 10^4\right)^2 = \left(3 \times 10^5\right)\left(4 \times 10^8\right) = 12 \times 10^{13} = 1.2 \times 10^{14}$

79. $\left(2 \times 10^5\right)^3\left(3 \times 10^{-6}\right)^2 = \left(8 \times 10^{15}\right)\left(9 \times 10^{-12}\right) = 72 \times 10^3 = 7.2 \times 10^4$

81. $\dfrac{\left(4 \times 10^2\right)\left(5 \times 10^{-1}\right)^{-1}}{2 \times 10^0} = \dfrac{4 \times 10^2}{\left(2 \times 10^0\right)\left(5 \times 10^{-1}\right)^1} = \dfrac{4 \times 10^2}{\left(2 \times 10^0\right)\left(5 \times 10^{-1}\right)}$

$$= \dfrac{4 \times 10^2}{10 \times 10^{-1}} = \dfrac{4 \times 10^2}{1} = 4 \times 10^2$$

83. $\dfrac{\left(3 \times 10^5\right)^2\left(6 \times 10^3\right)^1}{9 \times 10^7} = \dfrac{\left(9 \times 10^{10}\right)\left(6 \times 10^3\right)}{9 \times 10^7} = \dfrac{6 \times 10^{13}}{1 \times 10^7} = 6 \times 10^6$

85. $\dfrac{\left(2 \times 10^5\right)^{-3}}{\left(8 \times 10^7\right)^{-2}} = \dfrac{\left(8 \times 10^7\right)^2}{\left(2 \times 10^5\right)^3} = \dfrac{64 \times 10^{14}}{8 \times 10^{15}} = 8 \times 10^{-1}$

87. $\dfrac{\left(1 \times 10^8\right)^{-2}}{1 \times 10^{-1}} = \dfrac{1}{\left(1 \times 10^{-1}\right)\left(1 \times 10^8\right)^2} = \dfrac{1}{\left(1 \times 10^{-1}\right)\left(1 \times 10^{16}\right)} = \dfrac{1}{1 \times 10^{15}} = 1 \times 10^{-15}$

89. $\dfrac{9 \times 10^3}{\left(3 \times 10^{-4}\right)^{-1}} = \dfrac{\left(9 \times 10^3\right)\left(3 \times 10^{-4}\right)^1}{1} = \left(9 \times 10^3\right)\left(3 \times 10^{-4}\right) = 27 \times 10^{-1} = 2.7 \times 10^0$

---

## Chapter 3 Exercise 3.1

1. 4 has coefficient 4 and degree 0.       3. $-5x$ has coefficient $-5$ and degree 1.

5. $7y^3$ has coefficient 7 and degree 3.       7. $8x^2y^3$ has coefficient 8 and degree 5 $(= 2 + 3)$.

9. $\dfrac{10x^6}{11} = \dfrac{10}{11}x^6$ has coefficient $\dfrac{10}{11}$ and degree 6.

11. $-\dfrac{5y^{12}}{3} = -\dfrac{5}{3}y^{12}$ has coefficient $-\dfrac{5}{3}$ and degree 12.

13. $3x^2 + 5x - 6$ is a polynomial. The coefficients of the terms are 3, 5 and $-6$.

15. $\dfrac{y^2}{9} - \dfrac{7y}{3} + 8 = \dfrac{1}{9}y^2 - \dfrac{7}{3}y + 8$ is a polynomial. The coefficients of the terms are $\dfrac{1}{9}$, $-\dfrac{7}{3}$ and 8.

17. $-5t^4 + \dfrac{2}{t^2}$ is not a polynomial, since $\dfrac{2}{t^2}$ is not a monomial.

19. $\dfrac{2xy}{7} - \dfrac{3x^2}{7y}$ is not a polynomial, since $-\dfrac{3x^2}{7y}$ is not a monomial.

21. $\dfrac{6x^2 - 14}{3} = \dfrac{6x^2}{3} - \dfrac{14}{3} = 2x^2 - \dfrac{14}{3}$ is a polynomial. The coefficients of the terms are 2 and $-\dfrac{14}{3}$.

23. $\dfrac{x^2 + 12y^2 - 24}{12} = \dfrac{x^2}{12} + \dfrac{12y^2}{12} - \dfrac{24}{12} = \dfrac{1}{12}x^2 + y^2 - 2$ is a polynomial. The coefficients of the terms are $\dfrac{1}{12}$, 1 and $-2$.

25. $4 + 6x = 6x + 4$ has leading term $6x$, leading coefficient 6 and degree 1.

27. $8 - 3x = -3x + 8$ has leading term $-3x$, leading coefficient $-3$ and degree 1.

29. $5x^2 + 8 - 12x = 5x^2 - 12x + 8$ has leading term $5x^2$, leading coefficient 5 and degree 2.

31. $t^2 - 4t^3 + \dfrac{2}{7} = -4t^3 + t^2 + \dfrac{2}{7}$ has leading term $-4t^3$, leading coefficient $-4$ and degree 3.

33. $6 - \dfrac{8}{3}x - x^2 = -x^2 - \dfrac{8}{3}x + 6$ has leading term $-x^2$, leading coefficient $-1$ and degree 2.

35. $\dfrac{8x^4}{13} + 3x - \dfrac{1}{10}x^3 = \dfrac{8}{13}x^4 - \dfrac{1}{10}x^3 + 3x$ has leading term $\dfrac{8}{13}x^4$, leading coefficient $\dfrac{8}{13}$ and degree 4.

37. $5x = 5x^1$ is of degree 1, so it is linear.        39. $-4a = -4a^1$ is of degree 1, so it is linear.

41. $3x^2$ is of degree 2, so it is quadratic.        43. $2x - 5$ is of degree 1, so it is linear.

45. $6 - 10x = -10x + 6$ is of degree 1, so it is linear.        47. $7x + 4$ is of degree 1, so it is linear.

49. $y^2 + 6y - 2$ is of degree 2, so it is quadratic.        51. $8 + 8x^2 = 8x^2 + 8$ is of degree 2, so it is quadratic.

53. $4x^2 + 8x + 9x^3 = 9x^3 + 4x^2 + 8x$ is of degree 3, so it is neither.

55. $\dfrac{2x^2 - 8x + 1}{2} = \dfrac{2x^2}{2} - \dfrac{8x}{2} + \dfrac{1}{2} = x^2 - 4x + \dfrac{1}{2}$ is of degree 2, so it is quadratic.

57. $x + 5y - \underbrace{4x^2}_{\text{degree 2}}$ has degree 2.        59. $\underbrace{6y^3}_{\text{degree 3}} - \underbrace{x^3}_{\text{degree 3}} - 7x$ has degree 3.

61. $x^2 + \underbrace{8x^2 y}_{\text{degree 3}} - y^2$ has degree 3.        63. $2s^4 + \underbrace{8s^3 t^3}_{\text{degree 6}} + 9t^4$ has degree 6.

65. $a^3 b^4 + 3bc^2 + 8a^3 c^4 - \underbrace{a^2 b^3 c^4}_{\text{degree 9}}$ has degree 9.

## Chapter 3 Exercise 3.2

1. $9x + 4x = 13x$       3. $-8y^2 + 3y^2 = -5y^2$       5. $-5x - 5x = -10x$

7. $4ab^3 + (-7ab^3) = -3ab^3$       9. $(-16ab) - (-2ab) = -14ab$       11. $4x^2 + 6x^2 - 13x^2 = -3x^2$

13. $3n - 7n + n + 9n = 6n$       15. $(9a + 7) + (-3a + 1) = 6a + 8$

17. $\left(a^2 - 2a - 1\right) + \left(4a^2 - 5a + 3\right) = 5a^2 - 7a + 2$

19. $\left(-x^2 - 2xy + 14y^2\right) + \left(-x^2 + 2xy - 8y^2\right) = -2x^2 + 6y^2$

21. $(4a - 5b - 2) + (12b - 6ab + 4) = 4a + 7b - 6ab + 2$       23. $\left(a^2 - b^2\right) + \left(a^2 + 11ab + b^2\right) = 2a^2 + 11ab$

25. $(9x + 1) - (3x + 4) = 9x + 1 - 3x - 4 = 6x - 3$       27. $(-3a + 8b) - (4a - b) = -3a + 8b - 4a + b = -7a + 9b$

29. $\left(-x^2 + 10x + 3\right) - \left(3x^2 - 2x - 1\right) = -x^2 + 10x + 3 - 3x^2 + 2x + 1 = -4x^2 + 12x + 4$

31. $\left(5a^2 - 7ab + b^2\right) - \left(-3a^2 + 9b^2\right) = 5a^2 - 7ab + b^2 + 3a^2 - 9b^2 = 8a^2 - 7ab - 8b^2$

33. $(12p + pq - q) - \left(-3p + 2pq - 9q^2\right) = 12p + pq - q + 3p - 2pq + 9q^2 = 15p - pq - q + 9q^2$

35. $\left(-4x^2 + 12\right) - \left(12 - 3x^2 + 6y^2\right) = -4x^2 + 12 - 12 + 3x^2 - 6y^2 = -x^2 - 6y^2$

37. $(7x + y) + (5x - 3y) + (-2x + 2y) = 10x$

39. $\left(5x^2 - 9x\right) + \left(-x^2 + 7\right) + (8x + 9) = 4x^2 - x + 16$

41. $(8m + 3) + (9m - 1) - (-5m + 4) = 8m + 3 + 9m - 1 + 5m - 4 = 22m - 2$

43. $\left(x^2 + 5x + 9\right) + \left(x^2 - 5\right) - (-8x + 16) = x^2 + 5x + 9 + x^2 - 5 + 8x - 16 = 2x^2 + 13x - 12$

45. $\left(y^2 - 6\right) - \left(4y^2 + 2y - 2\right) + (y + 1) = y^2 - 6 - 4y^2 - 2y + 2 + y + 1 = -3y^2 - y - 3$

47. $\left(6t^2 + 12\right) - \left(-t^2 - 11t\right) - (7t - 14) = 6t^2 + 12 + t^2 + 11t - 7t + 14 = 7t^2 + 4t + 26$

49. The additive inverse of $6x$ is $-6x$.       51. The additive inverse of $2n - 7$ is $-(2n - 7) = -2n + 7$.

53. The additive inverse of $-a^2 + 2a - 3$ is $-\left(-a^2 + 2a - 3\right) = a^2 - 2a + 3$.

55. The additive inverse of $8t^2 + 3st - s^2$ is $-\left(8t^2 + 3st - s^2\right) = -8t^2 - 3st + s^2$.

## Chapter 3 Exercise 3.3

1. $\left(3x^2\right)\left(6x^3\right) = 18x^{2+3} = 18x^5$       3. $\left(-6a^5\right)\left(-9a^2\right) = 54a^{5+2} = 54a^7$

5. $\left(-\dfrac{\overset{1}{\cancel{5}}}{\cancel{6}}y^3\right)\left(\dfrac{\overset{2}{\cancel{12}}}{\cancel{25}}y^8\right) = -\dfrac{2}{5}y^{3+8} = -\dfrac{2}{5}y^{11}$       7. $(-8y^2)\left(\dfrac{-9}{16}y^2\right) = \left(\dfrac{\overset{1}{-\cancel{8}}}{1}y^2\right)\left(\dfrac{-9}{\underset{2}{\cancel{16}}}y^2\right) = \dfrac{9}{2}y^{2+2} = \dfrac{9}{2}y^4$

9. $\left(3a^3b^6\right)\left(-ab^2\right) = -3a^{3+1}b^{6+2} = -3a^4b^8$       11. $\left(\dfrac{9x^{14}y^{19}}{\underset{1}{\cancel{8}}}\right)\left(\dfrac{-\overset{3}{\cancel{24}}x^5y^2}{11}\right) = -\dfrac{27x^{14+5}y^{19+2}}{11} = -\dfrac{27x^{19}y^{21}}{11}$

13. $4a(5a+7) = 4a\,(5a) + 4a\,(7) = 20a^2 + 28a$   15. $8x^3(9x^4 - 2x) = 8x^3\,(9x^4) + 8x^3\,(-2x) = 72x^7 - 16x^4$

17. $-3x^5(8x^2 - 10x^4) = -3x^5\,(8x^2) + (-3x^5)\,(-10x^4) = -24x^7 + 30x^9$

19. $6x^3y^4(2x^2y^5 - 5xy^2) = 6x^3y^4\,(2x^2y^5) + 6x^3y^4\,(-5xy^2) = 12x^5y^9 - 30x^4y^6$

21. $5(3a^2 + 6a - 2) = 5\,(3a^2) + 5\,(6a) + 5\,(-2) = 15a^2 + 30a - 10$

23. $8x^2(4x^3 - 5x^2 - 11) = 8x^2\,(4x^3) + 8x^2\,(-5x^2) + 8x^2\,(-11) = 32x^5 - 40x^4 - 88x^2$

25. $-3x^4y^3(5x^2 - 7x^2y^2 + 9y^2) = -3x^4y^3\,(5x^2) + (-3x^4y^3)\,(-7x^2y^2) + (-3x^4y^3)\,(9y^2)$
$$= -15x^6y^3 + 21x^6y^5 - 27x^4y^5$$

27. $9a^3b^2(-a^4b^2 + 9a^2b^5 - 4a^6b^7) = 9a^3b^2\,(-a^4b^2) + 9a^3b^2\,(9a^2b^5) + 9a^3b^2\,(-4a^6b^7)$
$$= -9a^7b^4 + 81a^5b^7 - 36a^9b^9$$

29. $2xy^4z^5(x^3y + 4xy^6 - 5yz^{10}) = 2xy^4z^5\,(x^3y) + 2xy^4z^5\,(4xy^6) + 2xy^4z^5\,(-5yz^{10})$
$$= 2x^4y^5z^5 + 8x^2y^{10}z^5 - 10xy^5z^{15}$$

31. $(x+4)\,(x+1) = x^2 \underbrace{+x + 4x} +4 = x^2 + 5x + 4$   33. $(y-3)\,(y+8) = y^2 \underbrace{+8y - 3y} -24 = y^2 + 5y - 24$

35. $(t-7)\,(t-8) = t^2 \underbrace{-8t - 7t} +56 = t^2 - 15t + 56$

37. $(2y+5)\,(3y+1) = 6y^2 \underbrace{+2y + 15y} +5 = 6y^2 + 17y + 5$

39. $(6x-7)\,(2x+3) = 12x^2 \underbrace{+18x - 14x} -21 = 12x^2 + 4x - 21$

41. $(12-3n)\,(3+4n) = 36 \underbrace{+48n - 9n} -12n^2 = 36 + 39n - 12n^2$

43. $(8-7t)\,(2-3t) = 16 \underbrace{-24t - 14t} +21t^2 = 16 - 38t + 21t^2$

45. $(4x^2+5x)\,(2x+3) = 8x^3 \underbrace{+12x^2 + 10x^2} +15x = 8x^3 + 22x^2 + 15x$

47. $(-6a^2+3)\,(8a-3) = -48a^3 + 18a^2 + 24a - 9$

49. $(n^3-7n)\,(6n-2) = 6n^4 - 2n^3 - 42n^2 + 14n$   51. $(x+2)\,(x-2) = (x)^2 - (2)^2 = x^2 - 4$

53. $(7-y)\,(7+y) = (7)^2 - (y)^2 = 49 - y^2$   55. $(3x+1)\,(3x-1) = (3x)^2 - (1)^2 = 9x^2 - 1$

57. $(10a-3b)\,(10a+3b) = (10a)^2 - (3b)^2 = 100a^2 - 9b^2$

59. $(x+1)^2 = (x)^2 + 2\,(x)\,(1) + (1)^2 = x^2 + 2x + 1$   61. $(p-7)^2 = (p)^2 - 2\,(p)\,(7) + (7)^2 = p^2 - 14p + 49$

63. $(3y+2)^2 = (3y)^2 + 2\,(3y)\,(2) + (2)^2 = 9y^2 + 12y + 4$

65. $(5x-8y)^2 = (5x)^2 - 2\,(5x)\,(8y) + (8y)^2 = 25x^2 - 80xy + 64y^2$

67. $(11-4x)^2 = (11)^2 - 2\,(11)\,(4x) + (4x)^2 = 121 - 88x + 16x^2$

69. $(x+3)\left(x^2-2x+2\right)$

$$
\begin{array}{r}
x^2-2x+2 \\
x+3 \\
\hline
3x^2-6x+6 \\
x^3-2x^2+2x \\
\hline
x^3+\ x^2-4x+6
\end{array}
$$

71. $(2y-3)\left(y^2-2y-1\right)$

$$
\begin{array}{r}
y^2-2y-1 \\
2y-3 \\
\hline
-3y^2+6y+3 \\
2y^3-4y^2-2y \\
\hline
2y^3-7y^2+4y+3
\end{array}
$$

73. $(4b+2)\left(16b^2-8b+4\right)$

$$
\begin{array}{r}
16b^2-8b+4 \\
4b+2 \\
\hline
32b^2-16b+8 \\
64b^3-32b^2+16b \\
\hline
64b^3\qquad\quad +8
\end{array}
$$

75. $(x+2y+5)\left(6x-5\right)$

$$
\begin{array}{r}
x+2y+5 \\
6x-5 \\
\hline
-5x-10y-25 \\
6x^2+12xy+30x \\
\hline
6x^2+12xy+25x-10y-25
\end{array}
$$

77. $(t-2)^3 = \underbrace{(t-2)(t-2)}(t-2) = \left(t^2-2t-2t+4\right)(t-2) = \left(t^2-4t+4\right)(t-2)$

$$= t^3-2t^2-4t^2+8t+4t-8 = t^3-6t^2+12t-8$$

79. $(2m+3n)^3 = \underbrace{(2m+3n)(2m+3n)}(2m+3n) = \left(4m^2+6mn+6mn+9n^2\right)(2m+3n)$

$$= \left(4m^2+12mn+9n^2\right)(2m+3n) = 8m^3+12m^2n+24m^2n+36mn^2+18mn^2+27n^3$$

$$= 8m^3+36m^2n+54mn^2+27n^3$$

81. $(x-3)^2(x+3) = (x-3)\ \underbrace{(x-3)(x+3)}_{\text{easier to do these first}} = (x-3)\left((x)^2-(3)^2\right)$

$$= (x-3)\left(x^2-9\right) = x^3-9x-3x^2+27$$

83. $\underbrace{(2a+1)(3a-2)}(a+2) = \left(6a^2-4a+3a-2\right)(a+2) = \left(6a^2-a-2\right)(a+2)$

$$= 6a^3+12a^2-a^2-2a-2a-4 = 6a^3+11a^2-4a-4$$

85. $(2x - 3y + 1)^2 = (2x - 3y + 1)(2x - 3y + 1)$

$$
\begin{array}{r}
2x - 3y + 1 \\
2x - 3y + 1 \\
\hline
2x - 3y + 1 \\
- 6xy + 9y^2 \qquad - 3y \\
4x^2 - 6xy \qquad + 2x \\
\hline
4x^2 - 12xy + 9y^2 + 4x - 6y + 1
\end{array}
$$

87. $2(5x + 3) + 8(2x - 1) = 10x + 6 + 16x - 8 = 26x - 2$

89. $-7a^2(a - 5) + 6a^2(3a + 1) = -7a^3 + 35a^2 + 18a^3 + 6a^2 = 11a^3 + 41a^2$

91. $2p^2(-p^2 + 4p - 2) - 5p(5p^2 - p) = -2p^4 + 8p^3 - 4p^2 - 25p^3 + 5p^2 = -2p^4 - 17p^3 + p^2$

93. $7x(4x - 1) + 4x(-x + 3) - 8(x^2 - 9) = 28x^2 - 7x - 4x^2 + 12x - 8x^2 + 72 = 16x^2 + 5x + 72$

95. $\underbrace{(x - 1)(x + 3)} + \underbrace{(x + 9)(x + 2)} = (x^2 + 3x - x - 3) + (x^2 + 2x + 9x + 18) = 2x^2 + 13x + 15$

97. $\underbrace{(2a - 5)(a + 1)} - \underbrace{(a + 2)(2a - 3)} = (2a^2 + 2a - 5a - 5) - (2a^2 - 3a + 4a - 6)$
$$= 2a^2 + 2a - 5a - 5 - 2a^2 + 3a - 4a + 6 = -4a + 1$$

99. $\underbrace{(y - 5)(y + 5)} + \underbrace{(y - 7)(y + 7)} = \left((y)^2 - (5)^2\right) + \left((y)^2 - (7)^2\right) = (y^2 - 25) + (y^2 - 49) = 2y^2 - 74$

101. $\underbrace{(2b - 3)(2b + 3)} - \underbrace{(6 + 3b)(6 - 3b)} = \left((2b)^2 - (3)^2\right) - \left((6)^2 - (3b)^2\right) = (4b^2 - 9) - (36 - 9b^2)$
$$= 4b^2 - 9 - 36 + 9b^2 = 13b^2 - 45$$

103. $\underbrace{(r - 3)^2} + \underbrace{(r + 7)^2} = \left((r)^2 - 2(r)(3) + (3)^2\right) + \left((r)^2 + 2(r)(7) + (7)^2\right)$
$$= (r^2 - 6r + 9) + (r^2 + 14r + 49) = 2r^2 + 8r + 58$$

105. $\underbrace{(x - 6)^2} - \underbrace{(x + 1)^2} = \left((x)^2 - 2(x)(6) + (6)^2\right) - \left((x)^2 + 2(x)(1) + (1)^2\right)$
$$= (x^2 - 12x + 36) - (x^2 + 2x + 1) = x^2 - 12x + 36 - x^2 - 2x - 1 = -14x + 35$$

107. $\underbrace{(2x - 5)^2} - \underbrace{(x + 1)(x - 4)} = \left((2x)^2 - 2(2x)(5) + (5)^2\right) - (x^2 - 4x + x - 4)$
$$= (4x^2 - 20x + 25) - (x^2 - 3x - 4)$$
$$= 4x^2 - 20x + 25 - x^2 + 3x + 4$$
$$= 3x^2 - 17x + 29$$

## Chapter 3 Exercise 3.4

1. $(9x^6) \div (3x^3) = \dfrac{9x^6}{3x^3} = 3x^3$      3. $(-16a^{14}) \div (4a^5) = \dfrac{-16a^{14}}{4a^5} = -4a^9$

5. $(-25y^{18}) \div (-5y^{12}) = \dfrac{-25y^{18}}{-5y^{12}} = 5y^6$      7. $(54x^9y^5) \div (9xy^4) = \dfrac{54x^9y^5}{9xy^4} = 6x^8y^1 = 6x^8y$

9. $(28s^5t^9) \div (-7s^3t^2) = \dfrac{28s^5t^9}{-7s^3t^2} = -4s^2t^7$      11. $(-7x^3y^7) \div (14x^3y^5) = \dfrac{-7x^3y^7}{14x^3y^5} = \dfrac{-y^2}{2} = -\dfrac{y^2}{2}$

13. $(-6a^2b^3) \div (-16a^7b) = \dfrac{\overset{3}{\cancel{-6}}a^2b^3}{\underset{8}{\cancel{-16}}a^7b} = \dfrac{3b^2}{8a^5}$     15. $(-25xy^6) \div (30x^7y^4) = \dfrac{\overset{5}{\cancel{-25}}xy^6}{\underset{6}{\cancel{30}}x^7y^4} = \dfrac{-5y^2}{6x^6} = -\dfrac{5y^2}{6x^6}$

17. $(9x + 15) \div 3 = \dfrac{9x + 15}{3} = \dfrac{9x}{3} + \dfrac{15}{3} = 3x + 5$

19. $(4x^2 - 12x) \div (4x) = \dfrac{4x^2 - 12x}{4x} = \dfrac{4x^2}{4x} - \dfrac{12x}{4x} = x - 3$

21. $(-8x^3 + 24x^2) \div (-4x) = \dfrac{-8x^3 + 24x^2}{-4x} = \dfrac{-8x^3}{-4x} + \dfrac{24x^2}{-4x} = 2x^2 - 6x$

23. $(42x^3 + 18x^2 - 12x) \div (6x) = \dfrac{42x^3 + 18x^2 - 12x}{6x} = \dfrac{42x^3}{6x} + \dfrac{18x^2}{6x} - \dfrac{12x}{6x} = 7x^2 + 3x - 2$

25. $(-9a^5 - 24a^4 + 3a^2) \div (-3a^2) = \dfrac{-9a^5 - 24a^4 + 3a^2}{-3a^2} = \dfrac{-9a^5}{-3a^2} - \dfrac{24a^4}{-3a^2} + \dfrac{3a^2}{-3a^2} = 3a^3 + 8a^2 - 1$

27. $(16x^2 + 15x) \div (8x) = \dfrac{16x^2 + 15x}{8x} = \dfrac{16x^2}{8x} + \dfrac{15x}{8x} = 2x + \dfrac{15}{8}$

29. $(6x^3 - 8x^2 + 12x) \div (-6x) = \dfrac{6x^3 - 8x^2 + 12x}{-6x} = \dfrac{6x^3}{-6x} - \dfrac{\overset{4}{\cancel{8}}x^2}{\underset{3}{\cancel{-6}x}} + \dfrac{12x}{-6x} = -x^2 + \dfrac{4x}{3} - 2$

31. $(-36x^6y^9 - 24x^4y^8 + 16x^{12}y^{10}) \div (-12x^3y^4) = \dfrac{-36x^6y^9 - 24x^4y^8 + 16x^{12}y^{10}}{-12x^3y^4}$

$$= \dfrac{-36x^6y^9}{-12x^3y^4} - \dfrac{24x^4y^8}{-12x^3y^4} + \dfrac{\overset{4}{\cancel{16}}x^{12}y^{10}}{\underset{3}{\cancel{-12}}x^3y^4}$$

$$= 3x^3y^5 + 2xy^4 - \dfrac{4x^9y^6}{3}$$

33. $(16s^4t^5 - 18s^6t^{10} - 24s^4t^9) \div (8s^{12}t^9) = \dfrac{16s^4t^5 - 18s^6t^{10} - 24s^4t^9}{8s^{12}t^9}$

$$= \dfrac{16s^4t^5}{8s^{12}t^9} - \dfrac{\overset{9}{\cancel{18}}s^6t^{10}}{\underset{4}{\cancel{8}}s^{12}t^9} - \dfrac{24s^4t^9}{8s^{12}t^9}$$

$$= \dfrac{2}{s^8t^4} - \dfrac{9t}{4s^6} - \dfrac{3}{s^8}$$

35. $(x^2 + 6x + 5) \div (x + 1) = x + 5$

$$\begin{array}{r}
x + 5 \phantom{0} \\
x + 1 \overline{)\ x^2 + 6x + 5\phantom{0}} \\
\underline{-\ \ x^2 +\ x\phantom{ + 5000}} \\
5x + 5 \\
\underline{-\ \ \ \ \ \ \ \ 5x + 5} \\
0
\end{array}$$

37. $\left(x^2 - x - 6\right) \div (x + 2) = x - 3$

$$
\begin{array}{r}
x - 3 \\
x + 2 \overline{) \, x^2 - x - 6} \\
\underline{- \quad x^2 + 2x} \\
-3x - 6 \\
\underline{- \qquad -3x - 6} \\
0
\end{array}
$$

39. $\left(x^2 + 8x - 20\right) \div (x - 2) = x + 10$

$$
\begin{array}{r}
x + 10 \\
x - 2 \overline{) \, x^2 + 8x - 20} \\
\underline{- \quad x^2 - 2x} \\
10x - 20 \\
\underline{- \qquad 10x - 20} \\
0
\end{array}
$$

41. $\left(x^2 + 4x + 2\right) \div (x + 1) = x + 3 \text{ R } -1$

$$
\begin{array}{r}
x + 3 \text{ R } -1 \\
x + 1 \overline{) \, x^2 + 4x + 2} \\
\underline{- \quad x^2 + \ x} \\
3x + 2 \\
\underline{- \qquad 3x + 3} \\
-1
\end{array}
$$

43. $\left(y^2 - 8y + 4\right) \div (y + 4) = y - 12 \text{ R } 52$

$$
\begin{array}{r}
y - 12 \text{ R } 52 \\
y + 4 \overline{) \, y^2 - 8y + 4} \\
\underline{- \quad y^2 + 4y} \\
-12y + 4 \\
\underline{- \qquad -12y - 48} \\
52
\end{array}
$$

45. $\left(a^2 - 6a - 8\right) \div (a + 4) = a - 10 \text{ R } 32$

$$
\begin{array}{r}
a - 10 \text{ R } 32 \\
a + 4 \overline{) \, a^2 - 6a - 8} \\
\underline{- \quad a^2 + 4a} \\
-10a - 8 \\
\underline{- \qquad -10a - 40} \\
32
\end{array}
$$

47. $\left(x^2 + 9x - 7\right) \div (x - 3) = x + 12 \text{ R } 29$

$$
\begin{array}{r}
x + 12 \text{ R } 29 \\
x - 3 \overline{)\, x^2 + 9x - 7\phantom{0}} \\
-\ \underline{x^2 - 3x\phantom{0000000}} \\
12x - 7\phantom{0} \\
-\ \underline{12x - 36\phantom{0}} \\
29
\end{array}
$$

49. $\left(p^2 - 3p - 16\right) \div (p + 4) = p - 7 \text{ R } 12$

$$
\begin{array}{r}
p - 7 \text{ R } 12 \\
p + 4 \overline{)\, p^2 - 3p - 16\phantom{0}} \\
-\ \underline{p^2 + 4p\phantom{0000000}} \\
-7p - 16\phantom{0} \\
-\ \underline{-7p - 28\phantom{0}} \\
12
\end{array}
$$

51. $\left(3x^2 + x + 2\right) \div (x + 5) = 3x - 14 \text{ R } 72$

$$
\begin{array}{r}
3x - 14 \text{ R } 72 \\
x + 5 \overline{)\, 3x^2 + \phantom{0}x + 2\phantom{0}} \\
-\ \underline{3x^2 + 15x\phantom{00000}} \\
-14x + \phantom{0}2\phantom{0} \\
-\ \underline{-14x - 70\phantom{0}} \\
72
\end{array}
$$

53. $\left(7y^2 - 3y + 1\right) \div (y + 3) = 7y - 24 \text{ R } 73$

$$
\begin{array}{r}
7y - 24 \text{ R } 73 \\
y + 3 \overline{)\, 7y^2 - 3y + 1\phantom{0}} \\
-\ \underline{7y^2 + 21y\phantom{00000}} \\
-24y + 1\phantom{0} \\
-\ \underline{-24y - 72\phantom{0}} \\
73
\end{array}
$$

55. $\left(8m^2 - 2m - 5\right) \div (m - 2) = 8m + 14 \text{ R } 23$

$$
\begin{array}{r}
8m + 14 \text{ R } 23 \\
m - 2 \overline{)\, 8m^2 - 2m - 5\phantom{0}} \\
-\ \underline{8m^2 - 16m\phantom{00000}} \\
14m - 5\phantom{0} \\
-\ \underline{14m - 28\phantom{0}} \\
23
\end{array}
$$

57. $\left(2x^2 + 3x - 4\right) \div (2x + 1) = x + 1 \text{ R} -5$

$$
\begin{array}{r}
x + 1 \text{ R } -5 \\
2x + 1)\overline{\,2x^2 + 3x - 4\,} \\
\underline{-\ 2x^2 +\ x\quad} \\
2x - 4 \\
\underline{-\qquad 2x + 1} \\
-5
\end{array}
$$

59. $\left(3a^2 - 6a + 5\right) \div (3a - 4) = a - \frac{2}{3} \text{ R } \frac{7}{3}$

$$
\begin{array}{r}
a - \dfrac{2}{3} \text{ R } \dfrac{7}{3} \\
3a - 4)\overline{\,3a^2 - 6a + 5\,} \\
\underline{-\ 3a^2 - 4a\quad} \\
-2a + 5 \\
\underline{-\qquad -2a + \dfrac{8}{3}} \\
\dfrac{7}{3}
\end{array}
$$

61. $\left(5t^2 - 10t - 3\right) \div (5t - 2) = t - \frac{8}{5} \text{ R } -\frac{31}{5}$

$$
\begin{array}{r}
t - \dfrac{8}{5} \text{ R } - \dfrac{31}{5} \\
5t - 2)\overline{\,5t^2 - 10t - 3\,} \\
\underline{-\ 5t^2 -\ 2t\quad} \\
-8t - 3 \\
\underline{-\qquad -8t + \dfrac{16}{5}} \\
-\dfrac{31}{5}
\end{array}
$$

63. $\left(4y^2 + 2y + 3\right) \div (4y - 1) = y + \frac{3}{4} \text{ R } \frac{15}{4}$

$$
\begin{array}{r}
y + \dfrac{3}{4} \text{ R } \dfrac{15}{4} \\
4y - 1)\overline{\,4y^2 + 2y + 3\,} \\
\underline{-\ 4y^2 -\ y\quad} \\
3y + 3 \\
\underline{-\qquad 3y - \dfrac{3}{4}} \\
\dfrac{15}{4}
\end{array}
$$

65. $\left(6n^2 - n + 4\right) \div (3n - 1) = 2n + \frac{1}{3} \text{ R } \frac{13}{3}$

$$
\begin{array}{r}
2n + \dfrac{1}{3} \text{ R } \dfrac{13}{3} \\[2pt]
3n - 1 \overline{)\, 6n^2 - n + 4} \\
-\ \underline{6n^2 - 2n} \\
n + 4 \\
-\ \underline{\quad n - \dfrac{1}{3}} \\
\dfrac{13}{3}
\end{array}
$$

67. $\left(x^3 + 2x^2 - 3x + 1\right) \div (x + 4) = x^2 - 2x + 5 \text{ R } -19$

$$
\begin{array}{r}
x^2 - 2x + 5 \text{ R } \ -19 \\
x + 4 \overline{)\, x^3 + 2x^2 - 3x + 1} \\
-\ \underline{x^3 + 4x^2 \quad\qquad} \\
-2x^2 - 3x + \ 1 \\
-\ \underline{-2x^2 - 8x \qquad} \\
5x + \ 1 \\
-\ \underline{5x + 20} \\
-19
\end{array}
$$

69. $\left(y^3 - 8y^2 - y + 2\right) \div (y + 3) = y^2 - 11y + 32 \text{ R } -94$

$$
\begin{array}{r}
y^2 - 11y + 32 \text{ R } \ -94 \\
y + 3 \overline{)\, y^3 - \ 8y^2 - \quad y + 2} \\
-\ \underline{y^3 + \ 3y^2 \qquad\qquad} \\
-11y^2 - \quad y + 2 \\
-\ \underline{-11y^2 - 33y \qquad} \\
32y + 2 \\
-\ \underline{32y + 96} \\
-94
\end{array}
$$

71. $\left(x^3 - 4x^2 - 3x + 2\right) \div (x - 2) = x^2 - 2x - 7 \text{ R } -12$

$$
\begin{array}{r}
x^2 - 2x - 7 \text{ R } \ -12 \\
x - 2 \overline{)\, x^3 - 4x^2 - 3x + 2} \\
-\ \underline{x^3 - 2x^2 \qquad\qquad} \\
-2x^2 - 3x + 2 \\
-\ \underline{-2x^2 + 4x \qquad} \\
-7x + 2 \\
-\ \underline{-7x + 14} \\
-12
\end{array}
$$

73. $\left(5a^3 + 3a^2 - a + 2\right) \div (a - 3) = 5a^2 + 18a + 53$  R 161

$$
\begin{array}{r}
5a^2 + 18a + 53 \ \text{R} \ \ 161 \\
a - 3 \overline{)\ 5a^3 + \ 3a^2 - \ \ \ a + \ \ 2} \\
-\quad \underline{5a^3 - 15a^2} \\
18a^2 - \ \ \ a + \ \ 2 \\
-\quad \underline{18a^2 - 54a} \\
53a + \ \ 2 \\
-\quad \underline{53a - 159} \\
161
\end{array}
$$

75. $\left(y^2 - 5\right) \div (y + 3) = y - 3$  R 4

$$
\begin{array}{r}
y - 3 \ \text{R} \ \ 4 \\
y + 3 \overline{)\ y^2 + 0y - 5} \\
-\quad \underline{y^2 + 3y} \\
-3y - 5 \\
-\quad \underline{-3y - 9} \\
4
\end{array}
$$

77. $\left(8t^2 + 2t\right) \div (t - 4) = 8t + 34$  R 136

$$
\begin{array}{r}
8t + 34 \ \text{R} \ \ 136 \\
t - 4 \overline{)\ 8t^2 + 2t + 0} \\
-\quad \underline{8t^2 - 32t} \\
34t + 0 \\
-\quad \underline{34t - 136} \\
136
\end{array}
$$

79. $\left(x^2 - 6x\right) \div \left(x^2 + 5\right) = 1$  R  $-6x - 5$

$$
\begin{array}{r}
1 \ \text{R} \ \ -6x - 5 \\
x^2 + 5 \overline{)\ x^2 - 6x + 0} \\
-\quad \underline{x^2 \qquad + 5} \\
-6x - 5
\end{array}
$$

81. $\left(9p^2 + 2\right) \div \left(p^2 - 4p\right) = 9$  R  $36p + 2$

$$
\begin{array}{r}
9 \ \text{R} \ \ 36p + 2 \\
p^2 - 4p \overline{)\ 9p^2 + 0p + 2} \\
-\quad \underline{9p^2 - 36p} \\
36p + 2
\end{array}
$$

83. $\left(4x^2 + 1\right) \div \left(x^2 - 6x\right) = 4$  R  $24x + 1$

$$
\begin{array}{r}
4 \ \text{R} \ \ 24x + 1 \\
x^2 - 6x \overline{)\ 4x^2 + 0x + 1} \\
-\quad \underline{4x^2 - 24x} \\
24x + 1
\end{array}
$$

85. $\left(x^3 - 3x + 4\right) \div (x - 2) = x^2 + 2x + 1$ R  6

$$
\begin{array}{r}
x^2 + 2x + 1 \ \text{R}\ \ 6 \\
x - 2{\overline{)\, x^3 + 0x^2 - 3x + 4}} \\
-\quad x^3 - 2x^2 \phantom{xxxxxxxx} \\
\hline
2x^2 - 3x + 4 \\
-\quad 2x^2 - 4x \phantom{xxxx} \\
\hline
x + 4 \\
-\quad x - 2 \\
\hline
6
\end{array}
$$

87. $\left(a^3 + 6a^2 + 2\right) \div (a + 5) = a^2 + a - 5$ R  27

$$
\begin{array}{r}
a^2 + a - 5 \ \text{R}\ \ 27 \\
a + 5{\overline{)\, a^3 + 6a^2 + 0a + 2}} \\
-\quad a^3 + 5a^2 \phantom{xxxxxxxx} \\
\hline
a^2 + 0a + 2 \\
-\quad a^2 + 5a \phantom{xxxx} \\
\hline
-5a + 2 \\
-\quad -5a - 25 \\
\hline
27
\end{array}
$$

89. $\left(4b^3 - b^2 + 3b\right) \div \left(b^2 + 3\right) = 4b - 1$ R  $-9b + 3$

$$
\begin{array}{r}
4b - 1 \ \text{R}\ \ -9b + 3 \\
b^2 + 3{\overline{)\, 4b^3 - b^2 + \ 3b + 0}} \\
-\quad 4b^3 \phantom{xxx} + 12b \phantom{xx} \\
\hline
-b^2 - \ 9b + 0 \\
-\quad -b^2 \phantom{xxx} - 3 \\
\hline
-\ 9b + 3
\end{array}
$$

91. $\left(x^4 + 5x^2 - 9\right) \div \left(x^2 - 1\right) = x^2 + 6$ R  $-3$

$$
\begin{array}{r}
x^2 + 6 \ \text{R}\ \ -3 \\
x^2 - 1{\overline{)\, x^4 + 0x^3 + 5x^2 + 0x - 9}} \\
-\quad x^4 \phantom{xxxxx} - \ x^2 \phantom{xxxxxxx} \\
\hline
6x^2 + 0x - 9 \\
-\quad 6x^2 \phantom{xxx} - 6 \\
\hline
-3
\end{array}
$$

93. $\left(8x^3 + 1\right) \div (2x + 1) = 4x^2 - 2x + 1$

$$
\begin{array}{r}
4x^2 - 2x + 1 \\
2x + 1{\overline{)\, 8x^3 + 0x^2 + 0x + 1}} \\
-\quad 8x^3 + 4x^2 \phantom{xxxxxxxx} \\
\hline
-4x^2 + 0x + 1 \\
-\quad -4x^2 - 2x \phantom{xxxx} \\
\hline
2x + 1 \\
-\quad 2x + 1 \\
\hline
0
\end{array}
$$

95. $\left(64a^3 - 27\right) \div (4a - 3) = 16a^2 + 12a + 9$

$$
\begin{array}{r}
16a^2 + 12a + 9 \\
4a - 3 \overline{)\ 64a^3 + 0a^2 + 0a - 27} \\
-\quad\ \ 64a^3 - 48a^2 \\
\hline
48a^2 + 0a - 27 \\
-\quad\quad\ \ 48a^2 - 36a \\
\hline
36a - 27 \\
-\quad\quad\quad\ \ 36a - 27 \\
\hline
0
\end{array}
$$

## Chapter 3 Exercise 3.5

1. $3x + 12 = 3\left(x + 4\right)$     3. $2a^2 + 6 = 2\left(a^2 + 3\right)$     5. $5x^2 + 10x - 20 = 5\left(x^2 + 2x - 4\right)$

7. $12x^2 + 8x = 4x\left(3x + 2\right)$     9. $3x^3 - 21x^2 = 3x^2\left(x - 7\right)$     11. $8q^3 + 12q^2 = 4q^2\left(2q + 3\right)$

13. $32y^4 - 16y^3 + 8y^2 = 8y^2\left(4y^2 - 2y + 1\right)$     15. $20a^2b^2 + 22ab^3 = 2ab^2\left(10a + 11b\right)$

17. $27p^5q^3 + 3p^4q^6 - 6p^6q = 3p^4q\left(9pq^2 + q^5 - 2p^2\right)$

19. $56a^5b^2c^3 - 14a^4b^3c^4 - 7a^5bc^7 = 7a^4bc^3\left(8ab - 2b^2c - ac^4\right)$

21. $36j^2k^5 - 27jk^6 + 18k^8 = 9k^5\left(4j^2 - 3jk + 2k^3\right)$

23. $-5x + 15 = -5\left(x - 3\right)$     25. $-9t - 36 = -9\left(t + 4\right)$     27. $-8y^2 - 16y + 40 = -8\left(y^2 + 2y - 5\right)$

29. $-5n^4 - 25n^3 - 5 = -5\left(n^4 + 5n^3 + 1\right)$     31. $-16t^2 + 32t + 64 = -16\left(t^2 - 2t - 4\right)$

33. $y^2 - 4 = (y)^2 - (2)^2 = \left(y + 2\right)\left(y - 2\right)$     35. $v^2 - 9 = (v)^2 - (3)^2 = \left(v + 3\right)\left(v - 3\right)$

37. $b^2 - 25 = (b)^2 - (5)^2 = \left(b + 5\right)\left(b - 5\right)$     39. $36 - x^2 = (6)^2 - (x)^2 = \left(6 + x\right)\left(6 - x\right)$

41. $64t^2 - 9 = (8t)^2 - (3)^2 = \left(8t + 3\right)\left(8t - 3\right)$  43. $4q^2 - 121 = (2q)^2 - (11)^2 = \left(2q + 11\right)\left(2q - 11\right)$

45. $a^2 - 81b^2 = (a)^2 - (9b)^2 = \left(a + 9b\right)\left(a - 9b\right)$  47. $36u^2 - 169v^2 = (6u)^2 - (13v)^2 = \left(6u + 13v\right)\left(6u - 13v\right)$

49. $y^2 - \dfrac{1}{9} = (y)^2 - \left(\dfrac{1}{3}\right)^2 = \left(y + \dfrac{1}{3}\right)\left(y - \dfrac{1}{3}\right)$     51. $\dfrac{36}{49} - 25d^2 = \left(\dfrac{6}{7}\right)^2 - (5d)^2 = \left(\dfrac{6}{7} + 5d\right)\left(\dfrac{6}{7} - 5d\right)$

53. $\dfrac{4}{9}a^2 - 100b^2 = \left(\dfrac{2}{3}a\right)^2 - (10b)^2 = \left(\dfrac{2}{3}a + 10b\right)\left(\dfrac{2}{3}a - 10b\right)$

55. $y^3 + 8 = (y)^3 + (2)^3 = \left(y + 2\right)\left((y)^2 - (y)(2) + (2)^2\right) = \left(y + 2\right)\left(y^2 - 2y + 4\right)$

57. $m^3 + 27 = (m)^3 + (3)^3 = \left(m + 3\right)\left((m)^2 - (m)(3) + (3)^2\right) = \left(m + 3\right)\left(m^2 - 3m + 9\right)$

59. $64 - y^3 = (4)^3 - (y)^3 = \left(4 - y\right)\left((4)^2 + (4)(y) + (y)^2\right) = \left(4 - y\right)\left(16 + 4y + y^2\right)$

61. $q^3 - 1,000 = (q)^3 - (10)^3 = (q - 10)\left((q)^2 + (q)(10) + (10)^2\right) = (q - 10)\left(q^2 + 10q + 100\right)$

63. $8p^3 + 1 = (2p)^3 + (1)^3 = (2p + 1)\left((2p)^2 - (2p)(1) + (1)^2\right) = (2p + 1)\left(4p^2 - 2p + 1\right)$

65. $27x^3 - y^3 = (3x)^3 - (y)^3 = (3x - y)\left((3x)^2 + (3x)(y) + (y)^2\right) = (3x - y)\left(9x^2 + 3xy + y^2\right)$

67. $1,000m^3 + 27 = (10m)^3 + (3)^3 = (10m + 3)\left((10m)^2 - (10m)(3) + (3)^2\right) = (10m + 3)\left(100m^2 - 30m + 9\right)$

69. $8x^3 + 125y^3 = (2x)^3 + (5y)^3 = (2x + 5y)\left((2x)^2 - (2x)(5y) + (5y)^2\right) = (2x + 5y)\left(4x^2 - 10xy + 25y^2\right)$

71. $216a^3 - 125b^3 = (6a)^3 - (5b)^3 = (6a - 5b)\left((6a)^2 + (6a)(5b) + (5b)^2\right) = (6a - 5b)\left(36a^2 + 30ab + 25b^2\right)$

73. $5x^2 - 20 = 5\left(x^2 - 4\right) = 5(x + 2)(x - 2)$    75. $3m^5 - 48m^3 = 3m^3\left(m^2 - 16\right) = 3m^3(m + 4)(m - 4)$

77. $\underbrace{4a^2 - 16 = 4\left(a^2 - 4\right)}_{\text{GCF first!}} = 4(a + 2)(a - 2)$    79. $\underbrace{16x^2 - 64y^2 = 16\left(x^2 - 4y^2\right)}_{\text{GCF first!}} = 16(x + 2y)(x - 2y)$

81. $2p^3 + 16 = 2\underbrace{\left(p^3 + 8\right)}_{(p)^3 + (2)^3} = 2(p + 2)\left(p^2 - 2p + 4\right)$    83. $5u^3 - 5 = 5\underbrace{\left(u^3 - 1\right)}_{(u)^3 - (1)^3} = 5(u - 1)\left(u^2 + u + 1\right)$

85. $7x^5 + 56x^2 = 7x^2\underbrace{\left(x^3 + 8\right)}_{(x)^3 + (2)^3} = 7x^2(x + 2)\left(x^2 - 2x + 4\right)$

87. $x^4y^2 - 1,000xy^2 = xy^2\underbrace{\left(x^3 - 1,000\right)}_{(x)^3 - (10)^3} = xy^2(x - 10)\left(x^2 + 10x + 100\right)$

89. $x^2 + 3x + 2 = (x + 1)(x + 2)$    91. $y^2 + 11y + 24 = (y + 8)(y + 3)$

93. $x^2 + 5x - 6 = (x + 6)(x - 1)$    95. $y^2 + 8y - 48 = (y + 12)(y - 4)$

97. $a^2 - 9a + 20 = (a - 5)(a - 4)$    99. $b^2 - 18b + 45 = (b - 15)(b - 3)$

101. $p^2 - 4p - 21 = (p + 3)(p - 7)$    103. $q^2 + 16q + 39 = (q + 13)(q + 3)$

105. $x^2 + 2x + 1 = (x + 1)(x + 1) = (x + 1)^2$    107. $m^2 - 16m + 64 = (m - 8)(m - 8) = (m - 8)^2$

109. $t^2 + 24t + 144 = (t + 12)(t + 12) = (t + 12)^2$    111. $x^2 - 10x + 25 = (x - 5)(x - 5) = (x - 5)^2$

113. $x^2 + 3x + 7$ is prime.    115. $y^2 - 9y + 3$ is prime.    117. $2x^2 + 3x + 1 = (2x + 1)(x + 1)$

119. $3y^2 + y - 2 = (3y - 2)(y + 1)$    121. $5a^2 - a - 4 = (5a + 4)(a - 1)$

123. $14x^2 + 11x + 2 = (7x + 2)(2x + 1)$    125. $4x^2 - 12x + 5 = (2x - 5)(2x - 1)$

127. $4p^2 - 23p + 15 = (4p - 3)(p - 5)$    129. $6y^2 + 17y + 12 = (2y + 3)(3y + 4)$

131. $8t^2 - 38t + 45 = (4t - 9)(2t - 5)$    133. $12p^2 - 32p - 35 = (6p + 5)(2p - 7)$

135. $9x^2 + 12x + 4 = (3x + 2)(3x + 2) = (3x + 2)^2$    137. $49x^2 - 56x + 16 = (7x - 4)(7x - 4) = (7x - 4)^2$

139. $16s^2 + 40s + 25 = (4s + 5)(4s + 5) = (4s + 5)^2$    141. $2x^2 + 5x + 1$ is prime.

143. $5a^2 - 2a - 11$ is prime.     145. $6x^2 - x + 8$ is prime.

147. $x^3 + x^2 + 2x + 2 = \left(x^3 + x^2\right) + \left(2x + 2\right) = x^2\underline{(x+1)} + 2\underline{(x+1)} = \underline{(x+1)}\left(x^2 + 2\right)$

149. $y^3 - 6y^2 + 4y - 24 = \left(y^3 - 6y^2\right) + \left(4y - 24\right) = y^2\underline{(y-6)} + 4\underline{(y-6)} = \underline{(y-6)}\left(y^2 + 4\right)$

151. $2a^3 + 8a^2 + 3a + 12 = \left(2a^3 + 8a^2\right) + \left(3a + 12\right) = 2a^2\underline{(a+4)} + 3\underline{(a+4)} = \underline{(a+4)}\left(2a^2 + 3\right)$

153. $16m^3 - 40m^2 - 6m + 15 = \left(16m^3 - 40m^2\right) + \left(-6m + 15\right) = 8m^2\underline{(2m-5)} - 3\underline{(2m-5)}$
$= \underline{(2m-5)}\left(8m^2 - 3\right)$

155. $x^5 + x^3 + 9x^2 + 9 = \left(x^5 + x^3\right) + \left(9x^2 + 9\right) = x^3\underline{\left(x^2+1\right)} + 9\underline{\left(x^2+1\right)} = \underline{\left(x^2+1\right)}\left(x^3 + 9\right)$

157. $11a^5 + 99a^3 - 5a^2 - 45 = \left(11a^5 + 99a^3\right) + \left(-5a^2 - 45\right) = 11a^3\underline{\left(a^2+9\right)} - 5\underline{\left(a^2+9\right)} = \underline{\left(a^2+9\right)}\left(11a^3 - 5\right)$

159. $2p^3 + p + 6p^2q + 3q = \left(2p^3 + p\right) + \left(6p^2q + 3q\right) = p\underline{\left(2p^2+1\right)} + 3q\underline{\left(2p^2+1\right)} = \underline{\left(2p^2+1\right)}\left(p + 3q\right)$

161. $80s^4 - 50s^2 - 24s^2y + 15y = \left(80s^4 - 50s^2\right) + \left(-24s^2y + 15y\right)$
$= 10s^2\underline{\left(8s^2-5\right)} - 3y\underline{\left(8s^2-5\right)} = \underline{\left(8s^2-5\right)}\left(10s^2 - 3y\right)$

163. $x^2 + 2x + 1 - y^2 = \underbrace{\left(x^2 + 2x + 1\right)}_{(x+1)(x+1)} - y^2 = \underbrace{(x+1)^2 - (y)^2 = (x+1+y)(x+1-y)}_{\text{Use } A^2 - B^2 = (A+B)(A-B) \text{ with } A=x+1 \text{ and } B=y.}$

165. $a^2 - 10a + 25 - 4b^2 = \underbrace{\left(a^2 - 10a + 25\right)}_{(a-5)(a-5)} - 4b^2 = \underbrace{(a-5)^2 - (2b)^2 = (a-5+2b)(a-5-2b)}_{\text{Use } A^2 - B^2 = (A+B)(A-B) \text{ with } A=a-5 \text{ and } B=2b.}$

167. $k^2 + 20k + 100 - 121l^2 = \underbrace{\left(k^2 + 20k + 100\right)}_{(k+10)(k+10)} - 121l^2 = \underbrace{(k+10)^2 - (11l)^2 = (k+10+11l)(k+10-11l)}_{\text{Use } A^2 - B^2 = (A+B)(A-B) \text{ with } A=k+5 \text{ and } B=11l.}$

169. $2x^2 + 6x + 4 = 2\left(x^2 + 3x + 2\right) = 2\left(x+2\right)\left(x+1\right)$

171. $4a^3 - 8a^2 - 60a = 4a\left(a^2 - 2a - 15\right) = 4a\left(a+3\right)\left(a-5\right)$

173. $5u^5 - 55u^4 + 150u^3 = 5u^3\left(u^2 - 11u + 30\right) = 5u^3\left(u-6\right)\left(u-5\right)$

175. $2x^2y^3 - 6x^2y^2 - 56x^2y = 2x^2y\left(y^2 - 3y - 28\right) = 2x^2y\left(y+4\right)\left(y-7\right)$

177. $27x^2 + 63x + 18 = 9\left(3x^2 + 7x + 2\right) = 9\left(3x+1\right)\left(x+2\right)$

179. $24y^2 - 24y - 18 = 6\left(4y^2 - 4y - 3\right) = 6\left(2y-3\right)\left(2y+1\right)$

181. $42k^4 - 75k^3 + 18k^2 = 3k^2\left(14k^2 - 25k + 6\right) = 3k^2\left(7k-2\right)\left(2k-3\right)$

183. $8m^3 - 48m^2 + 72m = 8m\left(m^2 - 6m + 9\right) = 8m\left(m-3\right)\left(m-3\right) = 8m\left(m-3\right)^2$

185. $18a^4 + 12a^3 + 2a^2 = 2a^2\left(9a^2 + 6a + 1\right) = 2a^2\left(3a+1\right)\left(3a+1\right) = 2a^2\left(3a+1\right)^2$

187. $6 + x - x^2 = -x^2 + x + 6 = -1\left(x^2 - x - 6\right) = -1\left(x+2\right)\left(x-3\right)$ or $-\left(x+2\right)\left(x-3\right)$

189. $-48 + 14t - t^2 = -t^2 + 14t - 48 = -1\left(t^2 - 14t + 48\right) = -1\left(t-6\right)\left(t-8\right)$ or $-\left(t-6\right)\left(t-8\right)$

191. $36 + 15x - 6x^2 = -6x^2 + 15x + 36 = -3\left(2x^2 - 5x - 12\right) = -3\left(2x+3\right)\left(x-4\right)$

193. $x^4 + 4x^2 + 4 = (x^2 + 2)(x^2 + 2) = (x^2 + 2)^2$  195. $y^6 + 14y^3 + 49 = (y^3 + 7)(y^3 + 7) = (y^3 + 7)^2$

197. $t^4 - 8t^2 + 16 = (t^2 - 4)(t^2 - 4) = \underbrace{(t+2)(t-2)}_{t^2-4}\underbrace{(t+2)(t-2)}_{t^2-4} = (t+2)^2(t-2)^2$

199. $x^4 - 81 = (x^2)^2 - (9)^2 = \underbrace{(x^2 + 9)}_{prime}(x^2 - 9) = (x^2 + 9)(x + 3)(x - 3)$

201. $x^6 + 2x^3 + 1 = (x^3 + 1)(x^3 + 1) = \underbrace{(x+1)(x^2 - x + 1)}_{x^3+1}\underbrace{(x+1)(x^2 - x + 1)}_{x^3+1} = (x+1)^2(x^2 - x + 1)^2$

203. $k^4 + 7k^2 - 8 = (k^2 + 8)(k^2 - 1) = (k^2 + 8)\underbrace{(k+1)(k-1)}_{k^2-1}$

205. $p^6 - 10p^3 + 16 = (p^3 - 8)(p^3 - 2) = \underbrace{(p-2)(p^2 + 2p + 4)}_{p^3-8}(p^3 - 2)$

207. $1 - x^6 = (1)^2 - (x^3)^2 = (1 + x^3)(1 - x^3) = \underbrace{(1+x)(1-x+x^2)}_{1+x^3}\underbrace{(1-x)(1+x+x^2)}_{1-x^3}$

209. $b^6 - 64 = (b^3)^2 - (8)^2 = (b^3 + 8)(b^3 - 8) = \underbrace{(b+2)(b^2 - 2b + 4)}_{b^3+8}\underbrace{(b-2)(b^2 + 2b + 4)}_{b^3-8}$

211. $3a^2 - 13ab - 10b^2 = (3a + 2b)(a - 5b)$  213. $25p^2 - 40pq + 16q^2 = (5p - 4q)(5p - 4q) = (5p - 4q)^2$

215. $8x^4y + 42x^3y^2 + 54x^2y^3 = 2x^2y(4x^2 + 21xy + 27y^2) = 2x^2y(4x + 9y)(x + 3y)$

---

## Chapter 4 Exercise 4.1

1. $\dfrac{3x^2}{4x} = \dfrac{3x}{4}$  3. $\dfrac{\overset{1}{\cancel{4}}x^2}{\underset{2}{\cancel{8}}x^5} = \dfrac{1}{2x^3}$  5. $\dfrac{\overset{3}{\cancel{24}}}{\underset{2}{\cancel{16}}x^7} = \dfrac{3}{2x^7}$  7. $\dfrac{5x^4}{x^{12}} = \dfrac{5}{x^8}$

9. $\dfrac{x^8y^3}{x^2y^7} = \dfrac{x^6}{y^4}$  11. $\dfrac{\overset{3}{\cancel{-6}}a^3b^4}{\underset{8}{\cancel{16}}ab^2} = -\dfrac{3a^2b^2}{8}$  13. $\dfrac{\overset{5}{\cancel{15}}m^2n^3}{\underset{2}{\cancel{6}}m^5n^9} = \dfrac{5}{2m^3n^6}$  15. $\dfrac{\overset{2}{\cancel{14}}a^5b^4c^7}{\underset{3}{\cancel{21}}a^2b^6c^2} = \dfrac{2a^3c^5}{3b^2}$

17. $\dfrac{\overset{9}{\cancel{18}}m^{12}n^{10}p^7}{\underset{4}{\cancel{8}}m^3n^{10}} = \dfrac{9m^9p^7}{4}$  19. $\dfrac{-56ab^7}{7a^8c^6} = -\dfrac{8b^7}{a^7c^6}$  21. $\dfrac{2x + 4}{3x + 6} = \dfrac{2\cancel{(x+2)}}{3\cancel{(x+2)}} = \dfrac{2}{3}$

23. $\dfrac{8y - 24}{6y - 18} = \dfrac{\overset{4}{\cancel{8}}(y-3)}{\underset{3}{\cancel{6}}(y-3)} = \dfrac{4}{3}$  25. $\dfrac{4t + 10}{4t - 10} = \dfrac{\cancel{2}(2t+5)}{\cancel{2}(2t-5)} = \dfrac{2t+5}{2t-5}$

27. $\dfrac{3x - 1}{2 - 6x} = \dfrac{1\cancel{(3x-1)}}{-2(\cancel{-1+3x})} = \dfrac{1}{-2} = -\dfrac{1}{2}$  29. $\dfrac{6x^2 - 12}{6 - 3x^2} = \dfrac{6\cancel{(x^2-2)}}{-3(\cancel{-2+x^2})} = \dfrac{2}{-1} = -2$

31. $\dfrac{4x^2 + 10}{-30 - 12x^2} = \dfrac{2\left(2x^2 + 5\right)}{-6\left(5 + 2x^2\right)} = \dfrac{1}{-3} = -\dfrac{1}{3}$

33. $\dfrac{3p^2 + 8p}{2p^2 - p} = \dfrac{p\left(3p + 8\right)}{p\left(2p - 1\right)} = \dfrac{3p + 8}{2p - 1}$

35. $\dfrac{10x^2 + 15x}{10x^2 + 10x} = \dfrac{\overset{1}{5x}\left(2x + 3\right)}{\underset{2}{10x}\left(x + 1\right)} = \dfrac{2x + 3}{2\left(x + 1\right)}$

37. $\dfrac{2x^3y^3 - 2x^2y^4}{12x^5y + 12x^4y^2} = \dfrac{2x^2y^3\left(x - y\right)}{12x^4y\left(x + y\right)} = \dfrac{y^2\left(x - y\right)}{6x^2\left(x + y\right)}$

39. $\dfrac{2t^3 + 6t^2}{-5t^4 - 15t^3} = \dfrac{2t^2\left(t + 3\right)}{-5t^3\left(t + 3\right)} = \dfrac{2}{-5t} = -\dfrac{2}{5t}$

41. $\dfrac{x^2 + 3x + 2}{3x + 6} = \dfrac{\left(x + 2\right)\left(x + 1\right)}{3\left(x + 2\right)} = \dfrac{x + 1}{3}$

43. $\dfrac{2x^2 - 8x}{3x^3 - 48x} = \dfrac{2x\left(x - 4\right)}{3x\left(x^2 - 16\right)} = \dfrac{2x\left(x - 4\right)}{3x\left(x + 4\right)\left(x - 4\right)} = \dfrac{2}{3\left(x + 4\right)}$

45. $\dfrac{x^3 + 1}{x^2 - 1} = \dfrac{\left(x + 1\right)\left(x^2 - x + 1\right)}{\left(x + 1\right)\left(x - 1\right)} = \dfrac{x^2 - x + 1}{x - 1}$

47. $\dfrac{4t^2 - 8t - 21}{4t^2 + 12t + 9} = \dfrac{\left(2t + 3\right)\left(2t - 7\right)}{\left(2t + 3\right)\left(2t + 3\right)} = \dfrac{2t - 7}{2t + 3}$

49. $\dfrac{16x^3 - 8x^2}{4x^2 - 1} = \dfrac{8x^2\left(2x - 1\right)}{\left(2x + 1\right)\left(2x - 1\right)} = \dfrac{8x^2}{2x + 1}$

51. $\dfrac{2x^4 - 8x^3 - 42x^2}{5x^6 - 45x^4} = \dfrac{2x^2\left(x^2 - 4x - 21\right)}{5x^4\left(x^2 - 9\right)} = \dfrac{2x^2\left(x - 7\right)\left(x + 3\right)}{5x^4\left(x + 3\right)\left(x - 3\right)} = \dfrac{2\left(x - 7\right)}{5x^2\left(x - 3\right)}$

## Chapter 4 Exercise 4.2

1. $\dfrac{4x^2y^5}{12x^3y^2} \cdot \dfrac{6x^8y^2}{5xy^7} = \dfrac{\left(4x^2y^5\right)\left(6x^8y^2\right)}{\left(12x^3y^2\right)\left(5xy^7\right)} = \dfrac{2x^{10}y^7}{5x^4y^9} = \dfrac{2x^6}{5y^2}$

3. $\dfrac{10a^3}{b^3c^7} \cdot \left(-\dfrac{2a^4b^6c^2}{5}\right) = -\dfrac{\left(\overset{2}{10a^3}\right)\left(2a^4b^6c^2\right)}{\left(b^3c^7\right)\left(\underset{1}{5}\right)} = -\dfrac{4a^7b^6c^2}{b^3c^7} = -\dfrac{4a^7b^3}{c^5}$

5. $\dfrac{3x + 9}{8x - 16} \cdot \dfrac{4x - 8}{5x + 15} = \dfrac{3\left(x + 3\right)}{\underset{2}{8}\left(x - 2\right)} \cdot \dfrac{\overset{1}{4}\left(x - 2\right)}{5\left(x + 3\right)} = \dfrac{3}{10}$

7. $\dfrac{3u^3 + 18u^2}{9u^2 - 18u} \cdot \dfrac{8u + 8}{4u + 24} = \dfrac{\overset{1}{3u^2}\left(u + 6\right)}{\underset{3}{9u}\left(u - 2\right)} \cdot \dfrac{\overset{2}{8}\left(u + 1\right)}{\underset{1}{4}\left(u + 6\right)} = \dfrac{2u\left(u + 1\right)}{3\left(u - 2\right)}$

9. $\dfrac{2a^2 - 2a - 12}{2a^2 + 10a + 12} \cdot \dfrac{3a - 9}{a + 1} = \dfrac{2\left(a^2 - a - 6\right)}{2\left(a^2 + 5a + 6\right)} \cdot \dfrac{3\left(a - 3\right)}{a + 1} = \dfrac{2\left(a + 2\right)\left(a - 3\right)}{2\left(a + 2\right)\left(a + 3\right)} \cdot \dfrac{3\left(a - 3\right)}{a + 1}$

$= \dfrac{a - 3}{a + 3} \cdot \dfrac{3\left(a - 3\right)}{a + 1} = \dfrac{3\left(a - 3\right)^2}{\left(a + 3\right)\left(a + 1\right)}$

11. $\dfrac{8y^3 - 8}{24y + 12} \cdot \dfrac{12y^2 + 12y + 3}{y^2 + y + 1} = \dfrac{8\left(y^3 - 1\right)}{12\left(2y + 1\right)} \cdot \dfrac{3\left(4y^2 + 4y + 1\right)}{y^2 + y + 1} = \dfrac{\overset{2}{8}\left(y - 1\right)\left(y^2 + y + 1\right)}{\underset{}{12\left(2y + 1\right)}} \cdot \dfrac{\overset{}{3}\left(2y + 1\right)\left(2y + 1\right)}{y^2 + y + 1}$

$= \dfrac{2\left(2y + 1\right)\left(y - 1\right)}{1} = 2\left(2y + 1\right)\left(y - 1\right)$

13. $\dfrac{x^2 - 36}{x^2 - 16} \cdot \dfrac{x^2 - 9x + 20}{x^2 + 10x + 24} = \dfrac{\left(x + 6\right)\left(x - 6\right)}{\left(x + 4\right)\left(x - 4\right)} \cdot \dfrac{\left(x - 4\right)\left(x - 5\right)}{\left(x + 4\right)\left(x + 6\right)} = \dfrac{\left(x - 6\right)\left(x - 5\right)}{\left(x + 4\right)\left(x + 4\right)} = \dfrac{\left(x - 6\right)\left(x - 5\right)}{\left(x + 4\right)^2}$

15. $\dfrac{4t^2 + 5t - 6}{6 - 8t} \cdot \dfrac{5t}{t+2} = \dfrac{(4t - 3)\,(t + 2)}{-2\,(-3 + 4t)} \cdot \dfrac{5t}{t + 2} = \dfrac{5t}{-2} = -\dfrac{5t}{2}$

17. $\dfrac{x^2}{4} \div \dfrac{x^4}{8} = \dfrac{x^2}{4} \cdot \dfrac{8}{x^4} = \dfrac{8x^2}{4x^4} = \dfrac{2}{x^2}$

19. $\left(\dfrac{-25}{3y^6}\right) \div \left(\dfrac{10}{-9y^2}\right) = \left(\dfrac{-25}{3y^6}\right) \cdot \left(\dfrac{-9y^2}{10}\right) = \dfrac{(-\overset{5}{25})(-\overset{3}{9}y^2)}{(3y^6)(10)} = \dfrac{15y^2}{2y^6} = \dfrac{15}{2y^4}$

21. $\left(\dfrac{a}{-15}\right) \div \dfrac{b^2}{6} = \left(\dfrac{a}{-15}\right) \cdot \dfrac{6}{b^2} = \dfrac{\overset{2}{6}a}{-\underset{5}{15}b^2} = -\dfrac{2a}{5b^2}$

23. $\dfrac{3x^6y^2}{5x^3y} \div \dfrac{15xy}{10x^4y^2} = \dfrac{3x^6y^2}{5x^3y} \cdot \dfrac{10x^4y^2}{15xy} = \dfrac{(\overset{1}{3}x^6y^2)(\overset{2}{10}x^4y^2)}{(\underset{1}{5}x^3y)(\underset{5}{15}xy)} = \dfrac{2x^{10}y^4}{5x^4y^2} = \dfrac{2x^6y^2}{5}$

25. $\left(\dfrac{-16u^3v}{15uv^3}\right) \div \left(\dfrac{8u^4v}{-10u^2v^5}\right) = \left(\dfrac{-16u^3v}{15uv^3}\right) \cdot \left(\dfrac{-10u^2v^5}{8u^4v}\right) = \dfrac{(-\overset{2}{16}u^3v)(-\overset{2}{10}u^2v^5)}{(\underset{3}{15}uv^3)(\underset{1}{8}u^4v)} = \dfrac{4u^5v^6}{3u^5v^4} = \dfrac{4v^2}{3}$

27. $\dfrac{5x}{6} \div \dfrac{x^2 + x}{12x + 12} = \dfrac{5x}{6} \cdot \dfrac{12x + 12}{x^2 + x} = \dfrac{5x}{\underset{1}{6}} \cdot \dfrac{\overset{2}{12}(x + 1)}{x(x + 1)} = \dfrac{10}{1} = 10$

29. $\dfrac{4t + 12}{5t + 15} \div \dfrac{9t - 54}{10t - 60} = \dfrac{4t + 12}{5t + 15} \cdot \dfrac{10t - 60}{9t - 54} = \dfrac{4\,(t + 3)}{\underset{1}{5}\,(t + 3)} \cdot \dfrac{\overset{2}{10}\,(t - 6)}{9\,(t - 6)} = \dfrac{8}{9}$

31. $\dfrac{x^2 - 3x - 4}{3x + 3} \div \dfrac{x^2 - 6x + 8}{5x + 10} = \dfrac{x^2 - 3x - 4}{3x + 3} \cdot \dfrac{5x + 10}{x^2 - 6x + 8} = \dfrac{(x + 1)\,(x - 4)}{3\,(x + 1)} \cdot \dfrac{5\,(x + 2)}{(x - 2)\,(x - 4)} = \dfrac{5\,(x + 2)}{3\,(x - 2)}$

33. $\dfrac{y^3 - 8}{4y^2 - 5y - 6} \div \dfrac{2y^2 + 4y + 8}{8y^2 - 22y - 21} = \dfrac{y^3 - 8}{4y^2 - 5y - 6} \cdot \dfrac{8y^2 - 22y - 21}{2y^2 + 4y + 8}$

$\qquad = \dfrac{(y - 2)\,(y^2 + 2y + 4)}{(4y + 3)\,(y - 2)} \cdot \dfrac{(4y + 3)\,(2y - 7)}{2\,(y^2 + 2y + 4)} = \dfrac{2y - 7}{2}$

35. $\dfrac{7t^3 + 2t^2 - 21t - 6}{35t + 10} \div \dfrac{14t^3 + 4t^2 + 7t + 2}{6t^3 + 3t} = \dfrac{7t^3 + 2t^2 - 21t - 6}{35t + 10} \cdot \dfrac{6t^3 + 3t}{14t^3 + 4t^2 + 7t + 2}$

$\qquad = \dfrac{(t^2 - 3)\,(7t + 2)}{5\,(7t + 2)} \cdot \dfrac{3t\,(2t^2 + 1)}{(2t^2 + 1)\,(7t + 2)} = \dfrac{3t\,(t^2 - 3)}{5\,(7t + 2)}$

37. $\dfrac{9x^2 + 38xy + 8y^2}{3x^2y^3 + 12xy^4} \div \dfrac{x^2 - 2xy + y^2}{27x^3y + 6x^2y^2} = \dfrac{9x^2 + 38xy + 8y^2}{3x^2y^3 + 12xy^4} \cdot \dfrac{27x^3y + 6x^2y^2}{x^2 - 2xy + y^2}$

$\qquad = \dfrac{(9x + 2y)\,(x + 4y)}{\underset{1}{3}xy^3\,(x + 4y)} \cdot \dfrac{\overset{1}{3}x^2y\,(9x + 2y)}{(x - y)\,(x - y)}$

$\qquad = \dfrac{x\,(9x + 2y)\,(9x + 2y)}{y^2\,(x - y)\,(x - y)} = \dfrac{x\,(9x + 2y)^2}{y^2\,(x - y)^2}$

## Chapter 4 Exercise 4.3

1. $\dfrac{3}{x} + \dfrac{2}{x} = \dfrac{3+2}{x} = \dfrac{5}{x}$

3. $\dfrac{6}{7b} + \dfrac{9}{7b} = \dfrac{6+9}{7b} = \dfrac{15}{7b}$

5. $\dfrac{8}{3y} - \dfrac{2}{3y} = \dfrac{8-2}{3y} = \dfrac{6}{3y} = \dfrac{2}{y}$

7. $\dfrac{1}{x+3} + \dfrac{x+4}{x+3} = \dfrac{1+(x+4)}{x+3} = \dfrac{x+5}{x+3}$

9. $\dfrac{3t+2}{7t-1} + \dfrac{4t}{7t-1} = \dfrac{(3t+2)+4t}{7t-1} = \dfrac{7t+2}{7t-1}$

11. $\dfrac{3a+5}{2a-6} + \dfrac{2a-9}{2a-6} = \dfrac{(3a+5)+(2a-9)}{2a-6} = \dfrac{5a-4}{2a-6} = \dfrac{5a-4}{2(a-3)}$

13. $\dfrac{2x+1}{x^2-4} - \dfrac{x-1}{x^2-4} = \dfrac{(2x+1)-(x-1)}{x^2-4} = \dfrac{2x+1-x+1}{x^2-4} = \dfrac{x+2}{x^2-4} = \dfrac{\overset{1}{\cancel{x+2}}}{\underset{1}{\cancel{(x+2)}}(x-2)} = \dfrac{1}{x-2}$

15. $\dfrac{6t-7}{9t-8} - \dfrac{t+7}{9t-8} = \dfrac{(6t-7)-(t+7)}{9t-8} = \dfrac{6t-7-t-7}{9t-8} = \dfrac{5t-14}{9t-8}$

17. $\dfrac{18t^2-8}{4t+1} - \dfrac{2t^2-7}{4t+1} = \dfrac{(18t^2-8)-(2t^2-7)}{4t+1} = \dfrac{18t^2-8-2t^2+7}{4t+1}$

$= \dfrac{16t^2-1}{4t+1} = \dfrac{\overset{1}{\cancel{(4t+1)}}(4t-1)}{\underset{1}{\cancel{4t+1}}} = \dfrac{4t-1}{1} = 4t-1$

19. $\dfrac{10x^2-x-2}{2x^2+4x-5} + \dfrac{-3x^2-3x+7}{2x^2+4x-5} = \dfrac{(10x^2-x-2)+(-3x^2-3x+7)}{2x^2+4x-5} = \dfrac{7x^2-4x+5}{2x^2+4x-5}$

21. $\underbrace{\dfrac{6x}{x-3} + \dfrac{7}{3-x} = \dfrac{6x}{x-3} - \dfrac{7}{x-3}}_{x-3 \text{ and } 3-x \text{ are additive inverses of each other.}} = \dfrac{6x-7}{x-3}$

23. $\underbrace{\dfrac{5u+3}{2u-9} - \dfrac{2u}{9-2u} = \dfrac{5u+3}{2u-9} + \dfrac{2u}{2u-9}}_{2u-9 \text{ and } 9-2u \text{ are additive inverses of each other.}} = \dfrac{(5u+3)+2u}{2u-9} = \dfrac{7u+3}{2u-9}$

25. $\underbrace{\dfrac{4x-5}{6-8x} + \dfrac{3x-4}{8x-6} = \dfrac{4x-5}{6-8x} - \dfrac{3x-4}{6-8x}}_{6-8x \text{ and } 8x-6 \text{ are additive inverses of each other.}} = \dfrac{(4x-5)-(3x-4)}{6-8x} = \dfrac{4x-5-3x+4}{6-8x}$

$= \dfrac{x-1}{6-8x} = \dfrac{x-1}{2(3-4x)}$

27. $\underbrace{\dfrac{7a+12}{3a-13} - \dfrac{7-5a}{13-3a} = \dfrac{7a+12}{3a-13} + \dfrac{7-5a}{3a-13}}_{3a-13 \text{ and } 13-3a \text{ are additive inverses of each other.}} = \dfrac{(7a+12)+(7-5a)}{3a-13} = \dfrac{2a+19}{3a-13}$

29. The LCM of 3 and 7 is $3 \times 7 = 21$.

31. The LCM of $36 = 3^2 \times 2^2$ and $24 = 3^1 \times 2^3$ is $3^2 \times 2^3 = 72$.

33. The LCM of $6 = 3^1 \times 2^1$ and $14 = 7^1 \times 2^1$ is $\underbrace{3^1 \times 7^1 \times 2^1}_{\text{Only put one 2.}} = 42$.

35. The LCM of $90 = 3^2 \times 2^1 \times 5^1$ and $75 = 3^1 \times 5^2$ is $3^2 \times 2^1 \times 5^2 = 450$.

37. The LCM of $2x^4$ and $5x^3$ is $10x^4$ (the LCM of 2 and 5 is 10).

39. The LCM of $12a^3b^2$ and $9ab^6$ is $36a^3b^6$ (the LCM of 12 and 9 is 36).

41. The LCM of $10x^2y^5$ and $10x^2y^6$ is $10x^2y^6$ (the LCM of 10 and 10 is 10).

43. The LCM of $2x$ and $11y$ is $22xy$ (the LCM of 2 and 11 is 22).

45. The LCM of $8x^2$ and $6y^2$ is $24x^2y^2$ (the LCM of 8 and 6 is 24).

47. The LCM of 18 and $xy^2$ is $18xy^2$.     49. The LCM of $x$ and $x-5$ is $x(x-5)$.

51. The LCM of $x$ and $x+h$ is $x(x+h)$.     53. The LCM of $7x^2$ and $8x+3$ is $7x^2(8x+3)$.

55. The LCM of $x+3$ and $x-3$ is $(x+3)(x-3)$.     57. The LCM of $3y+5$ and $y-1$ is $(3y+5)(y-1)$.

59. The LCM of $4x+8 = 4(x+2)^1$ and $7x+14 = 7(x+2)^1$ is $\underbrace{28(x+2)}_{\text{Only put one } (x+2).}$

61. The LCM of $x^2-3x = x^1(x-3)^1$ and $x^2+4x = x^1(x+4)^1$ is $\underbrace{x(x-3)(x+4)}_{\text{Only put one } x.}$

63. The LCM of $y^3+6y^2 = y^2(y+6)^1$ and $y^2-36 = (y+6)^1(y-6)^1$ is $\underbrace{y^2(y+6)(y-6)}_{\text{Only put one } (y+6).}$

65. The LCM of $x^2+5x+4 = (x+4)^1(x+1)^1$ and $x^2-3x-28 = (x+4)^1(x-7)^1$ is $\underbrace{(x+4)(x+1)(x-7)}_{\text{Only put one } (x+4).}$

67. The LCM of $\underbrace{3x^4-3x^3-18x^2 = 3x^2(x+2)^1(x-3)^1}_{\text{Factor completely.}}$ and $\underbrace{6x^3+30x^2+36x = 6x(x+2)^1(x+3)^1}_{\text{Factor completely.}}$ is

$6x^2(x+2)(x-3)(x+3)$.

69. The LCM of $\underbrace{18x^4(x-1)^2(x+1) \text{ and } 12x^2(x-1)(x+1)^2}_{\text{Both are already factored for us.}}$ is $36x^4(x-1)^2(x+1)^2$.

71. The LCM of $\underbrace{5a^2(3a+4)^3(a-6)^2 \text{ and } a^5(3a-4)^2(a-6)^2}_{\text{Both are already factored for us.}}$ is $5a^5(3a+4)^3(a-6)^2(3a-4)^2$.

73. The LCM of $\underbrace{2(x-3)^2(x^2+4)^2 \text{ and } 2(x-3)^2(x^2-3)}_{\text{Both are already factored for us.}}$ is $2(x-3)^2(x^2+4)^2(x^2-3)$.

75. $\underbrace{\dfrac{2x}{5}+\dfrac{7}{3}}_{\text{The LCM of 5 and 3 is 15.}} = \left(\dfrac{3}{3}\right)\dfrac{2x}{5}+\left(\dfrac{5}{5}\right)\dfrac{7}{3} = \dfrac{3(2x)+5(7)}{15} = \dfrac{6x+35}{15}$

77. $\underbrace{\dfrac{8y}{9}-\dfrac{5}{12}}_{\text{The LCM of 9 and 12 is 36.}} = \left(\dfrac{4}{4}\right)\dfrac{8y}{9}-\left(\dfrac{3}{3}\right)\dfrac{5}{12} = \dfrac{4(8y)-3(5)}{36} = \dfrac{32y-15}{36}$

79. $\underbrace{\dfrac{9}{4x}+\dfrac{5}{6}}_{\text{The LCM of } 4x \text{ and 6 is } 12x.} = \left(\dfrac{3}{3}\right)\dfrac{9}{4x}+\left(\dfrac{2x}{2x}\right)\dfrac{5}{6} = \dfrac{3(9)+2x(5)}{12x} = \dfrac{27+10x}{12x}$

81. $\underbrace{\dfrac{3}{x+7} + \dfrac{4}{x-2} = \left(\dfrac{x-2}{x-2}\right)\dfrac{3}{x+7} + \left(\dfrac{x+7}{x+7}\right)\dfrac{4}{x-2}}_{\text{The LCM of } x+7 \text{ and } x-2 \text{ is } (x+7)(x-2).} = \dfrac{3(x-2)+4(x+7)}{(x-2)(x+7)} = \dfrac{3x-6+4x+28}{(x-2)(x+7)}$

$$= \dfrac{7x+22}{(x-2)(x+7)}$$

83. $\underbrace{\dfrac{4a}{3a+1} - \dfrac{1}{5a-2} = \left(\dfrac{5a-2}{5a-2}\right)\dfrac{4a}{3a+1} - \left(\dfrac{3a+1}{3a+1}\right)\dfrac{1}{5a-2}}_{\text{The LCM of } 3a+1 \text{ and } 5a-2 \text{ is } (3a+1)(5a-2).} = \dfrac{4a(5a-2)-1(3a+1)}{(5a-2)(3a+1)}$

$$= \dfrac{20a^2-8a-3a-1}{(5a-2)(3a+1)} = \dfrac{20a^2-11a-1}{(5a-2)(3a+1)}$$

85. $\underbrace{\dfrac{t+2}{t-5} + \dfrac{t+1}{t-3} = \left(\dfrac{t-3}{t-3}\right)\dfrac{t+2}{t-5} + \left(\dfrac{t-5}{t-5}\right)\dfrac{t+1}{t-3}}_{\text{The LCM of } t-5 \text{ and } t-3 \text{ is } (t-5)(t-3).} = \dfrac{(t-3)(t+2)+(t-5)(t+1)}{(t-3)(t-5)}$

$$= \dfrac{\overbrace{t^2+2t-3t-6}^{(t-3)(t+2)}+\overbrace{t^2+t-5t-5}^{(t-5)(t+1)}}{(t-3)(t-5)}$$

$$= \dfrac{2t^2-5t-11}{(t-3)(t-5)}$$

87. $\underbrace{\dfrac{1}{4+h} - \dfrac{1}{4} = \left(\dfrac{4}{4}\right)\dfrac{1}{4+h} - \left(\dfrac{4+h}{4+h}\right)\dfrac{1}{4}}_{\text{The LCM of } 4 \text{ and } 4+h \text{ is } 4(4+h).} = \dfrac{4-1(4+h)}{4(4+h)} = \dfrac{4-4-h}{4(4+h)} = \dfrac{-h}{4(4+h)}$

89. $\underbrace{\dfrac{1}{(3+h)^2} - \dfrac{1}{9} = \left(\dfrac{9}{9}\right)\dfrac{1}{(3+h)^2} - \left(\dfrac{(3+h)^2}{(3+h)^2}\right)\dfrac{1}{9}}_{\text{The LCM of } 9 \text{ and } (3+h)^2 \text{ is } 9(3+h)^2.} = \dfrac{9-1(3+h)^2}{9(3+h)^2} = \dfrac{9-(9+6h+h^2)}{9(3+h)^2}$

$$= \dfrac{9-9-6h-h^2}{9(3+h)^2} = \dfrac{-6h-h^2}{9(3+h)^2} = \dfrac{h(-6-h)}{9(3+h)^2} \text{ or } \dfrac{-h(6+h)}{9(3+h)^2}$$

91. $\underbrace{\dfrac{2m-1}{3m+2} - \dfrac{m+2}{m-4} = \left(\dfrac{m-4}{m-4}\right)\dfrac{2m-1}{3m+2} - \left(\dfrac{3m+2}{3m+2}\right)\dfrac{m+2}{m-4}}_{\text{The LCM of } 3m+2 \text{ and } m-4 \text{ is } (3m+2)(m-4).} = \dfrac{(m-4)(2m-1)-(3m+2)(m+2)}{(m-4)(3m+2)}$

$$= \dfrac{\overbrace{2m^2-m-8m+4}^{(m-4)(2m-1)}-\overbrace{(3m^2+6m+2m+4)}^{(3m+2)(m+2)}}{(m-4)(3m+2)} = \dfrac{2m^2-m-8m+4-3m^2-6m-2m-4}{(m-4)(3m+2)}$$

$$= \dfrac{-m^2-17m}{(m-4)(3m+2)} = \dfrac{-m(m+17)}{(m-4)(3m+2)}$$

93. $\underbrace{\dfrac{1}{12xy} + \dfrac{6}{9y^2} = \dfrac{3y}{3y}\left(\dfrac{1}{12xy}\right) + \dfrac{4x}{4x}\left(\dfrac{6}{9y^2}\right)}_{\text{The LCM of } 12xy \text{ and } 9y^2 \text{ is } 36xy^2.} = \dfrac{3y(1)+4x(6)}{36xy^2} = \dfrac{3y+24x}{36xy^2}$

95. $\underbrace{\dfrac{6}{11a^2b} - \dfrac{10}{3ab^2} = \left(\dfrac{3b}{3b}\right)\dfrac{6}{11a^2b} - \left(\dfrac{11a}{11a}\right)\dfrac{10}{3ab^2}}_{\text{The LCM of } 11a^2b \text{ and } 3ab^2 \text{ is } 33a^2b^2.} = \dfrac{3b(6)-11a(10)}{33a^2b^2} = \dfrac{18b-110a}{33a^2b^2}$

97. $\underbrace{\dfrac{x}{18y^3} + \dfrac{5y}{6x^2}}_{\text{The LCM of } 18y^3 \text{ and } 6x^2 \text{ is } 18x^2y^3.} = \left(\dfrac{x^2}{x^2}\right)\dfrac{x}{18y^3} + \left(\dfrac{3y^3}{3y^3}\right)\dfrac{5y}{6x^2} = \dfrac{x^2\,(x) + 3y^3\,(5y)}{18x^2y^3} = \dfrac{x^3 + 15y^4}{18x^2y^3}$

99. $\underbrace{\dfrac{1}{x+2} + \dfrac{4}{x^2-4}}_{\text{The LCM of } x+2 \text{ and } x^2-4=(x+2)(x-2) \text{ is } (x+2)(x-2).} = \left(\dfrac{x-2}{x-2}\right)\dfrac{1}{x+2} + \dfrac{4}{(x+2)(x-2)} = \dfrac{(x-2)+4}{(x+2)(x-2)} = \dfrac{\overset{1}{\cancel{x+2}}}{\underset{1}{\cancel{(x+2)}}(x-2)} = \dfrac{1}{x-2}$

101. $\underbrace{\dfrac{6}{a^2-a} - \dfrac{9}{a^2-1}}_{\text{The LCM of } a^2-a=a(a-1) \text{ and } a^2-1=(a+1)(a-1) \text{ is } a(a+1)(a-1).} = \left(\dfrac{a+1}{a+1}\right)\dfrac{6}{a(a-1)} - \left(\dfrac{a}{a}\right)\dfrac{9}{(a+1)(a-1)} = \dfrac{6\,(a+1) - 9a}{a(a+1)(a-1)} = \dfrac{6a+6-9a}{a(a+1)(a-1)}$

$\qquad = \dfrac{-3a+6}{a(a+1)(a-1)} = \dfrac{-3\,(a-2)}{a(a+1)(a-1)}$

103. $\underbrace{\dfrac{a+3}{a^2-4a-5} + \dfrac{a}{a^2-8a+15}}_{\text{The LCM of } a^2-4a-5=(a+1)(a-5) \text{ and } a^2-8a+15=(a-3)(a-5) \text{ is } (a-3)(a+1)(a-5).} = \left(\dfrac{a-3}{a-3}\right)\dfrac{a+3}{(a+1)(a-5)} + \left(\dfrac{a+1}{a+1}\right)\dfrac{a}{(a-3)(a-5)}$

$\qquad = \dfrac{(a-3)(a+3) + a\,(a+1)}{(a-3)(a+1)(a-5)} = \dfrac{a^2-9 + a^2 + a}{(a-3)(a+1)(a-5)} = \dfrac{2a^2 + a - 9}{(a-3)(a+1)(a-5)}$

105. $\underbrace{\dfrac{3x-10}{2x^2-11x+5} - \dfrac{7x+8}{2x^2-7x-15}}_{\text{The LCM of } 2x^2-11x+5=(2x-1)(x-5) \text{ and } 2x^2-7x-15=(2x+3)(x-5) \text{ is } (2x+3)(2x-1)(x-5).} = \left(\dfrac{2x+3}{2x+3}\right)\dfrac{3x-10}{(2x-1)(x-5)} - \left(\dfrac{2x-1}{2x-1}\right)\dfrac{7x+8}{(2x+3)(x-5)}$

$= \dfrac{(2x+3)(3x-10) - (2x-1)(7x+8)}{(2x+3)(2x-1)(x-5)} = \dfrac{6x^2 - 20x + 9x - 30 - \left(14x^2 + 16x - 7x - 8\right)}{(2x+3)(2x-1)(x-5)}$

$= \dfrac{6x^2 - 20x + 9x - 30 - 14x^2 - 16x + 7x + 8}{(2x+3)(2x-1)(x-5)} = \dfrac{-8x^2 - 20x - 22}{(2x+3)(2x-1)(x-5)} = \dfrac{-2\left(4x^2 + 10x + 11\right)}{(2x+3)(2x-1)(x-5)}$

107. $\underbrace{\dfrac{3m-1}{m^2+4m+4} + \dfrac{1}{m-3}}_{\text{The LCM of } m^2+4m+4=(m+2)^2 \text{ and } m-3 \text{ is } (m-3)(m+2)^2.} = \left(\dfrac{m-3}{m-3}\right)\dfrac{3m-1}{(m+2)^2} + \left(\dfrac{(m+2)^2}{(m+2)^2}\right)\dfrac{1}{m-3} = \dfrac{(m-3)(3m-1) + (m+2)^2}{(m-3)(m+2)^2}$

$= \dfrac{\overbrace{3m^2 - m - 9m + 3}^{(m-3)(3m-1)} + \overbrace{m^2 + 2m + 2m + 4}^{(m+2)^2=(m+2)(m+2)}}{(m-3)(m+2)^2} = \dfrac{4m^2 - 6m + 7}{(m-3)(m+2)^2}$

109. $\underbrace{\dfrac{1}{x} + \dfrac{3x+2}{x+1} - \dfrac{2}{x-2}}_{\text{The LCM of } x, \; x+1 \text{ and } x-2 \text{ is } x(x+1)(x-2).} = \left(\dfrac{(x+1)(x-2)}{(x+1)(x-2)}\right)\dfrac{1}{x} + \left(\dfrac{x(x-2)}{x(x-2)}\right)\dfrac{3x+2}{x+1} - \left(\dfrac{x(x+1)}{x(x+1)}\right)\dfrac{2}{x-2}$

$= \dfrac{(x+1)(x-2) + x(x-2)(3x+2) - 2x(x+1)}{x(x+1)(x-2)}$

$= \dfrac{\overbrace{x^2 - 2x + x - 2}^{(x+1)(x-2)} + x\overbrace{\left(3x^2 + 2x - 6x - 4\right)}^{(x-2)(3x+2)} - 2x^2 - 2x}{x(x+1)(x-2)}$

$= \dfrac{x^2 - 2x + x - 2 + 3x^3 + 2x^2 - 6x^2 - 4x - 2x^2 - 2x}{x(x+1)(x-2)} = \dfrac{3x^3 - 5x^2 - 7x - 2}{x(x+1)(x-2)}$

111. The LCM of $x^2 + 4x = x(x+4)$, $x^2 - 5x = x(x-5)$ and $x+3$ is $x(x-5)(x+3)(x+4)$. Therefore,

$$\frac{2}{x^2+4x} + \frac{3}{x^2-5x} + \frac{1}{x+3} = \left(\frac{(x-5)(x+3)}{(x-5)(x+3)}\right)\frac{2}{x(x+4)} + \left(\frac{(x+4)(x+3)}{(x+4)(x+3)}\right)\frac{3}{x(x-5)}$$

$$+\left(\frac{x(x+4)(x-5)}{x(x+4)(x-5)}\right)\frac{1}{x+3} = \frac{2(x-5)(x+3) + 3(x+4)(x+3) + x(x+4)(x-5)}{x(x-5)(x+3)(x+4)}$$

$$= \frac{2\overbrace{(x^2+3x-5x-15)}^{(x-5)(x+3)} + 3\overbrace{(x^2+3x+4x+12)}^{(x+4)(x+3)} + x\overbrace{(x^2-5x+4x-20)}^{(x+4)(x-5)}}{x(x-5)(x+3)(x+4)}$$

$$= \frac{2x^2+6x-10x-30 + 3x^2+9x+12x+36 + x^3-5x^2+4x^2-20x}{x(x-5)(x+3)(x+4)} = \frac{x^3+4x^2-3x+6}{x(x-5)(x+3)(x+4)}$$

113. $2 + \dfrac{3x-1}{2x+5} = \left(\dfrac{2x+5}{2x+5}\right)\dfrac{2}{1} + \dfrac{3x-1}{2x+5} = \dfrac{2(2x+5)+(3x-1)}{2x+5} = \dfrac{4x+10+3x-1}{2x+5} = \dfrac{7x+9}{2x+5}$

115. $8b - \dfrac{3}{b+1} = \left(\dfrac{b+1}{b+1}\right)\dfrac{8b}{1} - \dfrac{3}{b+1} = \dfrac{8b(b+1)-3}{b+1} = \dfrac{8b^2+8b-3}{b+1}$

117. $x^2 + 3x + \dfrac{2}{x} = \left(\dfrac{x}{x}\right)\dfrac{x^2+3x}{1} + \dfrac{2}{x} = \dfrac{x(x^2+3x)+2}{x} = \dfrac{x^3+3x^2+2}{x}$

119. $5u - 4 - \dfrac{10}{u-1} = \left(\dfrac{u-1}{u-1}\right)\dfrac{5u-4}{1} - \dfrac{10}{u-1} = \dfrac{(u-1)(5u-4)-10}{u-1}$

$$= \frac{\overbrace{5u^2-4u-5u+4}^{(u-1)(5u-4)}-10}{u-1} = \frac{5u^2-9u-6}{u-1}$$

## Chapter 4 Exercise 4.4

1. The LCM of the 'little denominators' 3, 4 and 6 is 12. Following the steps, we have

$$\frac{\frac{2}{3}-\frac{1}{4}}{\frac{1}{6}} = \left(\frac{\frac{2}{3}-\frac{1}{4}}{\frac{1}{6}}\right)\left(\frac{\frac{12}{1}}{\frac{12}{1}}\right) = \frac{\frac{2}{3}\left(\frac{\overset{4}{\cancel{12}}}{1}\right) - \frac{1}{4}\left(\frac{\overset{3}{\cancel{12}}}{1}\right)}{\frac{1}{\cancel{6}}\left(\frac{\overset{2}{\cancel{12}}}{1}\right)} = \frac{2(4)-3}{2} = \frac{8-3}{2} = \frac{5}{2}$$

3. The LCM of the 'little denominators' 10 and 5 is 10 (recall that we don't need to include the denominators of 1). Following the steps, we have

$$\frac{2-\frac{9}{10}}{3+\frac{1}{5}} = \left(\frac{2-\frac{9}{10}}{3+\frac{1}{5}}\right)\left(\frac{\frac{10}{1}}{\frac{10}{1}}\right) = \frac{2\left(\frac{10}{1}\right) - \frac{9}{\cancel{10}}\left(\frac{\overset{1}{\cancel{10}}}{1}\right)}{3\left(\frac{10}{1}\right) + \frac{1}{\cancel{5}}\left(\frac{\overset{2}{\cancel{10}}}{1}\right)} = \frac{2(10)-9}{3(10)+2} = \frac{20-9}{30+2} = \frac{11}{32}$$

5. The LCM of the 'little denominators' is 8.

$$\frac{3+\frac{5}{8}}{3} = \left(\frac{3+\frac{5}{8}}{3}\right)\left(\frac{\frac{8}{1}}{\frac{8}{1}}\right) = \frac{3\left(\frac{8}{1}\right) + \frac{5}{\cancel{8}}\left(\frac{\overset{1}{\cancel{8}}}{1}\right)}{3\left(\frac{8}{1}\right)} = \frac{3(8)+5}{3(8)} = \frac{24+5}{24} = \frac{29}{24}$$

7. The LCM of the 'little denominators' is 12.

$$\frac{2}{1-\frac{7}{12}} = \left(\frac{2}{1-\frac{7}{12}}\right)\left(\frac{\frac{12}{1}}{\frac{12}{1}}\right) = \frac{2\left(\frac{12}{1}\right)}{1\left(\frac{12}{1}\right) - \frac{7}{\cancel{12}}\left(\frac{\overset{1}{\cancel{12}}}{1}\right)} = \frac{2(12)}{1(12)-7} = \frac{24}{5}$$

9. The LCM of the 'little denominators' 36, 6 and 18 is 36. Therefore,

$$\frac{\frac{1}{36}+\frac{5}{6}}{\frac{7}{18}-\frac{1}{6}}=\left(\frac{\frac{1}{36}+\frac{5}{6}}{\frac{7}{18}-\frac{1}{6}}\right)\left(\frac{36}{\frac{36}{1}}\right)=\frac{\frac{1}{36}\left(\frac{\overset{1}{\cancel{36}}}{1}\right)+\frac{5}{\cancel{6}}\left(\frac{\overset{6}{\cancel{36}}}{1}\right)}{\frac{7}{\cancel{18}}\left(\frac{\overset{2}{\cancel{36}}}{1}\right)-\frac{1}{\cancel{6}}\left(\frac{\overset{6}{\cancel{36}}}{1}\right)}=\frac{1+5(6)}{7(2)-6}=\frac{1+30}{14-6}=\frac{31}{8}$$

11. The LCM of the 'little denominators' $3x$ and $9x$ is $9x$. Therefore,

$$\frac{\frac{1}{3x}-2}{\frac{4}{9x}+1}=\left(\frac{\frac{1}{3x}-2}{\frac{4}{9x}+1}\right)\left(\frac{\frac{9x}{1}}{\frac{9x}{1}}\right)=\frac{\frac{1}{3x}\left(\frac{\overset{3}{\cancel{9x}}}{1}\right)-2\left(\frac{9x}{1}\right)}{\frac{4}{9x}\left(\frac{\overset{1}{\cancel{9x}}}{1}\right)+1\left(\frac{9x}{1}\right)}=\frac{3-2(9x)}{4+1(9x)}=\frac{3-18x}{4+9x}=\frac{3(1-6x)}{4+9x}$$

13. The LCM of the 'little denominators' $y+1$, $y-2$ and $y^2-y-2=(y+1)(y-2)$ is $(y+1)(y-2)$.

$$\frac{\frac{2}{y+1}-\frac{3}{y-2}}{\frac{5}{y^2-y-2}}=\left(\frac{\frac{2}{y+1}-\frac{3}{y-2}}{\frac{5}{(y+1)(y-2)}}\right)\left(\frac{\frac{(y+1)(y-2)}{1}}{\frac{(y+1)(y-2)}{1}}\right)=\frac{\frac{2}{\cancel{y+1}}\left(\frac{\cancel{(y+1)}(y-2)}{1}\right)-\frac{3}{\cancel{y-2}}\left(\frac{(y+1)\cancel{(y-2)}}{1}\right)}{\frac{5}{\cancel{(y+1)(y-2)}}\left(\frac{\cancel{(y+1)(y-2)}}{1}\right)}$$

$$=\frac{2(y-2)-3(y+1)}{5}=\frac{2y-4-3y-3}{5}=\frac{-y-7}{5}\text{ or }-\frac{y+7}{5}$$

15. The LCM of the 'little denominators' $12x^2$, $4x$ and $3x^2$ is $12x^2$.

$$\frac{\frac{1}{12x^2}-\frac{5}{4x}}{\frac{2}{3x^2}}=\left(\frac{\frac{1}{12x^2}-\frac{5}{4x}}{\frac{2}{3x^2}}\right)\left(\frac{\frac{12x^2}{1}}{\frac{12x^2}{1}}\right)=\frac{\frac{1}{12x^2}\left(\frac{\overset{1}{\cancel{12x^2}}}{1}\right)-\frac{5}{4x}\left(\frac{\overset{3x}{\cancel{12x^2}}}{1}\right)}{\frac{2}{3x^2}\left(\frac{\overset{4}{\cancel{12x^2}}}{1}\right)}=\frac{1-5(3x)}{2(4)}=\frac{1-15x}{8}$$

17. The LCM of the 'little denominators' $y^2+3y=y(y+3)$, $y^2-9=(y+3)(y-3)$ and $y^2-3y=y(y-3)$ is $y(y+3)(y-3)$.

$$\frac{\frac{2}{y^2+3y}+\frac{3y}{y^2-9}}{\frac{4}{y^2-3y}}=\left(\frac{\frac{2}{y(y+3)}+\frac{3y}{(y+3)(y-3)}}{\frac{4}{y(y-3)}}\right)\left(\frac{\frac{y(y+3)(y-3)}{1}}{\frac{y(y+3)(y-3)}{1}}\right)=\frac{\frac{2}{\cancel{y(y+3)}}\left(\frac{\cancel{y(y+3)}(y-3)}{1}\right)+\frac{3y}{\cancel{(y+3)(y-3)}}\left(\frac{y\cancel{(y+3)(y-3)}}{1}\right)}{\frac{4}{\cancel{y(y-3)}}\left(\frac{y(y+3)\cancel{(y-3)}}{1}\right)}$$

$$=\frac{2(y-3)+3y(y)}{4(y+3)}=\frac{2y-6+3y^2}{4(y+3)}=\frac{3y^2+2y-6}{4(y+3)}$$

19. The LCM of the 'little denominators' is $x-6$.

$$\frac{-x+3+\frac{1}{x-6}}{x+2}=\left(\frac{-x+3+\frac{1}{x-6}}{x+2}\right)\left(\frac{\frac{x-6}{1}}{\frac{x-6}{1}}\right)=\frac{-x\left(\frac{x-6}{1}\right)+3\left(\frac{x-6}{1}\right)+\frac{1}{\cancel{x-6}}\left(\frac{\overset{1}{\cancel{x-6}}}{1}\right)}{x\left(\frac{x-6}{1}\right)+2\left(\frac{x-6}{1}\right)}=\frac{-x(x-6)+3(x-6)+1}{x(x-6)+2(x-6)}$$

$$=\frac{-x^2+6x+3x-18+1}{x^2-6x+2x-12}=\frac{-x^2+9x-17}{x^2-4x-12}$$

21. The LCM of the 'little denominators' is $2(x-9)$.

$$\frac{\frac{7}{2}+\frac{3}{x-9}}{4x-12}=\left(\frac{\frac{7}{2}+\frac{3}{x-9}}{4x-12}\right)\left(\frac{\frac{2(x-9)}{1}}{\frac{2(x-9)}{1}}\right)=\frac{\frac{7}{\cancel{2}}\left(\frac{\cancel{2}(x-9)}{1}\right)+\frac{3}{\cancel{x-9}}\left(\frac{2\cancel{(x-9)}}{1}\right)}{(4x-12)\left(\frac{2(x-9)}{1}\right)}=\frac{7(x-9)+3(2)}{(4x-12)(2(x-9))}$$

$$=\frac{7x-63+6}{4(x-3)(2(x-9))}=\frac{7x-57}{8(x-3)(x-9)}$$

23. The LCM of the 'little denominators' is $5\,(5+h)$.

$$\frac{\frac{1}{5+h}-\frac{1}{5}}{h} = \left(\frac{\frac{1}{5+h}-\frac{1}{5}}{h}\right)\left(\frac{\frac{5(5+h)}{1}}{\frac{5(5+h)}{1}}\right) = \frac{\frac{1}{5+h}\left(\frac{5(5+h)}{1}\right)-\frac{1}{5}\left(\frac{5(5+h)}{1}\right)}{h\left(\frac{5(5+h)}{1}\right)} = \frac{5-(5+h)}{5h(5+h)}$$

$$= \frac{5-5-h}{5h(5+h)} = \frac{-\overset{1}{h}}{5\overset{1}{h}(5+h)} = \frac{-1}{5(5+h)}$$

25. The LCM of the 'little denominators' $9$ and $(3+h)^2$ is $9\,(3+h)^2$.

$$\frac{\frac{1}{(3+h)^2}-\frac{1}{9}}{h} = \left(\frac{\frac{1}{(3+h)^2}-\frac{1}{9}}{h}\right)\left(\frac{\frac{9(3+h)^2}{1}}{\frac{9(3+h)^2}{1}}\right) = \frac{\frac{1}{(3+h)^2}\left(\frac{9(3+h)^2}{1}\right)-\frac{1}{9}\left(\frac{9(3+h)^2}{1}\right)}{h\left(\frac{9(3+h)^2}{1}\right)}$$

$$= \frac{9-(3+h)^2}{9h\,(3+h)^2} = \frac{9-\left(9+6h+h^2\right)}{9h\,(3+h)^2} = \frac{9-9-6h-h^2}{9h\,(3+h)^2} = \frac{-6h-h^2}{9h\,(3+h)^2}$$

$$= \frac{-\overset{1}{h}\,(6+h)}{9\overset{1}{h}\,(3+h)^2} = \frac{-\,(6+h)}{9\,(3+h)^2} = -\frac{6+h}{9\,(3+h)^2}$$

27. First simplify $\dfrac{1}{1+\frac{1}{3}}$ as follows:

$$\frac{1}{1+\frac{1}{3}} = \left(\frac{1}{1+\frac{1}{3}}\right)\left(\frac{\frac{3}{1}}{\frac{3}{1}}\right) = \frac{1\left(\frac{3}{1}\right)}{1\left(\frac{3}{1}\right)+\frac{1}{3}\left(\frac{3}{1}\right)} = \frac{3}{3+1} = \frac{3}{4}$$

Now, $1+\dfrac{1}{1+\frac{1}{3}} = 1+\frac{3}{4} = \frac{4}{4}+\frac{3}{4} = \frac{7}{4}$.

29. First simplify $\dfrac{x}{1+\frac{x}{x+3}}$ as follows:

$$\frac{x}{1+\frac{x}{x+3}} = \left(\frac{x}{1+\frac{x}{x+3}}\right)\left(\frac{\frac{x+3}{1}}{\frac{x+3}{1}}\right) = \frac{x\left(\frac{x+3}{1}\right)}{1\left(\frac{x+3}{1}\right)+\frac{x}{x+3}\left(\frac{x+3}{1}\right)} = \frac{x\,(x+3)}{1\,(x+3)+x} = \frac{x\,(x+3)}{2x+3}$$

Now, $x-\dfrac{x}{1+\frac{x}{x+3}} = x-\dfrac{x\,(x+3)}{2x+3} = \left(\dfrac{2x+3}{2x+3}\right)\dfrac{x}{1}-\dfrac{x\,(x+3)}{2x+3} = \dfrac{x\,(2x+3)-x\,(x+3)}{2x+3}$

$$= \frac{2x^2+3x-x^2-3x}{2x+3} = \frac{x^2}{2x+3}.$$

31. First simplify $\dfrac{1}{1+\frac{a}{3}}$ as follows:

$$\frac{1}{1+\frac{a}{3}} = \left(\frac{1}{1+\frac{a}{3}}\right)\left(\frac{\frac{3}{1}}{\frac{3}{1}}\right) = \frac{1\left(\frac{3}{1}\right)}{1\left(\frac{3}{1}\right)+\frac{a}{3}\left(\frac{3}{1}\right)} = \frac{3}{3+a}$$

Now, $\dfrac{a}{5+\frac{1}{1+\frac{a}{3}}} = \dfrac{a}{5+\frac{3}{3+a}} = \left(\dfrac{a}{5+\frac{3}{3+a}}\right)\left(\dfrac{\frac{3+a}{1}}{\frac{3+a}{1}}\right) = \dfrac{a\left(\frac{3+a}{1}\right)}{5\left(\frac{3+a}{1}\right)+\frac{3}{3+a}\left(\frac{3+a}{1}\right)} = \dfrac{a\,(3+a)}{5\,(3+a)+3}$

$$= \frac{a\,(3+a)}{15+5a+3} = \frac{a\,(3+a)}{18+5a}.$$

33. First simplify $\dfrac{1}{1+\frac{1}{x+1}}$ as follows:

$$\frac{1}{1+\frac{1}{x+1}} = \left(\frac{1}{1+\frac{1}{x+1}}\right)\left(\frac{\frac{x+1}{1}}{\frac{x+1}{1}}\right) = \frac{1\left(\frac{x+1}{1}\right)}{1\left(\frac{x+1}{1}\right)+\frac{1}{x+1}\left(\frac{x+1}{1}\right)} = \frac{x+1}{(x+1)+1} = \frac{x+1}{x+2}$$

Now, $1+\dfrac{1}{1+\frac{1}{x+1}} = 1+\dfrac{x+1}{x+2} = \left(\dfrac{x+2}{x+2}\right)\dfrac{1}{1}+\dfrac{x+1}{x+2} = \dfrac{(x+2)+(x+1)}{x+2} = \dfrac{2x+3}{x+2}$.

35. $\dfrac{2^{-1}+5^{-1}}{10^{-1}} = \dfrac{\frac{1}{2}+\frac{1}{5}}{\frac{1}{10}} = \left(\dfrac{\frac{1}{2}+\frac{1}{5}}{\frac{1}{10}}\right)\left(\dfrac{\frac{10}{1}}{\frac{10}{1}}\right) = \dfrac{\frac{1}{2}\left(\frac{\overset{5}{\cancel{10}}}{1}\right)+\frac{1}{5}\left(\frac{\overset{2}{\cancel{10}}}{1}\right)}{\frac{1}{\cancel{10}}\left(\frac{\cancel{10}}{1}\right)} = \dfrac{5+2}{1} = 7$

37. $\dfrac{-2+4^{-2}}{1-8^{-1}} = \dfrac{-2+\frac{1}{16}}{1-\frac{1}{8}} = \left(\dfrac{-2+\frac{1}{16}}{1-\frac{1}{8}}\right)\left(\dfrac{\frac{16}{1}}{\frac{16}{1}}\right) = \dfrac{-2\left(\frac{16}{1}\right)+\frac{1}{16}\left(\frac{\overset{1}{\cancel{16}}}{1}\right)}{1\left(\frac{16}{1}\right)-\frac{1}{8}\left(\frac{\overset{2}{\cancel{16}}}{1}\right)} = \dfrac{-32+1}{16-2} = \dfrac{-31}{14}$

39. $\dfrac{x+x^{-1}}{x^{-2}} = \dfrac{x+\frac{1}{x}}{\frac{1}{x^2}} = \left(\dfrac{x+\frac{1}{x}}{\frac{1}{x^2}}\right)\left(\dfrac{\frac{x^2}{1}}{\frac{x^2}{1}}\right) = \dfrac{x\left(\frac{x^2}{1}\right)+\frac{1}{\cancel{x}}\left(\frac{\overset{x}{\cancel{x^2}}}{1}\right)}{\frac{1}{\cancel{x^2}}\left(\frac{\cancel{x^2}}{1}\right)} = \dfrac{x\left(x^2\right)+x}{1} = x^3+x$

41. $\dfrac{1+5a^{-1}+a^{-2}}{1-5a^{-1}-a^{-2}} = \dfrac{1+\frac{5}{a}+\frac{1}{a^2}}{1-\frac{5}{a}-\frac{1}{a^2}} = \left(\dfrac{1+\frac{5}{a}+\frac{1}{a^2}}{1-\frac{5}{a}-\frac{1}{a^2}}\right)\left(\dfrac{\frac{a^2}{1}}{\frac{a^2}{1}}\right) = \dfrac{1\left(\frac{a^2}{1}\right)+\frac{5}{\cancel{a}}\left(\frac{\overset{a}{\cancel{a^2}}}{1}\right)+\frac{1}{\cancel{a^2}}\left(\frac{\cancel{a^2}}{1}\right)}{1\left(\frac{a^2}{1}\right)-\frac{5}{\cancel{a}}\left(\frac{\overset{a}{\cancel{a^2}}}{1}\right)-\frac{1}{\cancel{a^2}}\left(\frac{\cancel{a^2}}{1}\right)} = \dfrac{a^2+5a+1}{a^2-5a-1}$

43. $\dfrac{x^{-1}+x^{-1}}{x^{-1}} = \dfrac{\frac{1}{x}+\frac{1}{x}}{\frac{1}{x}} = \left(\dfrac{\frac{1}{x}+\frac{1}{x}}{\frac{1}{x}}\right)\left(\dfrac{\frac{x}{1}}{\frac{x}{1}}\right) = \dfrac{\frac{1}{\cancel{x}}\left(\frac{\cancel{x}}{1}\right)+\frac{1}{\cancel{x}}\left(\frac{\cancel{x}}{1}\right)}{\frac{1}{\cancel{x}}\left(\frac{\cancel{x}}{1}\right)} = \dfrac{1+1}{1} = 2$

Another method: notice that the numerator contains like terms and can be combined. By doing so, we obtain

$$\frac{x^{-1}+x^{-1}}{x^{-1}} = \frac{2x^{-1}}{x^{-1}} = 2.$$

---

## Chapter 5 Exercise 5.1.1

1. $\sqrt{4}=2$    3. $\sqrt{0}=0$    5. $-\sqrt{49}=-7$    7. $\sqrt{7^2}=\sqrt{49}=7$

9. $\sqrt{(-13)^2}=\sqrt{169}=13$    11. $-\sqrt{8^2}=-\sqrt{64}=-8$    13. $-\sqrt{-8^2}=-\sqrt{-64}$ is not a real number.

15. $\sqrt{(25)(25)}=\sqrt{25}\sqrt{25}=5\cdot 5=25$    17. $\sqrt{(121)(4)}=\sqrt{121}\sqrt{4}=11\cdot 2=22$

19. $\sqrt{-16}\sqrt{121}$ is not a real number, since $\sqrt{-16}$ is not a real number.    21. $\sqrt{\dfrac{1}{9}}=\dfrac{\sqrt{1}}{\sqrt{9}}=\dfrac{1}{3}$

23. $\sqrt{\dfrac{64}{25}}=\dfrac{\sqrt{64}}{\sqrt{25}}=\dfrac{8}{5}$    25. $\sqrt{\dfrac{100}{121}}=\dfrac{\sqrt{100}}{\sqrt{121}}=\dfrac{10}{11}$    27. $-\sqrt{\dfrac{144}{49}}=-\dfrac{\sqrt{144}}{\sqrt{49}}=-\dfrac{12}{7}$

29. $\sqrt{(16)\left(\dfrac{4}{81}\right)} = \sqrt{16} \cdot \sqrt{\dfrac{4}{81}} = 4 \cdot \dfrac{2}{9} = \dfrac{4}{1} \cdot \dfrac{2}{9} = \dfrac{8}{9}$

31. $\sqrt{4x^2} = \sqrt{4}\sqrt{x^2} = 2\,|x| = 2x$, since $x$ represents a positive number.

33. $\sqrt{64a^2} = \sqrt{64}\sqrt{a^2} = 8\,|a| = 8a$, since $a$ represents a positive number.

35. $\sqrt{(-3x)^2} = |-3x| = |-3| \cdot |x| = 3x$, since $x$ represents a positive number.

37. $\sqrt{(8y)^2} = |8y| = |8| \cdot |y| = 8y$, since $y$ represents a positive number.

39. $\sqrt{(14a^2b)^2} = |14a^2b| = |14| \cdot |a^2b| = 14a^2b$, since $a$ and $b$ represent positive numbers.

41. $\sqrt{\dfrac{y^2}{36}} = \dfrac{\sqrt{y^2}}{\sqrt{36}} = \dfrac{|y|}{6} = \dfrac{y}{6}$, since $y$ represents a positive number.

43. $\sqrt{\dfrac{100}{t^2}} = \dfrac{\sqrt{100}}{\sqrt{t^2}} = \dfrac{10}{|t|} = \dfrac{10}{t}$, since $t$ represents a positive number.

45. $\sqrt{\dfrac{(7x)^2}{100}} = \dfrac{\sqrt{(7x)^2}}{\sqrt{100}} = \dfrac{|7x|}{10} = \dfrac{|7| \cdot |x|}{10} = \dfrac{7x}{10}$, since $x$ represents a positive number.

47. $\sqrt{\left(\dfrac{3}{16x^4}\right)^2} = \left|\dfrac{3}{16x^4}\right| = \dfrac{|3|}{|16x^4|} = \dfrac{3}{16x^4}$, since $x$ represents a positive number.

49. $\sqrt{1}$ is rational.     51. $\sqrt{15}$ is irrational.     53. $\sqrt{\dfrac{25}{36}}$ is rational.     55. $-\sqrt{\dfrac{5}{8}}$ is irrational.

57. $\sqrt{0.09}$ is rational (note that $0.09 = \frac{9}{100}$).     59. $\sqrt{0.3}$ is irrational (note that $0.3 = \frac{3}{10}$).

61. $\sqrt{1.21}$ is rational (note that $1.21 = \frac{121}{100}$).

## Chapter 5 Exercise 5.1.2

1. $\sqrt{8} = \sqrt{4 \cdot 2} = \sqrt{4} \cdot \sqrt{2} = 2\sqrt{2}$     3. $\sqrt{20} = \sqrt{4 \cdot 5} = \sqrt{4} \cdot \sqrt{5} = 2\sqrt{5}$

5. $\sqrt{24} = \sqrt{4 \cdot 6} = \sqrt{4} \cdot \sqrt{6} = 2\sqrt{6}$     7. $-\sqrt{50} = -\sqrt{25 \cdot 2} = -\sqrt{25} \cdot \sqrt{2} = -5\sqrt{2}$

9. $\sqrt{32} = \sqrt{16 \cdot 2} = \sqrt{16} \cdot \sqrt{2} = 4\sqrt{2}$     11. $\sqrt{54} = \sqrt{9 \cdot 6} = \sqrt{9} \cdot \sqrt{6} = 3\sqrt{6}$

13. $-\sqrt{300} = -\sqrt{100 \cdot 3} = -\sqrt{100} \cdot \sqrt{3} = -10\sqrt{3}$     15. $-\sqrt{63} = -\sqrt{9 \cdot 7} = -\sqrt{9} \cdot \sqrt{7} = -3\sqrt{7}$

17. $\underbrace{\sqrt{y^5} = y^2\sqrt{y}}_{5 \div 2 = 2 \text{ R } 1}$     19. $\underbrace{\sqrt{x^4} = x^2}_{4 \div 2 = 2 \text{ R } 0}$     21. $\underbrace{\sqrt{b^{11}} = b^5\sqrt{b}}_{11 \div 2 = 5 \text{ R } 1}$     23. $\sqrt{25y} = 5\sqrt{y}$

25. $\sqrt{49y^4} = 7y^2$, since $\sqrt{49} = 7$ and $\underbrace{\sqrt{y^4} = y^2}_{4 \div 2 = 2 \text{ R } 0}$.

27. $\sqrt{8a^2b^9} = 2ab^4\sqrt{2b}$, since $\sqrt{8} = \sqrt{4}\sqrt{2} = 2\sqrt{2}$, $\sqrt{a^2} = a$ and $\underbrace{\sqrt{b^9} = b^4\sqrt{b}}_{9 \div 2 = 4 \text{ R } 1}$.

29. $\sqrt{6m^8n^3} = m^4n\sqrt{6n}$, since $\sqrt{6}$ is simplified, $\underbrace{\sqrt{m^8} = m^4}_{8 \div 2 = 4 \text{ R } 0}$ and $\underbrace{\sqrt{n^3} = n\sqrt{n}}_{3 \div 2 = 1 \text{ R } 1}$.

31. $-\sqrt{80xy^5} = -4y^2\sqrt{5xy}$, since $\sqrt{80} = \sqrt{16}\sqrt{5} = 4\sqrt{5}$, $\sqrt{x}$ is simplified and $\underbrace{\sqrt{y^5} = y^2\sqrt{y}}_{5 \div 2 = 2 \text{ R } 1}$.

33. $\sqrt{68x^{14}y^{11}z} = 2x^7y^5\sqrt{17yz}$, since $\sqrt{68} = \sqrt{4}\sqrt{17} = 2\sqrt{17}$, $\underbrace{\sqrt{x^{14}} = x^7}_{14 \div 2 = 7 \text{ R } 0}$, $\underbrace{\sqrt{y^{11}} = y^5\sqrt{y}}_{11 \div 2 = 5 \text{ R } 1}$ and $\sqrt{z}$

   is simplified.

## Chapter 5 Exercise 5.1.3

1. $\sqrt{3} \cdot \sqrt{2} = \sqrt{3 \cdot 2} = \sqrt{6}$    3. $\sqrt{7} \cdot \sqrt{6} = \sqrt{7 \cdot 6} = \sqrt{42}$    5. $\sqrt{5} \cdot \sqrt{10} = \sqrt{5 \cdot 10} = \sqrt{50} = \sqrt{25} \cdot \sqrt{2} = 5\sqrt{2}$

7. $\sqrt{8} \cdot \sqrt{8} = \sqrt{8 \cdot 8} = \sqrt{64} = 8$    9. $\sqrt{12} \cdot \sqrt{5} = \sqrt{12 \cdot 5} = \sqrt{60} = \sqrt{4} \cdot \sqrt{15} = 2\sqrt{15}$

11. $\sqrt{10} \cdot \sqrt{2} = \sqrt{10 \cdot 2} = \sqrt{20} = \sqrt{4} \cdot \sqrt{5} = 2\sqrt{5}$    13. $\sqrt{y^5} \cdot \sqrt{y^4} = \sqrt{y^5 \cdot y^4} = \underbrace{\sqrt{y^9} = y^4\sqrt{y}}_{9 \div 2 = 4 \text{ R } 1}$

15. $\sqrt{xy^2} \cdot \sqrt{x^3y^2} = \sqrt{xy^2 \cdot x^3y^2} = \underbrace{\sqrt{x^4y^4} = x^2y^2}_{4 \div 2 = 2 \text{ R } 0}$

17. $\sqrt{5a^3b^3} \cdot \sqrt{a^4b} = \sqrt{5a^3b^3 \cdot a^4b} = \underbrace{\sqrt{5a^7b^4} = a^3b^2\sqrt{5a}}_{7 \div 2 = 3 \text{ R } 1 \text{ and } 4 \div 2 = 2 \text{ R } 0.}$

19. $\sqrt{8x^2y} \cdot \sqrt{5x^3y^2} = \sqrt{8x^2y \cdot 5x^3y^2} = \underbrace{\sqrt{40x^5y^3} = 2x^2y\sqrt{10xy}}_{5 \div 2 = 2 \text{ R } 1 \text{ and } 3 \div 2 = 1 \text{ R } 1.}$

21. $\sqrt{7a^6b^3} \cdot \sqrt{7a^2b} = \sqrt{7a^6b^3 \cdot 7a^2b} = \underbrace{\sqrt{49a^8b^4} = 7a^4b^2}_{8 \div 2 = 4 \text{ R } 0 \text{ and } 4 \div 2 = 2 \text{ R } 0.}$

23. $\sqrt{6s^3t} \cdot \sqrt{6s^2t} = \sqrt{6s^3t \cdot 6s^2t} = \underbrace{\sqrt{36s^5t^2} = 6s^2t\sqrt{s}}_{5 \div 2 = 5 \text{ R } 1 \text{ and } 2 \div 2 = 1 \text{ R } 0.}$    25. $\dfrac{\sqrt{50}}{\sqrt{2}} = \sqrt{\dfrac{50}{2}} = \sqrt{25} = 5$

27. $\dfrac{\sqrt{40}}{\sqrt{2}} = \sqrt{\dfrac{40}{2}} = \sqrt{20} = \sqrt{4}\sqrt{5} = 2\sqrt{5}$    29. $\dfrac{\sqrt{16x^5}}{\sqrt{8x^4}} = \sqrt{\dfrac{16x^5}{8x^4}} = \sqrt{2x}$

31. $\dfrac{\sqrt{49y^{12}}}{\sqrt{7y^5}} = \sqrt{\dfrac{49y^{12}}{7y^5}} = \underbrace{\sqrt{7y^7} = y^3\sqrt{7y}}_{7 \div 2 = 3 \text{ R } 1}$    33. $\dfrac{\sqrt{200x^{15}y^4}}{\sqrt{4x^8y^4}} = \sqrt{\dfrac{200x^{15}y^4}{4x^8y^4}} = \underbrace{\sqrt{50x^7} = 5x^3\sqrt{2x}}_{\sqrt{50} = 5\sqrt{2} \text{ and } 7 \div 2 = 3 \text{ R } 1.}$

35. $\dfrac{\sqrt{7a^3b^2}}{\sqrt{63a^2b^4}} = \sqrt{\dfrac{7a^3b^2}{63a^2b^4}} = \underbrace{\sqrt{\dfrac{a}{9b^2}} = \dfrac{\sqrt{a}}{3b}}_{2 \div 2 = 1 \text{ R } 0}$    37. $\dfrac{\sqrt{11x^6yz^9}}{\sqrt{5x^6y^2z^7}} = \sqrt{\dfrac{11x^6yz^9}{5x^6y^2z^7}} = \underbrace{\sqrt{\dfrac{11z^2}{5y}} = \dfrac{z\sqrt{11}}{\sqrt{5y}}}_{2 \div 2 = 1 \text{ R } 0} = z\sqrt{\dfrac{11}{5y}}$

## Chapter 5 Exercise 5.1.4

1. $2\sqrt{3} + 6\sqrt{3} = 8\sqrt{3}$    3. $3\sqrt{10} - 8\sqrt{10} = -5\sqrt{10}$    5. $5\sqrt{5} + 9\sqrt{5} - 13\sqrt{5} = 1\sqrt{5} = \sqrt{5}$

7. $-3\sqrt{7} + 6\sqrt{7} - \sqrt{7} = 2\sqrt{7}$    9. $\underbrace{\sqrt{3} + \sqrt{27} = \sqrt{3} + 3\sqrt{3}}_{\sqrt{27} = \sqrt{9}\sqrt{3} = 3\sqrt{3}} = 4\sqrt{3}$

11. $\underbrace{5\sqrt{6} - 3\sqrt{72} = 5\sqrt{6} - 3\left(6\sqrt{2}\right)}_{\sqrt{72}=\sqrt{36}\sqrt{2}=6\sqrt{2}} = 5\sqrt{6} - 18\sqrt{2}$ do not combine into a single square root.

13. $\underbrace{-2\sqrt{18} - 8\sqrt{8} = -2\left(3\sqrt{2}\right) - 8\left(2\sqrt{2}\right)}_{\sqrt{18}=\sqrt{9}\sqrt{2}=3\sqrt{2} \text{ and } \sqrt{8}=\sqrt{4}\sqrt{2}=2\sqrt{2}.} = -6\sqrt{2} - 16\sqrt{2} = -22\sqrt{2}$

15. $\underbrace{10\sqrt{5} + \sqrt{20} - 18\sqrt{45} = 10\sqrt{5} + 2\sqrt{5} - 18\left(3\sqrt{5}\right)}_{\sqrt{20}=\sqrt{4}\sqrt{5}=2\sqrt{5} \text{ and } \sqrt{45}=\sqrt{9}\sqrt{5}=3\sqrt{5}.} = 10\sqrt{5} + 2\sqrt{5} - 54\sqrt{5} = -42\sqrt{5}$

17. $4\sqrt{5} + \sqrt{2}$ do not combine into a single square root.

19. $\underbrace{-4\sqrt{3} + 2\sqrt{40} + 9\sqrt{243} = -4\sqrt{3} + 2\left(2\sqrt{10}\right) + 9\left(9\sqrt{3}\right)}_{\sqrt{40}=\sqrt{4}\sqrt{10}=2\sqrt{10} \text{ and } \sqrt{243}=\sqrt{81}\sqrt{3}=9\sqrt{3}.} = -4\sqrt{3} + 4\sqrt{10} + 81\sqrt{3} = 77\sqrt{3} + 4\sqrt{10}$

21. $\underbrace{8\sqrt{4} - \sqrt{7} + \sqrt{63} + 2\sqrt{121} = 8\left(2\right) - \sqrt{7} + 3\sqrt{7} + 2\left(11\right)}_{\sqrt{4}=2, \ \sqrt{63}=\sqrt{9}\sqrt{7}=3\sqrt{7} \text{ and } \sqrt{121}=11.} = 16 - \sqrt{7} + 3\sqrt{7} + 22 = 38 + 2\sqrt{7}$

23. $\dfrac{2\sqrt{7} + 8\sqrt{28}}{9} = \dfrac{2\sqrt{7} + 8\left(2\sqrt{7}\right)}{9} = \dfrac{2\sqrt{7} + 16\sqrt{7}}{9} = \dfrac{\overset{2}{\cancel{18}}\sqrt{7}}{\underset{1}{\cancel{9}}} = \dfrac{2\sqrt{7}}{1} = 2\sqrt{7}$

25. $\dfrac{6\sqrt{4} - 5\sqrt{25}}{23} = \dfrac{6\left(2\right) - 5\left(5\right)}{23} = \dfrac{12 - 25}{23} = \dfrac{-13}{23} = -\dfrac{13}{23}$

27. $\dfrac{10 + \sqrt{32}}{2} = \dfrac{10 + 4\sqrt{2}}{2} = \dfrac{\overset{1}{\cancel{2}}\left(5 + 2\sqrt{2}\right)}{\underset{1}{\cancel{2}}} = \dfrac{5 + 2\sqrt{2}}{1} = 5 + 2\sqrt{2}$

29. $\dfrac{8\sqrt{3} - 12\sqrt{2}}{4} = \dfrac{\overset{1}{\cancel{4}}\left(2\sqrt{3} - 3\sqrt{2}\right)}{\underset{1}{\cancel{4}}} = \dfrac{2\sqrt{3} - 3\sqrt{2}}{1} = 2\sqrt{3} - 3\sqrt{2}$

31. $\dfrac{2 + \sqrt{8}}{2} = \dfrac{2 + 2\sqrt{2}}{2} = \dfrac{\overset{1}{\cancel{2}}\left(1 + \sqrt{2}\right)}{\underset{1}{\cancel{2}}} = \dfrac{1 + \sqrt{2}}{1} = 1 + \sqrt{2}$

33. $\dfrac{-12 - \sqrt{18}}{-6} = \dfrac{-12 - 3\sqrt{2}}{-6} = \dfrac{\overset{1}{\cancel{-3}}\left(4 + \sqrt{2}\right)}{\underset{2}{\cancel{-6}}} = \dfrac{4 + \sqrt{2}}{2}$

## Chapter 5 Exercise 5.1.5

1. $\sqrt{3}\left(5\sqrt{3}\right) = 5\sqrt{9} = 5\left(3\right) = 15$         3. $\left(7\sqrt{2}\right)\left(3\sqrt{2}\right) = 21\sqrt{4} = 21\left(2\right) = 42$

5. $\left(-6\sqrt{5}\right)\left(2\sqrt{5}\right) = -12\sqrt{25} = -12\left(5\right) = -60$     7. $\left(4\sqrt{8}\right)\left(3\sqrt{2}\right) = 12\sqrt{16} = 12\left(4\right) = 48$

9. $\left(4\sqrt{12}\right)\left(3\sqrt{2}\right) = \underbrace{12\sqrt{24} = 12\left(2\sqrt{6}\right)}_{\sqrt{24}=\sqrt{4}\sqrt{6}=2\sqrt{6}} = 24\sqrt{6}$   11. $\left(2\sqrt{25}\right)\left(-3\sqrt{2}\right) = \underbrace{-6\sqrt{50} = -6\left(5\sqrt{2}\right)}_{\sqrt{50}=\sqrt{25}\sqrt{2}=5\sqrt{2}} = -30\sqrt{2}$

13. $\left(4\sqrt{7}\right)\left(\sqrt{20}\right) = \underbrace{4\sqrt{140} = 4\left(2\sqrt{35}\right)}_{\sqrt{140}=\sqrt{4}\sqrt{35}=2\sqrt{35}} = 8\sqrt{35}$    15. $\left(-10\sqrt{8}\right)\left(-3\sqrt{7}\right) = \underbrace{30\sqrt{56} = 30\left(2\sqrt{14}\right)}_{\sqrt{56}=\sqrt{4}\sqrt{14}=2\sqrt{14}} = 60\sqrt{14}$

17. $\left(3\sqrt{6}\right)^2 = \left(3\sqrt{6}\right)\left(3\sqrt{6}\right) = 9\sqrt{36} = 9\,(6) = 54$

19. $\left(-5\sqrt{5}\right)^2 = \left(-5\sqrt{5}\right)\left(-5\sqrt{5}\right) = 25\sqrt{25} = 25\,(5) = 125$

21. $2\sqrt{3}\left(7\sqrt{3}-5\right) = 2\sqrt{3}\left(7\sqrt{3}\right) + 2\sqrt{3}\,(-5) = 14\sqrt{9} - 10\sqrt{3} = 14\,(3) - 10\sqrt{3} = 42 - 10\sqrt{3}$

23. $3\sqrt{3}\left(4\sqrt{3}+5\sqrt{27}\right) = 3\sqrt{3}\left(4\sqrt{3}\right) + 3\sqrt{3}\left(5\sqrt{27}\right) = 12\sqrt{9} + 15\sqrt{81} = 12\,(3) + 15\,(9) = 36 + 135 = 171$

25. $-2\sqrt{6}\left(5\sqrt{3}+4\sqrt{2}\right) = -2\sqrt{6}\left(5\sqrt{3}\right) + \left(-2\sqrt{6}\right)\left(4\sqrt{2}\right)$
$$= \underbrace{-10\sqrt{18} - 8\sqrt{12} = -10\left(3\sqrt{2}\right) - 8\left(2\sqrt{3}\right)}_{\sqrt{18}=\sqrt{9}\sqrt{2}=3\sqrt{2} \text{ and } \sqrt{12}=\sqrt{4}\sqrt{3}=2\sqrt{3}.} = -30\sqrt{2} - 16\sqrt{3}$$

27. $2\sqrt{3}\left(7\sqrt{3}-\sqrt{6}+4\sqrt{10}\right) = 2\sqrt{3}\left(7\sqrt{3}\right) + 2\sqrt{3}\left(-\sqrt{6}\right) + 2\sqrt{3}\left(4\sqrt{10}\right)$
$$= \underbrace{14\sqrt{9} - 2\sqrt{18} + 8\sqrt{30} = 14\,(3) - 2\left(3\sqrt{2}\right) + 8\sqrt{30}}_{\sqrt{9}=3 \text{ and } \sqrt{18}=\sqrt{9}\sqrt{2}=3\sqrt{2}.} = 42 - 6\sqrt{2} + 8\sqrt{30}$$

29. $\left(2\sqrt{3}-\sqrt{5}\right)\left(\sqrt{3}-\sqrt{5}\right) = \left(2\sqrt{3}\right)\left(\sqrt{3}\right) + \left(2\sqrt{3}\right)\left(-\sqrt{5}\right) + \left(-\sqrt{5}\right)\left(\sqrt{3}\right) + \left(-\sqrt{5}\right)\left(-\sqrt{5}\right)$
$$= 2\left(\sqrt{3}\right)^2 - 2\sqrt{15} - \sqrt{15} + \left(\sqrt{5}\right)^2 = 2\,(3) - 3\sqrt{15} + 5$$
$$= 6 - 3\sqrt{15} + 5 = 11 - 3\sqrt{15}$$

31. $\left(8\sqrt{3}+4\sqrt{7}\right)\left(2\sqrt{3}-2\sqrt{7}\right) = \left(8\sqrt{3}\right)\left(2\sqrt{3}\right) + \left(8\sqrt{3}\right)\left(-2\sqrt{7}\right) + \left(4\sqrt{7}\right)\left(2\sqrt{3}\right) + \left(4\sqrt{7}\right)\left(-2\sqrt{7}\right)$
$$= 16\left(\sqrt{3}\right)^2 - 16\sqrt{21} + 8\sqrt{21} - 8\left(\sqrt{7}\right)^2 = 16\,(3) - 8\sqrt{21} - 8\,(7)$$
$$= 48 - 8\sqrt{21} - 56 = -8 - 8\sqrt{21}$$

33. $\underbrace{\left(\sqrt{5}+\sqrt{7}\right)^2 = \left(\sqrt{5}\right)^2 + 2\left(\sqrt{5}\right)\left(\sqrt{7}\right) + \left(\sqrt{7}\right)^2}_{\text{use the formula } (A+B)^2=A^2+2AB+B^2 \text{ with } A=\sqrt{5} \text{ and } B=\sqrt{7}.} = 5 + 2\sqrt{35} + 7 = 12 + 2\sqrt{35}$

35. $\underbrace{\left(\sqrt{10}-4\sqrt{3}\right)^2 = \left(\sqrt{10}\right)^2 - 2\left(\sqrt{10}\right)\left(4\sqrt{3}\right) + \left(4\sqrt{3}\right)^2}_{\text{use the formula } (A-B)^2=A^2-2AB+B^2 \text{ with } A=\sqrt{10} \text{ and } B=4\sqrt{3}.} = 10 - 8\sqrt{30} + 4^2\left(\sqrt{3}\right)^2 = 10 - 8\sqrt{30} + 16\,(3)$
$$= 10 - 8\sqrt{30} + 48 = 58 - 8\sqrt{30}$$

37. $\underbrace{\left(\sqrt{x}-4\right)^2 = \left(\sqrt{x}\right)^2 - 2\left(\sqrt{x}\right)(4) + (4)^2}_{\text{use the formula } (A-B)^2=A^2-2AB+B^2 \text{ with } A=\sqrt{x} \text{ and } B=4.} = x - 8\sqrt{x} + 16$

39. $\left(8 + \sqrt{y}\right)\left(6 - \sqrt{y}\right) = (8)\,(6) + (8)\left(-\sqrt{y}\right) + \left(\sqrt{y}\right)(6) + \left(\sqrt{y}\right)\left(-\sqrt{y}\right)$
$$= 48 - 8\sqrt{y} + 6\sqrt{y} - \left(\sqrt{y}\right)^2 = 48 - 2\sqrt{y} - y$$

41. $\underbrace{\left(\sqrt{6}-\sqrt{3}\right)\left(\sqrt{6}+\sqrt{3}\right) = \left(\sqrt{6}\right)^2 - \left(\sqrt{3}\right)^2}_{\text{use the formula } (A+B)(A-B)=A^2-B^2 \text{ with } A=\sqrt{6} \text{ and } B=\sqrt{3}.} = 6 - 3 = 3$

43. $\underbrace{\left(2\sqrt{3}+4\right)\left(2\sqrt{3}-4\right) = \left(2\sqrt{3}\right)^2 - (4)^2}_{\text{use the formula } (A+B)(A-B)=A^2-B^2 \text{ with } A=2\sqrt{3} \text{ and } B=4.} = 2^2\left(\sqrt{3}\right)^2 - 16 = 4\,(3) - 16 = 12 - 16 = -4$

45. $\underbrace{\left(-6\sqrt{2}+5\right)\left(-6\sqrt{2}-5\right)=\left(-6\sqrt{2}\right)^2-(5)^2}$    $=(-6)^2\left(\sqrt{2}\right)^2-25=\underbrace{36\,(2)}_{72}-25=47$

     use the formula $(A+B)(A-B)=A^2-B^2$ with $A=-6\sqrt{2}$ and $B=5$.

47. $\underbrace{\left(\sqrt{x}-3\right)\left(\sqrt{x}+3\right)=\left(\sqrt{x}\right)^2-(3)^2}$    $=x-9$

     use the formula $(A+B)(A-B)=A^2-B^2$ with $A=\sqrt{x}$ and $B=3$.

49. $\underbrace{\left(2\sqrt{x}+7\right)\left(2\sqrt{x}-7\right)=\left(2\sqrt{x}\right)^2-(7)^2}$    $=(2)^2\left(\sqrt{x}\right)^2-49=4x-49$

     use the formula $(A+B)(A-B)=A^2-B^2$ with $A=2\sqrt{x}$ and $B=7$.

## Chapter 5 Exercise 5.1.6

1. $\dfrac{1}{\sqrt{6}}=\dfrac{1}{\sqrt{6}}\left(\dfrac{\sqrt{6}}{\sqrt{6}}\right)=\dfrac{\sqrt{6}}{\left(\sqrt{6}\right)^2}=\dfrac{\sqrt{6}}{6}$      3. $\dfrac{8}{\sqrt{3}}=\dfrac{8}{\sqrt{3}}\left(\dfrac{\sqrt{3}}{\sqrt{3}}\right)=\dfrac{8\sqrt{3}}{\left(\sqrt{3}\right)^2}=\dfrac{8\sqrt{3}}{3}$

5. $\dfrac{13}{\sqrt{26}}=\dfrac{13}{\sqrt{26}}\left(\dfrac{\sqrt{26}}{\sqrt{26}}\right)=\dfrac{13\sqrt{26}}{\left(\sqrt{26}\right)^2}=\dfrac{\overset{1}{\cancel{13}}\sqrt{26}}{\underset{2}{\cancel{26}}}=\dfrac{\sqrt{26}}{2}$

7. $\dfrac{18}{\sqrt{10}}=\dfrac{18}{\sqrt{10}}\left(\dfrac{\sqrt{10}}{\sqrt{10}}\right)=\dfrac{18\sqrt{10}}{\left(\sqrt{10}\right)^2}=\dfrac{\overset{9}{\cancel{18}}\sqrt{10}}{\underset{5}{\cancel{10}}}=\dfrac{9\sqrt{10}}{5}$

9. $\underbrace{\dfrac{10}{\sqrt{8}}=\dfrac{10}{2\sqrt{2}}}=\dfrac{5}{\sqrt{2}}=\dfrac{5}{\sqrt{2}}\left(\dfrac{\sqrt{2}}{\sqrt{2}}\right)=\dfrac{5\sqrt{2}}{\left(\sqrt{2}\right)^2}=\dfrac{5\sqrt{2}}{2}$

     $\sqrt{8}=\sqrt{4}\sqrt{2}=2\sqrt{2}$

11. $\underbrace{\dfrac{8}{3\sqrt{20}}=\dfrac{8}{3\left(2\sqrt{5}\right)}}=\dfrac{4}{3\sqrt{5}}=\dfrac{4}{3\sqrt{5}}\left(\dfrac{\sqrt{5}}{\sqrt{5}}\right)=\dfrac{4\sqrt{5}}{3\left(\sqrt{5}\right)^2}=\dfrac{4\sqrt{5}}{3\,(5)}=\dfrac{4\sqrt{5}}{15}$

     $\sqrt{20}=\sqrt{4}\sqrt{5}=2\sqrt{5}$

13. $\underbrace{\dfrac{-12}{5\sqrt{24}}=\dfrac{-12}{5\left(2\sqrt{6}\right)}}=\dfrac{-6}{5\sqrt{6}}=\dfrac{-6}{5\sqrt{6}}\left(\dfrac{\sqrt{6}}{\sqrt{6}}\right)=\dfrac{-6\sqrt{6}}{5\left(\sqrt{6}\right)^2}=\dfrac{-\cancel{6}\sqrt{6}}{5\,(\cancel{6})}=\dfrac{-\sqrt{6}}{5}$

     $\sqrt{24}=\sqrt{4}\sqrt{6}=2\sqrt{6}$

15. $\sqrt{\dfrac{1}{5}}=\dfrac{\sqrt{1}}{\sqrt{5}}=\dfrac{1}{\sqrt{5}}=\dfrac{1}{\sqrt{5}}\left(\dfrac{\sqrt{5}}{\sqrt{5}}\right)=\dfrac{\sqrt{5}}{\left(\sqrt{5}\right)^2}=\dfrac{\sqrt{5}}{5}$

17. $\sqrt{\dfrac{10}{7}}=\dfrac{\sqrt{10}}{\sqrt{7}}=\dfrac{\sqrt{10}}{\sqrt{7}}\left(\dfrac{\sqrt{7}}{\sqrt{7}}\right)=\dfrac{\sqrt{70}}{\left(\sqrt{7}\right)^2}=\dfrac{\sqrt{70}}{7}$

19. $\sqrt{\dfrac{11}{12}}=\underbrace{\dfrac{\sqrt{11}}{\sqrt{12}}=\dfrac{\sqrt{11}}{2\sqrt{3}}}=\dfrac{\sqrt{11}}{2\sqrt{3}}\left(\dfrac{\sqrt{3}}{\sqrt{3}}\right)=\dfrac{\sqrt{33}}{2\left(\sqrt{3}\right)^2}=\dfrac{\sqrt{33}}{2\,(3)}=\dfrac{\sqrt{33}}{6}$

     $\sqrt{12}=\sqrt{4}\sqrt{3}=2\sqrt{3}$

21. $\dfrac{3}{\sqrt{x}}=\dfrac{3}{\sqrt{x}}\left(\dfrac{\sqrt{x}}{\sqrt{x}}\right)=\dfrac{3\sqrt{x}}{\left(\sqrt{x}\right)^2}=\dfrac{3\sqrt{x}}{x}$

23. $\dfrac{2}{3\sqrt{2x}} = \dfrac{2}{3\sqrt{2x}}\left(\dfrac{\sqrt{2x}}{\sqrt{2x}}\right) = \dfrac{2\sqrt{2x}}{3\left(\sqrt{2x}\right)^2} = \dfrac{2\sqrt{2x}}{3\,(2x)} = \dfrac{2\sqrt{2x}}{6x}$

25. $\dfrac{1}{\sqrt{2}+1} = \underbrace{\dfrac{1}{\sqrt{2}+1}\left(\dfrac{\sqrt{2}-1}{\sqrt{2}-1}\right) = \dfrac{\sqrt{2}-1}{\left(\sqrt{2}\right)^2 - (1)^2}}_{\text{use the formula } (A+B)(A-B)=A^2-B^2 \text{ with } A=\sqrt{2} \text{ and } B=1.} = \dfrac{\sqrt{2}-1}{2-1} = \dfrac{\sqrt{2}-1}{1} = \sqrt{2}-1$

27. $\dfrac{1}{\sqrt{5}-2} = \underbrace{\dfrac{1}{\sqrt{5}-2}\left(\dfrac{\sqrt{5}+2}{\sqrt{5}+2}\right) = \dfrac{\sqrt{5}+2}{\left(\sqrt{5}\right)^2 - (2)^2}}_{\text{use the formula } (A+B)(A-B)=A^2-B^2 \text{ with } A=\sqrt{5} \text{ and } B=2.} = \dfrac{\sqrt{5}+2}{5-4} = \dfrac{\sqrt{5}+2}{1} = \sqrt{5}+2$

29. $\dfrac{2}{\sqrt{5}-3} = \underbrace{\dfrac{2}{\sqrt{5}-3}\left(\dfrac{\sqrt{5}+3}{\sqrt{5}+3}\right) = \dfrac{2\left(\sqrt{5}+3\right)}{\left(\sqrt{5}\right)^2 - (3)^2}}_{\text{use the formula } (A+B)(A-B)=A^2-B^2 \text{ with } A=\sqrt{5} \text{ and } B=3.} = \dfrac{2\left(\sqrt{5}+3\right)}{5-9} = \dfrac{\overset{1}{\cancel{2}}\left(\sqrt{5}+3\right)}{\underset{-2}{\cancel{-4}}} = \dfrac{\sqrt{5}+3}{-2}$

31. $\dfrac{1+\sqrt{2}}{2-\sqrt{2}} = \underbrace{\dfrac{1+\sqrt{2}}{2-\sqrt{2}}\left(\dfrac{2+\sqrt{2}}{2+\sqrt{2}}\right) = \dfrac{\left(1+\sqrt{2}\right)\left(2+\sqrt{2}\right)}{(2)^2 - \left(\sqrt{2}\right)^2}}_{\text{use the formula } (A+B)(A-B)=A^2-B^2 \text{ with } A=2 \text{ and } B=\sqrt{2}.} = \dfrac{2+\sqrt{2}+2\sqrt{2}+\left(\sqrt{2}\right)^2}{4-2} = \dfrac{4+3\sqrt{2}}{2}$

33. $\dfrac{\sqrt{5}-\sqrt{2}}{\sqrt{5}+\sqrt{2}} = \underbrace{\dfrac{\sqrt{5}-\sqrt{2}}{\sqrt{5}+\sqrt{2}}\left(\dfrac{\sqrt{5}-\sqrt{2}}{\sqrt{5}-\sqrt{2}}\right) = \dfrac{\left(\sqrt{5}-\sqrt{2}\right)\left(\sqrt{5}-\sqrt{2}\right)}{\left(\sqrt{5}\right)^2 - \left(\sqrt{2}\right)^2}}_{\text{use the formula } (A+B)(A-B)=A^2-B^2 \text{ with } A=\sqrt{5} \text{ and } B=\sqrt{2}.} = \dfrac{\overset{5}{\overbrace{\left(\sqrt{5}\right)^2}} - \sqrt{10} - \sqrt{10} + \overset{2}{\overbrace{\left(\sqrt{2}\right)^2}}}{5-2}$

$= \dfrac{7-2\sqrt{10}}{3}$

35. $\dfrac{-2\sqrt{6}+3}{3\sqrt{2}+\sqrt{6}} = \underbrace{\dfrac{-2\sqrt{6}+3}{3\sqrt{2}+\sqrt{6}}\left(\dfrac{3\sqrt{2}-\sqrt{6}}{3\sqrt{2}-\sqrt{6}}\right) = \dfrac{\left(-2\sqrt{6}+3\right)\left(3\sqrt{2}-\sqrt{6}\right)}{\left(3\sqrt{2}\right)^2 - \left(\sqrt{6}\right)^2}}_{\text{use the formula } (A+B)(A-B)=A^2-B^2 \text{ with } A=3\sqrt{2} \text{ and } B=\sqrt{6}.} = \dfrac{-6\sqrt{12}+2\left(\sqrt{6}\right)^2 + 9\sqrt{2}-3\sqrt{6}}{3^2\left(\sqrt{2}\right)^2 - 6}$

$= \dfrac{-6\left(2\sqrt{3}\right)+2\,(6)+9\sqrt{2}-3\sqrt{6}}{9\,(2)-6} = \dfrac{-12\sqrt{3}+12+9\sqrt{2}-3\sqrt{6}}{18-6} = \dfrac{-12\sqrt{3}+12+9\sqrt{2}-3\sqrt{6}}{12}$

$= \dfrac{\overset{1}{\cancel{3}}\left(-4\sqrt{3}+4+3\sqrt{2}-\sqrt{6}\right)}{\underset{4}{\cancel{12}}} = \dfrac{-4\sqrt{3}+4+3\sqrt{2}-\sqrt{6}}{4}$

37. $\dfrac{4+\sqrt{x}}{2-\sqrt{x}} = \underbrace{\dfrac{4+\sqrt{x}}{2-\sqrt{x}}\left(\dfrac{2+\sqrt{x}}{2+\sqrt{x}}\right) = \dfrac{\left(4+\sqrt{x}\right)\left(2+\sqrt{x}\right)}{(2)^2 - \left(\sqrt{x}\right)^2}}_{\text{use the formula } (A+B)(A-B)=A^2-B^2 \text{ with } A=2 \text{ and } B=\sqrt{x}.} = \dfrac{8+4\sqrt{x}+2\sqrt{x}+\left(\sqrt{x}\right)^2}{4-x} = \dfrac{8+6\sqrt{x}+x}{4-x}$

39. $\dfrac{\sqrt{7}}{2} = \dfrac{\sqrt{7}}{2}\left(\dfrac{\sqrt{7}}{\sqrt{7}}\right) = \dfrac{\left(\sqrt{7}\right)^2}{2\sqrt{7}} = \dfrac{7}{2\sqrt{7}}$

41. $\underbrace{\dfrac{\sqrt{12}}{3} = \dfrac{2\sqrt{3}}{3}}_{\sqrt{12}=\sqrt{4}\sqrt{3}=2\sqrt{3}} = \dfrac{2\sqrt{3}}{3}\left(\dfrac{\sqrt{3}}{\sqrt{3}}\right) = \dfrac{2\left(\sqrt{3}\right)^2}{3\sqrt{3}} = \dfrac{2(\overset{1}{\cancel{3}})}{\underset{1}{\cancel{3}}\sqrt{3}} = \dfrac{2}{\sqrt{3}}$

43. $\dfrac{2\sqrt{3}}{\sqrt{5}} = \dfrac{2\sqrt{3}}{\sqrt{5}}\left(\dfrac{\sqrt{3}}{\sqrt{3}}\right) = \dfrac{2\left(\sqrt{3}\right)^2}{\sqrt{15}} = \dfrac{2\,(3)}{\sqrt{15}} = \dfrac{6}{\sqrt{15}}$

45. $\underbrace{\dfrac{\sqrt{8}}{\sqrt{7}}}_{\sqrt{8}=\sqrt{4}\sqrt{2}=2\sqrt{2}} = \dfrac{2\sqrt{2}}{\sqrt{7}} = \dfrac{2\sqrt{2}}{\sqrt{7}}\left(\dfrac{\sqrt{2}}{\sqrt{2}}\right) = \dfrac{2\left(\sqrt{2}\right)^2}{\sqrt{14}} = \dfrac{2\,(2)}{\sqrt{14}} = \dfrac{4}{\sqrt{14}}$

47. $\sqrt{\dfrac{5}{9}} = \dfrac{\sqrt{5}}{\sqrt{9}} = \dfrac{\sqrt{5}}{3} = \dfrac{\sqrt{5}}{3}\left(\dfrac{\sqrt{5}}{\sqrt{5}}\right) = \dfrac{\left(\sqrt{5}\right)^2}{3\sqrt{5}} = \dfrac{5}{3\sqrt{5}}$

49. $\dfrac{\sqrt{x}}{3} = \dfrac{\sqrt{x}}{3}\left(\dfrac{\sqrt{x}}{\sqrt{x}}\right) = \dfrac{\left(\sqrt{x}\right)^2}{3\sqrt{x}} = \dfrac{x}{3\sqrt{x}}$

51. $\dfrac{2+\sqrt{6}}{4} = \underbrace{\dfrac{2+\sqrt{6}}{4}\left(\dfrac{2-\sqrt{6}}{2-\sqrt{6}}\right) = \dfrac{(2)^2-\left(\sqrt{6}\right)^2}{4\left(2-\sqrt{6}\right)}}_{\text{use the formula }(A+B)(A-B)=A^2-B^2\text{ with }A=2\text{ and }B=\sqrt{6}.} = \dfrac{4-6}{4\left(2-\sqrt{6}\right)} = \dfrac{\overset{-1}{\cancel{-2}}}{\underset{2}{\cancel{4}}\left(2-\sqrt{6}\right)} = \dfrac{-1}{2\left(2-\sqrt{6}\right)}$

53. $\dfrac{\sqrt{2}-\sqrt{5}}{\sqrt{3}} = \underbrace{\dfrac{\sqrt{2}-\sqrt{5}}{\sqrt{3}}\left(\dfrac{\sqrt{2}+\sqrt{5}}{\sqrt{2}+\sqrt{5}}\right) = \dfrac{\left(\sqrt{2}\right)^2-\left(\sqrt{5}\right)^2}{\sqrt{3}\left(\sqrt{2}+\sqrt{5}\right)}}_{\text{use the formula }(A+B)(A-B)=A^2-B^2\text{ with }A=\sqrt{2}\text{ and }B=\sqrt{5}.} = \dfrac{2-5}{\sqrt{6}+\sqrt{15}} = \dfrac{-3}{\sqrt{6}+\sqrt{15}}$

55. $\dfrac{\sqrt{6}+4}{\sqrt{6}-4} = \underbrace{\dfrac{\sqrt{6}+4}{\sqrt{6}-4}\left(\dfrac{\sqrt{6}-4}{\sqrt{6}-4}\right) = \dfrac{\left(\sqrt{6}\right)^2-(4)^2}{\left(\sqrt{6}-4\right)\left(\sqrt{6}-4\right)}}_{\text{use the formula }(A+B)(A-B)=A^2-B^2\text{ with }A=\sqrt{6}\text{ and }B=4.} = \dfrac{6-16}{\underbrace{\left(\sqrt{6}\right)^2}_{6}-4\sqrt{6}-4\sqrt{6}+16}$

$= \dfrac{-10}{22-8\sqrt{6}} = \dfrac{\overset{-5}{\cancel{-10}}}{\underset{1}{\cancel{2}}\left(11-4\sqrt{6}\right)} = \dfrac{-5}{11-4\sqrt{6}}$

57. $\dfrac{\sqrt{x}+9}{\sqrt{x}-3} = \underbrace{\dfrac{\sqrt{x}+9}{\sqrt{x}-3}\left(\dfrac{\sqrt{x}-9}{\sqrt{x}-9}\right) = \dfrac{\left(\sqrt{x}\right)^2-(9)^2}{\left(\sqrt{x}-3\right)\left(\sqrt{x}-9\right)}}_{\text{use the formula }(A+B)(A-B)=A^2-B^2\text{ with }A=\sqrt{x}\text{ and }B=9.} = \dfrac{x-81}{\left(\sqrt{x}\right)^2-9\sqrt{x}-3\sqrt{x}+27}$

$= \dfrac{x-81}{x-12\sqrt{x}+27}$

59. $\dfrac{\sqrt{7+h}-\sqrt{7}}{h} = \underbrace{\dfrac{\sqrt{7+h}-\sqrt{7}}{h}\left(\dfrac{\sqrt{7+h}+\sqrt{7}}{\sqrt{7+h}+\sqrt{7}}\right) = \dfrac{\left(\sqrt{7+h}\right)^2-\left(\sqrt{7}\right)^2}{h\left(\sqrt{7+h}+\sqrt{7}\right)}}_{\text{use the formula }(A+B)(A-B)=A^2-B^2\text{ with }A=\sqrt{7+h}\text{ and }B=\sqrt{7}.}$

$= \dfrac{7+h-7}{h\left(\sqrt{7+h}+\sqrt{7}\right)} = \dfrac{\overset{1}{\cancel{h}}}{\underset{1}{\cancel{h}}\left(\sqrt{7+h}+\sqrt{7}\right)} = \dfrac{1}{\sqrt{7+h}+\sqrt{7}}$

## Chapter 5 Exercise 5.2

1. $\sqrt[3]{8} = 2$       3. $-\sqrt[3]{-8} = -(-2) = 2$       5. $\sqrt[3]{-64} = -4$       7. $\sqrt[3]{\dfrac{1}{27}} = \dfrac{1}{3}$

9. $-\sqrt[3]{-\dfrac{1}{27}} = -\left(-\dfrac{1}{3}\right) = \dfrac{1}{3}$       11. $\sqrt[3]{-\dfrac{216}{125}} = -\dfrac{6}{5}$       13. $\sqrt[3]{(27)(125)} = \underbrace{\sqrt[3]{27}}_{3}\cdot\underbrace{\sqrt[3]{125}}_{5} = 3\cdot 5 = 15$

15. $\left(\sqrt[3]{9}\right)^3 = 9$       17. $\left(\sqrt[3]{-11}\right)^3 = -11$       19. $\sqrt[3]{\left(9^3\right)(8)} = \underbrace{\sqrt[3]{9^3}}_{9}\cdot\underbrace{\sqrt[3]{8}}_{2} = 9\cdot 2 = 18$

21. $\sqrt[3]{24} = \sqrt[3]{8\cdot 3} = \sqrt[3]{8}\cdot\sqrt[3]{3} = 2\sqrt[3]{3}$       23. $\sqrt[3]{-24} = \sqrt[3]{-8\cdot 3} = \sqrt[3]{-8}\cdot\sqrt[3]{3} = -2\sqrt[3]{3}$

25. $\sqrt[3]{54} = \sqrt[3]{27 \cdot 2} = \sqrt[3]{27} \cdot \sqrt[3]{2} = 3\sqrt[3]{2}$        27. $\sqrt[3]{-54} = \sqrt[3]{-27 \cdot 2} = \sqrt[3]{-27} \cdot \sqrt[3]{2} = -3\sqrt[3]{2}$

29. $\sqrt[3]{4,000} = \sqrt[3]{1,000 \cdot 4} = \sqrt[3]{1,000} \cdot \sqrt[3]{4} = 10\sqrt[3]{4}$        31. $\sqrt[3]{x^3} = x$        33. $\underbrace{\sqrt[3]{y^7} = y^2\sqrt[3]{y}}_{7 \div 3 = 2\ R\ 1}$

35. $\underbrace{\sqrt[3]{t^{17}} = t^5\sqrt[3]{t^2}}_{17 \div 3 = 5\ R\ 2}$        37. $\underbrace{\sqrt[3]{9x^5y^6} = xy^2\sqrt[3]{9x^2}}_{5 \div 3 = 1\ R\ 2\ \text{and}\ 6 \div 3 = 2\ R\ 0.}$        39. $\underbrace{\sqrt[3]{-40x^8y^5} = -2x^2y\sqrt[3]{5x^2y^2}}_{\sqrt[3]{-40} = \sqrt[3]{-8}\sqrt[3]{5} = -2\sqrt[3]{5},\ 8 \div 3 = 2\ R\ 2\ \text{and}\ 5 \div 3 = 1\ R\ 2.}$

41. $2\sqrt[3]{4} + 5\sqrt[3]{4} = 7\sqrt[3]{4}$        43. $8\sqrt[3]{9} - 6\sqrt[3]{9} = 2\sqrt[3]{9}$

45.  $\underbrace{\sqrt[3]{16} + 2\sqrt[3]{24} = 2\sqrt[3]{2} + 2\left(2\sqrt[3]{3}\right)}_{\sqrt[3]{16} = \sqrt[3]{8}\sqrt[3]{2} = 2\sqrt[3]{2}\ \text{and}\ \sqrt[3]{24} = \sqrt[3]{8}\sqrt[3]{3} = 2\sqrt[3]{3}.}$  $= 2\sqrt[3]{2} + 4\sqrt[3]{3}$ do not combine.

47. $5\sqrt[3]{2} - 12\sqrt[3]{16} + 6\sqrt[3]{54} = 5\sqrt[3]{2} - 12\left(2\sqrt[3]{2}\right) + 6\left(3\sqrt[3]{2}\right) = 5\sqrt[3]{2} - 24\sqrt[3]{2} + 18\sqrt[3]{2} = -1\sqrt[3]{2} = -\sqrt[3]{2}$
$\underbrace{\phantom{5\sqrt[3]{2} - 12\sqrt[3]{16} + 6\sqrt[3]{54} = 5\sqrt[3]{2} - 12\left(2\sqrt[3]{2}\right) + 6\left(3\sqrt[3]{2}\right)}}_{\sqrt[3]{16} = \sqrt[3]{8}\sqrt[3]{2} = 2\sqrt[3]{2}\ \text{and}\ \sqrt[3]{54} = \sqrt[3]{27}\sqrt[3]{2} = 3\sqrt[3]{2}.}$

49.  $\underbrace{6x\sqrt[3]{5x} + \sqrt[3]{40x^4} = 6x\sqrt[3]{5x} + 2x\sqrt[3]{5x}}_{\sqrt[3]{40x^4} = 2x\sqrt[3]{5x}\ \text{since}\ \sqrt[3]{40} = \sqrt[3]{8}\sqrt[3]{5} = 2\sqrt[3]{5}\ \text{and}\ 4 \div 3 = 1\ R\ 1.}$  $= 8x\sqrt[3]{5x}$        51. $\left(\sqrt[3]{2}\right)\left(\sqrt[3]{4}\right) = \sqrt[3]{8} = 2$

53. $\left(-\sqrt[3]{3}\right)\left(\sqrt[3]{9}\right) = -\sqrt[3]{27} = -3$        55. $\left(\sqrt[3]{4}\right)\left(\sqrt[3]{10}\right) = \sqrt[3]{40} = \sqrt[3]{8}\sqrt[3]{5} = 2\sqrt[3]{5}$

57. $\left(\sqrt[3]{8}\right)^2 = (2)^2 = 4$        59. $\left(\sqrt[3]{4}\right)^2 = \left(\sqrt[3]{4}\right)\left(\sqrt[3]{4}\right) = \sqrt[3]{16} = \sqrt[3]{8}\sqrt[3]{2} = 2\sqrt[3]{2}$

61. $\sqrt[3]{2}\left(\sqrt[3]{3} + 6\right) = \sqrt[3]{2}\left(\sqrt[3]{3}\right) + \sqrt[3]{2}\,(6) = \sqrt[3]{6} + 6\sqrt[3]{2}$

63. $\sqrt[3]{16}\left(\sqrt[3]{2} + 5\sqrt[3]{3}\right) = \sqrt[3]{16}\left(\sqrt[3]{2}\right) + \sqrt[3]{16}\left(5\sqrt[3]{3}\right) = \underbrace{\sqrt[3]{32} + 5\sqrt[3]{48} = 2\sqrt[3]{4} + 5\left(2\sqrt[3]{6}\right)}_{\sqrt[3]{32} = \sqrt[3]{8}\sqrt[3]{4} = 2\sqrt[3]{4}\ \text{and}\ \sqrt[3]{48} = \sqrt[3]{8}\sqrt[3]{6} = 2\sqrt[3]{6}.}$ $= 2\sqrt[3]{4} + 10\sqrt[3]{6}$

65. $\left(\sqrt[3]{2} - 1\right)\left(\sqrt[3]{2} + 2\right) = \left(\sqrt[3]{2}\right)\left(\sqrt[3]{2}\right) + \left(\sqrt[3]{2}\right)(2) + (-1)\left(\sqrt[3]{2}\right) + (-1)(2) = \sqrt[3]{4} + 2\sqrt[3]{2} - \sqrt[3]{2} - 2 = \sqrt[3]{4} + \sqrt[3]{2} - 2$

67.  $\underbrace{\left(\sqrt[3]{4} + 5\right)^2 = \left(\sqrt[3]{4}\right)^2 + 2\left(\sqrt[3]{4}\right)(5) + (5)^2}_{\text{use the formula}\ (A+B)^2 = A^2 + 2AB + B^2\ \text{with}\ A = \sqrt[3]{4}\ \text{and}\ B = 5.}$  $= \underbrace{\sqrt[3]{16} + 10\sqrt[3]{4} + 25 = 2\sqrt[3]{2} + 10\sqrt[3]{4} + 25}_{\sqrt[3]{16} = \sqrt[3]{8}\sqrt[3]{2} = 2\sqrt[3]{2}}$

69. $\left(\sqrt[3]{x} + 3\right)\left(\sqrt[3]{x} + 4\right) = \left(\sqrt[3]{x}\right)\left(\sqrt[3]{x}\right) + \left(\sqrt[3]{x}\right)(4) + (3)\left(\sqrt[3]{x}\right) + (3)(4)$
$= \sqrt[3]{x^2} + 4\sqrt[3]{x} + 3\sqrt[3]{x} + 12 = \sqrt[3]{x^2} + 7\sqrt[3]{x} + 12$

71. $\left(\sqrt[3]{x^2} - 6\right)\left(\sqrt[3]{x^5} - 2\right) = \left(\sqrt[3]{x^2}\right)\left(\sqrt[3]{x^5}\right) + \left(\sqrt[3]{x^2}\right)(-2) + (-6)\left(\sqrt[3]{x^5}\right) + (-6)(-2)$
$= \sqrt[3]{x^7} - 2\sqrt[3]{x^2} - 6\sqrt[3]{x^5} + 12$
$= x^2\sqrt[3]{x} - 2\sqrt[3]{x^2} - 6x\sqrt[3]{x^2} + 12$

## Chapter 5 Exercise 5.3

1. $\sqrt[4]{16} = 2$        3. $\sqrt[5]{32} = 2$        5. $\sqrt[5]{-32} = -2$        7. $\sqrt[6]{64} = 2$

9. $\sqrt[4]{\dfrac{16}{81}} = \dfrac{\sqrt[4]{16}}{\sqrt[4]{81}} = \dfrac{2}{3}$        11. $\sqrt[4]{48} = \sqrt[4]{16 \cdot 3} = \sqrt[4]{16} \cdot \sqrt[4]{3} = 2\sqrt[4]{3}$

13. $-\sqrt[4]{162} = -\sqrt[4]{81 \cdot 2} = -\sqrt[4]{81} \cdot \sqrt[4]{2} = -3\sqrt[4]{2}$    15. $\sqrt[5]{8^5} = 8$    17. $\sqrt[7]{(-20)^7} = -20$

19. $\sqrt[5]{-64} = \sqrt[5]{-32 \cdot 2} = \sqrt[5]{-32} \cdot \sqrt[5]{2} = -2\sqrt[5]{2}$    21. $\underbrace{\sqrt[6]{x^{17}} = x^2 \sqrt[6]{x^5}}_{17 \div 6 = 2 \text{ R } 5}$

23. $\underbrace{\sqrt[5]{a^8 b^{14}} = ab^2 \sqrt[5]{a^3 b^4}}_{8 \div 5 = 1 \text{ R } 3 \text{ and } 14 \div 5 = 2 \text{ R } 4.}$    25. $\underbrace{\sqrt[7]{x^3 y^{20}} = y^2 \sqrt[7]{x^3 y^6}}_{3 \div 7 = 0 \text{ R } 3 \text{ and } 20 \div 7 = 2 \text{ R } 6.}$    27. $\underbrace{\sqrt[4]{48 x^7 y^8} = 2xy^2 \sqrt[4]{3x^3}}_{\sqrt[4]{48} = \sqrt[4]{16} \sqrt[4]{3} = 2\sqrt[4]{3}, \ 7 \div 4 = 1 \text{ R } 3 \text{ and } 8 \div 4 = 2 \text{ R } 0.}$

29. $\sqrt[5]{3}\left(2\sqrt[5]{3} + 8\right) = \sqrt[5]{3}\left(2\sqrt[5]{3}\right) + \sqrt[5]{3}(8) = 2\sqrt[5]{9} + 8\sqrt[5]{3}$

31. $\sqrt[7]{10}\left(3\sqrt[7]{10} - 6\sqrt[7]{5}\right) = \sqrt[7]{10}\left(3\sqrt[7]{10}\right) + \sqrt[7]{10}\left(-6\sqrt[7]{5}\right) = 3\sqrt[7]{100} - 6\sqrt[7]{50}$

33. $\left(\sqrt[5]{3} + 1\right)\left(\sqrt[5]{3} - 2\right) = \left(\sqrt[5]{3}\right)\left(\sqrt[5]{3}\right) + \left(\sqrt[5]{3}\right)(-2) + (1)\left(\sqrt[5]{3}\right) + (1)(-2) = \sqrt[5]{9} - 2\sqrt[5]{3} + \sqrt[5]{3} - 2 = \sqrt[5]{9} - \sqrt[5]{3} - 2$

35.  $\underbrace{\left(\sqrt[7]{6} + 3\right)^2 = \left(\sqrt[7]{6}\right)^2 + 2\left(\sqrt[7]{6}\right)(3) + (3)^2}_{\text{use the formula } (A+B)^2 = A^2 + 2AB + B^2 \text{ with } A = \sqrt[7]{6} \text{ and } B = 3.} \quad = \overbrace{\sqrt[7]{36}}^{\sqrt[7]{6}\,\sqrt[7]{6}} + 6\sqrt[7]{6} + 9$

37.  $\underbrace{\left(\sqrt[5]{2} + 9\right)\left(\sqrt[5]{2} - 9\right) = \left(\sqrt[5]{2}\right)^2 - (9)^2}_{\text{use the formula } (A+B)(A-B) = A^2 - B^2 \text{ with } A = \sqrt[5]{2} \text{ and } B = 9.} \quad = \overbrace{\sqrt[5]{4}}^{\sqrt[5]{2}\,\sqrt[5]{2}} - 81$

39. $\left(\sqrt[3]{x} + 2\right)\left(\sqrt[3]{x} + 3\right) = \left(\sqrt[3]{x}\right)\left(\sqrt[3]{x}\right) + \left(\sqrt[3]{x}\right)(3) + (2)\left(\sqrt[3]{x}\right) + (2)(3)$
$\qquad\qquad = \sqrt[3]{x^2} + 3\sqrt[3]{x} + 2\sqrt[3]{x} + 6 = \sqrt[3]{x^2} + 5\sqrt[3]{x} + 6$

41.  $\underbrace{\left(\sqrt[7]{x} + y\right)^2 = \left(\sqrt[7]{x}\right)^2 + 2\left(\sqrt[7]{x}\right)(y) + (y)^2}_{\text{use the formula } (A+B)^2 = A^2 + 2AB + B^2 \text{ with } A = \sqrt[7]{x} \text{ and } B = y.} \quad = \sqrt[7]{x^2} + 2y\sqrt[7]{x} + y^2$

43.  $\underbrace{\left(\sqrt[5]{a} - \sqrt[5]{b}\right)\left(\sqrt[5]{a} + \sqrt[5]{b}\right) = \left(\sqrt[5]{a}\right)^2 - \left(\sqrt[5]{b}\right)^2}_{\text{use the formula } (A+B)(A-B) = A^2 - B^2 \text{ with } A = \sqrt[5]{a} \text{ and } B = \sqrt[5]{b}.} \quad = \sqrt[5]{a^2} - \sqrt[5]{b^2}$

45. $\sqrt[5]{x^2}\left(\sqrt[5]{x^3} - 3x\right) = \sqrt[5]{x^2}\left(\sqrt[5]{x^3}\right) + \sqrt[5]{x^2}(-3x) = \sqrt[5]{x^5} - 3x\sqrt[5]{x^2} = x - 3x\sqrt[5]{x^2}$

47. $3\sqrt[5]{x^3}\left(x + 6\sqrt[5]{x^2}\right) = 3\sqrt[5]{x^3}(x) + 3\sqrt[5]{x^3}\left(6\sqrt[5]{x^2}\right) = 3x\sqrt[5]{x^3} + 18\sqrt[5]{x^5} = 3x\sqrt[5]{x^3} + 18x$

---

## Chapter 6 Exercises

1. $9^{\frac{1}{2}} = \sqrt{9} = 3$    3. $49^{\frac{1}{2}} = \sqrt{49} = 7$    5. $25^{\frac{3}{2}} = \left(\sqrt{25}\right)^3 = 5^3 = 125$

7. $64^{\frac{3}{2}} = \left(\sqrt{64}\right)^3 = 8^3 = 512$    9. $8^{\frac{1}{3}} = \sqrt[3]{8} = 2$    11. $64^{\frac{2}{3}} = \left(\sqrt[3]{64}\right)^2 = 4^2 = 16$

13. $1,000^{\frac{1}{3}} = \sqrt[3]{1,000} = 10$    15. $16^{\frac{3}{4}} = \left(\sqrt[4]{16}\right)^3 = 2^3 = 8$    17. $-9^{\frac{1}{2}} = -\sqrt{9} = -3$

19. $(-8)^{\frac{1}{3}} = \sqrt[3]{-8} = -2$    21. $-27^{\frac{2}{3}} = -\left(\sqrt[3]{27}\right)^2 = -(3)^2 = -9$    23. $(-4)^{\frac{3}{2}} = \left(\sqrt{-4}\right)^3$ is undefined

25. $16^{-\frac{1}{2}} = \dfrac{1}{\sqrt{16}} = \dfrac{1}{4}$    27. $27^{-\frac{1}{3}} = \dfrac{1}{\sqrt[3]{27}} = \dfrac{1}{3}$    29. $1,000^{-\frac{2}{3}} = \dfrac{1}{\left(\sqrt[3]{1,000}\right)^2} = \dfrac{1}{10^2} = \dfrac{1}{100}$

31. $81^{-\frac{3}{4}} = \dfrac{1}{\left(\sqrt[4]{81}\right)^3} = \dfrac{1}{3^3} = \dfrac{1}{27}$   33. $\left(\dfrac{81}{4}\right)^{\frac{1}{2}} = \sqrt{\dfrac{81}{4}} = \dfrac{9}{2}$   35. $\left(\dfrac{125}{216}\right)^{\frac{2}{3}} = \left(\sqrt[3]{\dfrac{125}{216}}\right)^2 = \left(\dfrac{5}{6}\right)^2 = \dfrac{25}{36}$

37. $\left(\dfrac{1}{8}\right)^{-\frac{1}{3}} = \left(\dfrac{8}{1}\right)^{\frac{1}{3}} = \sqrt[3]{8} = 2$    39. $\left(\dfrac{1,000}{27}\right)^{-\frac{2}{3}} = \left(\dfrac{27}{1,000}\right)^{\frac{2}{3}} = \left(\sqrt[3]{\dfrac{27}{1,000}}\right)^2 = \left(\dfrac{3}{10}\right)^2 = \dfrac{9}{100}$

41. $-25^{-\frac{1}{2}} = -\dfrac{1}{\sqrt{25}} = -\dfrac{1}{5}$    43. $-8^{-\frac{1}{3}} = -\dfrac{1}{\sqrt[3]{8}} = -\dfrac{1}{2}$    45. $(-64)^{-\frac{2}{3}} = \dfrac{1}{\left(\sqrt[3]{-64}\right)^2} = \dfrac{1}{(-4)^2} = \dfrac{1}{16}$

47. $4^{\frac{3}{2}} \cdot 9^{\frac{1}{2}} = \left(\sqrt{4}\right)^3 \cdot \sqrt{9} = (2)^3 \cdot 3 = 8 \cdot 3 = 24$    49. $81^{\frac{1}{4}} \cdot 36^{-\frac{1}{2}} = \dfrac{81^{\frac{1}{4}} \cdot 36^{-\frac{1}{2}}}{1} = \dfrac{81^{\frac{1}{4}}}{36^{\frac{1}{2}}} = \dfrac{\sqrt[4]{81}}{\sqrt{36}} = \dfrac{3}{6} = \dfrac{1}{2}$

51. $\dfrac{36^{-\frac{1}{2}}}{27^{\frac{1}{3}}} = \dfrac{1}{27^{\frac{1}{3}} \cdot 36^{\frac{1}{2}}} = \dfrac{1}{\sqrt[3]{27} \cdot \sqrt{36}} = \dfrac{1}{3 \cdot 6} = \dfrac{1}{18}$    53. $\dfrac{25^{\frac{1}{2}}}{64^{-\frac{1}{3}}} = \dfrac{25^{\frac{1}{2}} \cdot 64^{\frac{1}{3}}}{1} = \sqrt{25} \cdot \sqrt[3]{64} = 5 \cdot 4 = 20$

55. $\dfrac{16^{-\frac{3}{4}}}{100^{-\frac{1}{2}}} = \dfrac{100^{\frac{1}{2}}}{16^{\frac{3}{4}}} = \dfrac{\sqrt{100}}{\left(\sqrt[4]{16}\right)^3} = \dfrac{10}{(2)^3} = \dfrac{\overset{5}{\cancel{10}}}{\underset{4}{\cancel{8}}} = \dfrac{5}{4}$

57. $\dfrac{4^{\frac{1}{2}} + 8^{-\frac{1}{3}}}{9^{-\frac{1}{2}} + 27^{\frac{1}{3}}} = \dfrac{\sqrt{4} + \frac{1}{\sqrt[3]{8}}}{\frac{1}{\sqrt{9}} + \sqrt[3]{27}} = \dfrac{2 + \frac{1}{2}}{\frac{1}{3} + 3} = \left(\dfrac{2 + \frac{1}{2}}{\frac{1}{3} + 3}\right)\left(\dfrac{\frac{6}{1}}{\frac{6}{1}}\right) = \dfrac{2\left(\frac{6}{1}\right) + \frac{1}{2}\left(\frac{6}{1}\right)}{\frac{1}{3}\left(\frac{6}{1}\right) + 3\left(\frac{6}{1}\right)} = \dfrac{12 + 3}{2 + 18} = \dfrac{\overset{3}{\cancel{15}}}{\underset{4}{\cancel{20}}} = \dfrac{3}{4}$

59. $x^{\frac{1}{2}} = \sqrt{x}$    61. $y^{\frac{1}{6}} = \sqrt[6]{y}$    63. $a^{\frac{2}{3}} = \sqrt[3]{a^2}$    65. $b^{\frac{3}{5}} = \sqrt[5]{b^3}$

67. $t^{\frac{5}{9}} = \sqrt[9]{t^5}$    69. $x^{-\frac{1}{2}} = \dfrac{1}{\sqrt{x}}$    71. $m^{-\frac{2}{3}} = \dfrac{1}{\sqrt[3]{m^2}}$    73. $y^{-\frac{2}{9}} = \dfrac{1}{\sqrt[9]{y^2}}$

75. $x^{\frac{1}{2}} y^{\frac{1}{2}} = \sqrt{x}\sqrt{y} = \sqrt{xy}$    77. $16^{\frac{1}{2}} m^{\frac{1}{2}} = \sqrt{16}\sqrt{m} = 4\sqrt{m}$    79. $x^{\frac{1}{2}} y^{\frac{2}{3}} = \sqrt{x}\sqrt[3]{y^2}$

81. $m^{\frac{3}{4}} n^{\frac{2}{5}} = \sqrt[4]{m^3}\sqrt[5]{n^2}$    83. $x(x+1)^{\frac{1}{2}} = x\sqrt{x+1}$    85. $x^2(x-5)^{-\frac{1}{2}} = \dfrac{x^2(x-5)^{-\frac{1}{2}}}{1} = \dfrac{x^2}{\sqrt{x-5}}$

87. $\dfrac{1}{2}x^{-\frac{1}{2}} = \dfrac{1}{2}\left(\dfrac{1}{\sqrt{x}}\right) = \dfrac{1}{2\sqrt{x}}$    89. $\dfrac{1}{5}(x^2 - 2x + 8)^{-\frac{4}{5}} = \dfrac{1}{5}\left(\dfrac{1}{\sqrt[5]{(x^2 - 2x + 8)^4}}\right) = \dfrac{1}{5\sqrt[5]{(x^2 - 2x + 8)^4}}$

91. $\left(\dfrac{x}{25}\right)^{\frac{1}{2}} = \sqrt{\dfrac{x}{25}} = \dfrac{\sqrt{x}}{\sqrt{25}} = \dfrac{\sqrt{x}}{5}$    93. $\dfrac{x^{\frac{1}{2}}}{25} = \dfrac{\sqrt{x}}{25}$    95. $\left(\dfrac{a}{16}\right)^{-\frac{1}{2}} = \left(\dfrac{16}{a}\right)^{\frac{1}{2}} = \sqrt{\dfrac{16}{a}} = \dfrac{\sqrt{16}}{\sqrt{a}} = \dfrac{4}{\sqrt{a}}$

97. $\left(\dfrac{x}{125}\right)^{-\frac{2}{3}} = \left(\dfrac{125}{x}\right)^{\frac{2}{3}} = \left(\sqrt[3]{\dfrac{125}{x}}\right)^2 = \left(\dfrac{\sqrt[3]{125}}{\sqrt[3]{x}}\right)^2 = \left(\dfrac{5}{\sqrt[3]{x}}\right)^2 = \dfrac{25}{\sqrt[3]{x^2}}$

99. $\dfrac{x^{-\frac{2}{3}}}{125} = \dfrac{1}{125x^{\frac{2}{3}}} = \dfrac{1}{125\sqrt[3]{x^2}}$    101. $\sqrt{a} = a^{\frac{1}{2}}$    103. $\sqrt[3]{x^2} = x^{\frac{2}{3}}$

**105.** $\sqrt[4]{m} = m^{\frac{1}{4}}$    **107.** $\sqrt[5]{n^3} = n^{\frac{3}{5}}$    **109.** $\sqrt{a}\,\sqrt[3]{b} = a^{\frac{1}{2}}b^{\frac{1}{3}}$    **111.** $\sqrt{\dfrac{x}{3}} = \left(\dfrac{x}{3}\right)^{\frac{1}{2}}$

**113.** $\dfrac{\sqrt{x}}{3} = \dfrac{x^{\frac{1}{2}}}{3}$    **115.** $\left(\sqrt[5]{u^2 v}\right)^2 = (u^2 v)^{\frac{2}{5}}$    **117.** $x\sqrt[6]{y} = xy^{\frac{1}{6}}$    **119.** $\left(\sqrt[3]{\dfrac{m}{9}}\right)^2 = \left(\dfrac{m}{9}\right)^{\frac{2}{3}}$

**121.** $x^{\frac{1}{2}} \cdot x^{\frac{2}{3}} = x^{\frac{1}{2}+\frac{2}{3}} = x^{\frac{3}{6}+\frac{4}{6}} = x^{\frac{7}{6}}$    **123.** $a^{-\frac{4}{5}} \cdot a^{\frac{1}{5}} = a^{-\frac{4}{5}+\frac{1}{5}} = a^{-\frac{3}{5}} = \dfrac{1}{a^{\frac{3}{5}}}$

**125.** $y^{-\frac{5}{6}} \cdot y^{-\frac{1}{9}} = y^{-\frac{5}{6}+\left(-\frac{1}{9}\right)} = y^{-\frac{15}{18}-\frac{2}{18}} = y^{-\frac{17}{18}} = \dfrac{1}{y^{\frac{17}{18}}}$

**127.** $\left(x^{\frac{2}{3}}\right)\left(x^{-\frac{1}{6}}\right)\left(x^{\frac{5}{3}}\right) = x^{\frac{2}{3}+\left(-\frac{1}{6}\right)+\frac{5}{3}} = x^{\frac{4}{6}-\frac{1}{6}+\frac{10}{6}} = x^{\frac{13}{6}}$

**129.** $\dfrac{u^{\frac{3}{8}}}{u^{\frac{1}{8}}} = u^{\frac{3}{8}-\frac{1}{8}} = u^{\frac{2}{8}} = u^{\frac{1}{4}}$    **131.** $\dfrac{n^{\frac{1}{2}}}{n^{-\frac{1}{4}}} = n^{\frac{1}{2}-\left(-\frac{1}{4}\right)} = n^{\frac{2}{4}+\frac{1}{4}} = n^{\frac{3}{4}}$

**133.** $\dfrac{p^{-\frac{4}{5}}}{p^{-\frac{2}{15}}} = p^{-\frac{4}{5}-\left(-\frac{2}{15}\right)} = p^{-\frac{12}{15}+\frac{2}{15}} = p^{-\frac{10}{15}} = p^{-\frac{2}{3}} = \dfrac{1}{p^{\frac{2}{3}}}$

**135.** $\left(x^{\frac{1}{2}}\right)^2 = x^{\left(\frac{1}{2}\right)\left(\frac{2}{1}\right)} = x^1 = x$    **137.** $\left(s^{\frac{6}{7}}\right)^{14} = s^{\left(\frac{6}{7}\right)\left(\frac{14}{1}\right)} = s^{12}$

**139.** $\left(a^2 b^4\right)^{\frac{3}{2}} = \left(a^2\right)^{\frac{3}{2}}\left(b^4\right)^{\frac{3}{2}} = a^{\left(\frac{2}{1}\right)\left(\frac{3}{2}\right)}b^{\left(\frac{4}{1}\right)\left(\frac{3}{2}\right)} = a^3 b^6$

**141.** $\left(x^{\frac{6}{5}}y^{\frac{1}{3}}\right)^{\frac{10}{3}} = \left(x^{\frac{6}{5}}\right)^{\frac{10}{3}}\left(y^{\frac{1}{3}}\right)^{\frac{10}{3}} = x^{\left(\frac{6}{5}\right)\left(\frac{10}{3}\right)}y^{\left(\frac{1}{3}\right)\left(\frac{10}{3}\right)} = x^4 y^{\frac{10}{9}}$

**143.** $\left(m^{-3}n^{10}\right)^{-\frac{4}{5}} = \left(m^{-3}\right)^{-\frac{4}{5}}\left(n^{10}\right)^{-\frac{4}{5}} = m^{\left(-\frac{3}{1}\right)\left(-\frac{4}{5}\right)}n^{\left(\frac{10}{1}\right)\left(-\frac{4}{5}\right)} = m^{\frac{12}{5}}n^{-8} = \dfrac{m^{\frac{12}{5}}n^{-8}}{1} = \dfrac{m^{\frac{12}{5}}}{n^8}$

**145.** $\left(\dfrac{p^{\frac{2}{5}}}{q^{-\frac{3}{5}}}\right)^{\frac{1}{4}} = \dfrac{\left(p^{\frac{2}{5}}\right)^{\frac{1}{4}}}{\left(q^{-\frac{3}{5}}\right)^{\frac{1}{4}}} = \dfrac{p^{\left(\frac{2}{5}\right)\left(\frac{1}{4}\right)}}{q^{\left(-\frac{3}{5}\right)\left(\frac{1}{4}\right)}} = \dfrac{p^{\frac{1}{10}}}{q^{-\frac{3}{20}}} = \dfrac{p^{\frac{1}{10}}q^{\frac{3}{20}}}{1} = p^{\frac{1}{10}}q^{\frac{3}{20}}$

**147.** $\left(\dfrac{x^2 y^{\frac{1}{3}}}{z^{-\frac{2}{5}}}\right)^{\frac{1}{6}} = \dfrac{\left(x^2\right)^{\frac{1}{6}}\left(y^{\frac{1}{3}}\right)^{\frac{1}{6}}}{\left(z^{-\frac{2}{5}}\right)^{\frac{1}{6}}} = \dfrac{x^{\left(\frac{2}{1}\right)\left(\frac{1}{6}\right)}y^{\left(\frac{1}{3}\right)\left(\frac{1}{6}\right)}}{z^{\left(-\frac{2}{5}\right)\left(\frac{1}{6}\right)}} = \dfrac{x^{\frac{1}{3}}y^{\frac{1}{18}}}{z^{-\frac{1}{15}}} = \dfrac{x^{\frac{1}{3}}y^{\frac{1}{18}}z^{\frac{1}{15}}}{1} = x^{\frac{1}{3}}y^{\frac{1}{18}}z^{\frac{1}{15}}$

**149.** $\left(\sqrt{x}\right)\left(\sqrt[3]{x}\right) = \left(x^{\frac{1}{2}}\right)\left(x^{\frac{1}{3}}\right) = x^{\frac{1}{2}+\frac{1}{3}} = x^{\frac{3}{6}+\frac{2}{6}} = x^{\frac{5}{6}} = \sqrt[6]{x^5}$

**151.** $\left(\sqrt[3]{x^2}\right)\left(\sqrt[6]{x^5}\right) = \left(x^{\frac{2}{3}}\right)\left(x^{\frac{5}{6}}\right) = x^{\frac{2}{3}+\frac{5}{6}} = x^{\frac{4}{6}+\frac{5}{6}} = x^{\frac{9}{6}} = x^{\frac{3}{2}} = \sqrt{x^3} = x\sqrt{x}$

**153.** $\left(\sqrt[4]{a}\right)\left(\sqrt[4]{a}\right) = \left(a^{\frac{1}{4}}\right)\left(a^{\frac{1}{4}}\right) = a^{\frac{1}{4}+\frac{1}{4}} = a^{\frac{2}{4}} = a^{\frac{1}{2}} = \sqrt{a}$

**155.** $\dfrac{\sqrt[5]{m^2}}{\sqrt[10]{m}} = \dfrac{m^{\frac{2}{5}}}{m^{\frac{1}{10}}} = m^{\frac{2}{5}-\frac{1}{10}} = m^{\frac{4}{10}-\frac{1}{10}} = m^{\frac{3}{10}} = \sqrt[10]{m^3}$

**157.** $\left(\sqrt[7]{x^2}\right)^{14} = \left(x^{\frac{2}{7}}\right)^{14} = x^{\left(\frac{2}{7}\right)\left(\frac{14}{1}\right)} = x^4$    **159.** $\sqrt[15]{a^5} = a^{\frac{5}{15}} = a^{\frac{1}{3}} = \sqrt[3]{a}$

**161.** $\sqrt[18]{t^6} = t^{\frac{6}{18}} = t^{\frac{1}{3}} = \sqrt[3]{t}$    **163.** $\sqrt{\sqrt{x}} = \left(x^{\frac{1}{2}}\right)^{\frac{1}{2}} = x^{\left(\frac{1}{2}\right)\left(\frac{1}{2}\right)} = x^{\frac{1}{4}} = \sqrt[4]{x}$

165. $\sqrt[3]{\sqrt[3]{b}} = \left(b^{\frac{1}{3}}\right)^{\frac{1}{3}} = b^{\left(\frac{1}{3}\right)\left(\frac{1}{3}\right)} = b^{\frac{1}{9}} = \sqrt[9]{b}$      167. $\sqrt[6]{\sqrt[4]{x^{12}}} = \left(x^{\frac{12}{4}}\right)^{\frac{1}{6}} = x^{\left(\frac{12}{4}\right)\left(\frac{1}{6}\right)} = x^{\frac{1}{2}} = \sqrt{x}$

169. $\left(\sqrt[7]{x^4} \cdot \sqrt[14]{x^3}\right)^7 = \left(x^{\frac{4}{7}} \cdot x^{\frac{3}{14}}\right)^7 = \left(x^{\frac{4}{7}+\frac{3}{14}}\right)^7 = \left(x^{\frac{8}{14}+\frac{3}{14}}\right)^7 = \left(x^{\frac{11}{14}}\right)^7$
$$= x^{\left(\frac{11}{14}\right)\left(\frac{7}{1}\right)} = x^{\frac{11}{2}} = \sqrt{x^{11}} = x^5\sqrt{x}$$

171. $\left(\dfrac{\sqrt[3]{a}}{\sqrt[6]{a}}\right)^{12} = \left(\dfrac{a^{\frac{1}{3}}}{a^{\frac{1}{6}}}\right)^{12} = \left(a^{\frac{1}{3}-\frac{1}{6}}\right)^{12} = \left(a^{\frac{2}{6}-\frac{1}{6}}\right)^{12} = \left(a^{\frac{1}{6}}\right)^{12} = a^{\left(\frac{1}{6}\right)\left(\frac{12}{1}\right)} = a^2$

173. $\left(\dfrac{\sqrt{m} \cdot \sqrt[3]{m}}{\sqrt[6]{m^5}}\right)^9 = \left(\dfrac{m^{\frac{1}{2}} \cdot m^{\frac{1}{3}}}{m^{\frac{5}{6}}}\right)^9 = \left(m^{\frac{1}{2}+\frac{1}{3}-\frac{5}{6}}\right)^9 = \left(m^{\frac{3}{6}+\frac{2}{6}-\frac{5}{6}}\right)^9 = \left(m^0\right)^9 = (1)^9 = 1$

175. $\sqrt{\sqrt[3]{x^2} \cdot \sqrt[4]{x^3}} = \left(x^{\frac{2}{3}} \cdot x^{\frac{3}{4}}\right)^{\frac{1}{2}} = \left(x^{\frac{2}{3}+\frac{3}{4}}\right)^{\frac{1}{2}} = \left(x^{\frac{8}{12}+\frac{9}{12}}\right)^{\frac{1}{2}} = \left(x^{\frac{17}{12}}\right)^{\frac{1}{2}} = x^{\left(\frac{17}{12}\right)\left(\frac{1}{2}\right)} = x^{\frac{17}{24}} = \sqrt[24]{x^{17}}$

---

## Chapter 7 Exercise 7.1

1. $6(-1) - 8 = -6 - 8 \overset{\checkmark}{=} -14$, so it is a solution.

3. $-(2)^3 + 7(2) + 5 = -8 + 14 + 5 \overset{\checkmark}{=} 11$, so it is a solution.

5. $\sqrt{3(6) - 2} = \sqrt{18 - 2} = \sqrt{16} \overset{\checkmark}{=} 4$, so it is a solution.

## Chapter 7 Exercise 7.2

1. $x + 4 = 7$

$$\begin{aligned} x + \cancel{4} &= 7 \\ -\cancel{4} \quad &\, -4 \\ \hline x \quad\;\; &= 3 \end{aligned}$$

3. $y - 7 = 12$

$$\begin{aligned} y - \cancel{7} &= 12 \\ +\cancel{7} \quad &\, +7 \\ \hline y \quad\;\; &= 19 \end{aligned}$$

5. $p - 8 = -6$

$$\begin{aligned} p - \cancel{8} &= -6 \\ +\cancel{8} \quad &\, +8 \\ \hline p \quad\;\; &= 2 \end{aligned}$$

7. $x + 5 = -9$

$$\begin{array}{rcl} x + \cancel{5} &=& -9 \\ -\cancel{5} & & -5 \\ \hline x & =& -14 \end{array}$$

9. $2x = 6$

$$\frac{\cancel{2}x}{\cancel{2}} = \frac{6}{2}$$
$$x = 3$$

11. $-3y = 24$

$$\frac{\cancel{-3}y}{\cancel{-3}} = \frac{24}{-3}$$
$$y = -8$$

13. $-7k = -49$

$$\frac{\cancel{-7}k}{\cancel{-7}} = \frac{-49}{-7}$$
$$k = 7$$

15. $\frac{4}{5}x = 6$

$$\frac{5}{4}\left(\frac{4}{5}x\right) = \frac{5}{\cancel{4}_2}\left(\frac{\overset{3}{\cancel{6}}}{1}\right)$$
$$x = \frac{15}{2}$$

17. $\frac{5}{2}t = -10$

$$\frac{2}{5}\left(\frac{\cancel{5}}{\cancel{2}}t\right) = \frac{2}{\cancel{5}}\left(\frac{-\overset{2}{\cancel{10}}}{1}\right)$$
$$t = -4$$

19. $-\frac{5}{6}y = -7$

$$-\frac{\cancel{6}}{\cancel{5}}\left(-\frac{\cancel{5}}{\cancel{6}}y\right) = -\frac{6}{5}\left(\frac{-7}{1}\right)$$
$$y = \frac{42}{5}$$

21. $2x + 3 = 9$

$$\begin{array}{rcl} 2x + \cancel{3} &=& 9 \\ -\cancel{3} & & -3 \\ \hline \dfrac{2x}{\cancel{2}} & =& \dfrac{6}{2} \\ x &=& 3 \end{array}$$

23. $4y - 7 = 11$

$$
\begin{aligned}
4y - \cancel{7} &= 11 \\
+\cancel{7} \quad &+ 7 \\
\hline
\frac{\cancel{4}y}{\cancel{4}} &= \frac{18}{4} \\
y &= \frac{9}{2}
\end{aligned}
$$

25. $-x + 17 = 25$

$$
\begin{aligned}
-x + \cancel{17} &= 25 \\
-\cancel{17} \quad &- 17 \\
\hline
\frac{\cancel{-} x}{\cancel{-} 1} &= \frac{8}{-1} \\
x &= -8
\end{aligned}
$$

27. $-3q + 8 = -21$

$$
\begin{aligned}
-3q + \cancel{8} &= -21 \\
-\cancel{8} \quad &- 8 \\
\hline
\frac{\cancel{-3}q}{\cancel{-3}} &= \frac{-29}{-3} \\
q &= \frac{29}{3}
\end{aligned}
$$

29. $2\,(3b + 4) - 6 = 16$

$$
\begin{aligned}
2\,(3b + 4) - 6 &= 16 \\
6b + 8 - 6 &= 16 \\
6b + \cancel{2} &= 16 \\
-\cancel{2} \quad &- 2 \\
\hline
\frac{\cancel{6}b}{\cancel{6}} &= \frac{\cancel{14}^{\,7}}{\cancel{6}_3} \\
b &= \frac{7}{3}
\end{aligned}
$$

31. $1 + 9\,(d - 3) = 13$

$$
\begin{aligned}
1 + 9\,(d - 3) &= 13 \\
1 + 9d - 27 &= 13 \\
9d - 2\cancel{6} &= 13 \\
+2\cancel{6} \quad &+ 26 \\
\hline
\frac{\cancel{9}d}{\cancel{9}} &= \frac{\cancel{39}^{\,13}}{\cancel{9}_3} \\
d &= \frac{13}{3}
\end{aligned}
$$

33. $8a - 9 = 5a + 3$

$$
\begin{aligned}
8a - 9 &= 5\cancel{a} + 3 \\
-5a \quad &- \cancel{5}a \\
\hline
3a - \cancel{9} &= \quad 3 \\
+\cancel{9} \quad &+ 9 \\
\hline
\frac{\cancel{3}a}{\cancel{3}} &= \frac{12}{3} \\
a &= 4
\end{aligned}
$$

35. $-13a + 2 = -a - 22$

$$-\cancel{13}a + 2 = -a - 22$$
$$\underline{+ \cancel{13}a \qquad\quad + 13a}$$
$$2 = 12a - \cancel{22}$$
$$\underline{+22 \qquad\quad + \cancel{22}}$$
$$\frac{24}{12} = \frac{\cancel{12}a}{\cancel{12}}$$
$$a = 2$$

37. $5y - 6 = 12(2y + 1) - 2$

$$5y - 6 = 12(2y + 1) - 2$$
$$5y - 6 = 24y + 12 - 2$$
$$5\cancel{y} - 6 = 24y + 10$$
$$\underline{- 5\cancel{y} \qquad\quad - 5y}$$
$$-6 = 19y + 1\cancel{0}$$
$$\underline{-10 \qquad\quad - \cancel{10}}$$
$$\frac{-16}{19} = \frac{1\cancel{9}y}{1\cancel{9}}$$
$$y = -\frac{16}{19}$$

39. $\dfrac{1}{2}x + 5 = 3x - \dfrac{1}{2}$

$$\frac{1}{2}x + 5 = 3x - \frac{1}{2}$$
$$\frac{2}{1}\left(\frac{1}{2}x + 5\right) = \frac{2}{1}\left(3x - \frac{1}{2}\right)$$
$$\cancel{x} + 10 = 6x - 1$$
$$\underline{- \cancel{x} \qquad\quad - x}$$
$$10 = 5x - \cancel{1}$$
$$\underline{+1 \qquad\quad \cancel{+1}}$$
$$\frac{11}{5} = \frac{\cancel{5}x}{\cancel{5}}$$

41. $\dfrac{1}{4}p + \dfrac{2}{5} = \dfrac{3}{5}p - \dfrac{1}{5}$

$$\frac{1}{4}p + \frac{2}{5} = \frac{3}{5}p - \frac{1}{5}$$
$$\frac{20}{1}\left(\frac{1}{4}p + \frac{2}{5}\right) = \frac{20}{1}\left(\frac{3}{5}p - \frac{1}{5}\right)$$
$$5\cancel{p} + 8 = 12p - 4$$
$$\underline{- \cancel{5}p \qquad\quad - 5p}$$
$$8 = 7p - \cancel{4}$$
$$\underline{+4 \qquad\quad + \cancel{4}}$$
$$\frac{12}{7} = \frac{7p}{7}$$

43. $\frac{5}{6}y - \frac{1}{8} = \frac{2}{3}y + \frac{1}{16}$

$$\frac{5}{6}y - \frac{1}{8} = \frac{2}{3}y + \frac{1}{16}$$

$$\frac{48}{1}\left(\frac{5}{6}y - \frac{1}{8}\right) = \frac{48}{1}\left(\frac{2}{3}y + \frac{1}{16}\right)$$

$$40y - 6 = 32y + 3$$

$$\underline{-32y \qquad\quad -32y}$$

$$8y - 6 = \qquad 3$$

$$\underline{\quad +6 \qquad\quad +6}$$

$$\frac{8y}{8} = \quad \frac{9}{8}$$

45. $\frac{4}{5}u + \frac{2}{5} = -\frac{9}{5}$

$$\frac{4}{5}u + \frac{2}{5} = -\frac{9}{5}$$

$$\frac{5}{1}\left(\frac{4}{5}u + \frac{2}{5}\right) = \frac{5}{1}\left(-\frac{9}{5}\right)$$

$$4u + 2 = -9$$

$$\underline{\quad -2 \quad\quad -2}$$

$$\frac{4u}{4} = \frac{-11}{4}$$

47. $\frac{3}{x+1} + \frac{2}{x-1} = \frac{9}{x^2-1}$

$$\frac{3}{x+1} + \frac{2}{x-1} = \frac{9}{x^2-1}$$

$$\frac{(x+1)(x-1)}{1}\left(\frac{3}{x+1} + \frac{2}{x-1}\right) = \frac{(x+1)(x-1)}{1}\left(\frac{9}{(x+1)(x-1)}\right)$$

$$3(x-1) + 2(x+1) = 9$$

$$3x - 3 + 2x + 2 = 9$$

$$5x - 1 = 9$$

$$\underline{\quad +1 \quad +1}$$

$$\frac{5x}{5} = \frac{10}{5}$$

$$x = 2$$

49. $\frac{2}{y-4} - \frac{3}{y+5} = \frac{6}{y^2+y-20}$

$$\frac{2}{y-4} - \frac{3}{y+5} = \frac{6}{y^2+y-20}$$

$$\frac{(y-4)(y+5)}{1}\left(\frac{2}{y-4} - \frac{3}{y+5}\right) = \frac{(y-4)(y+5)}{1}\left(\frac{6}{(y-4)(y+5)}\right)$$

$$2(y+5) - 3(y-4) = 6$$

$$2y + 10 - 3y + 12 = 6$$

$$-y + 22 = 6$$

$$\underline{\quad -22 \quad -22}$$

$$\frac{-y}{-1} = \frac{-16}{-1}$$

$$y = 16$$

51. $\dfrac{1}{p^2 + 6p + 9} + \dfrac{4}{p+3} = \dfrac{8}{p^2 + 6p + 9}$

$$\dfrac{1}{p^2 + 6p + 9} + \dfrac{4}{p+3} = \dfrac{8}{p^2 + 6p + 9}$$

$$\dfrac{\cancel{(p+3)}\cancel{(p+3)}}{1}\left(\dfrac{1}{\cancel{(p+3)}\cancel{(p+3)}}\right) + \dfrac{\cancel{(p+3)}(p+3)}{1}\left(\dfrac{4}{\cancel{p+3}}\right) = \dfrac{\cancel{(p+3)}\cancel{(p+3)}}{1}\left(\dfrac{8}{\cancel{(p+3)}\cancel{(p+3)}}\right)$$

$$1 + 4(p+3) = 8$$
$$1 + 4p + 12 = 8$$
$$\cancel{13} + 4p = 8$$
$$\underline{-\cancel{13} \qquad -13}$$
$$\dfrac{\cancel{4}p}{\cancel{4}} = \dfrac{-5}{4}$$

53. $\dfrac{7}{x^2 - 7x} - \dfrac{8}{x^2 - 9x + 14} = \dfrac{3}{x^2 - 2x}$

$$\dfrac{7}{x^2 - 7x} - \dfrac{8}{x^2 - 9x + 14} = \dfrac{3}{x^2 - 2x}$$

$$\dfrac{x\,(x-7)\,(x-2)}{1}\left(\dfrac{7}{x\,(x-7)} - \dfrac{8}{(x-7)\,(x-2)}\right) = \dfrac{x\,(x-7)\,(x-2)}{1}\left(\dfrac{3}{x\,(x-2)}\right)$$

$$7(x-2) - 8x = 3(x-7)$$
$$7x - 14 - 8x = 3x - 21$$
$$-\cancel{x} - 14 = 3x - 21$$
$$\underline{+\cancel{x} \qquad\qquad + x}$$
$$-14 = 4x - 21$$
$$\underline{+21 \qquad\qquad + 21}$$
$$\dfrac{7}{4} = \dfrac{\cancel{4}x}{\cancel{4}}$$

55. $\dfrac{4x}{x-2} + 1 = \dfrac{8}{x-2}$

$$\dfrac{4x}{x-2} + 1 = \dfrac{8}{x-2}$$

$$\dfrac{x-2}{1}\left(\dfrac{4x}{x-2} + 1\right) = \dfrac{x-2}{1}\left(\dfrac{8}{x-2}\right)$$

$$4x + (x-2) = 8$$
$$5x - \cancel{2} = 8$$
$$\underline{+\cancel{2} \quad +2}$$
$$\dfrac{\cancel{5}x}{\cancel{5}} = \dfrac{10}{5}$$
$$x = 2$$

Notice that if we check $x = 2$, we obtain

$$\dfrac{4(2)}{2-2} + 1 \overset{?}{=} \dfrac{8}{2-2}$$
$$\dfrac{8}{0} + 1 \overset{?}{=} \dfrac{8}{0}$$

which is invalid since zero denominators appear. Therefore, the equation has no solution.

57. $\dfrac{6m}{m^2 - 4} + \dfrac{1}{m - 2} = \dfrac{3}{m + 2}$

$$\dfrac{6m}{m^2 - 4} + \dfrac{1}{m - 2} = \dfrac{3}{m + 2}$$

$$\dfrac{(m+2)(m-2)}{1}\left(\dfrac{6m}{(m+2)(m-2)} + \dfrac{1}{m-2}\right) = \dfrac{(m+2)(m-2)}{1}\left(\dfrac{3}{m+2}\right)$$

$$6m + (m + 2) = 3(m - 2)$$

$$7m + 2 = 3m - 6$$

$$\underline{-3m \qquad\quad -3m}$$

$$4m + 2 = \qquad -6$$

$$\underline{\quad -2 \qquad\quad -2}$$

$$\dfrac{4m}{4} = \dfrac{-8}{4}$$

$$m = -2$$

Notice that if we check $m = -2$, we obtain

$$\dfrac{6(-2)}{(-2)^2 - 4} + \dfrac{1}{(-2) - 2} \overset{?}{=} \dfrac{3}{(-2) + 2}$$

$$\dfrac{-12}{0} + \dfrac{1}{-4} \overset{?}{=} \dfrac{3}{0}$$

which is invalid since zero denominators appear. Therefore, the equation has no solution.

59. $\dfrac{2y - 3}{y + 1} = \dfrac{4}{5}$

$$\dfrac{2y - 3}{y + 1} = \dfrac{4}{5}$$

$$5(2y - 3) = 4(y + 1)$$

$$10y - 15 = 4y + 4$$

$$\underline{-4y \qquad\quad -4y}$$

$$6y - 15 = \qquad 4$$

$$\underline{\quad +15 \qquad +15}$$

$$\dfrac{6y}{6} = \dfrac{19}{6}$$

61. $\dfrac{5a + 2}{4} = \dfrac{-a + 3}{3}$

$$\dfrac{5a + 2}{4} = \dfrac{-a + 3}{3}$$

$$3(5a + 2) = 4(-a + 3)$$

$$15a + 6 = -4a + 12$$

$$\underline{+4a \qquad\quad +4a}$$

$$19a + 6 = \qquad 12$$

$$\underline{\quad -6 \qquad\quad -6}$$

$$\dfrac{19a}{19} = \dfrac{6}{19}$$

63. $\dfrac{3k-8}{7k-2}=3$

$$\dfrac{3k-8}{7k-2}=\dfrac{3}{1}$$
$$1\,(3k-8)=3\,(7k-2)$$
$$3k-8=21k-6$$
$$\underline{-3k\qquad\quad -3k}$$
$$-8=18k-6$$
$$\underline{+6\qquad\quad +6}$$
$$\dfrac{-2}{18}=\dfrac{18k}{18}$$
$$k=-\dfrac{1}{9}$$

65. $\dfrac{-2}{s+3}=\dfrac{12}{s^2-9}$

$$\dfrac{-2}{s+3}=\dfrac{12}{s^2-9}$$
$$\dfrac{(s+3)(s-3)}{1}\left(\dfrac{-2}{s+3}\right)=\dfrac{(s+3)(s-3)}{1}\left(\dfrac{12}{(s+3)(s-3)}\right)$$
$$-2\,(s-3)=12$$
$$-2s+6=12$$
$$\underline{\qquad -6\quad -6}$$
$$\dfrac{-2s}{-2}=\dfrac{6}{-2}$$
$$s=-3$$

Checking this answer yields

$$\dfrac{-2}{(-3)+3}\overset{?}{=}\dfrac{12}{(-3)^2-9}$$
$$\dfrac{-2}{0}\overset{?}{=}\dfrac{12}{0}$$

Therefore, there is no solution for this equation.

67. $(x+3)(x-4)=(x+2)(x+1)$

$$(x+3)(x-4)=(x+2)(x+1)$$
$$x^2-4x+3x-12=x^2+x+2x+2$$
$$x^2-x-12=x^2+3x+2$$
$$\underline{-x^2\qquad\qquad -x^2}$$
$$-x-12=3x+2$$
$$\underline{+x\qquad\quad +x}$$
$$-12=4x+2$$
$$\underline{-2\qquad\quad -2}$$
$$\dfrac{-14}{4}=\dfrac{4x}{4}$$
$$x=-\dfrac{7}{2}$$

69. $(a+7)^2 = (a+8)(a+2)$

$$(a+7)^2 = (a+8)(a+2)$$
$$(a+7)(a+7) = (a+8)(a+2)$$
$$a^2 + 7a + 7a + 49 = a^2 + 2a + 8a + 16$$
$$a^2 + 14a + 49 = a^2 + 10a + 16$$
$$\underline{-a^2 \qquad\qquad\quad -a^2}$$
$$14a + 49 = 10a + 16$$
$$\underline{-10a \qquad\qquad -10a}$$
$$4a + 49 = 16$$
$$\underline{-49 \qquad -49}$$
$$\frac{4a}{4} = \frac{-33}{4}$$

71. $\dfrac{k-2}{k+3} = \dfrac{k+7}{k-1}$

$$\frac{k-2}{k+3} = \frac{k+7}{k-1}$$
$$(k-2)(k-1) = (k+3)(k+7)$$
$$k^2 - k - 2k + 2 = k^2 + 7k + 3k + 21$$
$$k^2 - 3k + 2 = k^2 + 10k + 21$$
$$\underline{-k^2 \qquad\qquad -k^2}$$
$$-3k + 2 = 10k + 21$$
$$\underline{+3k \qquad\qquad +3k}$$
$$2 = 13k + 21$$
$$\underline{-21 \qquad\qquad -21}$$
$$\frac{-19}{13} = \frac{13k}{13}$$

73. $\dfrac{3p+11}{6p} = \dfrac{p+1}{2p}$

$$\frac{3p+11}{6p} = \frac{p+1}{2p}$$
$$2p(3p+11) = 6p(p+1)$$
$$6p^2 + 22p = 6p^2 + 6p$$
$$\underline{-6p^2 \qquad\qquad -6p^2}$$
$$22p = 6p$$
$$\underline{-6p \qquad\qquad -6p}$$
$$\frac{16p}{16} = \frac{0}{16}$$
$$p = 0$$

Notice that when $p = 0$, both denominators in the equation become zero. Therefore, $p = 0$ is invalid and there is no solution.

75. $-8(y-2) = 4y + 3 - 3(4y+7)$

$$-8(y-2) = 4y + 3 - 3(4y+7)$$
$$-8y + 16 = 4y + 3 - 12y - 21$$
$$-8y + 16 = -8y - 18$$
$$\underline{+8y \qquad\qquad +8y}$$
$$16 = -18 \quad ???$$

Since $16 \neq -18$, this equation has no solution.

77. $7b - 12 = 6(b - 2) + b$

$$
\begin{array}{l}
7b - 12 = 6(b - 2) + b \\
7b - 12 = 6b - 12 + b \\
7b - 12 = 7b - 12 \\
\underline{-7b \qquad\quad -7b} \\
\quad -12 = -12 \ \ ???
\end{array}
$$

Since $-12 \overset{\vee}{=} -12$, there are infinitely many solutions. In fact, any real number is a solution to the equation.

## Chapter 7 Exercise 7.3

1. $x + y = 4$, for $x$

$$
\begin{array}{l}
x + y = 4 \\
\underline{\ -y \quad -y} \\
x \quad\quad = 4 - y
\end{array}
$$

3. $a - 3b = 7$, for $a$

$$
\begin{array}{l}
a - 3b = 7 \\
\underline{+3b \quad +3b} \\
a \quad\quad = 7 + 3b
\end{array}
$$

5. $5p = q$, for $p$

$$
\frac{5p}{5} = \frac{q}{5}
$$

7. $V = lwh$, for $w$

$$
\frac{V}{lh} = \frac{lwh}{lh}
$$

9. $7m + 5 = 4n$, for $m$

$$
\begin{array}{l}
7m + 5 = 4n \\
\underline{\ -5 \quad\ -5} \\
\dfrac{7m}{7} = \dfrac{4n - 5}{7}
\end{array}
$$

11. $y = -4x + 2$, for $x$

$$
\begin{array}{l}
y = -4x + 2 \\
\underline{-2 \qquad\quad -2} \\
\dfrac{y - 2}{-4} = \dfrac{-4x}{-4}
\end{array}
$$

13. $10a + 2b = 1$, for $a$

$$10a + 2b = 1$$
$$\underline{\quad\;\; -2b \;\; -2b}$$
$$\frac{10a}{10} = \frac{1 - 2b}{10}$$

15. $-5j + k = 7$, for $j$

$$-5j + k = 7$$
$$\underline{\quad\; -k \;\; -k}$$
$$\frac{-5j}{-5} = \frac{7 - k}{-5}$$

17. $4(a + 3b) - 2a = 7a + 1$, for $a$

$$4(a + 3b) - 2a = 7a + 1$$
$$4a + 12b - 2a = 7a + 1$$
$$2a + 12b = 7a + 1$$
$$\underline{-2a \qquad\qquad -2a}$$
$$12b = 5a + 1$$
$$\underline{\;\; -1 \qquad -1}$$
$$\frac{12b - 1}{5} = \frac{5a}{5}$$

19. $a(x + y) + 4 = y$, for $x$

$$a(x + y) + 4 = y$$
$$ax + ay + 4 = y$$
$$\underline{\quad -ay - 4 \qquad - ay - 4}$$
$$\frac{ax}{a} = \frac{y - ay - 4}{a}$$

21. $6j - 2k = 9j + 3k$, for $j$

$$6j - 2k = 9j + 3k$$
$$\underline{-6j \qquad\quad - 6j}$$
$$-2k = 3j + 3k$$
$$\underline{-3k \qquad\quad - 3k}$$
$$\frac{-5k}{3} = \frac{3j}{3}$$

23. $ax + 2x = 1$, for $x$

$$ax + 2x = 1 \qquad\qquad \text{group the } x\text{'s}$$
$$x(a + 2) = 1 \qquad\qquad \text{factor out the } x$$
$$\frac{x(a + 2)}{a + 2} = \frac{1}{a + 2} \qquad\qquad \text{divide both sides by } (-)$$

25. $ay + by = cy + 2$, for $y$

$$ay + by = cy + 2$$
$$\underline{-cy \quad -cy}$$   group the $y$'s
$$ay + by - cy = 2$$
$$y(a + b - c) = 2$$   factor out the $y$
$$\frac{y\,\cancel{(a + b - c)}}{\cancel{a + b - c}} = \frac{2}{a + b - c}$$   divide both sides by (−)

27. $\dfrac{3}{4}x - \dfrac{1}{2}y = \dfrac{7}{2}x + \dfrac{1}{4}y$, for $x$

$$\frac{3}{4}x - \frac{1}{2}y = \frac{7}{2}x + \frac{1}{4}y$$
$$\frac{4}{1}\left(\frac{3}{4}x - \frac{1}{2}y\right) = \frac{4}{1}\left(\frac{7}{2}x + \frac{1}{4}y\right)$$
$$3x - 2y = 14x + y$$
$$\underline{-3x \qquad\quad -3x}$$
$$-2y = 11x + y$$
$$\underline{-y \qquad -y}$$
$$\frac{-3y}{11} = \frac{\cancel{11}x}{\cancel{11}}$$

29. $\dfrac{1}{3x} + \dfrac{1}{2x} = \dfrac{4}{y}$, for $x$

$$\frac{1}{3x} + \frac{1}{2x} = \frac{4}{y}$$
$$\frac{6xy}{1}\left(\frac{1}{3x} + \frac{1}{2x}\right) = \frac{6xy}{1}\left(\frac{4}{y}\right)$$
$$2y + 3y = 24x$$
$$\frac{5y}{24} = \frac{\cancel{24}x}{\cancel{24}}$$

31. $\dfrac{2}{u} + \dfrac{3}{v} = \dfrac{6}{w}$, for $u$

$$\frac{2}{u} + \frac{3}{v} = \frac{6}{w}$$
$$\frac{uvw}{1}\left(\frac{2}{u} + \frac{3}{v}\right) = \frac{uvw}{1}\left(\frac{6}{w}\right)$$
$$2vw + 3uw = 6uv$$
$$\underline{-3uw \quad - 3uw}$$   group the $u$'s
$$2vw = 6uv - 3uw$$
$$2vw = u(6v - 3w)$$   factor out the $u$
$$\frac{2vw}{6v - 3w} = \frac{u\,\cancel{(6v - 3w)}}{\cancel{6v - 3w}}$$   divide both sides by (−)

33. $3 = \dfrac{1}{m} - \dfrac{1}{n}$, for $m$

$$3 = \frac{1}{m} - \frac{1}{n}$$
$$\frac{mn}{1}(3) = \frac{mn}{1}\left(\frac{1}{m} - \frac{1}{n}\right)$$
$$3mn = n - m$$
$$\underline{+m \quad +m}$$   group the $m$'s
$$3mn + m = n$$
$$m(3n + 1) = n$$   factor out the $m$
$$\frac{m\,\cancel{(3n + 1)}}{\cancel{3n + 1}} = \frac{n}{3n + 1}$$   divide both sides by (−)

35. $\dfrac{a}{x+2} + \dfrac{b}{x-2} = \dfrac{4}{x^2-4}$, for $x$

$$\dfrac{a}{x+2} + \dfrac{b}{x-2} = \dfrac{4}{x^2-4}$$

$$\dfrac{(x+2)(x-2)}{1}\left(\dfrac{a}{x+2} + \dfrac{b}{x-2}\right) = \dfrac{(x+2)(x-2)}{1}\left(\dfrac{4}{(x+2)(x-2)}\right)$$

$$a(x-2) + b(x+2) = 4$$

$$ax - 2a + bx + 2b = 4$$

$$\underline{+2a \qquad -2b \qquad +2a - 2b} \qquad \text{group the } x\text{'s}$$

$$ax + bx = 4 + 2a - 2b$$

$$x(a+b) = 4 + 2a - 2b \qquad \text{factor out the } x$$

$$\dfrac{x\,\cancel{(a+b)}}{\cancel{a+b}} = \dfrac{4+2a-2b}{a+b} \qquad \text{divide both sides by } (-)$$

37. $(x+p)(x+q) = x(x+p)$, for $x$

$$(x+p)(x+q) = x(x+p)$$

$$x^2 + qx + px + pq = x^2 + px$$

$$\underline{-x^2 \qquad\qquad\qquad\qquad -x^2}$$

$$qx + px + pq = px$$

$$\underline{-qx - px \qquad\qquad -qx - px}$$

$$\dfrac{pq}{-q} = \dfrac{-qx}{-q}$$

$$-p = x$$

39. $\dfrac{2Q}{5Q-3} = P$, for $Q$

$$\dfrac{2Q}{5Q-3} = \dfrac{P}{1}$$

$$1(2Q) = P(5Q-3)$$

$$2Q = 5PQ - 3P$$

$$\underline{-5PQ \quad -5PQ}$$

$$2Q - 5PQ = -3P \qquad \text{group the } Q\text{'s}$$

$$Q(2-5P) = -3P \qquad \text{factor out the } Q$$

$$\dfrac{Q\,\cancel{(2-5P)}}{\cancel{2-5P}} = \dfrac{-3P}{2-5P} \qquad \text{divide both sides by } (-)$$

41. $A = \dfrac{bh}{2}$, for $h$

$$\dfrac{A}{1} = \dfrac{bh}{2}$$

$$2A = bh$$

$$\dfrac{2A}{b} = \dfrac{\cancel{b}h}{\cancel{b}}$$

43. $S = \dfrac{a}{1-r}$, for $r$

$$\dfrac{S}{1} = \dfrac{a}{1-r}$$

$$S(1-r) = 1(a)$$

$$S - Sr = a$$

$$\underline{-S \qquad\qquad -S}$$

$$-Sr = a - S$$

$$\dfrac{-\cancel{S}r}{-\cancel{S}} = \dfrac{a-S}{-S}$$

**Chapter 7 Exercise 7.4**

1. $x^2 - 7x + 12 = 0$

$$x^2 - 7x + 12 = 0$$
$$(x-4)(x-3) = 0$$

| $x - 4 = 0$ | $x - 3 = 0$ |
|---|---|
| $+4 \quad +4$ | $+3 \quad +3$ |
| $x = 4$ | $x = 3$ |

3. $y^2 - 9y + 14 = 0$

$$y^2 - 9y + 14 = 0$$
$$(y-2)(y-7) = 0$$

| $y - 2 = 0$ | $y - 7 = 0$ |
|---|---|
| $+2 \quad +2$ | $+7 \quad +7$ |
| $y = 2$ | $y = 7$ |

5. $t^2 + 5t - 36 = 0$

$$t^2 + 5t - 36 = 0$$
$$(t+9)(t-4) = 0$$

| $t + 9 = 0$ | $t - 4 = 0$ |
|---|---|
| $-9 \quad -9$ | $+4 \quad +4$ |
| $t = -9$ | $t = 4$ |

7. $2x^2 - 11x - 21 = 0$

$$2x^2 - 11x - 21 = 0$$
$$(2x+3)(x-7) = 0$$

| $2x + 3 = 0$ | $x - 7 = 0$ |
|---|---|
| $-3 \quad -3$ | $+7 \quad +7$ |
| $\dfrac{2x}{2} = \dfrac{-3}{2}$ | $x = 7$ |

9. $4m^2 - 29m + 30 = 0$

$$4m^2 - 29m + 30 = 0$$
$$(4m-5)(m-6) = 0$$

| $4m - 5 = 0$ | $m - 6 = 0$ |
|---|---|
| $+5 \quad +5$ | $+6 \quad +6$ |
| $\dfrac{4m}{4} = \dfrac{5}{4}$ | $m = 6$ |

11. $x^2 + 5x = 0$

$$x^2 + 5x = 0$$
$$x(x+5) = 0$$

| $x = 0$ | $x + 5 = 0$ |
|---|---|
| | $-5 \quad -5$ |
| | $x = -5$ |

13. $3y^2 - 24y = 0$

$$3y^2 - 24y = 0$$
$$3y(y-8) = 0$$

| $3y = 0$ | $y - 8 = 0$ |
|---|---|
| $y = 0$ | $+8 \quad +8$ |
| | $y = 8$ |

15. $a^2 - 9 = 0$

$$a^2 - 9 = 0$$
$$(a+3)(a-3) = 0$$

| $a + 3 = 0$ | $a - 3 = 0$ |
|---|---|
| $-3 \quad -3$ | $+3 \quad +3$ |
| $a = -3$ | $a = 3$ |

17. $4t^2 - 49 = 0$

$$4t^2 - 49 = 0$$
$$(2t+7)(2t-7) = 0$$

| $2t + 7 = 0$ | $2t - 7 = 0$ |
|---|---|
| $-7 \quad -7$ | $+7 \quad +7$ |
| $\dfrac{2t}{2} = \dfrac{-7}{2}$ | $\dfrac{2t}{2} = \dfrac{7}{2}$ |

19. $p^2 = 5p$

$$p^2 = 5p$$
$$\underline{-5p \quad -5p}$$
$$p^2 - 5p = 0$$
$$p(p-5) = 0$$

| $p = 0$ | $p - 5 = 0$ |
|---|---|
| | $+5 \quad +5$ |
| | $p = 5$ |

21. $k(k+15) = -36$

$$k(k+15) = -36$$
$$k^2 + 15k = -36$$
$$\underline{+36 \quad +36}$$
$$k^2 + 15k + 36 = 0$$
$$(k+12)(k+3) = 0$$

| $k + 12 = 0$ | $k + 3 = 0$ |
|---|---|
| $-12 \quad -12$ | $-3 \quad -3$ |
| $k = -12$ | $k = -3$ |

23. $x(5x+3) = 2$

$$x(5x+3) = 2$$
$$5x^2 + 3x = 2$$
$$\underline{-2 \quad -2}$$
$$5x^2 + 3x - 2 = 0$$
$$(5x-2)(x+1) = 0$$

| $5x - 2 = 0$ | $x + 1 = 0$ |
|---|---|
| $+2 \quad +2$ | $-1 \quad -1$ |
| $\dfrac{5x}{5} = \dfrac{2}{5}$ | $x = -1$ |

25. $x - 10 = -\dfrac{21}{x}$

$$x - 10 = -\frac{21}{x}$$

$$\frac{x}{1}(x - 10) = \frac{\overset{1}{\cancel{x}}}{1}\left(-\frac{21}{\underset{1}{\cancel{x}}}\right)$$

$$x^2 - 10x = -21$$

$$\underline{\phantom{x^2 - 10x} +21 \quad\quad +21}$$

$$x^2 - 10x + 21 = 0$$

$$(x - 7)(x - 3) = 0$$

| $x - 7 = 0$ | $x - 3 = 0$ |
|---|---|
| $+7 \quad +7$ | $+3 \quad +3$ |
| $x = 7$ | $x = 3$ |

27. $x^2 = 4$

$$x^2 = 4$$
$$x = \pm\sqrt{4} = \pm 2$$

29. $t^2 = 18$

$$t^2 = 18$$
$$t = \pm\sqrt{18} = \pm\sqrt{9}\sqrt{2} = \pm 3\sqrt{2}$$

31. $y^2 - 64 = 0$

$$y^2 - 64 = 0$$
$$\underline{\phantom{y^2} +64 \quad\quad +64}$$
$$y^2 \phantom{xxxx} = 64$$
$$y = \pm\sqrt{64} = \pm 8$$

33. $m^2 - 100 = 0$

$$m^2 - 100 = 0$$
$$\underline{\phantom{m^2} +100 \quad\quad +100}$$
$$m^2 \phantom{xxxx} = 100$$
$$m = \pm\sqrt{100} = \pm 10$$

35. $a^2 - 5 = 0$

$$a^2 - 5 = 0$$
$$\underline{\phantom{a^2} +5 \quad\quad +5}$$
$$a^2 \phantom{xxx} = 5$$
$$a = \pm\sqrt{5}$$

37. $p^2 - 32 = 0$

$$p^2 - 32 = 0$$
$$\underline{\phantom{p^2} +32 \quad\quad +32}$$
$$p^2 \phantom{xxx} = 32$$
$$p = \pm\sqrt{32} = \pm\sqrt{16}\sqrt{2} = \pm 4\sqrt{2}$$

39. $3k^2 - 48 = 0$

$$
\begin{aligned}
3k^2 - 48 &= 0 \\
+48 \quad\ &+48 \\
\hline
\frac{3k^2}{3} &= \frac{48}{3} \\
k^2 &= 16 \\
k = \pm\sqrt{16} &= \pm 4
\end{aligned}
$$

41. $2x^2 - 150 = 0$

$$
\begin{aligned}
2x^2 - 150 &= 0 \\
+150 \quad\ &+150 \\
\hline
\frac{2x^2}{2} &= \frac{150}{2} \\
x^2 &= 75 \\
x = \pm\sqrt{75} = \pm\sqrt{25}\sqrt{3} &= \pm 5\sqrt{3}
\end{aligned}
$$

43. $(x+2)^2 = 3$

$$
\begin{aligned}
(x+2)^2 &= 3 \\
x + 2 &= \pm\sqrt{3} \\
-2 \quad\ &-2 \\
\hline
x &= -2 \pm \sqrt{3}
\end{aligned}
$$

45. $(a-7)^2 = 4$

$$
\begin{aligned}
(a-7)^2 &= 4 \\
a - 7 &= \pm\sqrt{4} \\
a - 7 &= \pm 2 \\
+7 \quad\ &+7 \\
\hline
a &= 7 \pm 2
\end{aligned}
$$

The solution set is $\{7-2, 7+2\} = \{5, 9\}$.

47. $\left(m + \dfrac{1}{2}\right)^2 = \dfrac{1}{4}$

$$
\begin{aligned}
\left(m + \frac{1}{2}\right)^2 &= \frac{1}{4} \\
m + \frac{1}{2} &= \pm\sqrt{\frac{1}{4}} \\
m + \frac{1}{2} &= \pm\frac{1}{2} \\
-\frac{1}{2} \quad\ &-\frac{1}{2} \\
\hline
m &= -\frac{1}{2} \pm \frac{1}{2}
\end{aligned}
$$

The solution set is $\left\{ -\dfrac{1}{2} - \dfrac{1}{2}, \ -\dfrac{1}{2} + \dfrac{1}{2} \right\} = \{-1, \ 0\}$.

49. $\left(x - \dfrac{1}{4}\right)^2 = \dfrac{3}{16}$

$$\left(x - \frac{1}{4}\right)^2 = \frac{3}{16}$$

$$x - \frac{1}{4} = \pm\sqrt{\frac{3}{16}}$$

$$x - \frac{1}{4} = \pm\frac{\sqrt{3}}{4}$$

$$+\frac{1}{4} \quad +\frac{1}{4}$$

$$\overline{\phantom{xxxxxxxxxx}}$$

$$x = \frac{1}{4} \pm \frac{\sqrt{3}}{4}$$

The solution set is $\left\{\dfrac{1}{4} - \dfrac{\sqrt{3}}{4}, \ \dfrac{1}{4} + \dfrac{\sqrt{3}}{4}\right\}.$

51. $b = 4$ gives us $\dfrac{b}{2} = \dfrac{4}{2} = 2$ and $\left(\dfrac{b}{2}\right)^2 = (2)^2 = 4$. Therefore, $x^2 + 4x + 4 = (x+2)^2$.

53. $b = -6$ gives us $\dfrac{b}{2} = \dfrac{-6}{2} = -3$ and $\left(\dfrac{b}{2}\right)^2 = (-3)^2 = 9$. Therefore, $t^2 - 6t + 9 = (t-3)^2$.

55. $b = 3$ gives us $\dfrac{b}{2} = \dfrac{3}{2}$ and $\left(\dfrac{b}{2}\right)^2 = \left(\dfrac{3}{2}\right)^2 = \dfrac{9}{4}$. Therefore, $p^2 + 3p + \dfrac{9}{4} = \left(p + \dfrac{3}{2}\right)^2$.

57. $b = -9$ gives us $\dfrac{b}{2} = \dfrac{-9}{2}$ and $\left(\dfrac{b}{2}\right)^2 = \left(\dfrac{-9}{2}\right)^2 = \dfrac{81}{4}$. Therefore, $m^2 - 9m + \dfrac{81}{4} = \left(m - \dfrac{9}{2}\right)^2$.

59. $b = \dfrac{2}{3}$ gives us $\dfrac{b}{2} = \dfrac{\frac{2}{3}}{2} = \dfrac{2}{6} = \dfrac{1}{3}$ and $\left(\dfrac{b}{2}\right)^2 = \left(\dfrac{1}{3}\right)^2 = \dfrac{1}{9}$. Therefore, $y^2 + \dfrac{2}{3}y + \dfrac{1}{9} = \left(y + \dfrac{1}{3}\right)^2$.

61. $b = -\dfrac{3}{7}$ gives us $\dfrac{b}{2} = \dfrac{-\frac{3}{7}}{2} = -\dfrac{3}{14}$ and $\left(\dfrac{b}{2}\right)^2 = \left(-\dfrac{3}{14}\right)^2 = \dfrac{9}{196}$. Therefore,

$$k^2 - \frac{3}{7}k + \frac{9}{196} = \left(k - \frac{3}{14}\right)^2.$$

63. $x^2 + 3x + 2 = 0$

We have $a = 1$, $b = 3$, and $c = 2$.

$$x = \frac{-b \pm \sqrt{b^2 - 4ac}}{2a} = \frac{-3 \pm \sqrt{(3)^2 - 4(1)(2)}}{2(1)} = \frac{-3 \pm \sqrt{9 - 8}}{2}$$

$$= \frac{-3 \pm \sqrt{1}}{2} = \frac{-3 \pm 1}{2} = \left\{ \begin{array}{l} \dfrac{-3 + 1}{2} = \dfrac{-2}{2} = -1 \\[2mm] \dfrac{-3 - 1}{2} = \dfrac{-4}{2} = -2 \end{array} \right\}$$

65. $y^2 - 6y + 8 = 0$

We have $a = 1$, $b = -6$, and $c = 8$.

$$y = \frac{-b \pm \sqrt{b^2 - 4ac}}{2a} = \frac{-(-6) \pm \sqrt{(-6)^2 - 4(1)(8)}}{2(1)} = \frac{6 \pm \sqrt{36 - 32}}{2}$$

$$= \frac{6 \pm \sqrt{4}}{2} = \frac{6 \pm 2}{2} = \left\{ \begin{array}{l} \frac{6+2}{2} = \frac{8}{2} = 4 \\[2mm] \frac{6-2}{2} = \frac{4}{2} = 2 \end{array} \right\}$$

67. $x^2 - x - 20 = 0$

We have $a = 1$, $b = -1$, and $c = -20$.

$$x = \frac{-b \pm \sqrt{b^2 - 4ac}}{2a} = \frac{-(-1) \pm \sqrt{(-1)^2 - 4(1)(-20)}}{2(1)} = \frac{1 \pm \sqrt{1 + 80}}{2}$$

$$= \frac{1 \pm \sqrt{81}}{2} = \frac{1 \pm 9}{2} = \left\{ \begin{array}{l} \frac{1+9}{2} = \frac{10}{2} = 5 \\[2mm] \frac{1-9}{2} = \frac{-8}{2} = -4 \end{array} \right\}$$

69. $y^2 + 8y + 16 = 0$

We have $a = 1$, $b = 8$, and $c = 16$.

$$y = \frac{-b \pm \sqrt{b^2 - 4ac}}{2a} = \frac{-8 \pm \sqrt{(8)^2 - 4(1)(16)}}{2(1)} = \frac{-8 \pm \sqrt{64 - 64}}{2}$$

$$= \frac{-8 \pm \sqrt{0}}{2} = \frac{-8 \pm 0}{2} = \left\{ \begin{array}{l} \frac{-8+0}{2} = \frac{-8}{2} = -4 \\[2mm] \frac{-8-0}{2} = \frac{-8}{2} = -4 \end{array} \right\}$$

71. $p^2 - 10p + 25 = 0$

We have $a = 1$, $b = -10$, and $c = 25$.

$$p = \frac{-b \pm \sqrt{b^2 - 4ac}}{2a} = \frac{-(-10) \pm \sqrt{(-10)^2 - 4(1)(25)}}{2(1)} = \frac{10 \pm \sqrt{100 - 100}}{2}$$

$$= \frac{10 \pm \sqrt{0}}{2} = \frac{10 \pm 0}{2} = \left\{ \begin{array}{l} \frac{10+0}{2} = \frac{10}{2} = 5 \\[2mm] \frac{10-0}{2} = \frac{10}{2} = 5 \end{array} \right\}$$

73. $3y^2 + 10y + 8 = 0$

We have $a = 3$, $b = 10$, and $c = 8$.

$$y = \frac{-b \pm \sqrt{b^2 - 4ac}}{2a} = \frac{-10 \pm \sqrt{(10)^2 - 4(3)(8)}}{2(3)} = \frac{-10 \pm \sqrt{100 - 96}}{6}$$

$$= \frac{-10 \pm \sqrt{4}}{6} = \frac{-10 \pm 2}{6} = \left\{ \begin{array}{l} \frac{-10+2}{6} = \frac{-8}{6} = -\frac{4}{3} \\[2mm] \frac{-10-2}{6} = \frac{-12}{6} = -2 \end{array} \right\}$$

75. $5t^2 + 4t = 0$

We have $a = 5$, $b = 4$, and $c = 0$.

$$
\begin{aligned}
t &= \frac{-b \pm \sqrt{b^2 - 4ac}}{2a} = \frac{-4 \pm \sqrt{(4)^2 - 4(5)(0)}}{2(5)} = \frac{-4 \pm \sqrt{16 - 0}}{10} \\
&= \frac{-4 \pm \sqrt{16}}{10} = \frac{-4 \pm 4}{10} = \left\{ \begin{array}{l} \dfrac{-4 + 4}{10} = \dfrac{0}{10} = 0 \\[2mm] \dfrac{-4 - 4}{10} = \dfrac{-8}{10} = -\dfrac{4}{5} \end{array} \right\}
\end{aligned}
$$

77. $x^2 - 16 = 0$

We have $a = 1$, $b = 0$, and $c = -16$.

$$
\begin{aligned}
x &= \frac{-b \pm \sqrt{b^2 - 4ac}}{2a} = \frac{-(0) \pm \sqrt{(0)^2 - 4(1)(-16)}}{2(1)} = \frac{0 \pm \sqrt{0 + 64}}{2} \\
&= \frac{0 \pm \sqrt{64}}{2} = \frac{0 \pm 8}{2} = \left\{ \begin{array}{l} \dfrac{0 + 8}{2} = \dfrac{8}{2} = 4 \\[2mm] \dfrac{0 - 8}{2} = \dfrac{-8}{2} = -4 \end{array} \right\}
\end{aligned}
$$

79. $x^2 + 9 = 0$

We have $a = 1$, $b = 0$, and $c = 9$.

$$
\begin{aligned}
x &= \frac{-b \pm \sqrt{b^2 - 4ac}}{2a} = \frac{-(0) \pm \sqrt{(0)^2 - 4(1)(9)}}{2(1)} \\
&= \frac{0 \pm \sqrt{0 - 36}}{2} = \frac{0 \pm \sqrt{-36}}{2}
\end{aligned}
$$

There are no real solutions since $\sqrt{-36}$ is not a real number.

81. $y^2 + 2y - 4 = 0$

We have $a = 1$, $b = 2$, and $c = -4$.

$$
\begin{aligned}
y &= \frac{-b \pm \sqrt{b^2 - 4ac}}{2a} = \frac{-2 \pm \sqrt{(2)^2 - 4(1)(-4)}}{2(1)} \\
&= \frac{-2 \pm \sqrt{4 + 16}}{2} = \underbrace{\frac{-2 \pm \sqrt{20}}{2} = \frac{-2 \pm 2\sqrt{5}}{2}}_{\sqrt{20} = \sqrt{4}\sqrt{5} = 2\sqrt{5}} \\
&= -\frac{\overset{1}{\cancel{2}}}{\underset{1}{\cancel{2}}} \pm \frac{\overset{1}{\cancel{2}}\sqrt{5}}{\underset{1}{\cancel{2}}} = -1 \pm \sqrt{5}
\end{aligned}
$$

83. $x^2 - 8x - 2 = 0$

We have $a = 1$, $b = -8$, and $c = -2$.

$$
\begin{aligned}
x &= \frac{-b \pm \sqrt{b^2 - 4ac}}{2a} = \frac{-(-8) \pm \sqrt{(-8)^2 - 4(1)(-2)}}{2(1)} \\
&= \frac{8 \pm \sqrt{64 + 8}}{2} = \underbrace{\frac{8 \pm \sqrt{72}}{2} = \frac{8 \pm 6\sqrt{2}}{2}}_{\sqrt{72} = \sqrt{36}\sqrt{2} = 6\sqrt{2}} \\
&= \frac{\overset{4}{\cancel{8}}}{\underset{1}{\cancel{2}}} \pm \frac{\overset{3}{\cancel{6}}\sqrt{2}}{\underset{1}{\cancel{2}}} = 4 \pm 3\sqrt{2}
\end{aligned}
$$

85. $2t^2 + t - 2 = 0$

We have $a = 2$, $b = 1$, and $c = -2$.

$$
\begin{aligned}
t &= \frac{-b \pm \sqrt{b^2 - 4ac}}{2a} = \frac{-1 \pm \sqrt{(1)^2 - 4(2)(-2)}}{2(2)} \\
&= \frac{-1 \pm \sqrt{1 + 16}}{4} = \frac{-1 \pm \sqrt{17}}{4}
\end{aligned}
$$

87. $4m^2 - 2m - 3 = 0$

We have $a = 4$, $b = -2$, and $c = -3$.

$$
\begin{aligned}
m &= \frac{-b \pm \sqrt{b^2 - 4ac}}{2a} = \frac{-(-2) \pm \sqrt{(-2)^2 - 4(4)(-3)}}{2(4)} \\
&= \frac{2 \pm \sqrt{4 + 48}}{8} = \underbrace{\frac{2 \pm \sqrt{52}}{8} = \frac{2 \pm 2\sqrt{13}}{8}}_{\sqrt{52} = \sqrt{4}\sqrt{13} = 2\sqrt{13}} \\
&= \frac{\overset{1}{\cancel{2}}}{\underset{4}{\cancel{8}}} \pm \frac{\overset{1}{\cancel{2}}\sqrt{13}}{\underset{4}{\cancel{8}}} = \frac{1}{4} \pm \frac{\sqrt{13}}{4}
\end{aligned}
$$

89. $-2y^2 + 3y + 4 = 0$

We have $a = -2$, $b = 3$, and $c = 4$.

$$
\begin{aligned}
y &= \frac{-b \pm \sqrt{b^2 - 4ac}}{2a} = \frac{-3 \pm \sqrt{(3)^2 - 4(-2)(4)}}{2(-2)} \\
&= \frac{-3 \pm \sqrt{9 + 32}}{-4} = \frac{-3 \pm \sqrt{41}}{-4} \text{ or } \frac{3 \pm \sqrt{41}}{4}
\end{aligned}
$$

91. $x^2 + 5x + 9 = 0$

We have $a = 1$, $b = 5$, and $c = 9$.

$$
\begin{aligned}
x &= \frac{-b \pm \sqrt{b^2 - 4ac}}{2a} = \frac{-5 \pm \sqrt{(5)^2 - 4(1)(9)}}{2(1)} \\
&= \frac{-5 \pm \sqrt{25 - 36}}{2} = \frac{-5 \pm \sqrt{-11}}{2}
\end{aligned}
$$

There are no real solutions since $\sqrt{-11}$ is not a real number.

93. $4m^2 - m + 6 = 0$

We have $a = 4$, $b = -1$, and $c = 6$.

$$m = \frac{-b \pm \sqrt{b^2 - 4ac}}{2a} = \frac{-(-1) \pm \sqrt{(-1)^2 - 4(4)(6)}}{2(4)}$$

$$= \frac{1 \pm \sqrt{1 - 96}}{8} = \frac{1 \pm \sqrt{-95}}{8}$$

There are no real solutions since $\sqrt{-95}$ is not a real number.

95. $\frac{1}{4}x^2 + \frac{3}{2}x - 3 = 0$

First, clear the fractions.

$$\frac{1}{4}x^2 + \frac{3}{2}x - 3 = 0$$

$$\frac{4}{1}\left(\frac{1}{4}x^2 + \frac{3}{2}x - 3\right) = \frac{4}{1}(0)$$

$$x^2 + 6x - 12 = 0$$

We have $a = 1$, $b = 6$ and $c = -12$.

$$x = \frac{-b \pm \sqrt{b^2 - 4ac}}{2a} = \frac{-6 \pm \sqrt{(6)^2 - 4(1)(-12)}}{2(1)}$$

$$= \frac{-6 \pm \sqrt{36 + 48}}{2} = \underbrace{\frac{-6 \pm \sqrt{84}}{2} = \frac{-6 \pm 2\sqrt{21}}{2}}_{\sqrt{84} = \sqrt{4}\sqrt{21} = 2\sqrt{21}}$$

$$= -\frac{\overset{3}{\cancel{6}}}{\underset{1}{\cancel{2}}} \pm \frac{\overset{1}{\cancel{2}}\sqrt{21}}{\underset{1}{\cancel{2}}} = -3 \pm \sqrt{21}$$

97. The discriminant of $x^2 + 4x - 2 = 0$ is $b^2 - 4ac = (4)^2 - 4(1)(-2) = 16 + 8 = 24$. Therefore, the roots are real and unequal.

99. The discriminant of $y^2 + y - 3 = 0$ is $b^2 - 4ac = (1)^2 - 4(1)(-3) = 1 + 12 = 13$. Therefore, the roots are real and unequal.

101. The discriminant of $x^2 + 6x + 9 = 0$ is $b^2 - 4ac = (6)^2 - 4(1)(9) = 36 - 36 = 0$. Therefore, the roots are real and equal.

103. The discriminant of $3x^2 - x - 4 = 0$ is $b^2 - 4ac = (-1)^2 - 4(3)(-4) = 1 + 48 = 49$. Therefore, the roots are real and unequal.

105. The discriminant of $4t^2 - 20t + 25 = 0$ is $b^2 - 4ac = (-20)^2 - 4(4)(25) = 400 - 400 = 0$. Therefore, the roots are real and equal.

107. $x^2 + 6x - 3 = 0$

$$x^2 + 6x - 3 = 0$$
$$\underline{\phantom{x^2 + 6x}\; +3 \quad +3}$$
$$x^2 + 6x = 3$$
$$x^2 + 6x + 9 = 3 + 9$$
$$(x + 3)^2 = 12$$
$$x + 3 = \pm \sqrt{12}$$
$$x = -3 \pm \sqrt{12} = -3 \pm 2\sqrt{3}$$

109. $x^2 - 12x + 4 = 0$

$$x^2 - 12x + 4 = 0$$
$$\underline{\phantom{x^2 - 12x}\; -4 \quad -4}$$
$$x^2 - 12x = -4$$
$$x^2 - 12x + 36 = -4 + 36$$
$$(x - 6)^2 = 32$$
$$x - 6 = \pm \sqrt{32}$$
$$x = 6 \pm \sqrt{32} = 6 \pm 4\sqrt{2}$$

111. $y^2 + 3y + 1 = 0$

$$y^2 + 3y + 1 = 0$$
$$\underline{\phantom{y^2 + 3y}\; -1 \quad -1}$$
$$y^2 + 3y = -1$$
$$y^2 + 3y + \frac{9}{4} = -1 + \frac{9}{4}$$
$$\left(y + \frac{3}{2}\right)^2 = \frac{5}{4}$$
$$y + \frac{3}{2} = \pm \sqrt{\frac{5}{4}}$$
$$y = -\frac{3}{2} \pm \sqrt{\frac{5}{4}} = -\frac{3}{2} \pm \frac{\sqrt{5}}{2}$$

113. $4y^2 + 4y - 5 = 0$

$$4y^2 + 4y - 5 = 0$$
$$\underline{\phantom{4y^2 + 4y}\; +5 \quad +5}$$
$$4y^2 + 4y = 5$$
$$\frac{4y^2}{4} + \frac{4y}{4} = \frac{5}{4}$$
$$y^2 + y + \frac{1}{4} = \frac{5}{4} + \frac{1}{4}$$
$$\left(y + \frac{1}{2}\right)^2 = \frac{6}{4}$$
$$y + \frac{1}{2} = \pm \sqrt{\frac{6}{4}}$$
$$y = -\frac{1}{2} \pm \sqrt{\frac{6}{4}} = -\frac{1}{2} \pm \frac{\sqrt{6}}{2}$$

115. $3m^2 - 12m - 2 = 0$

$$3m^2 - 12m - 2 = 0$$
$$\underline{\phantom{3m^2 - 12m} +2 \quad +2}$$
$$3m^2 - 12m = 2$$

$$\frac{3m^2}{3} - \frac{12m}{3} = \frac{2}{3}$$

$$m^2 - 4m + 4 = \frac{2}{3} + 4$$

$$(m - 2)^2 = \frac{14}{3}$$

$$m - 2 = \pm\sqrt{\frac{14}{3}}$$

$$m = 2 \pm \sqrt{\frac{14}{3}} = 2 \pm \frac{\sqrt{14}}{\sqrt{3}} = 2 \pm \frac{\sqrt{42}}{3}$$

117. $5k^2 + k + 4 = 0$

$$5k^2 + k + 4 = 0$$
$$\underline{\phantom{5k^2 + k} -4 \quad -4}$$
$$5k^2 + k = -4$$

$$\frac{5k^2}{5} + \frac{k}{5} = \frac{-4}{5}$$

$$k^2 + \frac{1}{5}k + \frac{1}{100} = -\frac{4}{5} + \frac{1}{100}$$

$$\left(k + \frac{1}{10}\right)^2 = -\frac{79}{100} \quad ???$$

There are no real solutions.

## Chapter 7 Exercise 7.5

1. $\sqrt{-4} = 2i$     3. $\sqrt{-49} = 7i$     5. $\sqrt{-144} = 12i$     7. $\sqrt{-32} = 4\sqrt{2}i$

9. $\sqrt{-45} = 3\sqrt{5}i$     11. $\sqrt{-30} = \sqrt{30}i$     13. $\sqrt{-55} = \sqrt{55}i$     15. $\sqrt{-200} = 10\sqrt{2}i$

17. $(1 + 4i) + (2 + 3i) = 3 + 7i$     19. $(3 - 7i) + (8 + 9i) = 11 + 2i$     21. $(-12 - 15i) + (4 - i) = -8 - 16i$

23. $(5 + 10i) - (3 + 6i) = 5 + 10i - 3 - 6i = 2 + 4i$     25. $(-4 + 6i) - (2 - 7i) = -4 + 6i - 2 + 7i = -6 + 13i$

27. $(-1 - 7i) - (-17 - 3i) = -1 - 7i + 17 + 3i = 16 - 4i$     29. $(9 + 5i) + (3 - 18i) + (7 - 12i) = 19 - 25i$

31. $(4 - 3i) + (-6 + 5i) - (7 - 4i) = 4 - 3i - 6 + 5i - 7 + 4i = -9 + 6i$

33. $(2 + 2i) - (-1 + 5i) - (9 - 3i) = 2 + 2i + 1 - 5i - 9 + 3i = -6$

35. $(3i)(7i) = 21i^2 = 21(-1) = -21$     37. $(-2i)(9i) = -18i^2 = -18(-1) = 18$

39. $(-4i)(-11i) = 44i^2 = 44(-1) = -44$    41. $4(-1 + 2i) = -4 + 8i$    43. $-8(3 - 6i) = -24 + 48i$

45. $2i(1 + 6i) = 2i + 12i^2 = 2i + 12(-1) = 2i - 12 = -12 + 2i$

47. $8i(7 - 5i) = 56i - 40i^2 = 56i - 40(-1) = 56i + 40 = 40 + 56i$

49. $-i(12 - 13i) = -12i + 13i^2 = -12i + 13(-1) = -12i - 13 = -13 - 12i$

51. $(1 + 5i)(2 + 3i) = 2 + 3i + 10i + 15i^2 = 2 + 13i + 15(-1) = 2 + 13i - 15 = -13 + 13i$

53. $(7 - 2i)(4 + 5i) = 28 + 35i - 8i - 10i^2 = 28 + 27i - 10(-1) = 28 + 27i + 10 = 38 + 27i$

55. $(6 - 8i)(3 - i) = 18 - 6i - 24i + 8i^2 = 18 - 30i + 8(-1) = 18 - 30i - 8 = 10 - 30i$

57. $(2 + 6i)^2 = (2 + 6i)(2 + 6i) = 4 + 12i + 12i + 36i^2 = 4 + 24i + 36(-1) = 4 + 24i - 36 = -32 + 24i$

59. $(1 - 5i)^2 = (1 - 5i)(1 - 5i) = 1 - 5i - 5i + 25i^2 = 1 - 10i + 25(-1) = 1 - 10i - 25 = -24 - 10i$

61. $(4 + 9i)(4 - 9i) = (4)^2 + (9)^2 = 16 + 81 = 97$

63. $i^2 = -1$    65. $i^4 = 1$    67. $\underbrace{i^{15} = (i^4)^3 \cdot i^3}_{15 \div 4 = 3 \text{ R3}} = 1^3 \cdot i^3 = i^3 = -i$    69. $\underbrace{i^{39} = (i^4)^9 \cdot i^3}_{39 \div 4 = 9 \text{ R3}} = 1^9 \cdot i^3 = i^3 = -i$

71. $\dfrac{1 + 2i}{3 + i} = \left(\dfrac{1 + 2i}{3 + i}\right)\left(\dfrac{3 - i}{3 - i}\right) = \dfrac{(1 + 2i)(3 - i)}{(3 + i)(3 - i)} = \dfrac{3 - i + 6i - 2i^2}{(3)^2 + (1)^2} = \dfrac{3 - i + 6i - 2(-1)}{(3)^2 + (1)^2}$

$= \dfrac{3 + 5i + 2}{(3)^2 + (1)^2} = \dfrac{5 + 5i}{10} = \dfrac{5}{10} + \dfrac{5}{10}i = \dfrac{1}{2} + \dfrac{1}{2}i$

73. $\dfrac{3 - 7i}{3 + 2i} = \left(\dfrac{3 - 7i}{3 + 2i}\right)\left(\dfrac{3 - 2i}{3 - 2i}\right) = \dfrac{(3 - 7i)(3 - 2i)}{(3 + 2i)(3 - 2i)} = \dfrac{9 - 6i - 21i + 14i^2}{(3)^2 + (2)^2} = \dfrac{9 - 6i - 21i + 14(-1)}{(3)^2 + (2)^2}$

$= \dfrac{9 - 27i - 14}{(3)^2 + (2)^2} = \dfrac{-5 - 27i}{13} = -\dfrac{5}{13} - \dfrac{27}{13}i$

75. $\dfrac{10 + 3i}{2 - 3i} = \left(\dfrac{10 + 3i}{2 - 3i}\right)\left(\dfrac{2 + 3i}{2 + 3i}\right) = \dfrac{(10 + 3i)(2 + 3i)}{(2 - 3i)(2 + 3i)} = \dfrac{20 + 30i + 6i + 9i^2}{(2)^2 + (3)^2} = \dfrac{20 + 30i + 6i + 9(-1)}{(2)^2 + (3)^2}$

$= \dfrac{20 + 36i - 9}{(2)^2 + (3)^2} = \dfrac{11 + 36i}{13} = \dfrac{11}{13} + \dfrac{36}{13}i$

77. $\dfrac{-5 - 6i}{4 - i} = \left(\dfrac{-5 - 6i}{4 - i}\right)\left(\dfrac{4 + i}{4 + i}\right) = \dfrac{(-5 - 6i)(4 + i)}{(4 - i)(4 + i)} = \dfrac{-20 - 5i - 24i - 6i^2}{(4)^2 + (1)^2}$

$= \dfrac{-20 - 5i - 24i - 6(-1)}{(4)^2 + (1)^2} = \dfrac{-20 - 29i + 6}{(4)^2 + (1)^2} = \dfrac{-14 - 29i}{17} = -\dfrac{14}{17} - \dfrac{29}{17}i$

79. $\dfrac{-8 + i}{-7 + 4i} = \left(\dfrac{-8 + i}{-7 + 4i}\right)\left(\dfrac{-7 - 4i}{-7 - 4i}\right) = \dfrac{(-8 + i)(-7 - 4i)}{(-7 + 4i)(-7 - 4i)} = \dfrac{56 + 32i - 7i - 4i^2}{(-7)^2 + (4)^2}$

$= \dfrac{56 + 32i - 7i - 4(-1)}{(-7)^2 + (4)^2} = \dfrac{56 + 25i + 4}{(-7)^2 + (4)^2} = \dfrac{60 + 25i}{65} = \dfrac{60}{65} + \dfrac{25}{65}i = \dfrac{12}{13} + \dfrac{5}{13}i$

81. $\dfrac{i}{11+i} = \left(\dfrac{i}{11+i}\right)\left(\dfrac{11-i}{11-i}\right) = \dfrac{i\,(11-i)}{(11+i)\,(11-i)} = \dfrac{11i-i^2}{(11)^2+(1)^2} = \dfrac{11i-(-1)}{122}$

$\qquad = \dfrac{1+11i}{122} = \dfrac{1}{122} + \dfrac{11}{122}i$

83. $x^2 + 4 = 0$

$$\begin{array}{rl} x^2 + 4 &= 0 \\ -4\quad &-4 \\ \hline x^2\quad &= -4 \end{array}$$
$$x = \pm\sqrt{-4} = \pm 2i$$

85. $a^2 + 121 = 0$

$$\begin{array}{rl} a^2 + 121 &= 0 \\ -121\quad &-121 \\ \hline a^2\quad &= -121 \end{array}$$
$$a = \pm\sqrt{-121} = \pm 11i$$

87. $9y^2 + 25 = 0$

$$\begin{array}{rl} 9y^2 + 25 &= 0 \\ -25\quad &-25 \\ \hline \dfrac{9y^2}{9}\quad &= \dfrac{-25}{9} \end{array}$$
$$y^2 = -\dfrac{25}{9}$$
$$y = \pm\sqrt{-\dfrac{25}{9}} = \pm\dfrac{5}{3}i$$

89. $p^2 + 12 = 0$

$$\begin{array}{rl} p^2 + 12 &= 0 \\ -12\quad &-12 \\ \hline p^2\quad &= -12 \end{array}$$
$$p = \pm\sqrt{-12} = \pm 2\sqrt{3}i$$

91. $m^2 + 27 = 0$

$$\begin{array}{rl} m^2 + 27 &= 0 \\ -27\quad &-27 \\ \hline m^2\quad &= -27 \end{array}$$
$$m = \pm\sqrt{-27} = \pm 3\sqrt{3}i$$

93. $x^2 + 300 = 0$

$$\begin{array}{rl} x^2 + 300 &= 0 \\ -300\quad &-300 \\ \hline x^2\quad &= -300 \end{array}$$
$$x = \pm\sqrt{-300} = \pm 10\sqrt{3}i$$

95. $4p^2 + 28 = 0$

$$4p^2 + 28 = 0$$
$$\underline{-28 \quad -28}$$
$$\frac{4p^2}{4} = \frac{-28}{4}$$
$$p^2 = -7$$
$$p = \pm\sqrt{-7} = \pm\sqrt{7}i$$

97. $3s^2 + 24 = 0$

$$3s^2 + 24 = 0$$
$$\underline{-24 \quad -24}$$
$$\frac{3s^2}{3} = \frac{-24}{3}$$
$$s^2 = -8$$
$$s = \pm\sqrt{-8} = \pm2\sqrt{2}i$$

99. $x^2 + x + 1 = 0$

We have $a = 1$, $b = 1$ and $c = 1$.

$$
\begin{aligned}
x &= \frac{-b \pm \sqrt{b^2 - 4ac}}{2a} = \frac{-1 \pm \sqrt{(1)^2 - 4(1)(1)}}{2(1)} \\
&= \frac{-1 \pm \sqrt{1 - 4}}{2} = \frac{-1 \pm \sqrt{-3}}{2} = \frac{-1 \pm \sqrt{3}i}{2} \\
&= -\frac{1}{2} \pm \frac{\sqrt{3}}{2}i
\end{aligned}
$$

101. $y^2 + 3y + 9 = 0$

We have $a = 1$, $b = 3$ and $c = 9$.

$$
\begin{aligned}
y &= \frac{-b \pm \sqrt{b^2 - 4ac}}{2a} = \frac{-3 \pm \sqrt{(3)^2 - 4(1)(9)}}{2(1)} \\
&= \frac{-3 \pm \sqrt{9 - 36}}{2} = \frac{-3 \pm \sqrt{-27}}{2} = \frac{-3 \pm 3\sqrt{3}i}{2} \\
&= -\frac{3}{2} \pm \frac{3\sqrt{3}}{2}i
\end{aligned}
$$

**103.** $3t^2 - 2t + 1 = 0$

We have $a = 3$, $b = -2$ and $c = 1$.

$$
\begin{aligned}
t &= \frac{-b \pm \sqrt{b^2 - 4ac}}{2a} = \frac{-(-2) \pm \sqrt{(-2)^2 - 4(3)(1)}}{2(3)} \\
&= \frac{2 \pm \sqrt{4 - 12}}{6} = \frac{2 \pm \sqrt{-8}}{6} = \frac{2 \pm 2\sqrt{2}i}{6} \\
&= \frac{\overset{1}{\cancel{2}}}{\underset{3}{\cancel{6}}} \pm \frac{\overset{1}{\cancel{2}}\sqrt{2}}{\underset{3}{\cancel{6}}}i = \frac{1}{3} \pm \frac{\sqrt{2}}{3}i
\end{aligned}
$$

**105.** $5m^2 - 2m + 2 = 0$

We have $a = 5$, $b = -2$ and $c = 2$.

$$
\begin{aligned}
m &= \frac{-b \pm \sqrt{b^2 - 4ac}}{2a} = \frac{-(-2) \pm \sqrt{(-2)^2 - 4(5)(2)}}{2(5)} \\
&= \frac{2 \pm \sqrt{4 - 40}}{10} = \frac{2 \pm \sqrt{-36}}{10} = \frac{2 \pm 6i}{10} \\
&= \frac{\overset{1}{\cancel{2}}}{\underset{5}{\cancel{10}}} \pm \frac{\overset{3}{\cancel{6}}}{\underset{5}{\cancel{10}}}i = \frac{1}{5} \pm \frac{3}{5}i
\end{aligned}
$$

**107.** $-2x^2 + 2x - 3 = 0$

We have $a = -2$, $b = 2$ and $c = -3$.

$$
\begin{aligned}
x &= \frac{-b \pm \sqrt{b^2 - 4ac}}{2a} = \frac{-2 \pm \sqrt{(2)^2 - 4(-2)(-3)}}{2(-2)} \\
&= \frac{-2 \pm \sqrt{4 - 24}}{-4} = \frac{-2 \pm \sqrt{-20}}{-4} = \frac{-2 \pm 2\sqrt{5}i}{-4} \\
&= \frac{\overset{1}{\cancel{-2}}}{\underset{2}{\cancel{-4}}} \pm \frac{\overset{1}{\cancel{2}}\sqrt{5}}{\underset{2}{\cancel{4}}}i = \frac{1}{2} \pm \frac{\sqrt{5}}{2}i
\end{aligned}
$$

**109.** $-4y^2 + 4y - 5 = 0$

We have $a = -4$, $b = 4$ and $c = -5$.

$$
\begin{aligned}
y &= \frac{-b \pm \sqrt{b^2 - 4ac}}{2a} = \frac{-4 \pm \sqrt{(4)^2 - 4(-4)(-5)}}{2(-4)} \\
&= \frac{-4 \pm \sqrt{16 - 80}}{-8} = \frac{-4 \pm \sqrt{-64}}{-8} = \frac{-4 \pm 8i}{-8} \\
&= \frac{\overset{1}{\cancel{-4}}}{\underset{2}{\cancel{-8}}} \pm \frac{\overset{1}{\cancel{8}}}{\underset{-1}{\cancel{-8}}}i = \frac{1}{2} \pm i
\end{aligned}
$$

## Chapter 8 Exercises

1. Let $a = 4$ and $b = 3$. We want to find $c$.

$$a^2 + b^2 = c^2$$
$$4^2 + 3^2 = c^2$$
$$16 + 9 = c^2$$
$$25 = c^2$$
$$c = \sqrt{25} = 5$$

The hypotenuse has length 5 inches.

3. Let $a = 5\sqrt{2}$ and $b = 1$. We want to find $c$.

$$a^2 + b^2 = c^2$$
$$\left(5\sqrt{2}\right)^2 + 1^2 = c^2$$
$$50 + 1 = c^2$$
$$51 = c^2$$
$$c = \sqrt{51}$$

The hypotenuse has length $\sqrt{51}$ feet.

5. Let $a = 2$ and $c = 8$. We want to find $b$.

$$a^2 + b^2 = c^2$$
$$2^2 + b^2 = 8^2$$
$$4 + b^2 = 64$$
$$-4 \qquad\qquad -4$$
$$b^2 = 60$$
$$b = \sqrt{60} = 2\sqrt{15}$$

The leg has length $2\sqrt{15}$ yards.

7. Let $a = 2\sqrt{2}$ and $c = 6\sqrt{3}$. We want to find $b$.

$$a^2 + b^2 = c^2$$
$$\left(2\sqrt{2}\right)^2 + b^2 = \left(6\sqrt{3}\right)^2$$
$$8 + b^2 = 108$$
$$-8 \qquad\qquad -8$$
$$b^2 = 100$$
$$b = \sqrt{100} = 10$$

The leg has length 10 meters.

9. Let $a = 9$ and $b = 9$. We want to find $c$.

$$a^2 + b^2 = c^2$$
$$9^2 + 9^2 = c^2$$
$$81 + 81 = c^2$$
$$162 = c^2$$
$$c = \sqrt{162} = 9\sqrt{2}$$

The hypotenuse has length $9\sqrt{2}$ feet.

11. Yes, since $6^2 + 8^2 = 10^2$.                13. Yes, since $7^2 + 24^2 = 25^2$.

15. No, since $2^2 + 7^2 \neq 12^2$.              17. No, since $6^2 + 3^2 \neq 8^2$.

19. Yes. Notice that $30 = 10 \times 3$, $40 = 10 \times 4$, $50 = 10 \times 5$ and $\{3,\ 4,\ 5\}$ is a Pythagorean triple.

21  Letting $s = 7$ inches, we have $P = 4s = 4\,(7\text{ inches}) = 28$ inches.

23. Letting $l = 2$ yards and $w = 5$ yards, we have $A = lw = (2\text{ yards})\,(5\text{ yards}) = 10$ square yards or 10 yd$^2$.

25. Letting $b = 5\sqrt{5}$ inches and $h = 4\sqrt{5}$ inches, we have $A = \dfrac{1}{2}bh = \dfrac{1}{2}\underbrace{\left(5\sqrt{5}\text{ inches}\right)\left(4\sqrt{5}\text{ inches}\right)}_{20(5)=100}$

$$= \frac{1}{2}\,(100\text{ square inches}) = 50\text{ in}^2.$$

27. Letting $r = 14$ feet, we have $A = \pi r^2 = \pi\,(14\text{ feet})^2 = 196\pi$ ft$^2$.

29. Letting $r = 8\sqrt{10}$ feet, we have $C = 2\pi r = 2\pi\left(8\sqrt{10}\text{ feet}\right) = 16\sqrt{10}\pi$ ft.

31. We are given $P = 16$ inches and we want $s$.

$$P = 4s$$
$$16\text{ inches} = 4s$$
$$\frac{16\text{ inches}}{4} = \frac{\cancel{4}s}{\cancel{4}}$$
$$4\text{ inches} = s$$

The length of each side is 4 inches.

33. We are given $P = 46$ inches and $w = 8$ inches. We want to find $l$.

$$P = 2l + 2w$$
$$46\text{ inches} = 2l + 2\,(8\text{ inches})$$
$$46\text{ inches} = 2l + 1\cancel{6}\text{ inches}$$
$$\underline{-16\text{ inches} \qquad\quad -\cancel{1}6\text{ inches}}$$
$$30\text{ inches} = 2l$$
$$\frac{30}{2}\text{ inches} = \frac{\cancel{2}l}{\cancel{2}}$$
$$15\text{ inches} = l$$

The length of the rectangle is 15 inches.

35. Letting $b = 7$ yards and $h = 8$ yards, we have $A = \dfrac{1}{2}bh = \dfrac{1}{2}\,(7\text{ yd})\,(8\text{ yd}) = \dfrac{1}{2}\left(56\text{ yd}^2\right) = 28$ yd$^2$.

37. Letting $b = \sqrt{11}$ mi and $h = 5\sqrt{11}$ mi, we have $A = \dfrac{1}{2}bh = \dfrac{1}{2}\underbrace{\left(\sqrt{11}\text{ mi}\right)\left(5\sqrt{11}\text{ mi}\right)}_{5(11)=55} = \dfrac{1}{2}\left(55\text{ mi}^2\right)$

$$= \frac{55}{2}\text{ square miles.}$$

39. We are given $A = 36\pi$ ft$^2$ and we want $r$ and $d$.

$$A = \pi r^2$$
$$36\pi\text{ ft}^2 = \pi r^2$$
$$\frac{36\cancel{\pi}\text{ ft}^2}{\cancel{\pi}} = \frac{\cancel{\pi}r^2}{\cancel{\pi}}$$
$$36\text{ ft}^2 = r^2$$
$$r = \sqrt{36}\text{ ft}^2 = 6\text{ ft}$$

The radius is 6 feet and the diameter is $d = 2r = 2\,(6\text{ ft}) = 12$ feet.

41. We are given $A = 54\pi$ yd$^2$ and we want $r$ and $d$.

$$A = \pi r^2$$
$$54\pi \text{ yd}^2 = \pi r^2$$
$$\frac{54\cancel{\pi} \text{ yd}^2}{\cancel{\pi}} = \frac{\cancel{\pi} r^2}{\cancel{\pi}}$$
$$54 \text{ yd}^2 = r^2$$
$$r = \sqrt{54 \text{ yd}^2} = 3\sqrt{6} \text{ yd}$$

The radius is $3\sqrt{6}$ yards and the diameter is $d = 2r = 2\left(3\sqrt{6} \text{ yd}\right) = 6\sqrt{6}$ yards.

43. Letting $s = 5$ ft, we have $V = s^3 = (5 \text{ ft})^3 = 125 \text{ ft}^3$ and $A = 6s^2 = 6\left(5 \text{ ft}\right)^2 = 150 \text{ ft}^2$.

45. Letting $r = 2$ yd, we have $V = \frac{4}{3}\pi r^3 = \frac{4}{3}\pi\left(2 \text{ yd}\right)^3 = \frac{32}{3}\pi \text{ yd}^3$ and $A = 4\pi r^2 = 4\pi\left(2\right)^2 = 16\pi \text{ yd}^2$.

47. Letting $l = 3$ ft, $w = 1$ ft and $h = 3$ ft, we have $V = lwh = (3 \text{ ft})(1 \text{ ft})(3 \text{ ft}) = 9 \text{ ft}^3$ and

$$
\begin{aligned}
A &= 2lw + 2wh + 2lh \\
&= 2\left(3 \text{ ft}\right)\left(1 \text{ ft}\right) + 2\left(1 \text{ ft}\right)\left(3 \text{ ft}\right) + 2\left(3 \text{ ft}\right)\left(3 \text{ ft}\right) \\
&= 6 \text{ ft}^2 + 6 \text{ ft}^2 + 18 \text{ ft}^2 = 30 \text{ ft}^2.
\end{aligned}
$$

49. We are given that $l = 2$ in., $w = 2$ in. and $A = 90$ in.$^2$. We want to find $h$.

$$
\begin{aligned}
A &= 2lw + 2wh + 2lh \\
90 \text{ in.}^2 &= 2\left(2 \text{ in.}\right)\left(2 \text{ in.}\right) + 2\left(2 \text{ in.}\right)h + 2\left(2 \text{ in.}\right)h \\
90 \text{ in.}^2 &= 8 \text{ in.}^2 + (4 \text{ in.})h + (4 \text{ in.})h \\
90 \text{ in.}^2 &= 8 \text{ in.}^2 + (8 \text{ in.})h \\
\underline{-8 \text{ in.}^2 \quad -8 \text{ in.}^2} & \\
\frac{72 \text{ in.}^2}{8 \text{ in.}} &= \frac{(8 \text{ in.})h}{8 \text{ in.}} \\
9 \text{ in.} &= h
\end{aligned}
$$

The height is 9 inches.

51. Letting $r = 3$ mi and $h = 18$ mi, we have $V = \pi r^2 h = \pi\left(3 \text{ mi}\right)^2\left(18 \text{ mi}\right) = 162\pi$ cubic miles.

53. Letting $r = 9\sqrt{2}$ m and $h = 4$ m, we have $V = \pi r^2 h = \pi \underbrace{\left(9\sqrt{2} \text{ m}\right)^2}_{81(2)=162}\left(4 \text{ m}\right) = \pi\left(162 \text{ m}\right)\left(4 \text{ m}\right) = 648\pi$

cubic meters.

---

## Chapter 9 Exercise 9.1

1. $X = \{x \mid x > 5\}$ is the set of all real numbers greater than 5.

3. $Y = \{y \mid y < 0\}$ is the set of all real numbers less than 0.

5. $E = \{k \mid k \text{ is an even number}\}$ is the set of all even numbers.

7. $A = \{a \mid a - 4 = 11\}$ is the set consisting of the number 15 (since $15 - 4 = 11$).

9. $\{x \mid x \text{ is an integer and } x > 1\}$ is the set of integers $\{2, \ 3, \ 4, \ 5, ...\}$.

11. $\{p \mid p$ is a natural number and $p \leq 6\}$ consists of the numbers $\{1, 2, 3, 4, 5, 6\}$.

13. $A = \{-2, -5, -1\} \subset N$        15. $C = \{-4, -6, -5\} \subset N$

17. $E = \{-1, -2, -8\} \not\subseteq N$, since $-8 \notin N$        19. $X = \{x \mid x + 4 = -2\} \subset N$, since $X = \{-6\}$

21. $A = B$        23. $M \neq N$        25. $X = Y$        27. $S \neq T$        29. $A \cap B = \{2, 5\}$

31. $X \cap Y = \{$Steve, Bill$\}$        33. $M \cap N = \{2\}$        35. $P \cap Q = \varnothing$

37. $A \cup B = \{1, 2, 4, 8, 3, 7\}$        39. $X \cup Y = \{$Frank, Ned, Vinny, Tony, Tom, Avram, Vinny$\}$

41. $P \cup Q = \left\{\dfrac{14}{5}, 2\right\}$        43. $S \cup T = \left\{-4, -6, -\dfrac{7}{3}\right\}$

## Chapter 9 Exercise 9.2

1. set notation: $\{x \mid x < 2\}$        interval notation: $(-\infty, 2)$

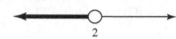

3. set notation: $\{t \mid t > 7\}$        interval notation: $(7, \infty)$

5. set notation: $\{a \mid a \leq 5\}$        interval notation: $(-\infty, 5]$

7. set notation: $\{x \mid x \geq -1\}$        interval notation: $[-1, \infty)$

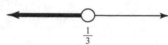

9. set notation: $\left\{p \mid p < \dfrac{1}{3}\right\}$        interval notation: $\left(-\infty, \dfrac{1}{3}\right)$

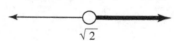

11. set notation: $\left\{x \mid x > \sqrt{2}\right\}$        interval notation: $(\sqrt{2}, \infty)$

13. set notation: $\{a \mid a \leq 5.927\}$        interval notation: $(-\infty, 5.927]$

15. set notation: $\{x \mid -4 \leq x \leq 0\}$        interval notation: $[-4, 0]$

17. set notation: $\{x \mid 0 \le x < 3\}$    interval notation: $[0, 3)$

19. set notation: $\{q \mid 0 < q < 2\}$    interval notation: $(0, 2)$

21. set notation: $\{x \mid -4 < x \le 4\}$    interval notation: $(-4, 4]$

23. set notation: $\{x \mid -\pi \le x \le \pi\}$    interval notation: $[-\pi, \pi]$

25. $(4, \infty)$ is written as $x > 4$.

27. $[-3, \infty)$ is written as $x \ge -3$.

29. $(-\infty, 6)$ is written as $x < 6$.

31. $(10, \infty)$ is written as $x > 10$.

33. $(-\infty, 3]$ is written as $x \le 3$.

35. $(-1, 1)$ is written as $-1 < x < 1$.

37. $[2, 8]$ is written as $2 \le x \le 8$.

39. $(0, 5]$ is written as $0 < x \le 5$.

41. $[-2\pi, 0)$ is written as $-2\pi \le x < 0$.

## Chapter 9 Exercise 9.3

1. If $x < y$ and $y < 4$, then $x < 4$.    3. If $p > q$ and $q > 1$, then $p > 1$.

5. If $x > y$ and $z < y$, then $z < x$.    7. $6^2 > 0$    9. $0 < (-4)^2$    11. $6^2 > -6^2$

13. If $x > 1$, then $x + 5 > 6$.    15. If $a \le 4$, then $a + 7 \le 11$.    17. If $p \ge -6$, then $p - 4 \ge -10$.

19. If $x > 3$, then $x - 9 > -6$.    21. If $x \le 5$, then $3x \le 15$.    23. If $a \ge -8$, then $\dfrac{a}{4} \ge -2$.

25. If $n < 16$, then $-2n > -32$.    27. If $x \le -\dfrac{2}{3}$, then $-9x \ge 6$.

## Chapter 9 Exercises 9.4

1. $x + 2 > 9$

$$
\begin{array}{r}
x + 2 > 9 \\
-2 \quad -2 \\
\hline
x > 7
\end{array}
$$

Set notation:  $\{x \mid x > 7\}$    Interval notation: $(7, \infty)$

3. $y - 6 \le 2$

$$
\begin{array}{r}
y - 6 \le 2 \\
+6 \quad +6 \\
\hline
y \le 8
\end{array}
$$

Set notation:  $\{y \mid y \le 8\}$    Interval notation: $(-\infty, 8]$

5. $3t \geq 15$

$$\frac{3t}{3} \geq \frac{15}{3}$$
$$t \geq 5$$

Set notation: $\{t \mid t \geq 5\}$     Interval notation: $[5, \infty)$

7. $-2a > 8$

$$-2a > 8$$
$$\frac{-2a}{-2} < \frac{8}{-2}$$
$$a < -4$$

Set notation: $\{a \mid a < -4\}$     Interval notation: $(-\infty, -4)$

9. $\frac{2}{5}x \geq 13$

$$\frac{2}{5}x \geq 13$$
$$\frac{5}{2}\left(\frac{2}{5}x\right) \geq \frac{5}{2}(13)$$
$$x \geq \frac{65}{2}$$

Set notation: $\left\{x \mid x \geq \frac{65}{2}\right\}$     Interval notation: $\left[\frac{65}{2}, \infty\right)$

11. $-\frac{1}{3}p > 14$

$$-\frac{1}{3}p > 14$$
$$-\frac{3}{1}\left(-\frac{1}{3}p\right) < -\frac{3}{1}(14)$$
$$p < -42$$

Set notation: $\{p \mid p < -42\}$     Interval notation: $(-\infty, -42)$

13. $3a + 7 \geq 16$

$$3a + 7 \geq 16$$
$$\underline{\quad -7 \quad -7}$$
$$\frac{3a}{3} \geq \frac{9}{3}$$
$$a \geq 3$$

Set notation: $\{a \mid a \geq 3\}$     Interval notation: $[3, \infty)$

15. $-2y + 1 < 7$

$$-2y + 1 < 7$$
$$\underline{\quad -1 \quad -1 \quad}$$
$$-2y < 6$$
$$\frac{-2y}{-2} > \frac{6}{-2}$$
$$y > -3$$

Set notation: $\{y \mid y > -3\}$      Interval notation: $(-3, \infty)$

17. $5y - 1 < 9y + 3$

$$5y - 1 < 9y + 3$$
$$\underline{-5y \qquad - 5y}$$
$$-1 < 4y + 3$$
$$\underline{-3 \qquad - 3}$$
$$\frac{-4}{4} < \frac{4y}{4}$$
$$-1 < y$$

Set notation: $\{y \mid -1 < y\}$      Interval notation: $(-1, \infty)$

19. $8b + 3 \le b - 7$

$$8b + 3 \le b - 7$$
$$\underline{-b \qquad - b}$$
$$7b + 3 \le -7$$
$$\underline{-3 \quad - 3}$$
$$\frac{7b}{7} \le \frac{-10}{7}$$
$$b \le -\frac{10}{7}$$

Set notation: $\left\{ b \mid b \le -\dfrac{10}{7} \right\}$      Interval notation: $\left( -\infty, -\dfrac{10}{7} \right]$

21. $-3a + 7 > -10a - 2$

$$-3a + 7 > -10a - 2$$
$$\underline{+10a \qquad + 10a}$$
$$7a + 7 > -2$$
$$\underline{-7 \quad - 7}$$
$$\frac{7a}{7} > \frac{-9}{7}$$
$$a > -\frac{9}{7}$$

Set notation: $\left\{ a \mid a > -\dfrac{9}{7} \right\}$      Interval notation: $\left( -\dfrac{9}{7}, \infty \right)$

23. $6m + 2(m - 9) < 26m$

$$6m + 2(m - 9) < 26m$$
$$6m + 2m - 18 < 26m$$
$$8m - 18 < 26m$$
$$\underline{-8m \qquad\quad -8m}$$
$$\frac{-18}{18} < \frac{18m}{18}$$
$$-1 < m$$

Set notation: $\{m \mid -1 < m\}$    Interval notation: $(-1, \infty)$

25. $\dfrac{1}{2}x + \dfrac{2}{3} \leq \dfrac{1}{6}x - \dfrac{1}{2}$

$$\frac{1}{2}x + \frac{2}{3} \leq \frac{1}{6}x - \frac{1}{2}$$
$$\frac{6}{1}\left(\frac{1}{2}x + \frac{2}{3}\right) \leq \frac{6}{1}\left(\frac{1}{6}x - \frac{1}{2}\right)$$
$$3x + 4 \leq x - 3$$
$$\underline{-x \qquad\quad -x}$$
$$2x + 4 \leq -3$$
$$\underline{\phantom{2x}\; -4 \qquad -4}$$
$$\frac{2x}{2} \leq \frac{-7}{2}$$
$$x \leq -\frac{7}{2}$$

Set notation: $\left\{x \mid x \leq -\dfrac{7}{2}\right\}$    Interval notation: $\left(-\infty, -\dfrac{7}{2}\right]$

27. $2 + \dfrac{1}{8}x \geq \dfrac{3}{4}x - 9$

$$2 + \frac{1}{8}x \geq \frac{3}{4}x - 9$$
$$\frac{8}{1}\left(2 + \frac{1}{8}x\right) \geq \frac{8}{1}\left(\frac{3}{4}x - 9\right)$$
$$16 + x \geq 6x - 72$$
$$\underline{-x \qquad -x}$$
$$16 \geq 5x - 72$$
$$\underline{+72 \qquad\quad +72}$$
$$\frac{88}{5} \geq \frac{5x}{5}$$

Set notation: $\left\{x \mid \dfrac{88}{5} \geq x\right\}$    Interval notation: $\left(-\infty, \dfrac{88}{5}\right]$

29. $\dfrac{6x + 3}{4} > 7$

$$\frac{6x + 3}{4} > 7$$
$$\frac{4}{1}\left(\frac{6x + 3}{4}\right) > \frac{4}{1}(7)$$
$$6x + 3 > 28$$
$$\underline{-3 \qquad -3}$$
$$\frac{6x}{6} > \frac{25}{6}$$

Set notation: $\left\{x \mid x > \dfrac{25}{6}\right\}$    Interval notation: $\left(\dfrac{25}{6}, \infty\right)$

31. $\dfrac{-2a+3}{5} < 6$

$$\frac{-2a+3}{5} < 6$$

$$\frac{\cancel{5}}{1}\left(\frac{-2a+3}{\cancel{5}}\right) < \frac{5}{1}(6)$$

$$-2a+\cancel{3} < 30$$

$$\underline{\phantom{-2a}-\cancel{3}\phantom{abc}-3}$$

$$-2a < 27$$

$$\frac{\cancel{-2}a}{\cancel{-2}} > \frac{27}{-2}$$

$$a > -\frac{27}{2}$$

Set notation: $\left\{ a \mid a > -\dfrac{27}{2} \right\}$     Interval notation: $\left(-\dfrac{27}{2},\ \infty\right)$

33. $\dfrac{-x+2}{-6} \le 5$

$$\frac{-x+2}{-6} \le 5$$

$$\frac{\cancel{-6}}{1}\left(\frac{-x+2}{\cancel{-6}}\right) \ge \frac{-6}{1}(5)$$

$$-x+\cancel{2} \ge -30$$

$$\underline{\phantom{-x}-\cancel{2}\phantom{abc}-2}$$

$$-x \ge -32$$

$$\frac{-x}{-1} \le \frac{-32}{-1}$$

$$x \le 32$$

Set notation: $\{x \mid x \le 32\}$     Interval notation: $(-\infty,\ 32]$

35. $\dfrac{-9y+2}{-12} > 4$

$$\frac{-9y+2}{-12} > 4$$

$$\frac{\cancel{-12}}{1}\left(\frac{-9y+2}{\cancel{-12}}\right) < \frac{-12}{1}(4)$$

$$-9y+\cancel{2} < -48$$

$$\underline{\phantom{-9y}-\cancel{2}\phantom{abc}-2}$$

$$-9y < -50$$

$$\frac{\cancel{-9}y}{\cancel{-9}} > \frac{-50}{-9}$$

$$y > \frac{50}{9}$$

Set notation: $\left\{ y \mid y > \dfrac{50}{9} \right\}$     Interval notation: $\left(\dfrac{50}{9},\ \infty\right)$

37. $5 < 2x + 1 < 7$

$$5 < 2x + \cancel{1} < 7$$

$$\underline{-1\phantom{abcd}-\cancel{1}\phantom{abcd}-1}$$

$$\frac{4}{2} < \frac{\cancel{2}x}{\cancel{2}} < \frac{6}{2}$$

$$2 < x < 3$$

Set notation: $\{x \mid 2 < x < 3\}$     Interval notation: $(2,\ 3)$

39. $-3 < 4y + 9 \le 5$

$$
\begin{array}{ccccc}
-3 & < & 4y + 9 & \le & 5 \\
-9 & & -9 & & -9 \\
\hline
\dfrac{-12}{4} & < & \dfrac{4y}{4} & \le & \dfrac{-4}{4} \\
-3 & < & y & \le & -1
\end{array}
$$

Set notation: $\{y \mid -3 < y \le -1\}$        Interval notation: $(-3, -1]$

41. $0 \le 7y - 3 < 11$

$$
\begin{array}{ccccc}
0 & \le & 7y - 3 & < & 11 \\
+3 & & +3 & & +3 \\
\hline
\dfrac{3}{7} & \le & \dfrac{7y}{7} & < & \dfrac{14}{7} \\
 & \dfrac{3}{7} & \le y < 2
\end{array}
$$

Set notation: $\left\{y \mid \dfrac{3}{7} \le y < 2\right\}$        Interval notation: $\left[\dfrac{3}{7}, 2\right)$

43. $-2 \le 6a + 1 \le 12$

$$
\begin{array}{ccccc}
-2 & \le & 6a + 1 & \le & 12 \\
-1 & & -1 & & -1 \\
\hline
\dfrac{-3}{6} & \le & \dfrac{6a}{6} & \le & \dfrac{11}{6} \\
-\dfrac{1}{2} & \le & a & \le & \dfrac{11}{6}
\end{array}
$$

Set notation: $\left\{a \mid -\dfrac{1}{2} \le a \le \dfrac{11}{6}\right\}$        Interval notation: $\left[-\dfrac{1}{2}, \dfrac{11}{6}\right]$

45. $3 < -2x + 3 < 9$

$$
\begin{array}{ccccc}
3 & < & -2x + 3 & < & 9 \\
-3 & & -3 & & -3 \\
\hline
0 & < & -2x & < & 6 \\
\dfrac{0}{-2} & > & \dfrac{-2x}{-2} & > & \dfrac{6}{-2} \\
0 & > & x & > & -3
\end{array}
$$

Set notation: $\{x \mid 0 > x > -3\}$        Interval notation: $(-3, 0)$

47. $-4 \le -m + 7 \le 0$

$$
\begin{array}{ccccc}
-4 & \le & -m + 7 & \le & 0 \\
-7 & & -7 & & -7 \\
\hline
-11 & \le & -m & \le & -7 \\
\dfrac{-11}{-1} & \ge & \dfrac{-m}{-1} & \ge & \dfrac{-7}{-1} \\
11 & \ge & m & \ge & 7
\end{array}
$$

Set notation: $\{m \mid 11 \ge m \ge 7\}$        Interval notation: $[7, 11]$

49. $2 < \dfrac{4y - 1}{6} \leq 4$

$$2 < \dfrac{4y - 1}{6} \leq 4$$

$$\dfrac{6}{1}(2) < \dfrac{6}{1}\left(\dfrac{4y - 1}{6}\right) \leq \dfrac{6}{1}(4)$$

$$12 < 4y - 1 \leq 24$$

$$\underline{+1 \qquad\qquad +1 \qquad +1}$$

$$\dfrac{13}{4} < \dfrac{4y}{4} \leq \dfrac{25}{4}$$

$$\dfrac{13}{4} < y \leq \dfrac{25}{4}$$

Set notation: $\left\{ y \mid \dfrac{13}{4} < y \leq \dfrac{25}{4} \right\}$    Interval notation: $\left( \dfrac{13}{4}, \dfrac{25}{4} \right]$

51. $7 \leq \dfrac{-4a + 5}{2} < 8$

$$7 \leq \dfrac{-4a + 5}{2} < 8$$

$$\dfrac{2}{1}(7) \leq \dfrac{2}{1}\left(\dfrac{-4a + 5}{2}\right) < \dfrac{2}{1}(8)$$

$$14 \leq -4a + 5 < 16$$

$$\underline{-5 \qquad\qquad -5 \qquad -5}$$

$$9 \leq -4a < 11$$

$$\dfrac{9}{-4} \geq \dfrac{-4a}{-4} > \dfrac{11}{-4}$$

$$-\dfrac{9}{4} \geq a > -\dfrac{11}{4}$$

Set notation: $\left\{ a \mid -\dfrac{9}{4} \geq a > -\dfrac{11}{4} \right\}$    Interval notation: $\left( -\dfrac{11}{4}, -\dfrac{9}{4} \right]$

53. $-2 < \dfrac{3}{2}x - \dfrac{1}{2} < 0$

$$-2 < \dfrac{3}{2}x - \dfrac{1}{2} < 0$$

$$\dfrac{2}{1}(-2) < \dfrac{2}{1}\left(\dfrac{3}{2}x - \dfrac{1}{2}\right) < \dfrac{2}{1}(0)$$

$$-4 < 3x - 1 < 0$$

$$\underline{+1 \qquad\quad +1 \qquad +1}$$

$$\dfrac{-3}{3} < \dfrac{3x}{3} < \dfrac{1}{3}$$

$$-1 < x < \dfrac{1}{3}$$

Set notation: $\left\{ x \mid -1 < x < \dfrac{1}{3} \right\}$    Interval notation: $\left( -1, \dfrac{1}{3} \right)$

55. $-6 \le \dfrac{t+3}{-4} \le 1$

$$-6 \le \frac{t+3}{-4} \le 1$$

$$\frac{-4}{1}(-6) \ge \frac{-4}{1}\left(\frac{t+3}{-4}\right) \ge \frac{-4}{1}(1)$$

$$24 \ge t+3 \ge -4$$

$$\underline{-3 \qquad -3 \qquad -3}$$

$$21 \ge t \ge -7$$

Set notation: $\{t \mid 21 \ge t \ge -7\}$        Interval notation: $[-7,\ 21]$

57. $2x + 5 < -1$ or $2x + 5 > 1$

$$
\begin{array}{cccc}
2x + 5 < -1 & \qquad \text{or} \qquad & 2x + 5 > 1 \\
\underline{\quad -5 \quad -5\quad} & & \underline{\quad -5 \quad -5 \quad} \\
\dfrac{2x}{2} < \dfrac{-6}{2} & & \dfrac{2x}{2} > \dfrac{-4}{2} \\
x < -3 & \text{or} & x > -2
\end{array}
$$

Set notation : $\{x \mid x < -3 \text{ or } x > -2\}$        Interval notation: $(-\infty,\ -3) \cup (-2,\ \infty)$

59. $\dfrac{1}{4}a - 1 < 0$ or $\dfrac{1}{4}a - 1 \ge 5$

$$
\begin{array}{ccc}
\dfrac{1}{4}a - 1 < 0 & \qquad \text{or} \qquad & \dfrac{1}{4}a - 1 \ge 5 \\
\underline{\qquad +1 \quad +1} & & \underline{\qquad +1 \quad +1} \\
\dfrac{1}{4}a < 1 & & \dfrac{1}{4}a \ge 6 \\
\dfrac{4}{1}\left(\dfrac{1}{4}a\right) < \dfrac{4}{1}(1) & & \dfrac{4}{1}\left(\dfrac{1}{4}a\right) \ge \dfrac{4}{1}(6) \\
a < 4 & \text{or} & a \ge 24
\end{array}
$$

Set notation : $\{a \mid a < 4 \text{ or } a \ge 24\}$        Interval notation: $(-\infty,\ 4) \cup [24, \infty)$

61. $-x - 5 \le 8$ or $-x - 5 \ge 12$

$$
\begin{array}{ccc}
-x - 5 \le 8 & \qquad \text{or} \qquad & -x - 5 \ge 12 \\
\underline{\quad +5 \quad +5} & & \underline{\quad +5 \quad +5} \\
-x \le 13 & & -x \ge 17 \\
\dfrac{-x}{-1} \ge \dfrac{13}{-1} & & \dfrac{-x}{-1} \le \dfrac{17}{-1} \\
x \ge -13 & \text{or} & x \le -17
\end{array}
$$

Set notation : $\{x \mid x \ge -13 \text{ or } x \le -17\}$        Interval notation: $[-13, \infty) \cup (-\infty, -17]$

63. $-7p + 2 \le -12$ or $-7p + 2 > 7$

$$
\begin{array}{ccc}
-7p + 2 \le -12 & \qquad \text{or} \qquad & -7p + 2 > 7 \\
\underline{\quad -2 \quad -2} & & \underline{\quad -2 \quad -2} \\
-7p \le -14 & & -7p > 5 \\
\dfrac{-7p}{-7} \ge \dfrac{-14}{-7} & & \dfrac{-7p}{-7} < \dfrac{5}{-7} \\
p \ge 2 & \text{or} & p < -\dfrac{5}{7}
\end{array}
$$

Set notation : $\left\{p \mid p \ge 2 \text{ or } p < -\dfrac{5}{7}\right\}$        Interval notation: $\left[2, \infty\right) \cup \left(-\infty, -\dfrac{5}{7}\right)$

65. $\dfrac{-3x+2}{5} < 0$ or $\dfrac{-3x+2}{5} > 2$

$$\dfrac{-3x+2}{5} < 0 \qquad \text{or} \qquad \dfrac{-3x+2}{5} > 2$$

$$\dfrac{5}{1}\left(\dfrac{-3x+2}{5}\right) < \dfrac{5}{1}(0) \qquad \dfrac{5}{1}\left(\dfrac{-3x+2}{5}\right) > \dfrac{5}{1}(2)$$

$$-3x+2 < 0 \qquad\qquad -3x+2 > 10$$

$$\underline{\quad -2 \;\; -2\quad} \qquad\qquad \underline{\quad -2 \;\; -2\quad}$$

$$-3x < -2 \qquad\qquad -3x > 8$$

$$\dfrac{-3x}{-3} > \dfrac{-2}{-3} \qquad\qquad \dfrac{-3x}{-3} < \dfrac{8}{-3}$$

$$x > \dfrac{2}{3} \qquad \text{or} \qquad x < -\dfrac{8}{3}$$

Set notation: $\left\{ x \mid x > \dfrac{2}{3} \text{ or } x < -\dfrac{8}{3} \right\}$ Interval notation: $\left( \dfrac{2}{3}, \infty \right) \cup \left( -\infty, -\dfrac{8}{3} \right)$

67. $\dfrac{x}{7} - \dfrac{6}{5} \le -3$ or $\dfrac{x}{7} - \dfrac{6}{5} > 3$

$$\dfrac{x}{7} - \dfrac{6}{5} \le -3 \qquad \text{or} \qquad \dfrac{x}{7} - \dfrac{6}{5} > 3$$

$$\dfrac{35}{1}\left(\dfrac{x}{7} - \dfrac{6}{5}\right) \le \dfrac{35}{1}(-3) \qquad \dfrac{35}{1}\left(\dfrac{x}{7} - \dfrac{6}{5}\right) > \dfrac{35}{1}(3)$$

$$5x - 42 \le -105 \qquad\qquad 5x - 42 > 105$$

$$\underline{\quad +42 \;\; +42\quad} \qquad\qquad \underline{\quad +42 \;\; +42\quad}$$

$$\dfrac{5x}{5} \le \dfrac{-63}{5} \qquad\qquad \dfrac{5x}{5} > \dfrac{147}{5}$$

$$x \le -\dfrac{63}{5} \qquad \text{or} \qquad x > \dfrac{147}{5}$$

Set notation: $\left\{ x \mid x \le -\dfrac{63}{5} \text{ or } x > \dfrac{147}{5} \right\}$ Interval notation: $\left( -\infty, -\dfrac{63}{5} \right] \cup \left( \dfrac{147}{5}, \infty \right)$

69. $\dfrac{-1}{6}y + \dfrac{1}{8} < 0$ or $\dfrac{-1}{6}y + \dfrac{1}{8} \ge 2$

$$\dfrac{-1}{6}y + \dfrac{1}{8} < 0 \qquad \text{or} \qquad \dfrac{-1}{6}y + \dfrac{1}{8} \ge 2$$

$$\dfrac{24}{1}\left(\dfrac{-1}{6}y + \dfrac{1}{8}\right) < \dfrac{24}{1}(0) \qquad \dfrac{24}{1}\left(\dfrac{-1}{6}y + \dfrac{1}{8}\right) \ge \dfrac{24}{1}(2)$$

$$-4y + 3 < 0 \qquad\qquad -4y + 3 \ge 48$$

$$\underline{\quad -3 \;\; -3\quad} \qquad\qquad \underline{\quad -3 \;\; -3\quad}$$

$$-4y < -3 \qquad\qquad -4y \ge 45$$

$$\dfrac{-4y}{-4} > \dfrac{-3}{-4} \qquad\qquad \dfrac{-4y}{-4} \le \dfrac{45}{-4}$$

$$y > \dfrac{3}{4} \qquad \text{or} \qquad y \le -\dfrac{45}{4}$$

Set notation: $\left\{ y \mid y > \dfrac{3}{4} \text{ or } y \le -\dfrac{45}{4} \right\}$ Interval notation: $\left( \dfrac{3}{4}, \infty \right) \cup \left( -\infty, -\dfrac{45}{4} \right]$

71. $x < 4$ and $x \le 5$ is simplified to $\{ x \mid x < 4 \}$. 73. $x \ge 6$ and $x \le 12$ is simplified to $\{ x \mid 6 \le x \le 12 \}$.

75. $y > -3$ and $y \le 0$ is simplified to $\{ y \mid -3 < y \le 0 \}$. 77. $y \le -1$ and $y \ge 5$ is simplified to $\varnothing$.

79. $t \le 0$ or $t \le -4$ is simplified to $\{t \mid t \le 0\}$.      81. $u > 1$ or $u > -9$ is simplified to $\{u \mid u > -9\}$.

83. $x \ge -8$ or $x \le 0$ is simplified to $\{x \mid -\infty < x < \infty\} = (-\infty,\ \infty)$ (the set of all real numbers).

85. $m \le 0$ or $m > 0$ is simplified to $\{m \mid -\infty < m < \infty\} = (-\infty,\ \infty)$ (the set of all real numbers).

---

**Chapter 10 Exercise 10.1**

Examples 1-19 odd

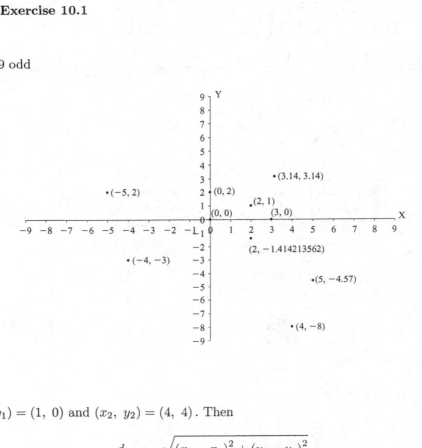

21. Let $(x_1,\ y_1) = (1,\ 0)$ and $(x_2,\ y_2) = (4,\ 4)$. Then

$$\begin{aligned} d &= \sqrt{(x_2 - x_1)^2 + (y_2 - y_1)^2} \\ &= \sqrt{(4 - 1)^2 + (4 - 0)^2} \\ &= \sqrt{(3)^2 + (4)^2} \\ &= \sqrt{9 + 16} = \sqrt{25} = 5 \end{aligned}$$

23. Let $(x_1,\ y_1) = (-2,\ 1)$ and $(x_2,\ y_2) = (4,\ 9)$. Then

$$\begin{aligned} d &= \sqrt{(x_2 - x_1)^2 + (y_2 - y_1)^2} \\ &= \sqrt{(4 - (-2))^2 + (9 - 1)^2} \\ &= \sqrt{(6)^2 + (8)^2} \\ &= \sqrt{36 + 64} = \sqrt{100} = 10 \end{aligned}$$

25. Let $(x_1, \, y_1) = (2, \, -6)$ and $(x_2, \, y_2) = (1, \, -1)$. Then

$$
\begin{aligned}
d &= \sqrt{(x_2 - x_1)^2 + (y_2 - y_1)^2} \\
&= \sqrt{(1 - 2)^2 + (-1 - (-6))^2} \\
&= \sqrt{(-1)^2 + (5)^2} \\
&= \sqrt{1 + 25} = \sqrt{26}
\end{aligned}
$$

27. Let $(x_1, \, y_1) = (0, \, -6)$ and $(x_2, \, y_2) = (4, \, 2)$. Then

$$
\begin{aligned}
d &= \sqrt{(x_2 - x_1)^2 + (y_2 - y_1)^2} \\
&= \sqrt{(4 - 0)^2 + (2 - (-6))^2} \\
&= \sqrt{(4)^2 + (8)^2} = \sqrt{16 + 64} \\
&= \sqrt{80} = \sqrt{16}\sqrt{5} = 4\sqrt{5}
\end{aligned}
$$

29. Let $(x_1, \, y_1) = (7, \, -2)$ and $(x_2, \, y_2) = (-3, \, -2)$. Then

$$
\begin{aligned}
d &= \sqrt{(x_2 - x_1)^2 + (y_2 - y_1)^2} \\
&= \sqrt{(-3 - 7)^2 + (-2 - (-2))^2} \\
&= \sqrt{(-10)^2 + (0)^2} \\
&= \sqrt{100 + 0} = \sqrt{100} = 10
\end{aligned}
$$

31. Let $(x_1, \, y_1) = (-6, \, 5)$ and $(x_2, \, y_2) = (-6, \, -7)$. Then

$$
\begin{aligned}
d &= \sqrt{(x_2 - x_1)^2 + (y_2 - y_1)^2} \\
&= \sqrt{(-6 - (-6))^2 + (-7 - 5)^2} \\
&= \sqrt{(0)^2 + (-12)^2} \\
&= \sqrt{0 + 144} = \sqrt{144} = 12
\end{aligned}
$$

33. Let $(x_1, \, y_1) = (3, \, 4)$ and $(x_2, \, y_2) = (1, \, 10)$. Then

$$
\begin{aligned}
\text{midpoint of } \overline{AB} &= \left( \frac{x_1 + x_2}{2}, \, \frac{y_1 + y_2}{2} \right) \\
&= \left( \frac{3 + 1}{2}, \, \frac{4 + 10}{2} \right) \\
&= \left( \frac{4}{2}, \, \frac{14}{2} \right) = (2, \, 7)
\end{aligned}
$$

35. Let $(x_1, \ y_1) = (-4, \ 6)$ and $(x_2, \ y_2) = (8, \ -6)$. Then

$$
\begin{aligned}
\text{midpoint of } \overline{PQ} \ &= \ \left( \frac{x_1 + x_2}{2}, \ \frac{y_1 + y_2}{2} \right) \\
&= \ \left( \frac{-4 + 8}{2}, \ \frac{6 + (-6)}{2} \right) \\
&= \ \left( \frac{4}{2}, \ \frac{0}{2} \right) = (2, \ 0)
\end{aligned}
$$

37. Let $(x_1, \ y_1) = (-11, \ -6)$ and $(x_2, \ y_2) = (-3, \ -1)$. Then

$$
\begin{aligned}
\text{midpoint of } \overline{ST} \ &= \ \left( \frac{x_1 + x_2}{2}, \ \frac{y_1 + y_2}{2} \right) \\
&= \ \left( \frac{-11 + (-3)}{2}, \ \frac{-6 + (-1)}{2} \right) \\
&= \ \left( \frac{-14}{2}, \ \frac{-7}{2} \right) = \left( -7, \ -\frac{7}{2} \right)
\end{aligned}
$$

39. Let $(x_1, \ y_1) = (-6, \ -6)$ and $(x_2, \ y_2) = (5, \ 6)$. Then

$$
\begin{aligned}
\text{midpoint of } \overline{PQ} \ &= \ \left( \frac{x_1 + x_2}{2}, \ \frac{y_1 + y_2}{2} \right) \\
&= \ \left( \frac{-6 + 5}{2}, \ \frac{-6 + 6}{2} \right) \\
&= \ \left( \frac{-1}{2}, \ \frac{0}{2} \right) = \left( -\frac{1}{2}, \ 0 \right)
\end{aligned}
$$

41. Let $(x_1, \ y_1) = \left( \frac{1}{2}, \ -\frac{1}{3} \right)$ and $(x_2, \ y_2) = \left( \frac{1}{4}, \ \frac{1}{6} \right)$. Then

$$
\begin{aligned}
\text{midpoint of } \overline{A_1 A_2} \ &= \ \left( \frac{x_1 + x_2}{2}, \ \frac{y_1 + y_2}{2} \right) \\
&= \ \left( \frac{\frac{1}{2} + \frac{1}{4}}{2}, \ \frac{-\frac{1}{3} + \frac{1}{6}}{2} \right) \\
&= \ \left( \frac{4 \left( \frac{1}{2} \right) + 4 \left( \frac{1}{4} \right)}{4 \, (2)}, \ \frac{6 \left( -\frac{1}{3} \right) + 6 \left( \frac{1}{6} \right)}{6 \, (2)} \right) \\
&= \ \left( \frac{2 + 1}{8}, \ \frac{-2 + 1}{12} \right) = \left( \frac{3}{8}, \ -\frac{1}{12} \right)
\end{aligned}
$$

43. Let $(x_1, \ y_1) = \left(-5, \ \dfrac{1}{10}\right)$ and $(x_2, \ y_2) = \left(\dfrac{1}{6}, \ -3\right)$. Then

$$
\begin{aligned}
\text{midpoint of } \overline{T_1 T_2} \ &= \ \left(\dfrac{x_1 + x_2}{2}, \ \dfrac{y_1 + y_2}{2}\right) \\[2mm]
&= \ \left(\dfrac{-5 + \dfrac{1}{6}}{2}, \ \dfrac{\dfrac{1}{10} + (-3)}{2}\right) \\[2mm]
&= \ \left(\dfrac{6\,(-5) + 6\left(\dfrac{1}{6}\right)}{6\,(2)}, \ \dfrac{10\left(\dfrac{1}{10}\right) + 10\,(-3)}{10\,(2)}\right) \\[2mm]
&= \ \left(\dfrac{-30 + 1}{12}, \ \dfrac{1 - 30}{20}\right) = \left(-\dfrac{29}{12}, \ -\dfrac{29}{20}\right)
\end{aligned}
$$

45. Let $A = (3, \ 0)$, $B = (0, \ 0)$, and $C = (0, \ 4)$.

The length of $\overline{AB}$ is (letting $(x_1, \ y_1) = A = (3, \ 0)$ and $(x_2, \ y_2) = B = (0, \ 0)$)

$$
\begin{aligned}
\text{length of } \overline{AB} \ &= \ \sqrt{(x_2 - x_1)^2 + (y_2 - y_1)^2} \\[1mm]
&= \ \sqrt{(0 - 3)^2 + (0 - 0)^2} \\[1mm]
&= \ \sqrt{(-3)^2 + (0)^2} \\[1mm]
&= \ \sqrt{9 + 0} = \sqrt{9} = 3
\end{aligned}
$$

The length of $\overline{AC}$ is (letting $(x_1, \ y_1) = A = (3, \ 0)$ and $(x_2, \ y_2) = C = (0, \ 4)$)

$$
\begin{aligned}
\text{length of } \overline{AC} \ &= \ \sqrt{(x_2 - x_1)^2 + (y_2 - y_1)^2} \\[1mm]
&= \ \sqrt{(0 - 3)^2 + (4 - 0)^2} \\[1mm]
&= \ \sqrt{(-3)^2 + (4)^2} \\[1mm]
&= \ \sqrt{9 + 16} = \sqrt{25} = 5
\end{aligned}
$$

The length of $\overline{BC}$ is (letting $(x_1, \ y_1) = B = (0, \ 0)$ and $(x_2, \ y_2) = C = (0, \ 4)$)

$$
\begin{aligned}
\text{length of } \overline{BC} \ &= \ \sqrt{(x_2 - x_1)^2 + (y_2 - y_1)^2} \\[1mm]
&= \ \sqrt{(0 - 0)^2 + (4 - 0)^2} \\[1mm]
&= \ \sqrt{(0)^2 + (4)^2} \\[1mm]
&= \ \sqrt{0 + 16} = \sqrt{16} = 4
\end{aligned}
$$

The sides of this triangle measure 3, 5 and 4. Since $(3)^2 + (4)^2 = (5)^2$, this is a right triangle.

47. Let $A = (2, \ -1)$, $B = (3, \ 1)$, and $C = (0, \ -2)$.

The length of $\overline{AB}$ is (letting $(x_1, \ y_1) = A = (2, \ -1)$ and $(x_2, \ y_2) = B = (3, \ 1)$)

$$
\begin{aligned}
\text{length of } \overline{AB} &= \sqrt{(x_2 - x_1)^2 + (y_2 - y_1)^2} \\
&= \sqrt{(3 - 2)^2 + (1 - (-1))^2} \\
&= \sqrt{(1)^2 + (2)^2} \\
&= \sqrt{1 + 4} = \sqrt{5}
\end{aligned}
$$

The length of $\overline{AC}$ is (letting $(x_1, \ y_1) = A = (2, \ -1)$ and $(x_2, \ y_2) = C = (0, \ -2)$)

$$
\begin{aligned}
\text{length of } \overline{AC} &= \sqrt{(x_2 - x_1)^2 + (y_2 - y_1)^2} \\
&= \sqrt{(0 - 2)^2 + (-2 - (-1))^2} \\
&= \sqrt{(-2)^2 + (-1)^2} \\
&= \sqrt{4 + 1} = \sqrt{5}
\end{aligned}
$$

The length of $\overline{BC}$ is (letting $(x_1, \ y_1) = B = (3, \ 1)$ and $(x_2, \ y_2) = C = (0, \ -2)$)

$$
\begin{aligned}
\text{length of } \overline{BC} &= \sqrt{(x_2 - x_1)^2 + (y_2 - y_1)^2} \\
&= \sqrt{(0 - 3)^2 + (-2 - 1)^2} \\
&= \sqrt{(-3)^2 + (-3)^2} = \sqrt{9 + 9} \\
&= \sqrt{18} = \sqrt{9}\sqrt{2} = 3\sqrt{2}
\end{aligned}
$$

The sides of this triangle measure $\sqrt{5}$, $\sqrt{5}$ and $3\sqrt{2}$. Since $\left(\sqrt{5}\right)^2 + \left(\sqrt{5}\right)^2 \neq \left(3\sqrt{2}\right)^2$, this is not a right triangle.

49. Let $A = (6, \ 3)$, $B = (-2, \ -3)$, and $C = (-5, \ 1)$.

The length of $\overline{AB}$ is (letting $(x_1, \ y_1) = A = (6, \ 3)$ and $(x_2, \ y_2) = B = (-2, \ -3)$)

$$
\begin{aligned}
\text{length of } \overline{AB} &= \sqrt{(x_2 - x_1)^2 + (y_2 - y_1)^2} \\
&= \sqrt{(-2 - 6)^2 + (-3 - 3)^2} \\
&= \sqrt{(-8)^2 + (-6)^2} \\
&= \sqrt{64 + 36} = \sqrt{100} = 10
\end{aligned}
$$

The length of $\overline{AC}$ is (letting $(x_1, \ y_1) = A = (6, \ 3)$ and $(x_2, \ y_2) = C = (-5, \ 1)$)

$$
\begin{aligned}
\text{length of } \overline{AC} &= \sqrt{(x_2 - x_1)^2 + (y_2 - y_1)^2} \\
&= \sqrt{(-5 - 6)^2 + (1 - 3)^2} \\
&= \sqrt{(-11)^2 + (-2)^2} = \sqrt{121 + 4} \\
&= \sqrt{125} = \sqrt{25}\sqrt{5} = 5\sqrt{5}
\end{aligned}
$$

The length of $\overline{BC}$ is (letting $(x_1,\ y_1) = B = (-2,\ -3)$ and $(x_2,\ y_2) = C = (-5,\ 1)$)

$$
\begin{aligned}
\text{length of } \overline{BC} &= \sqrt{(x_2 - x_1)^2 + (y_2 - y_1)^2} \\
&= \sqrt{(-5 - (-2))^2 + (1 - (-3))^2} \\
&= \sqrt{(-3)^2 + (4)^2} = \sqrt{9 + 16} \\
&= \sqrt{25} = 5
\end{aligned}
$$

The sides of this triangle measure $10$, $5\sqrt{5}$ and $5$. Since $(10)^2 + (5)^2 = \left(5\sqrt{5}\right)^2$, this is a right triangle.

**Chapter 10 Exercise 10.2**

1. Yes, since $1 \overset{\vee}{=} 2\,(1) - 1.$     3. Yes, since $3 \overset{\vee}{=} -2\,(-4) - 5.$     5. No, since $0 \neq \dfrac{2}{3}\,(-2) + 4.$

7. Yes, since $5\,(3) - 4\,(3) - 3 \overset{\vee}{=} 0.$     9. Yes, since $-\dfrac{5}{6}\,(-12) + \dfrac{1}{10}\,(10) - 11 \overset{\vee}{=} 0.$

11. Let $(x_1,\ y_1) = (1,\ 6)$ and $(x_2,\ y_2) = (2,\ 9)$. Then

$$
m = \frac{y_2 - y_1}{x_2 - x_1} = \frac{9 - 6}{2 - 1} = \frac{3}{1} = 3.
$$

13. Let $(x_1,\ y_1) = (9,\ -2)$ and $(x_2,\ y_2) = (3,\ -10)$. Then

$$
m = \frac{y_2 - y_1}{x_2 - x_1} = \frac{-10 - (-2)}{3 - 9} = \frac{-8}{-6} = \frac{4}{3}.
$$

15. Let $(x_1,\ y_1) = (-1,\ -12)$ and $(x_2,\ y_2) = (0,\ -2)$. Then

$$
m = \frac{y_2 - y_1}{x_2 - x_1} = \frac{-2 - (-12)}{0 - (-1)} = \frac{10}{1} = 10.
$$

17. Let $(x_1,\ y_1) = (4,\ 2)$ and $(x_2,\ y_2) = (-6,\ -5)$. Then

$$
m = \frac{y_2 - y_1}{x_2 - x_1} = \frac{-5 - 2}{-6 - 4} = \frac{-7}{-10} = \frac{7}{10}.
$$

19. Let $(x_1,\ y_1) = (4,\ 9)$ and $(x_2,\ y_2) = (-3,\ 9)$. Then

$$
m = \frac{y_2 - y_1}{x_2 - x_1} = \frac{9 - 9}{-3 - 4} = \frac{0}{-7} = 0.
$$

21. Let $(x_1,\ y_1) = (5,\ 7)$ and $(x_2,\ y_2) = (5,\ -3)$. Then

$$
m = \frac{y_2 - y_1}{x_2 - x_1} = \frac{-3 - 7}{5 - 5} = \frac{-10}{0} \text{ is undefined.}
$$

23. Let $(x_1,\ y_1) = \left(\dfrac{1}{2},\ -\dfrac{1}{3}\right)$ and $(x_2,\ y_2) = \left(\dfrac{3}{4},\ \dfrac{2}{3}\right)$. Then

$$m = \frac{y_2 - y_1}{x_2 - x_1} = \frac{\dfrac{2}{3} - \left(-\dfrac{1}{3}\right)}{\dfrac{3}{4} - \dfrac{1}{2}} = \frac{\dfrac{3}{3}}{\dfrac{3}{4} - \dfrac{1}{2}} = \frac{4\,(1)}{4\left(\dfrac{3}{4}\right) - 4\left(\dfrac{1}{2}\right)} = \frac{4}{3-2} = \frac{4}{1} = 4.$$

25. Let $(x_1,\ y_1) = \left(-\dfrac{2}{5},\ -\dfrac{1}{9}\right)$ and $(x_2,\ y_2) = \left(\dfrac{3}{10},\ -\dfrac{5}{6}\right)$. Then

$$m = \frac{y_2 - y_1}{x_2 - x_1} = \frac{-\dfrac{5}{6} - \left(-\dfrac{1}{9}\right)}{\dfrac{3}{10} - \left(-\dfrac{2}{5}\right)} = \frac{-\dfrac{5}{6} + \dfrac{1}{9}}{\dfrac{3}{10} + \dfrac{2}{5}} = \frac{90\left(-\dfrac{5}{6}\right) + 90\left(\dfrac{1}{9}\right)}{90\left(\dfrac{3}{10}\right) + 90\left(\dfrac{2}{5}\right)} = \frac{-75 + 10}{27 + 36} = \frac{-65}{63} = -\frac{65}{63}.$$

27. $m = 1$, $x_1 = 4$ and $y_1 = 2$. Our equation is

$$
\begin{aligned}
y - y_1 &= m\,(x - x_1) \\
y - 2 &= 1\,(x - 4) \\
y - 2 &= x - 4 \\
\underline{+2 \qquad\quad +2\phantom{x}} & \\
y &= x - 2
\end{aligned}
$$

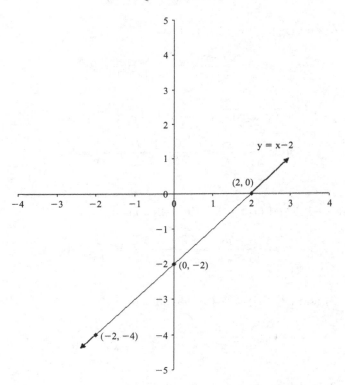

29. $m = 4$, $x_1 = -1$ and $y_1 = 3$. Our equation is

$$
\begin{aligned}
y - y_1 &= m\,(x - x_1) \\
y - 3 &= 4\,(x - (-1)) \\
y - 3 &= 4\,(x + 1) \\
y - 3 &= 4x + 4 \\
\underline{+3 \qquad\quad +3\phantom{x}} & \\
y &= 4x + 7
\end{aligned}
$$

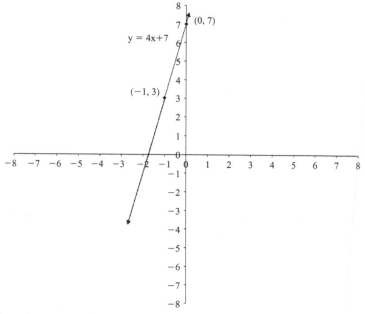

31. $m = 7$, $x_1 = -2$ and $y_1 = -7$. Our equation is

$$y - y_1 = m\,(x - x_1)$$
$$y - (-7) = 7\,(x - (-2))$$
$$y + 7 = 7\,(x + 2)$$
$$y + 7 = 7x + 14$$
$$\underline{\phantom{y +}{-7}\qquad\quad {-7}}$$
$$y = 7x + 7$$

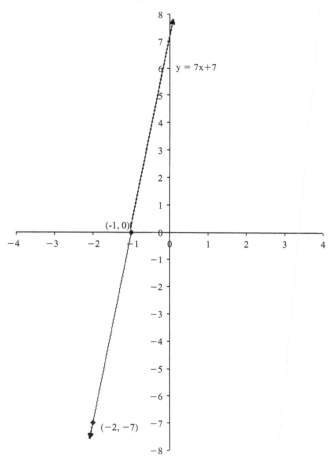

33. $m = \dfrac{1}{2}$, $x_1 = 0$ and $y_1 = 4$. Our equation is

$$y - y_1 = m\left(x - x_1\right)$$
$$y - 4 = \frac{1}{2}\left(x - 0\right)$$
$$y - 4 = \frac{1}{2}x$$
$$\underline{\phantom{y-}+4\phantom{=\frac{1}{2}x}+4}$$
$$y = \frac{1}{2}x + 4$$

Another way to find the equation is to notice that $m = \dfrac{1}{2}$ and $b = 4$ (since the given point is the $y$-intercept). Therefore, $y = mx + b$ yields $y = \dfrac{1}{2}x + 4$.

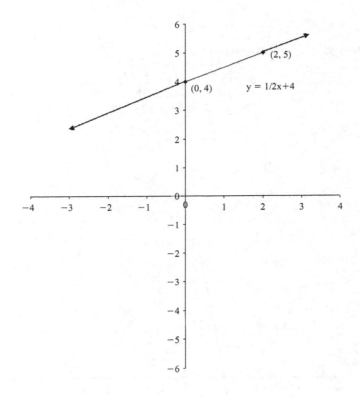

35. $m = -\dfrac{1}{8}$, $x_1 = -3$ and $y_1 = 0$. Our equation is

$$y - y_1 = m\left(x - x_1\right)$$
$$y - 0 = -\frac{1}{8}\left(x - (-3)\right)$$
$$y = -\frac{1}{8}\left(x + 3\right)$$
$$y = -\frac{1}{8}x - \frac{3}{8}$$

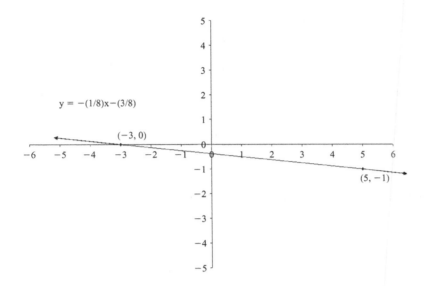

$$y = -(1/8)x - (3/8)$$

$(-3, 0)$

$(5, -1)$

37. $m = -\dfrac{4}{5}$, $x_1 = -8$ and $y_1 = 2$. Our equation is

$$y - y_1 = m(x - x_1)$$
$$y - 2 = -\frac{4}{5}(x - (-8))$$
$$y - 2 = -\frac{4}{5}(x + 8)$$
$$y - 2 = -\frac{4}{5}x - \frac{32}{5}$$
$$\underline{+2 \qquad\qquad +2}$$
$$y = -\frac{4}{5}x - \frac{22}{5}$$

$(-8, 2)$
$$y = -(4/5)x - 22/5$$

$(-3, -2)$

39. $m = \dfrac{3}{14}$, $x_1 = -9$ and $y_1 = -1$. Our equation is

$$y - y_1 = m(x - x_1)$$
$$y - (-1) = \frac{3}{14}(x - (-9))$$
$$y + 1 = \frac{3}{14}(x + 9)$$
$$y + 1 = \frac{3}{14}x + \frac{27}{14}$$
$$\underline{-1 \qquad\qquad -1}$$
$$y = \frac{3}{14}x + \frac{13}{14}$$

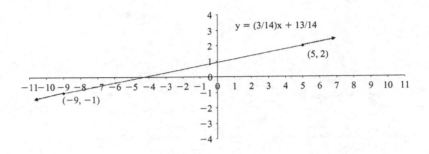

41. Since $m = 0$ and $y_1 = -6$, the equation of the line is $y = -6$.

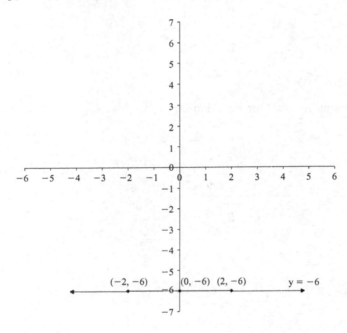

43. Since the line has no slope and $x_1 = -3$, the equation of the line is $x = -3$.

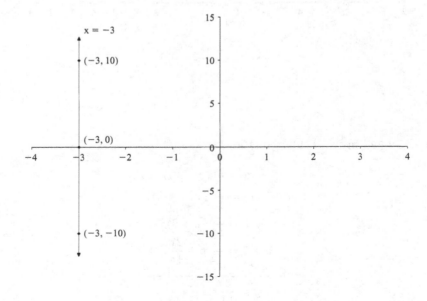

45. $y = 2x + 5$ has slope 2 and $y$-intercept $(0, 5)$.   47. $y = -4x + 8$ has slope $-4$ and $y$-intercept $(0, 8)$.

49. $y = \frac{1}{5}x - 3$ has slope $\frac{1}{5}$ and $y$-intercept $(0, -3)$.

51. First, get $3x + 4y - 6 = 0$ in slope-intercept form.

$$3x + 4y - 6 = 0$$
$$\underline{\quad -4y \qquad\qquad -4y}$$
$$\frac{3x - 6}{-4} = \frac{4y}{4}$$
$$\frac{3x}{-4} + \frac{-6}{-4} = y$$
$$-\frac{3}{4}x + \frac{3}{2} = y$$

The slope is $-\dfrac{3}{4}$ and the $y$-intercept is $\left(0, \dfrac{3}{2}\right)$.

53. First, get $y - 2 = 5(x - 3)$ in slope-intercept form.

$$y - 2 = 5(x - 3)$$
$$y - 2 = 5x - 15$$
$$\underline{+2 \qquad\qquad +2}$$
$$y = 5x - 13$$

The slope is 5 and the $y$-intercept is $(0, -13)$.

55. First, get $-8x + y - 3 = 0$ in slope-intercept form.

$$-8x + y - 3 = 0$$
$$\underline{+8x \qquad +3 \qquad +8x + 3}$$
$$y = 8x + 3$$

The slope is 8 and the $y$-intercept is $(0, 3)$.

57. First, get $x + y = 8$ in slope-intercept form.

$$x + y = 8$$
$$\underline{-x \qquad\qquad -x}$$
$$y = -x + 8$$

The slope is $-1$ and the $y$-intercept is $(0, 8)$.

59. First, get $x - y - 2 = 0$ in slope-intercept form.

$$x - y - 2 = 0$$
$$\underline{+y \qquad +y}$$
$$x - 2 = y$$

The slope is 1 and the $y$-intercept is $(0, 2)$.

61. $y = 5$ has slope 0 and $y$-intercept $(0, 5)$.       63. $x = 3$ has no slope and no $y$-intercept.

65. For the $y$-intercept, you set $x = 0$ and solve for $y$.

$$4(0) + y - 12 = 0$$
$$y - 12 = 0$$
$$\underline{+12 \quad +12}$$
$$y = 12$$

The $y$-intercept is $(0,\ 12)$. For the $x$-intercept, you set $y=0$ and solve for $x$.

$$4x + (0) - 12 = 0$$
$$4x - 12 = 0$$
$$\underline{+12\quad +12}$$
$$\frac{4x}{4} = \frac{12}{4}$$
$$x = 3$$

The $x$-intercept is $(3,\ 0)$.

67. For the $y$-intercept, you set $x=0$ and solve for $y$.

$$-(0) - 2y + 6 = 0$$
$$-2y + 6 = 0$$
$$\underline{-6\quad -6}$$
$$\frac{-2y}{-2} = \frac{-6}{-2}$$
$$y = 3$$

The $y$-intercept is $(0,\ 3)$. For the $x$-intercept, you set $y=0$ and solve for $x$.

$$-x - 2(0) + 6 = 0$$
$$-x + 6 = 0$$
$$\underline{+x\qquad +x}$$
$$6 = x$$

The $x$-intercept is $(6,\ 0)$.

69. For the $y$-intercept, you set $x=0$ and solve for $y$.

$$8(0) - 5y - 7 = 0$$
$$-5y - 7 = 0$$
$$\underline{+7\qquad +7}$$
$$\frac{-5y}{-5} = \frac{7}{-5}$$
$$y = -\frac{7}{5}$$

The $y$-intercept is $\left(0,\ -\dfrac{7}{5}\right)$. For the $x$-intercept, you set $y=0$ and solve for $x$.

$$8x - 5(0) - 7 = 0$$
$$8x - 7 = 0$$
$$\underline{+7\quad +7}$$
$$\frac{8x}{8} = \frac{7}{8}$$

The $x$-intercept is $\left(\dfrac{7}{8},\ 0\right)$.

71. For the $y$-intercept, you set $x=0$ and solve for $y$.

$$2(0) - y = 0$$
$$-y = 0$$
$$y = 0$$

The $y$-intercept is $(0,\ 0)$. This is also the $x$-intercept since the origin lies on both axes.

73. For the $y$-intercept, notice that the equation is in slope-intercept form and $b = 7$. Hence, the $y$-intercept is $(0,\ 7)$. For the $x$-intercept, you set $y = 0$ and solve for $x$.

$$
\begin{array}{r}
0 = -\tfrac{1}{2}x + 7 \\
\underline{-7 \qquad\qquad -7} \\
-7 = -\tfrac{1}{2}x \\
\tfrac{-2}{1}\,(-7) = \tfrac{-2}{1}\left(-\tfrac{1}{2}x\right) \\
14 = x
\end{array}
$$

The $x$-intercept is $(14,\ 0)$.

75. For the $y$-intercept, notice that the equation is in slope-intercept form and $b = -17$. Hence, the $y$-intercept is $(0,\ -17)$. For the $x$-intercept, you set $y = 0$ and solve for $x$.

$$
\begin{array}{r}
0 = -3x - 17 \\
\underline{+17 \qquad\qquad +17} \\
\dfrac{17}{-3} = \dfrac{-3x}{-3} \\
-\dfrac{17}{3} = x
\end{array}
$$

The $x$-intercept is $\left(-\dfrac{17}{3},\ 0\right)$.

77. $x = -4$ has an $x$-intercept $(-4,\ 0)$ and no $y$-intercept.

79. $y = 10$ has an $y$-intercept $(0,\ 10)$ and no $x$-intercept.

81. Let $(x_1,\ y_1) = (1,\ 1)$ and $(x_2,\ y_2) = (2,\ 3)$. Then

$$
m = \frac{y_2 - y_1}{x_2 - x_1} = \frac{3 - 1}{2 - 1} = \frac{2}{1} = 2.
$$

Therefore, our equation is (using $x_1 = 1$, $y_1 = 1$ in the point-slope form)

$$
\begin{array}{r}
y - y_1 = m\,(x - x_1) \\
y - 1 = 2\,(x - 1) \\
y - 1 = 2x - 2 \\
\underline{+1 \qquad\qquad +1} \\
y = 2x - 1
\end{array}
$$

83. Let $(x_1,\ y_1) = (-2,\ 4)$ and $(x_2,\ y_2) = (2,\ 8)$. Then

$$
m = \frac{y_2 - y_1}{x_2 - x_1} = \frac{8 - 4}{2 - (-2)} = \frac{4}{4} = 1.
$$

Therefore, our equation is (using $x_1 = -2$, $y_1 = 4$ in the point-slope form)

$$
\begin{array}{r}
y - y_1 = m\,(x - x_1) \\
y - 4 = 1\,(x - (-2)) \\
y - 4 = x + 2 \\
\underline{+4 \qquad\qquad +4} \\
y = x + 6
\end{array}
$$

85. Let $(x_1,\ y_1) = (0,\ 6)$ and $(x_2,\ y_2) = (1,\ 0)$. Then

$$
m = \frac{y_2 - y_1}{x_2 - x_1} = \frac{0 - 6}{1 - 0} = \frac{-6}{1} = -6.
$$

Therefore, our equation is (using $x_1 = 0$, $y_1 = 6$ in the point-slope form)

$$y - y_1 = m\,(x - x_1)$$
$$y - 6 = -6\,(x - 0)$$
$$y - 6 = -6x$$
$$\underline{+6 \qquad\ + 6}$$
$$y = -6x + 6$$

87. Let $(x_1,\ y_1) = (-1,\ -7)$ and $(x_2,\ y_2) = (-5,\ -6)$. Then

$$m = \frac{y_2 - y_1}{x_2 - x_1} = \frac{-6 - (-7)}{-5 - (-1)} = \frac{1}{-4} = -\frac{1}{4}.$$

Therefore, our equation is (using $x_1 = -1$, $y_1 = -7$ in the point-slope form)

$$y - y_1 = m\,(x - x_1)$$
$$y - (-7) = -\frac{1}{4}\,(x - (-1))$$
$$y + 7 = -\frac{1}{4}\,(x + 1)$$
$$y + 7 = -\frac{1}{4}x - \frac{1}{4}$$
$$\underline{-7 \qquad\qquad\ -7}$$
$$y = -\frac{1}{4}x - \frac{29}{4}$$

89. The points $(3,\ -4)$ and $(-2,\ -4)$ have the same $y$-values. Therefore, the line is horizontal and its equation is $y = -4$.

91. The points $(9,\ 1)$ and $(9,\ 14)$ have the same $x$-values. Therefore, the line is vertical and its equation is $x = 9$.

93.

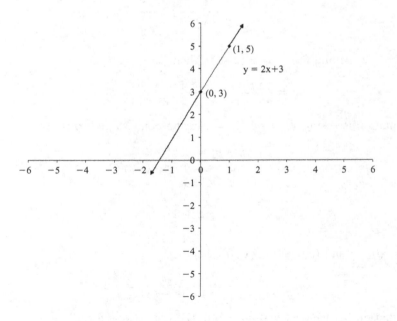

95.

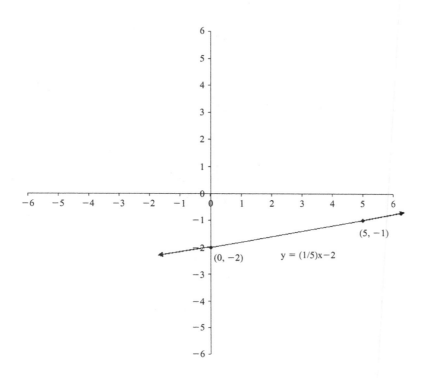

97.

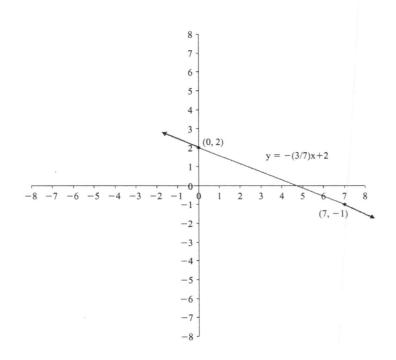

99.

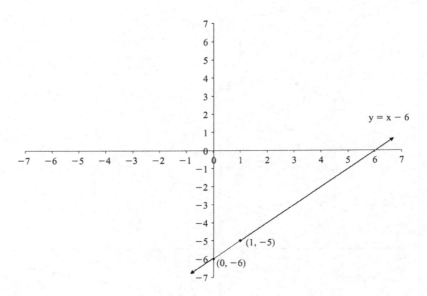

101.

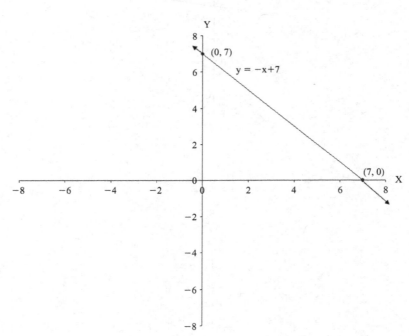

103.

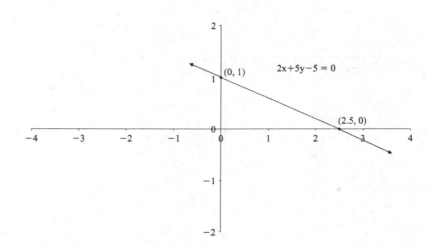

105.

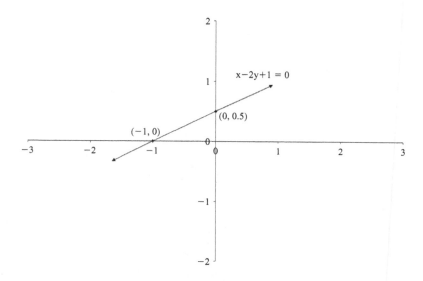

107.

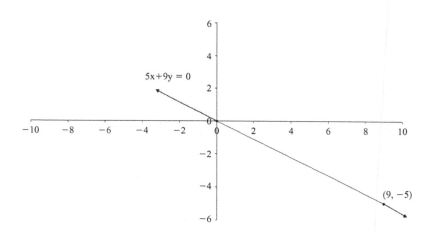

109.

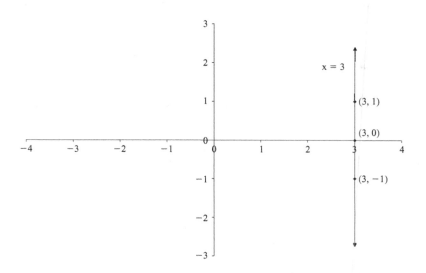

111.

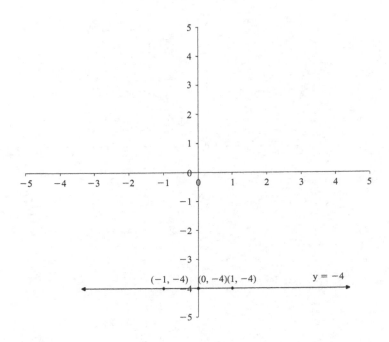

## Chapter 10 Exercise 10.3

1. $L_1 : y = 2x + 1$ has slope $m_1 = 2$ and $L_2 : y = 2x - 3$ has slope $m_2 = 2$. Moreover, they have different $y$-intercepts. Therefore the lines are parallel.

3. $L_1 : y = \frac{4}{5}x - 4$ has slope $m_1 = \frac{4}{5}$ and $L_2 : y = -\frac{5}{4}x - 9$ has slope $m_2 = -\frac{5}{4}$. Therefore the lines are perpendicular.

5. $L_1 : y = -4x + 3$ has slope $m_1 = -4$ and $L_2 : y = 4x + 6$ has slope $m_2 = 4$. The lines are neither parallel nor perpendicular.

7. $L_1 : y = 7x + 3$ has slope $m_1 = 7$ and $L_2 : y = 7x - 2$ has slope $m_2 = 7$. Moreover, they have different $y$-intercepts. Therefore the lines are parallel.

9. $L_1 : y = \frac{1}{6}x + 1$ has slope $m_1 = \frac{1}{6}$ and $L_2 : y = -6x - 7$ has slope $m_2 = -6$. Therefore the lines are perpendicular.

11. $L_1 : 2x - y + 4 = 0$ has slope $m_1 = 2$ and $L_2 : -6x + 3y - 1 = 0$ has slope $m_2 = 2$. Furthermore, they have different $y$-intercepts. Therefore the lines are parallel.

13. $L_1 : 7x - 3y + 15 = 0$ has slope $m_1 = \frac{7}{3}$ and $L_2 : -3x - 7y + 2 = 0$ has slope $m_2 = -\frac{3}{7}$. The lines are perpendicular.

15. $L_1 : 4x + 16y - 13 = 0$ has slope $m_1 = -\frac{1}{4}$ and $L_2 : 8x - 2y - 3 = 0$ has slope $m_2 = 4$. The lines are perpendicular.

17. $L_1 : y = 7$ and $L_2 : y = -5$ are parallel since both lines are horizontal.

19. $L_1 : x = -9$ and $L_2 : x = 1$ are parallel since both lines are vertical.

21. $L_1 : x = -4$ and $L_2 : x = 3$ are parallel since both lines are vertical.

23. $L_1 : y = 1$ and $L_2 : x = 2$ are perpendicular since one line is vertical and the other is horizontal.

25. $L_1 : y = -11$ and $L_2 : y = -11x + 1$ are neither parallel nor perpendicular, since $L_1$ is horizontal and $L_2$ is neither vertical nor horizontal.

27. Let $(x_1, y_1) = (1, 0)$. The slope of the given line is $m_{given} = 2$ and so the slope of the line we want is $m_{want} = 2$. Our equation is

$$y - y_1 = m (x - x_1)$$
$$y - 0 = 2 (x - 1)$$
$$y = 2x - 2$$

29. Let $(x_1, y_1) = (6, -4)$. The slope of the given line is $m_{given} = \dfrac{1}{2}$ and so the slope of the line we want is $m_{want} = \dfrac{1}{2}$. Our equation is

$$y - y_1 = m (x - x_1)$$
$$y - (-4) = \frac{1}{2} (x - 6)$$
$$y + 4 = \frac{1}{2}x - 3$$
$$\underline{\phantom{y + } -4 \qquad\qquad -4}$$
$$y = \frac{1}{2}x - 7$$

31. Let $(x_1, y_1) = (0, -4)$. Notice that $b = -4$, since the given point is the $y$-intercept. The slope of the given line is $m_{given} = 3$ and so the slope of the line we want is $m_{want} = 3$. Using the slope-intercept form, we have that

$$y = 3x - 4$$

33. Let $(x_1, y_1) = (-4, -2)$. The slope of the given line is $m_{given} = -6$ and so the slope of the line we want is $m_{want} = -6$. Our equation is

$$y - y_1 = m (x - x_1)$$
$$y - (-2) = -6 (x - (-4))$$
$$y + 2 = -6 (x + 4)$$
$$y + 2 = -6x - 24$$
$$\underline{\phantom{y + } -2 \qquad\qquad -2}$$
$$y = -6x - 26$$

35. Since $y = -8$ is a horizontal line, the line that we want is also horizontal. Moreover, it must contain the point $(0, 4)$. Therefore, the equation of our line is $y = 4$.

37. Since $x = 1$ is a vertical line, the line that we want is also vertical. Moreover, it must contain the point $(6, -8)$. Therefore, the equation of our line is $x = 6$.

39. Let $(x_1, y_1) = (0, 3)$. Notice that $b = 3$, since the given point is the $y$-intercept. The slope of the given line is $m_{given} = 2$ and so the slope of the line we want is $m_{want} = -\dfrac{1}{2}$. Using the slope-intercept form, we have that

$$y = -\frac{1}{2}x + 3$$

41. Let $(x_1, y_1) = (-5, 4)$. The slope of the given line is $m_{given} = 1$ and so the slope of the line we want is $m_{want} = -1$. Our equation is

$$y - y_1 = m\,(x - x_1)$$
$$y - 4 = -1\,(x - (-5))$$
$$y - 4 = -1\,(x + 5)$$
$$y - 4 = -x - 5$$
$$\underline{\phantom{y-}+4\phantom{xxxxxx}+4}$$
$$y = -x - 1$$

43. Let $(x_1, y_1) = (9, -2)$. The slope of the given line is $m_{given} = \dfrac{3}{2}$ and so the slope of the line we want is $m_{want} = -\dfrac{2}{3}$. Our equation is

$$y - y_1 = m\,(x - x_1)$$
$$y - (-2) = -\frac{2}{3}\,(x - 9)$$
$$y + 2 = -\frac{2}{3}x + 6$$
$$\underline{-2\phantom{xxxxxx}-2}$$
$$y = -\frac{2}{3}x + 4$$

45. Let $(x_1, y_1) = (-1, -10)$. The slope of the given line is $m_{given} = -6$ and so the slope of the line we want is $m_{want} = \dfrac{1}{6}$. Our equation is

$$y - y_1 = m\,(x - x_1)$$
$$y - (-10) = \frac{1}{6}\,(x - (-1))$$
$$y + 10 = \frac{1}{6}\,(x + 1)$$
$$y + 10 = \frac{1}{6}x + \frac{1}{6}$$
$$\underline{-10\phantom{xxxxxx}-10}$$
$$y = \frac{1}{6}x - \frac{59}{6}$$

47. Let $(x_1, y_1) = (7, -4)$. The slope of the given line is $m_{given} = -10$ and so the slope of the line we want is $m_{want} = \dfrac{1}{10}$. Our equation is

$$y - y_1 = m\,(x - x_1)$$
$$y - (-4) = \frac{1}{10}\,(x - 7)$$
$$y + 4 = \frac{1}{10}x - \frac{7}{10}$$
$$\underline{-4\phantom{xxxxxx}-4}$$
$$y = \frac{1}{10}x - \frac{47}{10}$$

49. Since $x = -4$ is a vertical line, the line that we want must be horizontal. Moreover, it contains the point $(2, 6)$. Therefore, the equation of our line is $y = 6$.

51. Since $y = 0$ is a horizontal line, the line that we want must be vertical. Moreover, it contains the point $(-4, -8)$. Therefore, the equation of our line is $x = -4$.

## Chapter 10 Exercise 10.4

1. The equation is $(x-2)^2 + (y-3)^2 = 2^2$ or $(x-2)^2 + (y-3)^2 = 4$.

3. The equation is $(x-5)^2 + (y-(-1))^2 = 3^2$ or $(x-5)^2 + (y+1)^2 = 9$.

5. The equation is $(x-(-2))^2 + (y-7)^2 = \left(\sqrt{7}\right)^2$ or $(x+2)^2 + (y-7)^2 = 7$.

7. The equation is $(x-(-8))^2 + (y-(-9))^2 = 1^2$ or $(x+8)^2 + (y+9)^2 = 1$.

9. The equation is $(x-0)^2 + (y-1)^2 = \left(2\sqrt{3}\right)^2$ or $x^2 + (y-1)^2 = 12$.

11. The equation is $(x-10)^2 + (y-0)^2 = 8^2$ or $(x-10)^2 + y^2 = 64$.

13. The equation is $(x-0)^2 + (y-0)^2 = 9^2$ or $x^2 + y^2 = 81$.

15. Comparing $(x-1)^2 + (y-3)^2 = 4$ to $(x-h)^2 + (y-k)^2 = r^2$, we have that $h=1$, $k=3$ and $r^2=4$ (so $r = \sqrt{4} = 2$). Therefore, the center is $(1,\ 3)$ and the radius is 2.

17. Comparing $(x+2)^2 + (y-7)^2 = 16$ to $(x-h)^2 + (y-k)^2 = r^2$, we have that $h=-2$, $k=7$ and $r^2 = 16$ (so $r = \sqrt{16} = 4$). Therefore, the center is $(-2,\ 7)$ and the radius is 4.

19. Comparing $(x+12)^2 + (y+10)^2 = 121$ to $(x-h)^2 + (y-k)^2 = r^2$, we have that $h=-12$, $k=-10$ and $r^2 = 121$ (so $r = \sqrt{121} = 11$). Therefore, the center is $(-12,\ -10)$ and the radius is 11.

21. Comparing $(x-3)^2 + y^2 = 8$ to $(x-h)^2 + (y-k)^2 = r^2$, we have that $h=3$, $k=0$ and $r^2 = 8$ (so $r = \sqrt{8} = 2\sqrt{2}$). Therefore, the center is $(3,\ 0)$ and the radius is $2\sqrt{2}$.

23. Comparing $x^2 + (y+8)^2 = 80$ to $(x-h)^2 + (y-k)^2 = r^2$, we have that $h=0$, $k=-8$ and $r^2 = 80$ (so $r = \sqrt{80} = \sqrt{16}\sqrt{5} = 4\sqrt{5}$). Therefore, the center is $(0,\ -8)$ and the radius is $4\sqrt{5}$.

25. Comparing $x^2 + y^2 = 3$ to $(x-h)^2 + (y-k)^2 = r^2$, we have that $h=0$, $k=0$ and $r^2 = 3$ (so $r = \sqrt{3}$). Therefore, the center is $(0,\ 0)$ and the radius is $\sqrt{3}$.

27.

$$(x-2)^2 + (y-1)^2 = 9$$
$$x^2 - 4x + 4 + y^2 - 2y + 1 = 9$$
$$x^2 + y^2 - 4x - 2y + 5 = \cancel{9}$$
$$\underline{\qquad\qquad\qquad -9 \quad -\cancel{9}}$$
$$x^2 + y^2 - 4x - 2y - 4 = 0$$

29.

$$(x+1)^2 + (y+7)^2 = 5$$
$$x^2 + 2x + 1 + y^2 + 14y + 49 = 5$$
$$x^2 + y^2 + 2x + 14y + 50 = \cancel{5}$$
$$\underline{\qquad\qquad\qquad -5 \quad -\cancel{5}}$$
$$x^2 + y^2 + 2x + 14y + 45 = 0$$

31.

$$x^2 + (y-12)^2 = 6$$
$$x^2 + y^2 - 24y + 144 = \cancel{6}$$
$$\underline{\qquad\qquad\qquad -6 \quad -\cancel{6}}$$
$$x^2 + y^2 - 24y + 138 = 0$$

33.

$$x^2 + y^2 = \cancel{16}$$
$$\underline{-16 \quad -\cancel{16}}$$
$$x^2 + y^2 - 16 = 0$$

35.

$$\left(x - \frac{1}{2}\right)^2 + \left(y + \frac{1}{2}\right)^2 = 16$$
$$x^2 - x + \frac{1}{4} + y^2 + y + \frac{1}{4} = 16$$
$$x^2 + y^2 - x + y + \frac{1}{2} = \cancel{16}$$
$$\underline{-16 \quad -\cancel{16}}$$
$$x^2 + y^2 - x + y - \frac{31}{2} = 0$$

37.

$$x^2 + y^2 - 4x - 6y + \cancel{12} = 0$$
$$\underline{\qquad \qquad -\cancel{12} \quad -12}$$
$$x^2 + y^2 - 4x - 6y = -12$$
$$x^2 - 4x + \underline{?} + y^2 - 6y + \underline{?} = -12 + \underline{?} + \underline{?}$$
$$\underbrace{x^2 - 4x + \underline{4}} + \underbrace{y^2 - 6y + \underline{9}} = -12 + \underline{4} + \underline{9}$$
$$(x - 2)^2 + (y - 3)^2 = 1$$
$$(x - 2)^2 + (y - 3)^2 = 1^2 \text{ is the standard form.}$$

39.

$$x^2 + y^2 + 10x - 2y - \cancel{10} = 0$$
$$\underline{\qquad \qquad +\cancel{10} \quad +10}$$
$$x^2 + y^2 + 10x - 2y = 10$$
$$x^2 + 10x + \underline{?} + y^2 - 2y + \underline{?} = 10 + \underline{?} + \underline{?}$$
$$\underbrace{x^2 + 10x + \underline{25}} + \underbrace{y^2 - 2y + \underline{1}} = 10 + \underline{25} + \underline{1}$$
$$(x + 5)^2 + (y - 1)^2 = 36$$
$$(x - (-5))^2 + (y - 1)^2 = 6^2 \text{ is the standard form.}$$

41.

$$x^2 + y^2 + 8x - \cancel{16} = 0$$
$$\underline{\qquad \qquad +\cancel{16} \quad + 16}$$
$$x^2 + y^2 + 8x = 16$$
$$x^2 + 8x + \underline{?} + y^2 = 16 + \underline{?}$$
$$\underbrace{x^2 + 8x + \underline{16}} + y^2 = 16 + \underline{16}$$
$$(x + 4)^2 + y^2 = 32$$
$$(x - (-4))^2 + (y - 0)^2 = \underbrace{\left(\sqrt{32}\right)^2} \text{ is the standard form.}$$
$$\text{or } \left(4\sqrt{2}\right)^2$$

43.

$$x^2 + y^2 - 4x + 6y + 12 = 0$$
$$\frac{-12 \quad -12}{x^2 + y^2 - 4x + 6y = -12}$$
$$x^2 - 4x + \underline{?} + y^2 + 6y + \underline{?} = -12 + \underline{?} + \underline{?}$$
$$\underbrace{x^2 - 4x + \underline{4}} + \underbrace{y^2 + 6y + \underline{9}} = -12 + \underline{4} + \underline{9}$$
$$(x - 2)^2 + (y + 3)^2 = 1$$

Therefore, $h = 2$, $k = -3$ and $r^2 = 1$ (so $r = \sqrt{1} = 1$). The center is $(2, \ -3)$ and the radius is 1.

45.

$$x^2 + y^2 - 8x - 4y - 4 = 0$$
$$\frac{+4 \quad +4}{x^2 + y^2 - 8x - 4y = 4}$$
$$x^2 - 8x + \underline{?} + y^2 - 4y + \underline{?} = 4 + \underline{?} + \underline{?}$$
$$\underbrace{x^2 - 8x + \underline{16}} + \underbrace{y^2 - 4y + \underline{4}} = 4 + \underline{16} + \underline{4}$$
$$(x - 4)^2 + (y - 2)^2 = 24$$

Therefore, $h = 4$, $k = 2$ and $r^2 = 24$ (so $r = \sqrt{24} = 2\sqrt{6}$). The center is $(4, \ 2)$ and the radius is $2\sqrt{6}$.

47.

$$x^2 + y^2 + 3y - 1 = 0$$
$$\frac{+1 \quad +1}{x^2 + y^2 + 3y = 1}$$
$$x^2 + y^2 + 3y + \underline{?} = 1 + \underline{?}$$
$$x^2 + y^2 + 3y + \underline{\frac{9}{4}} = 1 + \frac{9}{4}$$
$$x^2 + \underbrace{\left(y + \tfrac{3}{2}\right)^2} = \tfrac{13}{4}$$

Therefore, $h = 0$, $k = -\dfrac{3}{2}$ and $r^2 = \dfrac{13}{4}$, giving us $r = \sqrt{\dfrac{13}{4}} = \dfrac{\sqrt{13}}{2}$. The center is $\left(0, \ -\dfrac{3}{2}\right)$ and the radius is $\dfrac{\sqrt{13}}{2}$.

49.

$$x^2 + y^2 - 169 = 0$$
$$\frac{+169 \quad + 169}{x^2 + y^2 = 169}$$

Therefore, $h = 0$, $k = 0$ and $r^2 = 169$ (so $r = \sqrt{169} = 13$). The center is $(0, \ 0)$ and the radius is 13.

---

## Chapter 11 Exercises

1. It is a function.   3. It is not a function, since Anne $\longrightarrow$ seltzer and Anne $\longrightarrow$ lemonade.
5. It is a function.   7. It is a function.   9. It is a function.   11. It is a function.
13. It is not a function, since $b \longrightarrow 1$ and $b \longrightarrow 2$.
15. It is not a function, since $x \longrightarrow -4$ and $x \longrightarrow -5$.

17. $f(1) = 5\,(1) - 2 = 5 - 2 = 3$
  $f(-3) = 5\,(-3) - 2 = -15 - 2 = -17$
  $f(6) = 5\,(6) - 2 = 30 - 2 = 28$

19. $g(1) = 6\,(1) + 1 = 6 + 1 = 7$
  $g(-3) = 6\,(-3) + 1 = -18 + 1 = -17$
  $g(6) = 6\,(6) + 1 = 36 + 1 = 37$

21. $f(1) = (1)^2 - 7\,(1) + 2 = 1 - 7 + 2 = -4$
  $f(-3) = (-3)^2 - 7\,(-3) + 2 = 9 + 21 + 2 = 32$
  $f(6) = (6)^2 - 7\,(6) + 2 = 36 - 42 + 2 = -4$

23. $h(1) = -\,(1)^2 + 24 = -1 + 24 = 23$
  $h(-3) = -\,(-3)^2 + 24 = -9 + 24 = 15$
  $h(6) = -\,(6)^2 + 24 = -36 + 24 = -12$

25. $f(1) = \dfrac{5}{2\,(1) - 1} = \dfrac{5}{2 - 1} = \dfrac{5}{1} = 5$
  $f(-3) = \dfrac{5}{2\,(-3) - 1} = \dfrac{5}{-6 - 1} = -\dfrac{5}{7}$
  $f(6) = \dfrac{5}{2\,(6) - 1} = \dfrac{5}{12 - 1} = \dfrac{5}{11}$

27. $R(1) = \dfrac{2}{(1)^2 - 4\,(1) + 2} = \dfrac{2}{1 - 4 + 2} = \dfrac{2}{-1} = -2$
  $R(-3) = \dfrac{2}{(-3)^2 - 4\,(-3) + 2} = \dfrac{2}{9 + 12 + 2} = \dfrac{2}{23}$
  $R(6) = \dfrac{2}{(6)^2 - 4\,(6) + 2} = \dfrac{2}{36 - 24 + 2} = \dfrac{2}{14} = \dfrac{1}{7}$

29. $S(1) = \sqrt{2\,(1) + 7} = \sqrt{2 + 7} = \sqrt{9} = 3$
  $S(-3) = \sqrt{2\,(-3) + 7} = \sqrt{-6 + 7} = \sqrt{1} = 1$
  $S(6) = \sqrt{2\,(6) + 7} = \sqrt{12 + 7} = \sqrt{19}$

31. $f(1) = \sqrt{14 - 2\,(1)} = \sqrt{14 - 2} = \sqrt{12} = 2\sqrt{3}$
  $f(-3) = \sqrt{14 - 2\,(-3)} = \sqrt{14 + 6} = \sqrt{20} = 2\sqrt{5}$
  $f(6) = \sqrt{14 - 2\,(6)} = \sqrt{14 - 12} = \sqrt{2}$

33. $h(1) = \dfrac{6 - (1)}{\sqrt{(1) + 6}} = \dfrac{5}{\sqrt{7}}$
  $h(-3) = \dfrac{6 - (-3)}{\sqrt{(-3) + 6}} = \dfrac{9}{\sqrt{3}}$
  $h(6) = \dfrac{6 - (6)}{\sqrt{(6) + 6}} = \dfrac{0}{\sqrt{12}} = 0$

35. $p(1) = \dfrac{(1)^2}{\sqrt{(1)^2 + 3}} = \dfrac{1}{\sqrt{1 + 3}} = \dfrac{1}{\sqrt{4}} = \dfrac{1}{2}$
  $p(-3) = \dfrac{(-3)^2}{\sqrt{(-3)^2 + 3}} = \dfrac{9}{\sqrt{9 + 3}} = \dfrac{9}{\sqrt{12}} = \dfrac{9}{2\sqrt{3}}$
  $p(6) = \dfrac{(6)^2}{\sqrt{(6)^2 + 3}} = \dfrac{36}{\sqrt{36 + 3}} = \dfrac{36}{\sqrt{39}}$

37. The domain of $f(x) = 6x + 7$ is the set of all real numbers.

39. The domain of $h(x) = \dfrac{1}{9}x - 9$ is the set of all real numbers.

41. The domain of $g(x) = 8x^2 + x - 5$ is the set of all real numbers.

43. The domain of $P(x) = 6x^4 - 4x^2 + \dfrac{2}{3}x + 1$ is the set of all real numbers.

45. Setting the denominator to zero, we obtain $x = 0$. Therefore, the domain of $g$ is $\{x \mid x \neq 0\}$.

47. Setting the denominator to zero, we obtain $4x - 16 = 0$ and so $x = 4$. Therefore, the domain of $R$ is $\{x \mid x \neq 4\}$.

49. Setting the denominator to zero, we obtain $x^2 + 9x + 20 = 0$ and so $x = -5$, $x = -4$. Therefore, the domain of $g$ is $\{x \mid x \neq -5, \ -4\}$.

51. Setting the denominator to zero, we obtain $3x^2 - 27 = 0$ and so $x = -3$, $x = 3$. Therefore, the domain of $g$ is $\{x \mid x \neq -3, \ 3\}$.

53. Setting the denominator to zero, we obtain $x^2 + 4 = 0$ which has no real roots. Therefore, the domain of $g$ is the set of all real numbers.

55. Setting the denominator to zero, we obtain $x^2 + 2x + 4 = 0$ which has no real roots. Therefore, the domain of $f$ is the set of all real numbers.

57. Solving $x + 3 \geq 0$ yields $x \geq -3$. Therefore, the domain of $S$ is $\{x \mid x \geq -3\}$ or $[-3, \infty)$.

59. Solving $5x - 40 \geq 0$ yields $x \geq 8$. Therefore, the domain of $g$ is $\{x \mid x \geq 8\}$ or $[8, \infty)$.

61. Solving $18 - 22x \geq 0$ yields $x \leq \dfrac{9}{11}$. Therefore, the domain of $f$ is $\left\{x \mid x \leq \dfrac{9}{11}\right\}$ or $\left(-\infty, \dfrac{9}{11}\right]$.

63. Solving $\dfrac{2}{5}x - \dfrac{1}{10} \geq 0$ yields $x \geq \dfrac{1}{4}$. Therefore, the domain of $f$ is $\left\{x \mid x \geq \dfrac{1}{4}\right\}$ or $\left[\dfrac{1}{4}, \infty\right)$.

---

## Chapter 12 Exercises

1. Yes, since $-1 \overset{\checkmark}{=} -3 + 2$ and $-1 \overset{\checkmark}{=} 4(-3) + 11$.　　3. No, since $-1 \neq -7(-3) - 1$.

5. Yes, since $2(-3) - (-1) + 5 \overset{\checkmark}{=} 0$ and $3(-3) - 3(-1) + 6 \overset{\checkmark}{=} 0$.　　7. No, since $-3 - 5(-1) \neq 0$.

9. Yes, since $\frac{1}{2}(-3) + \frac{3}{2}(-1) + 3 \overset{\checkmark}{=} 0$ and $\frac{4}{5}(-3) - 2(-1) + \frac{2}{5} = 0$.

11. Yes, since $-1 \overset{\checkmark}{=} -(-3) - 4$ and $-3 \overset{\checkmark}{=} -3$.

13.

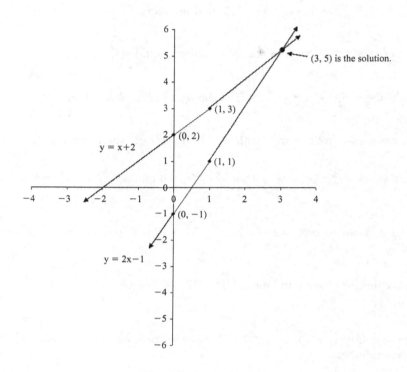

15.

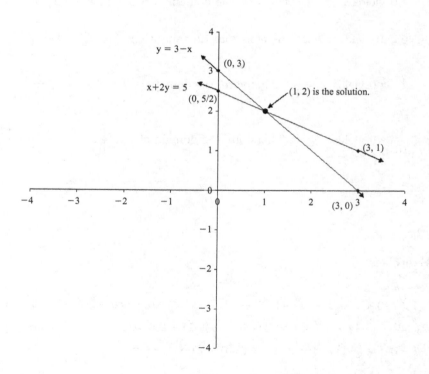

17.

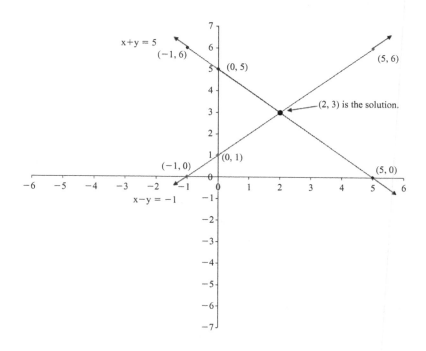

19.

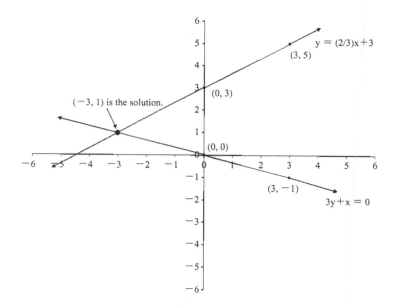

21.

$$x + 2\overbrace{(3x + 5)}^{y} = 17$$
$$x + 6x + 10 = 17$$
$$7x + 10 = 17$$
$$\underline{-10 \quad -10}$$
$$\frac{7x}{7} = \frac{7}{7}$$
$$x = 1$$

Plugging $x = 1$ into the first equation, we get

$$y = 3x + 5 = 8 = 3(1) + 5 = 8$$

The solution is $(1,\ 8)$.

23.

$$\overbrace{(7 + 4y)}^{x} + 3y - 4 = 0$$
$$3 + 7y = 0$$
$$\underline{-3 \qquad\quad -3}$$
$$\frac{7y}{7} = \frac{-3}{7}$$
$$y = -\frac{3}{7}$$

Plugging $y = -\dfrac{3}{7}$ into the first equation, we get

$$
\begin{aligned}
x &= 7 + 4y \\
&= 7 + \frac{4}{1}\left(-\frac{3}{7}\right) \\
&= 7 - \frac{12}{7} \\
&= \frac{49}{7} - \frac{12}{7} \\
&= \frac{37}{7}
\end{aligned}
$$

The solution is $\left(\dfrac{37}{7},\ -\dfrac{3}{7}\right)$.

25.

$$\overbrace{-4x}^{y} + 4 = 2x - 8$$
$$\underline{+4x \qquad\quad +4x}$$
$$4 = 6x - 8$$
$$\underline{+8 \qquad +8}$$
$$\frac{12}{6} = \frac{6x}{6}$$
$$2 = x$$

Plugging $x = 2$ into the first equation, we get

$$y = -4x + 4 = -4(2) + 4 = -4$$

The solution is $(2,\ -4)$.

27.

$$\frac{2}{3}\overbrace{(6y-1)}^{x}+\frac{4}{3}y+1=0$$
$$4y-\frac{2}{3}+\frac{4}{3}y+1=0$$
$$\frac{3}{1}\left(4y-\frac{2}{3}+\frac{4}{3}y+1\right)=\frac{3}{1}\,(0)$$
$$12y-2+4y+3=0$$
$$16y+1=0$$
$$\underline{\phantom{16y}-1\phantom{mmm}-1}$$
$$\frac{16y}{16}=\frac{-1}{16}$$
$$y=-\frac{1}{16}$$

Plugging $y=-\dfrac{1}{16}$ into the second equation, we get

$$
\begin{aligned}
x &= 6y-1 \\
&= 6\left(-\frac{1}{16}\right)-1 \\
&= -\frac{3}{8}-1 \\
&= -\frac{3}{8}-\frac{8}{8} \\
&= -\frac{11}{8}
\end{aligned}
$$

The solution is $\left(-\dfrac{11}{8},\ -\dfrac{1}{16}\right)$.

29.

$$-8x+2\overbrace{(4x+7)}^{y}+9=0$$
$$-8x+8x+14+9=0$$
$$15\neq 0$$

The system has no solution.

31.

$$16\overbrace{\left(\frac{7}{8}x-2\right)}^{y}=14x-32$$
$$14x-32=14x-32$$
$$\underline{-14x\phantom{mmmm}-14x}$$
$$-32=-32$$

The system has infinitely many solutions.

33.

$$
\begin{aligned}
&\phantom{+}\quad x+y=6 \\
+\ &\quad \underline{x-y=-2} \\
&\quad \frac{2x}{2}=\frac{4}{2} \\
&\quad \ \ x=2
\end{aligned}
$$

Find $y$ by plugging $x = 2$ into the first equation.

$$
\begin{aligned}
x + y &= 6 \\
2 + y &= 6 \\
-2 \qquad &-2 \\
\hline
y &= 4
\end{aligned}
$$

The solution is $(2,\ 4)$.

**35.**

$$
\begin{aligned}
x - 2y &= 10 \\
+ \quad 5x + 2y &= 8 \\
\hline
\frac{6x}{6} &= \frac{18}{6} \\
x &= 3
\end{aligned}
$$

Find $y$ by plugging $x = 3$ into the first equation.

$$
\begin{aligned}
x - 2y &= 10 \\
3 - 2y &= 10 \\
-3 \qquad &-3 \\
\hline
\frac{-2y}{-2} &= \frac{7}{-2} \\
y &= -\frac{7}{2}
\end{aligned}
$$

The solution is $\left( 3,\ -\dfrac{7}{2} \right)$.

**37.**

$$
\begin{array}{ccc}
4x + 6y = 8 & \text{becomes} & 4x + 6y = 8 \\
2(-2x - 5y) = 2(0) & & + \quad -4x - 10y = 0 \\
& & \hline \\
& & \dfrac{-4y}{-4} = \dfrac{8}{-4} \\
& & y = -2
\end{array}
$$

Plug $y = -2$ into the first equation to obtain

$$
\begin{aligned}
4x + 6y &= 8 \\
4x + 6(-2) &= 8 \\
4x - 12 &= 8 \\
+12 \quad &+12 \\
\hline
\frac{4x}{4} &= \frac{20}{4} \\
x &= 5
\end{aligned}
$$

The solution is $(5,\ -2)$.

**39.**

$$
\begin{array}{ccc}
2(-6x + 9y) = 2(4) & \text{becomes} & -12x + 18y = 8 \\
-3(-4x - 2y) = -3(3) & & + \quad 12x + 6y = -9 \\
& & \hline \\
& & \dfrac{24y}{24} = \dfrac{-1}{24}
\end{array}
$$

Plug $y = \dfrac{-1}{24}$ into the second equation to obtain

$$-4x - 2y = 3$$
$$-4x - 2\left(\dfrac{-1}{24}\right) = 3$$
$$-4x + \dfrac{1}{12} = 3$$
$$\dfrac{12}{1}\left(-4x + \dfrac{1}{12}\right) = \dfrac{12}{1}(3)$$
$$-48x + 1 = 36$$
$$\underline{\quad -1 \qquad -1 \quad}$$
$$\dfrac{-48x}{-48} = \dfrac{35}{-48}$$
$$x = -\dfrac{35}{48}$$

The solution is $\left(\dfrac{-1}{24},\ -\dfrac{35}{48}\right)$. Note that we could've found $x$ by doing another elimination (see the example from the text).

41. First let's clear out the fractions in the first equation.

$$\dfrac{6}{1}\left(\dfrac{2}{3}x - \dfrac{5}{6}y\right) = \dfrac{6}{1}(-4) \qquad \text{becomes} \qquad 4x - 5y = -24$$

Now we proceed as before.

$$\begin{array}{ll} 4x - 5y = -24 & \text{becomes} \\ -4(x + 3y) = -4(7) \end{array} \qquad + \begin{array}{l} 4x - 5y = -24 \\ -4x - 12y = -28 \\ \hline \dfrac{-17y}{-17} = \dfrac{-52}{-17} \\ y = \dfrac{52}{17} \end{array}$$

Plug $y = \dfrac{52}{17}$ into the second equation and obtain

$$x + 3y = 7$$
$$x + \dfrac{3}{1}\left(\dfrac{52}{17}\right) = 7$$
$$x + \dfrac{156}{17} = 7$$
$$\underline{\quad -\dfrac{156}{17} \qquad -\dfrac{156}{17} \quad}$$
$$x = 7 - \dfrac{156}{17}$$
$$= \dfrac{17}{17}\left(\dfrac{7}{1}\right) - \dfrac{156}{17}$$
$$= \dfrac{119}{17} - \dfrac{156}{17}$$
$$= -\dfrac{37}{17}$$

The solution to the system is $\left(-\dfrac{37}{17},\ \dfrac{52}{17}\right)$.

43. First we will multiply each equation by 10 to get rid of the decimal.

$$\begin{array}{ll} 10(1.5x + 3.5y) = 10(2) & \text{becomes} \\ 10(2x + 0.5y) = 10(4) \end{array} \qquad \begin{array}{l} 15x + 35y = 20 \\ 20x + 5y = 40 \end{array}$$

Now let's solve the new (equivalent) system.

$$15x + 35y = 20 \qquad \text{becomes} \qquad 15x + 35y = 20$$
$$-7(20x + 5y) = -7(40) \qquad\qquad + \;\underline{\;-140x - 35y = -280\;}$$
$$\frac{-125x}{-125} = \frac{-260}{-125}$$
$$x = \frac{52}{25}$$

To find $y$, I will replace $x$ in the first (new) equation by $\frac{52}{25}$.

$$15x + 35y = 20$$
$$\frac{15}{1}\left(\frac{52}{25}\right) + 35y = 20$$
$$\frac{156}{5} + 35y = 20$$
$$5\left(\frac{156}{5} + 35y\right) = 5(20)$$
$$156 + 175y = 100$$
$$\underline{-156 \qquad\qquad -156\;}$$
$$\frac{175y}{175} = \frac{-56}{175}$$
$$y = -\frac{8}{25}$$

The solution to the system is $\left(\dfrac{52}{25},\; -\dfrac{8}{25}\right)$.

45.

$$+ \;\; \begin{array}{r} 3x + y = 13 \\ \underline{-3x - y = -17} \\ 0 \neq -4 \end{array}$$

The system has no solution.

47.

$$8x - 2 = 6y \qquad \text{becomes} \qquad 8x - 2 = 6y$$
$$2(-4x + 5) = 2(-3y) \qquad\qquad + \;\underline{\;-8x + 10 = -6y\;}$$
$$8 \neq 0$$

The system has no solution.

49.

$$-6x - 9y + 12 = 0 \qquad \text{becomes} \qquad -6x - 9y + 12 = 0$$
$$-3(-2x - 3y + 4) = -3(0) \qquad\qquad + \;\underline{\;6x + 9y - 12 = 0\;}$$
$$0 = 0$$

The system has infinitely many solutions.

# Index